THE UNEMBARRASSED MUSE:

THE POPULAR ARTS IN AMERICA

TWO CENTURIES OF AMERICAN LIFE:
A BICENTENNIAL SERIES
HAROLD M. HYMAN, LEONARD W. LEVY, EDITORS

TWO CENTURIES OF AMERICAN LIFE:

A Bicentennial History

These thirty-one volumes, published or to be published between 1970 and 1976, represent the first comprehensive and systematic inquiry into United States history organized entirely on topical or institutional lines.

While TWO CENTURIES OF AMERICAN LIFE will represent the most recent and most comprehensive scholarship on each subject embraced, it is intended for a wide, general audience of readers, as well as for the academic community.

Daniel Boorstin THE HERO IN AMERICA • William R. Brock THE EVOLUTION OF AMERICAN DEMOCRACY • David Brody LABOR AND LABOR RELATIONS • D. W. Brogan THE PRESIDENCY • Stanley Coben AMERICAN NATIVISM, 1776–PRESENT • John Cogley THE HISTORY OF AMERICAN CATHOLICISM • Henry Steele Commager THE COURSE OF AMERICAN NATIONALISM, 200 YEARS OF THE SUPREME COURT • Lewis A. Coser THE INTELLECTUAL IN AMERICA • Carl N. Degler WOMEN AND THE FAMILY • John Duffy A HISTORY OF AMERICAN MEDICINE • Daniel J. Elazar 200 YEARS OF AMERICAN FEDERALISM • Charles Frankel AMERICAN PHILOSOPHY • Constance McLaughlin Green URBAN LIFE IN AMERICAN HISTORY • Oscar and Mary Handlin THE WEALTH OF THE AMERICAN PEOPLE • Grace and Fred M. Hechinger THE HISTORY OF AMERICAN EDUCATION • Ari Hoogenboom 200 YEARS OF AMERICAN BUREAUCRACY • Seymour Martin Lipset PARTIES, VOTERS AND ELECTIONS • Roy Lubove ENVIRONMENT AND CULTURE IN AMERICA: AN ECOLOGICAL PERSPECTIVE • Arthur Mann LOST CAUSES IN AMERICAN HISTORY • Martin E. Marty RIGHTEOUS EMPIRE: THE PROTESTANT EXPERIENCE IN AMERICA • Ernest R. May INCIDENTS IN AMERICAN DIPLOMACY • George Mowry 200 YEARS IN AMERICAN CONSERVATISM • Roy Franklin Nichols A HISTORY OF THE DEMOCRATIC PARTY • Russel Nye THE UNEMBARRASSED MUSE: THE POPULAR ARTS IN AMERICA • Moses Rischin A HISTORY OF IMMIGRATION • Robert Rutland 200 YEARS OF AMERICAN JOURNALISM • Ben B. Seligman THE POTENTATES: BUSINESS AND BUSINESSMEN IN

AMERICAN HISTORY • William R. Taylor THE HIS-
TORY OF EVANGELICALISM IN AMERICA • June and
Stephen Toulmin 200 YEARS OF AMERICAN SCIENCE •
T. Harry Williams HISTORY OF AMERICA'S WARS.

GENERAL EDITORS
Harold M. Hyman, William P. Hobby Professor of American
History, Rice University; Leonard W. Levy, Professor of Ameri-
can History, Claremont Graduate School

BY RUSSEL NYE

THE UNEMBARRASSED MUSE: THE POPULAR ARTS IN AMERICA

The Dial Press, New York

PREFACE

This book is a study of certain of the popular arts in American society, that is, the arts in their customarily accepted genres. *Popular* is interpreted to mean "generally dispersed and approved"—descriptive of those artistic productions which express the taste and understanding of the majority and which are free of control, in content and execution, from minority standards of correctness. The *arts*, as the term is used in this study, are works in literature, music, drama, and other artistic and broadly humanistic forms, produced for and expressive of the convictions, tastes, values, and feelings of the general public; intended, that is, for mass consumption. The most highly visual of the arts—painting and architecture—demand a picture book of their own, while their special relationships with their audiences, and their historical dependency on the technology of reproduction and distribution deserve separate treatment. This is, to repeat, a historical study of certain American popular arts, the arts of commercial entertainment.

RUSSEL NYE
East Lansing, Michigan
January, 1970

CONTENTS

CONTENTS

ACKNOWLEDGMENTS

Grateful acknowledgment is made to the following for permission to reprint from copyrighted material:

The Aberbach Group: for "Sixteen Tons" by Merle Travis. Copyright 1947 by Rumbalero Music, Inc., Elvis Presley Music, Inc., Gladys Music, Inc. and Norma Music, Inc. All rights administered by Rumbalero Music, Inc. Used by permission.

Arc Music: for "Back Door Man" by W. Dixon and C. Barnett. © 1961 Arc Music Corp. Used by permission of the publisher.

The Bobbs-Merrill Company, Inc.: for "When the Frost Is on the Punkin" and "An Old Sweetheart of Mine" from the Biographical Edition of *The Complete Works of James Whitcomb Riley*, copyright 1913 by James Whitcomb Riley, 1940 by Lesley Payne, Elizabeth E. Miesse and Edmund H. Eitel. Reprinted by permission of the publishers, The Bobbs-Merrill Company, Inc.

Boston Music Company: for "A Perfect Day" by Carrie Jacobs-Bond. Used by permission of Boston Music Company, Boston, Mass., agents for the copyright owners.

Dodd, Mead & Company, Inc., The Ryerson Press, Toronto and Ernest Benn Ltd., London: for "The Spell of the Yukon" and "The Shooting of Dan McGrew: from *The Collected Poems of Robert Service*.

Zane Grey, Inc.: for *The U.P. Trail* and *The Lone Star Ranger* by Zane Grey. Copyright Zane Grey, Inc.

Harcourt, Brace & World, Inc.: for "Mia Carlotta" from *Selected Poems of T. A. Daley*, copyright, 1936, by Harcourt, Brace & World, Inc.; renewed, 1964, by Thomas A. Daley, Jr. and reprinted by permission of the publisher.

Hawthorn Books, Inc.: for *The Covered Wagon* by Emerson Hough, published by Appleton-Century-Crofts.

Houghton Mifflin Company: for excerpts from *Collected Poems* by Edward
Roland Sill.

Alfred A. Knopf, Inc.: for excerpts from *This Is My Beloved* by Walter Benton
and *The Maltese Falcon* by Dashiell Hammet.

Little, Brown and Company: for "Tonight" from *Poems and Sonnets* (1909)
by Louise Chandler Moulton.

Lothrop, Lee & Shepard Co.: for excerpts from "The Coming American" from
The Coming American by Sam Walter Foss. Reprinted by permission.
For excerpts from "The House by the Side of the Road" from *Dreams in
Homespun* by Sam Walter Foss. Reprinted by permission.

Scott Meredith Literary Agency, Inc.: for *Double, Double* by Ellery Queen.
Copyright © 1950 by Little, Brown and Company; reprinted by per-
mission of the author and his agents, Scott Meredith Literary Agency,
Inc., 580 Fifth Avenue, New York, New York 10036.

Michigan State University Press; for *The Poetry of the Civil War* by Lee
Steinmetz. Copyright 1960, Michigan State University Press.

Pantheon Books, a Division of Random House, Inc.: for *America Rebels* by
Richard Dorson.

Random House, Inc. and the author: for the Preface by Henry Wilson Allen
to *The Last Warpath*.

Random House, Inc. and Rod McKuen Enterprises: for *Listen to the Warm* by
Rod McKuen.

Charles Scribner's Sons: for *The Canary Murder Case* by S. S. Van Dine.
"Four Things" is reprinted with the permission of Charles Scribner's Sons
from *The Builders* by Henry Van Dyke (1897). "Bachelor's Hall" and
"Little Boy Blue" are reprinted from COLLECTED WORKS by Eugene
Field.

H. N. Swanson Inc.: for *The Guns of Hanging Lake* by Luke Short. A
Bantam Book. Copyright 1968 by Frederick D. Glidden.

THE POPULAR ARTS AND
THE POPULAR AUDIENCE

*The arts that have most validity for the greatest part of the population
are not considered arts at all.*

—JOHN DEWEY

The term "the popular arts" cannot be used accurately to describe a cultural situation in Western civilization prior to the late eighteenth century. Certainly large numbers of people before that time found pleasant and rewarding ways of cultural diversion, but not until the emergence of mass society in the eighteenth century—that is, until the incorporation of the majority of the population into society—could either popular culture or popular art be said to exist.

Obviously, there had always been two artistic traditions—the high and low comedy of Greece, the drama and circuses of Rome, medieval cathedral plays and street fairs, Renaissance court-drama and tavern farces—separated by lay and ecclesiastical controls. The appearance of a predominantly middle-class civilization in the Western world, accompanied by the decrease in size and importance of the so-called elite and lower classes, drastically changed the cultural pattern. The eighteenth century thus saw the establishment of a triple artistic tradition—the folk and high art of the past, plus a new popular level of art (although the lines of demarcation were never so clear cut). Prior to the eighteenth century the serious artist created for a relatively small minority on whom his subsistence depended. Though Sam Johnson looked for a patron, he succeeded without one, for by his time the elite no longer could legislate culturally for the powerful middle class.

The primary condition for the emergence of popular culture was a great leap in population growth in Europe and the Americas, and the subsequent concentration of people into cohesive urban or near-urban units with common social, economic, and cultural characteristics. The result was the creation of a huge market for entertainment, with identifiable desires and responses. The existence of what is now called "the entertainment industry" can be easily recognized as early as 1750, when marketable cultural goods began to be manufactured in quantity to meet the needs of this mass public, to the profit of those who produced them.

After revolution broke the domination of cultural standards by the upper classes, the spread of education and literacy through the great middle class and below created a new audience which represented the tastes of the population at large. Control of the means of cultural production and transmission passed from a previously privileged elite to the urbanized, democratized middle classes. By the middle of the nineteenth century nearly everyone in the United States (except slaves and Indians) was minimally literate; by the middle of the twentieth three-quarters of American adults possessed a high school education or better. This mass society had much more leisure time, much more disposable income, and it needed a new art—neither folk nor elite—to use the one and fill the other.

Popular culture was also a product of modern technology and its new techniques for duplicating and multiplying materials (high speed presses, cheaper paper, new ways of graphic representation) along with much more efficient methods of production and distribution. Print became pervasive in nineteenth-century society, as machines widened and cheapened the public's access to the printed page. The twentieth century opened other channels of cultural communication to even larger audiences by introducing quite revolutionary methods of reproducing and transmitting sound and image—the phonograph, film, radio, television. Print is no longer the chief means of contact between artist and public, for the mass of today's population is accessible in a variety of ways. The average American between his second and his sixty-fifth year spends three thousand entire days, almost nine years of his life, watching television; by the time the average five-year-old enters kindergarten, he has spent more time before the family television set than the average college student has spent in classrooms over a four-year span.

The growth of a large popular audience, increasingly accessible through the mass media, caused in turn a demand for artists to satisfy its cultural needs. To these artists success lay not in pleasing a rich patron and his small, aristocratic, cultural circle, but in satisfying an increasingly broad "popular" audience. By the middle of the eighteenth century a large number of artists, especially novelists and dramatists (genres most adaptable to mass consumption) aimed their work directly at this new, general audience. The popular artist had to make his own tradition by investigating his market, calculating its desires, and evolving devices (many of which he adapted from folk art) for reaching it. He became a kind of professional (personified clearly, for example, by Daniel Defoe in England), who created for profit the kind of art that the public wanted.

The appearance of a *popular* artistic tradition, therefore, derives from a shift—initiated in the eighteenth century and completed during the nineteenth—from the patronage of the arts by the restricted upper classes to the support offered by a huge, virtually unlimited, middle-class audience, within the context of great technological, social, and political change. Modern mass society was fully formed by the middle of the nineteenth century; the modern mass media, in various stages of development, already provided the dominant forms of communication. Popular culture developed with it. The twentieth century established both more securely.

Although rather clear boundaries lie between popular and folk art on the one hand, and elite art on the other, the line between the first two is vague and easily crossed. The folk artist is usually satisfied with somewhat more anonymity; he is less concerned with aesthetic context, and less with specifically aesthetic purpose, though he wants to satisfy his audience, as does the popular artist. His art, however, tends to be thematically simple and technically uncomplicated, its production—the folksong, the duck decoy, the tavern sign, the circus act—not so strongly influenced by technological factors.

Popular art is folk art aimed at a wider audience, in a somewhat more self-conscious attempt to fill that audience's expectations, an art more aware of the need for selling the product, more consciously adjusted to the median taste. It is an art trying to perfect itself, not yet complete, not yet mature.

Elite art is produced by known artists within a consciously aesthetic context and by an accepted set of rules, its attainment (or failure) judged by reference to a normative body of recognized classics. The subjective element—that is, the presence of the creator or performer—is vital to its effectiveness. Elite art is exclusive, particular, individualistic; its aim is the discovery of new ways of recording and interpreting experience. Technical and thematic complexity is of much greater value in elite art than in folk or popular art; in fact, technique may become a vehicle for thematic expression, or may simply become an end in itself.

Popular art, aimed at the majority, is neither abstruse, complicated, or profound. To understand and appreciate it should require neither specialized, technical, nor professional knowledge. It is relatively free of corrective influences derived from minority sources; its standards of comprehension and achievement are received from consensus; it must be commonly approved, pervasive in the population, "popular" in the sense that the majority of people like and endorse it and will not accept marked deviations from its standards and conventions. More individualized than folk art, but less so than elite art, popular art tends to be more dependent than either on the skill of the performer.

Popular art confirms the experience of the majority, in contrast to elite art, which tends to explore the new. For this reason, popular art has been an unusually sensitive and accurate reflector of the attitudes and concerns of the society for which it is produced. Because it is of lesser quality, aesthetically, than elite art, historians and critics have tended to neglect it as a means of access to an era's—and a society's—values and ideas. The popular artist corroborates (occasionally with great skill and intensity) values and attitudes already familiar to his audience; his aim is less to provide a new experience than to validate an older one. Predictability is important to the effectiveness of popular art; the fulfillment of expectation, the pleasant shock of recognition of the known, verification of an experience already familiar—as in the detective story, the Western, the popular song, the Edgar Guest poem.

Popular art must be adaptable to mass production, and to diffusion through the mass media. It is irretrievably tied to the technology of duplication; to the popular artist the machinery of production and distribution may be as important—or more so—to what he does than either technique or content. Popular art, therefore, must be produced under conditions which make it possible to reach the widest possible audience in the most efficient way, a fact of life which the popular artist must accept as one of the stipulations of his craft.

Popular art assumes its own particular kind of audience, huge, heterogeneous, bewilderingly diverse in its combination of life styles, manners, interests, tastes, and economic and educational levels. This audience is much less self-conscious than an elite art audience; its standards are less clearly defined, its expectations less consistent and integrated. The audience for elite art possesses commonly held aesthetic and intellectual standards and has its own specialized idiom of appreciation and criticism. But those who respond to the popular arts are not sure why. Their standards are never precisely formulated or articulated and they are flexible and impermanent to a much greater degree than those of the audience for folk or elite art.

The relation of the popular artist to his audience is unique. The elite artist knows that his audience views his art in a context of certain predispositions; he anticipates success or failure within a definable framework of theory and achievement. His audience is acutely aware of him as an individual, knowing that his primary concern is the interpretation of his individual experience, and that he is personally involved with the content and technique of his product. The popular artist, however, works under no such set of rules, with a much less predictable audience, and for much less predictable rewards. His relationship with his public is neither direct nor critical, for between him and his audience stand editors, publishers, sponsors, directors, public relations men, wholesalers, exhibitors, merchants, and others who can and often do influence his product.

The elite artist is governed by traditional conventions of genre and technique, and knows that he will be judged by them. Since his accomplishment is measured by comparison with what others have done or are doing at his artistic level, he clearly understands the objectives and standards set for him by his critics and fellow artists. The popular artist, however, is subject primarily to the law of supply and demand; his aim is to win the largest possible audience in the marketplace. Neither what others have done, nor what critics say must be done, will necessarily guarantee success. The criterion of his success is contemporary, commercial, measured in terms of the size and response of his public. He competes not with his medium, nor with a preconceived set of critical standards, nor even with other popular artists, but with the audience under whose indirect control he must work—a notoriously fickle audience of unknown size and composition.

The popular artist must communicate with his audience through the mass media—with their interminably recurrent need for materials, unalterable publication deadlines, and vast amounts of empty space and time to be filled—which tends to depersonalize him, to remove him from close involvement with his art. The novelist writing for the little magazine or the prestige publisher, and the Western specialist writing for the mass-circulation weekly stand at completely different positions in relation to their materials and audiences, because they reach their audiences through media which make quite different demands and impose quite different conditions upon them.

The elite and popular arts are also distributed to their audiences in quite different ways, which in turn influence their product. Galleries, concerts, the quality press, the hardback book trade, academic discussion, self-improvement clubs and societies are not for the popular artist; he finds his public via the newsstand, the movie screen, the television, the paperback. His audience sees him less as an individual than as its own surrogate; his personal vision takes on meaning and effectiveness only when it reflects a wider, majority experience. He expresses not only what he feels, but also what many others feel.

The popular audience expects entertainment, instruction, or both, rather than an "aesthetic experience." To create for such an audience means that the popular artist cannot take into consideration the individualities and preferences of minority groups. Since the popular arts aim at the largest common denominator, they tend to standardize at the median level of majority expectation. The popular artist cannot disturb or offend any significant part of his public: though the elite artist may and should be a critic of his society, the popular artist cannot risk alienation.

The popular artist, then, hopes to do the very best he artistically can within the rigorous limits set by his situation. His accomplishment is measured by his skill and effectiveness in operating within the boundaries of the majority will and the requirements of the mass media. Since he hopes to make money, he aims at one thing—the largest possible audience —and whether it be a best seller, a high program rating, a four-star feature, or a "golden disc," his talents (which may be considerable) are directed toward mass response.

This does not mean that what the popular artist does is not worth doing, or personally unsatisfying, or aesthetically bad, or commercially cheap. It merely means that he must develop certain kinds of specialized skills to accomplish it, for his product must pay the medium and show a profit. And since popular art, to be successful, must be immediately popular, the artist must use those forms and media to which his audience has easiest access—movies, radio, television, the phonograph record, the magazine, the paperback book, the popular song, the newspaper, the comic book, and so on—and which it can most easily understand.

The fact that the mass audience exists, and that the popular artist must create for it, are simply the primary facts of life for the popular arts. Popular art can depend on no subsidy, state, or patron; it has to pay its way by giving the public what it wants, which may not always agree with what the artist may feel to be the most aesthetically apt. Satisfying a large audience involves no less skill than pleasing a smaller or more sophisticated one; popular artists can and do develop tremendous expertise and real talent. A best-selling paperback is not *ipso facto* bad; a song is not necessarily worthless because people hum it; a painting is neither bad because many look at it with pleasure nor good because few do.

Sometimes, with skill and talent alone, a popular artist may transmute mediocre material into something much better than it is, something even good; the gradual improvement over the years of standards of performance in the popular arts provides sufficient proof of this. A brief glance at the almost unbelievable banalities and ineptitudes of early movies, radio, television, fiction, or popular theater, in comparison with today's products, makes it abundantly clear that contemporary popular artists have developed tremendous technical skill, and that their sophistication and subtleties of performance are much greater than those of their predecessors. The distance between the movies of William S. Hart or Mary Pickford (or even of some Chaplin), between the comedy of Gallagher and Shean or Amos and Andy, between the music of the Wolverines or Paul Whiteman, and today's equivalents is incredibly wide. Over the years, the simple literalness of Tom Mix and Edward G. Robinson has become the symbolic, multileveled popular art of *High Noon* and *Bonnie and Clyde*.

PART ONE

POPULAR FICTION AND POETRY

God will not have any human being know what will sell.

—SAMUEL BUTLER

STORIES FOR THE PEOPLE

This story is for easy reading. It does not require any effort to under-stand it. It is a love story and appeals to the human heart.

—ADVERTISEMENT FOR *Florabel's Lover,*
LAURA JEAN LIBBEY, 1859.

The English colonists in America read neither more nor less than English-men who stayed at home, and they read much the same things. The list of books imported by John Usher, a Boston bookseller of the 1680's, indi-cates fairly well what his patrons bought and in what proportion—a thou-sand religious books, four hundred Bibles, a thousand schoolbooks (as one might expect) but also one hundred and sixty-two "romances," eighty-one books of poetry, and twenty-eight jest books. The colonial set-tlers liked novelty and adventure in their reading. The virgin country, filled with innumerable marvels and wonders; the strange plants and ani-mals; Indians (the first savages most of them had ever seen); the hazards and adventures of life in the wilderness; these furnished fresh materials for a new and American popular literature.

Early "relations," "reports of newes," chronicles and journals pro-vided storehouses of material for popular literature, with Indians, ship-wrecks, pirates, "providences," earthquakes, floods, wars, captivities and escapes, and nearly everything else. John Josselyn, for example, within a few months of his arrival in 1638, picked up tales of a mysterious lion, a sea-serpent, and a merman, as well as reports of a witches' revel, a spec-tral voice, a strange flame above the trees, and "the birth of a monster at Boston," and Josselyn was only one of many reporters.

The settlers brought with them an oral storytelling tradition that reached the colonies in undiminished strength. Since books were few and there was much to tell, the storyteller became a familiar figure in colonial communities. Everyone who kept a journal wrote down the stories he heard; sermons and chronicles recorded events and tales as remarkable and suspenseful as anything in the Bible, Hakluyt, or Defoe. Though he may have distrusted fiction, Cotton Mather advised ministers in his *Manuductio* that they ought to have "an Inexhaustible Store of Stories" and "the Skill of telling them Handsomely" if they were to be successful in their profession. Many of these were ancient folktales put into an American setting. Mermaids, St. Elmo's fire, ghostly appearances, heavenly displays, spectral ships, and other familiar motifs, common to European folklore for centuries, appeared in colonial diaries and journals, recorded by such men as Winthrop, Morton, Wood, Josselyn, and the Mathers.

Stories about unfamiliar animals and plants naturally bulked large, constituting a kind of American bestiary of whale, snake, wolf, and other stories, usually variants of British originals. John Lawson reported a horn snake in Carolina with a poisonous spur in its tail; James Kenny told of wild horses so large they slept leaning on tall trees; Cotton Mather sent a letter to the Royal Society describing a rattlesnake that bit a chunk out of a broadaxe. Lawson heard of a tulip tree so large that a man moved his furniture into it and lived inside; Beverley described a "love flower" of startlingly phallic appearance; he also told how chewing "Jamestown weed" (which survives as "jimson weed") sent men out of their minds.

Specters appeared very early in the colonies and continued to do so, beginning a long tradition of ghost sightings that provided material for American writers. Reports appeared in diaries, histories, and oral tales, later in newspapers and magazines, literally by the hundreds. A spectral ship visited New Haven harbor in 1647, while Sir Walter Raleigh's vessel was observed on the Carolina coast as late as 1709. Cavendish, Vermont, had a local ghost seen several times over a span of years from 1680 to 1790, while the ghost of a girl murdered by pirates in Marblehead harbor screamed in terror on the anniversary of her death for one hundred and fifty consecutive years.

Spectral appearances were very real, very much a part of the colonial imaginative experience. An account left by a bereaved father in his journal could have been duplicated a hundred times in any decade of the seventeenth or eighteenth century:

Thursday 29 (1735) of october my wife went into a chambur that was lock to seek candels that was in a half bushel under a bed and as shee kneled down and tock her candels and laid them on the beed and as shee thrust back the half bushel there came out a childs hand she saw the fingers the hand a striped boys cife or sleve and upon shurch there was no child in the chamber on thursday a fort nite aftar my stephen son henery died. the next thursday Ebenezar died the next monday morning his eldest son Stephen died.

The great witchcraft delusions that swept England, Europe, and the colonies in the seventeenth century created a body of witch and devil literature that persisted for three hundred years. The devil appeared very early in America and never left it. He was in Plymouth from the beginning, Bradford believed, and certainly at Merrymount at Morton's Maypole. He drank with a crony at Plymouth in 1670; he knocked off a minister's hat in Hopkinton in 1767; he stole Mr. Brainerd's axe at Braintree in 1771. He visited an elderly gentleman in Connecticut on a stormy night in 1732, but the old man fortunately saw his tail beneath his coat and drove him out of the house.

Stories of witches, and of their capture and trial, were regarded as no different from those of pirates, murderers, or other criminals. The colonies were filled with such tales; the first historians recorded them in the early days of settlement and never stopped. Susannah Trimmings, of Piscataqua, New Hampshire, for example, swore under oath in April 1685, that

On Lord's day 30th of March, at night, going home with Goodwife Barton, she separated from her at the freshet next her house. On her return, between Goodman Even's and Robert Davis's she heard a rustling in the woods, which she at first thought was occasioned by swine, and presently after there did appear to her a woman whom she apprehended to be old Goodwife Walford.

She asked me where my consort was. I answered, I had none. She said, Thy consort is at home by this time. Lend me a pound of cotton.

I told her I had but two pounds in the house, and I would not spare any to my mother. She said I had better have done it; that my sorrow was great already, and it should be greater—for I was going a great journey, but should never come there. She then left me, and I was struck as with a clap of fire on the back, and she vanished toward the waterside, in my apprehension in the shape of a cat. She had on her head a white linen hood tied under her chin, and her waistcoat and petticoat were red, with an old green apron and a black hat upon her head.

Accounts of witchcraft investigations and trials appeared in profusion, especially in the latter decades of the seventeenth century, some frankly sensational, others seriously done, such as Cotton Mather's *Wonders of the Invisible World* (1693) and Robert Calef's *More Wonders of the Invisible World* (1702). The devil-tale and the witch-tale were deep into the American consciousness before the eighteenth century and provided an important ingredient in the popular literature of the times.

So too were "providences," remarkable happenings which by their unusual character were believed to have some significant message or meaning. Providences were, of course, as old as folklore and common to all cultures, but for the Calvinist, who felt God's direction keenly, they were especially important. If God controlled all, then any deviation from the usual course of events ought to be analyzed and interpreted carefully. Within the providential framework the colonists recognized three varieties—those reflecting God's wrath and punishments, His prophecies and forewarnings, and His rewards and "deliverances." An Indian attack, a sick calf, a sudden plague of disease, a lost crop, a bolt of lightning, the death of a blasphemer—these were clearly judgments. John Winthrop told how in 1640 God handled certain "profane scoffers":

> July 27, 1640. Being the second day of the week, the *Mary Rose,* a ship of Bristol, of about two hundred tons, lying before Charlestown, was blown in pieces with her own powder, being twenty-one barrels; wherein the judgment of God appeared. For the master and company were many of them profane scoffers at us, and at the ordinances of religion here; so as our churches keeping a fast for our native country they kept aboard at their common service, when all the rest of the masters came to our assemblies; likewise the Lord's day following. And a friend of his going aboard next day and asking him why he came not on shore to our meetings, his answer was that he had a family of his own, and they had as good service aboard as we had on shore. Within two hours after this (being about dinner time) the powder took fire (no man knows how) and blew all up, viz., the captain and nine or ten of his men, and some four or five strangers.

A blazing comet, a strange dream, a spectral vision, a rain of frogs—these were portents, as in the experience reported by workmen in Connecticut in the 1760's:

> A report prevails that some unaccountable noises were lately heard near Hartford; and 'tis said, via Derby, that a few men being lately at work in a wood they were terrified with an extraordinary Voice, commanding them to read the seventh chap. of Ezekiel.

Mather reported that a red snow once preceded an Indian attack, allowing the colonists time to prepare a defense, while the Massachusetts militia refused to march during a partial eclipse of the moon in King

Philip's War. A school of fish at starving-time, a miraculous cure for illness, a smallpox epidemic that decimated hostile Indian tribes—these were obviously God's deliverances. Increase Mather's compilation of 1684, *Illustrious Providences,* remains one of the best of all such accounts. The belief that events had symbolic value was deeply ingrained in the colonial mind from the start, to take later root in popular poetry, novels, and drama.

The largest body of popular literary materials, however, was that which concerned the Indian. The English, who had few contacts with primitive peoples, found the "red savages" puzzling, dangerous, and absolutely fascinating. Every journal keeper, diarist, sermonizer, explorer, and historian who had any contact with Indians seemed to have written it down. They recorded customs, dress, manners, language, society, and appearances, speculated endlessly about the Indians' origins and history, killed them indiscriminately and were killed in turn. The colonists eagerly adopted their legends (America still is dotted with sites of sacrificed maidens, lover's leaps, and heroic braves who jumped from cliffs rather than surrender), used their herb-remedies, took some of their words, and copied their hunting methods and some of their cookery.

In a world dominated by witchcraft, providences, and supernaturalism (since the Indian was assumed to be in league with the Devil or one himself), the Indian shaman or sorcerer commanded much interest. Colonial Americans gathered many tales of Indian magic, rituals, and transformations; Passaconaway, for example, an actual Penacook "pawaw" or shaman whose deeds were noted by both William Wood and Thomas Morton, became a lengendary figure who appeared in many of the journals, newspapers, and historical accounts of the eighteenth century. At the same time the Indian's confrontation with the apparatus of an advanced society led to the creation in popular tales of an Indian booby, a redskinned comic who put gunpowder in the fire, looked down pistol barrels, and ran away in fright when an Englishman took off his wig. A good many of these folktales later were transferred to the Negro.

But as witches were Satan's emissaries, so were the Indians, whose depredations brought fear and sorrow to the settlements; Mather called them "miserable Salvages" whom "probably the Devil decoy'd hither" to destroy New England's Christian society. The seventeenth-century Indian wars produced a substantial body of writing, for these small conflicts were bitter and bloody reminders of the perils of frontier life. King Philip's War took the life of one of every sixteen New England males and destroyed thirty settlements, a story told well, and with anguished detail, in such narratives as William Hubbard's *Narrative of the Troubles with*

STORIES FOR THE PEOPLE

the Indians (1677), Cotton Mather's *Decennium Latuosum* (1699), and Thomas Prince's *History of King Philip's War* (1716).

The tale of Indian captivity took on quite early some of the qualities of the sermon, the novel, and the adventure story. Captain John Smith, in his story of Powhatan and Pocahontas, wrote the earliest of them all, but in its later manifestations the type took on a different cast. The point of the captivity narrative was neither excitement nor terror alone, but rather the struggle waged between the red servants of Satan and the captive Christian for his soul; it was a story of trial and victory, of suffering and martyrdom, complete with sentimentality, moralizing, psychological probings, and exciting adventure. Captivity stories—the first authentically popular American novels—mixed fact and fancy, religion and sensationalism, in highly satisfactory fashion. An ex-captive was virtually assured of a reading public; five hundred such accounts were published during the colonial period, and one, Mary Rowlandson's, ran through thirty-one editions. John Gyles of Maine, who spent the years 1689–1698 in captivity, authored one of the best known; John Williams of Deerfield, Massachusetts (whose daughter chose to stay with her Indian husband) wrote another in 1707; Elizabeth Harris' (1725) was a perennial bestseller. By far the most popular was *The Sovereignty and Goodness of God . . . , Being a Narrative of the Captivity and Restoration of Mrs. Mary Rowlandson*, an account of her capture during King Philip's War, published in its second edition in 1682.

"No one can imagine," Mrs. Rowlandson said, "what it is to be captivated and enslaved to such atheistical, proud, wild, cruel, barbarous, brutish (in one word) diabolicall creatures as these, the worst of heathen. . . ." She treated her captivity as a test of her faith, "for whom the Lord loveth he chasteneth," and instilled into her reader the values of high Christian ideals and faith in God. She also had an unerring sense of the right detail and a swift rushing style that never slowed the narrative pace. Her opening description of the raid, evoking all the terror and shock of its sudden savagery, still retains all its effectiveness after nearly three hundred years:

> On the tenth of February 1675, Came the Indians with great numbers upon Lancaster: Their first coming was about Sunrising; hearing the noise of some Guns, we looked out; several Houses were burning, and the Smoke ascending to Heaven. There were five persons taken in one house, the Father, and the Mother and a sucking Child, they knockt on the head; the other two they took and carried away alive. Their were two others, who being out of their Garison upon some occasion were set upon; one was knockt on the head, the

other escaped: Another their was who running along was shot and wounded, and fell down; he begged of them his life, promising them Money (as they told me) but they would not hearken to him but knockt him in head, and stript him naked, and split open his Bowels. Another seeing many of the Indians about his Barn, ventured and went out, but was quickly shot down. . . . At length they came and beset our own house, and quickly it was the dolefullest day that ever mine eyes saw. . . . Bullets seemed to fly like hail; and quickly they wounded one man among us, then another, and then a third, About two hours (according to my observation, in that amazing time) they had been about the house before they prevailed to fire it (which they did with Flax and Hemp, which they brought out of the Barn, and there being no defence about the House, only two Flankers at two opposite corners and one of them not finished) they fired it once and one ventured out and quenched it, but they quickly fired it again, and that took.

These tales of captivity, witchcraft, and danger furnished a base for a later formal American literature that included the Gothic novel, the romance of sensibility, and the frontier-Indian novel, as well as for a popular tradition that included the dime novel, the pulp adventure, the Western novel, and the cowboy-Western movie.

That new and immensely popular eighteenth-century literary genre, the novel, arrived in colonial America a trifle late. As they had in England, novels faced hostility in America from the orthodox Protestant sects, since, as clerics and critics agreed, they might "pollute the imagination," give "false ideas of life," and "contribute to female depravity." On the other hand, there were those who claimed that novels could "teach moral lessons . . . , blend instruction with amusement . . . , regale the imagination, and reform the heart."

The demand for fiction increased rapidly after 1750, and publishers printed more and more novels and tales, of which circulating libraries stocked greater numbers each year. Despite all the warnings, there was a large and lucrative market for fiction by the 1790's which American authors hoped to supply. In response to accusations of immorality, novelists claimed that their stories were really "moral lessons," usually appending a subtitle or preface to point out that their plots were "founded on fact" or were "truthful representations of human passions."

The American public maintained this ambivalent attitude toward fiction deep into the nineteenth century. As late as 1822 *The Christian Spectator* still argued that fiction, because of "its moral blemishes and unreal pictures of human life," ought to be read with caution. Writers, however, found novels an attractive and useful form of expression and, since the public obviously liked and bought them, a profitable one as well. It was agreed that excessive addiction to novels could be bad, and that *some* novels, at least, presented a false and delusive picture of life. On the other hand, *Pamela, Tom Jones, Roderick Random,* and *Tristram Shandy* (all of which appeared before 1770) seemed not to have corrupted England, and Americans read them as avidly as Englishmen.

The problem was, then, to separate good from bad novels, to read and write those which served the right purposes. Novelists therefore drew their stories from "real life" to show the consequences of irrationality, immorality, "mis-education," or bad judgment. Matthew Carey, a shrewd judge of public taste, endorsed such novels in his *American Museum* magazine because they were "true stories" which taught "moral lessons." The popular audience, so it seemed by the later eighteenth century, could have all the novels it wanted if they were written to this formula, and writers were quick to supply the market.

There were four major strains in the early American novel: the sentimental; the satiric; the Gothic; and the historical romance. All closely imitated the eighteenth- and early nineteenth-century British novel. The first of these, derived from Samuel Richardson and the British sentimentalists, was by far the most popular variety until displaced by the historical romances of Scott. It was natural for American writers to select Richardson from among the British novelists as their model, not only because of his great popularity but because his didacticism satisfied the American feeling that fiction should teach and elevate. American audiences, too, were prepared for the Richardsonian manner by long familiarity with the journal, of which Richardson's epistolary style was a sophisticated extension.

After 1770 Richardsonian sentimentalism covered America with a rainstorm of tears, deluging the public with sad tales of seduction, suicide, and sentiment. Women read Richardson's *Pamela* or *Clarissa* or *Sir Richard Grandison* voraciously and slept with them under their pillows. Richardson's novels, it was agreed, "cultivated the Principles of Virtue and Religion in the Minds of Youth of Both Sexes." Hundreds of imitations appeared in America, built to the master's formula, decorated with alluring subtitles such as "Female Frailty," "Delicate Embarrassments," or "Venial Trespasses." William Hill Brown's novel *The Power of Sympathy* (1789, long attributed to Sarah Morton) claimed to be "founded in truth" and, according to its preface, was intended "to expose the dangerous consequences of Seduction and to set forth the advantages of Female Education," which it did in a spectacular plot compounded of seduction, near-incest, kidnaping, attempted rape, and suicide.

Mrs. Susannah Rowson's *Charlotte Temple* (1791) was the queen of them all. Susannah Haswell, the daughter of a British naval officer, was born in England and came to America with her family shortly before the Revolution. After the war the Haswells returned to England, where Susannah in 1786 married William Rowson, a hardware merchant who was also a trumpeter in the Horse Guards. After his business failed, Rowson and his wife went on the stage with moderate success and came to Philadelphia until 1797, when Mrs. Rowson moved to Boston to open a girls' school. Thereafter she pursued a succesful career as schoolmistress, editor and contributor to magazines, poet, playwright, and Bostonian. She also translated Horace and Virgil, compiled a dictionary, wrote an opera, and published textbooks.

Mrs. Rowson wrote several novels before coming to America. *Charlotte Temple: A Tale of Truth,* based upon an actual experience in her family, appeared in London in 1791 and in an American edition in 1794. It began slowly, with three editions before the turn of the century, and then its popularity grew—fifty thousand copies sold before 1810, and ultimately some two hundred editions over the next century. She continued to write novels such as *Trials of the Human Heart, Reuben and Rachel,* and *Lucy Temple, or The Three Orphans* (the story of Charlotte's daughter), none of which approached *Charlotte*'s sales.

Mrs. Rowson had an inventive mind and more skill than most of her fellow practitioners. She had a knack for keeping her narrative moving, despite the rigidity imposed on her by the sentimental conventions, and the ability to endow unbelievable coincidences with a kind of spurious authenticity. *Charlotte* she told simply and directly. The daughter of respectable upper-middle-class parents and a student at Madame Du Pont's School for Girls in England, Charlotte meets Montraville, a young officer, shortly before his departure for the American wars. With the help of a devilish brother officer, Belcour, and a depraved Frenchwoman, Mademoiselle La Rue, the well-meaning but weak Montraville persuades Charlotte to elope with him to New York on promise of marriage. There he becomes enamored of Julia Franklin, a young American girl; and through the machinations of Belcour, who wants Charlotte for himself, abandons Charlotte and her illegitimate child. Belcour immediately loses interest, and the dying Charlotte sinks deeper into virtuous poverty until she finds refuge at the hut of a poor servant family. Here her true friend Mrs. Beauchamp, her grieving father, and Montraville find her, too late.

Charlotte opened the floodgates. The novels which inundated the

early decades of the nineteenth century followed Mrs. Rowson's pattern
to the letter and authors searched for ways to work ingenious changes
into her formula without violating it. In their plots young women had to
distinguish between "false" and "true" love; lovers had to surmount scandal, parental objection, and misunderstandings of heroic proportions.
Good people were deluded by false principles such as atheism, emotionalism, or irrationality; heroes had to choose between love and duty, honor
and affection, selflessness and humanity.

Short fiction of the same kind flourished in the magazines, which
bulged with sentimental stories; in the 1790's *The Philadelphia Minerva*,
The Massachusetts Magazine, The New York Magazine, and *The American Moral and Sentimental Magazine* published little else. The stories,
said *The Portfolio,* "furnish a means of instruction . . . of peculiar effectiveness," but they obviously also involved other things which appealed
more strongly to the popular taste, such as sensationalism, overemotion-
alism, and sex. Conventional and predictable as their plots were, they
reflected in their formalized, abstract way some of the real problems of
contemporary society. The sentimental-didactic strain remained a strong
current in the mainstream of popular American fiction and its formula
remains effective to the present day.

The sentimental novelists baited their hooks for the popular audience
with sex and moralism. The Revolutionary War furnished another kind
of lure, the patriotic adventure story, cast in the form of a narrative of
war or prison life, written during and after the Revolution by the dozens.
The Library of Congress still has over two hundred surviving examples,
some published fifty years after Yorktown. They were not exactly fiction,
nor were they quite fact, but, usually written in much the same kind of
prose as a novel, they provided a highly satisfactory alternative and often
sold equally well. These narratives augmented the Indian captivity tales
in the popular market, and (except for the elimination of the old-fashioned religious exhortations) followed much the same pattern, supplying
adventure, heroism, villainy, horror, and hairbreadth escapes in highly
satisfactory proportions.

The hero's opponents now were not redskins but redcoats; the victim's trial of captivity was not in an Indian village but in British prisons
at Dartmoor or Halifax, or on prison ships like *Jersey* or *Hunter.* Yet like
the Indian stories, prisoner tales illustrated how the individual, buttressed
by his bravery and dedication to a cause, stood up against suffering and
won out over temptation—as in Ethan Allen's story of the sick young
militiaman who chose to die in prison rather than take the Crown oath

and go free. Whereas the Indian captivity tale instilled a moral lesson in the reader, the prison narrative imparted a patriotic one.

The wartime narratives had sufficient details of violence, excitement, and suffering to satisfy the most lurid imagination. Jonathan Davis saw a Yankee prisoner beaten to death while "running the gauntlet" in Plymouth prison; John Shaw saw berserk British guards put a whole company of prisoners to the sword; David Perry saw a sailor, under sentence of eight hundred lashes, die at six hundred, the last two hundred laid on the bare bloody bones of his back. Thomas Dring, whose escape from the infamous *Jersey* is still a classic of its kind, told how the prisoners inoculated themselves for smallpox with a common pin and pus from the sores of a dying victim and strangely enough, survived. For the other side, the *Narrative of the Exertions and Sufferings of James Moody* (1783), recounting the imprisonment and escape of a Loyalist officer in the British army, was cut to exactly the same pattern and sold equally well in Boston and London.

A few of these wartime tales were written by educated men like Henry Laurens, who served as President of the Continental Congress, but most of them were plain, unvarnished tales, written with force, realism, and vigor by ordinary men. In them the reader heard authentic American voices speaking an American, not an English tongue. Ethan Allen, the hero of the Battle of Ticonderoga, spent three years as a prisoner, and in *A Narrative of Ethan Allen's Captivity* (1779), told about his experiences in soldierly prose. He reported thus on prisoners held captive by the British in New York:

The private soldiers who were brought to New York were crowded into churches and environed with slavish Hessian guards, a people of a strange language who were sent to America for no other design but cruelty and desolation, and at others by merciless Britons, whose mode of communicating ideas being intelligible in this country, served only to tantalize and insult the helpless and perishing; but above all was the hellish delight and triumph of the Tories over them, as they were dying by hundreds. This was too much for me to bear as a spectator, for I saw the Tories exulting over the dead bodies of their murdered countrymen. I have gone into the churches and seen sundry of the prisoners in the agony of death, in consequence of very hunger, and others speechless and very near death, biting pieces of chips; others pleading for God's sake for something to eat, and at the same time shivering with the cold. Hollow groans saluted my ears, and despair seemed to be imprinted on all of their countenances. The filth in these churches, in consequence of the fluxes, was almost beyond description. The floors were covered with excrements. I have carefully sought to direct my steps so as to avoid it, but could not. They would beg for God's sake for one copper, or morsel of bread. I have seen in one of these churches seven dead at the same time, lying among the excrements of their bodies.

It was a common practice with the enemy to convey the dead from these filthy places in carts, to be slightly buried, and I have seen whole gangs of Tories making derision, and exulting over the dead, saying, "There goes another load of damned rebels."

These wartime narratives, along with the still-popular Indian stories and the traditional "providence" tales of earlier America, constituted a large body of popular literature for post-war and nineteenth-century audiences.

The man who made respectable fiction popular in the United States, and popular fiction respectable, was Sir Walter Scott, whose tales of history, legend, adventure, folklore, scenery, love, and patriotism enthralled the early nineteenth century. American readers found in his strong Scottish nationalism a rationale for and reflection of their own; partly too, of course, his stories of excitement and derring-do were natural reactions against too much sentiment and too many tears. His popularity in the United States was immense. In Philadelphia alone at one point there were ten publishing houses engaged solely in reprinting Scott, and no doubt as many in New York. Americans bought his novels by the thousands (half a million volumes before 1823) and adapted, summarized, dramatized, and imitated them. In the South, where Scott's chivalric apparatus found an especially responsive audience, there were thirty-five towns named *Waverley*, sidewheel steamers named *Rob Roy* and *Marmion*, and hundreds of little girls named Rowena after the heroine of *Ivanhoe*.

Scott's fervent nationalism and his skillful use of historical materials were exactly what American authors hoped to emulate; why couldn't they, using their own past as Scott used his, create an art of equal value? Rufus Choate's oration at Salem in 1810, titled *The Importance of Illustrating New England History by a Series of Romances Like the Waverley Novels*, summarized popular opinion exactly. Many tried, among them such skillful writers as James Kirke Paulding, John Pendleton Kennedy, William Gilmore Simms and Daniel Thompson, to fit the Scott formula to American materials without marked success. But James Fenimore Cooper, after trying his hand at a Jane Austen-like novel of manners, wrote *The Spy* in 1821, which sold three thousand five hundred copies in two weeks, another five thousand in the next two months, and eventually a million copies over the next fifty years. In 1823 he wrote *The Pioneers*, the first of the "Leatherstocking" series which introduced frontiersman Natty Bumppo to the public; in 1826, *The Last of the Mohicans* (which eventually sold two million), and through the rest of the series to *The Deerslayer* in 1841. Using the term broadly, it is not inaccurate to call Cooper the first American best-selling novelist, if Mrs. Rowson is to be claimed by the English.

Cooper's success attracted imitators of lesser talent, such as Cheney's *A Peep at the Pilgrims*, Lydia Maria Child's *Hobomok* and *The Rebels*, Mrs. Catherine Sedgwick's *Hope Leslie*, Robert Montgomery Bird's *Nick of the Woods*, John Kennedy's *Rob of the Bowl*. The best-selling author of all of them, however, was Joseph Holt Ingraham, a self-effacing professor of languages at Jefferson College in Mississippi, who quit teaching to become the first great hackwriter of the American popular market. *The Pirate of the Gulf* (1836), a novel about Lafitte, was the first of perhaps a hundred similar and highly successful blood-and-thunder thrillers; probably every boy in the United States knew it, for it was still in print in 1900. A great admirer of Longfellow, Ingraham dedicated the novel to his idol—a doubtful honor, since Longfellow, after he read it, pronounced its author the worst novelist who ever lived.

His *Prince of the House of David* (1855), a religious novel, written after he entered the Episcopal Church, sold in the hundreds of thousands for decades; he followed it with others—*The Pillar of Fire*, *The Throne of David*, and so on—anticipating the popularity of Lew Wallace, Charles Sheldon, and Lloyd Douglas by a half-century. He preceded Alger with a story of the city streets, *Jemmy Daly, or, the Little News Vendor* (1843); and he was among the first practitioners of the melodramatic, narrow-escape school with *The Beautiful Cigar Girl, or The Mysteries of Broadway* (1856). *Bruising Bill* (1845), a story about Harvard, was the first popular novel to use a college locale.

But despite Ingraham's versatility, the writing of popular fiction in the forties and fifties was dominated by women. "America," Hawthorne wrote angrily, "is now wholly given over to a damned mob of scribbling women." He had a point. His *Mosses from an Old Manse* brought royalties in 1853 of $144.09; "Fanny Fern's" *Leaves*, however, sold 70,000 copies that year and showed no signs of weakening, while Susan Warner's *Wide, Wide World* (1850) earned her about $35,000 in royalties.

Hawkers and peddlers in colonial times sold cheap books along with pots, shoelaces, and ribbons as they traveled the country. Cotton Mather recorded buying books from one in 1683, and he was certainly not the first. For only sixpence a customer could read "The Affective Narrative of the Loss of the Merchant Ship *Sally* . . . , with the Miraculous Deliverance of the Suffering Survivors," or "The History of Simmons the Pirate, Hanged in Boston," in lurid paper covers. In fact, one of the books sold by John Usher in Boston in 1685, rather surprisingly, was *The London Jilt, or the Politick Whore: Shewing All The Artifices and Stratagems Which Ladies of Pleasure Make Use of* . . . , *Interwoven with Several Pleasant Stories of the Misses' Ingenious Performances,* a title which might still cause a stir on the newsstands.

These chapbooks, imported from Europe and widely imitated in the colonies, were the principal medium for popular literature in early America. The "book agent" (Parson Weems was one of the better known) who sold house to house, was a familiar figure on the American scene throughout the eighteenth and nineteenth centuries. Selling books by auction or "vendue" began in the early eighteenth century, when Boston held one in 1713. The subscription library (Franklin's in Philadelphia was the first) came not long after, the ancestor of the rental libraries that were widespread in the nineteenth century. Boston had a public library in 1653, but the public library movement did not begin to expand until the early nineteenth century. There were always bookstores of course—more than two thousand of them across the country by the eighteen-fifties.

The emergence of a popular book market naturally depended on the appearance of a mass popular audience, which in turn derived from the great population explosion between 1790 and 1830, when the American public doubled in size and doubled again by 1860. As opposed to the British and European public, this was an educated audience, more than ninety per cent literate, one that already had the reading habit. Reading in the United States was not restricted to the well educated, the wealthy, or even the upper classes. In 1772 an English traveler remarked that everybody in America seemed to have "a prevailing taste for books of every kind, that made almost every man a reader. . . ." A London bookseller, traveling in 1791, noted with surprise that in America "all ranks and degrees now READ." Boston had fifty bookstores by the seventeen-seventies, Philadelphia and New York thirty or more, and peddlers hawked books up to the edge of Indian country in the backwoods. By 1825 the libraries of the five largest cities in America had twenty times more books to *lend* than the entire country *owned* in Washington's time.

Booksellers and publishers, during the eighteen-twenties, developed a different kind of relationship than before, one more to their mutual advantage. Whereas previously they had worked together to produce and sell a book, the publisher now printed it and sold it to the bookseller, who resold it to the customer at a profit. Book publishing thus became a separate, professionalized business venture; by the thirties several of the great publishing houses—Harper, Matthew Carey, Thomas, Cummins and Hilliard—were established in the major cities. Meanwhile the invention of improved oil lamps (later gas) meant more reading hours per day for everyone; the expanding network of roads and railroads meant cheaper and wider distribution for reading matter of any kind. And there was a great deal of it. In 1860 there were 575 magazines published in the United States, 372 daily newspapers, 2,971 weekly newspapers, and ten million dollars' worth of books each year.

Publishers could never have produced the acres of print demanded by this huge audience, however, without the help of a succession of technological innovations in the mechanics of printing. New processes for making paper improved the product after 1800; from 150 paper mills in the country in 1830 the number went to 400 in 1840, 550 in 1860, 742 in 1880, and so on. Stereotyping came in 1811, electrotyping in 1841. David Prince in 1813 invented the cast-plate, replacing the old plate of handset type that had to be broken up and reset.

New machines and methods seemed to appear every few years. Cheap cloth bindings, which drastically reduced costs, came after 1812; an improved bookbinding machine came in 1823; folding and sewing machines in the fifties, a backing machine in 1870, a gathering machine in 1900. During the 1830's the Napier and Hoe cylinder presses made the flatbed press obsolete; with steam power they could spin out thousands of impressions per hour from plates set by the new typesetters. The publishing industry by the eighteen-thirties could turn out books as rapidly and efficiently as shirts, nails, or matches.

The first revolution in cheap publishing came in the 1840's. The depression of 1837 nearly wiped out the book market, forcing publishers to try new methods of getting it back. One way to lower publishing costs, and thus price, was to use newspaper presses; a news sheet folded once, to make four pages, made a cheap book-like format. Furthermore, newspapers paid no special tax, were granted special mailing rates, and—in the person of the postmen—had free delivery service. Even subscription payments could be franked free in the mails.

Taking advantage of this, Rufus Griswold and Park Benjamin founded a weekly periodical in New York called *Brother Jonathan;* although they called it a newspaper, it was really a collection of fiction. Their success brought on the flood—*The New Yorker, The New World, The Corsair* (which openly pirated books), and a dozen others. Book publishers and regular newspapers retaliated with "supplements" on newsprint, selling them first at fifty cents, then at twenty-five cents, later at six-and-a-quarter cents. A few of the better papers sold actual twenty-cent books, printed on regular presses: Curry and Company, for example, printed Cooper, Scott, Dickens, and *The American Encyclopaedia* in this form. Some supplements had bright colored covers which in effect made them paperbound books; most were shipped unbound and coverless to avoid higher postal rates.

These "papers" and "supplements" might appear in editions from five to forty thousand, in competition with the regular book trade and particularly in competition with each other. After a time it all became somewhat ridiculous. Prices came down to five and six cents; issues increased in size and unwieldiness until a paper like *The Boston Notion* offered 104 square feet of reading for a nickel. After stealing material from everywhere and straining the energies of the hackwriting profession, the papers began to pall on the public. "Literature is now a drug," editorialized *Brother Jonathan* in 1843. "All the markets are over-stocked."

That same year, in April, the Post Office Department changed the situation by charging book rates for papers and supplements and took the bottom out of the market, but cheap books remained. The major publishing houses, among them Harper, Lea and Blanchard, Post, and others, kept their paper-covered books on the market for twenty-five to seventy-five cents, bringing out new ones from time to time. Never again was the American reading public without a low-priced, mass-produced book.

The domination of popular fiction by the so-called domestic novel during the mid-nineteenth-century decades reflected the recent appearance of women as a cultural, social, and economic force in American society. Woman, said the Boston *Token of Friendship* in 1844, is to life "the luminary that enlightens, and the talisman that endures"; she is, wrote editor James Buckingham, a goddess of "domestic fidelity, social cheerfulness, unostentatious hospitality, and moral and religious benevolence," possessed of stronger moral sense than man, "superior to him in aesthetic judgment." Nevertheless, as women constantly reminded men, they had really no more rights than the slaves; they were, as one feminist said, "superior *moral* beings with *inferior* legal and economic status."

When the profession of letters opened to women after 1830, many of them found it a source of considerable income and influence. Mary Agnes Fleming, for example, received a $15,000 yearly retainer from the *New York Weekly* for two stories a year; a writer of Mrs. Southworth's stature could virtually set her own price. The burgeoning of women's magazines —*Godey's, The National Magazine, The Casket, The Token,* and others—

demanded hundreds of sketches, stories and essays each month. What the market required was fiction that spoke directly to women, dealt with their problems, and instructed them in handling their affairs. The domestic novels, over and above their plots, taught women how to run a home and handle a husband. It was no accident that many of the best-selling female novelists also conducted household-hints columns or advice-and-counsel departments in the magazines, while some edited cookbooks, etiquette books, and guides to child care. The center of all this female literary activity, as one publisher put it succinctly, was "Home and Jesus."

These domestic novels were useful weapons in women's undeclared war against a male-oriented society. They were often anti-husband novels, written in a code quickly understood by the female reader, with plots built about husbands who drank, gambled, and chased, or they involved erring runaway daughters, sons who strayed, or sickness, poverty, and insecurity.

The aim of the domestic novel was simple, no different from Sarah Morton's or Samuel Richardson's: to teach a moral lesson. It combined three powerful elements—sex, sentiment, and religion—in a potent mixture. Sex was very much there, realistically though delicately handled. The books taught that conventional sexual morality was best, that deviation from it was dangerous, that immorality was punished by terrifying results. Sentimentalism soaked the novels in tears. "Take a brokenhearted Georgia beauty," wrote Rose Terry Cooke, who disliked the whole school of female novelists, "a fairy princess—a consumptive school mistress—an elderly lady with a drunken husband—a young woman dying of the perfidy of her lover," and you had the essentials. Religion in the novels was simple and uncomplicated; "the religion of the heart," as *The Lamplighter* called it, furnished the solution to almost any problem.

Whatever their sentimentality and didacticism, the novels also could exhibit spine-chilling realism. Often subtitled "Founded on Fact," or "Drawn From Real Life," or "A True History," they dealt with grasping landlords, grinding poverty, debtor's courts, devilish grog-shops, delirium tremens, prostitution, gambling dens, prison, suicide. Other social issues received little or no notice at all. One could read dozens of the domestic novels written between 1850 and 1870 without being aware of the slavery question, labor unrest, the settlement of the West, urban problems, or any issues of political importance. Caroline Lee Hentz, writing of Southern society in *Marcus Warland,* passed over Negro slavery quickly by calling it "a dark thread" which "lent a kind of lustre" to Southern life, whose "most beautiful lights and shades . . . are owing to the blending in of these sable filaments." To Sylvester Judd (one of the few males in this female-dominated field of fiction), Massachusetts mill girls lived "like princesses in an abode of enchantment," working twelve hours a day at their looms "as in the warmth, quiet, and beauty of a summer day." That life outside the novel was not always what the story said it was made little difference to the reader, so long as it focused on domestic issues.

Inside the home, however, the heroine, though grievously tried by events, nearly always established control if she did the right things. Mary Agnes Fleming's *Out of the Wreck* (1857); her twenty-fourth book, illustrated this pattern. Thomas Marshall, a wealthy and happily married businessman, suddenly takes to drink, gambling, and loose women. His wife, driven beyond endurance, takes the three children and leaves him, sets up a millinery shop, and prospers by hard work and good planning. She makes new friends, educates her children, and establishes a secure place for herself in society. When Marshall reappears, broke and dying, she dutifully nurses him through his last illness and—needing him no more—simply forgets about him while she continues her rise to riches and respectability. Perhaps the most characteristic and predictable theme of the domestic novel was the assurance that it gave to wives and mothers that they won out in the end, no matter what the world and husbands might do to them.

The domestic novel neither needed nor encouraged originality. Readers wanted no surprises, but confirmation of what they believed—that right won and wrong lost—and instruction in how to meet domestic crises such as drink, violence, improvidence, and misfortune. The novels soon developed a roster of stock characters: the Other Woman; the Loose Woman; the Handsome Seducer; the Sick Husband; the Crude Husband; the Weak Husband; the Brave Wife; the Old Sweetheart; the Dying Child; the Martyred Wife; the Woman of Finer Feelings, and so on, who still appear in women's magazines without noticeable change.

There were four basic plots. The Decline and Rise Plot traced the fall from fortune of a wife who struggled against great odds back toward security and happiness. The Pursuit Plot, which might involve an orphan girl, a widow, or a defenseless virgin, showed (as Richardson had in *Pamela*) that it was hard to be good, but worth it. In The Renunciation Plot the heroine gave up something—a lover, a fortune, a career—for something of much greater value, usually a husband and a home. The Domestic Tragedy Plot dealt with erring husbands, broken homes, tragic illnesses, and adversity. Like the stage melodramas and the Gothic romances, these plots used all the traditional devices—forged letters, birthmarks, disguises, accidental meetings, mistaken identities, babies exchanged in the cradle, drugs that brought on a trance, newly-discovered wills, lost heirs—without the slightest restraint or embarrassment.

Mrs. Catherine Maria Sedgwick's *Redwood* (1824) was one of the earliest successful domestic novels, but the great ones came in the fifties. Susan Warner's *Wide, Wide World* (1850) had everything, including an angelic heroine, a struggling poor family, good and bad fortune, tears and smiles, the rewards of faith and Christianity. The book did more good, wrote a reviewer, "than any book outside the Bible," went through fourteen editions in two years, and continued to sell for another forty. "Fanny Fern," or Sarah Payson Willis, (N. P. Willis' sister and the wife of biographer James Parton) wrote essays and stories for the magazines which she collected in *Fern Leaves from Fanny Fern's Portfolio* in 1850, which sold 100,000 copies its first year. In 1855 alone she published three books, each selling more than 75,000 copies.

In 1854 Maria Susan Cummins' *The Lamplighter*, the story of an orphan girl who grew up to find her long-lost father and marry a rich husband, swept the market. Mary Jane Holmes's books (and she averaged a book a year from 1854 to 1907) were published in editions of 50,000; some of her books, in fact, were still in print in the 1930's. Mrs. Marion Harland, whose *Alone* appeared in 1864, wrote sentimental historical romances year after year; *Alone* sold 100,000 a year for five years.

Augusta Jane Evans, of Mobile, Alabama, contributed *St. Elmo* (1866), a throwback to *Pamela*, in which a virtuous and likeable girl, Edna Earl, not only reforms and marries her rich, witty, dangerously attractive guardian, but persuades him to enter the ministry. Written with more than ordinary skill, *St. Elmo* still ranks among the thirty most popular novels published in the United States. The Queen of the Domestic Novel, however, was probably Mrs. E. D. E. N. (Emma Dorothy Eliza Nevite) Southworth, whose first novel, *Retribution*, sold 200,000 copies and who wrote sixty-one others; "every one," remarked the *Atlantic's* book editor, "a separate astonishment." Her combination sentimental-domestic-mystery novel, *The Hidden Hand*, appeared in forty dramatized versions and remained in print continuously for sixty-two years.

As Mrs. Southworth ruled the domestic novel by sheer volume if not by craft in the sixties and seventies, so Laura Jean Libbey ruled in the eighties and nineties. Under contract to six publishers at once, she enjoyed a yearly income of at least $75,000. It was she who brought the working-girl novel to its highest development—her contribution was an updated urban version of *Pamela*—in which a bright young clerk, typist, or seamstress fought off seduction and eventually married well. Mrs. Libbey, who knew exactly what her public wanted, gave the shopgirls books like *She Loved Him Last; The Price of a Kiss; Only a Mechanic's Daughter; The Romance of the Jolliest Girl at the Book Bindery; Madcap Laddie; Plot and Passion.* Since her total sales seem to have exceeded sixteen million books, she can be pardoned for writing in the preface to one, "By Laura Jean Libbey, the world's greatest living novelist, whose stories no author has ever been able to equal and whose fame as the favorite writer of the people has never been surpassed."

The domestic novel and its companions lost ground, after the Civil War, to local color stories and later to the historical romance, but it remained (and still remains) a powerful strain in popular fiction. The blend of sex, domestic life, adventure, and current problems that the lady novelists discovered never lost its appeal to the popular audience for which it was written. These novels were not art. They were accessible, inexpensive entertainment, the nineteenth-century's equivalent of Hollywood, daytime radio, and television. They did little harm apparently, if little good, but to millions of people leading humdrum lives they brought excitement, sentiment, and possibly more than a temporary sense of morality.

No male writer of the mid-century period approached the women authors in sales, though the closest was probably Sylvanus T. Cobb, a New Englander who could write women's novels as well as they could. In 1850 he began the full-time manufacture of fiction, maintaining a prodigious output to the day of his death twenty-three years later. Cobb had the formula so well in hand—melodrama, morality, sentiment, and romance—that Robert Bonner hired him to write exclusively for his New York *Ledger*, to which Cobb eventually contributed 2,305 items. Cobb's lifetime total, by his own count, was 122 novels, 937 pieces of shorter fiction, and 2,143 essays and sketches. All of his books sold well, and his best novel, a sentimental-historical story, *The Gunmaker of Moscow* (1888), remained popular for many years.

Neither Timothy Shay Arthur nor George Lippard tried to compete with the women in their chosen specialty. Arthur's formula for reform novels, half-narrative and half-tract, hit the market exactly right. He chose a timely issue (temperance, imprisonment for debt, gambling, juvenile delinquency), built a simple plot around it, and closed the story with a moral. In a burst of energy, he produced fifty books in eight years (1842–1850) and then settled down to editing three magazines and publishing twenty-five more novels.

Arthur's *Ten Nights in a Barroom: and What I Saw There* (1854), published at the height of the temperance crusade, was the biggest seller of the era, second only to *Uncle Tom's Cabin*. Bound in black and gold, with a picture on the cover of a little girl grasping her father's arm and saying, "Father, come home!" the book sold a steady 100,000 a year for twenty years; turned into a play in 1858, it stayed on the stage for another fifty. The novel was a triple story: of Joe Morgan, an honest workman ruined by drink; of Frank Slade, who murdered his father in a drunken rage; and of Judge Hammond, driven by drink from bench to gutter. Naïve, badly written, and dripping with emotion, Arthur's book nevertheless had a ring of sincerity that his audience found extremely effective.

George Lippard left both the law and the ministry to become a police-court reporter in Philadelphia. He published his first novel in 1842, and in 1844 began a serial, *The Monks of Monk Hill* (later called *The Quaker City*), a half-fictional exposé of vice in the city. Its enormous sales encouraged Lippard to make it into a play, banned by the Philadelphia authorities, which he moved to New York with great success. Not a specialist, he wrote whatever would sell—sentimental romance (*Bel of Prairie Eden*), historical fiction (*Washington and His Men*), mysteries (*The Man with the Mask*)—while contributing stories and sketches each week to four magazines.

The semi-fictional, journalistic, sensational novel, as Lippard practiced it, had a long and honorable history, reaching back to Fielding's *Jonathan Wild* and Defoe's *Moll Flanders*. Lippard happened to be its most expert practitioner at the time, but similar books appeared in profusion throughout the fifties and sixties, with titles like *The Libertine Enchanters; or the Adventures of Lucinda Hartley; Confessions of a Washington Belle; The Beautiful Creole of Austria; The Adventures of Anna, A New York Belle; The Child of Passion;* or *The Amorous Foundling*—ancestors of the lurid sex novels that filled paperback racks a century later.

E. Z. C. Judson ("Ned Buntline"), wrote an early successful one, *The Curse: a Tale of Crime and its Retribution, Founded on Real Life*, in 1847, and others such as *The Death Mystery: A Crimson Tale of Life in New York* (1861) and *The Lady Thief* (1866). He was best known, however, for *The Mysteries and Miseries of New York* (1848, patterned after Eugène Sue's *Mysteries of Paris*) a collection of stories, Judson said, "drawn from *life, too-real life*, written with the ink of truth." In New York there were, he claimed, 18,000 prostitutes, 5000 thieves, 5000 grog shops, 2000 gambling halls, and 1000 brothels. His stories may well have been real, and were certainly lurid: a thug serves as secretary to a rich old man so that he may rob and murder him; a clerk gambles his way into hopeless debt, embezzles, murders, and finally kills himself; a working girl who supports a widowed mother tries to protect her honor from a rascally rich man. In the last instance, Angelina rejected her pursuer in Judson's richest dramatic dialogue:

> "Sir, I do not love you. No man living can claim my hand who does not possess my heart; No, not were he possessed of uncounted gold, and I had to work the hand that refused him to the bare bones."
> "Oh, do not speak so! You shall be mine!"
> "Never, never, sir, *never*," she replied proudly and firmly. "If it is this which has caused your bounty to my poor mother, take it back. We can return to our cellar, we can work, and earn enough to keep us alive."
> "Foolish girl, you know not what you refuse. Beware how you push my love from you, for you can be made to feel that a slighted lover may become a bitter enemy."
> "I care not, sir! My trust is in God! You cannot harm me, for He, the All-Powerful, is my protector!"

The book named names, provided addresses of gambling places and brothels, and included a glossary of "flash" underworld slang. It was so successful that Judson followed it with a similar exposé of New Orleans in 1851.

Lippard's and Judson's "inside" books attracted many imitators, among them Edward Crapsey's *The Nether Side of New York* (1872), C. E. Rogers' *The Secret Sins of Society* (1882), J. G. Grant's ("The Pinkerton Man") *The Evils of San Francisco* (1884), and George Stevens' *Chicago: Wicked City* (1896). A hardy perennial, this kind of novel flowered decade after decade in the popular market, and still persists in the "confidential" books of today.

St. Elmo, with its heavy religious emphasis, became the progenitor of a particular kind of religious novel, constructed around either a principle or a person. In the first instance it might be, as in Elizabeth Stuart Phelps' *Gates Ajar* (1868), an affirmation of immortality. Mrs. Phelps' novel, the first of three on the same theme, showed that the soul and personality of the departed lived forever in an almost literal Heaven that resembled a happy home on earth, a message of great solace to a generation that had lost a million young men in war. The doubts and skepticisms raised by agnostics like Ingersoll and scientists like Darwin and Huxley, added to the restlessness and violence of a changed postwar society, disturbed many Americans who found in novels like the Reverend E. P. Roe's *Barriers Burned Away* (1872) the solidity and reassurance of faith they needed. Roe, a Presbyterian minister, used the Chicago fire as background for the story of a young man's conversion from doubt to faith; the book was so successful that Roe turned to writing full time, using the formula with variations in eighteen more novels, all successful. Without Roe, neither Harold Bell Wright nor Lloyd Douglas would have found such an eager public, though of course Mrs. Humphry Ward's English novel, *Robert Elsemere* (1880), also helped to popularize the theme.

The great religious novel of the century, and quite likely the greatest of its kind of all time, was Lew Wallace's *Ben Hur: A Tale of the Christ,* which appeared in 1880, and is still selling today. Wallace, a Civil War general who later served as governor of New Mexico Territory and minister to Turkey, was inspired by Prescott's *History of Mexico* to write *The Fair God,* a best-selling historical novel in 1873. He apparently also had a biblical novel in mind when a chance conversation with Robert Ingersoll, the era's best known agnostic, shocked him into writing it.

After a slow start *Ben Hur* suddenly caught on, reaching a quarter-million people in its first decade, a million during its second, and eventually between four and five million in total sales. A nationwide survey in 1896 showed that eight of every ten libraries circulated *Ben Hur* more than any other book. A spectacular stage version in 1889 fixed it permanently in the all-time best-seller list; Sears, Roebuck, and Company sold over a million copies by mail order, the stage version ran for thirty-five years, and movies produced it three times.

Wallace's book was the perfect mixture of religion, adventure, romance, and melodrama. The narrative concerned an aristocratic young Jew who became a Roman officer, battled his false friend Messala for success and survival, and eventually was converted to Christianity by Jesus' example. The focus of the novel is on Ben Hur's conversion from arrogant doubter to humble Christian; the swift-moving action of the story (emphasized in the stage and movie versions) centers on his rivalry with Messala, climaxed in the famous chariot race. To Wallace's generation the book's affirmation of Christianity and its evangelical tone held great appeal, but long after the religious message lost its impact, *Ben Hur* kept selling as a historical novel.

Ben Hur pointed the way toward the historical romance, *sans* message, really a recrudescence of the Scott-Cooper strain popularized half a century earlier. If Wallace could make biblical history exciting, why not use the American Revolution, or the Civil War, or the French Revolution, or the Roman conquest, or medieval chivalry, or the Indian wars? Francis Marion Crawford (a nephew of Julia Ward Howe) chose Europe, usually Italy, as the setting for forty-five novels which the public eagerly bought. Crawford, a superb storyteller, believed that the purpose of the novel

was "to amuse and interest" the reader, not to instruct him or to "paint
reality." Since the most characteristic human emotion was love, Crawford
explained, this ought to be the subject of the "romance"; the novelist's
function was that of "public amuser," to write about "things as we should
like them to be. . . ." So while William Dean Howells was developing
the realistic novel that would lead to Stephen Crane, Frank Norris, and
Theodore Dreiser, Crawford was writing novels such as *A Cigarette-
Maker's Romance; A Roman Singer; Children of the King;* and *Don
Orsino,* for which he could get a minimum advance of $10,000. Crawford
knew precisely what the public wanted—not what he called "the dissatis-
factions of life," but good stories, well told, that neither exhorted nor reformed and came out right in the end.

The historical romance dominated popular fiction until the 1920's and
still remains one of the three most popular types of American fiction.
Imports from Europe competed with the American product in the nineties and after, among them Ouida's *Under Two Flags* (1867, with its
soiled heroine, Cigarette, later played in the movies by Claudette Colbert); Rider Haggard's great imaginative-fantasy novels of Africa, *King
Solomon's Mines* (1887) and *She* (1887); Blackmore's *Lorna Doone* (1869).
Many of the novels oversimplified history, made much of candlelight,
wigs, snuff boxes, and swords, and copied Scott, Thackeray, and each other
endlessly. Charles Major's *When Knighthood Was in Flower* (1898), a
blend of Scott and Malory set "in olde Englande," ran away with the market that year and later became a successful movie.

Paul Leicester Ford's *Janice Meredith* (1899), a novel about the
American Revolution by a distinguished historian, sold a quarter-million
copies and inspired a fashionable hair style, the "Janice curl," which hung
over the right shoulder. Maurice Thompson, an Indiana lawyer, wrote
Alice of Old Vincennes, an adventure-love story set against George
Rogers Clark's Indiana campaign of 1779. Mary Johnston, a Virginia lady
who eventually wrote twenty-three historical romances, mostly Southern,
published *To Have and To Hold* (1900), based on the Virginia colony of
1621, in which the hero rescued an innocent English girl from a villain
with the unlikely name of Lord Carnal.

Archibald Clavering Gunter, a chemist who made a fortune as a
stockbroker, evolved a different pattern for the romance. To him history
was less important than cultural contrast (as it was to Henry James), so
he invented a brash, cheerful American named Mr. Barnes (a descendant
of Twain's Connecticut Yankee) who kept getting involved in foreign
intrigues, fighting his way out, and winning the girl. He first appeared in
Mr. Barnes of New York in 1887, which sold so well that Gunter used the

formula again in thirty-eight more books in which his hero (a crack shot, trained surgeon, champion athlete, expert hunter, shrewd diplomat, scholarly scientist, or whatever he needed to be) triumphed over scheming, inferior foreigners. Gunter could see no reason to share royalties with a publisher, so he organized his own company and published exactly two books a year. Though he invented another character, a dashing American millionaire named F. N. Fresh, he never replaced "the incredible Mr. Barnes" in the public's affections.

The tremendous success of Anthony Hope's *Prisoner of Zenda*, a British novel that went through twenty-six printings in its American edition of 1897, created the cloak and sword romance, or pseudo-historical novel. Hope set his swashbuckling, sentimental story of adventure and love in the mythical kingdom of Ruritania, with a highly colored history of its own. (The book appeared in a new quarter-million edition in 1946 and is still found on paperback racks.) A number of Americans imitated him, including oldtimer F. Marion Crawford, but the most successful of them was a newspaperman, George Barr McCutcheon, who invented the kingdom of Graustark in his novel of the same name in 1901. McCutcheon's badly-written and naïvely-conceived novels had yet a touch of inspiration; he took Gunter's athletic American hero, put him through Hope-like adventures in the romantic land of Graustark, and let him marry the Princess after beating the decadent aristocrats at their shady game. *Graustark* sold 150,000 copies in six months, while McCutcheon's publishers were besieged with requests for maps of the country by enthralled readers who wanted to go there. McCutcheon wrote fifty more novels, most of which sold in the hundreds of thousands, and for a long time made "Graustark" a part of the language.

To Americans at the turn of the century these books brought escape from the troubles of an uncertain, restless society. Their heroes were brave, handsome and resourceful; heroines were beautiful and pure; endings were happy and virtues familiar and simple. Not all of these novels were mediocre. Winston Churchill, by far the best of the popular novelists of the period, brought his considerable talents to bear on the historical novel in *Richard Carvel* (1899), a story of the American Revolution that remained high on best-seller lists for ten years. Churchill did historical romances well: *The Crisis* (1901) was one of the better Civil War novels, and *The Crossing* (1904), about the westward migration, still has historical validity.

Churchill's two political-problem novels, *Coniston* (1906) and *Mr. Crewe's Career* (1913), were excellent specimens of another popular contemporary strain, the novel that, like contemporary muckraking journalism, "told the truth." The father of them all, Upton Sinclair's *The Jungle*, shook the public in 1906, a book about the Chicago meatpacking industry that Sinclair began as a socialist tract but which turned out to be a brutally realistic exposure of big business. Sinclair kept on with novels exposing journalism, oil, politics, the church, and the courts, while *The Jungle* became a kind of American classic, still in print and still read widely in the schools. David Graham Phillips, a more expert novelist than Sinclair, who had already begun to mine this vein with *The Master Rogue* (1903, banking) and *The Deluge* (1905, Wall Street), continued with *The Light Fingered Gentry* (1907, insurance), to a total of twenty-three novels. A consistent favorite, the "muckraking" or "exposé" novel moved into the 1920's without losing any of its popularity.

The bad historical romance faded after 1900, when the public began to accept only the better ones. The imitators and unskilled dropped out, unpublished manuscripts were put away, and the popular audience looked for a new favorite. Elinor Glyn's *Three Weeks* (1907) indicated what that might be. Mrs. Glyn, an Englishwoman, created a "Graustarkian" kingdom, provided it with a beautiful princess, and then gave her three weeks of torrid lovemaking with a handsome young Englishman, including a famous seduction scene on a tiger-skin rug. This was Hope and McCutcheon with sex, and the public loved it; banned in Boston, the book sold 50,000 copies the first month, 100,000 within six months, and a steady two hundred and fifty a day for several years.

Her sales quickly brought Mrs. Glyn to the United States to capitalize on the book, which she did with great skill, writing articles, feature stories, novels, and movie scripts for Rudolph Valentino and Gloria Swanson. She had a hilarious interview with Mark Twain, who was impressed by the fact that "the Englishman and the queenlet," as he called them, not only "obeyed the natural demands of passion" in that lonely house in the mountains but "kept on obeying them, while the process of obeying them is described several times, almost exhaustively, but not quite." He wrote later that "it was one of the damnedest conversations I ever had with a beautiful stranger of her sex."

Mrs. Glyn, however, stayed in fashion for a good many years, and in 1927, in a magazine article, defined sexual appeal as "It," which soon became a national byword and a successful movie starring Clara Bow, "the It Girl." *Three Weeks*, which sold steadily, pointed in one direction toward the bad-girl, flapper novels of the twenties, and in another toward the bosom-and-bravado historical novels of the thirties. Probably the worst novelist after Sylvanus Cobb, Mrs. Glyn nevertheless occupies a permanent place in the history of American popular fiction.

Swashbuckling romance and titillating sex, however, did not displace the average novel reader's interest in simple things and old-fashioned values. The American's long-standing distrust of the city, deriving from the agrarianism of Jefferson's time and the "nature" writings of the Romantic poets, reappeared with renewed vigor in the nineties, when writers like Stephen Crane and Frank Norris (with the help of reformers like Jacob Riis and Jane Addams) made the problems of the cities seem almost insoluble. The nation's nostalgia for simpler times evoked a whole school of "country life" novels, affirming the virtue and placidity of small town and rural life. Though James Lane Allen's mystical, sentimental stories of the bluegrass country, *A Kentucky Cardinal* (1894) and *The Choir Invisible* (1897) made a tentative beginning, F. Hopkinson Smith had already created the popular character of "Colonel Carter," a charming and courtly rustic gentleman, in *Colonel Carter of Cartersville* (1891). Edward Westcott, an upstate New York banker, established the type permanently with *David Harum: A Story of American Life*, in 1898. A novel about wise and gentle country folk who settle problems with Christian kindness, the book recalled a simpler, purer idealized society whose image appealed powerfully to the times.

Harum, a Yankee horsetrader descended from a long line of stage Jonathans, soon became virtually a folklore figure, while the book sold three-quarters of a million copies within two years; later, with Will Rogers in the title role, it was a highly successful movie. Westcott died shortly before his book appeared, but Irving Bacheller's *Eben Holden*, copied directly from Harum, sold 250,000 on its own in 1900. John Fox Jr., another Kentuckian, combined local color regionalism and rural sentiment in two popular novels, *The Little Shepherd of Kingdom Come* (1903) and *The Trail of the Lonesome Pine* (1908), both of which made even more successful stage plays.

But nothing could displace the older domestic novel as a steady favorite; it simply adapted itself to a changing society. Laura Jean Libbey kept on writing and selling, challenged only by Grace Livingston Hill, who wrote her first novel in 1882 and her eightieth just before her death in 1947. In the interval Mrs. Hill's others sold more than four million; they were pleasant, relaxing, wholesome novels absolutely free of ideas, perfect for hammock, bed, or parlor reading. Her heroines tended not to use lipstick and after a few romantic adventures, quietly found, as Dora did, "a way of life that brings happiness, satisfaction, and inspiration." They had enough suspense to maintain the reader's interest, liberal quantities of quite conventional courtship and love, and uniformly satisfactory endings, "inspiring faith, nobility of spirit, and a ringing sense of life's beauty," in the words of an admirer. *The Best Man,* a little more active than most, was "the story of a young hero pursued by desperate criminals straight into the arms of a pale and enigmatic girl who calls him her husband." *Ariel Custer* concerned "the wisdom and courage of a fragile Virginia beauty who wins the respect of a suspicious mother and a high-born rival when danger threatens the man they all love." In *Crimson Roses* "a young girl discovers the thrill of romance when a secret admirer enters her solitary life." Twenty-one years after her death there were fifteen of her novels in print, a boxed set of eight for four dollars. Critics and males may not recognize her name, but Mrs. Hill's novels have been to three generations of women one of the eternal verities, like the change of seasons. In 1968 she still had ten books on the list of paperback best sellers, and a guaranteed sale of 200,000 for any re-issued novel.

The sentimental-domestic novel as Mrs. Hill wrote it differed in at least one important respect from that of her predecessors—it was suffused with determined cheerfulness, smiles instead of tears, games instead of crises. Happiness will come, her message read, if you expect it. Alice Hegan Rice, in *Mrs. Wiggs of the Cabbage Patch* (1901), which despite its title was set in a city slum, was the first to appropriate Mrs. Hill's cheerfulness and make it a major theme of the "glad books." Mrs. Wiggs' philosophy of life, "Looks like evr'thing in the world comes out right, if we jes' wait long enough," became a popular catch phrase while the book sold 40,000 copies a month for the next three years, appeared in seven stage dramatizations, four times in the movies, and became a radio serial in the thirties.

Kate Douglas Wiggin's *Rebecca of Sunnybrook Farm,* written two years later, outsmiled even Mrs. Wiggs. The story of a bright, happy orphan girl raised on a farm by her aunts, *Rebecca* played for years on the stage and emerged in the movies with Mary Pickford. Lucy Montgomery's *Anne of Green Gables* (1908), written by a Canadian lady, followed the same pattern, while Eleanor Porter, who wrote as "Eleanor Stewart," produced the ultimate in *Pollyanna, The Glad Girl* in 1913, whose name eventually achieved dictionary status as a synonym for blind optimism.

Gene Stratton-Porter, a druggist's wife who lived in northern Indiana at the edge of the Limberlost forest, joined the cheerfulness of the glad books with a love story and added a third element, the nature-loving sentimentality of the currently popular outdoor school of John Muir, John Burroughs, Ernest Thompson Seton, and Theodore Roosevelt. She began with an incredibly mawkish story about love and marriage among the birds, *The Song of the Cardinal* (1903), an immediate hit. Sensing that she had something valuable, she followed with *Freckles* (1904), an orphan boy in the Limberlost. Her formula was a good one—sentimentality, faith and optimism, innocence and trust, nostalgia for country life, the curative and educational powers of Nature (with a capital N). She followed *Freckles* with nineteen books, among them *The Girl of the Limberlost* (1909), *The Harvester* (1911), *Laddie* (1913), *Michael O'Halloran* (1915), and on to the last, *The Keeper of the Bees,* published a year after her death, in 1925.

Five of Mrs. Porter's books sold more than five million copies; perhaps half her books are still in print. Called "molasses fiction" by critics and ridiculed for their sentimentality, her novels nonetheless became, someone said, public institutions like the national park system, and her home in Indiana a tourist shrine. She received thousands of letters from discouraged, hopeless readers which she answered with graceful sincerity. "I shall keep straight on writing of the love of joy and of life I have found in the world," she said, "and when I have used the last drop of molasses, I shall stop writing."

The "happy" novels satisfied one segment of the popular market; the "man story" appealed to another. Usually advertised as "action packed" or "powerfully adventurous," they provided clerks, bookkeepers, grocers, schoolteachers, and stay-at-homes with the escape they needed from the pettinesses of life. Tailored to masculine tastes, these stories dealt in melodrama of the "great outdoors" of lumbering, mining, sailing, ranching, exploration, and hunting. Filled with violence and love unsullied by sex, usually set in some woodsy or exotic locale, they flooded the market after 1900.

The Call of the Wild (1903) and *The Sea Wolf* (1904) placed Jack London among the best known writers in the field, where he still remains; both novels are still in print and have sold over a million copies each. London made the masculine novel peculiarly his own, drawing on his colorful, violent, and ultimately tragic life for his plots. Laid in Alaska, the South Seas, the prize ring, the West, the waterfront, wherever there was action and adventure, London's best novels were nearly first-rate; his worst, turned out by the ream to satisfy his creditors, were merely hackwork. Yet he produced more than enough good stories to belong at the head of the list of those who specialized in men-with-the-bark-on novels.

Rex Beach, capitalizing on the gold rush, specialized in the Klondike —*The Barrier* (1908), *The Silver Horde* (1909), *The Net* (1912), and his most popular, *The Spoilers* (1906), famous for its description of a bloody fight. *The Spoilers* was made into a movie four times, with William Farnum in 1914, Milton Sills in 1922, Gary Cooper in 1930, and John Wayne in 1942. James Oliver Curwood wrote twenty-six books—the best known *The Valley of Silent Men* (1920)—about lumbering, fishing, and hunting. Stewart Edward White, who ranked second only to London in production, divided his fifty books between adventure tales laid in the gold and lumber camps, Mexico, the mountains, and Africa, among them *The Blazed Trail* (1903), *The Riverman* (1908), *The Cabin* (1910), and *The Land of Footprints* (1912). Owen Wister opened the West to popular fiction. An Easterner, he used a brief stay at a Wyoming ranch as the base for *The Virginian* in 1902. A wholesome, vigorous novel, centered on the soft-spoken, chivalric, and thoroughly masculine hero-figure of the Virginian, the book passed a million copies in 1920; it went into the movies twice, and still in print, it has since provided the title (and nothing else) for a television serial. Even by contemporary standards of popular fiction, *The Virginian* was not a particularly good book; its fame derived almost wholly from its subject matter—the cowboy West—and its chief service was to pave the way for Zane Grey.

The man who put it all together—sentiment, love, masculine conflict, moral message, and the outdoors—was Harold Bell Wright, a minister of the Disciples of Christ, a gentle, simple man with a great understanding of the public taste in fiction. E. P. Roe, Charles Sheldon, and Mrs. Humphry Ward prepared the public for the religious novel; Lew Wallace added action and melodrama; Wright put the two together with apt if unconscious skill. *That Printer of Udell's* (1903), his first book, sold well; "an inspiring and uplifting novel," the reviews said, "with a valuable message for the times." The message, which appeared in much the same form in all of Wright's subsequent novels, was simple and clear—believe in Christ's principles, live by Christian faith, and most of life's problems will fade away. His books were awkward, mawkish, and ingenuous. His characters sermonized, his plots creaked, and he repeated all the melodramatic clichés—rascally villains, pure heroines, suffering orphans, unbelievably virtuous heroes—but the public forgave him all his flaws.

The sale of Wright's second novel, *The Shepherd of the Hills* (1907), exceeded his first; by the time of *The Calling of Dan Matthews* in 1909 any novel he published was an automatic best seller. His first three books passed the half-million mark in 1910; his next, *The Winning of Barbara Worth* (1911), carried an advertising budget of $75,000, marking the beginnings of modern sales promotion in popular fiction. Wright also developed other sales techniques, among them a postcard inserted in each copy of a book, which the reader could send to a friend, recommending it or another Wright novel as "one of the best I have ever read." The postcard contained useful quotations from the novel, and booksellers were provided with stacks of them, so that a collector could obtain the entire series. Wright also gladly sold the rights to his novels to tent-show playwrights, whose adaptations played to millions of people who were likely to buy the book after having seen the play.

Wright, who shrewdly calculated his market potential, owned half of the firm which published his books, and settled down to one novel every two years, each carefully advertised in advance, a schedule he maintained until 1934. Although the sales of his novels were never spectacular—*The Recreation of Brian Kent* (1919) was his last big success at 900,000 copies—they sold well until the thirties. Changing popular tastes and the appearance of writers with a better sense of the market reduced the sales of his biennial books sharply, so that his last, *The Man Who Went Away* (1942) went virtually unnoticed.

Wright was one of the five most popular novelists during the first quarter of the twentieth century; he wrote four books which sold over a million copies, and his nineteen books sold a total of over ten million. What he had to say he said honestly and directly, albeit with incredible naïveté and oversimplification—return to the verities of Christian faith, take responsibility for your neighbor, find satisfaction in service. "Behind the melodrama, the sentimentality, and the mawkishness of a Wright novel," wrote a critic somewhat grudgingly in *The Bookman* in 1915, "we do glimpse life, human nature, genuine joy . . . , and the standards of religion, morals, and practical living for the majority of people."

When America entered World War I the best-selling popular novelists were Winston Churchill, Gene Stratton-Porter, Harold Bell Wright, Zane Grey, and Mary Roberts Rinehart, whose first mystery story appeared in 1908 and last in 1953. At the close of the war, the main categories of American popular fiction were fully established, and still remain: the novel of adventure, including war and Western stories (descended from the "man's story" school); the love story with varying admixtures of sex (from Laura Jean Libbey and the working-girl school); the moral or religious novel (from Roe, Stratton-Porter, and Wright); the historical romance (from Churchill, McCutcheon, and the rest); the domestic novel (from Grace Livingston Hill and the home-life school); the exposé (from Lippard, Phillips, and Sinclair); and the mystery-detective (out of Poe, Conan Doyle, and Mary Roberts Rinehart).

NOVELS IN THE MARKETPLACE

Sex is what this great big book is all about and it's going to be a great big best seller.

—PUBLISHER'S ADVERTISEMENT, 1968.

Changes in American public tastes, temperament, and morals after 1918 were immediately reflected in the materials and attitudes of popular fiction. Many of the old favorites still sold, but the facts of a new society, influenced deeply by war, the assembly line, prosperity and depression, permissive psychology, and new kinds of communications media (movies, radio, and later television) demanded new variations within the traditional framework of popular fiction. The Supreme Court ruling on *Ulysses* in 1919 and a succession of subsequent rulings marked significant changes in moral standards which writers were quick to sense and quick to capitalize on.

The most obvious ingredient added to popular fiction after 1920 was sex, treated openly and aggressively, in contrast to the indirection and implication by which it was introduced into the popular fiction of the nineties. As James Hart pointed out in his study of popular books, the first choice for the new Modern Library reprint series in 1918 was Oscar Wilde's *Picture of Dorian Grey,* a book considered indecent when it was published in 1891. In the twenties *True Story* magazine, the chief periodical purveyor of sex to the masses, grew from 300,000 to a million circulation in three years. What Dreiser, Crane, Norris, and the "realists" did in the serious novel had its effects on the popular story; what Hollywood did with its amazingly suggestive "epics" of the twenties augmented it; what Elinor Glyn started in 1907 invited more and shrewder practitioners.

The great publishing innovation of the twentieth century—the paper-bound book—had its origins actually in the mid-nineteenth. Erastus Beadle, the shrewd publisher of dime novels, proved that cheap, paper-backed novels would sell like the proverbial hot cakes during the Civil War, when he sold four million copies in the army camps. After the war publishers plunged into the paperback market and their sales boomed for the rest of the century; in 1877 there were fifteen such series selling from ten to sixty cents each. To avoid paying postal rates, publishers made arrangements with news companies to place their books on news-stands, opening up a new channel of distribution.

The next marketing innovation came not in price but in format—the "pocket size" book, which appeared first in 1879. This handy-sized volume dominated the popular market for the next twenty years, not with "dime shockers," which still sold well at the lower market levels, but with a better grade of fiction. In 1887 *The American Bookseller* reported twenty-six "pocket libraries" in regular publication, sold everywhere from book-stores to department stores. Funk and Wagnalls, for that matter, sold its series by mail to a list of 16,000 subscribers who received two books a month, thereby becoming the first of the book clubs. But as it had in the forties, the tide of cheap books began to overwhelm the public. "I am conscious of a feeling of nausea at the mere sight of a row of paperbacks," wrote an editor in 1888, and furthermore, the International Copyright Act of 1891 halted publishing piracy and changed the nature of reprint pub-lishing.

The cheap cloth-bound book (whether published in series, individ-ually, or as a reprint) and the paper-covered, pocket-sized book consti-tuted the mainstays of the popular, mass market over the first thirty years of the twentieth century. The third publishing revolution, like the first, followed a depression—this time in 1929—which once more severely dam-aged the book market, once more saved by the intervention of new technological and marketing techniques. The industry developed methods of printing book pages on the same high speed presses designed for maga-zines, as well as methods of making durable laminated covers; new syn-thetic glues made "perfect" binding possible, that is, a binding in which each sheet is held firmly to each other single sheet. These and other devices lowered production costs considerably, so that the paperback book came rushing back into the mass market along with new and aggres-sive merchandizing methods.

Several series of paperbacks originated in the thirties—Bonibooks, Modern Age Books, Triangle Books, the American Mercury series, the Whitman series—but Robert de Graff's Pocket Books, selling at twenty-five cents, broke the market wide open in June, 1939, with a reprint of Pearl Buck's *The Good Earth*. Admittedly a gamble, it paid off; Higbee's department store in Cleveland, for example, sold 2,000 copies in the first six hours, and that was only a beginning. Within ten years Pocket Books (fifty-two of which sold a million each) had sold six hundred titles and 260 million books.

As they did in the Civil War, the armed forces in World War II devoured them by the millions; special Armed Forces Editions, distributed free to servicemen at the rate of fifty titles a week, made readers out of hundreds of thousands of young men. And as they had in the eighties, paperback publishers distributed their books through wholesalers and news companies, widening the market eventually to include drugstores, grocery stores, gas stations, airports, railroad stations, and so on. Although there were fewer than 5,000 bookstores in the country in the sixties, there were about 100,000 establishments of one sort or another selling low-priced books. In 1968 there were approximately 585 publishers selling 63,000 paperback titles to the amount of a sixty-six million dollars a year.

The first of the new-style popular sex novelists after Elinor Glyn was an Englishwoman, Edith M. Hull. *The Sheik* (1921), the story of an innocent English girl, kidnapped and initiated into the pleasures of love by a glamorous Arab chief, was hidden under pillows in dormitories and smuggled into boudoirs by the thousands. Attacked for its suggestiveness (*The Literary Review* called it "poisonously salacious") *The Sheik* sold 1,200,000 copies and led the bestseller list for two years. Made into a movie starring Rudolph Valentino, it encouraged thousands of young men to copy the exotic masterful Latin look and added a word to the current vocabulary.

Mrs. Hull followed with *The Son of the Sheik* (1925) and was herself followed by a spate of imitators for the next several years. An outrageously bad book, *The Sheik* nevertheless introduced millions of readers to more or less passionate sexual descriptiveness, sufficiently removed geographically from the American scene to make it the more fascinating. Gertrude Atherton's *Black Oxen*, the sensation of 1923, reported in detail the sexual rejuvenation of an elderly heroine by means of a gland transplant, giving vicarious pleasure to thousands of aging women and hope to thousands of younger ones.

The public read Michael Arlen's flippant tale of nymphomania, *The Green Hat* (1924), for its lurid passages, but Percy Marks' *The Plastic Age*, published the same year, caused an explosion. A novel of college life which exposed (and tacitly approved) sexual promiscuity, the book was among the first to use words like "petting" and "jazz" with sexual connotations, contained "damn" and "hell," and made open reference to venereal disease, eliciting both angry attacks and solemn approval from clergy, educators, parents, students, and the public at large. Marks, an instructor at Brown University, turned to writing as his vocation and published more than a dozen subsequent novels exploring contemporary manners and morals, though never again with the same success.

Viña Delmar put sex into the lives of Laura Jean Libbey's working girls; *Bad Girl* (1928) not only contained a casual love affair but a realistic description of pregnancy. Miss Delmar continued the sexual saga of career girls in *Loose Ladies* (1929), *Kept Women* (1929), *Women Live Too Long* (1932), and *The Marriage Racket* (1932). Her numerous short stories became staple fare in women's magazines, and after a twenty-year absence she returned to write four more novels in the fifties, some of which still sell moderately well. Fanny Hurst, in a number of novels and especially in *Back Street* (1931) improved on Viña Delmar's stories of secretaries and clerks, but not by much.

Pearl Buck's *The Good Earth* (1932) and Charles Morgan's *The Fountain* (1932) helped readers to find hope and affirmation during the depression years. The most popular spokesman for faith was an Englishman, James Hilton, whose *Lost Horizon* (1933) was a tale of a tired, disillusioned man's discovery of a peaceful Utopia in Tibet. To a generation facing depression at home, the cloud of fascism in Europe, and the threat of war, Hilton's novel said exactly the right thing, and "Shangri-La," the name of the Tibetan monastery where the novel's protagonist found peace and personal fulfillment, replaced "utopia" in the public's vocabulary. *Lost Horizon*, which sold only 3,300 copies its first year, suddenly spurted to 6,000 a month in 1934; and its choice as one of the first titles of a new twenty-five cent paperbound series put it in the hands of thousands of readers. Hilton's story of a kindly schoolmaster, *Goodbye, Mr. Chips* (1934) again led the best-seller lists, and so did his next five books. Book clubs distributed more than two million Hilton novels, making him one of the most popular writers of the thirties and forties, to which his slightly sentimental, deeply affirmative narratives had especial appeal.

Popular fiction in the thirties, however, was dominated by the historical romance, its saleability undiminished from the days of Major, McCutcheon, and Mary Johnston, but with an added sexual explicitness they would hardly have approved. Since the public clearly wanted sex in its novels, it was easy to add it to history. Hervey Allen's *Anthony Ad-*

verse, published in 1933, was actually a throwback to the ancient and honorable picaresque tradition, tracing a handsome young hero through the wars and bedrooms of the Napoleonic era in 1,200 pages of quite expertly-tailored narrative. The first novel to be advertised by weight, *Anthony Adverse* sold 275,000 copies within the year (in the midst of the depression), passed the million mark in 1939, two million in 1946, and is approaching three million in a 1968 reissue.

But even Anthony's success paled before Margaret Mitchell's *Gone With the Wind* (1936), a book nearly as long as Allen's and a more adroit mixture of romance, war, sex, and history, told with considerable skill and accuracy. Although it bore traces of the magnolia-and-happy-darkies school of southern fiction, it also had tough realism of its own. Scarlett O'Hara, the book's heroine, done in the tradition of Thackeray's Becky Sharp, and Rhett Butler, the dangerously handsome Byronic villain (expertly played by Clark Gable in the movie version of 1939) were fictional creations of some validity. At the time of her accidental death in 1949, Mrs. Mitchell's single novel had sold eight million copies (a year after publication it still sold at the rate of 50,000 copies a day), and a two-volume paper edition, reissued in 1967, sold another 150,000.

The second publishing phenomenon of the decade was Lloyd Douglas' religious novel, *Magnificent Obsession* (1929), a fictionalized sermon directly descended from Harold Bell Wright, preaching service to one's fellow man and confidence in Christian living. A Congregational clergyman who did not begin writing novels until he was fifty, Douglas' sales never approached Margaret Mitchell's, but his five subsequent books nevertheless sold consistently well. *Green Light* (1935), and *The Big Fisherman* (1948) were among the best sellers, while his historical novel, *The Robe* (1942) spent three years on the list. So too did other novels with a religious message, among them A. J. Cronin's *Keys of the Kingdom* (published in 1941 and selling well twenty-five years after) and Russell Janney's *Miracle of the Bells* (1947).

After the forties there were few changes in the style of popular fiction. Each year since 1931 has seen at least one best-selling historical novel, so that about ten per cent of all books published in paperback today are historical romances or variants thereof. Kathleen Winsor's *Forever Amber* (1944) sold one and a half million copies in three years by making Restoration England even more sexually active than it was; Mika Waltari's *The Egyptian* (1949) did the same with ancient Egypt.

Thomas Costain, beginning with *The Black Rose* (1945) and *The Silver Chalice* (1952), continued with *The White and the Gold* and *The*

Son of a Thousand Kings; Samuel Shellabarger, Marguerite Stern, Daphne du Maurier and others kept the species alive and vigorous. James Michener used Hawaiian history as the backdrop for *Hawaii* (1959); then, like Lew Wallace, turned to early Christianity in *The Source* (1965), which by 1968 had reached fifteen printings and a million copies.

Sergeanne Golon (actually a French husband-and-wife writing team) appeared in the American market with an 800-page historical novel, *Angélique,* in 1958, featuring the honey-blonde, green-eyed daughter of a seventeenth-century nobleman. She makes her way through the boudoirs and salons of Louis XIV's France with a good deal of wit and zest, a story continued in *Angélique and the King, Angélique in Revolt, Angélique in Love,* and so on, which have sold upwards of two million copies. Although Angélique is often in someone's bed, sex in the books is comparatively mild; they are written with light good humor and are soundly researched, filled with information about the social, political, and literary life of the times. Georgette Heyer, "England's Mistress of Romance," has produced a somewhat similar series of costume novels set in Regency England, extending to forty novels, of which about half are sold widely on American paperback racks.

The most successful novelist of all, however, has been Frank Yerby, an American Negro who lives in Spain, who after *The Foxes of Harrow* in 1946 published twenty-two novels (three made into successful movies) which have sold a total of twenty million copies. Yerby has made the best-seller lists eight times, more than any other American novelist since 1900 except Mary Roberts Rinehart.

Christopher Morley's *Kitty Foyle* (1939), a cut above Fannie Hurst and Viña Delmar, continued the tradition of the working-girl novel; Betty Smith's *A Tree Grows in Brooklyn* (1943), *Tomorrow Will Be Better* (1948), and *Joy in the Morning* (1963), all best sellers, continued the domestic strain with more than usual skill. Her first novel, a sensitively-told story of a Brooklyn childhood, sold two million copies within two years, not counting a half million in an edition for the armed forces.

Although it was first assumed that radio and television daytime serials might drain away some of the domestic novel's female audience, the competition seemed to have little effect on the work of three women—Edna Ferber, Frances Parkinson Keyes, and Taylor Caldwell—who have maintained steady sales over thirty years. In fact, the combined sales of the three, in 1960, already had reached twenty-six millions, about evenly divided among them. None of them believed in either blatant sex or excessive violence; as Mrs. Keyes put it, no author "has the right to intrude into the boudoir," although by implication sex plays an important part, certainly, in the novels of all three.

Miss Ferber, who began writing in 1911, produced eighteen novels, eight plays, and eleven volumes of short stories. Her first interest was woman in the business world, the "new woman" in the society of the competitive, emancipated postwar years—*Roast Beef Medium* (1913), *Personality Plus* (1914), *Emma McChesney and Co.* (1915), all collections of short stories. She then embarked on a series of novels based on keen observation and adroit characterization of American social life, putting adventurous female and male characters into picturesque, challenging settings like Alaska, Texas, the Mississippi River, Oklahoma. Her books were popular in the marketplace and also written with skill and craftsmanship. *So Big* (1924) deservedly won a Pulitzer Prize; eleven of her novels appeared as successful movies, particularly *Cimarron* (1958), *Showboat* (1936), and *Giant* (1952). Although much of Miss Ferber's work belonged with the thirties, eight of her novels were still in print in 1969, with thirty-three of Mrs. Keyes', and twenty-five of Mrs. Caldwell's.

Mrs. Keyes, Virginia-born and the widow of a former Governor and Senator, specializes in the high social novel dealing with the international scene, Washington or New York society, or the aristocratic South. Short on plot, her books are long on character and atmosphere. Once an associate of *Good Housekeeping*, she had produced forty-six books, among them a best-selling cookbook, an edition of poems, an autobiography, and a play. Taylor Caldwell writes much tougher novels than either; her thirty-three books abound with rivalries, passions, and animosities. A skillful if occasionally untidy plotmaker, she comes closer to violence than any of the other female novelists. Mrs. Caldwell's first major novel in ten years, *Testimony of Two Men* (1968) proved that her work had lost none of its popular appeal, since it sold 550,000 in hardcover editions over nine months and was the choice of four book clubs. The story of a young doctor's war against an angry and divided Pennsylvania town, it successfully combined the doctor-formula with sex, violence, and the conflict between selfishness and idealism.

Beginning in the forties, the "suspense" novel emerged as a separate entity, directly descended from the nineteenth-century Gothic novel and from the continuously popular novels of Mary Roberts Rinehart. The tremendous sales of Daphne du Maurier's *Rebecca* (1938), a powerful novel in the old Gothic tradition, attracted so many imitators that several publishers established "Gothic" or "suspense" series to supply the market on a regular basis. Victoria Holt, first in the field with a series which included titles such as *Bride of Pendoric, King of the Castle,* and *The Mistress of Mellyn,* set a successful pattern (seven titles in print in 1969 and total sales of four million), followed by others like Charlotte Armstrong, Josephine Edgar, and Mary Stewart, who after *Nine Coaches Waiting* (1958) continued with twelve more books and total sales by 1969 of over ten million. Her *Gabriel Hounds* (1967) stayed for six months on the *Times* best-seller list.

"Gothics" are almost always issued in paperback (appearing at the rate of fifty different titles per month), run about 60,000 to 90,000 words each, and have an initial print run of 100,000 copies. They are written by women—or under female pseudonyms—and display on the cover, more often than not, a stylized castle or shadowed old house with a light shining in the window. (Norman Daniels writes as "Dorothy Daniels," Dan Ross as "Marilyn Ross.") They emphasize atmosphere and mystery (with the castle or old country house as a locale), always involve a woman as the central character, and always have a strong romantic subplot built about a darkly attractive male figure. Heroes (as actual count has shown) tend to have names such as Jon, Robin, Noël, Rudolf, and Jonathan, even in one case Saint Clair Legrand. *Nine Coaches Waiting,* for example, sends Linda Martin, a pretty and ingenuous young English governess, into an old French chateau where "a strange terror lay coiled behind its brooding elegance," and where, after a series of adventures of "heartstopping suspense," she finds love in the arms of a handsome, mysterious Frenchman named Raoul.

The acknowledged queen of the modern Gothic is undoubtedly Emilie Loring, a New England-born lady who produced a steady stream of novels which have sold equally steadily over a twenty-five year period. Although she died in 1961, there were still forty-three of her books in print in 1969, rated by paperback publishers among the first dozen best sellers, with a total sale of seventeen million books. Mrs. Loring specialized in domestic novels with a Gothic-suspense touch, combining love and mystery in exactly the right proportions. Smoothly written, with a somewhat greater sophistication than either Mrs. Rinehart or Grace Livingston Hill, her novels maintain a devoted following among readers of women's magazines. A Loring title in paperback will still predictably sell 150,000 or more; along with Mrs. Hill's novels and those of Georgette Heyer, Mrs. Loring's are sold by number so that buyers who forget the titles of those they have read can avoid duplication when they purchase new ones. "Ladies buy 'em by the numbers," according to one publisher, "and can't get enough of 'em."

Not all Gothic novels, however, conform to the female-magazine pattern. The two most distinguished writers in the genre are Margaret Millar (whose husband, Kenneth Millar, writes detective stories as "Ross Macdonald") and Cornell Woolrich. Mrs. Millar's books (nineteen by 1969) are intense, mature, and expertly written. *How Like an Angel* (1962), *Beast in View* (1956), and *The Fiend* (1964) are psychological studies that deserve serious consideration as something more than Gothic suspense stories. Woolrich has done at least seventeen books under his own name and seventeen more as "William Irish." *The Bride Wore Black* (1940), the first of his "Black Series" (*Black Alibi, Black Curtain, Black Angel,* and *Rendezvous in Black*), and *Phantom Lady* (1942), the first of his "Irish" books (*Dead Man Blues, Strangler's Serenade,* and *Nightmare*) are recognized as classics in the suspense genre. *Rear Window* (1954), made into a movie by Alfred Hitchcock, is still one of the most effective suspense stories ever written, an excellent example of Woolrich's ability to suggest the utter terror that lies beneath commonplace daily life.

Grace Metalious, by inundating the domestic novel with waves of open, unblushing, prurient sex, overwhelmed the field. *Peyton Place,* which appeared in 1956, sold nine million copies over its first twelve years, its popularity reinforced by movies and television. Her epic of fornication in a small New England town invited dozens of imitations and the name of her novel's locale soon became synonymous with hypocritical sin. When death closed her career, Harold Robbin's clever combinations of topical interest with soft-core pornography continued the strain. Beginning with *The Dream Merchants* in 1949, a "sensational behind-the-scenes story of the motion picture business," Robbins has produced a steady series of massively sexual novels, among them *Never Leave Me* (1954, thirty-three printings, one million sales), *Stiletto* (1960, "a scorching novel of international intrigue"), *The Carpetbaggers* (1961, set in Reno, New York, and Hollywood where "men and women sin and claw their way to success"), *Where Love Has Gone* (1962, adult nymphomania, adolescent promiscuity), *The Adventurers* (1966, "the glittering world" of international playboys, laid in South America, the Riviera, London, Paris, New York, China, Hollywood, and Texas). In many paperback racks, Robbins occupies a row to himself, as well he might, since he has sold twenty-eight million books over a twenty-year span. The straight sexual novel of the Metalious-Robbins variety, thinly veiled by plot and setting, is probably the most consistently successful genre in present-day popular fiction. "Sex is what the book is all about," read an advertisement in *The New York Times* for a *Peyton Place*-type 1968 novel, "and this one is going to be a great big whopping bestseller." It was.

The religious novel has fallen far off its former pace. Henry Morton Robinson's *The Cardinal* (1950) and Morris West's *The Shoes of the Fisherman* (1963) were successful, but their sales were far short of Wright or Douglas. (However, the redoubtable, best-selling *Judas, My Brother* by Frank Yerby, which started with a prepublication printing of a quarter-million in 1968, may reactivate the type.) It was partially replaced by a succession of reassuring nonfiction "guides to living" written by men of the cloth—Joshua Liebman's *Peace of Mind* (1946); Norman Vincent Peale's *Guide to Confident Living* (1948); and Monsignor Fulton Sheen's triple successes, *Peace of Soul, The Power of Love*, and *The Way to Happiness*.

A great deal of the popularity once enjoyed by the religious novel has been transferred to the medical novel—the minister replaced by the doctor as glamor-symbol and guide-figure—so much so that paperback racks often display separate sections labeled "Doctor and Nurse." (There is not a single novel about glamorous dentists.) Sinclair Lewis's *Arrowsmith* (1925) was a straw in the wind; "Max Brand" (Frederick Faust) who created "Young Dr. Kildare," the adventurous intern, established a pattern that others eagerly followed. Morton Thompson's *Not As a Stranger* (1954) was among the later successes of the type and the fiction industry has averaged three to four each year since; Stanley Winduster's *The Practice* (1967, "Behind Locked Doors The Doctors See Their Women") and Elsa Lee's *Doctor's Office* (1968, "Raw Edges of Tension and Hot Fires of Passion in the Doctor's Office") are examples that can be multiplied by twelve in any publishing year. Frank G. Slaughter, who has sold twenty-four million books, has based a long and eminently successful career on the doctor novel, with a succession of books such as *The Healer, Spencer Brade M.D., Epidemic!, That None Should Die*, and so on. Slaughter has put medical men, uniformly heroic and self-sacrificing (though also capable of deep emotion and powerful love) into almost every conceivable situation, including the Army (*Battle Surgeon*), The Air Force (*Air Surgeon*), and the Civil War (*In a Dark Garden*).

The male or "hairy-chested" novel has lost none of its vitality or appeal. James Jones's *From Here to Eternity*, a novel of peacetime army life, won the National Book Award in 1951 and sold four million copies. Leon Uris's *Battle Cry* (1953) about the Marines, *Exodus* (1959), about the settlement of Israel, and *Topaz* (1968), about an international spy ring, have all reached best-seller status quickly; his total sales, in fact, have exceeded seven million. Kyle Onstott's *Mandingo* (1957), a "lusty, violent, cruel, mighty" novel, set a new pattern—interracial sex combined with violence, safely placed in the antebellum South. It sold three million copies and spawned a succession of imitators, usually recognized by the blurb "In the tradition of Mandingo" or "Bigger than Mandingo!" accompanied by a picture of a beautiful white woman surrendering to a muscular Negro slave. (A few imitators have tried it the other way around, which apparently does not sell so well.) MacKinlay Kantor's *Beauty Beast* (1960), advertised as "a rich sensual novel of a woman's forbidden love for a magnificent young slave, bringing to life the passion, the decadence, and the savagery of the Old South" is a good example of what has happened to *Gone With the Wind*. At least one such "lusty, brawling, virile" novel, that "pulls no punches" and "shocks you with unrestrained violence and magnificent romance" (to quote a typical advertisement) reaches the best-selling lists each year.

The most popular kind of fiction today, however, is the "inside" novel which derives from Lippard and his nineteenth-century companions in the exposé, usually focused on a topic of current interest, disclosing what it is "really like." Sloan Wilson's *Man in the Grey Flannel Suit* (1955), and Cameron Hawley's *Executive Suite* (1966) told what it was "really like" inside big business, repeated endlessly since. Allen Drury's "inside politics" books, *Advise and Consent* (1960), *A Shade of Difference* (1962), and *Capable of Honor* (1966) sold over a million each. Arthur Haley, who took his readers inside a hotel in *Hotel* (1965) and an airport in *Airport* (1968), had both of his books on best-seller lists for fifty weeks. Irving Wallace built sex into current events—such as the Kinsey Report (*The Chapman Report,* 1960); the possibility of a Negro President (*The Man,* 1964); and an international summit meeting (*The Plot,* 1967), which "nothing short of a paper shortage," remarked the Chicago *Tribune* quite accurately, "will keep from selling a million copies." The list of places inside which novelists have taken readers is almost endless, as a quick inspection of any paperback rack will show, although the ultimate was probably reached by Gore Vidal's inside Hollywood story, *Myra Breckinridge* (1968), which managed to involve homosexuality, heterosexuality, transvestism, and change of sex. No exposé, it would seem, could offer more.

A highly successful variation on the exposé novel appeared in 1966, Jacqueline Susann's *Valley of the Dolls*. Her device was to pattern her book fairly closely (but not close enough for libel) on the lives and adventures of famous contemporaries, thus "exposing" what "really happens" in the higher echelons of society, especially in show business.

Aimed directly at the great audience that reads movie magazines, gossip columns, true stories, and publicity handouts, *Valley of the Dolls,* one reviewer remarked, "was like reading a very long, absolutely delicious gossip column full of nothing but blind items; the fact that the names were changed and the characters disguised just made it more fun." The book's phenomenal success immediately produced imitations. David Slavitt, writing as "Henry Sutton," produced *The Exhibitionist* (1968) presumably about a famous movie star and his family, which sold 2,100,-000 copies in eleven months; his next, *The Voyeur* (1969) sold its first printing of 50,000 copies before publication and its second of 250,000 in two months. Morton Cooper's *The King* (1967), obviously patterned on the escapades of a famous singing star, and William Woolfolk's *The Beautiful Couple* (1968) about a well-known show business marriage, were equally successful.

Miss Susann demonstrated her mastery of the type, however, with *The Love Machine* (1969), which dealt with "the spectacular professional triumphs and dazzling sexual conquests" of a television executive in "the world of raw power and even rawer sex . . . , of uninhibited orgies . . . , of 'gay' parties in Hollywood, of sordid deals in which love and sex are coldly bartered." One publisher paid a quarter-million dollars for the hard-cover rights, another a quarter of a million for the paperback rights, while Miss Susann turned down as inadequate a million dollar bid for the movie rights, before publication.

The unremitting successes in the marketplace of the Metalious-Robbins-Susann group and their imitators drove Mike McGrady of the Long Island *Newsday* staff to retaliate by proposing in 1966 to a hundred friends that they collaborate on the worst possible book in the popular exposé-sex-high life tradition. Eventually twenty-five of them produced, under Grady's supervision and the pseudonym of "Penelope Ashe, a demure Long Island housewife," a monumentally bad novel titled *Naked Came the Stranger,* which dealt with the adulteries in show business, suburban Long Island, television studios, and elsewhere. Featuring "unremitting emphasis on sex" and "absolutely no excellence in writing" (McGrady sent chapters that were well written back for revision) the book was unsuspectingly published in 1969 by a reputable publisher, sold 20,000 copies in three weeks, made the best-seller list, and drew inquiries from ten film companies. Exposure of the hoax, however, simply increased the sales immediately and elicited interest from eight more movie producers. Exactly what point McGrady made remains debatable; there is the strong possibility that he analyzed and executed the formula far too well.

The question, "What makes a popular American novel?" cannot be answered. "Best seller" lists, originated in the nineteen-twenties, are compiled primarily from bookstores, department stores, and publishers' reports, and do not accurately reflect the situation in popular fiction. There are always books of literary quality by recognized authors that have appeared on these lists—by Sinclair Lewis, John Steinbeck, F. Scott Fitzgerald, Thornton Wilder, Pearl Buck, J. D. Salinger, Mary McCarthy, John P. Marquand, Irwin Shaw, James Gould Cozzens, Ernest Hemingway, and Katherine Anne Porter, to name a few. But what sells in cigar stores, newstands, drug stores, hotel lobbies, and bus stations is not likely to be reflected in so-called "best seller" compilations. Erskine Caldwell, who probably outsells any of these authors any month of any year, does not appear in these compilations at all.

Grace Metalious's sexual epic of a small New England town, *Peyton Place* (1956), has outsold Hemingway, Faulkner, Melville, Dreiser, and Fitzgerald combined. At over nine and a half million copies it has sold more than any other single American novel in modern times and is the fourth most popular book ever published in the United States (excepting the Bible), outsold only by Dr. Spock's *Child and Baby Care, The Better Homes and Gardens Cookbook,* and *The Pocket Atlas.* The second most popular novel is Erskine Caldwell's ironic shocker of poor-white life, *God's Little Acre,* with slightly more than eight million copies sold. Except for English novelist D. H. Lawrence's *Lady Chatterley's Lover,* the next seven places are occupied by Mickey Spillane's seven "tough guy" novels of violence and sex, each of which have sold nearly five million copies.

The five most popular fiction writers over the first quarter of the twentieth century were Winston Churchill, Zane Grey, Harold Bell Wright, Gene Stratton-Porter, and Mary Roberts Rinehart. The five most popular of the second quarter of the century (plus an extra decade or so) have been Grace Metalious, Mickey Spillane, Erskine Caldwell, Erle Stanley Gardner, and Frank Yerby. Yet the writer who has made the best-seller list most often in the twentieth century is Mary Roberts Rinehart (eleven times, with seventeen books still in print) followed by Zane Grey, Booth Tarkington, and Sinclair Lewis. The author who has made it most frequently since 1940 is Frank Yerby, with eight appearances.

In terms of total sales, *Publishers' Weekly's* 1969 compilations of sales figures (restricted to twentieth-century authors) places Gardner first (135 million), Spillane second (49 million) and Caldwell third (43.8 million). Fourth place, interestingly enough, is occupied by Charles Schulz's cartoon creation, "Peanuts," with 36 million books in print. John

Steinbeck leads among the better writers, with 28.8 million books, distributed among 21 titles; John O'Hara has 21 million with 21 titles; Pearl Buck 13 million with 23 titles. James Michener, with only two titles —*Hawaii* and *The Source*—has sold 13.4 million books.

Exactly what these figures mean in terms of a best-seller formula is unclear. E. Haldeman-Julius, whose "Little Blue Books" once blanketed the country with sales of over five hundred million, once wrote that the most saleable subjects were (more or less in order) love, sex, religion, self-improvement or education, and humor. Frank Luther Mott, at the conclusion of his book on American best sellers, named religion as their most popular common ingredient (about one-third have had some kind of religious component) with love (merging into sex), adventure, and morality as additional elements of nearly equal value. Granville Hicks, after analyzing forty popular twentieth-century novels, concluded that they all had a "romantic" theme, an active plot, conventional characters, and a message or thesis, neither disturbing nor profound. Edward Weeks rated timeliness—"reaching the public at precisely the time we are ready for it"—worth 45 per cent in making a book popular, emotionalism or sentimentalism 25 per cent, characterization 15 per cent, invention 10 per cent, and advertising 5 per cent, this last an estimate current commentators would place much higher.

On the other hand, the persistent myth that public relations and advertising make a book popular is no more than a myth. There have been such successes—Jacqueline Susann's *Valley of the Dolls* for one— but nearly always temporary. It must be remembered that 98 percent of all books published each year are *not* best sellers, despite advertising budgets, and that if there is anything a publisher would like to know, it is why they are not. Advertising does play a part (the amount spent often determines the profit from sales in a rough ratio), and so do the effects of a filmed version or the availability of the book in paperback.

The most effective merchandising innovation of the past fifty years, and one that has had direct effect on best-seller lists, has been the book club, selling books by mail order at regular intervals to a list of subscribers. The Book-of-the-Month Club, founded in 1926, added two successful devices unknown to its nineteenth-century forerunners: first, it served only as a distributive middleman between publisher and buyer, publishing nothing itself; and second, it selected its books by using a panel of prominent "judges" whose tastes presumably guaranteed high-quality books. With the Literary Guild, founded in 1927, the Book-of-the-Month-Club dominated the popular market at once.

Within ten years the Book-of-the-Month-Club reported that it distributed eleven and a half millions of books annually (about one and a half times the contents of the Library of Congress) and ten years after that there were sixty book clubs with a total membership of nearly four millions, aimed at every conceivable interest—a Labor Book Club, Catholic Children's Book Club, Teen Age Book Club, Family Book Club, Non-Fiction Book Club, History Book Club, Civil War Book Club, Executive Book Club, Yachtsman's Book Club, Garden Book Club, Fisherman's Book Club, Jewish Book Club, The Cookbook-of-the-Month Club, and even a Surprise Book Club. Sears, Roebuck and Company's Peoples Book Club, initiated in 1948 to select books "readable by every member of the family, without blushing," was the largest for nearly a decade, its place taken by the Readers' Digest Book Club. As of the late sixties, the Dollar Book Club distributed about 825,000 copies of each book it issued, the Literary Guild 650,000, the Book-of-the-Month Club a million, and the Readers' Digest Club two and a half millions, or more than the other three combined.

The rise of book clubs elicited strong argument in the book trade. If, on the one hand, they sold books to millions of people who would not ordinarily buy them, they obviously increased the market for books; if, on the other, they tended to reduce everything to the lowest common denominator of taste, they obviously lowered the market for *good* books. Whatever the justice of the claims, there is no doubt that such clubs have had tremendous influence on the popular market. Amid twentieth-century America's great increase in population, given a vastly increased number of sales outlets and intensified merchandising techniques, the average sale of books has risen spectacularly since the thirties. There are more people in the United States to buy books than ever before, with more money to do it with, and more places to buy them. A novel that sells a million copies in hardback and paperback editions today is no longer a rarity. The popular market seems to have no future limit.

James D. Hart, in his study of *The Popular Book* in 1950, listed six factors which, in his overall estimate, could carry considerable weight in popularity. To be popular, he writes, an author must first clarify ideas already in circulation or explain a change—as Thomas Paine's *American Crisis;* second, his plot and characters must be concerned with emotional attitudes and ethical values which engage the large majority of his readers—as Harriet Beecher Stowe's *Uncle Tom's Cabin;* third, he must provide entertainment at an acceptable level, neither above nor below the moral boundaries of the middle class—as in Erle Stanley Gardner's mysteries; fourth, his book must guide or elevate the reader with a message or thesis; fifth, what he says must confirm and reassure, rather than disturb, the reader's belief in the normal democratic, American system. Obviously, no one book can do all these things at once. And obviously, exceptions spring to mind so rapidly that the rules seem overgeneralized. It is difficult to fit *Peyton Place, God's Little Acre,* or *I, The Jury* into this pattern.

Any survey of popular fiction shows that a distinction should be made between best sellers and consistent sellers, counting the element of longevity as a factor in determining popularity. *Forever Amber,* a quick and easy best seller, sold more than *Ben Hur;* yet *Ben Hur* has stayed in print for eighty-eight years and *Forever Amber* lasted about ten. Total sales, then, may not alone be a sufficient index of popularity; the history of popular fiction is filled with best sellers few remember—Anne Parris, *The Perennial Bachelor;* Warwick Deeping, *Sorrell and Son;* Vicki Baum, *Grand Hotel;* Stark Young, *So Red The Rose;* Marcia Davenport, *Valley of Decision;* Mary Jane Ward, *The Snake Pit;* William Brinkley, *Don't Go Near the Water.* Some books may hit the public mood at exactly the right time, sell wildly, and disappear. Eugene Burdick's and Harvey Wheeler's *Fail Safe* (1962), dealing with the possibility of accidental nuclear war, is an excellent example of a book which made best-selling status because of its coincidence with a contemporary issue; so too Robert Serling's *The President's Plane Is Missing!* (1968), which capitalized on the possibility of presidential mishap against the background of deep popular concern in the sixties about political violence.

To try to define what makes a novel popular by analyzing its contents is frustrating, for changing tastes and times nullify any such generalizations. What was in *The Wide, Wide World* made it popular in the mid-nineteenth century; what was in Elia Kazan's *The Arrangement* made it a best seller in the mid-twentieth. To reduce popular fiction to a set of formulae or techniques is equally unsatisfactory, for the exceptions not only test the rules but annul them as well.

However, there are certain themes in popular fiction which seem to maintain perennial interest. One is nostalgia, the appeal of "better days and simpler times," the pervasive memory of the past, of childhood, of innocence not yet lost, of times free of the taint of contemporaneity. Another is the fairy-tale theme of romantic incongruity, the surprise of things which are not what they seem—the commoner who is nobler than nobility; the prostitute with the heart of gold; the tough truckdriver who is a gentle lover, the million-dollar-baby in a five-and-ten-cent store. Another is the sacrifice theme, the "far, far better thing that I do" theme that emphasizes the values of devotion, generosity, heroic selflessness. A fourth is the romanticism of the commonplace; investing ordinary experience with larger meaning, value, glamour (even sin); finding significance in such mundane places as hotels, airports, department stores, colleges, lawyer's offices, banks, and nurses' dormitories. And last, of course, are the basic emotional themes of love and danger, sex and violence, hope and fear, whether muted or explicit—with always the pleasant potentialities of the one in contest with the unhappy possibilities of the other.

FOR IT WAS INDEED HE: BOOKS FOR THE YOUNG

"You are a cheap cad," said Frank, evenly. "I shall thank you to apologize. You are not worthy of the Fardale team."

—*Frank Merriwell's Grit*

The belief that books may be used as tools for instilling virtue in the young is an old and honored one. Since ancient times literature (using the term loosely) has served as a medium for instructing youth in the manners and morals of society, and for introducing them to the major problems of adult life. The books young people read, therefore, often provide reflections of what society assumes to be valuable, and of the standards it holds. Certainly in America, where the Calvinistic heritage and the popularity of the sentimental-didactic novel combined justify it, a juvenile literature which amused, taught, and exhorted needed no encouragement.

By the close of the eighteenth century there was a thriving market for books whose purpose was to introduce young people to their culture and to provide them with minimal equipment to fit into it—books such as the Reverend Thomas Day's British classic, *Sandford and Merton* (1783–89), still being reprinted 125 years later, or the popular American equivalent, the Reverend Enos Hitchcock's *Farmer's Friend* (1793). These and other books like them were hardy perennials, given as Sunday-school prizes or by doting aunts, grimly didactic, primly moralistic, and no doubt fearsomely dull to children. Yet what they taught—piety, work, thrift, self-sacrifice, humility—represented deeply held and unanimously respected American virtues.

Books available to boys and girls during the early nineteenth century

were no different, for the most part, than their predecessors. Jacob Abbott's "Rollo" series, begun in 1834 (all twenty-eight volumes were still in
print fifty years later), taught its young readers geography, history, and
art appreciation by having Rollo, a New England farm boy, tour Europe
interminably with his Uncle George, who pointed out "lessons of self-
improvement, honesty, and industry" every step of the way. The author
of over two hundred juveniles in all, Abbott's colorful descriptions and
faintly exciting plots helped to convince parents that fiction for children
might be made pleasant as well as moral.

What radically changed the character of American juvenile fiction
was its discovery of the frontier and the Indian. The captivity and pioneer
tales of the previous century, as they emerged from the treatment administered by Cooper, Simms, Bird, and others, contributed a new kind
of literary subject matter to the juvenile market. What Cooper did for
adult readers, Joseph Holt Ingraham did at a lower level, creating blood-
and-thunder Western and pirate tales in their full glory. Ingraham, one
might easily argue, with his sure sense of the cliché, his acute use of the
sensational, and his barbarously Gothic style, was the grandfather of the
dime novel.

It is with the dime novel, of course, that the juvenile tradition begins,
and the dime novel begins with the publishing house of Beadle and
Adams, formed in 1856 by the Beadle brothers and a young Irishman,
Robert Adams. The company did not do well until in 1860 (the year of
Ingraham's death) it published a paperbound novel which sold for ten
cents, titled *Malaeska; The Indian Wife of The White Hunter*. Beadle
and Adams opened the floodgates, and for the next forty years these
books (later reduced to a nickel) poured from the presses by tons. Erasmus Beadle, the P. T. Barnum of the early juvenile trade, simply applied
big business methods to publishing. Millions of these paper thrillers were
bought by boys whose mothers and fathers and pastors gave them Rollo
books for Christmas and Bible stories as Sunday school prizes. (Tom
Sawyer's reading, as Twain faithfully reported it, represented the juvenile
literary level of the period.) What parents objected to in the dime novels
was not their morality, but their emphasis on sensationalism, violence,
and overwrought emotionalism, especially as the type began to degenerate in the seventies and eighties.

But what was of more importance, the Indian-killing, train-robbing
violence of the paper shockers had begun by the sixties to lose its relevance to American society. Even in their most popular period, the dime
novels found their juvenile market deeply cut by a new kind of story,
better fitted to the times—"Oliver Optic's" stories of adventure, "Harry

Castlemon's" tales of youthful derring-do, and Horatio Alger's stories of success.

William Taylor Adams, a Massachusetts schoolteacher who began writing under the "Optic" pseudonym in the fifties, left the profession and not long after became the first real entrepreneur in the juvenile field, editing a number of magazines—*Oliver Optic's Magazine, Student and Schoolmate, Our Boys and Girls, Our Little Ones,* and others—and introducing mass production methods into it. He gave Alger, among others, his start, and to a large extent developed the formulae followed by boys' books for the next half-century. His books conveyed "correct views of moral and social duties" to the young reader, but they also embodied them in "stories full of dash and vigor" as Rollo's were not. Adams himself specialized in sea stories (being a great believer in "the ship as an educational and reformatory institution") like *All Aboard, A Brave Old Salt, The Yankee Middy,* and *Outward Bound.* "Harry Castlemon" (Charles A. Fosdick) was less interested in preaching than in plain adventure, which he kept within more or less believable bounds. His *Gunboat Series* (1864–68), *Rocky Mountain Series* (1867–71) and *Rod and Gun Series* (1883–84), totaling fifty-eight volumes, were filled with sturdy prose like that of "Frank on a Gunboat":

> "Surrender, now, you infernal Yankees. Shoot down the first one who resists or attempts to escape!" he said, turning to his men.
> "Stand by your guns, my lads!" shouted Captain Wilson. "Don't give an inch!"
> The sailors, accustomed to obedience, gathered round their officers and poured a murderous fire upon the advancing enemy.

The Homer of the juveniles, however, was Horatio Alger, Jr., a failed clergyman who took up writing for boys in the early sixties. A series he wrote for *Student and Schoolmate* caught the attention of Adams, who encouraged A. K. Loring Company to publish it as a book in 1865 called *Ragged Dick.* From that point on Alger was always among the best sellers in the field until twenty years after his death, the author of somewhere between one hundred and eighteen and one hundred and twenty books (varying with admittedly unreliable figures) totaling between seventeen and twenty million words.

His stories of poor boys who succeeded in business, of country boys who (like Dick Whittington) confronted and conquered the city—boys bound to rise to fame and fortune—related much more directly to the ideals and aspirations of changing American society. Alger helped to provide boys with something the dime novels could not, and which the young American badly needed; that is, some grasp of the changes in nineteenth-century social and economic values, some understanding of the new forces of contemporary society and how to control them.

Alger's contributions to his age were numerous, but four deserve to be remembered: he explained and reemphasized the traditional American faith in self-reliance; he instructed his contemporaries in the complexities of a new kind of society; he reaffirmed the social values of middle-class virtues; and he, more than any other of his fellow-authors, recognized the changed nature of American urban life. He caught the meaning of what had been taking place in the postwar United States, and served the youth of the country well by explaining it in understandable terms. What he did, in effect, was to exemplify in his books many of the prevailing concepts of what American life was like, and how some of the traditional American beliefs functioned within it.

Alger restated what Franklin told his age, and what Emerson, in somewhat more exalted terms, told his. In an era of urbanization and industrialization, undergoing a real but unnoticed population explosion, the individual was in danger of submerging himself in a swiftly developing mass society. Alger's boy-heroes reaffirmed in highly satisfactory terms all the old values of Puritan and Franklinian individualism. It was perfectly clear that the poor boy who was honest and tipped his hat, saved his money and took baths, would probably become very successful and marry a wealthy girl.

The standard Alger plot concerns a boy of fifteen or so, usually fatherless, who has to make his own way, often in the city, against heavy financial and social odds. Sometimes he has to support a widowed mother, tormented by the village squire who holds a mortgage on her little cottage or scrabble farm. Whatever the circumstances, the boy has to stand on his own two feet and face the practical problem of getting on in the world and finding a place in it. The titles of the Alger books play variations on this theme of self-reliance—*Work and Win, Strive and Succeed, Facing the World, Do and Dare, Adrift in New York, Struggling Upward, Striving for Fortune, Making His Way, Try and Trust, Sink or Swim, Risen from the Ranks.* Tom Thatcher (of *Tom Thatcher's Fortune*) was a typical Alger hero:

> "Is supper ready, mother? I'm hungry as a bear."
> The speaker was a sturdy boy of sixteen, with bright eyes and a smiling, sunburned face. His shirt sleeves were rolled up, displaying a pair of muscular arms. His hands were brown, and soiled with labor. It was clear that here was no whitehanded young aristocrat. His clothes alone would have shown that. They were of

coarse, durable cloth, made without any special regard for the prevailing fashion.

Tom Thatcher, for this was his name, had just come home from the shoe factory, where he was employed ten hours a day pegging shoes, for the lucrative sum of fifty cents a day. I may as well state here that he is the hero of my story, and I hope that none of my readers will think any the worse of him for working in a shoe shop. Tom, having a mother and a little sister to support, could not choose his employment.

"Supper will be ready in five minutes, Tom," replied his mother, a rather delicate-looking woman of refined appearance, notwithstanding that she was dressed in a cheap calico.

One knows from the first few pages exactly what obstacles the boy faces, and the excitement of the narrative (such as it is) lies in how he comes to grips with his world and subdues it. Alger usually explains in scrupulously precise terms what these problems are. In *Do and Dare,* for example, the young hero's mother, the village postmistress, made exactly $398.50 the preceding year. Her mortgage, held by the rascally squire, is $481 at about 8 per cent; she owes him on installment plus interest. Thus the reader can figure for himself, when young Tom, Jack, Luke, Ben, Andy, or Dick gets a clerking job at $3 a week and also contracts to tutor the rich man's son in Latin, exactly how much progress he can make toward making that payment on time. What it takes for the boy to succeed, of course, are piety, courage, thrift, alertness, punctuality, morality, hard work, and the rest of the constellation of virtues surrounding self-reliance. "Have you got grit?" his employer asks the young hero of *Strive and Succeed.* "Do you generally succeed in what you undertake? Grit weighs heavily in this world." Alger's plots presented a simplified version of the great and abiding American belief in the ultimate success of individual effort; and whatever his shortcomings as a writer, which were many and grievous, he presented it with tremendous effectiveness to his generation.

Second, Alger's books provided boys with their first intelligible picture of contemporary economic life. His was the era of American business expansion, when businessmen worked hard, took daring risks, built giant corporations and amassed incredible fortunes. One must not forget that Russell Conwell's famous lecture, "Acres of Diamonds," repeated hundreds of times during these years, exhorted its listeners, "Get rich! Get rich! I say you have no right to be poor!" Alger's boys had no illusions about what happened to you when you had money and when you didn't, and were extremely conscious of the symbols of wealth—gold

watches, overcoats, watchchains, waistcoats, and the like. Tom Temple, in
Tom Temple's Career, who finds that his friends simply reject him when
he loses his estate, accepts it all realistically—"Tom had always understood that they cared for him only because he was rich, and he was
neither astonished nor disappointed at the change." In *Brave and Bold*,
when Halbert Davis falls on evil days,

> The wealth and position upon which he had based his aristo-
> cratic pretension vanished, and in bitter mortification he found him-
> self reduced to poverty. He could no longer flaunt his cane and
> promenade the streets in kid gloves, and he was glad to accept a
> position in the factory store, where he was compelled to dress accord-
> ing to his work.

This was the age of Rockefeller, Carnegie, Vanderbilt, Guggenheim,
Harriman, Gould, Fisk, and other multiple millionaires to whom riches
came so suddenly and in such profusion that simply how to control
wealth became one of the pressing ethical, political, and social problems
of the time. Alger knew this, and the majority of his books deal with
questions raised by money—how one gets it, what one does with it, what
happens when one does not have it. To Alger the pursuit of wealth could
be challenging, exciting, and satisfying, as indeed it was to his generation,
and his hero's progress toward his first million was the thread which held
the majority of Alger's plots together. In the background of Alger's books
was the story of Carnegie's rise from bobbin-boy to steel king, of Buck
Duke selling tobacco on the road, of Edison hawking papers on Michigan
trains. Alger's books were made real to his readers by life itself, for they
embodied the great American dream that any right-thinking and right-
acting American boy could by *Struggling Upward* succeed in *Finding
a Fortune*.

How did one get rich in Alger's books? Here the legend is at variance
with the facts. The Alger hero is honest, manly, cheerful, intelligent, self-
reliant, ambitious, moral, frugal, and all else that he need be, but it is not
by reason of any of these attributes, admirable as they are, that he becomes rich. The fact is that wealth in Alger comes by reason of the lucky
break, by seizure of the chance opportunity. Ragged Dick saves his
pennies, but when he rescues a child from the river her father turns out
to be a rich banker who gives Dick a job. Phil the Fiddler, ground under
the padrone system, falls exhausted in a snowstorm at the door of a
wealthy old physician who has lost a son of Phil's age. Tom Thatcher
catches a runaway horse, and in the buggy is the golden-haired daughter
of a wealthy Wall Street broker. Sam, in *Sam's Chance*, finds a gold nug-

get approximately the size of a basketball; the hero of *Bound to Rise* befriends a lonely old man who gives him a sizable packet of downtown Tacoma real estate. Worthless mining stock in Alger stories always turns out to be worth hundreds of thousands; wealthy merchants, saved from robbery by the young heroes, invariably give them good jobs and rich rewards. Frank the Cash Boy saves his meager salary, but he is really set on his way to wealth by capturing a thief; Alger remarks, "It is precisely to such lucky chances that men are often indebted for their advancement." An acute observer of the life around him, Alger knew better than to make wealth a matter of either luck or work alone; to him success was made out of labor plus the breaks, of ability plus the opportunity to capitalize on it.

Alger's boys are such model youths, and they save their money so carefully, that the modern reader is likely to miss the point. His message is not that you can save a great deal of money on a small salary, or that you ought to chase runaway buggies. The lesson is that money will come to him who is able to capitalize on the lucky opportunity—work and save, but watch for the break that may come only once to any man. In effect, one may say with some reason that the real heroes of the books are not the bootblacks and newsboys and store clerks, but the rich bankers, merchants, and stockbrokers who have seized their chances, and whom these boys hope to emulate. Alger made a clear distinction among rich men. There were small-town, minor-league rich men who foreclosed mortgages, dispossessed widows, and threatened young men with ruin. There were useless rich men, snobbish, idle parasites who, like Augustus Fitz-Herbert in Alger's poem, *Nothing to Do,*

> . . . cherishes deep and befitting disdain,
> For those who don't live in the Fifth Avenue,
> As entirely unworthy the notice of thought,
> Of the heir of two millions and nothing to do.

They are often represented in Alger by the rich boys who try every dirty trick in the book to win the big boat race, who fly into temper tantrums when foiled, and who are punished for their arrogance by a sudden plunge into poverty. However, the good rich men in Alger are consistently kind, generous, and virtuous, and we know that Frank the Cash Boy, or Mark Manning the Match Boy, will be like them when he has made his millions. Alger perceived, as Carnegie did, the ethical values of the Gospel of Wealth and the responsibilities of Christian stewardship. The boys who read Alger set out to become richer and also better men, for Alger saw, as his age did, a relationship between virtue and wealth, money and morality, and he made this crystal clear to his readers.

Alger's third contribution to an assessment of his times lay in his reaffirmation of the validity of American middle-class virtue. His books celebrated, in unmistakable terms, the values of individualism, self-reliance, and alertness to opportunity, and it was noticeable to his readers that success came to good boys, not bad ones. The old-fashioned virtues paid off in Alger's plots; it was not always exactly clear why, but they did, and the boy who was honest, punctual, respectable, and who honored his parents and his employer found success. The youth who grew up in the Alger tradition learned that work meant happiness, and that a busy life was a virtuous one, that it was best to stay out of debt and pay cash, that he who produced wealth was a useful citizen. As Alger wrote in one of his doggerel poems:

> Strive and Succeed, the world's temptations flee,
> Be Brave and Bold, and Strong and Steady be.
> Go Slow and Sure, and prosper then you must,
> With Fame and Fortune, while you Try and Trust.

Bound to Rise; or Up The Ladder (1873) is an excellent example of how Alger handled the relationship between success and virtue. He wrote in his introduction,

> Harry Walton and Luke Harris were two country boys who had the same opportunities to achieve success. Harry Walton by his efforts succeeded, and Luke Harris's life was a failure. Read this story and you will see what qualities in the one brought about his success, and what in the other caused his downfall.

Alger is not quite specific in detailing these qualities, but it is obvious by the end of the book that Harry succeeded by pursuing his education, paying his debts, dressing modestly, giving his best efforts to his job, and helping his indigent parents. Luke plays billiards, borrows more than he can repay, spends too much time on his clothes, and never reads a book. Harry continually revises his aims upward, inspired by a life of Benjamin Franklin which he wins as a school prize. Luke drifts, with apparently no aims at all. When his break comes, Harry is ready for it. Harry's lucky opportunity, however, raises an ethical point which Alger neatly avoids. Harry is robbed of his overcoat and forty dollars; the thief, however, leaves his own overcoat behind and Harry finds in it the loot from its owner's previous robberies, totaling ninety-seven dollars, which gives him a clear profit of fifty-seven dollars and starts him on his way. The pattern is a familiar one in Alger, who was constantly reassuring his readers that traditional virtues still meant something in the competitive, industrialized, urbanized society of the late nineteenth century. Alger had neither the intellectual equipment to formulate it, nor the literary skill to articulate it, but what he was trying to say was that there was a purposeful life and a pointless life, that there was a right way and a wrong way to live, and that the standards which determined them were still operative in times of great and unsettling change. Alger plots and Alger heroes gave the boys of the seventies and eighties an anchor to tie to in the era of Darwin, Sumner, Coxey, Ingersoll, Donnelly, Spencer, and the other movers and shakers of contemporary society.

Fourth, Alger almost alone among his fellow writers of juveniles, perceived the changing quality of city life and suggested how his readers might handle the problems it presented to the youth who had to make his way in it. He recognized the need of the city boy, or the country boy who came to the city, for guidelines to lead him successfully into this new, dangerous, and frightening urban environment. The New York street urchins Alger knew, and the farm boys who streamed into the cities from the upstate hamlets, each determined to go from rags to riches as swiftly as possible, had little equipment with which to deal with the harsh facts of the city's life. Alger's view of it was fundamentally realistic; his books include thieves and sharpers, gangs, temptation and vice, drunkenness, cruelty, and the pitfalls of fashion and irresponsibility. They included also a good deal of practical information on living and working in the metropolis, on rooms, food, jobs, costs, recreation, and the like. This was the same kind of city that Jacob Riis and Stephen Crane and Theodore Dreiser and Jane Addams and the muckrakers saw, and Alger, in his minor way, gave his youthful readers information about how to cope with it.

Alger's characters had no subtleties, and the young reader was able to distinguish good boys from bad in their very first words. When Andy Grant, a poor boy, meets Conrad Carter, a rich squire's son (evidence in itself), Andy says to him, "That's a new bicycle, isn't it?" to which Conrad replies, "Yes, I got tired of the old one. This is a very expensive bicycle. Wouldn't you like to have a new bicycle?" "Yes," replied Andy. "Of course," said Conrad, "you never will." But if they lack subtlety, Alger characters have the virtue of clarity. The reader is never at a loss to know what characters think and is never uncertain of their motives. Alger's dialogue never evades; if it is like nothing spoken on earth by normal people, it *is* clear. For example, when young Rufus, in *Rufus and Rose*, wishes to invite Miss Manning for an evening out, he goes at it this way:

"Miss Manning," said Rufus, "have you an engagement this evening?"

"It is hardly necessary to ask, Rufus," she replied. "My company is not in very great demand."

"You have heard of the Japanese jugglers at the Academy?" asked Rufus.

"Yes, said Miss Manning. "Mrs. Florence was speaking of them. They are very entertaining."

"We shall go this evening," said Rufus. "See, I have got tickets," and he drew out the tickets he had purchased that morning.

"Thank you very much," said Miss Manning. "I should like very much to go. It is a long time since I have been to any place of amusement. How much did the tickets cost?"

"A dollar and a half apiece," replied Rufus.

"Isn't that rather extravagant?" asked Miss Manning.

"Yes," said Rufus, "it would be if we went every week, but I do not plan to do this often."

Nor can one mistake the intentions of the villainous Curtis Waring toward Florence Linden, a poor orphan girl, in *Adrift in New York*:

"She is in the toils! She cannot escape me!" he muttered. "But I"— and here his brow darkened—"it vexes me to see how she repels my advances, as if I were some loathsome thing. Can there be a rival? But no! We live so quietly that she has met no one who could win her affections. Why can she not turn to me? Surely, I am not so ill-favored, and though twice her age, I am still a young man. Nay, it is only a young girl's caprice. She shall yet come to my arms, a willing captive."

None of this, of course, was parody, for Alger was a serious man; when he intended to be humorous, there was no mistake.

"Haven't I seen you somewhere?" asked Tom.

"Perhaps," replied Ned, "that's where I usually am."

It seems incredible that Alger, who stood eighth in his class at Harvard, could write such incredibly bad prose as he did for forty years, but he accomplished it. His great contribution to the tradition of bad juvenile prose was the flailing of the obvious, in such things as "Tom Thatcher, for such was his name," or "Five years have passed. Walter, now older . . . ," or his masterpiece from *Ragged Dick*, who is rescued after leaping into the river to save a little girl:

Strong hands seized Dick and his youthful burden and drew them into the boat, both dripping with water.

Alger plots, apparently made up hurriedly, were often wildly complicated, though his readers seemed not to care. In *Frank and Fearless* the
action very nearly got out of hand. The widowed father of Jasper, the
hero, marries the mother of Nicholas, the bully, who pretends to be her
nephew. When Jasper's father dies, his stepmother immediately cheats
Jasper out of the estate; mistreated while Nicholas flourishes, he soon
runs away to make his fortune but is robbed and abandoned in St. Louis.
Taking refuge in a deserted house, he finds a kidnapped child, held
captive by his stepmother's criminal brother Dick. After Jasper returns
the child to its father, a wealthy lawyer, he obtains a job with the firm
as a messenger. However, Dick, Nicholas, and the wicked stepmother
have followed him to St. Louis, capture him, and hold him in another
abandoned house (of which St. Louis seemed to have had more than its
share) for weeks before his escape. Sent West by his employer with a
bank deposit, Jasper is rescued from certain death at the hands of
brigands by a beautiful Indian princess named Minima, who incon-
veniently falls in love with him. In a swift denouement, however, Alger
kills the stepmother, sends Dick and Nicholas to prison and pays off
Minima with a gold watch, leaving Jasper free to return to St. Louis to
marry a wealthy heiress.

Although girls appeared faintly in the background of Alger books, he
was true to the code of the juvenile in his avoidance of anything remotely
resembling sex. There were no love scenes in Alger, and (so far as anyone
has yet discovered) but one kiss. When Harry Raymond returned from
Australia with a fortune of $15,525 (Alger is quite precise), he was
greeted by little Maud Lindsay, "a bright, handsome girl of thirteen,"
who flung her arms about him, while "Harry, somewhat embarrassed at
the unexpected warmth of his reception, felt it would be rather impolite
not to kiss Maud in return, and accordingly did so." In his only book
about a girl, *Helen Ford*, Alger came close to a love story; at the end of
the book Helen is friendly to a young man of great virtue and respectability, but Alger removes both from danger by sending him as a mis-
sionary to Africa for the next thirteen years. What the reader waited for
was not kisses, but the great confrontation scene when the boy came
home, sprouting greenbacks and sporting a large gold watch, just as the
rascally squire was preparing to foreclose the mortgage. It is even better
when Jed, The Poorhouse Boy, badly treated by Miss Holbrook (who
ran the orphanage in which he stayed as a child), turns out to be the
long-lost son of a British earl:

> Miss Maria Holbrook, who was surprised at Jed's improved appear-
> ance when he entered, eyed him with suspicion.

"Where are you staying?" she inquired. "Have you a situation?"

"I am staying at the Windsor Hotel," replied Jed, "and I have no situation."

"Then how can you afford to stay at a first-class hotel?" Miss Holbrook asked in surprise.

"I am with my mother, Lady Fenwick," replied Jed. "Allow me to present you with my card."

And Jed placed in her hand a card on which was engraved the name

SIR ROBERT FENWICK, BARONET

By the time of Alger's death in 1899, the popularity of the Alger strain in juvenile books was fast fading out. The things Alger boys strove for, the obstacles they faced, and the heroes they emulated were no longer the same. The rags-to-riches billionaire was becoming scarce; it took money to make money in 1900, and the sudden stroke of luck that in 1870 might take a poor boy from nothing to a million now needed plenty of capital to take advantage of it. The legend of Alger persisted, but the opportunities for making great wealth were narrowing fast; a boy needed technological skill, education, scientific talent, and highly-organized business know-how to struggle upward—not just energy, sobriety, and the rescue of the boss's daughter. Alger's theory, that opportunity lay everywhere, was obsolete, and American boys knew it. Juvenile readers were much more sophisticated in their attitudes toward social and economic values, and more familiar with city codes of behavior which had gradually ceased to hold terror for them.

There were also new publishing techniques, assembly-line authorship and new sales tricks, as juvenile publishing became big business under the aegis of such firms as A. L. Burt, Street and Smith, Cupples and Leon, Hurst and Company, or Grossett and Dunlap. Cupples and Leon, for example, printed a coupon on the book's dust jacket; filled with the names of ten friends, the coupon entitled the sender to a free catalog of all Cupples and Leon publications. At one time they had more than a half million boys' names on their mailing lists. Writers developed the habit of dovetailing a series, so that a boy might buy a copy of *Jack Out West* to find on page 1 that Jack had just completed a thrilling adventure in Brazil, while on the last page he was told that the young hero was about to embark on an even more thrilling one in Africa. Either way the reader was hooked. (There is a legend that Grosset and Dunlap printed all the titles of a series on the dust jacket with the words, "Uniform with this Edition." Thousands of earnest boys wrote in to say, "I bought the book. Where's the uniform?") Nor did the Alger formula satisfy the needs of a new decade. Cleverer men than he were in the field, men who caught much more precisely and accurately the spirit of the times. Two of these were Gilbert M. Patten, who wrote under the name of "Burt L. Standish," and Edward Stratemeyer, who wrote under so many names that some of them are not yet known.

Patten, who already had experience in writing dime-novel shockers, in 1895 received an offer from Street and Smith to begin a series about a youngster at prep school, and Frank Merriwell, student at Fardale Academy, came into being the next year. Patten produced 208 Merriwell books over the next twenty-odd years, detailing Frank's career at Fardale and Yale, his younger brother Dick's, and even part of Frank Junior's, to total sales of approximately 125 million copies. The Merriwell plots, whose details were familiar to an entire generation between 1900 and 1920, were frantically athletic. Frank won every big game in Fardale's history and Yale's, and so did Dick after him. Each was at Yale nine years, and each graduated with honors. (Toward the end of his career, Patten, who never went to Yale, or any other college, received a varsity "Y" from a group of Yale alumni.) Both were fullbacks, both were pitchers, both stroked the crew—Frank threw a "doubleshoot" ball that curved twice before it reached the plate, while Dick possessed a "jump ball" that rose a full foot as it approached the batter. In track meets the Merriwells ran the dashes, the half mile, the mile, did the pole vault, the broad jump, the high jump, and threw the hammer. In vacation periods they hunted big game, punched cows, explored the jungle, mined gold, and so on. Frank also left Yale for a time, during which he worked for a railroad, settled a strike, wrote a hit play, played major league baseball, beat the Irish boxing champion, bought a horse that won the English Derby, and broke the course record at St. Andrews.

The Merriwells were surrounded with a group of active, recognizably normal friends—Harry Nettleton, who stuttered (always good for a laugh), loyal Bart Hodge and Jack Diamond, Barney Mulloy (an Irish comic), and Ephraim the Vermont farmboy with a down-East accent. Rather daringly, Patten provided the Merriwells with girl friends, Frank with Inza Burrage (a brunette) and Elsie Bellwood (a blonde) in alternate books and Dick with Doris Templeton. (After an eighteen-year courtship, Frank finally married Inza.)

In focusing his stories on school and college life and on athletics, Patten opened up for his young readers a world that Alger never knew. During the nineties, and especially after 1900, athletics turned professional. Baseball and football became mass spectator sports and increasingly big business. Instead of the bankers and merchants of Alger's books,

Patten's series reflected a boy's secret desire to be Home Run Baker, Christy Mathewson, Pudge Heffelfinger, or Three-finger Mordecai Brown. This was also the era of Theodore Roosevelt, the Boy Scouts, the outdoors of Ernest Thompson Seton, and "the strenuous life," when hunting, exploring, mining, ranching, and athletics were made to seem exciting and glamorous activities—even prizefighting with its plug-uglies and gentlemen such as Sullivan, Corbett, Kilrain, and Ruby Robert Fitzsimmons. Patten caught the spirit of this emergent cult of mass sport in his books, tailoring them to the pattern of the new sets of heroes whom boys held in respect, and the new interests of a frenetically physical time.

The Merriwells tied morality and athletics together in highly satisfactory fashion. Patten, a pious man himself, felt that the series gave him "an opportunity to preach—by example—the doctrine of a clear mind in a clean and healthy body" and he took full advantage of it. "I did my best," he wrote later of his books, "to keep them clean, and make them beneficial without allowing them to become namby-pamby or Horatio Algerish." The Merriwells did not smoke, drink, or swear, because such habits were unhealthy and unathletic; thus Patten avoided the moral issue in his preaching and convinced his readers that morals and manliness went together. Frank once played a game of pool, but only to defeat a pool shark who hoped to victimize one of Frank's friend. As for whiskey— "'I do not want liquor,' Frank's voice remained on an even keel, 'and I will thank you to put away that flask. Don't you know that you can't drink *that* and play good baseball?'" Dick Merriwell put the case against cigarettes thus: "Cigarettes dull the faculties, stunt and retard the physical development, unsettle the mind, and rob the persistent user of will power and the ability to concentrate." It is no wonder that parents who objected to the adventures of Rattlesnake Ned and Jesse James approved of the Merriwells.

Implicit in the Merriwell books is a concept of success markedly different from that stated in Alger. The Alger hero's rise is measurable in accountable material terms; we know where our hero starts, where he will end, and we can measure his progress in the size of his wallet. The Merriwell books recognize success as something quite different, in terms of the personal satisfaction of excellence, of the assumption of authority through virtue, of establishing leadership by example, of excelling under the rules, of "doing the right thing" and "playing the game." This was spectacularly illustrated by a thug hired to break Frank's arm before the big ball game. Frank felled his attacker and then helped him to his feet and befriended him, leading to the thug's unforgettable line, "Gee, I don't know w'y it is, but jes' bein' wid youse makes me want ter do de square t'ing."

As Alger equated wealth and virtue, so the Merriwells equated virtue with the discipline of sport—the books were intended, Patten said, "to fire a boy's ambition to become a good athlete, in order that he may develop into a strong, vigorous, and right-thinking man." Using the athletic contest as his central device, Patten stressed success as self-improvement, self-realization, self-control, self-conquest. "It is possible for every boy," Dick Merriwell once said, "to improve himself, to become handsomer, stronger, manlier." The Merriwells' morals are those of the game, their enemies' vices those allied to poor sportsmanship, lack of control, false ambition. Villainy in the Merriwell world derived from evasion, distrust, hypocrisy, conceit, self-indulgence; virtue involved friendship, sincerity, frankness, true humility, regard for the rules. Chester Arlington, the villain of the Dick Merriwell series, although strong, handsome, athletic, and intelligent, has

> too much pride, too much conceit, too little sympathy with others, and too little undeviating honesty . . . Chester's one great weakness was that he could not recognize his own weak spots. He believed it impossible that he should fail through any fault of his own.

The Merriwells "play fair," a theme stressed in all the books; they "play fair with themselves, and the rest of the world," Patten's implied rule for living. Again using the analogy of the playing field, he emphasized the virtues of the competitor who refuses to give up and who plays the string out. In *Dick Merriwell's Grit* he inserted an eloquent passage about the "quitter" that might have come directly from Theodore Roosevelt himself:

> Do not quit. Above all things else, do not be a quitter. The boys who have a large amount of stick-to-it-iveness invariably develop into men who persist against all obstacles and succeed in the struggle of life. They rise above their companions and surroundings, and are pointed out as successful men. Those who do not see beneath the surface often say that their success is nothing but luck; of course there is a singular something called luck, but in nine cases out of ten luck plays little or no part in the game of life. . . . Quitters become ordinary men, followers of their more persistent and determined fellows. They form the rank and file of the laboring classes. They never rise to hold positions of trust and influence. At least, if one ever does rise through chance to hold such a position, it almost invariably happens that sometime his original weakness causes him to fail and fall. He is not a stayer.

Patten, like Alger, usually avoided the social issues of the day, but he allowed the Merriwells an occasional pointed comment. No Italians or

Jews or Poles appear in the books—the Merriwell companions are Irish, English, Dutch, Scots, and so on—but on the other hand Frank once outraged a crowd by shaking hands with a Negro jockey who had ridden a good race, and the books never, like those of many of his contemporaries, used Negro or Jewish types for low comedy purposes. (Patten later fought the Klan in New Jersey and in 1939 wrote a radio script for the Council Against Intolerance in which Frank Merriwell defended a Jewish ballplayer on the Fardale nine.) Sports, in Patten's view, basing their rewards on ability and discipline, were democracy at work. Frank, when he tried out for Yale's baseball team, found that he was judged on his skill alone, leading him to realize that "In athletics strength and skill win, regardless of money or family; so it happened that the poorest man in the university stood a show of becoming the lion and idol of the whole body of young men . . . ," a theme that Patten carried consistently through the series.

Neither Merriwell cared much for money; though the source of their income is always obscure, Frank is able to reply to an offer to hunt treasure in Peru, "I am so situated that the mere desire for riches might not be sufficient to induce me to participate in such a project." Noticeably, the young villains tend to be wealthy, idle, aristocratic young men, such as Roland Ditson, "a contemptible cur" whose parents "furnished him with plenty of loose change," and Chester Arlington, Dick's nemesis. Patten, in *Dick Merriwell's Choice*, gave his hero an eloquent passage about the meaning of wealth:

"My friend," said Dick, "you're about old enough to learn the lesson that money doesn't make the man."

"But money makes the mare go. Feller's got to have money to amount to anything in this world."

"Not always. Some of the greatest men the world has ever known were poor men."

"Don't believe it! Everybody is out for dough!"

"Not everybody," said Dick. "Even in these modern times there are men who are too busy to make money. There are men who follow their profession or careers with a certain lofty purpose, and refuse to give over their object, even for a short time, in order that they may make money."

The shift of values since Alger's time was never made more evident, for such a speech could never come from Ragged Dick. The Merriwells spoke to a different age and a different culture.

The athletic juvenile, as Patten wrote it, still remains a staple in the field, as the stories of John R. Tunis and Jackson Scholz testify. Rivals to the Merriwells appeared immediately, of course. Hurst and Company had

"Graham Forbes" writing about *The Boys of Columbia High*, a second series about Frank Armstrong, and a third about *Ben Stone at Oakdale*. Stratemeyer produced "Lester Chadwick," an authority on sports "unexcelled by any living author or coach," and *The Baseball Joe Series;* he also produced Jack Ranger who starred in every sport at Washington Hall and who hunted, explored, and caught criminals during vacations. Zane Grey brought his considerable talents to *The Young Pitcher* and *The Red-Headed Outfield;* the great Giant star, Christy Mathewson, wrote (with help from John Wheeler, a professional) *First-Base Faulkner, Second-Base Sloan*, and so on around the diamond. A cut above the rest were Ralph Henry Barbour and William Heyliger. Barbour broke into the market in 1899 with a superb football story, *The Half-Back*, followed by *The Crimson Sweater, Behind the Line, Merritt Leads the Nine*, and at least two books a year for the next thirty years. Barbour took the seasonal cycle of sports from baseball to football to hockey and basketball to baseball and track again at a school named Hillton, or Yardley, or something of the sort, and then changed schools and heroes for another round. Heyliger's *Captain of the Nine* (1912) was the first of a beautifully-written series of baseball books, filled with every boy's memories, he said, "of the wide free field, the smell of early grass, the ripple of soft breeze on flushed faces, the damp give of springy turf . . ."

Though Patten's books sold spectacularly, Edward Stratemeyer's syndicate dominated the juvenile field for more than a quarter of a century until his death in 1930. Stratemeyer, a graduate of Street and Smith's writing stable, published the first three books about the famous Rover boys—Dick, Tom, and Sam—in 1899, taking the Merriwells' adventures, adding a bit of Alger's morality, and creating an instantly successful series. In 1906 he took the Rover formula and added speed to make the Motor Boys series a runaway success, for the automobile was by then an accomplished fact and every boy dreamed of owning, as the Motor Boys did, a giant six-cylinder racer capable of forty miles an hour. Then Stratemeyer had an even better idea; he formed a syndicate and by 1908 he had at least ten juvenile series operating under ten different names, with a half-dozen or more hack-writers working for him. Mass production had been known before in publishing. But Stratemeyer's assembly-line technique soon made him the Henry Ford of the juvenile industry.

The Rover Boys and Motor Boys books, and the majority of other Stratemeyer productions, were built about adventure, action, humor, and suspense, with a minimum of instructive moralizing. Stratemeyer shrewdly recognized that what interested the general adult reading public would also interest youngsters, and so constructed his books that they fell just below the interest level of subnormal adult intelligence—that is, dealing with automobile, airplanes, sports, westerns, sea and war stories, exploring, and so on. They were, in effect, watered-down popular pulps, geared to the adolescent mind. A mild and moral man himself, Stratemeyer never allowed violence to get out of hand; his heroes used their fists, hot water, whitewash, stout sticks, and various other weapons to defeat villains, but never guns. Whether the books appeared under the name of "Arthur Winfield" (The Rovers), "Clarence Young" (The Motor Boys), "Captain Ralph Bonehill," "Frank V. Webster," "Roy Rockwood," "Jim Bowie," "Laura Lee Hope," "Carolyn Keene," "May Hollis Barton," or any other of the Stratemeyer pseudonyms, the formula remained that of the "action" pulp, diluted for youthful tastes. His formula called for exactly fifty jokes per book, no embracing or kissing girls, and either exclamation points or a question at the end of each chapter, such as, "What lay behind the mysterious wall?" or "Suddenly Tom and his father heard a tremendous explosion from the garage!"

Stratemeyer usually thought up the characters and plot outlines. An assistant (often Howard Garis, who wrote "Uncle Wiggly" on his own) filled in the outlines and passed them on to writers who did a section for twenty-five to one hundred dollars, depending on the writer's skill and the series' importance. The pieces then came back to the Stratemeyer offices where they were put together, scanned for discrepancies, and passed on to Stratemeyer, who gave final approval and sent them to the printer. He selected the names for the authors and copyrighted all major characters; he also retained possession of the plates, renting them to printers, not selling them. Exactly how many books were produced by the Stratemeyer syndicate cannot be verified. According to some estimates, Stratemeyer himself accounted for one hundred and sixty volumes under various pseudonyms, sixty or so under his own name, and devised plots for eight hundred others. By 1920 his production line was the country's largest single source of juvenile books, much to the despair of librarians, who disapproved of every one. The Motor Boys sold four million copies, the Rovers six million, Tom Swift perhaps six million and a half. So effective was his syndicate that in a survey of children in Illinois in 1926 ninety-eight per cent of those questioned named a Stratemeyer character as their favorite.

Stratemeyer learned his trade under the great ones—Edward Ellis, William Adams, Alger himself—and whenever a new demand appeared, he was in the market with a book for it. "Clarence Young" not only did *The Motor Boys* (Jerry, Bob, Ned, an eccentric inventor, Professor Snodgrass, and a motorized villain named Noddy Nixon) but *The Racer Boys* and *The Motor Girls,* the latter featuring Cora Kimball and her new touring car. "Frank V. Webster" (who wrote "much like the style of the boys' favorite author, the late lamented Horatio Alger, Jr.") carried on the master's tradition with titles like *Tom The Telephone Boy, Dick The Bank Boy, Bob Chester's Grit,* and *Jack The Runaway.* Stratemeyer had an *Old Glory Series,* a *Pan-American Series,* a *Colonial Series,* a *Civil War Series* and half a dozen others running simultaneously. *Bomba The Jungle Boy* competed with Tarzan; Dave Porter, Don Sturdy, and Jack Ranger with the Merriwells. "Victor Appleton" wrote *The Motion Picture Boys* and "Captain Wilbur Lawton" *The Boy Aviator Series,* about Frank and Harry Chester, "up-to-date gritty youths" who owned a $10,000 prize airship named The Golden Eagle.

For girls the syndicate had *The Moving Picture Girls,* Ruth and Alice DeVere, who went to Hollywood with their father, a prominent stage actor, when he lost his voice and had to enter the movies. There were also *The Outdoor Girls* who had adventures at camp, in the mountains, at the lake, in Florida, at Yellowstone, and elsewhere, and *The Girls at Central High* who had much the same kind of adventures at home. "Laura Lee Hope" wrote *Bunny Brown and His Sister Sue* for the under-ten group and was also responsible for the Bobbsey Twins Series, surely the most syrupy girls' books ever written. There were two sets of twins—Freddie and Bert, and Nan and Flossie—who along with Snap the Dog, Snoop the Cat, and Dinah the comic cook belonged to Mr. Bobbsey, who ran a lumberyard. Excitement in the Bobbsey household meant something like the disappearance of a favorite doll, Snoop caught up a tree, or the appearance of gypsies in town. Martha Finley's *Elsie Dinsmore* series, which stretched out into twenty-eight volumes from 1868 to 1905, and her *Mildred* series (seven volumes, 1876–94) may have been preferred by parents, but the girls preferred the adventures of the Moving Picture girls in Hollywood or Cora's trip to New York in her Hupmobile. Girls no doubt also read boys' books, borrowed from brothers and friends—but what boy wanted to be caught with the Bobbseys?

Whatever the literary level of Stratemeyer's products, no parent could complain of their morality. Some objected to their implied violence (though Stratemeyer was less at fault than many of his competitors); others objected to their obviously impossible plots (how many average boys ended up on Pershing's staff, were given command of a Navy destroyer, or captured bank-robber gangs by splashing them with whitewash?); others thought they did nothing for a boy's sense of language. The only real opposition Stratemeyer met came from Franklin K. Mathiews, chief librarian for the Boy Scouts of America, who claimed with some justification that the life of a Boy Scout in the popular books was nothing at all like what it really was in the Eagle Patrol of Ottumwa, Iowa. "One of the most valuable assets a boy has is his imagination," he wrote. "Story books of the right sort stimulate and conserve this noble faculty, while those . . . of the cheaper sort, by overstimulation, debauch and vitiate, as brain and body are debauched and destroyed by strong drink." To counteract stories of Scouts who broke rings smuggling Chinamen into California (*The Boy Scouts in The NorthWest; or Fighting Forest Fires*) and foiled plots to destroy Gatun Lock (*The Boy Scouts in the Canal Zone; or Fighting a Foreign Plot*) Mathiews and the Scouts commissioned Percy K. Fitzhugh to write one series about Tom Slade and another about Pee-Wee Harris, Scouts whose adventures were much more normal. Clarence Budington Kelland, a popular and skillful novelist, contributed Mark Tidd, a fat-boy detective who was at least the equal, in his way, of Philo Vance in erudition and intelligence. The Slade and Tidd books sold well, but so did "Lieutenant Howard Payson's" *Boy Scout Series* in which Bob Burke, leader of the Wolf Patrol, and his stalwart chums outwitted villains Jack Curtiss, Bill Bender, and Hank Handcraft in their various nefarious designs. It was hard for Slade to compete with Ned, the patrol leader in *Boy Scouts in the Mountains; or Finding A Lost Mine,* who crawled into a dark cave and suddenly found "one hand on a dead man's face and the other slipping in a pool of blood."

Of all the Stratemeyer productions, *The Rover Boys Series* was the most representative of the early twentieth-century juvenile; it was also Stratemeyer's favorite, written by him under the name of "Arthur M. Winfield." There were three Rovers, all perennial students at Putnam Hall, a military academy in New York State, all introduced to the reader on the second page of Chapter I:

> As old readers of this series know, the Rover boys were three in number, Dick being the oldest, fun-loving Tom the next, and sturdy-hearted Sam the youngest. They were the only offspring of Anderson Rover, a former traveler and mine-owner, who, at present, was living with his brother Randolph and his sister-in-law Martha, on their beautiful farm at Valley Brook, in the heart of New York State.

Dick's constant girl friend was Dora Stanhope, daughter of the Widow Stanhope, while two Laning sisters, Nellie and Grace, furnished companionship for Tom and Sam. The series included a rather large quota of villains, enough to provide relief for each other as one set served what Stratemeyer usually described as "a brief but richly-deserved jail sentence." The worst of the number was Dan Baxter, once a Putnam Hall student, "a fellow who had been a bully in school, but who was now a homeless wanderer on the face of the earth," a fallen juvenile angel dedicated solely to destroying the Rovers. Dan had his disciple, Mumps Fenwick, described tersely as "a bully's toady," and the help of his father, Arnold Baxter, a villain in his own right with his own toady, a small-time crook named Buddy McGurk. To round out the roster of enemies was an oily Machiavellian character named Josiah Crabtree, who seemed to have an almost hypnotic power over the Widow Stanhope and frequently kidnapped her. Wherever the Rovers were—On Land and Sea, In Southern Waters, Up The Amazon—one or more of the villains was certain to turn up, temporarily gain the upper hand, and finally retreat in disorder. Motivated by either money or revenge, they were vanquished by such things as a blow to the nose ("bringing a cry of pain and a flow of claret"), firm resistance (" 'I wouldn't touch liquor if I were starving!' cried Grace!"), or threat of exposure (" 'I shall call the police,' said Mr. Rover, at which Buddy cravenly turned tail and ran.") Yet at the end, unregenerate and unforgiving, Baxter and his cohorts remained to try another day:

> "Do you think we shall ever see Dan Baxter again?" questioned Sam.
> "I hardly think so," said Dick. "After what has happened he will not dare to show his face again."
> But Dan Baxter did show himself, and what he did to harm the Rover boys in the future will be told in another volume of this series, entitled "The Rover Boys at Camp; or The Rivals of Pine Island," in which we shall meet many of our old friends again.

Stratemeyer's admiration for Alger (he once wrote several bogus Algers under the old master's name) was clearly reflected in the characterization, and especially the prose, of the Rover series. Except for Alger himself, no writer of juvenile fiction had a more unerring sense of the hackneyed, nor did any other characters speak such unbelievable dialogue. Dick Rover, for example, on first viewing the Grand Canyon, remarks, "What a mighty upheaval of nature there must have once been at this place at some far distant time!" No Rover ever read a letter—he "perused its contents"—nor did a villain, when cornered, ever do anything but "tremble in his boots" and whine "Take all I have, but let me go!" Tied to a tree by a villain, a Rover predictably says, "Dan Baxter, you shall rue the day! Unloose me this instant!" It was all as formalized as Noh drama, so that the youthful reader knew exactly what to expect. And like Alger, Stratemeyer tended to belabor the obvious. In *The Rover Boys Out West*, for example, Crabtree tries to abduct the Widow Stanhope, wrecks the boys' stagecoach, and finally, cornered in a house, kicks one

Rover in the head, hits another with a club, fires three shots and leaps through a glass door to escape. As Dick, the last upright Rover, runs to pursue him, Tom shouts, "Take care of what you do! He may be in a desperate frame of mind!" Alger could have done no better.

The best of the Stratemeyer books was the *Tom Swift* series, much of which was written under the name of "Victor Appleton" by Howard Garis. Garis was a somewhat more resourceful writer than most of the Stratemeyer employees, and the Swift series was a distinct improvement over its companions, as well as the most popular syndicate property, since it sold six and a half million copies to the Rovers' six and the Motor Boys' four. There were forty Tom Swifts, published between 1910 and 1941, the last one eleven years after Stratemeyer died. Tom lives in Shipton, New York, and like his widowed father, is an inventor. His chum, Ned Newton, who works in a bank, is a fine, brave boy who serves as a kind of Boswell to Tom's genius. Feminine interest is supplied by Mary Nestor, a local girl "whose acquaintance Tom made after stopping a runaway horse" and to whom Tom remains engaged for thirty-one years. Mary, like Dora Stanhope, is every boy's dream of what his sister is not—sweet, admiring, pliable, always an appreciative audience. Humor is supplied by Mr. Wakefield Damon, "a wealthy, eccentric gentleman," who continually blesses some portion of his anatomy, clothing, or inanimate object ("Bless my shoelaces!" cried Mr. Damon), by Eradicate Simpson, a faithful Negro servant, and various dialect-speaking youngsters.

Like the Rovers, Tom has a number of enemies. The Happy Harry Gang, described vaguely as "a group of bad men," lurk about the Swift home, occasionally kidnapping Mary, Ned, or Mr. Damon. Addison Berg, a rival inventor and business agent, leads another gang when Happy Harry's group is temporarily imprisoned. Most important of all, however, is youthful Andy Foger, "a red-haired, squint-eyed, rich bully" who is always out to steal Tom's inventions, sabotage his dirigible, and thwart him in the big boat race.

Tom simply invents—almost everything one could think of—and the excitement of the plots lies in whether or not his invention will work, whether it can be protected from rival scientists or thieves, and whether it can be used to benefit one's friends, society, or nation.

In Tom Swift, Stratemeyer and Garis hit on a formula shrewdly designed to catch the interest of boys who were growing up in the midst of the twentieth century's great burst of invention and technology. Machines are always magic to the adolescent male, and Tom, the most prolific and imaginative inventor of them all, gave his readers one major invention and at least six minor ones in each book. Garis and Stratemeyer took the adventure story of the Rovers, combined it with Jules Verne, Thomas Edison, Ford, Marconi, and all the others who contributed to the excitement of the machine age, and mixed into it the greatest assortment of gadgets known to man.

The Swift books had the usual ingredients, a race, a chase, a capture, an escape, villainous villains, a decent respect for the proprieties. But what they had most of were machines—electric rifles, motorcycles, racing autos, various kinds of boats, television (in 1921), radios, eight different kinds of airplanes, guns, and a multitude of other things. Tom, in his private laboratory, casually solved problems that had stumped the world since Newton. What he invented was always *almost* plausible, just far enough around the corner to be visionary, not quite far enough to be absurd; many of his inventions, in fact, were only a year or so ahead of their real-life counterparts. A boy could read Tom Swift, a book at a time, feel that he was pretty well up on what was going on in science, and amaze his friends with bits of inaccurate but impressive scientific knowledge. Two of Tom's inventions have not yet been duplicated, his diamond-making machine (which made not industrial diamonds but blue-white gems as large as a golf-ball), and his silencer for airplane motors, which jet-plane manufacturers would dearly love to borrow. Stratemeyer and Garis were extremely clever in their use of pseudoscience, using convincing language and explaining processes in detail, except for a good deal of fuzziness about essentials. Tom's revolutionary storage battery, for example, which drove his electric runabout at thirty miles an hour, used oxide of nickel, steel, and iron oxide electrodes in a solution of lithium hydrate. It wouldn't work, of course, but it sounded so good that any boy who read the book could converse knowledgeably about nickel oxide and lithium hydrate with his friends until they read it too.

It is this faith in science, this admiration for the machine, that set Tom Swift apart from the financially minded Alger heroes, the hyperactive Merriwells, or the redoubtable Rovers, and made him a hero to the twentieth-century boy. Stratemeyer and Garis recognized the shift of values that took place in American society after 1900 and charted Tom's career accordingly. Alger's boys amassed fortunes by pluck and luck but, products of the Gilded Age that they were, to them material success seemed an end in itself. The athletic Merriwells, exponents of the ethics of the game, were proper heroes too, and the Rovers adventured in every part of the globe. Tom Swift had all of this and more. Though the books rarely mention money, Tom had $100,000 in the bank as early as 1914; he won dozens of races on land, sea, and in the air; he found adventures in tunnels, jungles, deserts, and at the bottom of the ocean and in the caves of ice. These were not the important things. What mattered was Tom's success at breaking through the barriers of the unknown. His books were filled, in their naïve way, with the excitement of a conquest of matter and space, the thrill of accomplishing with one's own brain and hands what others had hoped to do. It was not Rockefeller or Carnegie, Honus Wagner or Eddie Plank who were the implied heroes of the Swift books, but the Wright brothers, Steinmetz, Tesla, Edison, and the others who were pushing back the frontiers of knowledge and invention. Whereas Alger's boys faced the problems of an urbanized, acquisitive society, and the Merriwells the ethics of the competitive contest, Tom Swift grasped the technology of the machine age and brought it under control. He made scientific discovery exciting and technological advance adventurous, and most of all he made both seem useful and optimistic.

Even Tom could not go on forever. After Stratemeyer's death there was an obvious falling off in the quality of the series, and the last few were no more than weak science fiction. There was nothing much left by 1940 for Tom to invent. The scientific developments of midcentury were simply too much for his home laboratory, which could hardly compete with Oak Ridge, jet flight, and the exploration of space. A victim of technological unemployment, Tom ended his career in a house-trailer, a sad anticlimax to the speedy motorcycles and giant planes of his youth. In 1954 Grosset and Dunlap initiated a Tom Swift, Jr., series, in which Tom's son invented such things as Tomasite plastic (casings for nuclear reactors), a Swift Spectograph that analyzed anything in an instant, and a Damonscope (named after gentle, bumbling Mr. Damon) which detected fluorescence, or something, in space. But it was not the same.

The dividing line between the old tradition of juvenile fiction—from the Beadle books to Tom Swift—and the new can be placed approximately in the forties, a result of a number of factors. Improvements in school libraries and library training, the institution of better reading programs for adolescents, and the impact of child psychology on parents and teachers, all had powerful effects on the juvenile market. The competition of the comic book drastically changed the character of the audience. Television, later, simply made the whole Stratemeyer-Patten school of thought obsolete. The boy who can watch baseball and football on television, and to whom Africa, the South Seas, and the Sea of Tranquility are familiar territory on the television screen, finds little to excite him in the adventures of Dick Rover or Frank Merriwell. At the same time, growing sophistication, wider experience, and a rising set of expectations among mid-twentieth-century youth demanded higher levels of skill and conception from writers. It is not uncommon today to find on juvenile shelves in bookstores, historians like Daniel Boorstin and George Stewart, novelists like MacKinlay Kantor and Will Henry, or reporters like William K. Shirer and Hodding Carter. The gain in accuracy, depth, and relevance of information has been enormous. What has been lost is the pleasure of innocence—the joy of reading a peanut-butter smeared Merriwell in the attic on a rainy afternoon, or the delightful risk of finding out by flashlight, under the covers, how the Boy Scouts foiled a Japanese plot to dynamite the United States Navy.

Nonetheless, two survivors of the classic tradition remain—*The Hardy Boys* and *Nancy Drew,* both over forty years old. The Hardy Boys Series, now in its fiftieth volume, written by "Franklin W. Dixon" (at first Stratemeyer himself, then a succession of writers, and today Andrew E. Svenson and Harriet Stratemeyer Adams, the present syndicate partners) is nothing more than updated Rover. Students at Bayport High, Frank is eighteen, dark, and dependable, Joe seventeen, yellow-haired, impetuous. Chet Morton, a traditional fat-boy comic (described as "chunky and ever-hungry") provides the familiar chum-figure. His sister Iola ("dark and vivacious") furnishes companionship for Joe and her friend Callie Shaw, a taffy blonde who plays a guitar, for Frank. Hardy plots are frankly patterned after the detective story, bearing a more-than-accidental resemblance to Ellery Queen, since the boys' father, Fenton Hardy, is a retired New York police detective who runs his own agency with the help of excop Sam Radley and private pilot Jack Wayne. Mother Laura and spinster Aunt Gertrude complete the family. Whatever the boys' adventures, they all sound as if they came from Dave Porter, the Motor Boys, or the Boy Aviators—the Hardys trace an Aztec statue, settle a South American revolution, solve the sabotage of a bridge, find a lost mine, capture jewel thieves, and so on. The plot of *The Secret Agent on Flight 101,* for example, is vintage Don Sturdy or Jack Ranger with the addition of jets:

> Rarely do magicians reveal their professional secrets. Consequently Frank and Joe Hardy are amazed when a well-known magician, the Incredible Hexton, offers to reveal the secret of his "Vanishing Man Act" and invites Mr. Hardy to be the subject. When their detective father fails to reappear, his sons are convinced that something sinister is afoot, despite Hexton's insistence that Mr. Hardy is playing a joke on them.
>
> While desperately searching for their father, Frank and Joe find themselves working with SKOOL, a U.S. organization of crack secret agents pitted against UGLI, an international ring of spies stealing government secrets from the U.S. and other democratic countries.

In a lighthouse off the coast of New England and in Scotland, Frank and Joe and their pal Chet Morton grimly match wits with UGLI's evil agents. With cool daring the three boys invade the magician's Scottish castle, where an astounding surprise awaits them.

The young detectives' gripping adventures culminate in a dramatic climax when they unmask the secret agent on Flight 101.

The Hardys, like the Rovers, meet the unexpected with steady confidence. Held captive by an evil Hindu named Bangalore in *The Hooded Hawk Mystery*, the boys' skill at jujitsu pulls them through:

Frank and Joe were seized by four guards, while two others raised their whips. But the brothers did not flinch.

Instead, Frank leaned toward Joe. "Here we go again!" he whispered.

A knowing smile crossed Joe's face. The expression was a signal for action. Before the whips could descend, the Hardys, using a jujitsu twist, flung their would-be floggers to the floor, and with the speed of Bengal tigers, tore the whips from the men's hands. The guards shrank back as the boys raised the whips.

Bangalore's jaw dropped. "How did you do that?" he asked, amazed, then added, "I like your courage. My men are skilled in wrestling, but you took them by surprise. It will entertain me to have you demonstrate your skill. Perhaps it can save you a flogging—or maybe even your lives."

Needless to say, Frank and Joe defeat Bangalore's guards handily, finishing the last bout as Fenton Hardy and the State Police arrive in time to prevent Bangalore from forcing poison pellets down their throats.

More interesting, inventive, and fully-textured than the Hardys—and the only juvenile to outsell Swift and the Rovers—is Nancy Drew, another descendant of the Stratemeyer Syndicate written by "Carolyn Keene" (Harriet S. Adams). ("Carolyn Keene" also writes *The Dana Girls Series*, sisters whose adventures resemble but cannot match Nancy's.) Begun in 1930, the Nancy Drew series reached forty-five volumes in 1969, with no sign of termination. All are based on the mystery-adventure-Gothic pattern developed by Mary Roberts Rinehart, geared to the level of the early teen. Nancy lives in the upper-middle-class suburb of River Heights, the daughter of a prosperous, widowed lawyer named Carson Drew, who worries about her, pays her not inconsiderable bills, trusts her absolutely, and allows her to do exactly what she pleases—as an ideal Daddy should.

Sixteen, blonde, attractive but not beautiful, Nancy is very much her own girl (mothered occasionally by a crotchety old family retainer, Han-

nah), the product of a good school, ballet and piano lessons, and world
travel. She rides well, swims superbly (once beating an Olympic champion) and is an excellent shot with a pistol when necessary. With all her
accomplishments, and the recipient of constant praise ("Of course, you
are quite right!" cried Mrs. Chatham, marvelling at Nancy's cleverness),
Nancy's head is never turned:

> "And three cheers for Nancy Drew!" said Mr. Smith warmly.
> "She solved the mystery of my missing brother."
> "She succeeded in her quest for the lost half of the map," added
> Ned warmly.
> "And caught the villains!" put in Bill Tomlin. "She even————"
> "Oh, stop it!" cried Nancy, blushing to the roots of her hair. "I
> couldn't have done a thing without the help of every one of you."
> That was like the girl—to remain generous and unspoiled no
> matter how much praise was heaped upon her. This was to remain
> true as she solved her next mystery, "The Clue in the Jewel Box."
> "Come on, let's sing," Nancy urged.
> She started a familiar tune which the crowd took up. Their
> voices carried far across the water as the *Primrose* started for its
> home port. The adventure was at an end.

Her fiancé, Ned Nickerson, a sophomore at Emerson College, ap-
pears only when Nancy wishes him to. He has never been allowed a
single kiss in over thirty years of dating, and since he is in college during
the academic year and counselor at a boys' camp during the summer, he
is never in the way. Nancy blushes when Ned (who has very little time
between adventures to speak of such things) occasionally refers to the
fact that he expects to marry her some day, which is as close as the series
ever comes to sex. Ned, however, never importunes, invites her to all the
proms and fraternity dances, happily content to serve as attentive escort
and occasional rescuer.

"Carolyn Keene's" plots follow a predictable pattern. Nancy by accident stumbles into a mysterious situation, probes it, and is warned to
stay out. However, she continues to investigate, follows a series of puzzling clues, and after some dangerous moments solves the affair, which
usually involves money, wills, valuables, hidden jewels, lost documents,
old maps, forgeries, embezzlements, and the like. Each narrative includes
a chase, a kidnapping, or both, a hideout, a mysterious box or stairway
or chamber or code, and some violence (lightning, dynamite, landslides,
fires, storms, auto wrecks, wild animal attacks) which she barely escapes.
Nancy is assisted by two friends, George (so-named, and not Georgie)
Fayne, a masculine girl who cuts her hair short and wears mannish

An early American Horn Book.
CULVER PICTURES, INC.

Title page of Poor Richard's Almanac. CULVER PICTURES, INC.

Four early best sellers:
The Gunmaker of Moscow,
by Sylvanus T. Cobb;
St. Elmo, by Augusta J. Evans;
Three Weeks, by Elinor Glyn;
Bad Girl, by Viña Delmar.

An early Frank Merriwell cover. **CULVER PICTURES, INC.**

Three nineteenth-century poetry volumes: *The American Common Place Book of Poetry* (1831); *Poems,* by Lidia H. Sigourney (1844); *A Library of Poetry and Song* (1872).

One of the first Tom Swift titles by "Victor Appleton" (Howard Garis). **CULVER PICTURES, INC.**

clothes (facts which are absolutely not to be misconstrued in this context) and Bess Marvin, a frilly, bubbleheaded type who is always terrified when the chips are down.

The society in which Nancy moves is the orderly, suburban society of the thirties, untouched by depression, war, or trouble. There are no cigarettes at River Heights High, no high-jinks at Emerson College dances (where the high point of the evening is the crowning of the Queen) no makeup, no liquor—Nancy does not even drink coffee. In the earlier books there were Negroes named Uncle and Beulah who said "Yassum, Miss Nancy," and some comic foreigners and aggressive Jews, most of whom were written out of later editions. Nancy's appeal (a steady million copies a year) seems to be primarily to the eleven to fifteen age group, those too old for dolls and not yet ready for the drive-ins, who find in her what they hope soon to be—a poised, capable, self-sufficient girl in control of her life; one who can take care of herself and who needs neither guidance nor exhortation.

RHYMES FOR EVERYBODY

He is the greatest poet,
Who will renounce all art,
And take his heart and show it,
To every other heart.

—SAM WALTER FOSS

To the Puritan colonist, poetry was a useful but not especially important branch of rhetoric, a view also held by most of his non-Puritan contemporaries. He knew and respected the great English poetic tradition, but in the midst of the business of settling a new continent he had little time for that kind of poetry which, as Cotton Mather called it, was "meer Playing and Fiddling upon Words." Poetry which might enlighten, persuade, or instruct—this he approved and appreciated.

The colonists wrote a surprisingly large amount of poetry, public and private, for such useful purposes. The function of public poetry, they believed, was instructive; it dealt with historically important events, theological argument, funerals, commemorations, ordinations, and the like. *The Whole Booke of Psalmes, Faithfully Translated . . .* , published at Cambridge in 1640 and known as "The Bay Psalm Book," was exactly such poetry, intended to turn the psalms into metrical versions suitable to congregational singing. The translators made it eminently clear that they strove "for conscience rather than eloquence, fidelity rather than poetry," thereby making a distinction between poetry as high art and poetry as a functional art that remained clear throughout American literary history.

To the seventeenth-century settler, poetry of this second order taught moral lessons. To the eighteenth century it was not only educative but informative. The first popular verse in America was the broadside, a

sheet of paper printed on one side, containing verses designed to give
the maximum of information in the most quickly dispersed form. Sold
for a penny by street hawkers, the broadside—really a form of poetic
journalism—circulated swiftly news about crimes, domestic tragedies,
natural disasters, battles, funerals, sermons, proclamations, holidays, or
anything else of public interest. Anybody could write them. Young
Franklin, by no means a poet, dashed off doggerel like "Teach the Pirate" and "The Lighthouse Tragedy," to capitalize on the news. The
latter, written on reading of the drowning of Captain Worthilake (keeper
of the Boston Light) and his family, Franklin later called "wretched stuff
in the Grub Street style, but it sold wonderfully." A few stanzas of one
reputed version of the ballad testify to the accuracy of Franklin's judgment, though the poem was no worse, probably, than most such impromptu rhyming:

> With wild nor'wester came the morning,
>   Cold and clear the heartless sky.
> Come wife, take Ruth. The pull will be long,
>   So—into the boat I will take you home.
>
> Now they reach the open channel
>   Where the flood tide breasts the gale,
> Rears a topping wall of water,
>   Making Anne's cheeks grow pale.
>
> Quick the prow is upward borne:
>   George in Anne's arms is thrown.
> Husband, wife and child together
>   To the chilly waves have gone.
>
> Frenzied clasp of wife and daughter
>   Bears the sturdy swimmer down;
> Save the boat upon the water,
>   Nothing of their fate is known.

Popular broadside poetry tended to be factual, direct, minimally
metaphoric. Originality and polish were no virtues, for the verse was
aimed at providing information in palatable and easily remembered
form. Built about simple imagery, limited to a basic vocabulary, it was
nonetheless the most vigorous verse written in the eighteenth century,
and certainly the most widely read. It is impossible to calculate the circulation of broadsides, but the fact that they appeared steadily for a

hundred years, until the rise of newspapers in the late eighteenth century, testifies to their tenacity. Something like "The Victory of Captain Paul Jones," or "The Death of Major André" must have had tremendous sales.

Didacticism and information, the double aim of broadside verse, were to become the distinguishing characteristics of the American popular poetic tradition. The broadside account of the public hanging of Richard Wilson in Boston in 1732 accomplished both admirably:

> This day from gaol must Wilson be
> Conveyed in a cart'
> By Guards unto the Gallows Tree
> To die as his Desert;
> For being wicked overmuch
> There for a wicked crime,
> Must take his fatal Lot with such
> As die before their time.

"The Great Boston Fire of 1787" drew an authentic picture of panic:

> When refreshing feeble Nature
> Friends were sitting round the Board,
> Curling Smoak surrounds their Dwellings
> With Commission from the Lord.
> Fierce Aeolus spreads his Pinions,
> Howls along with hideous Groan;
> Flaming Arrows tare the Structures,
> All is in Confusion thrown.

Collections such as Tilden's *Miscellaneous Poems* (1716) or Benjamin Church's *Patriot Muse* (1764) reprinted the better examples of such popular verses, many of them dealing with the wars against the French and Indians. There were many on Braddock, and many on Wolfe; John Maylem and George Cockings, among others, wrote ballads about Louisburg, and there were dozens inspired by the Battle of Quebec. They ranged in sophistication from Nathaniel Niles' "The American Hero," done in difficult Sapphic meter, to the rustic doggerel of Peter St. John's "American Taxation":

> While I relate my story,
>   Americans give ear;
> Of Britain's fading glory
>   You presently shall hear;
> I'll give a true relation,

> Attend to what I say,
> Concerning the taxation
> Of North America.

As temperatures rose in the conflict with Britain, every Parliamentary act, Crown order, or Board of Trade directive tended to generate retaliatory ballads. The Tea Act, for example, elicited such poems as "The Blasted Herb," "The Fated Plant," "A Lady's Adieu to Her Tea-Table," "A New Song to an Old Tune," and "Virginia Banishing Tea, By a Lady," which began

> Begone, pernicious baleful Tea,
> With all Pandora's ills possessed,
> Hyson, no more beguiled by thee,
> My noble sons shall be oppressed.
> To Britain fly, where gold enslaves
> And venal men their birthright sell;
> Tell North and his brib'd clan of knaves,
> Their bloody acts were made in hell!

After Lexington and Concord, "The King's Own Rangers," "A New Story for the Grenadiers," "The Enemy's First Coming to Boston," "A Song for the Redcoats," "The Patriot's Prayer," and hundreds of other songs followed the progress of American arms. "The Present War" was typical:

> Britons grown big with pride
>   And wanton ease,
> And tyranny beside
>   They sought to please
> Their craving appetite;
> They strove with all their might,
> They vow'd to make us fight,
>   To make us bow.
> The plan they laid was deep,
>   Even like hell;
> With sympathy I weep
>   While here I tell
> Of that base murderous brood,
> Void of the fear of God,
> Who came to spill our blood
>   In our own land.

Particular battles and heroes brought other poems—Joseph Warren's death, Arnold's treason, Burgoyne's defeat, Howe's retreat, victories at Trenton or King's Mountain:

> T'was on a pleasant mountain
> The Tory heathens lay;
> With a doughty major at their head,
> One Ferguson they say,
> Cornwallis had detached him,
> A thieving for to go,
> And catch the Carolina men
> Or bring the rebels low. . . .

or the haunting "Hale in the Bush," which appeared after Nathan Hale's execution:

> The breezes went steadily through the tall pines,
> A-saying oh, hush! a-saying oh, hush!
> As stilly stole by a bold legion of horse,
> For Hale in the bush, for Hale in the bush.
> "Keep still" said the thrush as she nestled her young,
> In a nest by the road, in a nest by the road,
> "For the tyrants are near and with them appear,
> What bodes us no good, what bodes us no good."

Almanacs, those most prolific and indispensable books for the colonial household, provided another medium for the publication and distribution of popular poetry. Practically coterminous with settlement, almanacs began appearing in 1639, and by the late seventeenth century New York, Boston, Philadelphia and most other major cities had at least two or three almanac series in publication. (Franklin's famous *Poor Richard* began in 1733). Early American almanacs resembled their English counterparts, emphasizing mostly meteorological and astrological information; later almanacs expanded their offerings, including scattered bits of wisdom and fact, proverbs, jests, pieces of history, essays, and much verse.

By the mid-eighteenth century the almanac had an important function in American life as the most widely distributed medium of general information and, until the spread of journalism, the most influential. While almanac editors reprinted poetry from the English masters, they also printed a good deal of topical popular verse. Nathaniel Ames in 1729, for example, put in his almanac a witty reminder to his readers:

> Man was at first a perfect, upright creature,
> The lively image of his great Creator.
> When Adam fell, all men in him transgressed;
> And since that time they err that are the best.
> The printer errs; I err—much like the rest.

> Welcome's the man for to complain to me,
> Whose self and works are quite from error free.

An almanac of 1749, gave thanks for a year of peace following King George's War:

> No heroes' ghosts, with garments rolled in blood,
> Majestic stalk; the golden age renewed,
> No hollow drums in Flanders beat; the breath
> Of brazen trumpets rings no peals of death.
> The milder stars their peaceful beams afford,
> And sounding hammer beats the wounding sword
> To ploughshares now; Mars must to Ceres yield,
> And exiled Peace returns and takes the field.

Another poet, in Ames's edition of 1757, explained to his readers how "Grumbling" damaged a man's efficacy and told how to rid oneself of the habit:

> I choose to labor, rather than to fret;
> What's rage in some, in me goes off in sweat.
> If times are ill, and things seem never worse,
> Men, manners, to reclaim—I take my horse:
> One mile reforms 'em, or if aught remain
> Unpurged—'tis but to ride as far again.
> Thus on myself in toils I spend my rage:
> I pay the fine, and that absolves the age.
> Sometimes, still more to interrupt my ease,
> I take my pen, and write such things as these.

The hundreds of almanacs printed in America over the span of a century and a half included literally thousands of similar poems, ephemeral, modest, aimed at the public.

Though the rise of newspapers in the later eighteenth century obviated the need for broadside and almanac verse as a means of public communication, the early nineteenth century still recognized poetry as an important instrument of instruction. There were two kinds of poetry, critics explained—"great" or "high" poetry; and poetry that might guide, teach, and elevate the majority of people without being "great." No one would dispute the eminence of Shakespeare and Milton, but admittedly there were also lesser poets whose verse might, in its way, be equally valid and useful art. George B. Cheever, in the preface to his *American Common-Place Book of Poetry* (1831) distinguished rather carefully between poetry that is "stately and perfect . . . , containing throughout the true power of spirit and harmony . . . , deep and sublime emotion," and "common-place poetry . . . , quiet and unambitious, like a pleasant thought when such are wanted, sweet and chaste in moral influence."

This distinction between popular and "high" art remained perfectly clear in the history of American poetry, although academic critics have tended to confuse the two and blur the distinctions much more than the general public has. The nineteenth-century reader who was moved by Lydia Sigourney knew quite well that he was not reading Milton; the twentieth-century reader who liked Edgar Guest's *Just Folks* knew he was not reading T. S. Eliot's *Prufrock,* which appeared the same year. He was well aware that in reading Mrs. Sigourney and Guest he was not reading "poetry" as the critics defined it, but reading popular verse. (Guest, interestingly enough, never called himself a poet.) The reader had no suitable name for what he was reading, but he liked it, respected it, and was affected by it; it was to be read for a variety of purposes, but chiefly, as Cheever said, "to please and do good." This was, obviously, *popular* poetry in the cultural sense.

Editors of anthologies of popular verse after Cheever made this distinction abundantly clear. William Cullen Bryant, who served as consultant for the best-selling *Library of Poetry and Song* (1872), distinguished between poems "acknowledged by the intelligent to be great," and those which, "though less perfect than others in form, have, by some power of touching the heart, gained and maintained a sure place in the popular esteem." There is poetry of "common apprehension," Bryant wrote, for "mankind at large . . . , near to the common track of the human intelligence," and there is "great poetry" by "acknowledged masters." Both, he believed, were art. Henry M. Coates' *Fireside Encyclopedia of Poetry* (1879) included only poems which in Coates' opinion "through some peculiar power, have touched the popular heart"; Anne Brackett and Ida Elliott, choosing selections for *Poetry for Home and School* (1879) took only those "of practical value for school, home, and family . . . , poetry which applies to life and helps [one] to live it."

Frank McAlpine, who sold thousands of copies of his *Popular Poetic Pearls* by subscription in 1885, selected "poems that live in the popular mind" rather than those "uttered by the master poets." Slason Thompson's anthology of *The Humbler Poets* (1886) included those "which speak out from a mind . . . amid the multitude, and not from the heights of the masters." Charles Gayley's *Poetry of the People* (1904) picked "poetry most characteristic of the people . . . , poetry the people possess and occupy." Hazel Felleman, who supervised the "Queries and Answers" page of *The New York Times Book Review* for fifteen years, in 1936 anthologized "The Best Loved Poems of the American People," written by those whom Edwin Markham called "the nearby poets." All of them knew exactly what they were doing—distinguishing between popular and "great" poetry.

The poetry of Mrs. Lydia Sigourney, a Connecticut lady known as "The Sweet Singer of Hartford," dominated the first fifty years of nineteenth-century popular verse, conceding only to Longfellow in popularity. Her first book appeared in 1815, her last in 1865; in the half-century between she published sixty-nine books and two thousand articles. She never varied from the pattern established in her first book, nor did she need to; every poem, no matter its length, tone, or subject, taught a clear and understandable lesson.

Mrs. Sigourney drew her subjects from her daily life and the news. A fire, a death, an accident, a crime, or a disaster furnished the opportunity for a dozen stanzas telling the story, with one or two added to draw the moral. She always responded graciously to requests for "lines" to commemorate an occasion, such as "Scenes at the Deathbed of the Reverend Dr. Payson," or "The Death of Garalfi Mohabi." She liked death poems, she said, which made her readers "feel sad but not unhappy," since death presupposed resurrection, and she immortalized in elegaic song everything from a canary who died of starvation to a child drowned in a bushel of swine food.

Mrs. Sigourney's annual production for gift annuals and poetry collections brought her a comfortable income; in her best year she turned out nine books. She also wrote children's books, household hints, histories, essays, etiquette books, and guides to morality and deportment; she contributed, she said, to over three hundred periodicals, and during the thirties and forties something from her pen was likely to appear in almost every issue of all the leading magazines. Her *Letters to Young Ladies* went through twenty American and five English editions, while her *Letters to Mothers* had eighteen American and four English editions.

Anything she wrote was saleable. Only Mrs. Sigourney could have written a popular dramatic poem about Pocahontas, skipping the Smith story and emphasizing instead her "quiet domestic life, and early death, presented in an animated and sympathetic manner, frequently interrupted by passages of reflection." Only Mrs. Sigourney could have rhymed Lafayette with "tears are wet." Given to words like "glorious," "sublime," and "heartfelt," she evolved a vocabulary that her readers instantly identified as "poetic." Waves always "dash'd" against the shore, rivers were "swol'n," Death "stalk'd," thoughts "mused," heaven "smil'd," tears fell like "briny dew," in a kind of easily recognized code her audience came to know and appreciate. In the periphrastic manner of the time, she made potatoes into "tub'rous roots," sugar and butter into "saccharine and oleaginous matter," and a cat into "a quadruped member of our establishment."

Her range of subject matter was so wide that it is difficult to choose a representative poem, but "Death of an Infant" serves as an example of her most persistent theme, no doubt the result of the death of her own first three babies:

> Death found strange beauty on that cherub brow
> And dashed it out. There was a tint of rose
> On cheek and lip;—he touched the veins with ice,
> And the rose faded. Forth from those blue eyes
> There spake a wishful tenderness,—a doubt
> Whether to grieve or sleep, which innocence
> Alone can wear. With ruthless haste, he bound
> The silken fringes of their curtaining lids
> Forever. There had been a murmuring sound,
> With which the babe would claim its mother's ear,
> Charming her even to tears. The spoiler set
> His seal of silence. But there beamed a smile
> So fixed and holy from that marble brow,—
> Death gazed, and left it there;—he dared not steal
> The signet-ring of heaven.

No other poet of the period remotely touched Mrs. Sigourney's fame (except Longfellow) but there were other favorites. James Hillhouse, a bright and unstable young man, published a long, overheated dramatic tragedy, *Hadad,* in 1825, a blend of Jewish history, English balladry, romantic landscape verse, and reflective moralizing. *Hadad* attracted much attention, and cuttings from it, usually the biblically-flavored passages, dotted anthologies and giftbooks. *Hadad's* description of the City of David seen from afar, a popular anthology piece, was poetry in the grand manner preferred by the public:

> 'Tis so—the hoary harper sings aright:
> How beautiful is Zion! Like a queen,
> Armed with a helm in virgin loveliness,
> Her heaving bosom in a bossy cuirass,
> She sits aloft, begirt with battlements
> The bulwarks swelling from the rock, to guard
> The sacred courts, pavilions, palaces,
> Soft gleaming through the umbrage of the woods,

Which tuft her summit, and like raven tresses,
Wave their dark beauty round the tower of David!

His shorter poems, collected in 1839, furnished additional choices, especially a curious poem called "Extract from a Poem Written on Reading an Account of the Opinions of a Deaf and Dumb Child before She had Received Instruction: She was Afraid of the Sun, Moon, and the Stars." The darkly melancholic tone of Hillhouse's work, combined with the shock of his suicide in 1841, drew popular attention to his poetry for a decade after his death.

John Pierpont, a Boston minister and businessman, was the era's favorite "occasion" poet, much in demand for religious, patriotic, and civic celebrations. Few collections failed to include some of his numerous "Patriotic Odes," "Centennial Poems," "Stanzas in Commemoration of . . . ," or "Lines on Laying the Cornerstone of. . . ." Possessed of a talent for saying the right thing in a way people considered dignified and conventional, Pierpont was undoubtedly the best-known public poet of the day.

John G. C. Brainerd, the first of a long line of newspaper poets, collected his first volume of verses in 1825. "Tuning his pastoral pipe to the woodland lays and lyrics of his native state, Connecticut," a critic wrote of him, Brainerd wrote about family life, the farm, childhood, daily tasks, and nature, themes later more successfully exploited by his friend Whittier, who wrote an appreciative preface for a posthumous collection of his works. Brainerd's impressions of Niagara Falls, which inspired more verse than any other single phenomenon in American nature, were among the most famous of all Niagara poems:

The thoughts are strange that crowd into my brain,
While I look upward to thee. It would seem
As if God poured thee from his hollow hand,
And hung his bow upon thine awful front;
And spoke in that loud voice which seemed to him
Who dwelt in Patmos for his Saviour's sake,
"The sound of many waters;" and had bade
Thy flood to chronicle the ages back,
And notch His centuries in the eternal rocks.
Deep calleth unto deep. And what are we,
That hear the question of that voice sublime?
O, what are all the notes that ever rung
From war's vain trumpet, by thy thundering side!
Yea, what is all the riot man can make,
In his short life, to thy unceasing roar!
And yet, bold babbler, what art thou to Him,

> Who drowned a world, and heaped the waters far
> Above its loftiest mountains?—a light wave,
> That breaks, and whispers of its Maker's might.

James Gates Percival (who was also a geologist, physician, linguist, botanist, and chemist) wrote on a variety of subjects, almost invariably melancholy; everything reminded Percival, a cheerful man in his non-poetic life, of mutability and death, and the public liked it. "Contemplations of Religion to the Poor," a long poem combining sadness with religion and death in typical Percival fashion, is about a dying widow who on her deathbed "asks not wealth nor pleasure, begs no more than Heaven's delightful volume," her Bible, and who dies happily as "her faith sees a new world":

> A few short moments over, and the prize
> Of peace eternal waits her, and the tomb
> Becomes her fondest pillow; all its gloom
> Is scattered. What a meeting there will be
> To her and all she loved here! and the bloom
> Of new life from those cheeks shall never flee:
> Theirs is the health that lasts through all eternity.

Richard Henry Dana, Sr., who counted Mistress Anne Bradstreet among his ancestors, served in the Massachusetts legislature and edited the *North American Review* for a time. He wrote a relatively small amount of verse, but he enjoyed a wide reputation and his name appeared in most standard collections. Much of his poetic prestige rested on "The Buccaneer," an interminably long narrative poem built about the currently popular character of the "heroic villain"—a tale of "heart and conscience," wrote critic Evert Duyckinck, with "scenes of visionary horror and the supernatural" mixed with "touches of human feeling . . . , and lovely, peaceful scenes of nature." Since it was easily excerpted, portions of it appeared again and again under titles such as "The Effect of the Ocean and Scenery on the Mind," or "The Power of the Soul in Investing External Circumstances with the Hue of Our Feelings":

> And see we thus sent up, rock, sand, and wood,
> Life, joy and motion from the sleepy flood?
> The world, O man, is like that flood to thee:
> Turn where thou wilt, thyself in all things see
> Reflected back. . . .
> Soul, fearful is thy power which transforms
> All things into its likeness; heaves in storms
> The strong, proud sea or lays it down to rest,

> Like the hushed infant on its mother's breast—
> Which gives each outward circumstance its hue,
> And shapes all others' acts and thoughts anew,
> That so, they joy, or love, or hate, impart,
> As joy, love, hate, holds rule within the heart.

The career of Charles Sprague, a Boston banker whose name was well known throughout New England in the eighteen-twenties and thirties, is a lesson in the mutability of reputations. Sprague, a self-educated boy from Boston's poorer classes, was apprenticed to a merchant at thirteen, entered banking, rose to eminence in the city's financial circles, and wrote poetry in his spare time. He first attracted attention by writing prologues for plays, and soon became much in demand at civic celebrations —the opening of the Park Theater in 1821, Boston's Shakespeare memorial pageant, the bicentennial of Boston's founding, and lesser affairs like the Annual Meeting of the Massachusetts Society for the Suppression of Intemperance, or the Sixth Triennial Festival of the Massachusetts Mechanic Charitable Society.

Sprague's finest hour, certainly, was his selection as honorary poet by the Harvard Phi Beta Kappa Society in 1829; after that he was invited to write poems for dozens of civic events throughout New England. Sprague wrote a great deal of sentimental, melancholy verse in the tradition of Mrs. Sigourney, but his best-known compositions were variations on the ode, the loose, flexible form of poetic address favored by poets on public occasions, "elegant, polished compositions," wrote one critic, "always possessing a certain chaste eloquence." Critic H. T. Tuckerman, writing in 1852, ranked Sprague among America's five best poets; E. P. Whipple, another respected critic, flatly declared him the best writer of prologues since Pope. Usually rated in ability with Bryant, Halleck, and the New York group, Sprague even attracted favorable notice in London.

Whatever Sprague's contemporary reputation, it clearly rested on his willingness to serve the public with satisfactory poetry on demand, rather than on his limited and somewhat imitative talents. Successive editions of his poetry and prose, the last in 1850, sold well, but it is difficult to find more than a few memorable lines in his work; his most famous poem, "Curiosity," his Phi Beta Kappa ode, seems flat and uninspired in its concept and execution. Written to illustrate "in a series of pleasing pictures . . . the various means, low and elevated, taken for the gratification of this universal quality," the poem ran through a long list of professions and vocations in which curiosity played a part. His account of a burial at sea (prompted by curiosity about a mariner's life) furnishes a sample of his couplet style:

Wrapped in the raiment that it long must wear,
His body to the deck they slowly bear;
Even there the spirit that I sing is true,
The crew look on with sad, but curious view;
The setting sun flings round his farewell rays,
O'er the broad ocean not a ripple plays;
How eloquent, how awful in its power,
The silent lecture of death's sabbath-hour
One voice that silence breaks—the prayer is said,
And the last rite man pays to man is paid;
The plashing waters mark his resting-place,
And fold him round in one long, cold embrace;
Bright bubbles for a moment sparkle o'er,
Then break, like him, beheld no more.

The position of the poet in early nineteenth-century society was more elevated and secure than at any other period in American history. People read poetry for amusement, exhortation, and edification; the poet had a place in society which he knew and the public acknowledged. First of all, poetry had a domestic function, as part of a household-centered culture. Families read poetry aloud together around the fireside, children memorized it at school, young ladies sang poems (like Longfellow's "Serenade") set to music for the parlor piano. Almost every literate person between 1820 and 1900 had a fund of poetry stored in his memory, to be referred to on appropriate occasions, and the majority of the general public held a large body of verse in common. Houghton Mifflin Company, when it published the nineteenth-century poets in their popular series of "Household Editions" chose exactly the right term. Since life occasioned a constant series of decisions, poets were conceived of as "guides" or "mentors" whose poems could help the reader to make them properly. James Russell Lowell, for example, reported in a letter to Longfellow his encounter with a shoe salesman in 1867, who told him:

I have a feeling of personal obligation to Mr. Longfellow.
When I was in a state of deep personal depression, such as
I have never experienced before or since, when everything
looked dark and no chance of light, my daughter sat down by
my bedside and read "Evangeline" to me, then just published.
That gave me comfort, and sent light into my soul.

Readers expected poets to help them with life's problems, and they looked to poetry for assistance.

The popular poet had a public function as well. The programs for special occasions such as the laying of a cornerstone, the dedication of a

monument or building, a college graduation, the meeting of an association or society, or for holidays like the Fourth of July or Washington's
Birthday, almost always included the reading of a poem. Famous poets
like Bryant, Lowell, and Holmes, contributed and often read poems for
such occasions, but more often the verses were composed and presented
by the class poet, the local schoolmaster, the current favorite newspaper
versifier, or some other such person. Many were printed as part of the
proceedings or as separate pamphlets and lost their relevance when removed from the event. They were, as Holmes said, "something like the
firework frames on the morning of July 5," but it was important to the
nineteenth century that poetry be part of the public occasion.

The poet and the reader, then, in nineteenth-century society, treated
each other with respect. Mrs. Sigourney, who never turned down a request from a reader for another verse, knew her obligations to her fellow
men and discharged them well. So did Henry Wadsworth Longfellow,
the most famous of all American poets, the only one enshrined in Westminster Abbey, the only one whose birthday was celebrated by American
schools as a national holiday, and the only one whose face is still almost
instantly recognized by millions of his countrymen.

Longfellow's sales were phenomenal, even by modern standards. His
first collection *Voices of the Night* (1839) sold nine hundred copies the
first month, and eventually (until absorbed into *Collected Poems*) fifty
thousand copies. *Hiawatha* began with an advance sale of four thousand,
sold eleven thousand more the first month, ten thousand a month for the
next five, and settled down to a steady four thousand a month for ten
years. (Whitman's *Leaves of Grass*, which also appeared in 1855, sold
less than a thousand its first year; Emerson's collected poems sold eight
hundred in 1847). Forty-five years after its publication, *Hiawatha* had
sold more than a million copies, and *Evangeline* and *The Courtship
of Miles Standish* not many less. His books appeared in first printings of
15,000, and journals were happy to pay him as much as three thousand
dollars for a single poem.

Longfellow quietly accepted the responsibilities that such popularity
and public confidence brought. He wrote far too much (as Tennyson
did) because he took his role as poet seriously, dutifully producing verses
even when he had little to say—enough eventually to fill nine volumes.
To the American people he represented all that a poet should be—wise,
lyrical, sensitive, understanding, a teacher and guide, an interpreter of
common experience. And because Longfellow did his work well, "The
Psalm of Life" ("Let us then be up and doing . . . ,"), "The Village
Blacksmith," "The Old Clock on the Stair," "The Children's Hour," "Ex-

celsior," "Paul Revere's Ride," "The Bridge," "The Day Is Done," "The Wreck of the Hesperus," "Hymn to the Night," and a score of other poems became inseparable parts of the American poetic heritage, touchstones of the nation's cultural life.

The key to Longfellow's popularity was his consummate ability to make things clear, his skill at unwinding complexities. He could locate and express in artful, reflective verse all the homely, wholesome thoughts and feelings he shared with the great majority of men, whatever their nationality or occupation. (Ironically, he was by no means a man of the people but a wealthy, aristocratic, scholarly Cambridge professor.) He could write, and write well, for a discriminating, elite, literary audience —"poetry for Harvard yard," as Norman Holmes Pearson has remarked— as well as for the man on the street or the boy in the schoolroom. Without consciously trying to do so, Longfellow somehow struck exactly the right notes for everyone. His poetic aim was, he said, "to charm, to strengthen, and to teach," goals that fitted his society perfectly. Reading his poetry, one knew that life was real and not empty, that it had design and meaning if one trusted in it and in God.

"A Psalm of Life," one of the best-known poems in English, was an excellent example of Longfellow's genius for popular verse at work:

What the Heart of the Young Man Said to the Psalmist

>Tell me not, in mournful numbers,
>   Life is but an empty dream!—
>For the soul is dead that slumbers,
>   And things are not what they seem.

>Life is real! Life is earnest!
>   And the grave is not its goal;
>Dust thou art, to dust returnest,
>   Was not spoken of the soul.

>Not enjoyment, and not sorrow,
>   Is our destined end or way;
>But to act, that each tomorrow
>   Find us farther than today.

>Art is long, and Time is fleeting,
>   And our hearts, though stout and brave,
>Still, like muffled drums, are beating
>   Funeral marches to the grave.

In the world's broad field of battle,
In the bivouac of Life,
Be not like dumb, driven cattle!
Be a hero in the strife!

Trust no Future, howe'er pleasant!
Let the dead Past bury its dead!
Act,—act in the living Present!
Heart within, and God o'erhead!

Lives of great men all remind us
We can make our lives sublime,
And, departing, leave behind us
Footprints on the sand of time;

Footprints, that perhaps another
Sailing o'er life's solemn main,
A forlorn and shipwrecked brother,
Seeing, shall take heart again.

Let us, then, be up and doing,
With a heart for any fate;
Still achieving, still pursuing,
Learn to labor and to wait.

A poem of hope, courage, and optimism, written (as the subtitle shows) in reply to doubt, cynicism, and passivity, it affirms faith in immortality, progress, individual integrity, and each man's power to triumph over adversity, closing with a characteristically American exhortation to action. Its rhythmical pattern and rhyme scheme are easily read, recited, and remembered; its language is lucid and direct; its imagery fresh, interesting, drawn from the familiar. It is a highly quotable poem which places no intellectual strain on the reader; and as in all Longfellow's popular verse, there is never a clouded word nor a clouded thought.

John Greenleaf Whittier's appeal to the American public was different from Longfellow's. The gentle Quaker and his poetry symbolized a peaceful, quiet rural America fast disappearing in the city's rush and industry's smoke. A man of homely and simple tastes (although he wrote angry, strident poems against slavery) Whittier wrote of boyhood, church, the farm, and family love, in "The common unrhymed poetry/Of simple life and country ways." His poems of pastoral life aroused much nostalgia among urbanites, many of whom came from the farm, or who if they did not, liked to idealize it. Recalling boyhood's "painless play" and

youth's "time of June," Whittier's "Barefoot Boy" immortalized the remembered joys of boyhood:

> Blessings on thee, little man,
> Barefoot boy, with cheeks of tan!
> With thy turned-up pantaloons,
> And thy merry whistled tunes;
> With thy red lip, redder still
> Kissed by strawberries on the hill;
> With the sunshine on thy face,
> Through thy torn brims jaunty grace.
> From my heart I give thee joy—
> I was once a barefoot boy!

"Maud Muller," his most famous story poem, concerned a pretty
farm girl and an older judge, whose differences in age and social position
kept them apart and doomed each to an unhappy life; because the poem
rhymed "been" with "again" and "pen," "*For of all sad words of tongue
or pen,/The saddest are these, 'It might have been,'*" a perfectly familiar
rustic Yankee pronunciation, it caused some mirth among sophisticates.
"Telling the Bees," based on an old rural custom of dressing the hive in
mourning when there was a death in the family lest the swarm leave for
a new home, brought back a past already gone; "Indian Summer," "The
Pumpkin," and other rural poems caught bits of childhood memories
common to thousands of ex-farm boys and girls.

"Snowbound" (1866), Whittier's major poetic effort, the story of a
New England family housebound by a heavy snowstorm, had special
relevance to the city dweller:

> Dreaming in his city ways
> Of winter joys his boyhood knew.

Inviting the reader to

> Sit with me by the homestead hearth
> And stretch the hands of memory forth
> To warm them at the woodfire's blaze,

Whittier re-created the simple, kindly, loving family circle of his own
Quaker childhood and made his poem the classic picture of American
farm life. The poem sold 28,000 copies its first year, a phenomenal sale
for non-Longfellow poetry, eventually providing him with over $100,000
in royalties. "Barbara Frietchie" recounted a quite apocryphal incident
related to Stonewall Jackson's march through Frederick, Maryland, in
which he supposedly ordered his troops to fire on an American flag.

When the aged Barbara protected the flag with her body, crying " '*Shoot if you must this old grey head,/But spare your country's flag!' she said,*" Jackson's "nobler nature" asserted itself, and "with a blush of shame" he withdrew his order. Chosen as a recitation-day favorite by hundreds of schoolboy elocutionists, the poem was second in popularity only to Read's "Sheridan's Ride" among Civil War poems.

Bryant, who ranked third in public appreciation, possessed something of Longfellow's gift for sentimental moralism, but his range was much narrower. Though "Thanatopsis," his youthful death-poem, concluded with a positive message in Longfellow fashion, Bryant was more widely known as "nature's interpreter to man," like Wordsworth (whose poetry he knew well) the expositor of what the Romantics called "the power in nature that moves by suggestion, which excites in us emotion, imagination, or poignant association." The public knew Bryant's serious work, of course—his translations of Homer, his critical reviews, his editorial crusades—and respected it. But his popularity rested on his poems of common experience, as in his pleasant, deft lyric on spring as it comes to the city, "Spring in Town":

> The country ever has a lagging spring,
> Waiting for May to call its violets forth,
> And June its roses. Showers and sunshine bring
> Slowly the deepening verdure o'er the earth;
> To put their foliage out, the woods are slack,
> And one by one the singing birds come back.
> Within the city's bounds the time of flowers
> Comes earlier. Let a mild and sunny day,
> Such as full often, for a few bright hours,
> Breathes through the sky of March the airs of May,
> Shine on our roofs, and chase the wintry gloom—
> And lo, our borders glow with sudden bloom.
> For the wide sidewalks of Broadway are then
> Gorgeous as are a rivulet's banks in June,
> That overhung with blossoms, through its glen
> Slides soft away beneath the sunny noon;
> And they that search the untrodden wood for flowers,
> Meet in its depths no lovelier ones that ours.

In a fringed gentian, a hurricane, the evening wind, the pines of the forest, or a snow shower, or (most famous of all) the flight of a waterfowl across the evening sky, Bryant illustrated in competent verse the lessons Nature (always in his mind with a capital *N*) held for mankind. He believed firmly that poetry had a public purpose, that it should have an active role in American life "by infusing a moral sentiment into natural objects, and bringing images of visible beauty and majesty to heighten the effect of moral sentiment." His unerring sense of the majority mind and taste made him not only a popular poet, but a skillful anthologist, beginning with *Selections from the American Poets* (1840). His *Library of Poetry and Song* (1871) and his *New Library of Poetry and Song* (1876), standard library items for every home, were reissued yearly for the next twenty years.

Longfellow, Whittier, and Bryant established the range of themes and techniques that were to dominate American popular verse for the next century. What they wrote, it was clear, was what the public wanted: direct, unsophisticated poetry that had a message, presented with a minimum of irony, subtlety, or indirection; poetry that confirmed, reassured, and neither disturbed nor doubted; poetry that dealt sentimentally with basic things like home, mother, children, true love, country, Nature, and faith in God. It was this kind of poetry, wrote the Reverend Washington Gladden, one of the nation's better known ministers, in *Art and Morality* (1897), which served the nation by "putting the highest thoughts and the commonest feelings into poetic forms . . . ; [it] sets forth the facts of human life, and gives testimony to the divine presence in our hearts."

Josiah Gilbert Holland knew the formula and followed it expertly. A schoolteacher and physician, Holland drifted into the magazine market with novels, essays, and verse, eventually taking over the editorship of *Scribner's* to make it the best-selling magazine in its field. *Titcomb's Letters to Young People,* a book of moralizing sketches he published in 1858, went through fifty editions. *Bitter Sweet* (1858), a two-hundred-page narrative poem, sold equally well; a combination of New England scenery, Bryant-like nature poetry, and Longfellow-fashioned reflective platitudes, with a wildly melodramatic plot, there is nothing quite like it in the history of American poetry.

Holland moved easily from prose to verse and back again, and anything he wrote seemed to sell. With an uncanny sense of what the man in the shop and the woman at home liked, Holland never missed giving it to them. His *Life of Abraham Lincoln,* written hastily in 1865, sold 80,000 copies in eight months; *Kathrina: Her Life and Mine* (1867), a long poem about a rebellious young man who found faith, was reprinted fifty times in nine years.

Whether writing poetry or prose, short or long, Holland said essentially the same things—home is best, religion helps you, love is stability, a moral life is the happiest. His poetry, endlessly quoted and anthologized, said obvious, simple things obviously and simply. "Gradatim," his most popular short poem (except for "Where Shall Baby's Dimple Be?") was the kind of verse Holland could turn out effortlessly, stanza after stanza:

> Heaven is not reached at a single bound,
> But we build the ladder by which we rise,
> From the lowly earth to the vaulted skies,
> And we mount to its summit round by round.
>
> I count this thing to be grandly true
> That a noble deed is a step toward God—
> Lifting the soul from the common clod,
> To a purer air and a broader view.
>
> We rise by the things that are under feet;
> By what we have mastered of good and gain;
> By the pride deposed and the passion slain,
> And the vanquished ills that we hourly meet. . . .

The Cary Sisters, Alice and Phoebe, while no match for Holland in popular reputation, nevertheless had a large following, especially among women. Alice, the older of the two by a few years, even drew praise from Edgar Allan Poe, a notoriously hard-to-please critic, who thought her "Pictures of Memory" a "perfect lyric." Concerned with a child's death—rather than that of Poe's "beautiful woman"—the poem had a kind of simple effectiveness, as its closing stanzas illustrated:

> I once had a little brother,
>   With eyes that were dark and deep—
> In the lap of that old dim forest
>   He lieth in peace asleep;
> Light as the down of thistle,
>   Free as the winds that blow,
> We roved there the beautiful summers,
>   The summers of long ago:
> But his feet on the hills grew weary,
>   And one of the autumn eves,
> I made for my little brother
>   A bed of the yellow leaves.
>
> Sweetly his pale arms folded
>   My neck in a meek embrace,
> As the light of immortal beauty
>   Silently covered his face:

POPULAR FICTION AND POETRY

> And when the arrows of sunset
>   Lodged in the tree-tops bright,
> He fell, in his saint-like beauty,
>   Asleep by the gates of light.
> Therefore of all the pictures,
>   That hang on Memory's wall,
> The one of the old dim forest
>   Seemeth the best of all.

The sisters complemented each other well. Alice excelled in poems of death and meditation with Poe-like titles, "Lily Lee," "Ulalie," and "The Spirit Haunted." Phoebe's verse struck a more confident note; her 1866 collection bore the title *Poems of Faith, Love, and Hope,* one of which, "Our Heroes," praised the steadfast virtues in forthright fashion:

> Here's a hand to the boy who has courage
> To do what he knows to be right;
> When he falls in the way of temptation,
> He has a hard battle to fight.
> Who strives against self and his comrades
> Will find a most powerful foe,
> All honor to him if he conquers,
> A cheer for the boys who say "No . . . !"
> Be steadfast, my boy, when you're tempted,
> To do what you know to be right.
> Stand firm by the colors of manhood,
> And you will o'ercome in the fight.
> "The right," be your battle-cry ever
> In waging the warfare of life,
> And God, who knows who are the heroes,
> Will give you the strength for the strife.

John Godfrey Saxe, a contemporary of the Carys, wrote in a wholly different vein—the kind of sentimental, humorous poetry later done with greater skill and appeal by James Whitcomb Riley. A dry, witty Vermonter, Saxe specialized in light verse with a moral tag, as in his most famous production, "The Blind Men and the Elephant," a schoolboy elocution standard for years. As each blind man felt the elephant, each believed the animal to resemble the shape of the part he touched—a wall (the side), a spear (the tusk), a fan (the ear), a snake (the trunk), and so on, leading Saxe to conclude:

> And so these men of Industan
> Disputed loud and long,
> Each in his own opinion

> Exceeding stiff and strong,
> Though each were partly in the right,
> And all were in the wrong!
>
> So oft in theologic wars
> The disputants, I ween,
> Rail on in utter ignorance
> Of what each other mean,
> And prate about a elephant,
> *Not one of them has seen!*

After a public reading in 1858, Saxe discovered he had real talent as a performer and went on the lecture circuit, the first popular poet to take to the road and make money at it.

Nathaniel Parker Willis, the literary phenomenon of the Jacksonian generation, was a talented, elegant young man with a facile, mediocre mind. He used good looks, a colorful personality, and a shrewd sense of public relations to gain a national reputation as a literary lion. Skillfully playing the part of man-of-the-world sophisticate, he became as well known in Knickerbocker circles as Cooper or Irving. Willis could do many things well—criticism, travel sketches, essays, plays, novels, light and serious verse—in any style he chose. He wrote, he said quite honestly, "from present feelings for present gain," that is, for money and reputation, both of which he attained if only temporarily.

Publishing at least a poem a week for twenty-one years, Willis filled nine volumes with titles like "An Apology for Avoiding, After a Long Separation, A Woman Once Loved," or "To the Lady in the Black Chemisette with Black Buttons," or "Sunrise Thoughts at the Close of a Ball." He could produce on demand impish satire like "Love in a Cottage," or moralized reflections like "The Belfry Pigeon," or sermonizing nature-verse like "River at Night," or expertly tailored sentimental verse like "A Child's First Impression of a Star," which was Willis at his clever best:

> She had been told that God made all the stars
> That twinkled up in Heaven, and now she stood
> Watching the coming of the twilight on,
> As if it were a new and perfect world,
> And this were its first eve. How beautiful
> Must be the work of Nature to a child
> In its first fresh impression! Laura stood
> By the low window, with the silken lash
> Of her soft eye upraised, and her sweet mouth
> Half parted with that new and strange delight

> Of beauty which she could not comprehend,
> And had not seen before. The purple folds
> Of the low sunset clouds, and the blue sky
> That looked so still and delicate above,
> Filled her young heart with gladness, and the eve
> Stole on with its deep shadows, and she still
> Stood looking at the west with that half smile,
> As if a pleasant thought were at her heart.
> Presently, in the edge of the last tint
> Of sunset, where the blue was melted in
> To the faint golden yellowness, a star
> Stood suddenly. A laugh of wild delight
> Burst from her lips, and putting up her hands,
> Her simple thought broke forth expressively—
> "Father, dear father, God has made a star!"

But the vogue for Willis depended too much on Willis himself. After his death in 1867 not many remembered him.

The Civil War brought a great burst of poetic effort, more than any that accompanied other American military conflicts. Some poets (Whitman and Melville among them) devoted separate volumes of poetry to the war; others published war verses in newspapers, magazines, and anthologies. Not all who wrote poetry introduced the war into it (Longfellow, for example, though deeply touched by it, rarely mentioned the war) but Lee Steinmetz, who collected and edited a collection of Civil War verse in 1960, has estimated that at least two hundred volumes of poetry published during the sixties treated the war in one way or another. Written by schoolboys, lawyers, teachers, ministers, bankers, or anyone, amateur or skilled professional, these poems represented the feelings of the millions of people who were enmeshed in that brutal, bitter struggle.

Much Civil War poetry was in the prevailing sentimental, melodramatic mode. Some saw the war as a dramatic, excitingly emotional spectacle filled with acts of bravery and idealism, fought for a holy cause; others recognized it as a tragic force that tore society apart, shattered families, and sent thousands of young men to death. The Reverend Theodore Tilton's Northern ode, "God Save the Nation!" was set to music in twelve different versions and sung as a hymn; Harvard philosopher F. H. Hedge's "Our Country is Calling" supported the Union cause; George H. Boker, a leading playwright, contributed a popular ballad, "March Along!" To the South, Albert Pike, a prominent lawyer, editor, and poet, wrote "Southrons, Hear Your Country's Call!" while James Randall's

"Maryland" became a favorite Southern hymn. Francis Durivage's "The Cavalry Charge" exemplified the "war is glorious" school of military verse:

> With bray of the trumpet
>   And roll of the drum,
> And keen ring of bugle,
>   The cavalry come!
> Sharp clank the steel scabbards,
>   The bridle-chains ring,
> And foam from red nostrils
>   The wild chargers fling!
>
> Cut right! And cut left!
>   For the parry who needs?
> The bayonets shiver
>   Like wind-shattered reeds!
> Triumphant, remorseless,
>   Unerring as death—
> No saber that's stainless
>   Returns to its sheath!

But the poems of parting, loss, and sorrow—of which there were many—showed that war was not all heroism and cavalry charges. There were too many with titles like "Following the Drum," "The Soldier's Mother," "The Volunteer to his Wife," "Kiss me, Mother, and Let Me Go," "The Soldier's Dream of Home," or "He Sleeps Where He Fell" to maintain the illusion that war was glorious. "The Jacket of Grey," published anonymously in a Southern newspaper in 1863, had a different ring:

> Fold it up carefully, lay it aside;
> Tenderly touch it, look on it with pride;
> For dear must it be to our hearts evermore,
> The jacket of grey that our loved soldier boy wore.
>
> His fond mother blessed him and looked up above,
> Commending to heaven the child of her love;
> What anguish was hers, mortal tongue cannot say,
> When he passed from her sight in his jacket of grey.
>
> His young comrades found him and tenderly bore
> The cold lifeless form to his home by the shore;
> Oh dark were our hearts on that terrible day,
> When we saw our dead boy in his jacket of grey!

The war's popular verse ranged from rude ballads filled with invective, through sentimental songs, to ambitious verse epics. "Ole Secesh's" attack on Lincoln represented a kind of savage lampoon common to both sides:

> With a beard that was filthy and red,
>   His mouth with tobacco bespread,
> Abe Lincoln sat in the White House,
>   A-wishing that he was dead—
>   Lie, lie, lie!
>   I've lied like the very deuce
>   Lie, lie, lie!
>   As long as lies are of use!
> Brandy, and whiskey, and gin,
>   Sherry, champagne, and pop,
> I tipple, I guzzle, I suck 'em all in,
>   Till down dead-drunk I drop.

"L. M.," a fire-eating Southern belle, would have no part of a temporizer:

> If I ever consent to get married
> (And who could refuse a good mate?)
> The man whom I give my hand to,
> Must believe in the rights of the State.
>
> To a husband who quietly submits
> To the negro-equality sway,
> The true Southern girl will not barter
> Her heart and affections away.
>
> We girls are all for a Union,
> Where a marked distinction is made,
> Between the rights of the mistress,
> And those of the kinky-haired maid!

At the other extreme, Charles T. Daniel, a Kentucky lawyer, wrote a long sentimental verse-romance, *William and Annie, or A Tale of Love and War* (1864), about William, a Kentucky boy who married Annie on the eve of his departure for the army. When she died of loneliness and a broken heart, William rushed to throw himself on the Federal guns, so that he might be reunited with his sweetheart in death. John M. Dagnall's *Daisy Swain, or The Flower of the Shenandoah* (1866) took ten long books to tell a complicated story of love and danger involving a Virginia belle, a Northern officer, and a villainous Confederate guerilla chief that did not quite escape the ridiculous. Yet now and then, in the midst of the welter of pretentious, awkward verse that the Civil War brought, there came something like "Left on the Battlefield," a young wife's cry of pain as real and moving now as it was in 1864:

> Oh my darling! My darling! never to feel
>   Your hand going over my hair!
> Never to lie in your arms again—
>   Never to know where you are!
> It is but little I might have done
>   To lighten your parting pain;
> But 'tis bitter to think that you died alone
>   Out in the dark and rain.
> I am left alone, and the world is changed,
>   So dress me in bridal white,
> And lay me away in some quiet place,
>   Out of the hateful light.

Broadside poetry, out of the eighteenth-century tradition, became big business in the early nineteenth. Set to incidental music but more often read than sung, these poems were printed by the thousands, sold wholesale to dealers, and retailed by hawkers, book shops, and stationery stores. The cheaper ones, printed on a single sheet with an ornamental border, sold for a penny; some on better quality paper, with a colored border and a vignette, cost a nickel. "Popular" in every sense of the word, they filled the need of the moment. As one of the poets described their popularity,

> As you've walked through the town, on a fine Summer's day,
>   The subject I've got, you have seen I dare say:
> Upon fences and railings, wherever you go,
>   You'll see the penny-ballads sticking up, all in a row.

Broadside verse reached its peak, probably, during the bitter political campaigns of the fifties and during the Civil War; most of it had disappeared by the seventies, absorbed by the sheet-music market and the newspapers. Some of it doggerel, some little more than jingles, some stiffly formal verse, it covered the ephemeral topical interests of the day. 1849 naturally produced broadsides like "The California Emigrant" and "The Gold Digger's Lament." The Burdell murder case of 1857, in which a dentist was accused of murdering his wife in order to marry his sweetheart, who had apparently borne his child and then adopted it, inspired "The Bellevue Baby Mrs. Cunningham Adopted," and "Mrs. C. and the

Baby." A railroad tragedy in 1856 produced "Killed By Accident on the North Pennsylvania Railroad"; election year brought "Bell, Everett, and the Union," and "The Ninth Ward for Frémont."

The Civil War furnished hundreds of broadsides on the order of "Give Us Back Our Old Commander [McClellan]," "Grafted Into the Army," "Bring My Brother Back to Me," or savage lampoons such as "I Am Fighting for the Nigger":

> Three for Honest Abe, who will be a great man yet,
> Though he has loaded us with taxes and has burdened
>   us with debt;
> He tells his little jokes while pocketing our pelf,
> And at last has made the nigger the equal of himself.

The Heenan-Sayers fight, which pitted the American John C. Heenan against English heavyweight Tom Sayers, elicited poems like "The Fight for the Championship," and "Heenan the Champion of the World," although the fight was a draw. "No Irish Need Apply" provided a comment on contemporary prejudices:

> I'm a dacint boy just landed
>   from the town of Ballyfad;
> I want a situation, yis,
>   and want it mighty bad.
> I saw a place advertised—
>   It's the thing for me, says I,
> But the dirty spalpeen ended,
>   "No Irish need apply."

"Our Grandfather's Days" disapproved of the emancipation of women in the seventies:

> The gals didn't paint, stuff themselves up with cotton;
> They didn't wear hoops, patent bustles, or stays;
> Didn't smoke cigarettes or drink cocktails at Taylor's,
> That wasn't the style in our grandfather's days,

but it was among the last specimens of the type.

There was little new in the popular poetry of the later nineteenth century; younger men wrote it, but they wrote it in the Longfellow-Whittier-Bryant pattern. Thomas Bailey Aldrich, for example, known also for his fiction and criticism (he succeeded Howells as the *Atlantic Monthly* editor) wrote a great deal of extravagantly praised verse. He began his day, he said, "with a lyric or two" before going to the office;

those which did not resemble Longfellow's tended to resemble Bryant's. Edmund Clarence Stedman, another editor and critic whose verse was widely reprinted and anthologized, imitated Longfellow and Tennyson. Bret Harte, who made his reputation on a small body of "mining camp" verse—"Jim," "Plain Language from Truthful James," and "In the Tunnel" —wrote much more verse that sounded like Bayard Taylor.

Taylor, whose travel essays made him one of the better-known prose writers of the seventies, represented the popular concept of what the poet of the times should be. World traveler, intellectual, scholar of repute (professor of German at Cornell), translator of *Faust* (1870–71), biographer of Lincoln, editor, journalist, and public lecturer, his name appeared everywhere. He wrote four novels, five plays, several volumes of essays, and, as Stedman (who gave him equal status with Whitman) remarked, "did everything a man of letters could do with cheerfulness and facility."

Of Taylor's total output of fifty-three books, twelve were poetry, the most popular his *Poems of the Orient* (1854). These were translations and imitations of Arabic verse that thrilled readers with suggestions of exotic Eastern love, as in the oft-printed *Bedouin Love Song*:

> From the desert I come to thee,
> On a stallion shod with fire,
> And the winds are left behind,
> With the speed of my desire.
> Under thy window I stand,
> And the midnight hears my cry,
> I love thee, I love but thee,
> With a love that shall not die. . . .

His attempt at a poetic tour de force, a long narrative poem called *Lars, A Pastor of Norway* (mixing *Evangeline* with *Snowbound* in a Norwegian setting) failed. *The Masque of the Gods,* a religious drama, and *The Prophet,* a Mormon epic, were equally disastrous; but his shorter poems, especially his *Rhymes of Travel* and his translations, were widely read by both upper-class and general readers.

Richard Watson Gilder, who learned his trade from Holland on *Scribner's,* edited *The Century Magazine,* but he preferred to write verse, he said, over anything else. He eventually published sixteen volumes of Longfellow-touched poetry, much of it religious and most of it mediocre. His popularity, wrote his admirer James Onderdonk, derived from the fact that his poems "irradiated the dark clashes of death, pain, and sorrow, teaching the way that leads from darkness to the perfect day."

Thomas Buchanan Read, a Bohemian adventurer among the arts who was also a talented painter and sculptor (his was the famous painting of Longfellow's children) was generally assumed during the fifties and sixties to be a major American literary figure.

Poe, who hated Read, attacked his verse bitterly; on the other hand the British critic Coventry Patmore hailed him as America's best. Read's "New Pastoral" (1855), a two-hundred-and-fifty page blank verse epic of westward migration, attracted much attention, but he was better known for his shorter poems, in which he quite successfully imitated not only Bryant, Longfellow, and Whittier, but Scott, Wordsworth, Thomas Moore, and Mrs. Hemans. He wrote a great deal of popular lyric verse, and tried his hand once more at a frontier epic with "The Wagoner of the Alleghanies" (1862).

During the Civil War Read wrote enough war poetry to fill a volume. "Sheridan's Ride," written shortly after Sheridan's engagement with Early's Confederates at Winchester, Virginia, in 1864, became in a matter of days the most widely-known poem of the war. After its stirring opening,

> Up from the South at break of day,
> Bringing to Winchester fresh dismay,
>   The affrighted air with a shudder bore,
>   Like a herald in haste, to the chieftain's door,
>   The terrible grumble, rumble, and roar,
>   Telling the battle was on once more,
> And Sheridan twenty miles away,

the poem stanza by stanza brought Sheridan on his great black steed Rienzi back to the field to save the day. James Murdoch, one of the country's leading orators, gave readings of the poem throughout the North to raise funds for field hospitals, while reproductions of Read's painting of Sheridan and his horse sold hundreds of thousands. Despite his popularity, little remains of his three volumes of verse but "Sheridan's Ride," testimony to a lost reputation.

The homespun rural tradition of Whittier attracted a number of practitioners, chief among them Will Carleton, a Michigan newspaperman who collected his verse in *Farm Ballads* (1873), which sold forty thousand copies within the year. Carleton specialized in exactly the right blend of sentimentality, rustic humor, and dialect, "uttering in simple language," he said, "the homely sentiments of plain people." "Over The Hill to the Poorhouse," which treated the plight of the elderly and unwanted, became one of the half-dozen or so best-known poems of its era;

a plaque marking the site of the poem still stands in southern Michigan. It began,

> Over the hill to the poorhouse, I'm trudgin' my weary way—
> I—a woman of seventy and only a trifle gray—
> I, who am smart and chipper, for all the years I've told,
> As many another woman who's only half as old
> Over the hill to the poorhouse—I can't quite make it clear!
> Over the hill to the poorhouse—and it seems so horrid queer!
> Many's the step I've taken a-toilin' to and fro,
> But this is the sort of journey I never thought to go . . . ,

continuing for six more stanzas. Poems such as "Betsy and I Are Out" and "Betsy and I Are Back" (separation and reconciliation), "Gone With a Handsomer Man" (a runaway wife), and "Out of the Old House, Mary" (moving day for the dispossessed) struck wide response. Carleton followed with *Farm Legends* (1875) and eight more volumes which sold a total of a half-million during his lifetime. He also made a sizeable income from public readings.

But in this vein no one could equal James Whitcomb Riley. Born in Indiana and eventually made editor of the Indianapolis *Journal,* Riley began versifying in 1877. His collection, *The Old Swimmin' Hole and 'Leven More Poems,* in 1873, started him on a career as poet and lecturer that lasted without a break until his death in 1916. Riley's Hoosier dialect poems, among them "The Old Swimmin' Hole," "When The Frost is on the Punkin," "Little Orphant Annie," and "The Raggedy Man" swiftly became part of the public heritage. His straight nature-and-sentiment poems, such as "Knee Deep in June" and "An Old Sweetheart of Mine" were no less popular. A superb actor, Riley appeared at Chickering Hall in Boston on the same platform with Twain, George Washington Cable, and William Dean Howells, and virtually stole the show. After that, his annual tours with humorist Bill Nye became national events, while his books, which appeared in an endless stream, sold as well in Boston as in Bean Blossom, Indiana.

Though such an eminent critic as Professor Brander Matthews of Columbia praised Riley for "his elaborate metrical artistry and his dextrous command of sound," the public loved him for his frankly sentimental, gently humorous, and artfully artless treatment of tried-and-true themes of childhood, love and marriage, of honest work and wholesome play, and for his celebration of old-fashioned country values in a frantically competitive, urbanized society. To city folk, and farm folk too, his poetry was utterly genuine and completely theirs:

When the frost is on the punkin and the fodder's
    in the shock,
And you hear the kyouck and gobble of the
    struttin' turkey cock,
And the clackin' of the guineas and the cluckin'
    of the hens,
And the rooster's hallylooyer as he tiptoes on
    the fence;
O it's then's the times a feller is a-feelin'
    at his best,
With the risin' sun to greet him from a night of
    peaceful rest,
As he leaves the house, bareheaded, and goes out
    to feed the stock,
When the frost is on the punkin and the fodder's
    in the shock.

Colleges showered degrees on him, Indiana celebrated his birthday in 1911 with exercises in his honor in the schools, and his death in 1916 temporarily crowded war news from the front pages.

Riley's greatest assets were his sense of locality and his feeling for character. His poems epitomized the small-town, rural, old-fashioned Midwest, not simply by reason of his expert use of dialect, but because he knew intuitively how people of his time and place felt and thought. He populated his verse with real people—Orphant Annie, Tradin' Joe, Old Aunt Mary, Doc Sifers, and others, drawn with skill and authenticity. Riley's non-dialect verse, while less individualized than his more famous Hoosier poetry, was hardly less popular for its unabashed, homely sentimentality. "An Old Sweetheart of Mine," one of his best known verses, was exactly the proper mixture of nostalgia and love, reflection, plus a predictable surprise at the close when the "old sweetheart" enters the poet's study:

As one who cons at evening o'er an album, all alone,
And muses on the faces of the friends that he has known,
So I turn the leaves of fancy, till in a shadowy design,
I find the smiling features of an old sweetheart of mine.

The lamplight seems to glimmer with a flicker of surprise,
As I turn it low—to rest me of the dazzle in my eyes,
And light my pipe in silence, save a sigh that seems
    to yoke
Its fate with my tobacco and to vanish with my smoke. . . .

I can see the pink sunbonnet and the little checkered dress
She wore when first I kissed her and she answered the caress
With the written declaration that, "as surely as the vine,
Grew 'round the stump" she loved me—that old sweetheart
    of mine.

When I should be her lover, forever and a day
And she my faithful sweetheart till the golden hair was gray;
And we should be so happy that when either's lips were dumb
They would not smile in Heaven till the other's kiss
    had come—

But ah! my dream is broken by a step upon the stair,
And the door is softly opened and—my wife is standing
    there:
Yet with eagerness and rapture all my vision I resign—
To greet the living presence of that old sweetheart of mine.

No poet since Longfellow was so widely read and loved; no one rivaled his grasp of the common man's poetic needs until Edgar Guest.

Until nearly the close of the nineteenth century, popular poetry dealt with much the same areas of experience as the popular novel. Like the novel, it emphasized didacticism and sentimentality, moralized on nature, taught respect for old-fashioned values, found deeper meanings in ordinary life. But when fiction moved toward realism in the latter decades of the century, poetry did not move with it. Bryant saw it coming in the seventies, wondering if an age "occupied with politics, railroads, and steamboats" would want or need poetry at all. It did, of course, but chiefly as a defense against the forces of modernism, reform, and industrialism that Bryant observed.

There were neither realistic nor reform movements in American popular verse (notwithstanding the surprising reception of Edwin Markham's attack on exploited labor, "The Man With The Hoe," in 1899) but instead a deliberate emphasis on the retention of the older sentimental tradition. The "newspaper poets" who dominated popular verse after 1890 upset no applecarts. Poetry was "a thought for the day," a nostalgic reminiscence of childhood, an apostrophe to the simple life, an exhortation to work and succeed, a humorous glance at city living, and so on. These were the poets whose names dotted popular anthologies, and whose syndicated verse, as one critic wrote, guided people with "an unfailing gleam . . . in the drifting and difficult days" of war, unrest, and pessimism, "like a lighthouse in a dark night."

Few readers recognized their names (Major Sigourney, Mrs. C. F. Alexander, Kate Putnam Osgood, George Bungay, T. H. Robertson) and many were published anonymously. Slason Thompson, who compiled an anthology of newspaper and magazine verse in 1885 (which went through an edition a year for the next eleven years) collected over a thousand specimens, some of which had appeared a dozen times or more in various periodicals over the years—"Tired Mothers," "Christmas Bells," "Rain on the Roof," "The Water Wheel," The Frivolous Girl." Thompson finally chose four hundred for his anthology, divided into sixteen categories ranging from "The Little Folk" to "Comedy and Burlesque," a revealing cross section of contemporary popular taste in poetry.

Baby poetry, often written in excruciating baby-talk, was apparently popular, since Thompson gave over seventy-five pages to it, including such things as "Our New Baby,"

> Mozzer bought a baby!
>   'Ittle bitsy sing;
> Sinks I mos' could put him
>   Frou my yubber ying.
> Ain't he awful ugly?
>   Ain't he awful pink?
> "Just come down from heaven"—
>   Yat's a fib, I sink. . . .

Or, "Only a Baby,"

> Only a baby, 'thout any hair,
>   'Cep a little fuzz here and there.
> Only a baby, name you have none,
>   Barefoot and dimpled, sweet little one.
>   (*Baby replies*)
> Only a baby, what sood I be?
> Lots o' big folks been 'ittle 'ike me;
> Ain't dot any hair? 'Es I have too,
> Sposin' I hadn't, dess it tood drow. . . .

Love poems, such as "A Kiss in the Rain," "In the Hammock," "The Motto in the Ring," or "Askin' for a Kiss" tended to be humorous or sentimental, as in "Undowered," which must have reassured many girls from poor families and many typists and clerks:

> Thou hast not gold? Why, this is gold
>   All clustering round thy forehead white;
> And were it weighed, and were it told,
>   I could not say its worth tonight.

> Thou hast not wit? What, what is this
>   Wherewith thou capturest many a wight,
> Who doth forget a tongue is his,
>   As I well-nigh forgot tonight?
> Nor station? Well, ah, well, I own
>   Thou hast no place assured thee quite—
> So now I raise thee to a throne,
>   Begin thy reign, my Queen, tonight!

The Longfellow strain was strong in newspaper poetry, as in "Better to Climb and Fall":

> Give me a man with an aim,
>   Whatever that aim may be;
> Whether it's wealth or it's fame,
>   It matters not to me.
> Let him walk in the path of right,
>   And keep his aim in sight,
> And work and pray alway,
>   With his aim on the glittering height.
> Better to strive and climb,
>   And never reach the goal,
> Than to drift along with time,
>   An aimless, worthless soul.
> Ay, better to climb and fall,
>   Or sow, though the yield be small,
> Than to throw away day after day,
>   And never to strive at all!

Narrative poems, Thompson wrote, were especially well-received by editors. "The New Magdalen," he explained, was the story (in 24 stanzas)

> of a fallen woman in Memphis, Mollie Cooke by name,
> who, owning a gilded palace of sin, turned it into
> a hospital for yellow-fever sufferers, and with her
> hands nursed the sick and dying until at last she
> too fell prey to the fever.

"Bay Chaleur," another long narrative, told of the death by shipwreck of "a fisher-boy, young and fair," and of the girl who waited for him while

> The night comes on, the village sinks in slumber,
>   The rounded moon illumes the water's rim;
> Each evening hour she hears the old clock number,
>   But brings the evening no return of him—
>   From the Bay Chaleur.

Nature, of course, furnished moralistic inspiration to dozens of newspaper and magazine versifiers. "C. P. R.," of Jackson, Michigan, wrote
"The River" in traditional sonnet form, but with a typically Bryant-like
moral tag attached:

> The noble river widens as we drift,
> And the deep waters more brackish grow;
> We note the sea-birds flying to and fro,
> And feel the ocean-currents plainly lift
> Our bark and yet our course we would not shift:
> These are but signs by which the boatmen know
> They're drawing near the port to which they go
> To land their cargo or to bring their gift.
> So may our lives reach out on either hand,
> Broader and broader as the end draws near;
> So may we seek God's truths to understand,
> As the sea-birds shelter seek when storms appear;
> So may the currents from the heavenly sea
> Lift us and bear us to eternity.

Wartime verse still appeared regularly into the eighties, though in less
quantity than a decade earlier. "The Blue and the Gray," a perennial favorite, told of a mother whose sons enlisted on opposite sides, closing
with a well-known stanza:

> The shadows fall upon their graves; they fall
> upon my heart;
> And through the twilight of this soul, like dews
> the tears will start;
> The starlight comes so silently and lingers
> where they rest;
> So hope's revealing star-light sinks and shines
> within my breast.
> They ask not there, where yonder heaven,
> smiles with eternal day—
> Why Willie wore the loyal blue, and Harry wore the gray.

Newspaper "poet's corners" attracted a great deal of humorous verse,
much of it in Irish or Negro dialect, or as Thompson explained, parodies of
Poe, Swinburne, and especially Shakespeare. "Poker" is a good example:

> To draw or not to draw, that is the question.
> Whether 'tis safer in the player to take
> The awful risk of skinning to a straight,
> Or standing pat, to raise 'em to the limit,

> And thus by bluffing, get it. To draw, to skin—
> Ay, there's the rub, and by the skin to get a full,
> Or two pairs, or the fattest bouncing kings
> That luck is heir to. . . .

One of the standards was the pseudo-dialect classic, "I Wud Knot Dy in Wintur," which still has a strange, wild charm:

> I wud knot dy in wintur, when whiski punches flo,
> An when pooty gals is skatin o'er feelds ov ise and sno;
> When sassidge-meet is phyrin, and hickry knuts is thick;
> Owe! who kud think o' dighin, or even gettin sick?
>
> I wud knot dy in springtime, and miss the turnup greens,
> And the pooty songs ov leetle phraugs, or the ski-lark's
> airli skreems.
> When burds begin there wobblin, and tater's gin to sprout,
> When turkis go to gobblin, I wud knot then peg out.
>
> I wud knot dy in summer, and leave the garden sass,
> The roasted lam and buttermilk, the kool plase in the grass;
> I wud knot dy in summer, when everythin's so hot,
> An leave the whiski jewleps—Owe know! Ide ruther knot!
>
> I wud knot dy in ortum, with peeches fit for eatin,
> When wavy korn is gettin wripe and Kandidates is treetin;
> Phor these and other wreasons, Ide knot dy in the phall,
> And sinse I've thot it over, I wud knot dy at all.

The most successful newspaper poet of the era was Mrs. Ella Wheeler Wilcox. A published poet at fifteen, at sixteen she entered newspaper work, where she discovered she had a flair for putting the chastely erotic fancies of millions of women into simple verse. Though she actually preached a highly conservative morality, her poetry was daring enough so that her first collection, *Poems of Passion* (1876), was at first rejected by her publishers as immoral. When the Milwaukee papers took up her cause (she was a farm girl from Johnson Center, Wisconsin) with headlines like

TOO LOUD FOR CHICAGO
The Scarlet City by the Lake Shocked By
Badger Girl, Whose Verses Out-
Swinburne Swinburne and Out-
Whitman Whitman

publishers scrambled for her poems and the volume sold thousands. Her reputation made, Mrs. Wilcox went on to publish more than forty books over a span of forty-six years. Beginning in 1884 she wrote a poem a day for syndicated distribution, not including special assignments for particular occasions. She was commissioned to attend Queen Victoria's funeral, and during World War I toured army camps reading her poems and giving talks on morals.

Her aim, Mrs. Wilcox said, was "to raise the unhappy and guide those who need it." Her "passionate" verse actually made up a small part of her total output, which was chiefly hortatory and didactic. "I Love You," which like most of her "daring" love poems tended to promise more than it delivered, opened:

> I love your lips when they're wet with wine
> And red with a wild desire;
> I love your eyes when the lovelight lies
> Lit with a passionate fire.
> I love your arms when the warm white flesh
> Touches mine in a fond embrace;
> I love your hair when the strands enmesh
> Your kisses against my face.

But the first stanza of "Whatever Is" was much more representative of the bulk of her work:

> I know, as my life grows older,
> And mine eyes have clearer sight,
> That under each rank wrong somewhere,
> There lies the root of right;
> That each sorrow has its purpose,
> By the sorrowing oft unguessed,
> But as sure as the sun brings morning,
> Whatever is—is best.

Two of her lines attained permanency, "Laugh, and the world laughs, with you;/Weep, and you weep alone"; but many other quotable Wilcox verses appeared in scrapbooks, were pinned to bulletin boards, and were repeated in newspaper columns for another generation.

Eugene Field, a Chicago newspaperman, enjoyed a considerable public of a different kind. Joining the Chicago *Daily News* in 1883, Field wrote a column, "Sharps and Flats," in which he printed his own and others' poems. An odd, irrepressible man, fond of practical jokes, Field was also a first-rate scholar who did excellent translations of Heine, Béranger, and Horace. His satire was witty and shrewd; however, he had a strong streak of sentimentality, particularly where children were concerned, and his children's verses—"Little Boy Blue," and "Dutch Lullaby: Wynken, Blynken, and Nod" among them—were better known than the smooth, facile verse he published in *A Little Book of Western Verse* (1889) and *A Second Book of Verse* (1892). "Bachelor Hall," a sentimental poem about a lover and his dead sweetheart (but done much differently than Poe) represented Field's efforts at serious verse:

> It seems like a dream, that sweet wooing of old—
> Like a legend of fairies on pages of gold—
> Too soon the sweet story of loving was closed,
> Too rudely awakened the soul that reposed;
> I kissed the white lips that lay under the pall,
> And crept back to you, lonely Bachelor Hall.
> Mine eyes have grown dim and my hair has turned white,
> But my heart beats as warmly and gaily tonight . . . ,
> I see her fair face through a vapor of tears,
> And her sweet voice comes back thro' the desert of years,
> And I hear, oh so gently, the promise she spoke,
> And a soft spirit hand soothes the heart that is broke;
> So I fill up the flagon and drink—that is all—
> To the dead and the dying of Bachelor Hall.

He died suddenly in 1895, but "Little Boy Blue," written for a dead child, is still reprinted in "favorite poem" anthologies:

> The little toy dog is covered with dust,
> But sturdy and stanch he stands;
> And the little toy soldier is red with rust,
> And his musket molds in his hands.
> Time was when the little toy dog was new,
> And the soldier was passing fair,
> And that was the time that our Little Boy Blue
> Kissed them and put them there. . . .
> Ay, faithful to Little Boy Blue they stand,
> Each in the same old place,
> Awaiting the touch of a little hand,
> The smile of a little face;
> And they wonder, as waiting the long years through
> In the dust of that little chair,
> What has become of our Little Boy Blue,
> Who kissed them and put them there.

There were, of course, many other "favorite" or "best-loved" poems, as a glance at any anthology will attest. The nineteenth century had

Sarah Hale's "Mary Had a Little Lamb"; John Hay's "Jim Bludsoe"; Clement Moore's "Visit from St. Nicholas"; Hugh D'Arcy's "Face on the Barroom Floor"; Eugene Pullen's "Now I Lay Me Down to Sleep"; and Arthur Chapman's "Out Where The West Begins," to name a few. John Luckey McCreery, a government clerk in Washington, wrote "There Is No Death" for a newspaper in 1859 and spent the rest of his life trying to prove that Sir Edward Bulwer-Lytton, to whom it was ascribed, did not. Reprinted all over the world, translated into a dozen languages, put to music twelve times, inserted into the *Congressional Record,* and a standard in anthologies, the poem is still read at funeral services:

> There is no death! The stars go down
> To rise upon some other shore,
> And bright in heaven's jewelled crown,
> They shine for evermore. . . .

John Whittaker Watson's "Snow, The Beautiful Snow," written in 1858 and ascribed to seven other poets, appeared in newspaper columns during winter for the next sixty years, and still does occasionally. Ernest Thayer's rousing "Casey at the Bat," immortalized by vaudevillian De Wolfe Hopper's recitation of it, was written in 1888. William Allen Butler's satire on Flora McFlimsey, the wealthy girl who had "Nothing To Wear" to the ball while the poor shivered in the slums, sold 80,000 copies of the issue of *Harper's* that printed it and when published as a gift book, it sold 150,000 more. Elizabeth Akers' "Rock Me to Sleep," with its famous opening lines, *Backward, turn backward, O Time, in your flight,/ And make me a child again, just for tonight!* was set to music thirty different times, featured by the Christy Minstrels, sold thousands as an illustrated gift book, was sung on the stage for forty years, and was a standard recitation piece in elocution textbooks.

Edwin Markham's turn-of-the-century protest poem, "The Man with the Hoe," put him into anthologies between 1900 and 1925 with more entries than Whittier; "Joaquin" (Cincinnatus Heine) Miller, a Californian who affected long hair and sombreros, enjoyed popularity in the eighties after the appearance of *Songs of the Sierras* in 1871. Madison Cawein, a Kentuckian who produced thirty-five books of poetry between 1887 and 1915, was much admired for his nature verse, which like Bryant's was filled with lines like:

> When winds go organing through the pines
> On hill and headland darkly gleaming,
> Meseems I hear sonorous lines
> Of Iliads that the woods are dreaming.

Turn-of-the-century readers also liked H. C. Bunner, who wrote deft light verse like "Feminine":

> She might have known it in the earlier Spring—
> That all my heart with vague desire was stirred;
> And, ere the Summer winds had taken wing,
> I told her, but she smiled and said no word.
> The Autumn's eager hand his red gold grasped,
> And she was silent; till from skies grown drear
> Fell one fine, first snowflake, and she clasped
> My neck and cried, "Love, we have lost a year!"

and the misty melancholy of Louise Chandler Moulton's "Tonight":

> Bend low, O dusky Night,
> And give my spirit rest.
> Hold me to your deep breast,
> And put old cares to flight,
> Give back the lost delight
> That once my soul possest,
> When Love was loveliest—
> Bend low, O dusky Night!

Edward Rowland Sill wrote moralized nature verse in the Bryant tradition,

> The stars know a secret
> They do not tell,
> And morn brings a message
> Hidden well . . . ,

and hortatory verse in the Longfellow tradition. His "Fool's Prayer" was a standard elocution piece for school exercises, moving to the familiar climax of its colloquy between arrogant King and humble Jester,

> "Earth bears no balsam for mistakes;
> Men crown the knave, and scourge the tool
> That did his will; but Thou, O Lord,
> Be merciful to me, a fool!"

> The room was hushed; in silence rose
> The King, and sought his gardens cool,
> And walked apart, and murmured low,
> "Be merciful to me, a fool."

The best-known practitioner of the Longfellow school, however, was Henry van Dyke, a fashionable preacher and professor of literature at

Princeton. *The Builders* (1897) and *The White Bees* (1909), his most popular collections, reflected his background in their consistent sermonizing. His verses such as "Four Things" were widely quoted,

> Four things a man must learn to do
> If he would keep his record true:
> To think, without confusion, clearly;
> To love his fellowman, sincerely;
> To act from honest motives purely;
> To trust in God and Heaven securely,

because like Longfellow's, they were easily understood, easily remembered, and impeccably didactic.

The most surprising poetic phenomenon of the early twentieth century was Robert W. Service, English-born, Scottish-educated, an emigrant to Canada at twenty. Lured by the North, Service went to White Horse and Dawson in the Yukon, where he worked in a bank and gathered materials for poetry in the manner of Kipling, whom he idolized. *Songs of a Sourdough* (1907, retitled *The Spell of the Yukon* in later editions) contained "The Spell of the Yukon:"

> I wanted the gold and I sought it;
> I scrabbled and mucked like a slave.
> Was it famine or scurvy I fought it;
> I hurled my youth into a grave.
> I wanted the gold and I got it—
> Came out with a fortune last fall—
> Yet somehow life's not what I thought it,
> And somehow the gold isn't all.

It also contained "The Cremation of Sam McGee," a ballad based on an old joke about a miner in the frozen North who was never warm enough until they cremated him, a poem in which Service gained a questionable immortality by rhyming "crematorium" with "frozen chum." (The real Sam McGee, a White Horse businessman whose name Service borrowed for the poem, was annoyed the rest of his life by people asking if the weather was hot enough for him.) But most important, the collection included "The Shooting of Dan McGrew," one of the most famous poems ever written, with its ominous opening lines:

> A bunch of the boys were whooping it up
> in the Malemute saloon;
> The kid that handles the music box was
> hitting a jag-time tune;

> Back of the bar, in a solo game, sat
> Dangerous Dan McGrew,
> And watching his luck was his light-o'-love,
> The lady that's known as Lou.

Songs of a Sourdough went through seven printings almost at once, six more editions within the decade, and by the time of Service's death fifty-one years later, over a hundred. He followed up quickly with *Ballads of a Cheechako* (1909), composed chiefly of narrative poems about Yukon characters named Sailor Swede, The Dago Kid, Windy Ike, Muckluck Mag, and God, "The Last Recorder." His first two books brought in royalties of $30,000 which continued to accumulate while he wrote *Rhymes of a Rolling Stone* (1912), *Rhymes of a Red Cross Man* (1916, on the best seller list for two years) and *Ballads of a Bohemian* (1920), all of which increased his fortune. After World War I Service settled in France on the Riviera, living in comfort and continuing to write popular verse and undistinguished novels until World War II forced him back to Canada. As soon as peace was restored he returned to France, publishing his last collection, *Carols of an Old Codger*, in 1954, four years before his death.

Service's sales, by the time of his death, had approached three million, which placed him as one of the two (with Edgar Guest) best-selling poets of his times. He never broke away from the Kipling tradition nor did he care to, for a great part of his appeal derived from his Kiplingesque rhythms (one critic remarked you could hear "Boots" and "Gunga Din" behind every other Service poem and "If" behind the ones between) and his masculine, adventurous narratives. Like Jack London, Rex Beach, and the popular novelists, Service used the material of the North sentimentally and romantically, to illustrate old-fashioned values like pure love, clean living, hard work, and honest money.

The First World War produced far fewer poems of note than the Civil War, although *Stars and Stripes,* the A.E.F. newspaper, ran a well patronized poetry column. The two best known, given added poignancy by their authors' deaths, were Lt. Col. John McCrae's "In Flanders Fields," written by a young officer in France, and Alan Seeger's "I Have a Rendezvous With Death," by far the most anthologized of all poems of that war. Seeger, a young, rebellious aesthete who went to Paris to write in 1912, was strongly influenced by the nineteenth-century French decadents. A believer in the validity of sensation and the beauty of intense experience, he wanted always, he said, "to be present when the pulsations are liveliest." War, he explained to a friend, and possibly death, were obviously ultimate individual experiences, "the largest movement the planet allows . . . , a companionship to the stars."

Seeger enlisted in the French Foreign Legion immediately, one of the first fifty foreigners to do so, saying "How could I let millions of men know an emotion that I remained ignorant of?" and according to his letters found battle exciting and enjoyable. After he was killed on July 4, 1916, friends collected his poems and published them in 1916, rather conventional verses, as they turned out, by a talented, romantic, but immature boy. Nonetheless, his single surviving poem, with its intertwined imagery of Death and Spring, caught the tragedy of a generation of youth trapped by war, and rang true to thousands like him who were caught in it:

> I have a rendezvous with Death,
> At some disputed barricade,
> When Spring comes back with rustling shade
> And apple blossoms fill the air—
> I have a rendezvous with Death
> When Spring brings back blue days and fair. . . .

Joyce Kilmer, another war casualty, wrote "Trees," before the war, but it did not gain its practically permanent popularity until afterward, when it was set to music by Oscar Rasbach in 1922. Kilmer, who conducted poetry departments for *Current Literature, The Literary Digest,* and *The New York Times,* was already known as a critic, lecturer, and poet (strongly influenced by Yeats and the Irish school) when "Trees" appeared in *Poetry* magazine in 1913. The poem, which actually on examination proved to be little more than a sensitive rendering of Bryant's theme of God and Nature and Romanticism's theme of art as divinely inspired organic creation, became the title poem of his second collection in 1914, and he had readied a third when the United States entered the war. Kilmer enlisted and was killed in July, 1918, becoming (with Seeger) the symbol of poetic idealism, the Byronic adventurer, in the eyes of his generation. "Trees," which had no connection with the war, somehow in the public mind became part of the metaphoric meaning of the poet at war. The Army named Camp Kilmer, an embarkation post in New Jersey in World War II, after him, while the poem remains an anthology standard and in its musical version a tour de force for amateur vocalists. The lines "I think that I shall never see/A poem lovely as a tree" are a permanent part of the popular poetic heritage, quoted by conservationists, garden clubs, poetry groups, and millions of school children on Arbor Day.

The largest and most convenient outlet for popular verse after 1880 was the daily newspaper. Papers which did not subscribe to a syndicated poetry column often had their own; Wallace and Frances Rice's anthology of newspaper poetry, *The Humbler Poets* (1911) listed seventy-eight well-known poets, probably only a fraction of the total.

Several had national reputations and were in much demand on the lecture circuit. Sam Walter Foss, who wrote for the Boston *Globe, Judge, Puck, The Youth's Companion,* and other journals, wrote a poem a week for syndication between 1887 and 1893, and in 1893 began writing one a day, a schedule he maintained for twenty years. Foss, who called himself "a laughing philosopher," specialized in homespun, humorous, sentimental verse, aptly illustrated in his widely known

> Let me live in a house by the side of the road,
>   Where the race of men go by—
> The men who are good and the men who are bad,
>   As good and as bad as I.
> I would not sit in the scorner's seat,
>   Or hurl the cynic's ban—
> Let me live in a house by the side of the road,
>   And be a friend to man,

and by his equally famous "The Coming American" which began

> Bring me men to match my mountains,
> Bring me men to match my plains,
> And new eras in their brains
> Bring me men to match my prairies,
> Men to match my inland seas
> Men whose thoughts shall pave a highway
> Up to ampler destinies. . . .

Berton Braley, who began in *Puck* magazine, published his first collection in 1904. *Songs of a Workaday World* (1915) was his most popular book, but he continued writing into the nineteen-thirties, by his own count producing 10,000 poems, five-hundred articles, and three more anthologies. Braley specialized in "work" poems, much reprinted in house organs, with titles such as "Do It Now," "The Slacker," and "The Thinker," which celebrated "the clear-eyed man who knows . . . , the thinker who drives things through . . . , making the dream come true." The opening stanza of "Let Me Live Like a Regular Man," a favorite with YMCA clubs, represented Braley's brand of muscular verse:

> Lord, let me live like a Regular Man,
>   With Regular friends and true;

Let me play the game on the Regular plan,
And play it that way all through;
Let me win or lose with a Regular smile,
And never be known to whine;
For that is a Regular fellow's style,
And I want to make it mine!

T. A. (Thomas Augustus) Daly, however, made his fame with Irish and especially Italian dialect poetry. He published seven books of verse between 1906 and 1946, but his popularity rested on such verses as "Da Leetla Boy," and "Mia Carlotta," the story of the courtship of Carlotta by the author and Guiseppe the barber, to the latter's loss:

Guiseppe da barber, he gotta da cash,
He gotta da clothes and da bigga mustache;
He gotta da seely young girls for da 'mash'
    But notta—
    You bat my life notta—
    Carlotta.
    I gotta.

Daly's collection *Canzoni* (1906), sold 25,000 copies over ten years; *Carmina Madrigali* (1913) and *Little Polly's Poems* (1916) sold nearly as well.

The newspaper poet retained his popularity into the twentieth century, and the large daily or small weekly newspaper that does not publish some poetry now and then tends to be the exception. Athie Sale Davis, who compiled an annual anthology of newspaper verse from 1920 to 1942, noted that whereas in 1920 he looked over about 2500 poems each year, in 1942 he examined over five thousand, which he calculated represented perhaps a third of the total yearly output. He published about a thousand a year, chosen from newspapers which ranged from the Ada (Ohio) *Herald* to the Winthrop (Massachusetts) *Review*, most of them classifiable under the standard categories of current events, love and marriage, home and family, nature (including pets and travel), patriotism, and humorous. The majority of poems in his 1942 collection—with titles like "Just Plain Dog," "A Time for Work," "Our Flag," "Sunrise on Mount Wilson," "The Little Brown House," or "Thoughts of a Mother"—might as easily have appeared in 1872.

Of all newspaper poets, however, none has ever approached the popularity of Edgar A. Guest, who spent his entire career, from 1891 to 1959, on the Detroit *Free Press*. Guest began a verse column in 1899, writing seven poems a week for several decades; in addition he wrote greeting-card verse, Sunday features, anecdotes, epigrams and filler for the paper;

had a radio show for eight years; and read his verses before hundreds of clubs and lecture-series audiences. His total production, he once calculated, must have exceeded 11,000 poems. Guest was an unassuming, friendly man who preferred to call himself not a poet, but "a newspaper man who writes verses . . . ,"

> rhymes, doggerel, anything you like to call it.
> I take the simple, everyday things that happen to
> me and figure that they probably happen to a lot
> of other people and then I make simple rhymes out
> of them, and people seem to like them.

The appeal of his verses lay precisely in that—in their direct, simple, honest recapitulation of average experience. Very much an average man himself, he possessed a great gift for identifying himself with others, and for putting ordinary experiences and human feelings into easily understood verse. Guest once remarked, very perceptively, that the three basic principles of American life were Home, Work, and God. As for Home, the opening lines of his poem "Home," remain indelibly impressed on the American mind:

> It takes a heap o' livin' in a house t' make it home,
> A heap o' sun and shadder, an' ye sometimes have t' roam
> Afore ye really 'preciate the things ye lef' behind,
> And hunger fer 'em somehow, with 'em allus on yer mind.
>
> It don't make any differunce how rich ye get t' be,
> How much yer chairs an' tables cost, how much yer luxury;
> It ain't home t' ye, though it be the palace of a king,
> Until somehow yer soul is sort o' wrapped round everything.

As for Work, his poem "It Couldn't Be Done" is permanently familiar to hundreds of luncheon clubs,

> Somebody said that it couldn't be done
> But he with a chuckle replied,
> That maybe it couldn't but he'd be the one
> Who wouldn't say so till he tried,

with the triumphant ending, *It couldn't be done, but he did it!* As for God, the opening lines of "A Packet of Seed" furnished a text for dozens of sermons: *In this bright little package, isn't it odd?/You've a dime's worth of something known only to God.* The point of all he wrote, Guest said in 1919, was to "find in poetry, for the great mass of readers . . . , the mirror of themselves." Few have perceived more clearly the goal toward which all popular poets strive.

Three phenomena of the twentieth century remain to be noted—Kahlil Gibran, Walter Benton, and Rod McKuen, all poets of the young. Gibran, born in Palestine of Lebanese parents, came to the United States in 1911 and became famous as an Oriental mystic by reason of *The Forerunner* (1920), a cryptic mixture of fable, epigram, poetry, and drawings. Of his eleven subsequent books *The Prophet* (1923) was by far the best known; still in print, though Gibran died in 1931, it has sold nearly three million copies. His poems and aphorisms, according to his translator, hopefully lead his readers toward "a world of understanding, a world of logic and of positive thinking . . . , illumined by reason and understanding." His quasi-philosophical, quasi-poetical books, with an uncomplicated message of faith, self-confidence, and good will, have especial appeal to troubled adolescents. No matter what the college town, its bookstore will have a row of Gibran's books, with several youngsters paging through them.

Walter Benton's poetic reputation among youth rests chiefly on a thin, forty-two page volume, *This Is My Beloved*, published in 1943. A series of free-verse poems, reminiscent of the kind written by D. H. Lawrence and his followers in the twenties, it covers in detail the story of a highly passionate love affair that waxed and waned between April and November. Adorned with yellow, purple, and salmon covers, the book met an enthusiastic response from young people, its reputation built on imagery such as

> Your dress lies
> against the cheeks and hollows of your thighs like
> running water.

> Your breasts nod each step,
> your slow involute hips cradle the eternal synonym
> for God.

It went through thirty-four printings in twenty years, the last edition (1965) its thirty-seventh, still a staple in gift-book sections of university bookstores. *This Is My Beloved* consists simply of variations on a single explicitly erotic theme, the sexuality of love:

> What enslaving cocktail have I sucked
> from your mouth . . . to leave me so totally yours!
> The red pulp of your kisses is sweet on my tongue as
> the red ripe melon meat—yes, even now,
> Though remembered only . . . though you are marketing
> your love,
> I have looked too long upon you . . . too long . . .

and with so much love that strangers can see you
   in my face—
as the sun and vivid colors leave an after image
   in the eyes.

Benton's second collection, *Never A Greater Need* (1948), continued the story of passion rediscovered, even more frankly aimed at the youthful reader with lines like "All your incomparable body laughs to my touch," and "This, then, is you . . . , tender-eyed, nineteen . . . , mine."

Rod McKuen, musician, arranger, and singer, whose first three books of poetry had sold a million copies by 1968, was born in California and drifted from job to job, working as movie extra, disc jockey, reporter, and journeyman night club entertainer. Making his start as a composer and singer of rock-blues and pop songs in the fifties, he developed both his vocal and poetic styles in postwar Paris, returning to the United States to work as a writer and composer for various comedians, singers, and singing groups. His first book of verses, *Stanyan Street and Other Sorrows* (1954) steadily built up a following, with five printings by 1960, but his second book, *Listen to the Warm* (1963) rocketed immediately into the best-seller lists. His third book, *Lonesome Cities* (1967–68), appeared with an incredible first printing of 135,000 copies, and his fourth, *The World of Rod McKuen* (1968, actually a song book as well) with 190,000. Meanwhile he made thirty-five long-playing albums featuring his verse and songs, flavored with the warm, slightly salty taste of adolescence, and all in print in 1969. In 1968 McKuen's albums alone sold over two million copies. After much persuasion, McKuen in early 1969 consented to a television special, "The Loner," which drew one of the season's largest audiences.

McKuen's popularity was almost wholly concentrated in the fifteen to twenty-five age group. "It would be virtually impossible," remarked Albert Drake, a younger poet and critic, "for a mature adult of any sophistication to respond seriously to McKuen's verse, although his music probably has a much wider range of appeal." Written in simple, free verse form, his poems, he says, "speak honestly of people's need for one another," concerned almost wholly with what McKuen believes is the overwhelming problem of modern life, "love, loneliness, and alienation." His wistful expressions of this theme, recited on records in a gravelly baritone against a background of strings, are flavored with updated Ella Wheeler Wilcox-eroticism, with lines such as *I want to see the world within the circle of your arms,/And sail the wide seas of your thighs,* though by no means so explicitly detailed as Benton's.

McKuen's effectiveness with youthful readers, however, lies in his unabashedly confessional sentimentalism:

> I make rimes for people who won't hear
> some who will not turn their faces to mine.
> It is for me a kind of loving,
> A kind of loving, for me.

That this is effective with younger readers is without doubt; as a teen-aged girl wrote to the Detroit *Free Press* after McKuen's television special was roughly handled by adult reviewers,

> I was filled with compassion when I read the letter concerning Rod McKuen. I truly feel sorry for people who can't grasp the beauty and meaningfulness that he puts across. His poetry may not be looked upon as the best by English professors, but I may say, that to those human beings who love the simple, honest things in life, he communicates. I feel sometimes when I am listening to him that he is speaking the words that I feel in my heart. The only frauds in the world today are those who are afraid to speak how they feel inside.
> S.M.B., Hamtramck

His four books all deal directly and exclusively with his central theme, "people's inability to communicate with each other, the need of people to read one another, to share." His blend of message, love, and sentiment, presented in simple imagery and an almost primer-like vocabulary, lies clearly within the historical mainstream of the popular verse tradition.

As Mrs. Sigourney saw death as the (overwhelming) fact of life in her time, so McKuen saw loneliness and isolation in his—an observation which, to judge by the public's million-copy reaction, must have considerable validity. Confirming the principle that no poet of negation or despair has ever been an American favorite, McKuen offers (as Mrs. Sigourney did) hope for mankind's gradual realization of its need for brotherhood, in a mutual holding-of-hands against the dark of life:

> Each of us was made by God
> and some of us grew tall.
> Others stood out in the wind
> their branches bent and fell.
> Those of us who walk in light
> must help the ones in darkness up.
> For that's what life is all about
> and love is all there is to life.
>
> Each of us was made by God
> beautiful in His mind's eye.

Those of us that turned out sound
should look across our shoulders once
and help the weak ones to their feet.

It only takes an outstretched hand.

Longfellow wrote about this need with somewhat more formality—and
perhaps more maturity and skill—a century and a half ago.

Whatever the shifting fashions of poetry in the twentieth-century
marketplace, whether it be philosophy (Gibran), sex (Benton), or philosophy plus sex (McKuen), certain poets and poems remain popular;
the common taste does not change. The all-time best-selling book of
poetry is still Roy J. Cook's *One Hundred and One Famous Poems,* originally published in 1916, revised in 1929 (to include a prose supplement
containing the Gettysburg Address, the Declaration of Independence,
and similar documents), still in print in 1969, with a total sales record of
somewhat over six million copies. (Its closest rival, Speare's *Pocket Book
of Verse,* has sold 2,700,000 since 1940.) Cook's list of poems, selected
"to enrich, ennoble, and encourage" readers in "an age of hard faces and
hard highways, an age of steel and cement," ranges from Lucy Larcom
to Edna St. Vincent Millay, from Bryant to Robert Frost, from Shakespeare to Sam Walter Foss.

About two-thirds of Cook's authors are American, the rest British, a
reasonable proportion for American readers, with Longfellow (seven
poems) the most popular, followed by Shakespeare and Wordsworth
(five each.) Also popular are Kipling, Holmes, Emerson, Whittier, and
Eugene Field followed by Bryant, Poe, Tennyson, Burns, Byron, E. R.
Sill, Markham, and Vachel Lindsay. It would be difficult to fault Cook's
choices—"Hiawatha," "The Bells," "Thanatopsis," the "Mercy" speech from
The Merchant of Venice, "Little Boy Blue," "Crossing the Bar," "Rabbi Ben
Ezra," "The Chambered Nautilus," "Maud Muller," "If" Polonius' "Advice
to Laertes," "The Children's Hour," "A Man's a Man for A'That," "Concord
Hymn," and eighty-seven others, most of which the average American
recognizes with familiar surprise. These seem to be the verities.

PART TWO

THE POPULAR THEATER AND OTHER ENTERTAINMENTS

The theater is no place for painful speculation; it is a place for diverting representation.

—H. L. MENCKEN

AT THE OPERA HOUSE
TONIGHT

The public wants variety, well-cooked and well-served.

—CHARLES HOYT

Though the American colonies were settled at the height of the English theater's Golden Age, there was no perceptible Colonial theater for perhaps a century after the settlement. Drama, a peculiarly social art, required a kind of sophisticated, cohesive urban life that seventeenth-century America did not have. Actors and plays were viewed with mistrust and distaste in both Northern and Southern colonies. New England Calvinists, New York Dutch, and Pennsylvania Quakers all held strong objections to theatrical performances, which were believed to encourage idleness and immorality.

As late as 1750 the Massachusetts General Court reaffirmed the traditional Calvinistic objection to "public stage-plays, interludes, and other theatrical entertainments, which not only occasion great and unnecessary expenses, and discourage industry and frugality, but likewise tend generally to increase immorality, impiety, and a contempt for religion." Student and amateur performances were nevertheless tolerated and even encouraged, as were plays presented under the guise of "moral lectures" or "musical performances." In Virginia and the South bans against the theater were soon lifted, and with the growth of cities and the establishment of a wealthy, leisured class, life became richer in cultural and intellectual activities. New York, Philadelphia, Baltimore, Charleston, Boston, and other cities by the close of the seventeenth century contained a self-consciously cultivated society which could not only support a theater, but hoped to emulate the playgoing fashions of British aristocracy.

In the early eighteenth century itinerant English actors and companies made fairly regular tours of the Southern and Middle colonies, avoiding Puritan New England. Tony Aston, a comedian who advertised himself as "Gentleman, Lawyer, Poet, Actor, Soldier, Sailor, Exciseman, and Publican," made such a tour of the Carolinas in 1702–04, certainly one of the first to do so. Williamsburg built a theater in 1716, New York in 1732, Charleston in 1735 (or 1736), though plays were more often presented in ballrooms, taverns, and assembly halls.

Murray and Kean's company had great success in New York and Philadelphia in 1750, but the first professional company to play regularly to American audiences was Lewis Hallam's London company, which opened at Williamsburg in 1752 and moved later to New York and Philadelphia. To accommodate the Hallams and other companies, theaters sprang up in the 1760's, such as the Chapel Street Theater and the John Street Theater in New York City, and the Southwark in Philadelphia. Except for the accident of location, these companies were no different from British companies in England, drawing their talent from the London stage and playing Shakespeare, Otway, Addison, Cibber, Farquhar, Sheridan, and others from the standard English repertoire.

Like the English city theaters, colonial playhouses played to both ends of the social spectrum. The John Street Theater, for example, showed *Richard III, Hamlet, The Mock Doctor,* and *High Life Below Stairs* on successive bills. The theater was particularly popular in the South, not only in cultural centers such as Williamsburg, Annapolis, or Charleston, but in places such as Port Tobacco and Hob's Hole. George Washington's journals for 1771–72, for example, show that between fall and spring he went to the theater nineteen times; the season at Charleston in 1773–74 included fifty-eight different offerings, ranging from Shakespeare to ballad opera.

In 1774 Continental Congress asked for the suspension of "horseracing, gambling, cockfighting, exhibitions of shows, plays, and other expensive diversions and entertainments." In the cities, most of which were occupied by the British, there were a few theatricals for the amusement of resident British and local society, but most actors retired either to London or to the West Indies during the war. Immediately afterward they flocked back.

A hastily organized company played the 1782–83 season in Baltimore and New York. Lewis Hallam, Jr., arrived with another group in Philadelphia in 1784 and moved to New York in 1785. John Henry, a talented Irish actor, came to the United States at almost the same time to join Hallam and form the Old American Company, which dominated the

American theater for another decade. In 1794 Thomas Wignell withdrew from it to form a company of his own in Philadelphia, leaving the Old American players, now owned by Hallam and William Dunlap, in control of the New York stage.

Theological opposition to the theater gradually disappeared after the Revolution, though some prejudice remained. In 1788 in New England it was still necessary to advertise plays as "moral lectures"; managers therefore billed *Richard III* as "The Fate of Tyranny," *Hamlet* as "Filial Piety," and *She Stoops to Conquer* as "Improper Education." Since the actors were almost unanimously British, they too faced hostility as "foreign minions, lately the enemy." During the great yellow fever epidemics of the 1790's many citizens preferred to avoid crowds, and many also disliked the rowdiness of theatergoers, who sometimes shouted profanities and threw garbage. Theaters were also expensive; New York's Park Street Theater in 1798 charged two dollars for a box and one dollar for the gallery.

On the other hand, to an educated and sophisticated city gentry the traditional moral objections to popular plays seemed long outmoded. Wealthy gentlemen and their ladies in Boston, New York, Philadelphia, and Charleston, anxious to imitate London and Paris, attended plays with increasing frequency, and while city audiences were mixed, they were by no means unfashionable. Objections to the theater diminished in proportion to the rising social level of its patrons. Josiah Quincy of Boston noted with some surprise in 1773 that Charleston ladies of good family often went to plays, while after the war General Washington himself was known as an enthusiastic playgoer. Theater managers were quick to advertise the presence of well-known public figures or wealthy patrons.

That the theater had arrived in America was proved by the fact that new and elegant playhouses began to appear in the cities even before the Revolution. Annapolis had a new theater in 1771; Charleston's, opened in 1773, was larger than any in New York or Philadelphia. A Boston group built the Federal Street Theater (designed by Charles Bulfinch) and opened it in 1794, at almost the same time as Philadelphia's new Chestnut Street Theater. Charleston built its Church Street Theater in 1786, and New York's Park Theater was completed in 1798. Ten years after Yorktown the American theater was in good health. At least two permanent companies, the Old American and Wignell's Philadelphia group, gave professional performances probably equal to those of the better British troupes. Theaters usually gave three plays each week during their season, on Mondays, Wednesdays, and Fridays, beginning at six or seven o'clock; the bill usually included a play and an "afterpiece" which might be a farce, a ballet, or an operatic performance.

American theaters of the period, like their English counterparts, could be noisy, odorous, drab places. Occupants of the more expensive boxes were often more interested in seeing and being seen than in the play. In the pit, men lounged uneasily on the hard benches, hats and coats off, spitting tobacco juice or eating, and if the play lagged, harassing the actors, who if sufficiently provoked might step to the edge of the stage and shout insults back. (Ladies who attended sat with their escorts in the boxes; no woman who valued her safety sat in the pit.) In some theaters the third balcony was reserved for toughs and prostitutes. The acting was not always good, costumes were dirty more often than not, some actors were as famous for their alcoholic capacity as for their talent, and the plays were often ineptly staged. Nevertheless, despite all this, popular interest in the drama grew rapidly and theaters sprang up quickly in the cities. As theaters improved, so did audiences; the increasing splendor of the surroundings may have impressed and quieted some of the rowdies. William Dunlap, describing the remodeled Park Theater in New York in 1807, decorated by John Joseph Holland, remarked that it had

> . . . in the lower lobby, a colonnade with mirrors and fireplaces at each end, the whole lighted by glass lamps between the columns. . . . There are several coffee rooms, one of which is fitted in an elegant style for the accommodations of the ladies. The boxes will accommodate upwards of sixteen hundred persons and the pit and gallery about eleven hundred. The ceiling painted as a dome, with panels of light purple, and gold mouldings; the centre a balustrade and sky. The box fronts (except the fourth row) are divided into panels, blue ground with white and gold ornaments, a crimson festoon draping over each box. The lower boxes are lighted by ten glass chandeliers . . . , while a beautiful effect is produced by a large oval mirror at the end of the stage boxes, which reflects the whole of the audience in the first row.

London still provided nearly all the plays for the American stage, with two notable exceptions, Royall Tyler (1757–1826) and William Dunlap (1766–1839). Tyler, a Boston lawyer who later became Chief Justice of the Vermont Supreme Court, wrote a delightful Sheridan-like comedy of manners, *The Contrast,* first performed in 1787. Built about the theme of native American worth versus foreign affectations, the play contrasted Colonel Manly, an upstanding, true-blue American, with Billy Dimple, an Anglicized fop, much to the former's advantage. The character of Jonathan, a Yankee farmer, played to the hilt by Thomas Wignell, was a major theatrical creation and the first of a long line of comic rustics.

More important in the history of American drama, however, was William Dunlap, who helped to organize and stabilize the theater during its most chaotic period. He purchased a share of Hallam and Hodgkinson's Old American Company in 1796, managed it until its bankruptcy in 1805, and also managed New York's Park Theater for some years after 1798. In addition, Dunlap helped to found the National Academy of Design, taught painting, and wrote *The History of the American Theater* (1832) which, despite errors and personal bias, is still a landmark in American theatrical history.

Dunlap wrote and produced many bad and mediocre plays, yet he was not afraid to experiment, encouraged originality, and was himself a serious student of producing, acting, staging, and management. His collapse into bankruptcy illustrated the difficulties faced by the American theater in the decade before the War of 1812. Little hostility against the stage remained anywhere in the United States, but American drama needed a playgoing public accustomed to regular attendance, better playhouses, and a large number of good American playwrights.

By the beginning of the nineteenth century, the American stage nevertheless showed encouraging signs of strength and independence. Traveling companies after 1812 carried plays inland, down the Ohio and Mississippi and into the remote hamlets of the hinterland; amateur "Thespian" and "Aeolian" societies appeared in colleges and cities. The growing popularity of the stage is illustrated by the boom in theater-building between 1820 and 1830—the Bowery, Chatham, Lafayette, and the New Park in New York, Boston's Tremont, the New Chestnut Street and the Arch Street in Philadelphia, among others. Theaters also sprang up in smaller cities such as Buffalo, Rochester, Cincinnati, and Pittsburgh, and in Southern towns from Baltimore to Savannah. Where theaters did not exist, companies played in tents, taverns, ballrooms, barns, or anywhere an audience could find seats. A regular circuit developed for acting companies; touring groups in the forties might begin in New York, and play Philadelphia, Baltimore, Washington, Alexandria, Charleston, Savannah, and Columbus, swinging back via New Orleans, Mobile, St. Louis, Cincinnati, Pittsburgh, Buffalo, and Albany.

The new buildings reflected changes in both the size and the character of audiences. They were much larger than before—the second Park Theater in New York held 2,500, with a pit, three rows of boxes, and a huge gallery; the Bowery, built not long after, held 3,500; the Broadway, constructed in the forties, held 4,000. Theater prices came down at the same time. The Park, which charged two dollars for a box in 1800, now advertised a seventy-five cent top, whereas others held to a fifty-cent top, twelve-and-a-half cents for the gallery. Producers appealed not to the elite or the select; although first-rate plays and actors drew large crowds, the emphasis was clearly on mass entertainment. As an English traveler reported in the thirties, "society people" made up only a small part of an American audience; theaters were mostly "sustained by the middle and humbler ranks." The Olympic Theater in New York, in fact, reserved the pit on Saturday afternoons for newsboys, butcher boys, and apprentices.

Still, few actors, managers, companies, or producers could be called prosperous. Actors were so badly paid that managers were sometimes forced to hold "third nights" and "farewell tours" to augment stars' pay. Fees for playwrights were equally small; five hundred dollars for an original play was unusual, one hundred dollars for an adaptation generous. The plays themselves were often written in a matter of days, poorly rehearsed, and badly acted. Actor-producer Harry Watkins reported in the forties that he wrote a complete five-act drama in eight days, "the last two filled with considerable pain." The man who probably had more plays on the stage than anybody else was John Baldwin Buckingstone, who wrote more than one hundred and fifty, including two of the most popular farces in American drama, *The Pet of the Petticoats*, and *A Kiss in the Dark*.

One of the most difficult problems faced by the theater manager was that he had to try to please everybody, so that his theater might present Shakespeare one night, farce the next, and an equestrian-acrobatic troupe the next. (Edwin Booth once played his famous *Richelieu* as half of a double bill with a rowdy farce called *The Double-Bedded Room*.) Serious plays had to have "afterpieces," carried over from the eighteenth century, which entertained the crowd, either after the play or between the acts, with pantomimists, trained animals, dancers, singers, and the like.

The fact was that American society had lost many of the strong class distinctions of British and European society, and now possessed a large, affluent middle class. The theater, by the end of the eighteenth century, already showed many of the democratic, "popular" tendencies needed to attract that audience. "The rapid increase in population in the cities," an English actor commented somewhat ruefully after an American tour, "produces a style of patrons whose habits and associations afford no opportunity for the cultivation of the arts." This was not quite true. The rising middle class wanted its own kind of *popular* art in the theater, neither Shakespearean tragedy nor jugglers, something that would entertain as well as embody and reflect its tastes and values.

As a result, the early American stage developed two distinct theatrical traditions—an upper class "serious" theater, and a "popular" theater aimed at lower and middle social and economic groups. In New York the Bowery Theater, the People's, the Windsor, the Third Avenue, the National, the London—charging ten, twenty, and thirty-cent admissions, "the People's own prices"—catered to the popular taste. Chicago had a whole block of such theaters, and so did Philadelphia, St. Louis, San Francisco, and other cities. The combination of Shakespeare and acrobats (to choose extremes) could not last, for each pointed in a different direction. As an observer wrote in the forties, "Opera [comic opera] and burlesque, the melodrama and ballet, have literally swallowed up legitimate drama."

So it may have seemed, but what happened was that the formal theater of Shakespeare and Sheridan, of classic opera and symphony, continued to draw the same audiences it always had; while the other, popular audience wanted and got something else—spectacles, dioramas, comedies, "Living Tableaux" (with models in "diaphanous costumes"), moral plays, melodrama, and musicals. The majority of people knew of Forrest and Booth and Sir Henry Irving, but they also knew and loved James Hackett's Yankee, Joseph Jefferson's Rip, Chanfrau's Mose the Fireman, and Frank Mayo's Crockett. The likes and dislikes of the great American middle class turned the nineteenth-century theater into a medium for mass entertainment.

Americans used the popular drama (until it was displaced by the motion picture) as a way to explore the aims, ideals and problems of their society—as well as for entertainment. Few popular plays could claim dramatic or literary distinction, nor could they bear comparison with the formal, legitimate theater, which by the 1840's had developed a respectable body of talented actors, playwrights, and a healthy box office. Popular drama had its own design; it followed the public taste, showed people what they wanted to see and told them what they wanted to hear in terms they could easily understand. It was not drama of change or protest (with a few notable exceptions such as *Uncle Tom's Cabin* and *The Drunkard*) but one which, as a reviewer of Murdoch's *Davy Crockett* remarked in 1874, "must make the heart beat responsively . . . , and strike the linked chords of humanity . . . which join all people as one."

There were plays of real artistic merit, of course, which had long runs because they contained elements which appealed to a mass audience, or because they featured such stars as Edwin Forrest, Sarah Bernhart, Eleanora Duse, E. H. Sothern, or James O'Neill. But these were not "popular" drama. Robert Montgomery Bird's *The Gladiator* (1831), James Herne's *Shore Acres* (1892), or Langdon Mitchell's *New York Idea*

(1906), among others, were plays of distinction which happened also to have qualities of general appeal. This was not true of Joseph Jefferson's *Rip Van Winkle* (1866), or Dion Boucicault's *Octoroon* (1859), or Harrigan and Hart's romp, *The Mulligan Guard Ball* (1879), or David Belasco's melodramatic *Heart of Maryland* (1895), none of which made any pretensions to literary merit and which were frankly written to draw the largest possible crowd for the longest possible time. Plays such as these, literally thousands of them, made up the American popular drama.

Plays dealing with native materials appeared earliest on the scene and persisted longest. Patriotic drama, the product of wartime and postwar nationalism, emerged during the Revolutionary War; Hugh Henry Brackenridge's *Battle of Bunker Hill*, published in Philadelphia in 1776, was probably the first. John Burk did another Bunker Hill play in 1797, while William Dunlap's *André* (1798) was the best of the type on the post-Revolutionary stage. Dunlap's *Glory of Columbia* (1803) and *Battle of New Orleans* (1815) contained typical crowd-pleasing elements such as cannon, martial music, patriotic declarations, and marching armies. A. H. Quinn, in his historical study of American drama, listed twenty-one plays about the Revolution written between 1820 and 1860, testifying to its perennial popular appeal.

The War of 1812 produced plays like Mordecai Noah's *She Would Be a Soldier* (1819), a surefire pleaser about a girl masquerading as a man in the army, but the Mexican War attracted little theatrical attention. The Civil War went on the stage immediately. An enterprising producer had a play about Bull Run on the boards within a month of the battle; later, plays about particular engagements might appear within two weeks, made to order from a standard script.

After the war, however, the spate of plays about it dealt less with battles and leaders than with its melodramatic and sentimental aspects, following the pattern of Dion Boucicault's *Belle Lamar* (1874). To Boucicault, who knew his audiences, battles were secondary attractions, people the primary thing. With *Belle Lamar* he was among the first to put the Southern belle on stage, building his plot about the tried-and-true "star cross'd lover" theme of Southern girl and Northern soldier.

Boucicault's success attracted numerous imitators—William Gillett's *Held By The Enemy* (1886), Bronson Howard's *Shenandoah* (1888), and Belasco's *Heart of Maryland* (produced in 1895 as a vehicle for Mrs. Leslie Carter) and dozens of others. The patriotic theme, in its military and romantic aspects, continued directly into motion pictures like *The Big Parade, Lilac Time,* and *Hell's Angels,* down to Errol Flynn and John Wayne.

Indian plays were equally durable. Robert Rogers' story of the tragic fate of *Chief Ponteach* (1766) was the first American Indian play, but popular interest in the stage Indian did not appear until after the turn of the century, when James Nelson Barker recognized the romantic potential of the Pocahontas story and used it with great effectiveness in *The Indian Princess, or La Belle Sauvage,* a wild success in 1808. These two figures—the doomed chieftain and the dusky princess—became central characters in more than fifty Indian plays that appeared over the next thirty years. Easily the biggest hit of all was John Augustus Stone's *Metamora, or the Last of the Wampanoags,* produced in 1829 as a starring vehicle for Edwin Forrest. A mixture of romantic tragedy, sentimentality, and bombast, Stone's play lasted well into the eighties and evoked a dozen imitations. However, by the seventies *Metamora* and others were being burlesqued, a sure sign that the strain had run out. The dime novel and the Western adopted the chief but not the princess.

The roaring, swashbuckling frontiersman, another native product, appeared first in James K. Paulding's play, *The Lion of the West,* in 1831, as "Colonel Nimrod Wildfire" (possibly modeled on Davy Crockett), a part written for actor James Hackett. Rewritten several times and widely imitated, the play emerged again in 1833 as *A Kentuckian's Trip to New York.* Dressed in buckskin, coonskin hat, and boots, Hackett made a career out of his role as "a son of old Kentuck, a mite wolfy about the head and shoulders," who "needed a fight every ten days to keep in shape."

The Colonel and his sweetheart, Pat Snap from Salt Lick, held the stage until 1872 when Davy Crockett (played by Frank Mayo) in Frank Murdoch's play of the same name replaced him. Crockett, a rough but gentlemanly frontiersman, in contrast to the bumptious Wildfire, represented the pioneer as nature's nobleman; Murdoch combined Indians, wolves, blizzards, and a dastardly villain with the love story of brave hunter and city girl. When Crockett told his sweetheart, "I ain't fitten to breathe the same air with you; what am I, nothing but an ignorant backwoodsman?" there was hardly a dry eye in the house. Mayo played the part until 1896, over two thousand times, the last only two days before his death. James J. Jeffries played it later in a revival that somehow included a boxing match, but it was hardly the same.

The "Western" drama of the seventies was largely a continuation of Indian and frontier plays, but it was also directly related to the same popular interest in the newly-opened prairie West that produced the dime novel and the Wild West show. Colonel E. Z. C. Judson ("Ned Buntline" of dime novel fame) persuaded Buffalo Bill Cody and his friend Texas Jack to appear in a play called *The Scouts of the Prairie* in

Chicago in late 1872. Cody's debut was so successful—it included a temperance lecture, a lasso exhibition, a prairie fire, a lovely Indian princess (played by an Italian girl from Chicago), and a knife fight with ten Indians—that it obviously had to be repeated. After increasing the number of Indians to twenty-five, adding horses, and inserting a ballet by ten Indian maidens, Cody took the show on the road for one of the most successful tours in American theatrical history. The next year Wild Bill Hickok starred in *The Scouts of the Plains*, while Cody returned in 1876 with *The Red Right Hand, or Buffalo Bill's First Scalp for Custer*, who had just lost at Little Big Horn.

From then on, until it merged into the Western movie, the Western play was a popular dramatic staple. Cody went on tour almost every year, until he started his Wild West exhibitions in 1883, in more or less the same play under new titles—*The Knight of the Plains, Buffalo Bill at Bay, The Prairie Waif, Vera Vance, or Saved from the Sioux*—and so did a number of imitators. Unlike either the swaggering Wildfire or the noble Crockett, the Western hero, modeled on Cody and Hickok, was sharpshooter, Indian fighter, hunter, and lawman. When the movies came, the cowboy hero simply changed media.

The shrewd, homespun, comic Yankee, the most durable of all popular stage characters, derived from Royall Tyler's "Jonathan" in his comedy, *The Contrast* (1787), a part shaped for generations by actor Thomas Wignell, who played it first. Yankees appeared in at least five other plays within the next decade, and after dropping out of sight for a time, reappeared with new vigor in Samuel Woodworth's *The Forest Rose* (1825) as "Jonathan Ploughboy," a play which ran intermittently in both England and America for the next half-century. Cornelius Logan wrote two Yankee plays, both perennial favorites—*Yankee Land* (1834), featuring a character named Lot Sap Sago, and *The Vermont Wool Dealer* (1840), with Deuteronomy Dutiful. George Handel Hill played so many Downeast parts that he became known as "Yankee" Hill; when *The Forest Rose* was not on the boards, he simply played one of a dozen or so other Yankee parts—"Sy Saco," "Jedidiah Homebred," "Zachariah Dickerwell," "Industrious Doolittle," "Solomon Gundy," and so on. James Hackett played "Solomon Swap," Dan Marble "Sam Patch," Joshua Silsbee "Curtis Chunk," and Joe Jones "Solon Shingle."

Playwrights, to satisfy the Yankee industry, sent their rustic characters to Buffalo, London, Paris, the mountains, the Bowery, and a multitude of other places, including Italy and Poland, searching for some new comic device. Curiously enough, no other regional type was ever so successful on the stage as the Yankee. Even the Dutch Rip Van Winkle was transformed into a Yankee in his first appearance in 1829, played by Hackett. Hackett's success led to a second, improved version of the play in 1833 and a third in 1850. Joseph Jefferson, third in a distinguished line of actors, presented his *Rip* in 1859. He persuaded Dion Boucicault, the best re-write specialist of the period, to revise it in 1865, and opened it in New York in 1866. Jefferson's *Rip* replaced all previous Yankee plays; no one could play the part as he could, and he played it continuously for thirty-eight years. Though the play was intrinsically mediocre, *Rip Van Winkle* had real power in Jefferson's hands. An actor of consummate skill who never lost interest in the character he created, he made it into the most popular single role in the history of the American theater.

The popularity of the Yankee plays reflected something about the American's vision of himself, as honest, shrewd, sentimental, independent, and possessed of a heart of gold. Long after he left the stage, the same Yankee appeared again in a number of disguises—as David Harum, Scattergood Baines, Abe Martin, and the greatest of the moderns, Will Rogers.

The burgeoning of the city, where the bulk of the popular theater's audience lived, naturally attracted the attention of playwrights who, like their counterparts in London and Paris, recognized the great dramatic possibilities of urban society. A few of these plays began to appear in the eighteen-thirties and forties: *Life in Philadelphia* (1833), *The New York Merchant and His Clerks* (1843), *Fifteen Years in a Fireman's Life* (1841), and others patterned on French and British models. The first really popular city play was Benjamin Baker's *A Glance at New York* (1848), a potpourri of materials centered on the character of "Mose the Bowery Bhoy," an Irish volunteer fireman played by Frank Chanfrau with a plug hat, red shirt, turned-up trouser bottoms, and plastered-down hair like a Bowery dude. Mose was such a hit that he soon had a series of plays to himself, such as *Mose in a Muss, Mose in China, Mose's Visit to Philadelphia*, and many more, mostly played by Chanfrau, the Bowery's favorite actor, whose appearance invariably touched off wild demonstrations.

The popularity of Mose, impressive as it was, was less important than the fact that Baker and the Bowery plays opened a whole new vein of popular dramatic interest—the humor, joys, sorrows, people, manners, and society of urban America. Other plays quickly appeared, emphasizing not Mose but cross sections of city life; among them *New York as It Is, The Mysteries and Miseries of New York, Philadelphia as It Is,* and others in the forties. Dion Boucicault, who based his play *The Poor of New York* (1857) on a current French success, took a realistic look at the humorous world of Mose and produced a different and more meaningful play. He peopled his stage with rowdy comics, virtuous heroines, heroic heroes, and dastardly villains, and threw in a fire scene for effect; but he also presented real people—policemen, seamen, bankers, street boys, shopgirls, clerks. Like the skillful writer that he was, Boucicault gave the audience rattling drama, sentimental love, and plenty of stage business. He also gave them a reflection of their own lives.

Edward Harrigan picked up the city play from Boucicault. Harrigan, born on New York's East Side, got into stage life at sixteen, danced, played banjo, and told dialect stories in minstrel shows. In 1871 he teamed with Anthony Cannon, who changed his name to Hart, in variety sketches which Harrigan wrote. In 1876 they opened their own theater in New York, specializing in variety, and in 1878 Harrigan wrote *The Mulligan Guard Picnic*, a play about the Irish of Harrigan's own "Bloody Sixth" ward of tenements and saloons. Since it was moderately successful, he wrote *The Mulligan Guard Ball*, which opened in January, 1879 to run for more than a hundred performances, followed by six more Mulligan Guard plays within three years. The partnership with Hart broke up in 1885, but Harrigan continued his stream of successes with plays about Irish, Jewish, German, Italian, and Negro city types, returning to the Mulligans in 1901.

Harrigan knew little about playwriting and cared less, but he had an unerring sense of what the public wanted for entertainment. He put together songs, dances, slam-bang farce, witty dialogue, and sentimental sketches, along with sympathetic, accurate, and delightful vignettes of city life. The Mulligan plays brought howls of laughter (one character, looking out at the audience, remarked, "I see all the politicians here, so the city is safe until the play's over"), but they also dealt with politics, the police, domestic life in the tenements, the manners and mores of lower class society, and the constant clash of ethnic values and customs among the immigrant groups trying to become Americans.

Harrigan did for New York what Dickens had done for London. As he wrote in 1889,

> I try to be as realistic as possible. . . . Each drama is a series of photographs of life today in the Empire City. In constructing plots, I try to use one that is simple and natural, just like what happens around us every day . . . , to the poor, the workers, and the great middle class. Whoever puts them on the stage appeals to an audience of millions.

Harrigan took the materials tentatively explored by Baker and Boucicault and developed from them a body of popular social drama that still remains a considerable achievement. What he did pointed toward *Potash and Perlmutter, Abie's Irish Rose, Street Scene, Pal Joey,* and *West Side Story.*

Harrigan's forte was social satire, a strong strain in popular drama from its beginnings. Royall Tyler's contrast of true-blue American with Anglophile fop, in *The Contrast,* stated a theme that never lost its appeal for American audiences. The contrast of silly-ass Englishman, dancing French count, combative Irishman, comic Dutchman, or fiery Italian, with other native and foreign types, remained a stage staple for the next century. Satires of fashionable, pseudo-aristocratic society appealed to the American national spirit and to Jacksonian equalitarianism. They were not done in the witty, urbane tradition of Sheridan, but with cruder, earthier jibes that brought cheers from the cheaper seats. James Hackett's masterful portrait of "high society" in *A Trip to the Springs* (1831) and *Scenes at the Fair* (1833) were repeated in dozens of plays and sketches which contrasted the pretensions of the upper class with the sound democracy of the common man.

Anna Ogden Mowatt's *Fashion* (1845) became the classic of the type. A well-known writer for the women's magazines, Mrs. Mowatt took the old plot of the socially ambitious newly rich woman, Mrs. Tiffany (who hoped "to become one of the ee-light") and turned it into a devastingly clever study of social types, including the bogus French count, the worthless rich boy, the effeminate poet, the upstart clerk, and the honest American named Adam Trueman, mixing them all into an improbably farcical plot combined with a sentimental love story. Though she had no stage experience, she decided to act it herself, which she did with great skill over two hundred times its first year. Though she left the play after nine years, it remained in repertory until the nineties. *Fashion* inspired dozens of imitations, among the best and most successful British playwright Tom Taylor's *Our American Cousin* (1858) in which E. H. Sothern starred as Lord Dundreary, the comic, monocled Englishman.

Charles Hoyt, an expert writer of comic sketches, was the most prolific and talented of Mrs. Mowatt's successors. Hoyt, originally a drama critic, began as a sentimental playwright and found his metier with a successful farce, *A Bunch of Keys,* in 1882. For the next sixteen years he wrote and produced at least a play a year, most of them broad satires of American character types—senators, feminists, spiritualists, businessmen, tourists, artists, railroad men, anybody else who came under his critical eye.

He wanted always, Hoyt said, "to furnish an entertainment that would draw the public," but he liked to poke fun "at anything ludicrous, or at any type of individual that strikes me as eccentric, mean, or narrow-minded." Hoyt's satires, introducing such characters as Vilas Canby the plumber, Christian Berriel the undertaker, and the pious hypocrite Kneeland Pray, dominated the popular theater for years. His *Texas Steer* (1890), about a braggart Congressman, played a hundred straight nights; so did his prohibitionist sketch, *A Temperance Town* (1893), while *Trip to Chinatown* (1893), one of the best and earliest of musical comedies, ran for 650 consecutive performances. Nobody ever wrote better satires for the popular stage than Hoyt.

Despite their prejudices against the stage, even the Calvinist colonists were willing to use it for moral purposes, the model, of course, being that "great expositor of human nature" and "virtue's friend," William Shakespeare. Othello, therefore, taught the dangers of jealousy, Lear of selfishness, Macbeth and Richard III of ambition, the Merchant of Venice of greed, and so on. Reformers were well aware of the power of drama to instruct, and the nineteenth century had many messages to deliver.

The problem was, of course, to combine moralism with entertainment, or how to keep the play popular while using it to preach. Very few straight propaganda plays ever did well, but William Henry Smith's *The Drunkard, or the Fallen Saved,* which opened in 1844 (the first play in American theatrical history to run a hundred consecutive performances) combined sermon and stage with tremendous effectiveness.

Smith's play, billed as "a moral lecture" and endorsed by every temperance society in the country, drew audiences that would never have entered a theater under any other circumstances. Drunkenness was a very real problem to nineteenth-century society, the root of many of its social ills, so the play's message struck audiences directly at home. Though poorly written and constructed of shop-work materials, *The Drunkard* came across the footlights with undeniable power; the delirium-tremens scene, played hundreds of times separately as an actor's tour de force, was nearly as famous as Hamlet's soliloquy. C. W. Clarke, who played the role for years, gained such a wide national reputation for the role that he was known in the profession as "Drunkard" Clarke.

The Drunkard stayed on the boards for the next twenty years (at one point there were four New York theaters playing it simultaneously) and continued in road show repertories for another twenty. Some troupes specialized in it and played nothing else; Robinson's show played it across the continent for a year and a half to audiences of more than a quarter million. Other playwrights imitated it—Timothy Shaw Arthur's dramatized novel, *Ten Nights in a Barroom; One Glass More; The Drunkard's Warning,* and so on. It appeared in a variety of productions, among them one that included a parade of a thousand children marching across the stage singing temperance songs; another that featured a quadrille of forty-eight dancers; and another in California that exhibited a panorama "covering 3,000 square feet of canvas."

But no drama, moral or otherwise, ever matched *Uncle Tom's Cabin* or equaled its impact on the American people. After Mrs. Stowe's novel, which appeared in 1852, sold 300,000 copies within the year, it was of course inevitable that it would be adapted to the stage. Two such adaptations, one in Baltimore and one in New York, appeared immediately without much success. In September, however, a version by a young actor named George Aiken began a phenomenal hundred-performance run in Troy, New York.

The company then moved to New York City in 1853 for a run of two hundred consecutive days, toward the close presenting the play eighteen times a week, with the actors eating in costume between shows. Five other versions ran simultaneously in New York, one produced by P. T. Barnum himself, and others sprang up in other cities. No one can guess how many performances of *Uncle Tom's Cabin* have been given over the play's span of years, but it has been calculated that it was staged an average of four times a week for the next seventy-five years.

By 1854 there were companies on the road and in the cities playing nothing but *Uncle Tom's Cabin;* by the seventies there were forty-nine road shows; by the late eighties at least four hundred "Tom companies." Some actors spent their entire careers playing nothing else, specializing as "Legrees," "Marks," "Evas," and so on. Some companies might number six or less (one company did it with three), others had fifty actors and a five-hour show. Al Martin's Tom Show, one of the last, in 1907 had eighty actors, a twenty-piece band, a white drum and bugle corps, a Negro drum and bugle corps, forty horses, eighteen chariots, and fifteen bloodhounds.

Played in so many different versions, the play naturally underwent alterations, some wildly improbable. New characters were introduced, the plot endlessly changed, and specialties added, such as steamboat races, minstrel shows, jubilee singers, comic skits, dancers, panoramas, equestrian acts, anything that might draw a crowd. Bits such as the ascent of little Eva to Heaven, or Eliza crossing the ice (followed by bloodhounds, which had not occurred to Mrs. Stowe), or Legree's brutal beating of Tom, became standard spectacles. (One production in 1891 substituted an alligator for hounds in the Eliza scene.)

Peter Jackson, the Negro pugilist, concluded his performance as Uncle Tom with an exhibition round; John L. Sullivan, who had his own company, did the same. Double companies, featuring two Toms, two Evas, and so on, appeared in the nineties. Twenty Tom shows were still going in the nineteen-twenties; the last seems to have disappeared about 1930. But Edward Porter made a movie of the play for the Edison Company in 1903, followed by at least ten more film versions, leading up to Carl Laemmle's super-production in the twenties which used five thousand actors and 10,000 artificial magnolias.

Uncle Tom's Cabin exerted tremendous influence on the popular concept of the prewar South and the institution of slavery. Lincoln's famous remark to Mrs. Stowe, "So this is the little lady who wrote the big book that caused the big war!", while not entirely accurate, reflected the impact of her work on public opinion. The stage versions of the novel (which were responsible for many incorrect ideas about what the book actually said) presented to the world the most widely disseminated and accepted picture of the slave-holding South. Whatever its inaccuracies and oversimplifications, to millions of people the play represented actuality, and what it showed became the standard popular concept of an important segment of American history. Simon, Uncle Tom, Eva, and Topsy became part of the national heritage, like Leatherstocking and Huck Finn; the version of southern society they represented still remains deeply imbedded in the national consciousness.

Uncle Tom's Cabin, like *The Drunkard,* brought a new kind of audience into the theater. Quite shrewdly, the original New York production offered neither between-the-acts skits nor an afterpiece, in order to maintain the play's mood; soon other plays did the same thing, so that the play became an evening in itself. Because *Uncle Tom's Cabin* was considered, its producers said, "a moral, religious, and instructive play," written by a lady of impeccably Christian views, respectable people could and did come to see it, by millions.

The reviewer for the New York *Atlas,* who visited the National Theater's production in October, 1853, immediately noticed the difference in the audience. Instead of newsboys and apprentices piled on benches in the pit, he saw "many people who have been taught to look on the stage with horror and contempt . . . , Methodists, Presbyterians, and Congregationalists of the strait-laced school," and the gallery filled with "a heroic class of people, many of them in red woollen shirts, with countenances as hardy and rugged as the implements of industry employed by them in the pursuit of their vocation." (Significantly, he did not see one prostitute in the house, either.) These people, drawn from the middle class, provided a new kind of audience for the popular drama of the rest of the nineteenth century.

Melodrama, which dominated the popular theater from the middle to the close of the nineteenth century, was not a native form. Emotionalism and sentimentalism were common elements in drama since the sixteenth century; oversimplified and exaggerated motivation, stereotyped characters, and spectacular production devices had been part of the popular dramatic tradition in England and Europe for even longer. The Elizabethan "tragedies of blood" and the wildly sensational English, French, and German Gothic plays (which inundated the American stage in the 1790's) brought to the nineteenth century a full-blown dramatic type, free from rigid dramatic laws of cause and effect, characterized by coincidence and accident, intensified sentiment, and exaggerated emotionalism. Melodrama was especially well adapted to American audiences for its ability to present moral messages in easily-understood form while emotionally involving the audience, as *Uncle Tom's Cabin* and *The Drunkard* showed could be effectively done, if done right.

Techniques of melodramatic production were well known in America when William Dunlap presented his adaptation of the German playwright Kotzebue's *The Stranger* in 1803. Within a few years American playwrights and producers developed their own melodramatic style, using native materials such as *Captain Kyd, or the Witch of Hell Gate; The Black Hound, or the Hawks of Hawk Hollow;* and *Nick of the Woods, or The Jibbenainosay*, whose closing scene featured twelve bloody corpses. Melodramatic elements, of course, appeared in the legitimate theater too, but the pure type emerged after *Uncle Tom's Cabin* had drawn the new middle-class audience to the popular theater.

Melodrama was, despite its emotional excesses and its propensity to violence, fundamentally moral drama. In it virtue was rewarded, vice punished, evil defeated—a message designed to attract an audience which, though it might still have suspicions about the stage, nevertheless recognized its power as a moral and educational force. The basic plot situation of the melodramas showed that faith and love—the essential elements of a Christian life—provided the right guides for moral action, encouraged a democratic society, created happy homes, and triumphed over sin and wrong. Whether or not the world of melodrama accurately reflected the world in which the audience lived did not matter; what did matter was that it reflected their ideal of what the real world ought to be.

It would be difficult to identify the first American melodrama, but certainly the ubiquitous Dion Boucicault deserves to be recognized as a pioneer in the form. *The Poor of New York*, which opened in 1857, established much of the classic melodramatic pattern—a sensational plot, a dastardly villain, a brave hero, virtue rewarded and evil foiled, all set in a familiar, semirealistic framework. His greatest success, *The Octoroon*

(1859), which he adapted from a novel by Mayne Reid, *The Quadroon* (1856), combined the sentimental theme of tragic love (in this case between a white man and a free mulatto girl, a re-doing of the Pocahontas story) with all the elements of popular drama—a knife duel, a chase, a steamboat explosion, a slave auction, and two killings.

To do such a play in the explosive atmosphere of 1859 (the play opened in New York only two months after John Brown's raid on Harper's Ferry) required a good deal of courage. The play was, however, a tremendous success, for it shrewdly balanced pro-Northern and pro-Southern feeling so expertly that both elements of the audience could find reason to praise it. Joseph Jefferson, who played in it, remarked that it was "non-committal, the dialogue and the characters of the play made one feel for the South, but the action proclaimed against slavery, and called boldly for its abolition." Whatever one's political sympathies, the play had a great deal of power, as it proved when it was revived in 1961. In subsequent versions, Boucicault and others gave it alternate endings, including a happy conclusion for English audiences in which the star-crossed lovers were united in marriage.

Out of such elements Boucicault's successors fashioned a particular kind of play which filled the cheaper popular theaters (known as "ten-twent'-thirt'" houses because of their admission scale) year after year. From the point of view of dramatic literature, they were poorly written, artificially constructed plays, done hastily to meet the ephemeral tastes of a mass audience. They quickly developed a pattern which the playgoer expected to see followed; too much deviation from it was likely to draw boos, catcalls, and perhaps rougher forms of criticism. Yet within the confines of the tradition, the playwrights who wrote them often displayed great ingenuity and resourcefulness, and not a little skill. The melodrama, as it became standardized by the eighteen-seventies, was a four-act play that presented ten to twenty scenes, featuring one or more spectacular stage effects. The Milwaukee *Journal*, advertising the melodrama *Convict 999* at the Bijou Theater in January, 1900, noted that

> . . . its four acts will be found to contain no less than thirteen scenic settings. Some of the more notable are the Waldorf-Astoria Hotel, the Eighth Regiment Armory, the annual Social Ball, the criminal courtroom, three scenes of Sing Sing Prison, a ruined stone mill, its marvelous transformation to an immense cornfield in full bloom, a villa on the Hudson River, and a church wedding.

The spectacle, clearly, was a primary factor in attracting an audience. It always contained a virtuous, vulnerable heroine, threatened by danger (often sexual) from a villain (almost always a vile seducer, and not above rape) who combined sexuality with an overwhelming desire for money, power, or revenge. The hero, rigidly chaste in his attitude toward the heroine, was as a rule involved in a personal struggle with the villain while serving as her agent or protector. The plays quite often contained a kindly, philosophical father, uncle, or older man who served as commentator or lecturer. They also contained subordinate male and female comedy characters who acted as foils to the central love affair; and assorted comics drawn from servants, "rubes," Irish, Scotsmen, Yankees, Negroes, and so on.

A good writer could turn out two or three plays a month, with titles like *Dangers of the City, The Hidden Hand, The Silver King, The Overland Mail, The Black Flag*, or *Queen's Evidence*. Owen Davis authored more than three hundred of them, beginning with *Through the Breakers* in 1898. Specialized melodramas were written for persons in the news, such as Steve Brodie (who jumped from Brooklyn Bridge) or John L. Sullivan, or James J. Corbett. When Gentleman Jim, come to rescue the girl, slowly removed his top hat, stripped off his white gloves, and faced the whole kidnap gang in his graceful, classic boxing stance, theatrical history reached a high point.

Plot and dialogue, under such conditions, rapidly became stylized. Audiences expected a danger scene, a rescue scene, and a recognition or reunion scene. *The Phoenix* contributed to posterity the famous line, "And the villain still pursued her"; *The White Slave* the line "Rags are royal raiment when worn for virtue's sake"; and *The Ticket-of-Leave Man*, starring Hawkshaw the Detective and Jim Dalton the crook, contributed two, "Thou cur!" and "Curse you, Jim Dalton!" Dozens of writers tried to match the anguished maiden's pathetic prayer in *The Silver King*, "O God! Put back thy universe and give me yesterday!" but none succeeded.

Since the melodrama's effectiveness leaned heavily on stage effects, playwrights and producers vied in inventing situations and devices to surprise their audiences. Augustin Daly, perhaps the greatest of the experts and the author of ninety plays, tied a wounded soldier to a railroad track, to be rescued in the nick of time, in *Under The Gaslight* (1867). Later, in *The Red Scarf*, he tied the heroine to a log in the path of a buzz saw; still later, in *Saved From the Storm*, he tied the heroine to the track and rescued her with trained dogs, anticipating Rin-Tin-Tin and Lassie by a good many years.

Train wrecks, steamboat explosions, forest and prairie fires, earthquakes, tidal waves, floods, avalanches and other natural disasters became routine; the interest lay in how well they were done by the stage crews, who often drew much audience applause. Ingenious writers introduced variants on standard situations—the "leap for life" from a burn-ing building, the canoe over a waterfall, pursuit onstage by wolves, lions, even alligators. In *John Martin's Secret* (1898) a cable car fell into a canyon; in *The Fatal Land* (1895) an entire house collapsed onstage; David Belasco's *Heart of Maryland* (1895), an adaptation of "Curfew Shall Not Ring Tonight," swung the heroine on a huge bell clapper back and forth across the stage.

Melodrama during the eighties and nineties had plenty of violence, but none of a sexual nature, though the threat of rape hung over hun-dreds of heroines. In *Uncle Tom's Cabin,* the whippings, bloodhounds, and sexual overtones bore some relevance to the plot, but in the average melodrama violence became an end in itself. Duels, knife-fights, and savage beatings were crowd pleasers; even *The Two Orphans,* about a blind girl and her sister, had a knife fight in it and the suggestion of rape. *Michael Strogoff*, adapted from Jules Verne's novel, featured a blinding with white-hot swords, *The Bells* an onstage murder. *The Royal Slave* had a knife fight, a whip-and-machete duel, two kidnappings, a shark attack, a suicide, and a human sacrifice, while the murder of Nancy Sykes in Dickens' *Oliver Twist,* an all-time favorite, was undoubtedly the most brutal scene on the nineteenth-century American stage.

But there were also melodramas which combined morality and sen-timentality in a gentler vein. *East Lynne,* based on the English novel by Ellen Price Wood in 1863, was easily the most famous of the domestic melodramas. Billed quite accurately as "a moral, sensational play," *East Lynne* dealt with an erring wife, misunderstanding, injustice, and be-trayal, without violence and with great emotional power. Lucille Western, who made a career of acting Lady Isabel Vane, the tragic heroine, played the part nine hundred times in a single season. *The Two Orphans,* a widely copied tearjerker, played for one hundred and ninety consecutive performances in 1874 and was still on the road in 1920. Denman Thomp-son in 1886 wrote and starred in *The Old Homestead,* an updated Yankee play which contrasted homely rural virtue with big-city corruption, a theme of wide appeal to the times. In a variation of the prodigal son story, Joshua Whitcomb travels from New Hampshire to New York to find his son Reuben, a country boy adrift in the city, discovers him broke and drunk in the gutter, and brings him back to the old homestead and a better life.

Thompson's play attracted so many imitations (the best-known Jo-seph Arthur's *Blue Jeans*) that they were known in the trade as "Si shows" or "Uncle shows," with Thompson's Joshua turning up as "Jud Hawkins," "Seth Bascomb," "Uncle Hiram Spalding," or "Josh Spruceby," always with the same message—stay home, live right, the old-fashioned virtues are best. The last two of the Old Homestead melodramas, Charles Dazey's *In Old Kentucky* (1893) stayed in road company repertory for twenty-seven years, while Lottie Parker's story of rural temptation and betrayal, *Way Down East* (1898) ran for 361 consecutive performances in New York, went on the road, and entered the movies in 1910.

As Raymond Grimsted has pointed out, the importance of melodramas in American cultural history has been seriously underestimated, for they embodied many of contemporary society's fundamental attitudes toward morality, democracy, and domestic life. To sneer at these plays, as recent drama critics have, as "full of moral cant and social claptrap," is to miss their point and their significance completely. To the huge audiences that saw them, year after year, what they had to say was neither cant nor claptrap. They appealed to millions because they treated the lives and values of ordinary people with respect.

However poor the plays may have been artistically (though in the hands of Augustus Thomas and Bronson Howard they reached a rather high level of excellence) they were popular because they dealt with things people considered important—honesty, chastity, family ties, Christian virtues, personal integrity. Many of the situations presented in the melodrama often reflected real problems, quite familiar to their audiences. Drunkenness and gambling caused untold sorrow in nineteenth-century homes; country girls and boys *did* go wrong in the city, which was rapidly draining off the younger rural population; the clash between middle-class virtue and upper-class sophistication *was* clearly a moral issue in contemporary society. Melodramas reduced the complexities of the era to the kind of clear and simple rules society needed.

Though the movies absorbed many of melodrama's plots and devices, it still maintained a kind of theatrical identity up to the nineteen-twenties. It was not the same, of course. Twentieth-century playgoers demanded greater credibility of character and situation, and emotionalism had to be toned down; successful popular plays, however, still depended on melodrama's sentimental morality and spectacular staging, shaded for a more sophisticated audience. George Broadhurst's plays exemplified the new trend. After writing a number of farces in the nineties, he turned to a serious play about city politics, *The Man of the Hour* (1906), followed by *Bought and Sold* (1911), a study of the tinsel values of the idle rich, really a re-doing of the Old Homestead theme. Charles Klein, after his sentimental hit, *The Music Master* (1904), wrote *Daughters of Men* (1906), about labor unions; *The Third Degree* (1909), about the police;

and *The Gamblers* (1910), about high finance in the stock market. Eugene Walter's *Paid in Full* (1908), *The Easiest Way* (1908), and especially *Fine Feathers* (1913), dealing with a young man's attempt to cope with the materialism of contemporary life, combined old-fashioned morality with newer-style melodrama.

CHAPTER SIX

MINSTRELS
TO MUSICALS

It was not so much what the two-and-three-a-day favorites did, but how they said and did it.

—FRED ALLEN

The American minstrel show was a thoroughly native form of theatrical entertainment—and purely entertainment—with roots in neither dramatic nor folkloristic tradition. It helped to originate and perpetuate the utterly unreal, yet entertaining, picture of the American Negro slave as a singing, dancing, joking, well-adjusted element in American society, a stereotype that still persists, to some extent, in the American imagination.

The comic Negro appeared on the English stage in the early eighteenth century, usually in entr'actes and afterpieces; Lewis Hallam, in fact, did an impersonation of "a drunken darky" on the American stage in 1769. By 1800 there were several well-known Negro performers, among them Andrew Allen (who later went with Edwin Forrest's company); George Washington Dixon, who wrote "Old Zip Coon" (better known as "Turkey in the Straw"); and Picayune Butler, a New Orleans banjoist and singer. White comedians in blackface frequently appeared in variety shows and skits, telling dialect jokes and imitating what the public believed were Negro dances. While Southern plantation owners occasionally may have used talented slaves to perform for guests, neither Negro nor blackface comedians, singers, and dancers seem to have been influenced by such entertainments. The minstrel "darky" was primarily a stage creation who owed little or nothing to real life.

The most important figure in early blackface theatricals was Thomas "Daddy" Rice, born in New York City in 1808, who made his way in the traveling stage companies from property man to actor and writer. Cast as a comic Negro field hand in a Louisville production of Robinson's *The Rifle* in 1829, he inserted a song and dance which he called "Jim Crow." The sources of both song and dance are obscure, most theories favoring a crippled Negro stableboy Rice once saw in Louisville, Cincinnati, or Pittsburgh. Rice possibly composed (and certainly arranged) the music, wrote a number of verses, and developed the dance step, whose exact nature cannot be accurately reconstructed, though it seems to have contained a shuffle and a jump. As Rice's original refrain described it,

> First on de heel tap, den on de toe,
> Eberty time I wheel about I jump Jim Crow.
> Wheel about and turn about and do jis so,
> And eberty time I wheel about I jump Jim Crow.

Rice's interpolation was so successful that he made it into a separate act and took it to New York in 1832. He continued to "jump Jim Crow" until he died in 1860, attracting a number of imitators, among them Barney Williams, Jack Diamond, Bill Keller, Barney Burns, and Bob Farrell, who found that audiences paid well for watching white actors in burnt cork copying the popular conception of a type of Negro entertainment that did not exist. Daddy Rice's "Jim Crow" characterization provided the original core of the minstrel show tradition.

The next step was logical: that is, to build an evening's show about the Jim Crow character. Rice himself did exactly this in 1833 when he staged an "Ethiopian Opera" at New York's Bowery Theater, combined with other "Negro" specialty numbers. The minstrel show, however, as a unified show done in blackface, sprang full-blown from another famous performance, that of Dan Emmett and his group at the Bowery Theater in 1843, calling themselves "The Virginia Minstrels."

Emmett and three others (a banjo player, tambourine player, and bones player, with Emmett on fiddle) recruited some friends and presented a show called "The Essence of Old Virginny, with songs, dances, and comedy." A great success, Emmett's show played other New York theaters and went on the road. They improvised as they went along, and by the time they reached Boston they had developed a comic blackface dialogue, sat in a semicircle, and closed the show with a "walk-around" (Emmett later wrote "Dixie" for one), while their instrumentation became the minstrel show standard.

Edwin P. Christy, who formed a group resembling Emmett's at about the same time, had gathered by 1846 the scattered elements of blackface theatricals into the final form of the minstrel show. Christy's company went on to give more than twenty-seven hundred performances, and although he retired in 1856, his chief comedian, George Harrington, changed his name to Christy and took over the company.

Christy put a man with a tambourine at one end of the semicircle and a man with a pair of bones at the other, thereby creating the end-men, Tambo and Bones. He put the "Interlócutor" or master of ceremonies (without burnt cork) in the center, introduced harmony singing and choral effects, and conventionalized the show's pattern. The first half of a Christy show was devoted to singing, dancing, jokes, instrumental numbers and comic dialogue, closing with a rousing walkaround by the entire company. The dances, though influenced in the early shows by Negro dances, were more likely to be adaptations of Scotch reels, Irish jigs, and rural hoedowns, though done by Negro impersonators. The second act, borrowing from the variety show, introduced skits, "break-downs," and special numbers using whatever talents the members of the company might possess.

Later, burlesques and parodies, often done with skill, wit, and shattering effectiveness, were added as a third act. Lew Dockstader's version of Sir Henry Irving's Faust ruined the original for anyone who had seen it. The minstrel comedians' imitations of Forrest's Indian chieftain Metamora finally drove him out of the part; dancers like Fanny Ellsler and actresses like Sarah Bernhardt were natural targets. The third part might also contain an "Ethiopian Opera," with built-in farce numbers like "Bone Squash Diavolo," "The Black Cupid," or "Long Island Juba."

Within this general pattern different companies developed their own specialties and characters—the "wench" or female impersonator, the "Dixie Land" plantation scene, the steamboat scene, the white quartet and chorus, the sentimental ballad tenor, and so on. Another popular addition was the Negro sermon, an overblown rhetorical monologue made famous by men like "Senator" Frank Bell and Billy Rice.

The minstrel show was never sexually suggestive, obscene, or scatalogical. Its humor was occasionally rowdy, but never vulgar. It treated the Negro as an object of amusement, but its racism was never vicious or degrading. Negro impersonations fell into two classifications—the field hand type in ragged clothes, bare feet, straw hat, lazy, shiftless, grinning, avid for watermelon or chicken, ignorant but not stupid; and the Northern city Negro "dandy," resplendent in "long-tail blue" coat, cane, silk hat, fancy shirt, yellow shoes, with a vocabulary spilling over with malapropisms, unable to resist a crap game or a cakewalk.

The Negro woman was never an object of derision and the "mammy" type rarely appeared. The minstrel Negro was never assumed by either performer or audience to bear any resemblance to the real Negro; he was a stage type created by white men in burnt cork and wigs, a character who did not exist outside the show. There were a few *Negro* Negro minstrel companies (who played in burnt cork and wigs too) but of these only the Georgia Minstrels (organized in 1865), Jack's Creoles, and one or two others were successful. The minstrel show was popular entertainment by white performers for white audiences.

Always at the heart of the minstrel show, no matter how large or varied it became, was music, harking back to Daddy Rice's song-and-dance act and Emmett's four musicians. Emmett himself wrote many of the best early songs—"Old Dan Tucker," "Early in the Morning," and "The Boatman's Dance," among others. Minstrel show writers borrowed some tunes from the Negro, perhaps, but most of them came from everywhere else. Early shows copied a few plantation melodies, but minstrel music drew from jigs, reels, hymns, opera bouffe, sentimental balladry, and other white man's music. Minstrel songwriting, as Stephen Foster accurately called it, was simply "the Ethiopian business." Foster, whose career lay almost wholly within the minstrel show, wrote the best of them, but there were dozens of other talented songwriters in the business.

Born in Pittsburgh, Foster knew nothing about the South or the Negro except what he learned from minstrel shows and Negro servants; thus he could write in the minstrel idiom with perfect sincerity and without reference to any reality that would have complicated his music's appeal. He wrote some of his early songs with the help of and for "Daddy" Rice, later for E. P. Christy, who sang many of his best ones before they were published. (For a five dollar bonus Foster sometimes allowed Christy to list himself as composer.) Chiefly from Foster, of course, came the sentimentalized, romanticized picture of Southern life that still lingers about his songs. "Old Black Joe," "The Swanee River," and the "Old Kentucky Home" are imperishable creations, as permanent a part of the cultural heritage as Uncle Tom.

For the greater part of the nineteenth century, the minstrel show was the most important medium through which popular songs reached the public. Songbooks were filled with minstrel-show songs that everyone knew, sang, and played—"Darling Nelly Gray," "Polly Wolly Doodle," "Buffalo Girls," "The Old Folks at Home," "In the Evening by the Moonlight," and others no longer so well remembered but popular for years, such as "The Mellow Horn," "Way Down in Cairo," "Dandy Jim," "Stop Dat Knockin' At My Door," "Root, Hog, or Die," or "I'm Sittin' on de Rail, Dinah." This was America's popular music, hundreds upon hundreds of humorous, lively, sentimental, melodic songs. The banjo-bones-fiddle-tambourine combination, of course, gave way to twenty and forty-piece orchestras, and although "Negro" music remained a staple in the program, later shows used sentimental ballads, folk songs, band marches, operatic pieces, and anything the music director wished. The Irish tenor, in fact, was standard equipment in minstrel shows by the nineties.

Campbell's Minstrels were nearly as popular as Christy's in the fifties; Bryant's Minstrels, organized in 1857, played continuously for eighteen years. Eleven major minstrel companies operated throughout the sixties, and most cities had at least one theater and a resident company devoted to minstrel shows. New York had ten companies, Boston six. Callendar's Minstrels, The Gus Hill Minstrels, Richard's and Pringle's, The Georgia Minstrels, Buckley's Serenaders, Ordway's Aeolians, Hi Henry's Superb Operatic Minstrels, The Star Troupe Minstrels, Haverly's Mastodon Minstrels, The New Gigantic Minstrels, The Sable Brothers' Show, The Nightingale Serenaders, Primrose and West, were familiar names in the minstrel business. Road shows fanned out over the country, and the larger shows played England, the Continent, Australia, and New Zealand.

The minstrel show reached its height during the sixties, when there were a hundred companies playing nothing else. Later shows were bigger, but the rate of attrition grew higher—by the eighties there were about thirty remaining, playing what was more or less a standardized variety-vaudeville show with few of the original elements left. In 1896 there were ten shows, in 1920 three. The Al G. Fields Show, the last of the old companies, gave its last performance in 1921, forty years after its first. Amateur minstrel shows, put on by service clubs, community theaters, and civic organizations continued into the thirties, but few have appeared since in any form.

There were economic, social, and artistic reasons for the decline and disappearance of the minstrel show from the popular theatrical scene. The panic of 1873 and the depression after it put the majority of smaller companies out of business. The growth of "mammoth" and "gigantic" shows raised costs and payrolls, and killed the twenty-five-cent to fifty-cent admission. When the minstrel show had to compete with vaudeville and popular drama at the same price, it was no longer profitable; meanwhile the better performers went into vaudeville and musical shows for better salaries. Despite the obvious talent of many performers who worked in them, minstrel shows never really broke out of the format Christy originated in the forties, so that opportunities for originality and variation within it were severely limited. The all-male cast no doubt was another factor in its decline; although Sam Jack's all-Negro company introduced sixteen pretty girls, few others tried it, and burlesque did it better. After its first twenty years or so, minstrelsy had nothing new to offer.

The fact that the focus of the minstrel show—the stage Negro—was an artificial creation was its strength and eventually its fatal weakness. Since it never made any attempt to be authentic, the minstrel show could do anything it needed to do to entertain. Its great effectiveness as popular entertainment lay in its freewheeling, inventive spontaneity, but the Civil War and its aftermath changed the American attitude toward the Negro.

The Negro was one of the things the war was about; antislavery societies spent thirty years convincing the public that life under slavery was not like a minstrel show, and after the war there were a million young veterans who had seen plantations and slaves which looked nothing at all like the stage set for "Old Uncle Ned." It was difficult to relate the Ku Klux Klan to "Carry Me Back to Old Virginny," or to reconcile the actuality of Reconstruction with the stage version of Southern life. The blackface comedian persisted for a while in musical comedy and films, and in radio (where he could be heard but not seen), to disappear swiftly in World War II. In the end the great legacy of the minstrel show to American popular culture was its music.

The history of vaudeville stretched back to the traveling acrobats, jugglers, and magicians of antiquity, and more recently to the popular entertainments of England, transported to the American colonies with the settlers. The French "pieces de vaudeville," developed in eighteenth-century street fairs, had little to do with the American brand, which stemmed directly from the English variety shows imported from the home country. Tony Aston, the first professional actor to tour the American colonies, apparently also juggled and did variety turns between skits in the British music-hall tradition, and there were many who followed him. Acting companies, both native and imported, offered "entr'actes" and "afterpieces" of a similar nature, drawing on the extra talents of the actors.

Frontier communities, which had little theatrical entertainment of any kind, welcomed the jugglers, acrobats, singers, dancers, and comedians who filtered into the back country. Minstrel shows had "olios," made up of specialty acts; in the cities the dime museums offered similar programs as extra attractions; and traveling troupes played beer gardens, amusement parks, honky-tonks, and saloons. During the eighteen-forties theaters began to present shows which consolidated many of these acts into a regular performance. The Franklin Theater in New York, for example, advertised itself as a "variety theater" in 1842, featuring "J. Morris' Concert and Olio Company," with "Magic Lantern Slides, Comic Lectures, Chemistry, French Plays, Mesmeric Clairvoyance, and Beautiful Arithmetical Diagrams." During the next twenty years similar theaters and "concert saloons" appeared in the cities, providing a potpourri of acts, often suggestive, aimed at a predominantly male audience.

This was changed by Tony Pastor, a deeply moral man who, after serving his apprenticeship in show business as acrobat, boy soprano, actor, and circus performer, bought a variety theater in Paterson, New Jersey, in 1865. Pastor disapproved of the vulgarity of the customary variety bill and in 1881 opened his own Fourteenth Street Theater in New York, specializing in "straight, clean variety shows," he said, for a new kind of audience, the middle-class family trade. His first program included a serious singer and a popular balladeer, a comedian, an Irish act, an acrobatic pantomimist, and a lady who played concertina, banjo, and xylophone. Other theater managers followed him, so that within a few years "blue" performances had almost disappeared and the "vaudeville theater" (a term first used in 1881 but not of Pastor's invention) operated under informal but rather strict conventions.

To make this perfectly clear, theater managers invariably advertised their shows as "polite," "refined," "fashionable," "legitimate," or "family entertainment"—shows to which, comedian Fred Stone said, any child could bring his parents. What Pastor did was to make the variety theater respectable, middle class, mass entertainment, flexible and quickly adaptable to the public taste. The essential pattern of the vaudeville show was established in Pastor's Fourteenth Street Theater.

Vaudeville took over many of the acts long popular in the beer gardens and cleaned them up. Song and dance acts were especially popular, classified as "blackface, whiteface, Irish, neat, rough, plantation, acrobatic, and team," with endless variations involving different kinds of props such as eggs, sand, stairsteps, bottles, hats, wine glasses, tools, animals, and so on. Banjo players were favored in the eighties; in 1882 about fifty were on tour at the same time. Racial and ethnic comedy outplayed all other kinds—Irish, Jewish, Negro (white men in blackface), German (called "Dutch" in the trade), Italian. Irish comics tended to run in twos —Needham and Kelly, Kelly and Ryan, Kernell and Kernell, Rooney and Rogers—as did "Dutch" comics like Lessinger and Moore, Watson and Ellis, Murphy and Shannon (oddly enough, one of the best), and of course the team of Weber and Fields.

Blackface comics like J. W. Matthews, Frank Bell, McIntyre and Heath, Lew Dockstadter, and later Frank Tinney, were second only to the Irish as box office draws. There were only a few real Negro comedians, Bert Williams and "Honeyboy" Evans among them, but many

Jewish comics—Burt and Leon, Frank Bush, Ben Welch, Barney Bernard, and Julian Rose—while Gallagher and Shean combined Jewish and Irish comedy with great success. The Tramp comedian developed later in the hands of experts such as Hay Ward, Nat Wills, Lew Bloom, Charles Sweet, W. C. Fields, and the legendary tramp-bicyclist, Joe Jackson.

Almost anyone with something to do could get a showing in vaudeville, which constantly searched for ways to diversify the standard acts. As a result, shows featured some wild and curious specialties, like "The Speed Mechanics," who disassembled and reassembled a Ford onstage in eight minutes, "Bughouse Hamlets" who parodied Shakespeare; "bone soloists" who imitated cobblers, horses, and other sounds; rope dancers, hat spinners, knife-throwers, bird-whistle imitators, "living pictures" in tableaux, and quick-change specialists. There was also a man who played a "cat piano" by pretending to pull the tails of captive cats while imitating their yowls; an Englishman in Turkish costume who could whistle with his navel; Enoch the Fish Man who played trombone under water; and a tattooed man who made moving pictures by rippling his muscles in sequence. It was to such acts that Mark Twain referred when he spoke of the need for a net to protect the performers from an outraged audience.

By the eighteen-eighties vaudeville was easily the most popular form of theatrical entertainment. New York had ten vaudeville theaters, Philadelphia six, St. Louis three, Chicago five, San Francisco three, and every city of consequence at least one. The average bill consisted of twenty to thirty acts, and since each was allowed about only twelve to fifteen minutes, vaudeville demanded precision, polish, expert timing, and formidable skill. The best vaudevillians attracted huge audiences, had national reputations, and drew large salaries—Carmencita the Spanish dancer, Sandow the Strong Man, magicians Houdini and Blackstone, Pat Rooney the song-and-dance-man, Harry Lauder the Scotch monologist, stand-up comic Nat Goodwin, and female stars such as Lottie Collins, May Irwin, Lillian Russell, Lily Langtry, Vesta Victoria, and Yvette Guilbert, were quite literally household names.

To add "class," managers recruited stars from the legitimate stage, opera, and ballet, among them basso Édouard de Reszke (who was paid $3,000 a week) and Sarah Bernhardt, who collected $7,000 a week at the Palace in 1913, $500 of it paid in gold pieces after each performance. The typical bill, however, was usually built up with a song-and-dance team, a singer, a comedy sketch, a featured star, a musical number, an animal act (like Carr's Dogs, Rhinelander's Pigs, May Barkeley's Bulldogs, Tetchow's Cats, or Andress and His Goats), and any number of acts involving bicyclists, acrobats, roller skaters, jugglers, magicians, and other specialists. Edward Albee's Boston *Bijou* introduced the continuous show, running from 10 A.M. to 11 P.M.; prices, about 1900, ranged from fifty cents to two dollars, depending on the quality of the bill and the status of the theater.

When vaudeville became big business the individual theater owner soon disappeared. By 1900 the theaters were almost wholly owned by chains, each dominated by a single company, the performers controlled by a few powerful booking agencies. The Percy Williams chain operated in New York, Sylvester Poli in New England, Kohl and Castle in the Midwest, Alexander Pantages in the West. The giant was the Keith-Albee chain, formed by Benjamin Franklin Keith and Edward Franklin Albee, which by 1920 controlled more than four hundred theaters across the eastern half of the country, as well as the United Booking Agency (established in 1900, later National Vaudeville Artists) which eventually controlled more than 20,000 performers. Its only serious opposition came from Martin Beck's Orpheum circuit, west of Chicago.

Vaudeville's great years, a surprisingly short span, lasted from about 1890 to 1920, when crowds flocked into the theaters, and Martin Beck's New York *Palace*, built in 1913, represented the pinnacle of show business. New York had thirty-seven vaudeville houses, Philadelphia thirty, and Chicago twenty-two. Outside the cities, about two thousand smaller theaters also booked vaudeville; there were a dozen millionaires in vaudeville management; headliners could count on $1,000 a week and fifty weeks work a year. An opening act usually drew $150–$200 weekly, a middle-bill act $250, a next-to-closing act around $300–350, and the closing feature whatever the traffic would bear. Albert McLean's study of audiences shows that between 14 and 16 per cent of the urban population attended vaudeville at least once a week for an average theater gross of $20,000 per week. Vaudeville simply outdistanced every other kind of theatrical entertainment, drawing larger audiences than all others combined.

The composition of the average vaudeville bill after 1910, and the emergence of new stars and troupes, reflected the growing sophistication of the audiences. Pratfall comedy, dialect and ethnic humor and circus-juggling-acrobat acts disappeared or changed. The first bill at the Palace in 1913, in contrast to Pastor's in 1881, opened with a ballet, and continued with a Spanish violinist, a pantomimist, a skit by George Ade, a monologist, a wire act, and a cartoonist, closing with star comic Ed Wynn. Instead of blackface comedians there were "minstrel men," Eddie Leonard, Eddie Cantor, Al Jolson, and the like. "Society" dancers—the Cansinos, Castles, de Marcos, Astaires—replaced the knockabout hoofers of earlier days. As a measure of audience sophistication, Julian Eltinge, the great female impersonator, even had a theater named after him.

Comedians such as Eugene and Willie Howard, Joe Cook, Eddie Garr, Ed Wynn, Block and Sully, Imhoff and Corinne, Fannie Brice, Will Rogers, and Bobby Clark represented a wholly different brand of humor, and so did family acts like the Foys, the Cohans, and the Dixons. Sex came back with flamboyant female "belters" like Eva Tanguay ("It's All Been Done Before But Not The Way I Do It"), Maggie Cline ("Throw Him Down McCluskey"), Norah Bayes, May Irwin, Elsie Janis, and Sophie Tucker. Yet vaudeville, for all its imaginative variety and dazzling talent, was only mass-produced entertainment geared to the broadest denominator of middle-class taste. It had no pretensions to art, nor did it make any consistent appeal to a serious audience.

In the late nineties vaudeville theaters used a brief motion picture (usually something like "A Trip to Niagara" or "A View of Old Faithful") to "clear the house" for the next performance, an ironic foreshadowing of impending doom. Twenty years later theater managers were featuring full-length films and using added vaudeville acts to "clear the house." The growth of radio and the introduction of sound movies dealt vaudeville the final blow by draining off not only its audience but most of its talent. Practically every vaudeville star or act went into film and radio (some later into television) while the Palace lost $4,000 a week. In April, 1930, when the Palace was finally equipped for "talkies," there were fewer than a hundred theaters in the country showing vaudeville, and fewer than six hundred performers able to find a week's work per year. About all that was left was the resort hotel (or "borscht") circuit, night clubs, bars, and conventions. Without performers, theaters, or audiences, vaudeville was gone.

Vaudeville was the ultimate democratic theater, simple, uncomplicated, and direct, with neither continuity nor implication. The spectator was under no compulsion to supply either; he was asked only to look and listen.

While it lasted vaudeville reflected, and in turn to a considerable extent influenced, contemporary social and cultural patterns. That Americans could find entertainment in ethnic and racial stereotypes showed something about the assimilative process at work in an expanding, variegated society. That vaudeville was a distinctly citified form of popular theater, the first to use the city as its primary source of materials, reflected the rapidly urbanizing society it entertained. The great stars, most of them of lower middle class, immigrant origins, were men and women with whom these audiences could identify, and their talents were of the

kind the great majority of people could understand and appreciate. The
new media—film, radio, television—did not kill vaudeville, for the kind of
popular theater it represented was too hardy to die. They simply took it
over.

There were two kinds of burlesque theater, not to be confused. One
kind, the older, drew from the centuries-old low comedy tradition of
Europe, the circus, the minstrel show, and the variety skit. Used as afterpieces or between-the-acts, burlesques of popular plays and novels were
standard fare in the nineteenth-century theater. Shakespearean productions were favorite targets (see the excellent example in *Huckleberry
Finn*) while John Brougham's *Much Ado About a Merchant of Venice,
Poc-ca-hont-as,* and *Columbus* combined a spoof of three honorable theat-
rical favorites at once. George Fox's parody of Booth playing Macbeth,
Brougham's of Forrest's Metamora, called *Metamora, or the Last of the
Pollywogs* (featuring two Indians named Bad Enough and Worser) and
Charles Walcott's *Hiawatha, or Ardent Spirits and Laughing Water,* de-
lighted audiences for years. Nothing was safe. *Bad Breath, the Crane of
Chowder; Hamlet and Egglet; Roman Nose and Suet (Romeo and
Juliet); The Bohea Man's Girl; Old Dad's Cabin; Sarah Heartburn*
(Sarah Bernhardt); and other skits dotted playbills for years.

With this kind of burlesque, the other had little to do. It had flourished for years in the beer gardens, low-class theaters, honky-tonks (also
called "slabs," "dumps," and "free and easies") from the Bowery to San
Francisco. These shows might have as many as fifteen acts running from
dusk to dawn, featuring the cheapest performers, bare-knuckle bouts,
and "stag" skits with names like "The Bathing Girls," "In the Haystack,"
or "The Old Husband." When Pastor cleaned up the variety show and
made it into vaudeville, its rougher elements found a home immediately
in this kind of entertainment. There was nothing new about it; it was as
old as Boccaccio.

The event that changed the course of American burlesque for the
next forty years was the appearance at Niblo's Gardens in New York in
1866 of the musical extravaganza, *The Black Crook,* and its ballet corps
of a hundred girls in formfitting silk tights. The burning of the Academy of Music stranded a French ballet company scheduled to perform
there, so William Wheatley, Niblo's manager, put the troupe into a melodrama called *The Black Crook* with unexpected success. Since the show
ran for sixteen months and grossed over a million, it was obvious to enterprising theater managers that it had something the public wanted. What
it had was girls. It also had music, which pointed in the direction of

musical comedy; but it most certainly had girls. *The Black Crook* introduced the popular theater for the first time to the display of the female figure for its own sake, something which had little relationship to plot, theme, characterization, or any other dramatic element. This became the fundamental purpose of burlesque.

Capitalizing on the success of *The Black Crook*, Lydia Thompson brought her *British Blondes* troupe to the United States in 1868, the first authentic burlesque show in the modern sense. She introduced a few mild double-entendre songs and a number of statuesque poses of gauze-clad beauties, featuring Pauline Markham as Venus. Dozens of imitators appeared at once, but the hardy "Blondes" continued to travel over the country for the next twenty years, adding a few dances, a comic skit or two, and gradually establishing the basic pattern of burlesque. As a Chicago newspaper remarked of the Blondes in 1877, the girls "really had nothing to offer but their persons," which was precisely the point and quite sufficient.

Other companies, such as May Fiske's *English Blondes*, Mme. Rejani's *Female Minstrels*, Mable Snow's *Spectacular Burlesque Comedy*, and *The Night Owls*, followed the format with great success. By the nineties there were thirty to forty burlesque companies on tour, and in the cities some theaters specialized in nothing else. The proliferation of shows led to the organization of circuits or "wheels," with regular routes, centralized bookings, and standardized salaries. Tycoons of the trade appeared—Sam T. Jack, whose New York Theater was burlesque's equivalent of vaudeville's Palace, T. E. Miaco, Samuel Scribner, and later the famed Minsky brothers, whose Winter Garden Apollo, and Republic theaters in New York became the center of the business.

Some of the better companies made an attempt to provide a kind of variety-show entertainment in addition to the display of girls. The standard burlesque pattern of the nineties might include some singing and dancing acts, some slapstick, double-entendre comic sketches, and an "added attraction" like a "pugilistic exhibition" or a "sensational dance." The focus of the show, however, was always the girls who exhibited themselves in varying degrees of undress. No matter how camouflaged, the basic appeal of burlesque was sexual. Gradually the shows gave up all pretense of being anything but displays of commercialized sex. The booking agents of the Empire Circuit gave orders in 1900 to "give it as raw as it will come," which has been burlesque's purpose ever since.

To accomplish this, burlesque elected to emphasize two major elements of the earlier shows, dance and comedy. The "daring" or "exotic" dance was a staple ingredient in the shows of the nineties; Little Egypt's dance at the Columbian Exposition of 1893 elicited dozens of Fatimas, Cleos, Zazas, and Fifis. Under a multitude of names—hootchie-kootchie, cooch, Oriental, nautch, harem, belly, shimmy, tassle, and many others— the dance soon was the standard feature attraction of all burlesque shows.

Milly De Leon, the Philadelphia *North American* reported in 1909, capitivated audiences by "agitating the muscles of her body in a wavelike motion," and from there it was only a step toward continuing the agitation in less and less costume. Actually, burlesque had already featured "quick-change" acts in which girls changed costumes in more or less full view, so the combination of suggestive dance and increased exposure was easy and logical. The "stripper" per se appeared about 1917. Twenty years later there were somewhere between one hundred and fifty and two hundred strippers working the circuits. In addition, the fashion of short skirts in the twenties made the display of legs so routine that practically all female burlesque performers bared their breasts. *Variety* wrote accurately in 1923 that burlesque was "ninety nine percent strip with the other just to pad out the show."

The other one per cent (it was really more than that) was "blue" comedy out of the honky-tonks of the eighteen-fifties, ranging from double-entendre jokes to outright scatology. Most of the skits were constructed about two stock characters, the cuckolded husband and the racial comic, with endless variations—later expanded to include the homosexual and the prostitute. Billy "Beef Trust" Watson, the reigning comic of the pre-1900 era, seems to have been a vulgar (but not obscene) kind of genius, while other comics—Al Reeves, Dan McAvoy, Rice and Barton —gained wide reputations. Though burlesque povided a proving ground for aspiring comedians, the better ones left it as soon as possible. Weber and Fields made their reputation after leaving burlesque; so did Leon Errol, Jack Pearl, Abbott and Costello, Red Buttons, Rags Ragland, and Phil Silvers, among others.

Burlesque's connection with the popular theater was brief, and at most tenuous. Since burlesque's attraction derived always from sexual display and low comedy, it soon became stereotyped and repetitious. When burlesque was too good, it was no longer burlesque; when its performers were too talented, they left it. Attempts to depart from the formula were immediately rejected by audience and performer alike. Whatever opportunity burlesque had to become part of the popular theatrical tradition was lost in the display of flesh on which it came to depend. New York City's refusal to renew the licenses of burlesque theaters in 1942 marked the end, more or less. It still exists in a few cities, but what remains is now either cheap bar entertainment or "stag" acts, where it began.

Musical comedy is a particularly American kind of theatrical entertainment, developed in the twentieth century from a number of diverse dramatic and musical elements. These can be identified, but the mixture called musical comedy cannot be so accurately defined. Related, sometimes only indirectly, to early ballad opera, minstrel show, vaudeville, operetta, and burlesque, it is like and unlike all of these.

Musical comedy differs from comic opera and operetta in that it adheres to a less formalized and more vernacular style in its music, dialogue, and dances. It differs from vaudeville and variety (which may also contain music and dialogue) in that it possesses at least a rudimentary plot, and usually involves a much more elaborate production. It resembles more closely the nonnudity "burlesques" of the later nineteenth century in its association of music and comedy, but unlike them it is not restricted to imitation or parody. The critic in 1894 who said that the musical comedy he saw was "an indefinable melange of music and drama" probably came as close to a definition as anyone since.

The nineteenth century's burlesques and variety shows had both music and comedy; the minstrel show added dancing and so did vaudeville. The combination of music, dancing, plot, and girls (the final ingredient) that led eventually to musical comedy arrived in the United States with *The Black Crook*.

There was little relationship in the show among plot, songs, dances, and girls (a hundred of them in "closefitting flesh-colored tights and as little else as the law will permit," the press remarked) but the public liked it immensely. Since it presented a simple story line more or less integrated with music, that is, a "book" and a "score," *The Black Crook* deserves to be called the first step toward musical comedy. It fitted the theatrical space between vaudeville on one extreme, and operetta, opera, and serious drama on the other. It had, naturally, many imitators, the best of which was Nate Salisbury's production of *The Brook* (1879), which built its songs, dances, and skits about the device of a picnic and had a long run.

Meanwhile, the burlesque (not the "girlie" variety but the comic parody of a popular work) was in the process of putting together musical and comic elements in somewhat similar manner. In 1874 Edward Rice and J. G. Goodwin produced *Evangeline*, a hilarious spoof of Longfellow's poem, as a full-scale stage production with a comedy plot, songs, dances, skits, and an original musical score. Rice actually called it "musical comedy," among other terms, to differentiate it from the variety show. (*Evangeline*, which ran on the stage for years, first introduced the trick cow, later a horse, with two actors walking about under a draped cow costume.) Rice's and Goodwin's success led to other burlesque musicals like *Adonis, Little Christopher Columbus, Excelsior Junior,* and to an all-Negro musical produced by Rice in 1898 with a score by Negro composer Will Marion Cook (who studied with Anton Dvořák) and lyrics by Negro poet Paul Laurence Dunbar.

The burlesque furnished a source for the broad farces (first cousins to the later "revues") which played music halls in the nineties, with names like *Hurly-Burly, Twirly-Whirly,* and *Fiddle-de-dee,* and stars like Lillian Russell, DeWolfe Hopper, and Bessie Clayton. In the same vein, and more important as an influence on musical comedy, was Charles Hoyt's *A Trip to Chinatown* (which opened in 1893) whose light and frothy love plot, laid in New York's Chinatown, combined comedy and music in the typical musical comedy manner, introducing three magnificent songs, "After The Ball," "Reuben, Reuben," and "The Bowery." The next year Charles Lederer produced a spectacular show at New York's Casino called *The Passing Show,* which, by reason of its combination of girls, songs, sketches, and gaudy production numbers, was probably the first true example of the American musical comedy.

European operetta drew large audiences after the eighties—New York played eighty-nine of them between 1880 and 1900. Oskar Straus, Offenbach, Von Suppé, Franz Lehar, and Johann Strauss were familiar names on playbills, and in the nineties so were those of Reginald De Koven and Victor Herbert, who wrote American-style versions of Viennese operettas. Gilbert and Sullivan arrived in 1878 with *H.M.S. Pinafore,* which had one hundred companies on tour before the year was out.

It seemed quite clear at the turn of the century that a very vigorous new theatrical form called musical comedy had arrived, drawing from everything going on at the moment in the musical theater. It was in the process of acquiring a recognizable shape and a native identity, evolving some of the basic characteristics which would henceforth identify it. The key to the new form lay in closer integration of all these borrowed elements into a free, flexible whole. Skillfully written, imaginatively produced, performed by talented entertainers, these shows struck exactly the right level for popular entertainment.

Paul Tietjens and A. B. Sloan in 1903 wrote a musical version of L. Frank Baum's fantasy, *The Wizard of Oz,* that was a true musical comedy, featuring the dancing and songs of the famous team of Montgomery and Stone. George M. Cohan, a sort of one-man company who emerged from vaudeville, wrote and starred in a series 'of aggressively energetic productions like *Little Johnny Jones* (1904) and *George Washington Junior* (1906). Charles Dillingham hired Irving Berlin to write the score for "a syncopated musical show," *Watch Your Step,* in 1914, the first of many Berlin musicals.

Meanwhile operetta lost none of its audience. Herbert continued to write until 1922, the year of his last show, *Orange Blossoms;* in 1924 Rudolf Friml wrote *Rose Marie* with "Indian Love Call," and its famous "yoo, hoo hoo *hoo,* hoo hoo *hoo,*" and *The Vagabond King.* The unstoppable Sigmund Romberg started with *Blue Paradise* in 1915; his last operetta, *The Girl in Pink Tights,* was produced posthumously in 1954. Yet popular as these operettas were, they were not musical comedy; music and production were European in style and content, and nearly all the composers were born or trained in Europe.

The "revue," another popular form of musical theater, came directly from Harrigan and Hart, Hoyt's farces, and the Floradora Girls. Florenz Ziegfeld, who learned much from the Floradoras, produced his first *Follies* in 1907 (to continue for twenty-five years) and stabilized the pattern for the type. Revues depended on gags and girls, at a higher level than burlesque, and on dances and songs that were more sophisticated than vaudeville's. The revue served most effectively as a medium for popular songs and a showcase for individual performers, many of them transferred from vaudeville—Nora Bayes, Lillian Lorraine, Al Jolson; dancers like the Castles and Marilyn Miller and the Astaires; comedians like Fanny Brice, W. C. Fields, Leon Errol, and Fred Allen.

The sophistication, wit, and tunefulness of the revues appealed powerfully to the twenties, which had the best of them—the *Follies,* George White's *Scandals,* Earl Carroll's *Vanities,* the *Music Box Revues, The Little Shows,* the *Garrick Gaieties,* and others. However, by the thirties the emphasis on girls, costumes, and jokes seemed to pall. Zeigfeld died broke in 1932, the *Vanities* quit in 1931, the *Scandals* in 1939. *Pins and Needles,* an acidly humorous revue staged by the International Ladies Garment Workers Union in 1937, which ran for 1,180 performances, fitted the mood of the depression years much better.

For composers, librettists, and performers with more than ordinary talent, neither the musical comedy nor the revue provided much challenge. Both became quickly stereotyped, filled with musical and comic clichés, emphasizing gaudy productions and expensive costuming. Songwriter Jerome Kern, with librettists Guy Bolton and P. G. Wodehouse, in 1915 wrote *Very Good, Eddie,* the first of a series that included *Oh Boy!* (1917), and *Oh Lady! Lady!* (1918), known as the "Princess Theater Shows." These were, in effect, comedies with music, rather than musical comedies. They were, said Bolton, "straight, consistent comedy with the addition of music. Every song and lyric contributed to the action.

The humor was based on the situation, not interjected by the comedians."
He hoped, Bolton continued, to have "real plot and characters," and to
"get altogether away from irrelevant scenes . . . , to depend as much on
plot and character development for success as on the music." The idea,
of course, was not new. Tightening and disciplining the show by careful
attention to a good book and a relevant score were.

It was more than a decade, however, before the Kern-Bolton-Wode-
house formula received serious attention. Girls-gags-costume shows
glutted the twenties, most of them undistinguished and unremembered:
Always You (1920), *Sally, Irene, and Mary,* (1922), *Lady in Ermine* (1922),
and so on, many of which were nothing more than vehicles for popular stars
like Eddie Cantor in *Kid Boots* (1923) or Al Jolson in *Big Boy* (1925). The
turning point came in 1927 with *Show Boat,* Jerome Kern's score for Oscar
Hammerstein II's dramatization of Edna Ferber's novel. *Show Boat* was a
serious musical play, neither a comedy with music nor music with comedy;
book, score, characterization, production, chorus, and sets were consolidated into a dramatic whole in the manner of the legitimate stage. "No
other piece of its vintage," writes Cecil Smith, the historian of the musical
theater, "left so large a permanent legacy."

Two quite distinct types of musical theater emerged after *Show
Boat:* the musical play, as Kern and Hammerstein had created it; and
the musical comedy, as it had already developed in the twenties. The
movies took away much of musical comedy's mass audience, but it survived
and flourished nevertheless in shows like *The Girl Friend* (1926), *The
Connecticut Yankee* (1927), *Present Arms* (1928), and the fluff-and-
chorus shows which Buddy De Sylva, Lew Brown, and Ray Henderson
did so well—*Good News, Hold Everything, Follow Thru,* and *Flying
High.* These were expertly written and well produced, but Hollywood
began to do them better, bigger, and gaudier. For those who wanted "a
good show" with funny men, big production numbers, and hummable
tunes that rhymed "June" with "moon," the movies were the place to go.
Jolson's *Jazz Singer* (1927), the first sound-film musical, doomed the old-
style, gags-and-girls Broadway show. The audience that remained for
musical theater was smaller, definitely urban, much more upper class in
its interests and tastes.

The musical play, then, became Broadway and upper-strata oriented,
demanding a great deal more in talent, production, and execution than a
movie audience expected or wanted. No longer could the Broadway musical be called "popular entertainment" in the usual sense, for its appeal
was limited, its audience selective, its sights raised. The chorus line became ballet. Georges Balanchine came from the Ballet Russe in the thir-

ties to choreograph *On Your Toes* and *Babes in Arms;* Vera Zorina of the Ballet Russe de Monte Carlo danced in *I Married an Angel* in 1938; Agnes de Mille supervised the ballet in *Bloomer Girl* (1944). *South Pacific* (1944), which did not feature dancing, was essentially a straight dramatic play with music.

Show Boat, in adapting a serious novel for its book, started the search by musical theater writers for plots of greater substance. The standard sailors-on-shore-leave, or poor-boy-meets-rich-girl, or Kollege Kapers plot, which served musical comedy for years as a story line on which to hang songs, no longer sufficed. As a result, the great majority of musical plays became adaptations of pretested books, short stories, and plays by established authors: Eugene O'Neill (*New Girl in Town*); Shakespeare (*Kiss Me, Kate; West Side Story; Boys from Syracuse*); George Bernard Shaw (*My Fair Lady*); Sholom Aleichem (*Fiddler on the Roof*); Thornton Wilder (*Hello, Dolly!*), to name only a few; and of course Lynn Riggs' folk play, *Green Grow the Lilacs,* for *Oklahoma!* Creativity and originality in the musical theater have been expressed in scores and productions, not in narrative or characterization. Productions cost too much for backers to take chances on an untried story.

The two predominant strains of the American musical theater—plays and comedies—have developed about equally over the past thirty years. Many artists have successfully worked in both. George Gershwin, who began in musical comedy, changed his style when joined by his brother Ira for *Funny Face* (1927). *Strike up the Band* (1930), done with Morrie Ryskind, was a wry, witty, antiwar satire; *Of Thee I Sing* (1931), a penetrating satire of politics which won a Pulitzer Prize for drama, starred Victor Moore as sad, lost, little Vice President Alexander Throttlebottom. Increasingly interested in further developing the form, Gershwin wrote *Porgy and Bess* (1935) as a folk-opera, a curious blend of Broadway and what he believed to be serious music.

Musical plays in the depression-ridden thirties were heavy with messages—*As Thousands Cheer* (1933) by Berlin, Harris, and Hart, a scatter-gun satire on contemporary society; Rodgers' and Hart's *I'd Rather be Right* (1937), a satire on Roosevelt and the New Deal; Marc Blitzstein's *The Cradle Will Rock* (1935), such a bitter indictment of the social order that musicians refused to play for it and Blitzstein had to play the piano himself at its opening. The trend toward serious themes continued in the forties: *Pal Joey* (1940), an affair between a Broadway heel and a bored society woman; *South Pacific* (1944), love between an aging planter and a young nurse; *West Side Story* (1957), a Leonard Bernstein score for *Romeo and Juliet* in the ghetto. The most distinguished holdout against significance and seriousness was Cole Porter, who wrote chic, brittle, witty musical comedies in the twenties manner for years, from *Fifty Million Frenchmen* (1929) down to *Can-Can* (1953) and *Silk Stockings* (1954). Porter's "inside humor" and urban hauteur made his shows attractive to the *New Yorker* set, but he had nothing to say to popular audiences.

Oklahoma! (1943), written by Richard Rodgers and Oscar Hammerstein II, hit exactly the right combination. A good-natured play, swiftly paced, well-produced and with an assortment of superb songs, *Oklahoma!* did everything musical comedy had always done, but more skillfully. It had no message, criticized nobody, pretended to nothing more than entertainment, and ran so long (2,248 performances) that it became part of the American musical tradition. The plot, with a heavy villain, curly-haired hero, comic rube, and sweet country-girl heroine, was no more than updated melodrama, but twentieth-century audiences liked the formula as much as their grandfathers had. This was *popular* musical comedy at its best, and others followed its lead. The rowdy *Annie Get Your Gun* (1946), the romanticized *King and I* (1951), the misty, escapist *Camelot* (1960), the energetic fun of *Hello, Dolly!* (1963) and the frankly wholesome *Music Man* (1957) and *The Sound of Music* (1959) were all straight popular entertainment—good shows with tuneful songs.

In theme and tone, the difference between the Princess Theater shows of the World War I era and *Oklahoma!* is not so wide as the difference between them in level of conception, execution, and talent. After the sixties, American musical comedy, to succeed, must have a believable story line, strong characterization, imaginatively staged dancing, creative production, and high-skilled performers, all tied into a musical whole. The music of the musical comedy, in particular, has reflected the rising level of audience expectation. The songs of the twenties and thirties could be whistled while washing the car—thirty-two bar choruses in an AABA or ABAC pattern, like Youmans' *Tea for Two* or Berlin's *Let's Have Another Cup of Coffee.*

In the forties musical comedy music began a steady increase in complexity and sophistication, so that a score today may involve recitative, choral passages, contrapuntal duets, and long dramatic-musical passages. (The song "Cool" in *West Side Story*, for example, is actually a twelve-tone fughetto; *The Fantasticks,* curiously enough, used elements from the ancient arts of pantomime, opera bouffe, and morality play.) Yet the fact remains, and undoubtedly will remain, that good songs lie always at the heart of musical comedy's success as popular theatrical entertainment.

THE SHOW ON THE ROAD

We're in the entertainment business; if you're looking for art go some-where else. We simply want to give folks a good time for an evening.
                                                                    —TENT SHOW OWNER.

Audiences loved the spectacular in the theater since the days of the Greeks, and American audiences were never exceptions. In the popular theater, the play itself was sometimes little more than an excuse for ex-hibiting the playwright's daring and the stage technician's skill. As the Elizabethans did, American companies matched wits in executing new and startling effects to attract crowds, while playwrights knew it was an effective way of strengthening a weak story line or hiding actors' inade-quacies. Many a Shakespearean play got by on the movement of Birnam Wood to Dunsinane in *Macbeth,* the battle of Agincourt in *Henry V,* or a rousing duel between Hamlet and Laertes in *Hamlet.*

In the late eighteenth century "spectacles" were presented in Amer-ica, as in England, as separate theatrical exhibitions or as afterpieces to plays. Charles Willson Peale's Philadelphia pageant to celebrate the peace treaty in January, 1784, called for a triumphal arch to be lit at night by a thousand candles and climaxed by a hundred rockets; it exploded pre-maturely, but Peale built another at Annapolis. "The Battle of Bunker's Hill," staged at Boston in 1793, reproduced the entire engagement with troops, gunfire, burning houses, cannon, and a parade. That same year a theatrical company in Charleston used Shakespeare's *Tempest* to stage a storm at sea, including the sinking of an entire fleet and Neptune riding over the sea in a chariot of clam shells.

The most fanciful of all, however, was the spectacle produced by the French artist, Andin, who put on "The Apotheosis of Franklin; or His

A Louisville Fair, 1857. CULVER PICTURES, INC.

One of the last surviving tent shows.
The tent can be set up or taken down
by a minimum crew of three men
and two women. The canvas must be
replaced every five years.

Handbill for the eighteenth-century
play, *The Beggar's Opera*. COLONIAL
WILLIAMSBURG.

CULVER PICTURES, INC.

The Black Crook, backstage.
CULVER PICTURES, INC.

Lillian Russell in *Brigands.*
CULVER PICTURES, INC.

The Drunkard: "Have courage, child!"
CULVER PICTURES, INC.

Reception into the Elysian Fields," in Charleston in 1796, with scenes representing the River Styx, The Temple of Memory, The Elysian Fields, and so on, accompanied by pantomime and dialogue. Andin next moved to Boston, where he staged another Battle of Bunker Hill—on a real hill—and later supervised "The Taste of the Times," which had views of Mount Vernon, Beacon Hill, the State House, and other famous places of American history. "The Temple of American Independence" in New York in 1799 featured Yorktown and four other battles, plus a diorama of New York City.

Playwrights, of course, used on the stage whatever audience-pleasing spectacles they could, often with little relevance to the action. One Boston play in 1800 presented, in addition to the plot, the destruction of the Persian fleet, a volcano eruption, a broadsword duel, an army carried over a waterfall, and a "leap for life" from an eighteen-foot tower. Another play of the eighteen-twenties required that a bolt of lightning strike the villain at exactly the critical point in the plot, a trick that must have taxed the ingenuity of the stage manager. A typical stage direction for such a play was that attached to a single scene in *The Young Carolinian* (1818), in which the United States Navy lost an engagement to the Barbary pirates:

> The ocean—a ship sailing—a gun is fired—American ship hoists the US flag—an Algerine corsair approaches under Hamburg colors—fires another gun—hoists the bloody flag and puts out a boat, which rows to the ship—they attempt to board but are sometime repulsed by the Americans—The Americans are finally overpowered—Algerines hoist the crescent on board their prize, leaving some of the pirates to keep possession—the rest of the American sailors to row to the corsair—the vessel sails off.

Since the captured seamen were later rescued, at least one more such spectacle must have been required in the last act.

Effects that did not work sometimes aroused as much applause as those that did, for audiences appreciated a good try. The stage manager for *The Red Rover* in 1832 devised apparatus for sinking a ship onstage and for launching lifeboats in a rainstorm, simulated by waving curtains of gauze descending from above. But actors and boats were soon hopelessly entangled in gauze, which had to be drawn up out of the way, giving the astonishing effect of rain falling upward. The Philadelphia production of *The Last Days of Pompeii* in 1830 (which required twenty-two scenes) called for the eruption of Vesuvius, of course, but the carefully-laid powder trains would not ignite and the manager closed the curtains to light the fuse. The fireworks exploded properly but before the curtain could rise, so the audience saw only a dark stage, a few sparks, and clouds of choking smoke. *The Pirate's Signal,* produced at the Bowery Theater in 1840, actually sailed a huge model ship across stage in an immense water tank, while *Yankee in China* that year put two frigates in the tank, with men in their rigging firing at a fort. These efforts brought applause even when the tank leaked.

Since the public liked wild and extravagant staging, the popular theaters gave it to them. *The Cataract of the Ganges* put a complete waterfall on stage in 1824 with a "leap for life" across it by a lady on horseback. George Washington Parker Custis (the President's grandson) seems to have been the first to get a locomotive on stage, including steam and smoke, in 1830. Hamblin and Hackett's New York Bowery Theater, known as "The Bowery Slaughterhouse" for its blood-and-thunder plays, specialized in effects at which others quailed. Their production of *Mazeppa* in 1833 featured a scene in which Mr. Gale "is strapped to the back of a wild horse, while birds peck at his eyes, lightning destroys a tree on stage, and wolves pursue the horse." A later *Mazeppa* production featured fifty horses, while Captain C. J. Rogers somehow managed to get his entire troupe of twenty-one horses, each rider in correct equestrian costume, into a Shakespeare play for a half-hour riding exhibition.

An interesting variation of the spectacular appeared in the forties and fifties with "tableaux vivantes," imported from the Continent and inspired in part by the controversy stirred up in 1843 by the public exhibition of Hiram Powers' nude statue, "The Greek Slave." Enterprising theater managers recognized the dramatic possibilities of putting similar *living* statues on stage, so Palmo's New York Opera House presented a series of biblical tableaux posed by "men and women in almost the same state as Gabriel saw them in the Garden of Eden on the first morning of creation," which meant dressed in closefitting silk tights.

Within the year at least seven theaters in the city were showing tableaux, with others presented "in taverns, hotels, and saloons," the newspapers said, "for every price from sixpence up to fifty cents." The exhibitions favored themes from Greek mythology, biblical history (featuring Eve, Bathsheba, Susanna at the bath, and so on), or famous paintings such as "Venus Rising from the Sea." Clearly the main attraction was the display of the female figure in what the theaters called "semi-transparent drapery." Though the theaters stressed the educational value of such tableaux, a newspaper poet put it better when he spoke of the cultural pleasures of viewing

> Pretty tableaux vivantes,
> Of beautiful young ladies sans
> Both petticoats and pants.

These exhibitions were short-lived, however, and soon passed into variety shows, burlesque, and musical comedy in less exposed versions.

Popular theaters, a critic complained with some justification in 1847, were becoming "show-shops, filled with pasteboard pageantry, conflagrations, bombardments, springing of mines, blowing up castles, and suchlike accumulations of artful nursery horrors." However, the better playwrights made efforts to integrate such special effects into the play, and exerted great influence on stage design and production. In 1846 the distinguished British tragedian Charles Kean brought to America a production of *King John* that greatly impressed American producers. Its stage effects, though admittedly extravagant, were tastefully and expertly handled, and its accessories—helmets, armor, scenery, costumes—were done with scrupulous historical accuracy. Its panoramic view of Angers and the French camp, which occupied the entire stage, fascinated American theater technicians and spurred them to more restrained but artistically improved accomplishments.

The influence of the Shakespearean productions carried over quickly into popular theater. *The Black Crook*, staged by Richard Marston in 1866, featured a "transformation,"—a slowly-developing scene made up of gauze risers, tinseled "sinks," and posed ballet girls—which gradually changed colors before the audience's eyes and closed with a burst of red fire. *The White Fawn* in 1868 had a similar transformation scene, built by eighty carpenters and twenty gas men, which took twelve minutes to complete. The Kiralfy Brothers in 1875 found Jules Verne's *Around the World in Eighty Days* the perfect vehicle for a spectacular, since it allowed practically unlimited scope for the stage mechanic—the Taj Mahal, the Suez Canal with ships, the Great Wall of China, and so on. The Kiralfys became acknowledged masters of the craft, gaining a national reputation for such spectacles as *The Fall of Rome* and *The Duke's Moat*.

Popular interest in the spectacular never flagged, whether it was a part of a play or a separate presentation. Steele Mackaye planned a drama about Columbus, called *The World Finder*, for the Chicago Exposition of 1893 (but never staged) centered in a "Spectatorium" in which special effects, such as Columbus' fleet in a storm, could be most effectively presented. Audiences went by the thousands to see the chariot race in *Ben Hur*, Lew Wallace's novel, made into a play in 1894; it also had Cleopatra's barge, a galley filled with galley slaves, and gladiators battling in the Coliseum.

The Hippodrome, which opened in New York in 1905, specialized in spectaculars—*Andersonville* (1905); *Pioneer Days* (1906, with cowboys, Indians, cavalry, and the Mexican Army); *The Auto Race* (1907);

Sporting Days (1908, with an airplane battle); and the tried-and-true *Around the World in Eighty Days* again in 1909. *Under Many Flags* (1912) staged both an earthquake and a tornado; *Wars of the World* (1914) featured battles from the French Revolution, the War of 1812, and Mexican, Civil, and Spanish wars. The Winter Garden entered the competition in 1911 with shows involving sandstorms, city fires, and Hannibal's army with elephants crossing the Alps.

In the twenties, however, the movies, with their almost unlimited capacity for flexibility and illusion, stole the spectacular for its own. The great film extravaganzas of Laemmle and De Mille with their "cast of thousands" drove theaters like the Hippodrome out of business. The last real spectacular (except for circuses and rodeos, where the tradition still remains) was Billy Rose's *Jumbo* in 1935. Or so it seemed, until Ice Shows, beginning in 1948, revived the tradition and put it on skates.

Panoramas, dioramas, and cycloramas were almost as popular as stage spectaculars throughout the nineteenth century. The panorama, a device imported from London in the 1790's, was a painting stretched about the inside wall of a circular building, called a "rotunda." The spectator stood on a platform in the middle, surrounded by the painting, so that by turning about slowly he had a continuous view of the whole scene. The diorama (although the two terms were often used interchangeably) was a continuous strip of canvas, about 12 feet wide, cranked from one roller to another across a stage to make a kind of primitive moving picture. The cyclorama placed a painted scene and wax figures on a platform before the spectator, with a curved wall backdrop to give the illusion of distance—a technique still widely used in museums.

In a big panoramic rotunda spectators might sit on a moving platform which turned slowly, looking through framed openings at the scenes in succession, over a 360 degree circle. In the "cosmorama," a refinement of the cyclorama, the spectator looked through magnifying lenses at three-dimensional tableaux which moved across a platform before him. All such exhibitions were customarily accompanied by music, a lecturer, and detailed program notes. William Dunlap, for example, wrote a complete travelogue to accompany a diorama called *A Trip to Niagara or Travellers in America,* showing the Hudson from the Bowery to the Catskill landing, the journey to Buffalo, and a succession of views of the Falls.

The first such exhibition seems to have been a panorama of Jerusalem shown at Hyer's Tavern in New York in 1790. Panoramic views of cities proved to be the most popular; Westminster, Versailles, London,

Paris, Rome, New York, and Charleston (a painting 110 feet long and 20 feet high) were all on exhibition before 1815. Next most popular were battles. Robert Kerr Porter's *Alexandria* (1804) covered 3,000 square feet, while Niblo's Gardens in 1831 displayed a 20,000 square foot panorama of *Waterloo, St. Helena,* and *Napoleon's Funeral,* one of the largest ever shown. Each year, every major city introduced at least one new panorama or diorama, which later moved from city to city into special theaters built for the purpose. A panorama of the Liverpool and Manchester Railroad which opened in Brooklyn in 1834 moved to four different rotundas in New York before going on the road. The Panoramic Building in New York in the 1839–40 season showed Jerusalem, Niagara, Lima, Rome, New Zealand, and five others.

These exhibitions reached the crest of their popularity between 1840 and 1860. Travelogues presented as educational entertainment by lyceums and schools lasted longest of all. *The Mirror of the World,* for example, showed "a continuous pictorial voyage around the world, commencing and ending in Boston," carried with it a three hour lecture, a study guide, and illustrated program notes. The Bowery in 1833 featured "a grand moving panorama [actually a diorama] of the Banks of the Dneiper, the Confines of Tartary, Wolf's Hollow, a Mountain Torrent, and the Desert" as part of its stage production of *Mazeppa,* while in 1853 J. B. Booth's diorama covered a complete transcontinental trip beginning with "Views of New York" and ending at "The City Beside the Golden Gate."

Other popular titles included *A Voyage to Europe, China and Japan, A Journey on the Rhine, The Arctic Regions,* and *A Whaling Voyage.* Exhibitions of battles—such as *The Battle of Mexico* (1847) or *The Bombardment of Vera Cruz* (1848)—were sometimes accompanied by pyrotechnical displays; religious scenes, such as *The Creation of the World, A Panoramic Mirror of the Old Testament,* and *Journey through the Holy Land,* invariably drew capacity crowds.

River and lake dioramic trips were favorite fare, among them journeys on the Great Lakes, the Hudson, the St. Lawrence, and the Potomac. The Mississippi, naturally the best draw of all, was represented by six different dioramas painted between 1850 and 1887. John Barnard, who took his floating studio from New Harmony, Indiana, down the Wabash, the Ohio, and the Mississippi to New Orleans, eventually completed a diorama nearly three miles long, so accurate and detailed that Longfellow studied it to obtain background for *Evangeline.* His diorama drew 400,000 people on its first tour and even more in England, where he took it for another. John Rowson Smith painted two dioramas of the river, the second reputedly four miles long (although such claims are suspect), while Samuel Stockwell, Samuel Hudson, and Henry Lewis also painted it from source to Gulf.

The panoramic craze had run its course by 1860, though the Civil War temporarily revived it. A half-mile diorama of the war appeared in New York in 1868, the first of many to tour the country. Enery's Libby Prison Cyclorama (actually a diorama presented against a cycloramic background) toured the North in the eighties and nineties, combined with a drum and bugle corps parade and a spieler in a blue uniform to lend a quasi-military tone. The most famous survivor of the form is Paul Philippoteaux's painting of Gettysburg, completed in 1881 and still to be seen at Gettysburg.

Eventually, lantern slides, engravings, mass journalism, and photography made such exhibitions obsolete. They existed one at a time; they could not be duplicated for mass distribution nor standardized for popular tastes. Yet they were, for nearly half a century, a vital, popular kind of dramatic art. As William Dunlap pointed out, they appealed to "all classes of spectators . . . , for no study of cultivated taste is required fully to appreciate the merits of such representations."

The circus, despite its name, has its roots in England and not in Rome; the term, as applied to an animal show, seems to date from mid-eighteenth-century England, with its first American appearance recorded in 1791. Its American origins lie in the animal trainers, acrobats, jugglers, and itinerant actors who traveled through the colonies, and in the English equestrian shows of the late eighteenth century. Records show that somebody imported and displayed a lion in America in 1716, a camel in 1721, trained monkeys and other animals in the 1730's. Animal shows and itinerant performers were frowned upon by the pious because of their association with taverns and public houses, and with the brutal bull-baiting and dog-fighting entertainments of lower-class England.

By mid-century, however, a number of animal and acrobatic shows toured the colonies fairly regularly. The first successful equestrian shows, modeled after Philip Astley's famous London horse shows, were presented in Philadelphia in 1792 by John Bill Ricketts, an English horseman who built his own amphitheater the next year. Ricketts's show attracted large audiences, including George Washington, himself an expert horseman who once rode with Ricketts and who sold him a horse. Ricketts took his show to New York and Boston, added a tightrope walker, a clown, and some acrobats, and soon had competition from imitators and rival shows from England and Europe.

These early circuses were city entertainment, presented in buildings or arenas suited to the purpose. Hachaliah Baily of Somers, New York, took to the road in 1815 with a few animals and an elephant named Old Bet, exhibiting them in barns, open fields, and town squares. A surprised farmer shot Old Bet, but Baily imported more animals and returned to the road the next year, billing his show as an "educational exhibition," thereby subduing at least some rural fears and attracting larger crowds. Inspired by his prosperity, five other Somers citizens went into the business and soon the roads in the East were filled with traveling animal shows, most with a clown or two after the fashion of European shows. Where roads did not go, the shows went by boat; circuses appeared on the Ohio and Mississippi in the 1820's, and reached Detroit in 1830. Quite logically, these shows often teamed up with traveling acrobatic troupes and horse shows. For the next twenty years they exchanged performances and performers; animal shows might have acrobats, equestrian shows animals, and acrobatic troupes clowns.

Since few towns had buildings large enough to accommodate the larger troupes, and since open air performances depended on the weather, more prosperous shows began to use canvas walls, later tents. The first circus to travel under the "big top" was probably the Turner show in 1826, but within a few years tents were standard for all but the smallest shows. Copying the popular stage spectaculars, the shows introduced "specs," with parades, costumes, and pageants titled "Napoleon in Egypt," "Joan of Arc," "The Queen of Sheba," or "Solomon and His Host." Well aware of the popularity of the city's "dime museums," some added "side shows" with weird and unusual exhibits. By the fifties the basic pattern of the circus was fully established—acrobats and aerialists, freaks, animals, spectaculars, horses, and clowns—from which it has never varied.

The circus' biggest problem was transportation. The more affluent shows had specially built wagons, fancifully carved and painted—Phineas Barnum, naturally, owned the most elaborate and expensive, custom-built for $40,000. Tents grew larger and better; seating, advertising, accounting, ticket sales, and internal organization improved. Doc Spalding, of the Spalding and Rogers Circus, introduced new methods of striking and setting up tents in the forties and fifties, put in quarter poles to support larger tents, and used oil lamps for better lighting. Then, in 1856, he put his show into nine special railroad cars, the first to be rail-borne. As each circus worked out its own ways of doing things and exchanged information, the circus turned into a tightly-organized, efficient, specialized entertainment unit. The expansion of the railroad, of course, made it possible for circuses to penetrate into new territory and cover more of it, faster and with less cost. Dan Costello's Circus made the first cross-country tour, from Baltimore to San Francisco by way of New Orleans, in 1868–69.

The Golden Age of the circus lasted from about 1870 to 1914. Phineas Barnum, the most successful showman of them all, entered the field in 1871, bringing to it his vast experience and shrewd box office sense. He put two rings instead of one into his show, introduced advance ballyhoo and imaginative advertising, and made the sideshow into a major attraction with the first Bearded Lady, the first Wild Man from Borneo, and the first Siamese Twins. Circuses had elephants before Barnum, but he made his elephant, Jumbo, into a nationally-known attraction and added a word to the language.

By the early eighties Barnum's circus traveled in sixty-one special railroad cars and put on its show in a tent that held 20,000 people. His closest rival, James A. Bailey (who was actually named McGinnis) set up his circus in San Francisco in 1873 and bought out the Royal British Circus in 1877. After fevered competition that nearly ruined both, Barnum and Bailey merged in 1881, although Barnum sold out in 1885. William Cole's circus started in 1872, the Sells Brothers in 1878. The seven Ringling Brothers, who began in 1884, slowly built up their circus until it surpassed the rest, and when Bailey died in 1906, the Ringlings bought his show, keeping his and Barnum's names. In 1910, probably the peak year for circuses, there were thirty big shows on the road and fifty smaller ones, not counting "dog-and-pony" shows, animal-carnival shows, or fly-by-night outfits.

As circuses and audiences grew larger, the shows became much more complicated. Barnum's double ring became three, with five stages, surrounded by a "hippodrome" track for parades and races. Circuses took in the Wild West show and adopted elements of the rodeo, featured larger and more dangerous wild animal acts, increased the splendor of spectacles, introduced ballets, and poured money into acts and costumes. By 1910 a single circus program might include thirty acts, lasting from four to six hours.

It was not enough. Movies, phonographs, radios, and the automobile pointed toward the end of the road. There were still touring circuses after the First World War, and they still drew large audiences, but there were fewer of them and their ownership grew more concentrated as bigger shows drove out or bought out the smaller ones. The American Circus Corporation by 1921 owned seven, the Ringlings six. The toll of the depression was enormous—in 1932 only four circuses made it on tour, and

in 1934 only three. By the forties, out of the thirty major circuses that existed in 1910, only Ringling Brothers, Barnum and Bailey still survived,
while a few small shows tended more and more to play sport arenas, ball
parks, and country fairs.

Even the Ringlings, who traveled in a train of a hundred steel cars
and played in the world's biggest tent, had their troubles. A tragic fire
at Hartford, Connecticut, in July, 1944, very nearly put them out of
business. When smoke appeared at the sidewall of the tent, the ring-
master asked the crowd of seven thousand to file out quietly; the first
wave panicked, however, at finding the way blocked by a steel runway
for the next animal act, sending the entire audience into a hysterical rush
for the exit. Although the fire was out within fifteen minutes, there were
one hundred and sixty-eight dead and four hundred and eighty-seven
injured under the big top. Charges of involuntary manslaughter were
filed against six members of the Ringling management, hundreds of dam-
age suits dragged through the courts for years, and public confidence in
circus safety never really returned for another decade.

The Ringlings opened again in August, but the shadow of Hartford
remained. Rising costs and declining crowds plagued the circus until
1956, when the management decided to close the show four months ahead
of time. Their last show under canvas was given in Pittsburgh on July 15;
later the Ringlings reorganized and continued yearly performances, but
only indoors and only in the large cities. What exists today is urbanized,
Europeanized entertainment, quite different from the circus that, as
Hamlin Garland once wrote, came each year to the small towns with
tigers, tinsel, popcorn, and bands, "trailing clouds of glorified dust and
filling our minds with the color of romance."

The origins of the Wild West Show, completely and uniquely an
American product, had nothing to do with the circus. It began and ended
with one man, William F. "Buffalo Bill" Cody, who dominated it while it
existed. Cowboys in the sixties staged rodeo contests at spring roundups,
with steer riding, roping, broncho-busting, and the rest. Cody, already
famous as a stage star in melodrama Westerns, helped the promoters of
a Fourth of July rodeo at North Platte, Nebraska, 1882, directing all the
cowboy events himself. The show drew thousands of people from miles
around, convincing Cody that a similar show, taken on tour through the
East, could hardly fail.

Buffalo Bill worked through the year hiring cowboys and Indians,
renting horses and catching buffalo, and by April, 1883, had his company
gathered at Columbus, Nebraska. The "Wild West, Rocky Mountain, and

Prairie Exhibition" opened in Omaha on May 17, featuring running battles of scouts versus Indians, steer riding, rodeo contests, shooting exhibitions, an attack on a mail coach, and a dramatization of the Pony Express. As the show moved across the country toward its final performance at Coney Island, the crowds grew enormous.

The Wild West show was an instant national mania. Cody's show, which combined elements of the parade, the circus, the stage spectacular, the carnival and the melodrama, coincided exactly with current popular interest in the romantic West, and could hardly have been better qualified to appeal to the great American public. Nor was it a fake. Cody hired real cowboys, real Indians, and real marksmen. For that matter, he had been a Pony Express rider at thirteen, stagecoach driver, buffalo hunter, prospector, Union Army soldier, scout for Crook, Sheridan, Custer, and Miles, and he also held the Congressional Medal of Honor. Buffalo Bill was the genuine article.

Cody hired a business manager, Nate Salisbury, and in 1884 took to the road again with a hundred more Indians, a hundred more horses, and a new group of authentic Westerners, among them Buck Taylor, "King of the Cowboys"; Con Groner, "The Cowboy Sheriff of the Platte"; "Mustang Jack" the Indian scout; "Cowboy Kid" Johnny Baker, John Belson "The Squaw Man," and later sure-shot Annie Oakley and her husband Frank Butler. The show, now called "Buffalo Bill's Wild West Show," opened in St. Louis (attracting 35,000 people the first day), moved to Chicago (42,000 opening day), and across the country eastward, with every performance a sellout. Each year Cody added something new, a buffalo hunt, foot races, animal exhibitions; in 1885 he hired Sitting Bull, who sat in silent dignity watching the gawking spectators with hooded eyes.

Other shows sprang up in imitation, of course, such as Captain Jack Crawford's and Doc Carver's, but none ever matched the original. Cody's 1887 show toured England, France, Spain, and Italy—probably the most successful European tour ever made by any American company—to make "Buffalo Bill's" name a byword the world over. At one afternoon performance in England, during the Indian attack on the stagecoach, the Deadwood Coach carried four kings as passengers (Denmark, Greece, Belgium, and Saxony) with Buffalo Bill driving and the Prince of Wales riding shotgun—clearly a climax that no show would ever reach again.

As years passed, though the core of the show still remained cowboys and Indians, Cody's managers added other attractions. The 1899 show dropped the stagecoach attack and substituted the Battle of San Juan Hill; later shows featured a riding exhibition by the Royal Northwest

Mounted Police, scenes from the Boer War, a ship rescue by the Coast Guard, and circus-type wild animal acts. Other shows developed in the nineties to give Cody's fierce competition—Pawnee Bill's Show, the Miller Brothers 101 Ranch (which contributed both Buck Jones and Tom Mix to the movies), Adam Forepaugh's Show, the Gabriel Brothers, and a host of lesser ones down to ex-bandits Cole Younger's and Frank James' Wild West, featuring bank-robbing and hold-ups.

Many of these shows made little attempt at authenticity; they were entertainment and nothing else, with only a vague relationship to the West. Cowboys carried Spanish-American War surplus rifles; some Indians were bad arrow shots; marksmen cheated with birdshot; and one show even featured a football game between cowboys and Indians. By 1910, however, the Wild West show was clearly losing out to other forms of entertainment. Cody merged with Pawnee Bill that year, but in 1913 the show dissolved and Cody put the equipment up for sale. He toured for a time with the Sells Floto Circus, and later with 101 Ranch.

Old, ill, and tiring fast, Buffalo Bill made his last public appearance in November, 1916, and died a few months later. The circus and the movies absorbed what was left of the tradition. In 1910 the first movies of the West appeared, one- and three-reelers of Indians, horses, cowboys, and buffalo, and that same year Essanay started its "Bronco Billy" series with Bronco Billy Anderson, the first of the Western movie stars.

Brief as its history was, the Wild West show exerted a powerful and lasting influence on the American imagination. It embedded in the popular cultural tradition, as nothing else did, the great, romantic legend of the American West. The Wild West parade—a hundred Red Indians on ponies; cowboys, scouts, stage coaches; the U.S. Cavalry, with Sweeney's Cowboy Band riding on matched grey horses—this was a picture indelibly impressed on the memory of millions of Americans who saw it. And at the head of the parade sat the man who personified it all; Buffalo Bill, straight in the stirrups, with flowing white hair, fringed buckskin jacket, and broadbrimmed Stetson held aloft, his big white horse prancing to the music, symbol of a lost era.

Filmmakers took over many of the plays, actors, and techniques of the popular stage, so that many early movies were little more than screened versions of old stage favorites—*Way Down East, St. Elmo, Uncle Tom's Cabin.* Popular drama, however, went on as before, except that it took to the road—in the riverboats, repertory or "rep" companies, and tent-shows in which the same actors played the same old plays, or new plays in the same tradition, no matter what the movies did. These companies rarely played towns of more than 10,000, where people had formed the moviegoing habit, and made no attempt to compete with either motion pictures or the legitimate theater. Experiments in putting more sophisticated shows from Broadway on the road were swift and utter failures (as late as 1949) and "rep" show managers never tried them.

Theater companies traveled through the American colonies in the eighteenth century and followed the great westward migration in the early nineteenth, playing in barns, taverns, ballrooms, or anywhere they could. The early riverboats carried itinerant actors, musicians, and performers into the wilderness as soon as the new settlements sprang up. Samuel Drake's company left Pittsburgh in 1815 on a flatboat bound for New Orleans, presenting bits of Shakespeare, skits, and specialty acts along the way for two years. Others followed Drake, but the first boat built especially for theatrical entertainment was William Chapman's, built in Pittsburgh in 1831; after that the western rivers were never without showboats, except during the Civil War. The showboat era reached its height between 1890 and 1920, when twenty-six boats traveled the western waters. But by 1938 there were only five, and Farnsworth's *Water Lily*, which finally failed to leave the dock in 1942, seems to have been the last—although Indiana University, keeping the tradition alive, put its own showboat on the Ohio in the sixties.

The larger showboats played the upper Ohio in the spring; the lower Ohio and the upper Mississippi in the summer; and the lower Mississippi in the winter. Smaller boats swarmed over the tributaries of the big rivers whenever water levels and the seasons permitted. Unfortunately, so too did boats specializing in gambling, medicine-shows, and whiskey (some were practically floating saloons) which brought disrepute to the legitimate traveling companies. By the nineties the larger boats developed promotional techniques of their own, resembling those of the circus. A speed launch preceded the showboat with advertising posters and advance men. The arrival of the boat was heralded by a downriver steam calliope concert, audible for miles, a street parade of actors and musicians, and sometimes the presentation of a few bits from the program in the village square.

Showboats offered much the same programs as the land-based traveling shows; plays, acts, and performers were interchangeable. Most of them offered variety programs, such as Captain French's *Sensation #2* in 1898, which consisted of a comedy, songs illustrated by slides, three musical numbers, acrobats, a minstrel show, a magician, and an afterpiece. The Eisenbarth-Henderson *Floating Theater* played only straight drama; the *Reynolds Majestic* specialized in melodrama; *The Sunny South* presented musical comedy. In 1925 the *James Adams* put on a typical program with a musical, a mystery, two comedies, a melodrama, and a current hit, *Pollyanna.*

Over the years the showboat trade developed its own tycoons—Captain French, whose wife was also a licensed river pilot, built and ran five boats betwen 1878 and 1902; Captain Price owned eight, Captain Emerson nine. W. R. Marble operated the three biggest, *The Grand Floating Palace, The Sunny South,* and *The Goldenrod,* which seated 1,400. In their time the boats drew audiences from miles away, but good roads and movies reduced the last few in the thirties to playing ridiculous burlesques of the plays that once made them famous. But for nearly a century they furnished an important means of carrying popular drama to otherwise inaccessible audiences. What they presented was no different from what these audiences would have seen on land; the floating theater was merely another way of getting it to them.

Yankee Robinson's Opera Pavilion, of Rock Island, Illinois, was apparently the first theater company to tour under canvas, in 1855. The tent show remained largely a Midwestern, Southern, and Southwestern institution, even after theaters and "opera houses" appeared in the towns. By the time the movies arrived these traveling shows had developed a large and faithful following which the films could not take away. Rural and small-town audiences seemed to like the informal, circus-like atmosphere of the tent-show theater, and the specially designed tents provided good theatrical conditions. The average tent held 1,000–1,500 people, although the Harry Sadler Shows seated 3,000 in the nineteen-twenties.

Road-show companies played the older favorites, updated melodramas, and adaptations of popular novels. The tent show, as showman Harold Rosier defines it,

> was not a circus, or a carnival, or vaudeville (though it may have had some elements of these), but a family-type dramatic show with three-act plays, specialty acts, and sometimes an "after show" for a small extra charge, generally playing a town for three days to a week, and moving on. It was just entertainment; if you wanted culture, you didn't go.

Paychecks were unheard of, at least in the average company; actors simply split the take evenly at the end of the week. There were really no "stars," although some actors specialized in certain parts, like Marks the lawyer in "Uncle Tom's Cabin," or Sputters the stuttering cowboy, or the lost heiress in "Sundown." Any actor might play the butler on Monday, carry the leading role on Tuesday, take tickets on Wednesday, handle lights on Thursday, and so on.

Tent-show companies avoided the risqué, suggestive, or controversial. A manager's proudest boast was that the show contained "nothing you can't take your family to see," so that families who disapproved of "city theaters" and movie "spectacles" eagerly awaited the annual arrival of what tent-show bills tirelessly advertised as "shows you can see without blushing." The shows never tried to compete with the movies, even during the cinema's boom years in the twenties, but instead avoided larger towns and played the older plays with updated variations, deliberately aiming at an audience which the movies did not reach and which mistrusted Hollywood's values. "We gave the public a decent alternative," an old-time manager recalled, "to epics, orgies, sex, and horror."

Traveling "rep" companies usually prepared six to nine plays a season (enough for a week's engagement with substitutions), chiefly comedies but always also one serious play. There were possibly five hundred or so standard comedies (many of them variations of the same plot) to draw upon, with titles such as *Lazy Bones, A Night Out, Tamed and How, Up in Mable's Room, The Girl and the Tramp, Meet the Bride, Abie's Little Rose* (forerunner of the long-playing *Abie's Irish Rose* that Anne Nichols wrote later for the Broadway stage), or *Henry's Wedding*. Serious plays were *Lena Rivers* (from an 1860's novel by Mary Jane Holmes), *St. Elmo* (from Augusta Jane Evans's novel), *Stricken Blind, The Vendetta, In the Heart of the Sierras,* and *The Marriage Game.* There were also mysteries like *The House of a Thousand Candles* and *The Great Diamond Robbery.*

Each company carried one "feature," usually an adaptation of a current best-selling novel—*The Virginian, Freckles, The Trail of the Lonesome Pine, The Shepherd of the Hills*—or a time-tested favorite like *A Royal Slave* (from Lew Wallace's novel, *The Fair God*), *Jesse James,* or *Dr. Jekyll and Mr. Hyde.* Companies wrote new plays, or more often rewrote old ones, to fit the talents of their casts and the tastes of the area in which they traveled. Vern Slout and Neil Schaffner, for example, each wrote or adapted more than a hundred plays for his own troupe between 1910 and 1930. An old play like *The Awakening of John Slater* (actually a descendant of the "Yankee" plays of the days of Hackett), written about 1910, might reappear year after year; the Rosier Players in Michigan, in fact, staged it in 1968 as *Rubes in the City.* Vern Slout, who wrote *Whittlin'* in 1920, played it under six different titles with minor variations for twenty years.

The road show's unique contribution to popular drama, "Toby" the comic bumpkin, appeared around 1910 in the shows that toured the Midwest and upper South. It is difficult to name his inventor, but Fred Wilson, who noted the popularity of the character, built it into a specialty and others copied it. Toby, who might have a number of different names, was a rustic "shrewd boob" in the old Yankee tradition, who confused and defeated the city slickers who tried to bamboozle him and ended up ahead of the designing villain. He was, wrote Neil Schaffner, who played Toby for thirty-five years, "unlettered, awkward, with a native wit, shrewdness, and a great deal of common sense. He says what the man in the street wishes he could have thought of."

Rural and small-town audiences made Toby their own, and managers hastily wrote new Toby plays or inserted Toby parts in old ones. In 1916 there were at least two hundred Toby specialists in the traveling shows, each with his own way of playing the part. Toby makeup was standard—a red wig, freckles, a blacked out tooth, and "rube" clothes— but different characterizations emerged in different areas. In the Midwest Toby was a country hick, in the South a hillbilly, in Minnesota and the Dakotas a blond-wigged Swede; there was even a cowboy-type Toby for the West. Whatever the crisis or complication, Toby won out in the last act to nobody's surprise and everybody's satisfaction.

In 1925 there were about four hundred traveling tent-show companies, employing twenty thousand people. That year these shows visited 16,000 communities and played to a total audience of 76,800,000, or about twice as many as attended the legitimate theater. But the inroads of depression, construction of better roads, and the appearance of the radio and movies soon began to show up in the statistics. By the fifties, when television came, there were about thirty companies; by the sixties only six; in 1968 only three, the Sun Players of Iowa, the Jimmie Davis-Neil Schaffner Players of Illinois, and the Rosier Players of Michigan. The last regular season to be played by an American tent show may well have been that of the Harold Rosier company at Brighton, Michigan, in 1969, although both the Rosier and Davis-Schaffner companies hoped to open again in 1970. Harold Rosier, who played his first Toby role in 1930, played his last (probably the last appearance Toby will ever make on the tent-show circuit) in "Toby's on the Spot" during the week of July 6, 1969. Toby, however, went out in a blaze of heroics, outwitting and capturing a whole group of very dangerous Chicago gangsters.

The popular theater, as it developed over the nineteenth century and into the twentieth, eventually vanished into movies and television. Ex-

cept for the hardy road shows, the history of popular drama since about
1910 has been the history of Hollywood. A few plays out of the older
tradition appeared on the stage in ensuing years, all of them modernized
versions (sometimes not so modernized) of easily recognizable hits of the
past. J. Hartley Manners' *Peg o' My Heart* (1912, starring Laurette Taylor) was, as critic Burns Mantle shrewdly noted, "an old-fashioned comedy drama . . . , a frank reversion to the type of stage entertainment
that strikes at the fundamental emotions of common folk." The play, after
it left Broadway, of course became a tent-show standard.

Lightnin' (1918) a collaboration by Winchell Smith and Frank
Bacon, who took the title role, was simply an updated Rip, played by
Bacon in the honored tradition of Hackett and Jefferson. Bayard Veiller's
Within the Law (1912) and *The Thirteenth Chair* (1917), and George
M. Cohan's *Seven Keys to Baldpate* (1913) introduced the mystery-
melodrama, which reached its high point with *The Bat* (1920, 867 performances) by Avery Hopwood and Mary Roberts Rinehart, an old-
fashioned Gothic thriller with murders, a bank robbery, and a bruising
fight. *Abie's Irish Rose* (1922, 2,327 performances), a preposterously
naïve and sentimental play, was Harrigan and Hart plus love, tears, and
dialect.

Many plays since have set performance records—*Tobacco Road*
(3,182), *Life with Father* (3,224), *Arsenic and Old Lace* (1,444), *Harvey*
(1,775), *Born Yesterday* (1,642), *Mary, Mary* (1,572), and *The Fantasticks* (3,225 plus), but all of them have been plays written by expert
playwrights for minority, sophisticated audiences, the records themselves
confined to Broadway showings. None can be classed as "popular" drama
in the cultural definition of the term; none could have been, or would be,
successful on the traditional road show circuit with its Toby-oriented
audiences.

The plots, characters, themes, situations, and devices of popular
drama, with all of its emotionalism, sentimentalism, and moralism, have
passed into motion pictures and television, where any night you can see
them all on a screen.

PART THREE

THE POPULAR
ARTS ON
THE NEWSSTAND

If the public wants it that way, why not?
—"NED BUNTLINE" (E. Z. C. JUDSON) 1852

CHAPTER EIGHT

THE DIME NOVEL
TRADITION

The game is to give the ordinary guy what he wants, that is, the transitive verb—action, excitement, blood, love, a little humor, a taste of sex, a pepper of passion, a lot of escape.

—PULP MAGAZINE EDITOR

The dime novel sprouted in the eighteen-forties and fifties, flowered in the sixties and seventies, and drooped and died at the turn of the century. As a popular genre of fiction it was not particularly new, for the "story papers" and "yellow-covered romances" of the thirties and forties (like England's "penny dreadfuls") were already familiar to the public. Commercial hack-writers like Emerson Bennett, A. J. A. Duganne, and young Edward Ellis, with Cobb's and Ingraham's sentimental novels and the Indian stories of the magazine writers, had prepared the public for more of the same. Mrs. Mary Denison's *Chip the Cave Child,* Mrs. Metta Victor's *Backwoods Bride,* Colonel Duganne's *Massasoit's Daughter* and other novels were pre-Civil War best sellers; Mrs. Victor's *Maum Guinea and Her Children* (1862), a novel of slave life, sold 100,000 copies within the year; Lincoln and others who read it placed it not far behind *Uncle Tom's Cabin.* Maturin Ballou's and Frederick Gleason's publishing houses ground out novelettes to sell at a shilling (twelve and a half cents) through the forties and fifties, and Ballou published a series called *The Weekly Novelette,* each issue of which cost four cents and contained one-fifth of a story, so that one could buy a complete novel for twenty cents.

Competition among the publishers of these cheap novels was fierce and companies often short-lived. The Beadle brothers, Erasmus and Irwin, formed a shaky publishing house with Robert Adams in 1856 which existed on the edge of failure until, by shrewd reckoning and chance, they published a paperbound novel in 1860 called *Malaeska, The Indian Wife of the White Hunter,* by Ann Sophia Stephens, and sold it for a dime. The book sold 65,000 copies within a few months, a success Erasmus knew could be repeated. He hired Edward S. Ellis, a well-known hack-writer, to write another novel, *Seth Jones; or The Captives of the Frontier,* and decorated the East with placards asking, "Who is Seth Jones?" The public waited expectantly for the famous opening words of the novel, "How de do? How de do? Ain't frightened, I hope. It's nobody but me, Seth Jones of New Hampshire," and ultimately bought a half-million copies.

Beadle and Adams's contribution to publishing was one of merchandising, not content. They organized production, standardized the product, and did some shrewd guessing about the nature and extent of the market. Then they put 30,000 to 50,000 words of wild plot into a salmon-colored paper cover with a lurid illustration and sold it for a minimum price. The stories had been there for a long time—since the Indian captivity, pirate, and low-life tales of the eighteenth century—and Beadle simply applied mass production methods to them. His aim, he said, was "to see how much I could give for ten cents, cash sales, not credit." To a country with a million men under arms, the dime novel provided exactly what the army camps wanted; Beadle and Adams sold four million of them between 1861 and 1866.

Their success invited imitators. George Munro, Beadle's printing foreman, established his own firm in 1863 and for the next thirty years Munro's Ten-Cent Novels were real competition. Robert De Will started a series in 1867, publishing 1,118 novels over the next ten years. Norman Munro, George's brother, established his own firm in 1870; Frank Tousey entered the field in 1878; Street and Smith, the most successful of all, arrived in 1889. These five firms dominated the market until the nineties, when Beadle sold out, and the Munros quit business, and Street and Smith turned paper-covered novels into pulp magazines and absorbed Tousey. The last genuine dime novel publication was probably Street and Smith's *New Buffalo Bill Weekly* in 1912.

During the forty-odd years of the dime-novel's rise and fall, the industry poured out millions of novels. Not all of them sold for ten cents, for some cost as little as a nickel and others as much as a quarter. Printed in editions of 60,000 to 70,000, some went through ten or twelve editions a year; authors' fees ranged from fifty dollars to two hundred fifty dollars depending on the length of the novel, its type, and the writer's reputation. (Beadle and Adams supported a stable of nearly two hundred writers over the years.)

By the late seventies, the novels settled down into three classifications. Some were booklets selling at ten cents, seven inches by five, about a hundred pages, issued semimonthly. Others, at five cents, were eight-by-twelve inch booklets of about the same length, issued weekly or semimonthly. A third type, an actual paperbound book of two hundred to two hundred fifty pages, appeared in the eighties, selling at ten, fifteen, and twenty-five cents; Nick Carter, Buffalo Bill, "Bertha M. Clay" (a pseudonym for staff writers) and Horatio Alger appeared in this format. The best marketing device was the continuing series, wherein the reader followed a character or a particular plot line ad infinitum.

Between 1880 and 1890 there were 101 different series divided among the various companies; from 1890 to 1912 seventy-six. Within these series, separate titles often numbered in the thousands. Beadle's Dime series, beginning with Ann Stephen, issued 631 titles; its Pocket Novels series, begun in the seventies, reached 272; the Dime Library 1,103; the Half Dime Library 1,168. Tousey's Five Foot Wide-Awake Library listed 1,353 titles, his Wild West series 1,294, the Liberty Boys of '76 series 1,273, the Fame and Fortune series 1,193. Norman Munro's Old Cap Collier series contained eight hundred titles alone. In addition, some dime novel publishers issued weekly papers—Beadle's Banner (1872–97), Elverson's Saturday Night (1865–1902), George Munro's Fireside Companion (1866–1907), and Norman Munro's Family Story Paper (1873–1921).

Contrary to popular legend, not all dime novels were Westerns. They covered the Revolution, the War of 1812, the Mexican War, and the Civil War; they used pirate stories, sea stories, city stories of high and low life, crime stories, bandit stories, stories of exploration, adventure, history, love, romance, and many reprints of Cooper, Scott, and Dickens. Beadle's Popular Library series, for example, advertised "Wild West, Border, Mining, Ranching, Secret Service, Detective, Robber, City, and Sea Life" stories. Philip Durham's analysis of 1,500 Beadle novels published between 1860 and 1898 shows the two most popular types to be Western and detective, the latter introduced by George Munro's Old Sleuth series in 1885. He copyrighted the word "Sleuth," but Norman came on with Old Cap Collier, Frank Tousey with Old King Brady, and later Street and Smith with the great Nick Carter.

The better dime novels rarely attained the level of literary mediocrity, but they were highly conventional in their regard for contemporary standards of conduct. The action might be bloody and the heroes roughhewn, but the books were resolutely virtuous. Erasmus Beadle's regulations forbade "all things offensive to good taste . . . , subjects or characters that carry an immoral taint . . . , and what cannot be read with satisfaction by every right-minded person, young and old alike."

William Everett, in 1864, found Beadle publications "without exception unobjectionable morally, whatever fault be found with their literary style and composition. They do not even obscurely pander to vice, or excite the passions." Their heroes neither drank, smoked, or swore, and limited themselves to expletives like "Thunderation!" and "By the horns of Gabriel!" Good and bad men were instantly recognizable; women might be threatened by death, but never by a worse fate; there was absolutely no suggestion of sexuality, though the villain might "gaze into her white, lovely face with fiendish triumph." There was blood, bullets, and constant, frantic action, but no more.

What parents objected to in the dime novels was not their morality, but their emphasis on sensationalism, violence, and overwrought emotionalism, especially as the type began to degenerate in the seventies and eighties. The demand for ever-increasing suspense and action pushed authors ever closer to absurdity; the quality of the writing, never high, slipped into the very worst kind of shoddy prose. At first the writers drew heroes more or less from real life—Buffalo Bill, Daniel Boone, Texas Jack, Kit Carson, Big Foot Wallace, and so on—but when they ran out of material they soon invented lurid characters on the order of Deadwood Dick, Deadshot Dave, Rattlesnake Ned, or The Black Avenger. Within a few decades the stories were out of hand, filled with a disrespect for law and the proprieties that led to the canonization of train robbers, outlaws, and criminals such as Jesse James, the Youngers, Billy the Kid, and their fictional counterparts.

Ground out by weary hack-writers, the novels quickly developed a formula. Titles were divided by a semicolon, indicating the character and the nature of the narrative, so the reader knew exactly what he was buying—*Desperate Dan, the Dastard; or, The Pirates of the Pecos; Buffalo Bill's Fair, Square Deal; or the Duke of Dagger's Deadlock*. Characterization was simple and direct: "Silas Rogers was a man honest and upright after the fashion of frontiersmen. He was brave, and had shot two or three in brawls, but he was not regarded as quarrelsome." Style could be incredibly inflated. No one ever "went," but "traversed"; nothing was "named" but "derived its appellation." Dialogue could be excruciatingly bad. One pioneer scout, surprised by a sound in the forest, was given the line least likely to be spoken in the situation, "Hark, pard!" Two characters in another novel carried on this conversation after a mine slide:

"Are you hurt?"
"Who?"
"You."
"Me?"
"Yes."
"No."
"Oh!"

Most dime-novel dialogue, however, was set at the level of Bandit Burling Sharp's dying conversation with Scout Harold Tracy.

"Who fired? Who killed me?" cried the dying man. "Oh, God, it's too late!"

"Aye, too late," cried Harold Tracy. "I fired the bullet which found your life and I shall never regret the deed!"

"Oh had I but one minute more!" groaned the dying wretch, but he did not.

Not one present but felt as Trapper Ned, that Burling Sharp had met a just doom.

Whatever their shortcomings, dime-novel authors mastered the trick of catching attention. Colonel Prentiss Ingraham opened *Freelance the Pirate; or The Red Raiders of the Gulf* with blood and gunfire:

A rumbling cry of fury broke from the crew, and they hurled themselves on the captain while shots resounded through the cabin like thunderclaps. They were fired by a youth, and the bullets found the hearts of those they were aimed for, his two pistols spitting red in the dark, checking the rush of the maddened buccaneers.

"Freelance is dead!"

The cry came from the lips of the ringleader, as he rose to his feet, a drawn knife in his hand, stained crimson. . . .

Burke Brentford's *Rocky Mountain Sam; or The Windspecter of the Black Feet* emphasized ominous foreboding:

It was a wild and picturesque scene on the waters of the Upper Missouri; a wildly magnificent scene; and all bathed in the brilliant sunshine of a fresh spring morning; and yet in the midst of all the beauty and grandeur, a fearful tragedy was preparing. . . .

The writing could be uncomfortably vivid, and death was often gory. In one novel the hero stumbled on "the swollen, mutilated corpse of a man, covered with blood and clotted gore," noting that "the pain-distorted countenance was rendered doubly repulsive by the red streaks where mingled blood and brains had oozed from the shattered skull." Or death could be quick and casual, as when Young Wild West, after long pursuit, lassoed Buster Bill:

Straight up the street in the direction of the barracks rode Buster Bill.

And after him came Young Wild West, swinging his lasso. His companions remained well in the rear, knowing full well he could take care of the man.

Just as Buster Bill got in front of the barracks, Young Wild West let his lariat go.

It twisted through the air with a swishing noise and then settled about the neck of the border renegade.

Wild's well-trained horse came to a halt and braced himself.

Buster Bill was jerked from the saddle and landed in a heap on the ground.

"He won't get up," said Wild, as his friends rode up. "I heard his neck crack. It's a wonder his head was not yanked right off."

"It would have served him right," remarked Cheyenne Charlie. "Such a measly coyote as he is oughtn't to have a head on his shoulders, even after he is dead."

Twenty deaths per novel was not unusual, and the formula demanded at least one dangerous crisis per chapter. You began, said Robert Davis, who wrote dozens of Westerns for Street and Smith, with "a hero, a villain, dustbiting redskins, three Colts, thin air, and much desperado dialogue," and proceeded from there.

All laws of credibility were suspended, for dime-novel readers accepted anything. The cavalry was never late, the hero's gun never missed; Rocky Mountain Sam, at half a mile, once shot the flint and steel an Indian was about to use to light the torture fire right out of his hand. The Red, White, and Blue Series, for example, featured brothers on opposite sides of the Civil War (Phil Sterling for the South and Ralph Sterling for the North) on alternate weeks, until they finally discovered each other fighting side by side in the Boxer Rebellion. No one minded. Kit Carson, in his old age, on being shown the cover of a novel depicting him fighting off eight Indians with his right hand while protecting a fainting maiden with his left, adjusted his glasses, inspected the drawing, and remarked politely, "That there may have been the way it happened, but I don't recollect it."

The names of the best dime-novel authors, who wrote under their own and various others, were known to most boys and many adults across the land. Edward S. Ellis, the New Jersey schoolmaster who wrote *Seth Jones* for Beadle and Adams, wrote under at least seven pseudonyms; he also wrote a popular six-volume history of the United States (1896) that sold in the thousands. Captain Mayne Reid, an Irish adventurer who actually knew the West, was Beadle's highest paid writer for some years;

he received $750 for *The White Squaw,* or about double the normal rate for 55,000 words. Edward Wheeler, who wrote the Deadwood Dick series (the first masked rider, dressed in black), also wrote a series about Calamity Jane, another about Hurricane Nell, and others (he had an uncontrollable weakness for alliteration) about Sierra Sam, Nobby Nick, Corduroy Charlie, Rosebud Rob, High Hat Harry, and Blonde Bill.

Samuel S. Hall, who wrote as "Mayor Sam Hall" and "Buckskin Sam," created the great Diamond Dick (later written by George Jenks and others), Arizona Jack, Giant George, Desperate Duke, Rocky Mountain Al, and Nugget Hill. He also wrote semifictional accounts of real characters like Big Foot Wallace, Jim Bearfield, and Kit Carson. J. W. Musick wrote the James Boys; and Albert Aiken, who wrote a novel a week for twenty-one years, was responsible for Sol Ginger, The Giant Trapper; Injun Dick, Detective; and Lone Hand, The Shadow.

Colonel Prentiss Ingraham, the son of novelist Joseph Holt Ingraham, was even more prolific than his father. He knew Buffalo Bill Cody personally, and out of his seven hundred novels, devoted about two hundred to his friend. Thomas Harburgh did Kit Carson stories, a series about Navajo Dick, and mystery novels like *The Withered Hand.* Young Wild West, the most popular of the cowboy heroes except for Buffalo Bill, was written by various hands under the name of "Old Scout." Young West traveled with Cheyenne Charlie, "a government scout"; Jim Dart, "a Wyoming cowboy"; Ariette Murdock, his sweetheart; Eloise Gardner, Jim's sweetheart; and two comedy Chinese, Wing Wah and Hop Wah.

Edward Zane Carroll Judson, known as "Ned Buntline" and a dozen other names, was probably the king of them all. He wrote fewer novels than Ingraham (between three hundred and four hundred, and once under pressure a 610 page novel in sixty-two hours) but his colorful career eclipsed anything he wrote. He served in the Navy, won a reputation as a deadly duelist, went into the fur trade, edited magazines, wrote plays, and ground out novels. He spent a year in jail as one of the instigators of the Astor Place riots in New York in 1849, helped organize the viciously anti-Catholic and anti-foreign Know Nothing Party, was cashiered from the Army for drunkenness (claiming later to have been Grant's chief of scouts) and in the meantime founded his own magazine, *Ned Buntline's Own,* as a vehicle for lurid literature.

Twenty years before Beadle and Adams started, Judson was churning out cheap novels—one of the best known of all, *The Black Avenger of the Spanish Main,* Tom Sawyer's favorite—like *Magdalena, The Beautiful Mexican Maid; Stella De Lorme, or the Comanche's Dream;* and *The Gals of New York.* His great contribution to the dime novel was the Buffalo Bill story, and in a real sense, Buffalo Bill. Judson created the name and the character in *Buffalo Bill, King of the Border Men*, in 1869 after a brief talk with the then unknown Cody, who later adopted the costume and style of the dime-novel hero.

Buffalo Bill was undoubtedly the best known of all dime-novel Western heroes, of whom there were hundreds. Judson produced only fourteen Buffalo Bill novels, but practically every hack-writer of note had a hand in what became eventually the classic Western. Street and Smith, in fact, had a nickel weekly devoted to nothing but Buffalo Bill stories. There were many others like him, Comanche Bill, Young Scout Bill, Apache Charlie, Denver Dan, Prairie Sam, Buffalo Ned, Buffalo Ben, and so on, all cut to the same cloth, like Red River Bill, Prince of Scouts:

> A tall, spare figure, clothed in hunting costume, a face strikingly handsome, framed in heavy masses of chestnut hair that hung to his broad shoulders, the whole surmounted by a black felt hat from the crown of which drooped an ostrich feather. Two revolvers and a knife hung from his belt; he was indeed well armed, and apparently a man of steel nerve, as well as of great physical endurance.

Bill had several companions, but among the more popular were Wild Bill Hickok, "a veritable terror to bad men on the border," and Nick Wharton, "a redoubtable Indian fighter and hater of horse thieves." The emphasis was strictly on action:

> There was a wild, fierce yell, such as only Sioux throats could utter, as they leaped to their feet and made a dash toward him. Quick as was their movement, Bill had gained his feet ere the red devils gained the thicket. There was no time to use his Winchester, but the two six-shooters leaped from his belt, and the scout was soon surrounded by a sheet of flame as his deadly revolvers vomited leaden hail into the scarlet foe. The fight was short, sharp, and decisive, and was soon at an end, with seven scarlet bodies weltering in their blood under the midnight sky.

Although the Western strain in the dime novel never ran out, writers searched for alternatives to the prairie-Indian-scout formula and found one in the detective, probably inspired by the currently famous "Pinkerton men" of Allan Pinkerton's agency. George Munro introduced Old Sleuth to the public in 1885 and within the decade detectives began to outsell Westerns. The introduction of the detective into the dime novel opened up a whole new area of material—city low life—providing writers with a new arena of conflict between good and evil, a new kind of hero (presaged in Poe's Dupin) and a new set of adversaries for him.

The dime-novel detective story was not a mystery, but a cops-and-robbers story, intended to excite and entertain. There was never any doubt of who done it or why, and the question was simply *when* the criminals would be caught and punished. The reader knew from the first that the detective would escape the trap closed on him in the abandoned warehouse by Crime Queen Elmora, "a radiant creature with a jewelled stiletto," and her thirteen hired thugs. He read on to find out how.

Old Sleuth (written at first by Harlan Halsey) was actually a young detective who assumed the disguise of an old man; a master of masks, he never appeared as himself, or so the reader believed, in over six hundred novels covering his exploits. Norman Munro countered with Old Cap Collier, another master at disguise, in eight hundred novels. (Old Cap, in one novel, assumed eighteen different disguises, was shot at twelve times, won five fights against overwhelming odds, was apparently burned alive and blown up in a tunnel, and at the end captured twenty-one criminals in a shootout.) The New York Detective series reached eight hundred and so did Wheeler's Diamond Dick and Diamond Dick Junior. Frank Tousey's Old King Brady with his son Young King and (a daring innovation) Alice Montgomery, a pretty assistant, appeared in 1,374 novels.

Nick Carter solved more crimes (sometimes several in a single book), survived more desperate adventures, and captured more criminals than any other character in popular fiction. He appeared in 1886 in *The New York Weekly* (a year before Sherlock Holmes) as an apt pupil of his detective father, Old Sim Carter. Ormond Smith of Street and Smith invented the character and assigned it to John R. Coryell, one of his writers, but at least fifteen others contributed to the series which still survives in paperbacks and comic books to this day. The original series reached 1,500 titles, of which Frederick Van Rensselaer Dey claimed to have written about a thousand; although the number may be exaggerated, he and Coryell wrote the most.

What manner of man was the great detective?

Giants were like children in his grasp. He could fell an ox with one blow of his small, compact fist. Old Sim Carter had made the physical development of his son one of the studies of his life. Only one of the studies, however. Young Nick's mind was stored with knowledge—knowledge of a peculiar sort. His gray eye had, like an Indian's, been trained to take in minutest details fresh for use. His rich, full voice could run the gamut of sounds, from an old woman's broken, querulous squeak to the deep, hoarse notes of a burly ruffian. And his handsome face could, in an instant, be distorted into any one of a hundred types of unrecognizable ugliness. He was a master of disguise, and could so transform himself that even old Sim could not recognize him. And his intellect, naturally keen as a razor blade, had been incredibly sharpened by the judicious cultivation of the astute old man.

To assist him Nick had street-boy Chick, "a shock-headed ragged fellow, whose eyes shone with unusual brightness, with a face intelligent beyond his years, which could not have numbered beyond seventeen." (Years later, in the thirties, Nick would have a Filipino valet.) He also had bright little Patsy and Pedro the Dog Detective, "Nick Carter's Four-Footed Assistant." Together they foiled their perennial enemies, particularly the evil genius, Dr. Quartz:

> As powerful as a veritable giant; stronger even than the great detective himself; as keen as a razor; as quick as a flash; thoroughly educated; noted for his skill as a physician; as perfect and adept at disguises as Nick Carter; a scholar, and a man utterly without conscience or heart, he was one to whom even the keenest of all detectives—for Nick Carter had no peer—was forced to accord the old saying: "This is a foeman worthy of my steel."

Most criminals, however, simply gave up in despair when Nick confronted them:

> "Who—who are you?" ejaculated the fearstricken wretch.
> "Nick Carter."
> "Oh, Lord, I'm done for, then."
> Sharkey made a gesture of despair. Nick regarded him with cool satisfaction.

Nick never moralized, and neither he nor his brother sleuths ever instructed anybody about anything—except that it was useless to try to outwit, outfight, or outgun Nick Carter. Neither alienated knight-errant, nor lonely, troubled philosopher, Nick caught crooks because, as he said simply, "That is the profession I have followed."

The dime novel was absorbed by the comics, the movies, the magazines, and finally by paperbacks, radio, and television (Buffalo Bill and Nick Carter have appeared in all of them) which merely transferred the old cowboys-and-Indians and cops-and-robbers stories to different media. What the dime novels sold was entertainment—only that and no more—marketing vicarious thrills and a glorious counterfeit of life to millions of homebound country boys and anonymous city clerks.

Their heroes were self-reliant, resourceful, self-made men, whether frontier scouts, explorers, miners, pirates, detectives, or street urchins who rose to fame and fortune. They never whined and never gave up. They were plain, unsophisticated, "natural" men (some even illiterate) but unanimously virtuous, gentlemanly, and ethical by nature—cowboys, hunters, artisans, miners, policemen—with not an aristocratic dandy among them. (Nick Carter was an exceptional scholar, linguist, and scientist, but he wore his learning lightly and used it solely for professional purposes.) They represented the American ideal of democratic man, straight from Natty Bumppo to Gary Cooper's taciturn cowhands.

Dime-novel characters, plots, and style moved quickly into the pulp magazine, a relatively short-lived publishing phenomenon which served as a bridge between the popular novel of the nineteenth century and the magazine, paperback, and comic-book of the twentieth.

The pulp originated with Frank Munsey, who made *Argosy* into an adventure-story magazine in 1896 and printed it on rough woodpulp paper, making it eligible for second-class postal rates. Tousey, Street and Smith, and other publishers followed suit, so that the pulp magazine almost wholly supplanted the dime novel and the "story paper" before 1910. As it became standardized, the pulp was usually about 120 untrimmed pages, seven inches by ten, with a bright enameled color cover, carrying some advertising and selling for ten to twenty-five cents. Pulps were sold only at newsstands, never by subscription. During their best days—the late twenties and early thirties—they sold at the rate of twenty million per month.

Editors paid two cents a word for routine stories in the twenties (up to eight cents a word to their star writers) dropping to a cent a word in the late thirties. It took a professional to make a living at it. Harold Hersey, who spent thirty years as a pulp editor, once discussed the qualities a professional needed. Facility, of course, stood first, the ability to turn out quantities of material day in and day out, which also required rigid self-discipline. Second was consistency. In pulp-writing individuality was no virtue—a little, perhaps, but editors wanted the same product done in the same way time and again. The writer who got fancy most likely had to do it over. Third, the writer must have *limited* inventiveness; he could vary the standard plot elements a bit, but never enough to disturb the reader's expectations. Pulp readers, as Hersey put it, did not like to be surprised too much, for much of their pleasure came from anticipating correctly. Manufacturing daydreams for the millions, one had to be sure that the dream always came true. Top-liners like H. Bedford-Jones, Frank C. Robertson, Forbes Parkhill, W. C. Tuttle, and Allan Vaughan could repeat the formula expertly and endlessly.

Pulp stories were frankly mass production items, written to a rather rigid formula, never realistic, never disturbing, never disappointing. War could never be grim, a hero must never show fear, airplanes could never have accidents (though such might threaten), cowboy life had to be exciting, courtship must end in marriage.

Strong language was not allowed in the pulps, profanity never. Under stress of combat a soldier might say "Cripes!" but not "Gee!" or "Geez!" since that could be interpreted as blasphemy. *Western Story,* in its entire history, never once printed "Damn." Since no writer could be expert in all fields, writers exchanged information through a trade journal which printed glossaries of sea terms, airplane nomenclature, prison jargon, boxing rules, jockey terms, Hawaiian geography, ranch vocabulary, Spanish phrases (for cowboys), and the like. A New York writer who had never been west of Jersey City could therefore write westerns, while a Chicagoan who had never seen the Atlantic could write sea-stories.

Argosy, the most successful of the early pulps, claimed a half-million sales per issue in 1910. Munsey's *All-Story,* probably the next most popular, printed a few love stories to attract a wider audience, but stayed primarily with adventure. Street and Smith's *Popular Magazine* charged fifteen cents and expanded to 224 pages; *Monthly Story Magazine* and Munsey's *Cavalier* copied *Argosy's* format. Munsey's experimental pulp, *The Scrap Book* (1906) appeared in two simultaneous but different issues at two for a quarter, but later shifted to a single ten-cent pulp.

By 1915 there were about two dozen pulp magazines, most of them running general adventure stories, but in the early twenties Street and Smith established three new specialized magazines, *Love Story* (1921), *Detective Story* (1915), and *Western Story* (1919). These four categories remained standard until the pulps died out in the forties. Westerns were the most popular; there were thirty-two of them for sale in 1930, with names like *Lariat, Triple X, All-Western, Far West,* and *Golden West.* Butterick's *Adventure,* for example, in 1929 carried about one-third Westerns.

The Western formula called for a picaresque adventurer (usually a drifting cowhand with a buddy as a foil) who roved the West encountering Indians, rustlers, outlaws, raiders, sheriffs, and the like. W. Bert Foster wrote over a hundred stories about Homer of the Lazy D and his sidekick Poke Fellows; Allan Bosworth wrote two hundred about a muleskinner named Shorty Masters; Ray Nafziger wrote a long series about the Hooker Brothers of Canyon Lobo; H. H. Knibbs' Young Hardesty and his companions Bedrock and Bordan were familiar figures to thousands of pulp readers.

Gunfighter and range stories were popular; no Western pulp could sell without at least one dangerously quiet gunman, dressed in black, his right hand tanned and ungloved, stalking bad men. W. C. Tuttle's Cultus Collins was a good representative of the breed:

> Collins was several inches over six feet in height, bronzed as an Indian, with a long, gaunt face. Men said that he had the face of a gargoyle and the smile of a saint. He was long of arm, bony of wrist, and big of hand. His faded shirt seemed molded to his muscular torso. His huge bat-wing chaps were weathered and patched, as were his belt and holster; and the big black Colt in his holster was shiny from use. His horse, a tall, gaunt, smoke-grey animal with a snakelike head, walked with a swinging walk; a tireless, venomous-looking brute, which Cultus called "Amigo." They were well-known along the border, these two, and more than once had a price been placed on the head of Cultus Collins.

Although a few pulps rose above the hack-writer level, most of them were stock-formula dime-novel stories, marginally classifiable as Westerns chiefly because they used a few cowboy terms, some Spanish, and mentioned cows, horses, and guns.

Next most popular were love-pulps like *Real Love, Pocket Love, True Love, Thrilling Love, Love Romances, Sweetheart Stories,* and so on. (There were even *Ranch Romances* and *Western Love.*) Their stories were not about love, but about marriage. Many of their plots were stolen directly from the nineteenth-century domestic novels; Amita Fairgreave, who created *Love Story* for Street and Smith, read stacks of them before fashioning her magazine. The heroines were usually girls in their late teens or early twenties in noncareer jobs—stenographers, waitresses, clerks, maids, secretaries—from middle-class homes. In the rules laid down by the editor of one love magazine, the heroine was to be pretty, between eighteen and twenty-four, earning her own living, pure in thought and deed; she could not use tobacco or touch alcohol in any form, must not have a college education, allow kisses from anyone other than her parents or fiancé, or dress immodestly. The stories were aimed wholly at women, to show, one editor said, "Men as women wish they were, girls as they'd like to be, and stories you'd like to live," or, as an author commented, "to put in them what my maid misses in life."

The goal of each love story was husband, home, and security; the central question was, how do I find the right man, and what kind of man should he be? The right man, pulp authors agreed, undoubtedly had plenty of flaws, but he was kind, honest, and a good provider. He usually came from the upper levels of blue-collar employment, though not always. There was little "rich-boy-marries-poor-girl" or "clerk-marries-boss," which, attractive as the prospect was, the pulp audience knew was simply not credible. Basically, the message of the love-pulp to girls was work, wait, discriminate, keep control, and you should someday find security, stability, and possibly "romance."

Love-pulp stories did not differ essentially from what the girls' grandmothers read, except that they were shorter. They dealt almost wholly with courtship, ending in marriage or the guarantee thereof. Nor was courtship a matter of love; it involved strategy, manipulation, planning. The stories rested on the assumption that men were large and rather dangerous children, to be handled as such. It took wit, care, and perception to bring the affair to the right conclusion.

Each story had certain standard scenes and situations: the meeting in which boy discovers girl by accident or design; the quarrel and reconciliation; the threat of a less virtuous rival; the admission of male stupidity, insensitivity, or inferiority. (One editor demanded at least one scene in which the girl slapped the man's face, on the assumption, apparently correct, that every woman secretly desired to do exactly that.) Central to the story was the scene of female virtue tested by male impatience, the age-old feminine problem of how to maintain the promise without too early fulfillment. The girl always found ways, leading to a satisfactory if sometimes inarticulate proposal:

> Susan turned as he entered the door, and her heart gave a great leap, for she knew why he had come. She was wise, suddenly, in every woman's wisdom since time began.
> "Hello," he said.
> "Hello," she said.
> He stood there, uncertain, an odd shyness on his face, his hand plucking nervously at his coat, strong hands, yet capable of gentleness. The way his hair curled tugged at her heart. How like a little boy, she thought, and smiled secretly to herself.
> "I came . . . ," he said falteringly.
> She turned away and waited.
> "Yes?" she said.
> "I came to tell you . . . ," he said, but the words would not come.
> She turned toward him, and saw the glad relief and joy in his eyes as he started to her.
> She opened her arms to him.
> "Harold," she said.

In their heyday, the early thirties, two dozen or so love-pulps sold perhaps thirty million copies a year. Like other pulps, they were stiffly

virtuous; a study made in the thirties showed that they were more conservative in their morality than most of the quality magazines on such
things as sex out of wedlock, immodesty of dress, child discipline, money
matters, and the like, reflecting generations of Sunday-school lessons.

On the other hand, some publishers took advantage of the postwar
frankness about sex to introduce a different kind of pulp, the "snappy"
magazine that titillated without offending. "Snappy" did not mean obscene; it meant sex with a light touch, suggestive rather than explicit, as
the names of the magazines implied—*Snappy Stories, Spicy Stories, Saucy
Stories, La Parisienne* (the latter two published by no less than George
Jean Nathan and H. L. Mencken) and even one called *Spicy Western*—
none of them having much to do with love, as the love-pulps did, and
less with marriage.

After the Western and love-story pulps, the next most popular varieties were adventure and detective stories. The first lived on action—sea,
air, land, jungle, war, sport, exploration, hunting, fishing, history, or
whatever. *Argosy, Blue Book, Adventure,* and others used action stories
of any kind, but specialized pulps appeared in the twenties, among them
Sea Stories, Sport Stories, Air War, Flying Aces, Battle Stories, and *Spy
Stories.* The detective-pulp worked to a strict formula, allowing no humor, an infallible sleuth, at least one surprise gimmick, and a crook or
crooks with absolutely no redeeming qualities. The most common crime
was murder, the next theft; other crimes appeared infrequently as corol-
laries to the commission of the two most important.

The greatest of the crime fighters was Doc Savage (excepting Nick
Carter, who had a pulp of his own) who mixed adventure and fantasy
with his work. A strong, handsome, bronzed god with "strange, gold-
flaked eyes," the mind of a genius, and near-supernatural powers, Doc
had the help of Lt. Col. "Monk" Mayfair (the world's most brilliant
chemist), Major "Long Tom" Robert (the world's finest electrical expert), Colonel John Raymond (an engineering wizard), and General
"Ham" Brooks (America's best lawyer and best-dressed man). *Doc Savage* pulps sold 250,000 copies per month, and the publishers would send,
on request, the Doc Savage Plan of Living, "to build you up physically,
mentally, and morally . . . , for bigger things in life."

The Shadow, "mysterious avenger of crime and injustice," appeared
in nearly three hundred pulps, written mostly by "Maxwell Grant,"
Walter Gibson's pseudonym. Gibson turned out between twenty-four and
twenty-eight "Shadow" novels a year for seven years, then a novel a
month for the next eight, capturing the imagination of hundreds of thousands of readers, and of millions more in the radio version. Only The

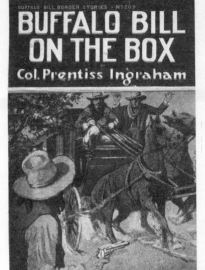

Two dime novel covers.
CULVER PICTURES, INC.

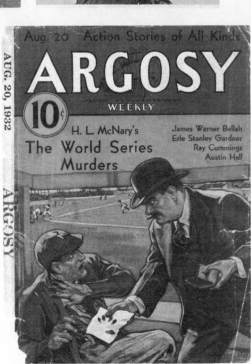

A 1932 issue of *Argosy*.
CULVER PICTURES, INC.

Four kinds of pulp magazines, 1930–1945.

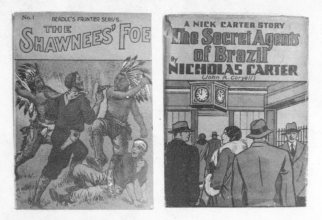

The evolution of the comic book cover: from a Beadle dime novel (circa 1875) to a Nick Carter hardcover detective jacket (circa 1900) to a World War II comic book, culminating in the Dali-influenced Nick Fury (Marvel Comics, 1969).

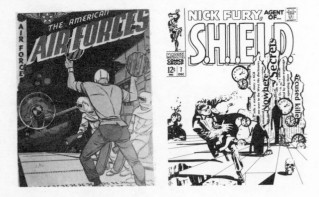

Shadow "knew the Evil that lurks within the hearts of men," and The Avenger and The Whisperer, pale imitations that sought to capitalize on the popularity of the original, were never serious rivals.

The Shadow appeared almost simultaneously in radio and in Street and Smith's pulp magazine in 1931. The radio series, originally written by Harry Charlot, was continued after his death by a number of writers. Though Walter Gibson and the radio writers borrowed frequently from each other, there were differences; the radio series, for example, introduced Margot Lane, the Shadow's constant "friend and companion" and a number of other characters who might appear in the novels. When Orson Welles, then only twenty-two, took over the radio part, the program became one of the air's prime favorites.

A famous aviator named Kent Allard, The Shadow used the identity of Lamont Cranston, a wealthy lawyer, as his cover in a relentless war on crime—a fact known only to his faithful Xinca Indian servants and his readers. He also disguised himself as the police-station janitor, and as Henry Arnaud, another mysterious figure. The Shadow, who wore a bat-like black cloak and a black hat, cracked crimes the police could not. He possessed the power of surrounding himself with darkness, and his "bloodchilling laugh," accompanied by two red-lit eyes glowing out of the dark, unhinged crooks and destroyed their will to resist. (In case they recovered too soon, The Shadow also carried four pistols.) In his entourage of crime-fighters were assistants Cliff, Hawkeye, and Harry; a reporter named Clyde Burke; cabdriver Moe Shrevnitz; Rutledge Mann, an insurance agent; and Burbank, who relayed messages from a secret communications center somewhere in Manhattan.

The pulp market reached its peak in the mid-thirties, when about two hundred pulps sold to an audience of more than ten million per issue. Clayton, Street and Smith, Doubleday-Page, Munsey, Butterick, Fiction House, and other publishers shipped them out in freight cars all over the country. Increased paper and production costs in the forties hit them hard; radio, television, and paperback books finished them off. Even as they died, however, another form of popular fiction took their place—the comic book, derived from the comic strip, which had developed to maturity a generation earlier.

FUN IN FOUR COLORS:
THE COMICS

*Are people's eyes to be debauched and diseased weekly, if not daily, by
these crude, discordant, ugly washes and messes of the cheapest colored
inks?*

—QUERY TO *The North American Review*, 1920

Narratives told by pictures, of course, are older than printing, but the
comic strip in its modern form originated in the cartoon sequences of late
nineteenth-century Europe. The Swiss cartoonist Rodolphe Töpfer drew
the adventures of M. Vieuxhois, M. Cryptogramme, and M. Jabot in 1846;
Wilhelm Busch's "Max und Moritz" dealt with the adventures of two
young German rascals in the 1880's; Georges Colomb drew the "Fenouil-
lard Family" in France during the 90's; W. F. Thomas created Weary
Willie and Tired Tim, two English tramps, at about the same time. In
the United States the appearance of magazines like *Judge* (1881), *Life*
(1883), and *Puck* (1887) stimulated interest in cartooning and provided
training for Americans. By the 1890's all the essential elements of the
comic "strip"—a narrative told by a sequence of related drawings containing the necessary dialogue to advance the action—were present, and
well advanced, in the United States.

The first American newspaper comic strip to be published on a regular basis was probably James Swinnerton's animal cartoon, "Little Bears
and Tigers," which ran in the San Francisco *Examiner* during 1892. Cartooning received its first great impetus, however, from the circulation
battle between Joseph Pulitzer's New York *World* and William Randolph
Hearst's New York *Journal* in 1895. Pulitzer, who introduced color printing as a circulation-getter, gave over a page of the Sunday issue to a staff
cartoonist, Richard Outcault, who drew a series about city slum life in

paper was a family reading project, involving children,
d adults, comics hopefully had to appeal to all of them.
ingle strip could do so; what a newspaper needed was a
several strips, each designed to attract different age and

seph Medill Patterson, who with his cousin Colonel Rob-
made comics a great circulation device at the Chicago
ed the New York market with a new tabloid, *The Daily*
Among his innovations at the new paper was a comic
ith the day-to-day life of an average (more or less) fam-
readers of all ages could identify. Patterson and McCor-
wd judges of their readers' tastes, were the first to recog-
comics had become—an integral part of the daily lives of
ple, reflecting their interests, dreams, and ideals. People
bout people like themselves, and they also liked reading
ot like themselves; the comics offered them the familiar
ected, reassurance and escape, pleasure and adventure.
McCormick saw to it that the comics, one way or another,
for everybody.
ly" strip, pioneered by Hershfield, caught on first. Sydney
s," first drawn in 1917, soon had an audience of millions.
her a good draftsman nor a good storyteller, but somehow
got across to the great mass of comic readers: Andy, not
htly pompous, chinless, a kind but bumbling husband and
is plain and practical wife; Uncle Bim, the eccentric mil-
g Chester, Andy's bright, stubbornly independent boy.
soon brought Fisher a contract of $100,000 a year for ten
ard-of price for a comic strip, which McCormick increased
year when he renewed it in the thirties. Gus Edson, who
isher's death in 1935, continued the strip until 1959, but it
lost its original appeal.
ng's "Gasoline Alley," begun in 1919, is the longest-lived
omics. It started as a strip about automobiles, that great
n for American families in the twenties, but in 1921 King
a narrative about the suburban family life of Walt Wallett,
s, and their adopted son Skeezix. King, in an inspired mo-
to let his characters age in natural chronological time,
ree of reader identification granted to no other strip. The
and the readers' families grew together; parents grew
grew up and married and had children of their own, boys
nd girls waited for them, while each generation recapitu-

places like "Hogan's Alley," "McGoogan's Alley," or "Casey's Alley," featuring in each a bald, gap-toothed, gamin dressed in a flour sack which, because of a mistake in inking, turned out a brilliant yellow. The appearance of "The Yellow Kid" on February 16, 1896, marked the real beginning of the comic strip.

The tough, vulgar Kid was a lucky hit. What Outcault drew was actually not a strip but a chaotic panel, filled with action, gags, puns, signs, and dialogue, with The Kid as a day-to-day continuing character. His grade of humor was relatively low (The Kid, on his first auto ride, exclaims, "Gee, dis beats de carpet, which is hard to beat!") and his drawing was crude. But The Yellow Kid was so popular that Hearst bought a color press and hired Outcault away from the *World*. Pulitzer bought him back, and after further offers and counteroffers Outcault stayed with the *World* to do another strip, "Buster Brown," about a mischievous boy and his faithful dog, so popular that parents bought Buster Brown shoes, clothes, toys, caps and the like for their children for years.

The Hearst-Pulitzer struggle made newspaper publishers acutely aware of the effects of comics on circulation. Hearst also hired Rudolph Dirks to draw a series about two German scamps (modeled on "Max und Moritz") named Hans and Fritz, or "The Katzenjammer Kids," which appeared in the *Journal* in 1897. 1899 brought another extraordinary character, Happy Hooligan, drawn by F. (Frederick Burr) Opper. These three—The Yellow Kid, The Katzenjammer Kids, and Happy Hooligan—opened the first great era of the comic strip. By 1900 cartoonists had fixed its traditional pattern, that is, the sequential narrative, the daily joke, the balloon for dialogue (making the words a part of the drawing rather than merely a caption) and had established its most important element, the central character or set of characters on whom continuity depended.

Outcault's "Yellow Kid" was an earthy, rough cartoon, rooted in rowdy humor; "Buster Brown" (1902) aimed at a higher level of sophistication but retained a good deal of Outcault's sardonic, nose-thumbing style. The Katzenjammer Kids (in German, "cat-yowling"), a pair of utter rebels against the authority of Der Captain, Mamma, and the world at large, left a trail of destruction behind them; their motto, "Society iss nix," expressed the mood of their daily assaults on law, order, and logic. Philosophical Mamma, however, tolerated their outrages, remarking that "Kindness mit kidlets iss der pinochle of life." Even the Captain, tormented beyond endurance by the devilish Kids, felt in rare moments of peace that "Ven all iss done and said dere ain't no dodrotted place like home." Hooligan, an amiable, gentle boob, was everybody's target. His tin-can hat, ragged pants, and sadly suffering smile were soon as familiar to the public as Chaplin's Little Tramp. Opper, a man of amazing inventiveness, later drew "Maud the Mule," a mean and independent creature who always got in the last kick, and "Alphonse and Gaston," two super-polite Frenchmen whose exaggerated manners led to insane disasters.

Charles Kahles' "Sandy Highflyer" (1903) concerned the adventures of a boy with a balloon, a forerunner of the next generation's air-adventure strips. (Kahles later drew "Hairbreadth Harry," a burlesque of stage and film melodrama.) Bud Fisher's "A. Mutt," (1907) a racetrack tout, met his short friend Jeff in 1908. The San Francisco *Examiner* printed "Mutt and Jeff" in a strip across the page, making it literally the first comic strip to last, though Clare Briggs briefly drew "A. Piker Clerk" in strip form for the Chicago *American* in 1904. Fisher's drawing and his humor were undistinguished; he drew his materials from burlesque, racetracks, pool halls, and joke books, but the pompous, girl-chasing little man with the top hat, and the big, dumb, friendly dupe with the checkered vest were lasting character creations. (Al Smith, who continued the strip after Fisher's death in 1954, followed the spirit of the original admirably.)

Winsor McKay, a talented artist, began his curiously imaginative fantasy, "Little Nemo," in 1905, concerning a small boy who each night entered Slumberland, a strange world with its own geography, history, and cast of characters like Flip the Dwarf, the Beautiful Princess, and Impy the Cannibal. "Little Nemo" (which McKay dropped after six years) was neither strip nor comic, but a beautifully-drawn dream adventure.

Harry Hershfield's "Abie the Agent" (1910) was the first to use ethnic humor (although it was common on the stage) in the person of a Jewish businessman, his wife Reba, and his fellow-competitors. Done with wit and good humor, "Abie" was a bundle of comic Jewish traits; he was also a gentle, warmhearted man, a useful citizen, and a constant puzzle to his *macher* wife Reba. Adult in concept and execution, Hershfield's was the first distinguished "family" strip, a type that bloomed in the twenties and thirties.

George Herriman in 1910 drew a strip in which a mouse picked up a stone and hit a cat. A year later he started "Krazy Kat" on a thirty-five year career. Still considered by its devotees as the best ever drawn, Herriman's strip featured Krazy, a gentle, sentimental dupe, and Ignatz the Mouse, a pugnacious, cynical, sharp-faced little con man who threw a brick with unerring aim. Offissa B. Pupp, a well-meaning but ineffectual policeman, vainly tried to keep order in and make sense out of Herriman's wild world, one that included not only mice who threw bricks at cats, but characters like Joe Bark, Mock Duck, Kristopher Kamel, Don

Koyote, the aristocratic Bum
Krazy, who had a touch of th
strange language (which poe
his epitaph for a day that went

My kittil of sou
My Kendill ha
The Dippest p
Is where I otta

Herriman's strip was a st
illogical love, exemplified by K
on a dark night and sang him
Krazy loved the world; Offissa
His answer to it all was the co
garde draftsmanship was a gr
the Arizona landscape, which
backdrop for Ignatz' eternal re

George McManus's "Bring
continuation of the comic as p
pow-zowie situation humor. H
forty-one years) concerned a n
and their adventures in high an
the continuing human conflict
ness, sincerity and falsity, den
Jiggs, the vulgar husband who
sive chord in male hearts ev
women readers.) His favorite
bage, which he preferred to al
in Mexico, choucroute in Fra
Manus never worked well with
line; he did best with a gag a
into a number of languages, "B
strip to gain an international aud

Syndication, which came t
Mass-distributed to audiences
ever the syndicates could sell t
the King Features Syndicate, th
Press's United Features domina
Naught came later. Naturally, s
part of their mass audience, w
tremes and aim at the largest c

Since the new
adolescents, a
Obviously no
combination o
interest groups

Captain J
ert McCormic
Tribune, inva
News, in 191
strip dealing
ily with which
mick, both shr
nize what the
millions of pe
liked reading
about people
and the unex
Patterson and
had something

The "fam
Fisher's "Gum
Fisher was ne
his characters
too bright, sli
father; Min,
lionaire; your
"The Gumps"
years, an unh
to $150,000 a
took over at
had long since

Frank Ki
of all family
new acquisiti
changed it to
his wife Phyl
ment, decide
gaining a de
Wallett fami
older, childre
were drafted

lated the average experience of the average family. Skeezix, who was left on Walt's doorstep in 1921, served in World War II and in 1969 worried about his own son in Viet Nam.

Other family strips appeared, some to last, many to disappear. Jimmy Murphy's "Toots and Casper" (1918), a family-style comedy strip, first introduced the likeable boob husband, the bright, cute wife, and the mischievous child. Emphasizing the comic aspects of family life, Murphy inspired a number of other strips, as well as family comedies on radio and in the movies. Sol Hess and W. A. Carlson drew "The Nebbs," (1923) with a cast of well-conceived characters, including Rudy, the optimist, and his friend Max, the wet blanket. Henry Tuthill's "Bungle Family," another twenties strip, was intelligently plotted, well drawn, and wryly humorous. Bungle, the world's most well intentioned man, constantly victimized by luck, weather, and woman, was a solid character creation.

Buster Brown and the Katzenjammers, the pioneer "kid strips," had their own descendants. Percy Crosby's "Skippy," the earliest of them, was also the best. Skippy, an insouciant, shrewd, sloppy kid with drooping socks and a checkered hat, had his own personal contest with the world and usually managed to outwit it by persistence and ingenuity. Crosby, an artist of repute (who had one-man shows in New York, Paris, and London) gave his strips a genuinely poetic quality matched by no other of his generation; old Skippy strips still excite professional admiration.

Walter Berndt's "Smitty" (1922) moved through adolescence and manhood into a family-life story; so did Merrill Blosser's "Freckles and his Friends." R. M. Brinkerhoff's "Little Mary Mixup" (1918) was among the first of the mischievous-little-girl comics; Gene Byrnes' "Reglar Fellers" and Ad Carter's "Just Kids" belonged with the "Peck's Bad Boy," "Tom Sawyer," and James Whitcomb Riley tradition of sentimentalized boyhood. Carl Anderson's "Henry" and Hank Ketcham's "Dennis the Menace" brought the type into the fifties and sixties.

The most durable and controversial of the "kid" comics was Harold Gray's "Little Orphan Annie," born in 1924 with her dog Sandy ("Arf, Arf!") and her fabulous billionaire guardian, Daddy Warbucks, who helped Annie win (as she always does) her continuous battle against a threatening society. Annie, more than a kid-adventure strip, served from its inception as an allegory of virtue versus wickedness, played out by Annie and her unbelievably good allies in conflict with her unbelievably bad enemies—crooks, Nazis, Orientals, hippies, socialists, bleeding-heart liberals, silly social workers, corrupt politicians and cops, and so on.

What Annie strives to protect is an America based on honesty, hard work, and old-fashioned morality; what threatens it is deceit, irresponsibility, corruption. The society that Gray's strip projects is modeled on Andrew Carnegie, the Social Gospel, and the Stewardship of Wealth; and there is always in the strip a nostalgic desire for the good old days of nineteenth-century, free-enterprise capitalism. In the ideology of the strip, decent people must constantly be on guard against a viciously irresponsible underground that wants to subvert and overthrow American society; Annie, a combination of Red Riding Hood and Horatio Alger, stands always in their way. Gray's strip has been extravagantly damned and praised since 1924, depending on the critic's political coloration, but it endures.

A third variety, the "girl strip," clearly belonged to the years after World War I when young women went to college, took jobs, shared apartments, and began to vote. All the new girl strips centered on an attractive, intelligent, independent girl who dramatized the changed role of young women in American society. Cliff Sterrett's "Polly and Her Pals," which came out slightly before the War, supplied a model for others to follow. Polly, a stylish, pretty girl with a mind of her own, was a constant source of trouble for Paw, who could not understand modern youth, and Maw, who understood her daughter but could not cope with her. Over the years "Polly" changed into a family-life strip, but she was the original "modern" girl.

There were many like her in the twenties. Winnie Winkle, drawn by Martin Branner, worked in an office to support her family—Pa, a pleasant bum; her old-fashioned mother; bright little brother Perry. Winnie's problems reflected those of thousands of typists, file clerks, and salesgirls who brought home their paychecks and held things together. (Later "Winnie," however, turned into a family-style strip). "Tillie the Toiler," Russ Westover's career girl strip, was more amusing than "Winnie." In it Westover set up the triangle later familiar in radio, movies, and television; that is, attractive girl, irascible boss, and comic boyfriend—in this case Mac, a born loser, who pursued Tillie with doglike devotion for forty years and always set a place for her at his lonely bachelor table, just in case. Tillie's problems were never very serious. To her living was fun, the world a happy place, and there was always Mac, hanging around. Westover dressed her in the latest and most tasteful styles, so that girls watched the strip carefully for fashion hints.

Charles Voight's "Betty," the most glamorous of the girls, was a leggy, shapely beauty, vainly pursued by Lester DePester, a comic shortstuff suitor. Edgar Martin's Boots, of "Boots and Her Buddies," originally a "flaming youth" flapper type, turned into a responsible young career girl, married, had children, and became the center of a family-life strip.

J. P. McEvoy's "Dixie Dugan," a showgirl in her early years, became a career girl too. Chic Young's "Dumb Dora" (who preceded his Blondie) was a fluffy flapper later drawn by Paul Fung. Larry Whittington (later Ernie Bushmiller) drew "Fritzi Ritz" a doll-faced, empty-headed flapper with a small niece Nancy, who in the forties took over the strip with Fritzi making only occasional appearances.

There were others, of course—Parker's "Flapper Fanny," Brewerton's "Pam," Jensen's "Syncopating Sue"—most of which lasted only so long as the bobbed-hair, Charleston, rolled-stocking set interested the public. For high-schoolers who met at the soda fountain there was Carl Ed's "Harold Teen" and his circle, the first of the strips to recognize teen-agers as a social group with its own style. As the raccoon coat phenomenon died out, Ed shifted his strip's focus toward family life. Another popular strip aimed at the same age group was Paul Robinson's "Etta Kett," which emphasized fashions, fads, parties, and young love.

Frank Willard's "Moon Mullins" (later drawn by Ferd Johnson) was a throwback to the raffish, pratfall humor of the first generation of cartoonists. Moon, a boastful poolroom hanger-on; Kayo, his roughneck little brother; Uncle Willie the bum; Lord Plushbottom the silly-ass Englishman; Emmy the ugly spinster; and Mamie the slatternly maid came out of burlesque and one-reeler movie comedies. Drawn with good-humored vitality and earthiness, Moon and his friends appealed to an audience that found nothing of interest in Tillie, Winnie, or Skeezix.

Two of the twenties' greater cartoon creations derived from the multi-leveled fantasy tradition of Herriman and the low-life tradition of Outcault and Opper—Elzie Segar's "Thimble Theater" (1919) and Billy DeBeck's "Barney Google" (1918). Segar's strip was unusual in that it was presented as a one act play, based on a single incident, presented on a stage with a curtain and a playbill. Its continuity over the first ten years depended on the Oyl family and its adventures, done in broad slapstick with added supporting characters like Fadewell the gambler and Berenice the Whiffle-Hen, the earliest of Segar's outlandish animals. The tone of the strip changed in January, 1929, with the introduction of Popeye, a blunt, affable sailor man who solved the problems of the Oyls, and of the world in general, with his heart and fists. After that "Thimble Theater" became primarily a tongue-in-cheek vehicle for the legendary adventures of Popeye, his unlovely sweetheart Olive Oyl, and his hamburger-loving friend Wimpy.

Segar's uninhibited imagination produced wildly unreal animals and people by the score, among them The Goon and The Jeep (which ate orchids and told only the truth), and he made spinach, the source of Popeye's fabulous strength, a national dish. (There is a statue to Popeye in the heart of Texas spinach country, and a hamburger is still known in England as a wimpy.) Drawn after Segar's death with great skill and imaginativeness by Bela Zaboly and others, Popeye stands with Tarzan and Mickey Mouse among the world's best-known comic creations.

Barney Google, DeBeck's little tinhorn gambler with the derby hat and saucer eyes, represented the sharper who was never quite sharp enough, the con man who never quite made it pay. The owner of Spark Plug, an outrageous horse who never won races; the suitor of Sweet Mama, who demanded always more money; and the possessor of a troublesome ostrich named Rudy, Google lived in perpetual crisis, always on the edge of disaster. In his confused world nothing held together for very long, and what attracted readers to DeBeck's strip was Barney's cheerful, persistent belief he could somehow, someday, bring it under control.

A rowdy, good-natured strip, continued after DeBeck's death by Fred Lasswell, "Barney" was eventually taken over by Snuffy Smith, a hillbilly character who entered it in 1934 and enriched the language with "jughaid," "shiftless skonk," "tetched in the haid," and that notable contribution to World War II, "yardbird." The modern strip closest to the old DeBeck and Segar tradition is Bill Holman's "Smoky Stover," a fireman who provides continuity for a stream of lunatic gags, outlandish puns, and wildly meaningless slogans. Holman's is one of the last and best of the old-style gag strips.

At the close of the twenties, the comic strip had found its final form. Cartoonists had perfected its continuity, improved the quality of its draftsmanship and story line, and introduced into it strong documentary, realistic elements. Its growing trend toward realism, both in drawing and narrative, to a large extent reflected the influence of the movies; more sophisticated strips cut from scene to scene, serialized the action in episodes, and used long shots, closeups, varied camera angles, and other cinematic techniques. While old-timers like McManus, Fisher, DeBeck, and Smith held their audiences with old-fashioned cartooning, the superior skills displayed by men like Crosby, Voight, and John Strieble (who drew "Dixie Dugan") indicated the changing nature of the business. It is doubtful if Sidney Smith's "Gumps" could have survived at all had it been introduced in the thirties.

The trends established in the twenties continued into the thirties, which turned out to be the golden years for comics. Chic Young's "Blondie" appeared in 1930 as a dizzy blonde, but in 1933, when she married her well-meaning, clumsy suitor Dagwood Bumstead, Young changed it into a family strip, the most popular of its kind ever to be drawn. The Bumsteads became the paradigm of The Great American Family—bumbling, well-meaning husband; efficient, sexy wife; irascible, driving boss; shrewd, quick-witted children; and all the pets, neighbors, postmen, clerks, mechanics, grocers, and door-to-door salesmen that baffle and bully the man of the house. Young's story line is simple and witty; his humor smacks of Laurel and Hardy and Harold Lloyd; his drawing is sprightly and clever. The most widely syndicated of all comics (more than 1600 newspapers), "Blondie" has already served as a movie series (forty pictures), a radio series, and a television series.

"Blondie" was, of course, a skillful refinement of a type already popularized in the twenties. Three new types of comics, however, did appear in the thirties: the adventure strip, the police-detective strip, and the satire-strip.

Roy Crane's "Wash Tubbs," featuring an amusing little fellow with wide eyes and a bow tie who fell into amusing and occasionally exciting adventures, commenced in 1924. The entry of Captain Easy, a handsome, resourceful soldier of fortune, however, changed the nature of the narrative; when Crane sent Easy and Wash on mysterious assignments that involved attractive women, dangerous villains, and exotic locales, he made it into a straight adventure strip. A superb draftsman, Crane used movie techniques with great skill and rather daringly introduced sex as a natural ingredient of the plot. When Crane dropped "Wash" to draw "Buz Sawyer," a similar strip, in 1943, Leslie Turner took it over.

Five years after "Wash Tubbs" appeared, Harold Foster transferred Tarzan to the comic page, done like Crane's strip with excellent drawing and sophisticated cinematic technique. "Tarzan" soon became the most popular adventure comic of the times; taken over by Bruce Hogarth and others after 1936, it maintained its position for years. "Buck Rogers" (drawn by Dick Calkins and written by Philip Nolan) also appeared in 1929, the first to adapt science-fiction themes to the comics. Buck, an Air Force officer transplanted into the twenty-fifth century (as he was in radio) engaged the gangster Killer Kane in a running battle for mastery of the universe, thus transferring the old dime-novel formula to space. Crane, Foster, and Calkins, by emphasizing action, draftsmanship, and movie-serial narrative, furnished the pattern for the adventure comic strip for years to come.

Milton Caniff's "Terry and the Pirates," begun in 1934, attracted more imitators than any other comic strip in history. Caniff put together Crane's adventure-sex-"male mag" formula with the exotic locales of "Tarzan," the movie serial's strong story line, and a handsome adventurer,

Pat Ryan. Then in 1937 he boldly sent his characters to the current Chinese-Japanese War, the first major comic to follow the headlines.

Caniff's drawing was superb and his narrative literate and sophisticated, but his great talent lay in characterization, especially of women. Readers never forgot The Dragon Lady, the most beautiful and dangerous villainess in comic history; pretty, tragic Normandie, trapped between her love for her husband and her attraction to young Pat Ryan; fresh-eyed April Kane, forever the sorority girl; Lieutenant Taffy Tucker, an efficient, intelligent, and very sexy WAC; mysterious, unpredictable Burma; or sensual, untrustworthy Rouge. What went on in the daily strip was exciting enough; the implications of what went on between strips was even more interesting. When his contract expired in 1947 Caniff created Steve Canyon, whose picaresque life involved beauties of similar potentialities—Madame Lynx, Princess Snowflower, Herself Muldoon, Feeta-Feeta. Caniff's strips, in their choice of story line, narrative technique, draftsmanship, and their unobtrusive but effective use of sex, influenced adventure comics for thirty years.

A second influential strip out of the thirties was Chester Gould's "Dick Tracy," suggested by Captain Patterson as a way of capitalizing on the drama of the gangster era, when Pretty Boy Floyd, Dillinger, Big Al, and the FBI were in the news, the "private-eye" stories of the *Black Mask* school were popular in magazines and movies, and the crusading D. A. appeared nightly on radio. Begun in 1931, "Tracy" marked the first appearance in the comics of real violence, although the dime-novel and the pulp had dealt in it for years. Gould kept guns and gore at a reasonable level but nonetheless his narratives had violent overtones.

Intended at first as a semiburlesque (as "Hawkshaw The Detective" burlesqued Sherlock Holmes) "Tracy" soon turned serious. Since Tracy was a professional detective, Gould emphasized the accuracy of police procedures and offered "crime-stopper" tips to his readers, giving the strip a kind of quasi-official air. Tracy himself became in the eyes of the public a kind of idealized J. Edgar Hoover; in 1964 a member of the House of Representatives, distrustful of recent Supreme Court rulings, observed for the *Record*, "If more members of the Court read Dick Tracy regularly and became aware of the growing crime rate in America, perhaps we would not have some of the decisions which have created such a flourishing climate for the crime rate." On the other hand, Gould has built a curious fantasy into his continuity, involving his quite authentic policemen with interplanetary travel, space pirates, science-fiction apparatus, and even romance with a Moon Maid. A man of impish imagination, Gould created a series of eerie, unbelievable crooks—Pruneface,

Flattop, Mumbles, Nothing Yonson, the Painted Lady—who got their just deserts in highly ingenious ways. The grandfather of all police and crime strips, Gould and Tracy continue with no sign of ennui or change.

Al Capp's "Li'l Abner" began as a comedy hillbilly in 1934, over the decade changed into a wonderfully inventive social comedy, and became over the second a relentless, sometimes savage critique of contemporary life. (Academics in particular have hailed Capp's later phase, mentioning names like Hogarth and Swift in his company, while John Steinbeck once suggested that he receive "serious consideration" for a Nobel Prize.) While working as Ham Fisher's assistant on "Joe Palooka," Capp concluded that comic strips were everything except comic, and that comedy (as others found before him) yielded a valuable corrective for much of humanity's folly, pomposity, and wrongheadedness. He began with the Yokum family (a combination of yokel and hokum) of Dogpatch, a hillbilly town somewhere in Appalachia, creating around the Yokums a society that served as a gallery of human types.

Abner's world existed (and still does) on two levels: as a burlesque American comedy, pitting the Great American Innocent against the forces of chicanery and hypocrisy; and as a satiric symbol of an irrational, often corrupt society that only the simple, honest, and incorruptible can master. Avowedly political, avowedly opinionated (as clearly as "Little Orphan Annie" but at the opposite pole) and avowedly personal, Capp's strip arouses strong feelings. His humor is broad, edged, and most of all purposeful. "Li'l Abner" teaches—it exposes fraud, folly, stupidity, ignorance, prejudice; its characters, animals, and even its places say something. In the sixties Capp himself took to the public forum on television, on the platform, and in print, to augment what his strip said daily.

Capp's talent for characterization, like Caniff's, is strong. Such people as narcissistic movie star Clark Bagel, Senator Phogbound the Southern demagogue, Marryin' Sam the phony evangelist, repulsive lover Adam Lazonga, Henry Cabbage Cod the Boston Brahmin, Lord Cesspool the silly Englishman, and dozens of other Capp creations live on in the memories of millions. It has been estimated that Capp introduced, over a thirty-year span, over four hundred original characters. *Life* magazine covered Abner's long-delayed marriage to nubile, luscious Daisy Mae; Sadie Hawkins Day, Dogpatch's holiday for the capture of reluctant males by pursuing females, is observed informally in colleges and high schools across the country; and two of Capp's animal creations, the Schmoo and the Kigmy, for a time became national symbols. The Schmoo, an obliging animal, supplied almost all of humanity's needs. The Kigmy, who took masochistic delight in punishment, absorbed all of man's hatreds and aggressions, Capp said, so "people wouldn't have to kick each other around."

The most popular comic form of the thirties, however, was the adventure strip, constructed about a central character (like Easy and Ryan) who by reason of his trade or temperament was involved in dangerous, violent action. Differences among the various adventure strips lay chiefly in their settings. "Jungle Jim" and "Tim Tyler's Luck" followed the Tarzan pattern. Alex Raymond chose Malaysia and India for the adventures of Jungle Jim Bradley, a hunter who traveled with a faithful Hindu servant named Kolu and a lissome girl assistant named Lil whose presence was never fully explained. Tim Tyler and his friend Spud, drawn by Lyman Young, served in an African colonial constabulary, pursuing ivory thieves, slavers, poachers, and revolutionaries.

Caniff's "Terry" produced picaresque heroes like "Scorchy Smith," "Vic Flint," "Johnny Hazard," and "Steve Roper," who moved over from another strip in the fifties. Caniff's own Steve Canyon (which he drew after leaving "Terry") was an ex-Air Force officer who accepted dangerous missions as a semiofficial investigator; Frank Martinek's "Don Winslow of the Navy" found adventure and excitement in a different branch of the service.

There were perhaps half a dozen Western comics in the thirties, a type not especially popular. Fred Harmon's "Red Ryder," the best of them, followed the trail of a restless, wandering cowhand; there were also "Way Out West," a cowboy strip; "Little Joe," a kid strip with a range locale; and the comic strip version of "The Lone Ranger," with Tonto, Silver, and Scout. Ed Dodd's "Mark Trail," an outdoor adventure that stressed conservation and woodcraft, was the only one of its kind. Air comics, of course, received a great boost from Lindbergh's flight and the beginnings of commercial air travel; running simultaneously for a time were "Ace Drummond" (with a script partly by Captain Eddie Rickenbacker), "Tailspin Tommy," "Smilin' Jack," "Barney Baxter," and "Skyroads."

Vincent Hamlin's "Alley Oop," a kind of anti-Tarzan, featured Oop, a caveman with a small brain and a good heart. Hamlin placed the action at first in the Kingdom of Moo, a Cro-Magnon Dogpatch, with a burlesque group of companions including Alley's curvaceous sweetheart Oola, the irascible King Guzzle I, and an assortment of low-comedy characters. Tiring of the single locale, Hamlin invented a time-machine that transplanted Oop to other eras and planets. A genuinely funny strip, "Alley Oop" belonged both with the pow-zap cartoon school and the Capp strain of satire, but was much gentler than either.

"Mandrake the Magician" (Lee Falk and Phil Davis, 1934) and "The Phantom" (Falk and Ray Moore, 1936) were mixed adventure with fantasy and science fiction. Mandrake used his supernatural powers to do good, particularly to frustrate the plans of an equally powerful but villainous magician, The Cobra. The Phantom, a masked man whose weapon was invisibility, dispensed justice in Africa much as The Lone Ranger had in the old West. The development of the supernaturally endowed hero however, reached its culmination in Siegel and Shuster's "Superman," who first appeared in comic books in 1938 and became a strip—one of the three or four most popular of all time—in 1939.

"Superman" outshone "Buck Rogers" and his followers, "Brick Bradford" (1933), and "Flash Gordon" (1934), the best of the three, drawn by Alex Raymond, who also drew "Jungle Jim." Harold Foster, after relinquishing "Tarzan," introduced an unusual variation on the space adventure strip by moving "Prince Valiant" backward into history, rather than into the future, choosing Arthurian England and sixth-century Scandinavia as his locale. Deriving much from Scott, Haggard, and Malory, Foster's Prince, drawn with scrupulous historical accuracy, is one of the few comics which can honestly be said to have educational value in the customary sense.

What "Dick Tracy" started, others continued—"Inspector Wade," "Radio Patrol," "In The Service of the Law," "Secret Agent X–9" (for which Dashiell Hammett wrote the script), "Bruce Gentry," and others. In 1943 Alfred Andriola gave up "Charlie Chan" to draw "Kerry Drake," a detective strip that stressed authentic police work, realistic narrative, and rather sophisticated characterization. Three years later Raymond introduced "Rip Kirby," a former Marine officer turned detective. Kirby, a rather bold innovation, was a thoughtful, intellectual man who used his head oftener than fists or guns, unlike the hard-boiled dicks of Hammett, Chandler, and the pulp school. Kirby played golf and chess, listened to good music, read good books, and wore glasses off duty; he also maintained a delicate, gentlemanly relationship with dark, exciting Pagan Lee, and with a blonde girl-next-door type named Honey Donan. Terminated by Raymond's death in 1956, "Rip Kirby" was the most adult and interesting of the detective comics.

A few new "girl strips" began in the forties. "Jane Arden, Girl Reporter" combined career with adventure; so did "Brenda Starr," another girl reporter drawn by Dale Messick. Harry Haenigsen's "Penny" and Lee Holley's "Ponytail" were aimed at the adolescent, and later Dick Brooks' "Jackson Twins." Jo Fischer's "From Nine to Five" and Andriola's "It's Me, Dilly" were bachelor-girl strips, while Bob Lubbers' "Long

Sam" rather successfully blended hillbilly humor and girl-adventure by bringing an innocent beauty from the hills into the city. Buford Tune's "Dottie Dripple" was another "Blondie" imitation. Raeburn Van Buren's "Abbie and Slats," originally an adventure story starring young Slats, turned into a pleasantly humorous family strip with the addition of a pretty girl, Becky, and her raffish father, Bathless Groggins. Jack Elrod's "The Ryatts," an old-fashioned family strip, came in the sixties.

Ham Fisher's "Joe Palooka," which he began in 1930, was a surprisingly successful comic strip made up from several popular types. Fisher got the idea for it from a kindly pugilist he knew in Pennsylvania, turning him into Joe, a strong, simple, honest "natural" who happened to be a boxer. Although Fisher depended on sports for his story line, the strip was not a sports comic; Joe won his bouts and kept his championship because his heart was pure and his ideals high.

When Joe married his childhood sweetheart, Anne Howe, "Palooka" became more or less a family strip; when it centered on the adventures of Knobby Walsh, Joe's cigar-chewing manager or on Jerry Leemy, his Brooklyn sharper friend, it resembled Bud Fisher's "Mutt and Jeff." Whatever the strip was during a given week, Joe, the archetypal B-movie hero, moved through it like a good-hearted, muscular Scout. Fisher, ironically, died a suicide in 1956, but "Palooka" continued in the hands of Moe Leff.

By the time of Pearl Harbor the larger city newspapers ran as many as twenty to thirty comic strips daily. The war took over most of them, of course. Orphan Annie organized the Junior Commandos, Tiny Tim contributed his dog to the K-9 Corps, and Tillie the Toiler joined the WACs. Tarzan demolished a submarine base, Superman smashed the Nazis' Atlantic defenses, "Terry and the Pirates" joined the Air Force, and most of the family strips had a boy in the service. Cartoons derived from Army life immediately appeared, among them George Baker's "Sad Sack," about a poor slob draftee; and Dave Breger's "G. I. Joe," a brightly witty narrative of civilian soldier life. After the war the strips demobilized too. Mort Wallace's "Beetle Bailey," an army-life strip which did not begin until 1950, struck home to a nostalgic generation of World War II veterans and later to Korean vets. The most successful strip based on military life yet to appear, it held its audience through Viet Nam as well.

The "soap opera" strip was an obvious adaptation to the comics of radio and television daytime drama. The oldest of them, "Mary Worth," originated as "Apple Mary," featuring a middle-aged, motherly character who helped people in trouble during the Great Depression. In 1938 Mary Orr, who developed the strip, was replaced by Dale Connor (another young woman) and artist Allen Saunders (later Ken Ernst). They moved Apple Mary into the upper middle class, changed her name to Mary Worth, and involved her in a series of complicated, melodramatic, self-contained episodes, much like a radio serial. Now a slimmer and more stylishly coifed widow, Mary still helped people, but they had much more modern problems. She helped a handsome, grizzled Naval officer to find happiness in retirement, taught a young executive's wife how to advance her husband's career, kept a bright young college professor from choosing the wrong girl, and so on. Serving as mother-confessor and wise counselor, Mary presided over what was, in effect, a soap opera in comic strip form.

Dr. Nicholas Dallas, a practicing psychiatrist, introduced the second soap opera in 1948, with "Rex Morgan, M. D.," the comic-page equivalent of the "doctor, hospital, nurse" books, movies, and radio dramas of the period. His "Judge Parker," a legal strip emphasizing the "human, dramatic side of the law," followed in 1952. Both strips, while retaining the time-tested melodramatic formula of fears, tears, and triumphs, tried to avoid being too sentimental and sensational.

Morgan and Parker, whose offices vibrate with daily drama, treated real human problems with some sense of their complexities and realities. Adoption, alcoholism, divorce, juvenile delinquency, compulsive gambling, paranoia, melancholia, and illegitimacy, are among the topics that have been examined in these strips. Nor are all problems happily solved. Not all episodes have happy endings, nor do the doctor and judge always have all the answers. Together "Rex Morgan" and "Judge Parker" represent the closest approach the comics have made to the novel and film in handling semidocumentary materials.

Career-girl strips remained a comic-page staple through the fifties and sixties. Messick's "Brenda Starr" turned toward the radio-television serial format as it grew older. Alex Kotzky's "Apartment 3-G," about three bachelor girls in a city apartment, and Leonard Starr's "On Stage," about the tribulations of a young actress, were only minor variations of the same theme. Stan Drake's "The Heart of Juliet Jones," begun in 1953, was virtually pure soap opera. Juliet, an attractive and capable young woman, keeps house for her widowed father, counsels her younger sister, and serves as target for an interminable succession of suitors. Displaying strong characterizations and well-conceived story lines, Drake's strip is "Mary Worth's" closest competitor.

The turning point in the "kid strip" came with Crockett Johnson's "Barnaby" in 1942, the first adult strip about children since Crosby's "Skippy." Barnaby, a bright small boy with an inventive mind, possessed two puzzled parents, a talking dog named Gorgon (who refused to talk before adults), and three unlikely acquaintances from the other world—a nasty, low-life goblin named Lancelot McSnoyd, a timid ghost named Gus, and most important of all, a genial, talkative, phony Irish leprechaun named Mr. O'Malley, who resembled the late W. C. Fields. Johnson (whose real name was David Johnson Leisk) drew and wrote the strip with gentle, delightfully subtle wit until he lost interest and dropped it in 1946. It finally disappeared in 1954, but nevertheless, the early "Barnaby" strip belongs with "Krazy Kat," "Pogo," and "Peanuts" as an example of the popular comic at its best.

Charles Schulz's "Peanuts" appeared the following year, soon to become the most discussed strip of its kind. Unusual in that its humor lies almost wholly in characterization, "Peanuts" has no adults, gags, puns, or kiddie pranks. The children who inhabit it are modern children with modern problems, deeply self-conscious, introspective, never (with a few exceptions) wholly secure, very much aware of the society they live in and very much a reflection of it.

Charlie Brown, the central figure, is uncertain, hesitant, baffled by the world; he wants only love, stability, and a few mild victories. The eternally put-upon man, Charlie's good will and faith in human nature are constantly tested and betrayed. ("I've developed a new philosophy," he once remarked. "I only dread one day at a time.") Linus needs the security of his blanket; Schroeder, the artist, finds fulfillment in playing Beethoven on his toy piano; Snoopy, the dog, lives in a self-generated world of delusion in which he is always the hero, a World War I ace, a champion skater, the best shortstop in the world. Self-possessed, domineering Lucy, who gives psychiatric help for a nickel, is always in control; for her nothing is a problem. ("I don't want any downs. I just want ups and ups and ups.") Pigpen, who will not wash and who refuses to recognize Dr. Spock and child psychology, rebels against it all.

Schulz's great talent lies in his concepts. His strip manages to convey a thoughtful, tolerant, bittersweet appreciation of the absurdity of the human condition that has led commentators on his work to mention names like Kierkegaard, Barth, and Bonhoeffer. "They call me everything," Schulz once told an interviewer.

> They call me philosopher, theologian, psychiatrist. But I'm not, or I wouldn't be doing what I do. I draw. Things come to me and I draw them, that's all. . . . No hidden motives or meanings. Whatever people get out of them, that's what's in them.

Nevertheless, as a lay preacher in the Church of God, Schulz puts more into "Peanuts" than mere entertainment. The strip is, as Schulz says, "about the dumb things I did when I was little," but it is also a parable, flavored by the same wry humor that characterized Herriman and Johnson. Syndicated in over a thousand newspapers, with an average of ninety million readers, it is one of the most popular strips in the world. "Peanuts" has also done equally well in book form; Schulz published *eighteen* Peanuts books between 1963 and 1969, which sold the incredible total of thirty-six million copies. It is significant that for the Apollo 10 moon shot in 1968, the astronauts chose the name of gentle Charlie Brown for their command ship, and for the lunar module that of Snoopy of the soaring imagination.

Walt (Walter Elias) Disney's "Mickey Mouse" appeared as a movie cartoon character in a short, "Steamboat Willie," in 1928 and entered comic strips in 1931. He belonged, of course, in a long line of anthropomorphic animals stretching back to Aesop and beyond, more recently observed in McKay's "Little Nemo" and Swinnerton's "Bears and Tigers." Mickey and his companions, Minnie, Goofy, Pluto, and particularly Donald Duck, soon were known all over the world; if it were possible to identify the world's most familiar cartoon character, it would very likely be Mickey Mouse. The style of the Disney strips, like his movies, was reminiscent of the older illustrators, quiet, gentle, and protected, like pictures in children's books at the turn of the century.

Disney's movie cartoons were made for children, and his comic strips retained the same quality. Mickey's is a child's world, safe (though occasionally scary), nonviolent, nonideological, where all the stories have happy endings. Characterization is strong and simple—Mickey is bright and friendly, Minnie eternally feminine, Goofy happily stupid, Donald of the terrible temper a raffish, likeable rascal. No Disney strip ever gave a child bad dreams or an adult anything to ponder. Mickey's whole existence is predicated on love and security for all; there are no philosophical overtones to his adventures, no meaning other than what the strip says, nothing more implied. (Ignatz would smother in Mickey's world.) The roots of Mickey's appeal lie in his continual reassurance that all's right with the world, that the meek will inherit, the innocent triumph. The mouse, the symbol of all that is weak, always wins in the end.

Few animal strips have been more than moderately successful, though several—"Felix the Cat," "Napoleon," "Porky Pig," "Spooky the Cat"—managed to last over a fairly long span. The popularity of Disney's strip has never flagged, but its audience has been primarily children. Disney's great success, beyond both his strip and his movies, has been in the shrewd marketing sense shown by the Disney organization, which entered the entertainment business in the sixties. Though Disney died in 1966, the valuation of the Disney enterprises has steadily increased until in

1969 its worth was calculated in excess of five hundred million dollars. One quarter of a billion people during 1968–69 saw one or more Disney movies, somewhere in the world; over a hundred million saw a Disney production on television; nearly one billion people bought a Disney book, toy, magazine, or other article; over seven million paid their way into Disneyland in California. Disney's Florida project, due to open in October, 1971, already has a waiting list of thirty million people. Walt Disney Productions covers the field of family entertainment like a blanket—movies, television, radio, amusement parks, outdoor recreation, merchandising, publishing, educational films, records, and so on. The empire built on Mickey Mouse has turned out to be one of the nation's largest businesses, an ironic accomplishment for a "comic" strip.

The single animal strip of distinction aimed at a mature audience is Walt Kelly's "Pogo," which Kelly, a former Disney animator, started somewhat inauspiciously in 1949. By 1951 "Pogo" comic books sold over two million per issue, and the strip ranked seventh in overall popularity with an estimated thirty-seven million readers. By 1960 it was in five hundred papers, read daily by at least sixty million people.

Pogo, a small possum who lives in Georgia's Okefenokee Swamp, is the center of a circle of animal friends (and a few enemies) who represent a cross section of human society. Kelly's strip (like Capp's, but much more subtle) carries within it a strong current of social satire. There are over one hundred identifiable, recurring animal characters in the strip, from Pogo down to Li'l Bug, each allegorically functional. Whatever Kelly wants to say about people and events, he can find somewhere in his gallery of characters a symbol through which to say it.

Pogo (a much more complex animal than Mickey Mouse) believes in live-and-let-live. He is an optimistic, practicing liberal, a committed humanitarian, a thoughtful observer of the passing show. Albert the Alligator, a cigar-chomping blusterer with a larcenous heart and a taste for the ladies, is Pogo's foil; he rings hollow, his public front is fake, but he now and then sees things with startling clarity. The other denizens of the swamp cover the range of human virtues and frailties—the untrustworthy Mr. Mole, crafty Seminole Sam the fox, Dr. Howland Owl the pompous fraud, Mamselle Hepsibah the coquettish French skunk, Beauregard the happy bloodhound who can't smell very well, Porkey the irritable, misanthropic porcupine, and many others.

"Pogo" is a direct descendant of Herriman's "Krazy Kat," infused with something of the same zany humor, gentle parody, and imaginative, suddenly surprising concepts. Like Herriman, Kelly experiments with language, puns, inversions, and extremely subtle rhythmic devices. Characters talk in mixtures of Georgia dialect, Elizabethan English, hillbilly language, Old Southern Demagogue, army slang, and a wild poetic tongue that echoes with metaphor, rhyme, and alliteration. Kelly uses different type faces for the conversations of different kinds of characters. Phineas Bridgeport, for example, a bear who serves as advance man for a circus, talks always in three-sheet poster type; others may talk in italics, capitals, black-face, Old English script, or whatever may be suited to the character and situation.

Like Krazy Kat, Pogo is a richly imaginative strip whose humor derives from the human comedy itself. Unlike Herriman, Kelly uses Pogo as a mouthpiece for editorial purposes. He ran for President in 1952 with a slogan that sounded suspiciously like "I Like Ike," and millions in the fifties noted the resemblance between Senator Joseph McCarthy and Okefenokee's resident jackal. Dr. Owl's attempt to make an atomic bomb and the community's indecision about what to do with it was an obvious mirror of contemporary life. Kelly has stated his positions on political and social issues in a number of essays and interviews, and it is also clear that he intends to use his pen as a weapon when he feels like it.

The distance, not only in time, between "Happy Hooligan" or "Mutt and Jeff," and "Barnaby" or "Rip Kirby," is very great. The older comics persist, for their appeal is perennial, but the intellectualized, sophisticated strip of the seventies is far removed from the days of The Yellow Kid. Audiences of the sixties liked adventure, soap opera, and gag strips, but the trend toward a higher level of draftsmanship, continuity, and concept was evident. Of thirty-nine new strips introduced in the sixties, thirty-two were so-called humorous strips, characterized by some kind of situational or ideological content as distinct from straight adventure, family, or fantasy.

Mell Lazarus' "Miss Peach," built about a teacher at Kelly Elementary School, used children somewhat as Schulz did, but with stronger narrative continuity. Frank O'Neal's "Short Ribs," Jerry Robinson's "Still Life" (which uses only objects), and Irving Phillips' "Strange World of Mr. Mum," all products of the fifties and sixties, made demands on their readers that Mary Worth never did. Johnny Hart's "B.C." and "Wizard of Id" (for which Brant Parker wrote the script) represent this trend most clearly. "B.C." concerns a prehistoric society (much more sophisticated than Alley Oop's) more or less analogous to our own. B.C. himself is a prehistoric Dagwood, surrounded by, and at silent war with, a talking rock, a philosophical anteater, an affectionate dinosaur, and a cast of unlikely characters that includes a rowdy one-legged poet, a vaguely existentialist philosopher, a monumentally inept inventor, and a windy politician. "The Wizard of Id" concerns a mean, egotistical little king who presides over a quite un-Arthurian medieval court of crafty knights, shifty ladies, an incompetent wizard, a drunken jester, and a thoroughly cowardly army.

The ultimate in sixties sophistication was probably Jules Feiffer's strip, simply named "Feiffer," a black humor creation composed entirely of an isolated monologue or dialogue, located nowhere, part of no story. Stuffed shirts, homosexuals, neurotics, hypocrites, and others from the dark underside of contemporary life (including many persons in the news) confess their sins and failures and shuffle out of the strip as baffled, or corrupt, or disturbed as they were before. Sharp-edged, occasionally vicious, "Feiffer" is an anticomic strip, a vehicle for deadly serious social criticism.

"Whatever it is," wrote Milton Caniff, "that makes a popular art effective—escape, or appeal to basic emotions, or audience identification—the funnies have it, and they have more of it than any of us ever suspected." Of course, they have all of these. "Terry and the Pirates" provides escape for millions of office-bound males; Daddy Warbucks, like all daddies, sees to it that justice is done; Tracy confirms our belief that crime never pays. Families everywhere identify with the Walletts and Bumsteads; "Blondie" once drew half a million replies to a request for the new baby's name.

No popular art, whatever the medium, is so pervasive and persistent in American society as the comics. Studies have continuously shown that they reach about half the total national population more or less regularly. The comic strip since its beginnings has produced from eight to twelve million drawings, by far the largest body of materials of any popular art. Furthermore, there are in the seventies at least two generations who have spent their entire lives with the same comics. The Katzenjammers lasted seventy years, Mutt and Jeff are in their sixties, Jiggs and Maggie covered forty-five. Parents still read Orphan Annie to their children, as their parents read the strip to them. A generation of young men went to war with Skeezix, returned, and watched their own sons go to Korea or Viet Nam. There are millions of adults who have known Li'l Abner, Dagwood, and Dick Tracy all their lives. Comics have provided for them a common experience through childhood, maturity, and old age, intertwined with memories of sorrow and happiness, courtship, marriage, parenthood, war and peace.

The rise of the newspaper comic strip in the twenties, combined with the erosion of the pulp magazine and cheap fiction market by movies, radio, general entertainment magazines, and later television, encouraged publishers to experiment with a new way of marketing comics on a broader scale. They took pulp magazine material, put it into comic-strip form, and sold it as a comic "book" for six to ten cents as a complete story unit. It was nothing more than an adaptation of the daily comic strip and the Sunday comic page; it was also, from the publishers' view, a logical development out of the pulp magazine, aimed at the same market. (The name "comic" book was a misnomer, of course, for its contents were seldom comic.) For several years, in fact, comic books maintained much the same categories—love, adventure, supernatural-science, Western, and crime-detective—as the pulps. They were published periodically, like magazines, often by the same publishers, and distributed through the same outlets. They told their stories by comic-strip techniques, merely translating pulp-magazine stories into cartoons.

The mass appeal of the comic book was no different from that of any of the forms of popular literature which preceded them. They emphasized (and still do) action, contemporaneity, and all the basic emotions; they were cheap, easy to understand, colorful, and easily available. They reflected what millions hoped and feared, what they wanted and rejected, and what they thought about things that mattered to them.

Cartoon narratives like "Jeremiah Saddlebags'" *Journey to the Gold Diggins*, sold in 1849, could perhaps be called the ancestors of comic books. The Chicago *American* offered bound reprints of Mutt and Jeff as a subscription premium in 1911, and occasionally similar pamphlets were given away with box tops and coupons. The modern version appeared when the publisher of *New Fun*, one such collection, put a price of ten cents on it and sold it in the twenties.

The first regularly issued comic book was probably Eastern Color Printing Company's *Famous Funnies*, priced at ten cents in 1934. Within a few years the product was standardized into a booklet seven and one-fourth by ten and one-fourth inches, about sixty four pages done in four colors, selling at six to ten cents, occasionally more. The Whitman Publishing Company experimented with "Big Little Books," which were only three inches by two inches, with stiff, colorful cardboard covers. They used newspaper comics, with one frame on the right and a typeset narrative on the facing lefthand page. A combination of story book and comic strip, they sold well in the thirties but soon yielded to regular-size comic books, which sold better. *Popular Comics* appeared in 1935, *Tip Top Comics* in 1936, *King Comics* the same year. *Detective Comics*, in 1937, was the first to specialize in one kind of story.

When Superman came out in *Action Comics* in 1938, the market exploded. There had been nothing like him since the early dime novels. He was created by comic books, and in turn he created a new genre of them —the supernaturally endowed hero who was judge, jury, and executioner, the crime-fighting god disguised, omnipotent, triumphant.

Jerry Siegel and Joe Shuster, who invented Superman while high school students in Cleveland, failed to sell him to the comic strips and after several years of disappointment, finally sold the idea to *Action Comics*. When circulation doubled within a few months, it was clear that Superman was a winner. The McClure Syndicate bought the strip and began publishing it in January, 1939; Superman went on the air in February, 1940, and shortly after into movies and movie cartoons. By 1941 the semimonthly comic book devoted entirely to his adventures reached a circulation of 1,400,000, while the comic strip version reached a combined newspaper audience of 20,000,000 daily. No other comic book, and few strips, ever attained such popularity.

In retrospect, it is easy to see why, for "Superman" put together (either accidentally or by shrewd design) most of the salient features of science fiction, adventure, gangster, and police comics with the appeal of fairy-tale fantasy. A migrant from the lost planet Krypton, sole survivor of a superrace possessed of infinite strength, unlimited knowledge, X-ray vision, and the power of flight, Superman enforced law, redressed wrongs, and defeated the forces of evil at home, abroad, and in space. Disguised as Clark Kent, a mild-mannered, chicken-hearted newspaperman, permanently subjected to the jibes of his girlfriend Lois Lane, Superman satisfied Everyman's dream of showing off.

The basic idea behind *Superman* was simple and tremendously effective—the shy, modest, undistinguished man with the glasses is really a supermuscled, superintelligent, superhandsome hero, right out of the mythic past; Apollo, Paul Bunyan, Beowulf, and Roland rolled into one. All shy, modest, bespectacled men in office-brown suits could identify with him and live vicariously through him. When Clark Kent slipped into the nearest phone booth to change swiftly into his flowing cape and tight-fitting suit with the letter "S" on his chest, millions of men changed with him. His incredible feats of strength (holding up a falling skyscraper, reversing the flow of Niagara Falls, pulling together a whole state split by an earthquake fissure) were less important, in the final analysis, than his quick, complete victories over most of the problems that plagued society —subversion, crime, war, disaster, injustice. It was not merely his strength that made Superman godlike, but his virtue.

During the forties a tide of comic books featuring superheroes rolled relentlessly over the country, inundating the adolescent and younger adult market. Superman's imitators numbered in the dozens—Skyman, Plastic Man, Doll Man, Hangman, Mr. Justice, The Comet, The Angel, and his most serious rival, Captain Marvel—along with variants like Batman, The Green Hornet (from radio), The Spirit, The Shadow, Superboy, and Superwoman. Tarzan moved over from radio and the comic strip, and new characters appeared, like Sheena the Queen of the Jungle, who adroitly combined the qualities of Tarzan and Superman with sex appeal.

The rise and fall of Batman, first drawn by Robert Kane for *Detective Comics* in 1939, is a unique chapter in comic book history. Like Superman a crusader for justice (dressed in a batlike costume) Batman was promoted to a magazine of his own in 1940 and in 1941 gained a young helper, Robin. Two years later he appeared as a daily cartoon strip and the same year as a movie serial. (In 1945, in one of radio's rarest occurrences, Batman and Superman joined forces on the same program, an alliance which lasted sporadically until 1952.) In January, 1966, however, after Batman went on television (Adam West played the part) he became a national mania. The program hit a 58.8 Trendex rating (one of every three viewers) and stayed in the top ten for months; within the year there were more than a thousand articles for sale with the Batman label, among them Batguns, Batpens, and Batguitars. (When a psychiatrist suggested that there were certain ambiguities in the Batman-Robin relationship, the writers hastily introduced Batgirl to make it a trio.) A nightspot in San Francisco featured a topless Batgirl dancer, and a girls' school in Montana rescheduled its Evening Rosary to avoid conflict with the program. But Batman faded fast, disappeared in 1968 (except for re-runs) and returned to the comic books, leaving behind thousands of Batmasks and Batpencils among the young.

There were sixty comic books issued regularly in 1939 and 168 in 1942, netting publishers an annual revenue of eight million dollars which increased to thirty-two millions in 1953. Sales in 1942 exceeded twelve million copies a month; in 1946 they passed sixty million. As dime novels sold in Civil War army camps, so did comic books in World War II; at post exchanges they outsold *Life, The Reader's Digest,* and *Saturday Evening Post* combined at ten to one. A readership survey in 1943 showed who provided the market. Ninety-five per cent of all boys and 91 per cent of all girls in the six to eleven age group read comic books regularly; 87 per cent and 81 per cent in the twelve to seventeen group; 40 per cent and 28 per cent in the eighteen to thirty bracket. Except for the daily newspaper, the comic book was probably the most widely read form of printed matter among people under thirty.

Comic books reached the climax of their popularity in 1953–54, when there were about 650 titles in print with a combined circulation of one hundred million copies per month. Categories broadened and subcategories multiplied. There were cartoon comics (*Mickey Mouse, Donald Duck*), war comics (*G.I. Joe*), comic strip comics (*Blondie, Mutt and Jeff*), romance comics (*Heart Throbs, Young Love*), detective comics (*G-Men, Crime Squad*), classic comics (simplified versions of Twain, Dickens, Shakespeare), Westerns (*Lone Ranger, Hopalong Cassidy*), and dozens of horror, supernatural, and fantasy-hero comics. In 1955 the tide began to recede. The number of regularly-issued comic books dropped to four hundred, then within a year or so to two hundred and fifty, where it has remained, more or less, ever since. Major comic books today sell at a fairly steady rate of about thirty-five million copies per year; publishers calculate, however, a "pass on" readership of three for each single copy sold.

Radio, and particularly television, obviously drained off a large portion of the comic book market, but by no means reduced it drastically. They also, again particularly television, diverted a good deal of criticism away from the comic book. Studies in the sixties, however, suggested that the most consistent television viewers were also likely to be the heaviest comic book readers. In January, 1969, *The Magazine and Paperback Sales Guide* listed 231 comic book titles, a figure which might vary by perhaps 10 per cent any given month since not all comic books publish regularly. The major subject matter categories remain virtually unchanged since the midfifties. (Only two detective comics appear, that genre having been absorbed by the "true" detective magazine and the paperback book.) By far the greater number fall into the Superman-Fantasy-Space Adventure category, including *Batman, Aquaman, Hawkman, Iron Man, Metal Man, Mandrake, Wonderwoman, Superboy, Captain Action, Captain Savage, Captain Marvel, Flash Gordon, Unknown, Dr. Strange, Unexpected, Spectre, Ghostly Tales, Space Adventure, Star Trek, The Invaders, Dr. Solar, Space Family Robinson,* and naturally, *Superman* himself.

The introduction in 1961 of *The Fantastic Four* by Marvel Group Comics marked a direction in comic book content, artwork, and concept that may prove to be as important as that initiated by *Superman* in 1938. Spiderman, a character introduced in 1968, had in fact nearly overtaken Superman in sales by 1969. Emphasizing a sophisticated story line, imaginative and psychedelic-influenced drawing, and dialogue with implied social and political significance, Marvel Comic plots have included young black characters as well as incidents involving rent eviction, ghetto problems, racism, war, and the like, subjects previously off-limits.

The emphasis in the Marvel Groups is on super-heroes—among them The Human Torch, Captain America, Iron Man, The Hulk, The Mighty Thor, The Silver Surfer, and of course Captain Marvel himself—for in the estimate of editorial director Stan Lee comic book superheroes have much the same meaning today that myths, romances, and legends did for earlier generations. (*Esquire* has called Marvel Comics "twentieth-century mythology.") These super beings, however, like the Greek gods, yet have human qualities, flaws, problems, joys and disappointments. The Hulk, a huge, pathetic monster of incredible strength, wants only peace and friendship in a world that, because of his difference, will not leave him alone. The Mighty Thor is a crippled doctor in real life, held in some contempt by his attractive nurse as a flawed weakling. Spiderman, who is really a youngster named Peter Parker, is a loner, an alienated outsider who has to find himself while he fights crime and injustice. The scripts strive for relevance and individuality; the language spoken by various characters is personalized, characters differentiated, a great deal of care given to motivations. The Fantastic Four (Reed Richards, Benjamin Grimm, Johnny Storm and his sister Sue) for example, emerge as four quite different, quite human people. The fifteen comics of the Marvel Group, aimed especially at young adults, may indicate an important trend for the market of the seventies.

PART FOUR

COPS, SPACEMEN, AND COWBOYS

I suppose we all get tired of being what we are every day, doing what we do every day, seeing what we do every day.

—MYSTERY STORY WRITER

CHAPTER TEN

MURDERERS AND
DETECTIVES

We do not live in a fragrant world.

—RAYMOND CHANDLER

The novel of intrigue and mystery is of comparatively recent origins, although its antecedents lie deep in antiquity. To solve puzzles and to see justice done have always been great human desires, as novelists have long been aware. The rogue novels of the eighteenth century, the Gothic and "low life" novels of the later eighteenth and early nineteenth (Defoe's *Moll Flanders,* Fielding's *Jonathan Wild,* Mary Shelley's *Frankenstein,* Godwin's *Caleb Williams,* and others) testified to the early popularity of the type.

The modern detective story, however, developed only after the establishment of the police as an official social agency. François Eugène Vidocq, a reformed thief, organized the first investigative unit (a forerunner of the detective bureau) of the Paris police in 1817. In 1829 he published five volumes of *Memoirs* which were widely read in England and the United States and extensively quarried by novelists for half a century after. That same year Sir Robert Peel, who organized the London police, placed his headquarters at Scotland Yard. The publication of memoirs, journals, and criminal cases soon reached flood proportions; obviously a market, potentially a huge one, existed for a new, popular literary genre.

Edgar Allan Poe created it in three stories, *The Murders in the Rue Morgue* (1841), *The Mystery of Marie Roget* (1842–43), and *The Purloined Letter* (1845). His detective (although he did not use the word),

C. Auguste Dupin, and his choice of a Parisian locale, indicated his debt to Vidocq. But Poe also created something completely new, a form of fiction so classically complete that the principles he established still to a large extent govern it. Dupin, the brilliant, eccentric amateur, solves by rational analysis a crime that baffled the police; he explains it to a puzzled friend who records it for the reader. Information is released to the reader in a carefully arranged sequence. He is given the account of the crime and of the unsuccessful methods of the police, while the detective, working from the same information, reaches a conclusion which proves to be correct. He then recapitulates the process by which he has arrived at the solution, showing where police and reader erred in their interpretations. Detached, fearsomely learned, ironically aware of the frailties and depravities of human nature, completely in command of himself and events, Dupin was the ancestor of multitudes of detectives.

Émile Gaboriau, who published *L'Affaire LeRouge,* knew Poe as well as Vidocq. His book, published in Paris in 1866, and in the United States as *The Crimson Crime,* was the first of a long series of novels which made him famous on both sides of the Atlantic. Combining Poe and Vidocq, he created a pair of detectives—LeCoq the amateur and Tabaret the professional—each brilliant, each resourceful, each supplying what the other lacked. Wilkie Collins, who wrote a best seller in *The Woman in White* (1860), wrote an even more popular one in *The Moonstone* (1868) which, when reprinted in a cheap edition, swept the American market. Except for Dickens, remarked *The New York Citizen and Round Table* on January 3, 1869, "there is no living novelist who enjoys a popularity which approaches that of Wilkie Collins." Like Poe, Collins drew on special fields of knowledge to assist the detective—law, medicine, chemistry, psychology—but unlike Poe he used an indirect, complicated narrative method, involving letters, journals, memoranda, and the like, partly for suspense, partly to create an air of authenticity.

The Moonstone invited American imitations, one of which, by a young lady named Anna Katherine Green, not only rivaled it but outstripped it in American sales. The daughter of a famous trial lawyer, Miss Green's interest in her father's cases produced *The Leavenworth Case,* which G. P. Putnam's Sons published in 1878, featuring an amiable, portly detective named Ebenezer Gryce whose fatherly appearance hid a shrewd mind. In 1893 Putnam's announced that they had worn out two sets of plates reprinting the novel and were making a third; it continued to sell for another thirty years.

Conan Doyle's Sherlock Holmes, of course, displaced Collins, Miss Green, and everyone else. Doyle's *Study in Scarlet* (1887) and *The Sign of the Four* (1890), both published in cheap bindings almost simultaneously in the United States, sold fairly well. (Old Sleuth had already appeared in Munroe's dime novels, with Old Cap Collier soon to come.) After Harper & Row published *The Adventures of Sherlock Holmes* in 1892, the great detective took over the field as completely as Nick Carter had the yellow-backed, dime-novel trade. Doyle was pirated in ten-cent editions, syndicated in the newspapers, and run endlessly in the magazines. "Sherlock" became synonymous with "detective"; "elementary, my dear Watson," was a catch-phrase everyone knew; fore-and-aft deerstalker caps (after the book's illustrations) were popular men's wear.

The conventions of the detective story had taken rather clear shape by 1900. Its point was the puzzle; the crime existed to be solved; the approach of both writer and reader to crime (as Dupin and Holmes showed) was detached, neutral, removed. Whatever the crime (even murder, the worst one), the point was that it disturbed and threatened social order and security. The detective's function, in which the reader shared, was to set the balance right again by solving the crime and repairing the intrusion. Poe and Doyle provided the detective-figure, the brilliantly logical, highly individualized amateur; they also provided the blundering police, the admiringly obtuse friend, and the almost equally brilliant criminal adversary. In addition they set the narrative pattern—the discovery of the crime, the gathering of evidence, the movement of the action toward a second crime, misdirected suspicion, the ruse of exposure, surprise solution, recapitulation and explanation. Subsequent writers did little more than play variations, some quite inventive, on these themes.

Jacques Futrelle's "Thinking Machine," Professor S. F. X. Van Deusen, appeared first in an adventure novel, *The Chase of the Golden Plate*, in 1906. The character interested Futrelle, who developed him further in a series of short stories collected in *The Thinking Machine* in 1907. Van Deusen, clearly, owed much to Holmes. A brilliant scientist, possessed of an M.D., M.D.S., F.R.S., and Ph.D., he solved everything by sheer logic. Since every chain of events had a beginning, the Professor searched it out, followed it to its logical conclusion, and there found the criminal waiting. The crime solved by the Thinking Machine was incidental to his way of solving it, which he believed absolutely the logical mind could do. "Nothing is impossible," he confidently told a doubter. "The mind is the master of all things"—a statement which Dupin and Holmes would have recognized instantly. Had Futrelle lived (he died on the *Titanic* in 1912) Professor Van Deusen might well have become much better known than he is in detective annals.

The Thinking Machine represented the ultimate extension of the deductive detective, beyond which it was difficult to go. A year after his appearance Mary Roberts Rinehart's *Circular Staircase* opened a new road for detective fiction, deriving as much, if not more, from the domestic novel and the old-fashioned Gothic story as from Holmes or Poe. Married to a physician whose comfortable fortune was swept away in the stock market crash of 1903, Mrs. Rinehart turned her talent for writing to verse, articles, and children's stories before trying crime novels in 1908. After that her place on the American best-seller list was nearly permanent. No other author in the twentieth century placed so many books there so many times.

In *The Circular Staircase* Mrs. Rinehart introduced several variations on the established formula. First of all, she combined the crime story with a parallel love story, or sentimental plot, much as if Grace Livingston Hill had collaborated with Doyle. Nearly every Rinehart novel ended not only with a solution to a crime but with a happy marriage in the offing. Second, she made it axiomatic that the first crime was only a prelude to others, thereby creating an atmosphere of continuous suspense, danger, and mystery.

Third, she used, and quite cleverly, the novelist's device of foreshadowing (sometimes called the "Had I but known" school of writing) to maintain the reader's interest. Fourth, she created an interesting, individualized narrator in the person of a middle-aged spinster, humorous, perceptive, warmly companionable, whose personal involvement with the other characters was easily transferred to the reader. Her novels were not detective stories, she insisted, but novels of detection; "the organized police play a very small part in any of my books, and indeed I know little about them."

Mrs. Rinehart's formula in *The Circular Staircase* was a good one. She used it again in *The Man in Lower Ten* (1909), and over and over again, down to *The Swimming Pool* in 1952. The society she wrote about was the comfortable, orderly society of 1912, temporarily disturbed by a crime but perfectly capable of rearranging itself after the guilty were apprehended. Cooks were Irish, chauffeurs Negro, gardeners crotchety old men named Amos, chambermaids not very bright and easily frightened. The clean-cut young people were named Jim and Judy, and the police who called were always Inspectors and Captains.

Mrs. Rinehart's style was old-fashioned and leisurely, fitted to long evenings of reading at home. *The Door* (1921), one of her most popular, opened with a fifteen-hundred word essay on the psychology of crime ("What is it that lies behind the final gesture of the killer?") followed by a three-thousand word description of the narrator's home, location, fur-

nishings, staff of five servants, and the ramifications of the family's relationships. The "Had I but known" theme is introduced quietly:

> It is one of the inevitable results of tragedy that one is always hark-
> ing back to it, wondering what could have been done to avert it. I
> find myself going over and over the events of that night, so simple
> in appearance, so dreadful in result. Suppose I had turned on Sarah's
> light that night? Would I have found her murderer in the room? Was
> the faint sound I heard the movement of her curtain in the wind, as
> I had thought, or something much more terrible?
>
> Again, instead of sending Joseph upstairs to search, what if I
> had had the police called and the house surrounded?
>
> Still, what could I have done for Sarah? Nothing. Nothing at all.

Her trademark was creating the initial atmosphere of foreboding, which
she did well, as in *The Confession:*

> Yet the Benton house undeniably made me uncomfortable. Per-
> haps it was because it had remained unchanged for so long. The old
> horsehair chairs, with their shiny mahogany frames, showed by the
> slightly worn places in the carpet before them that they had not de-
> viated an inch from their position for many years. The carpets—car-
> pets that reached to the very baseboards and gave under one's feet
> with the yielding of heavy padding beneath—were bright under beds
> and wardrobes, while in the centers of the rooms they had faded
> into the softness of old tapestry. . . . Looking back, there are a
> number of things that appear rather curious. Why, for instance, did
> Maggie, my old servant, develop such a dislike for the place? It had
> nothing to do with the house.
>
> "I've just got a feeling about it, Miss Agnes," she said. "I can't
> explain it, any more than I can explain a cold in the head, but it's
> there."

Mrs. Rinehart could make up her own rules for the detective story
when she wished. In *The Circular Staircase* the detective himself turned
out to be the criminal; in *The Door,* quite literally, the butler did it; in
The Red Lamp, she left two key incidents unexplained except as "ecto-
plasmic phenomena" or "clairvoyant visions." Her readers never complained. She wrote fifty short stories, twenty non-detection novels, and
dozens of magazine articles. *The Circular Staircase,* adapted to the stage
by Avery Hopwood as *The Bat* in 1920, ran for 867 consecutive performances in New York, stayed on the tent-show circuit for another decade,
was twice made into movies, and is still in print along with sixteen of her
other novels. Her imitators numbered in the dozens, but the most expert
was probably Carolyn Wells, who in 1909 introduced Fleming Stone (fea-

tured in seventy-five novels), a witty, urbane lawyer whose adventures
were a woman's-magazine staple for thirty-five years.

The school of Mrs. Rinehart asked little of the police, who usually
deferred to spinsters, family counselors, or helpful friends who solved
the crime with a minimum of professional help. Melville Davisson Post,
a successful West Virginia lawyer, contributed a different kind of detective to the tradition in the person of a somewhat shady lawyer who used
the intricacies of the law to frustrate justice. *The Strange Schemes of
Randolph Mason* (1906) proved popular with readers who wanted something different from the usual fare. In 1909 Post responded to requests
and put Mason on the right side of the law, in *Corrector of Destinies*, so
that he could use his tricky legal skills in bringing justice to seemingly
impossible cases.

Losing interest, Post dropped out of the game for several years before returning with a second character—Uncle Abner, an elderly, rustic,
Virginia squire who espoused the cause of the poor, the wronged, and
the unjustly accused. *Uncle Abner, Master of Mysteries* (1918) and other
Abner stories that appeared until the late twenties, established Post as an
important influence on the development of the detective story.

Post put Abner into the early nineteenth-century backwoods South,
where the machinery of law was not yet fully formed. His backgrounds
were carefully and accurately drawn; his plots were controlled and credible; his dialogue natural and authentic. He treated his characters as in-
dividuals and developed them carefully. Uncle Abner knew that to solve
a crime, one must understand the criminals' motives, how and why people thought as they did. He was, as Post drew him, the first American
detective to be more concerned with his responsibility to society than
with solving a puzzle.

Edwin Balmer and William McHarg collaborated on a series featuring "Luther Trent, Psychological Detective," in 1909, who used a battery
of laboratory apparatus—lie detectors, chronoscopes, galvanometers, and
so on—to trap and convict criminals. A shrewd innovation, reminiscent of
Poe (who used a kind of primitive ballistics and a rigged corpse in "Thou
Art the Man" in 1844), Trent's methods were unique in that the criminal
convicted himself by his own physical and psychological reactions, such
as hesitations, changes in blood pressure, respiration, and the like. Then
Arthur B. Reeve introduced "Craig Kennedy" in 1910, obviously modeled
on the Trent stories. Reeve, who had done a good deal of magazine writing about police work, brought a fund of information that the McHarg-
Balmer team did not have.

The Poisoned Pen, the first Kennedy collection in 1911, established

Reeve as the most successful writer of straight detection stories of his generation. He followed with *The Silent Bullet* (1912), *The Dream Doctor* (1917), and three more collections down to *Enter Craig Kennedy* in 1935, by then an old-fashioned, outmoded book. Reeve's most successful years were the twenties, when Kennedy appeared in three long movie serials and when Reeve himself was called in as consultant on the Lindbergh kidnapping case.

Except for a few additions and variations, the pattern of the detective story changed very little after 1920. The brilliant amateur, whose success depended on some kind of specialized knowledge of law, science, medicine, and so on, continued to hold the center of interest. The first real professional policeman to emerge in the American version was, surprisingly enough, a Chinese-Hawaiian detective named Charlie Chan of the Honolulu Police Department (modeled on a real detective named Chang Apana) in Earl Derr Biggers' *The House Without a Key,* in 1925. Chan, a wise, bright, round little man followed about by some rather thick-headed patrolmen, not only solved baffling crimes with Oriental élan, but left behind a trail of counterfeit Chinese epigrams—"Truth is rare fruit in garden of murder," "When tasting soup of crime, it is best to use long spoon," or "Patience are a lovely virtue,"—that stuck in the minds of his affectionate admirers for years. (A trace of Chan still remains in Agatha Christie's Hercule Poirot and Simenon's Inspector Maigret.) There were actually only six Chan books—the last, *The Keeper of the Keys,* in 1932— but the movie character, played by Warner Oland, became very much a part of American folklore.

Philo Vance appeared in *The Benson Murder Case* (1926) and *The "Canary" Murder Case* (1927), which broke all sales records for detective fiction up to that time. "S.S. Van Dine," the author, was Willard Huntington Wright, an art and drama critic for fashionable magazines like *Smart Set* and *Town Topics,* who began writing detective stories for diversion while recovering from an illness. Wright was an erudite snob, and so was Vance, an urbane, amusingly eccentric man-about-town who brought his imposing (and often pretentious) learning to bear on the problem at hand. Vance, wrote Wright, was "a young social aristocrat of amazing gifts and capabilities."

> He was an art collector in a small way, a fine amateur pianist, and a profound student of aesthetics and psychology. Although an American, he had largely been educated in Europe, and still retained a slight English accent and intonation. . . .
> Vance was not yet thirty-five, and, in a cold, sculptural fashion, was impressively good-looking. His face was slender and mobile;

but there was a stern, sardonic expression to his features, which acted as a barrier between him and his fellows. He was not emotionless, but his emotions were, in the main, intellectual. . . . He gave the impression of remaining remote from all mundane matters; and, in truth, he looked upon life like a dispassionate and impersonal spectator at a play, secretly amused and debonairly cynical at the meaningless futility of it all.

Wright developed the character of Vance with great detail. He dropped his g's in fashionable slang, collected Chinese prints, smoked imported Régie cigarettes, and relaxed in "an elaborately embroidered silk kimono and sandals." He used phrases like "My word!," "Allons-y!," and "Bien, mon vieux"; quoted Cato, Cowley, Chaucer and Chatterton (to choose examples beginning with C) and once, within twenty lines of dialogue in The "Canary" Murder Case, used Italian, French, German, and Latin. Wright sprinkled "in" New Yorker references through the text, including notes about himself and many of his friends which he explained to less sophisticated readers in footnotes. Both the crimes Vance solved and his methods of solving them tended to be somewhat esoteric; the key clue to the "Canary" case was a mislabeled record of Beethoven's Andante.

Nevertheless, the public bought Vance completely. Wright drew character well and maintained his narrative pace through complicated maneuverings; like Mrs. Rinehart he knew how to lead the reader from crime to crime in seemingly incongruous (but eventually logical) sequence. Though Wright once said that nobody "had more than six good detective novels in his system" he wrote twelve Philo Vance books, the last, The Winter Murder Case, published posthumously in 1939. Despite his humorless sophistication Vance still remains one of the early immortals of detective fiction.

His immediate successor was "Ellery Queen," the joint product of Frederic Dannay and Manfred Lee, who won a $7,500 prize in a contest sponsored by a publisher with The Roman Hat Mystery in 1929. Queen, whose career has spanned over forty years and over forty books, quickly eclipsed Vance to become one of the best-known names in the history of detective fiction. Dannay and Lee have authored twenty juveniles, two hundred articles, fifteen short story collections, and have edited thirty-five anthologies and a magazine. Queen books have been published by thirty American and a hundred foreign publishers, translated into every language of importance except Russian and Chinese, and have formed the basis of several radio and television series. Their total sales passed one hundred million in the fifties.

It is not hard to account for Queen's durability and popularity, for Dannay and Lee (no doubt by design) merged in one character nearly all the characteristics of popular detective fiction from Poe to Van Dine. (Their collection of crime fiction, perhaps the world's best, is housed at the University of Texas.) Queen is a gifted amateur, but he works with the police rather than as their adversary; his father, whose methods are standard but effective, is in fact Chief of New York's Homicide Division. Like Vance he is learned and perceptive but he carries his erudition gracefully, with no trace of the snob. Like Kennedy and Professor Van Deusen he depends on logic, scientific analysis, and all other intellectual and physical apparatus which may assist him—but he can make mistakes, and sometimes fails to correct them in time. Like Post's Abner, he finds answers in human nature; facts and deductions, while they may form a chain of logic, ultimately lead Queen to people, in whose motivations and actions the problem originates.

The early Queen novels stressed puzzles, sealed rooms, impossible crimes, ingeniously complicated plots, and the like; Dannay and Lee, in fact, introduced the custom of stopping the novel, when the clues were all in, to challenge the reader to anticipate Queen's solution. In later novels, however, they shifted the emphasis away from riddles toward greater interest in locale, atmosphere, and characterization. They were written with skill and perception, as in the description from *Double, Double* (1960), one of the Wrightsville series:

Dr. Dodd's appearance shocked him.

Ellery had visualized the beneficiary of Luke MacCaby's will as a rather sad-eyed little man with a workworn body and a halo of silvery hair—a slender, almost fragile, saint at peace with himself and the universe. The man who came swiftly, almost furtively, into the waiting room and stopped in his tracks in the archway was a harried brute. His great body was powerful and grossly fleshed; had he been smaller, he would have been fat. He was all but bald and his glossy skull was stippled with liverish-looking pigment, like the spots on his big, unsteady hands. His face was startling. It was a great jowled face, its jowls shaking. The eyes were buried in pits of deeply sagging flesh, like pouches, and the pouches quivered, too. They twitched and jerked. The eyes themselves, small and overbrilliant, were never still. They kept darting from side to side like minnows. And his skin was lifeless and of a yellow color, as if some poison was sapping its vitality.

Had his voice been in tune with his appearance, Dr. Dodd would have been monstrous, a vast obscenity. But when he spoke the sounds that came out of his throat were grave and sweet and slowly given. His voice was the only part of him with beauty. It suggested what he might have been, or what perhaps he once was.

At the opening of the thirties the books were filled with scientific detectives, gentlemen-detectives, amateurs-turned-detective and numerous combinations and mutations thereof. The rules, after half a century of practice, were well set, conventions agreed upon, the basic Poe-Doyle pattern accepted by author and reader without argument. A number of skillful practitioners continued doing (and some did it better) what others had done, finding no reason to change the formula.

Out of the crowd of popular but undistinguished detective-figures of the thirties, however, emerged two major creations: Rex Stout's Nero Wolfe and Erle Stanley Gardner's Perry Mason. Stout's Wolfe, the more complex and interesting of the two, bears strong resemblances to Holmes, Dupin, and the Thinking Machine. Of mysterious but apparently Montenegrin origin, Wolfe, who grows orchids, loves beer, is a gourmet of formidable proportions, and hates women, exercise, and automobiles, is interested primarily in solving crimes so that he can indulge some expensive tastes which need to be financed by high fees. His wisecracking, girl-chasing assistant Archie Goodwin, an able operative in his own right, serves as an effective foil to the static Wolfe, who like Dupin prefers to solve the puzzle from his own secluded study.

Stout began as a pulp-magazine factory hand in 1912, grinding out saleable fiction at the prime rate of two cents a word. Nero Wolfe, who appeared first in 1934 in *Fer-de-lance,* soon developed as a kind of anti-Philo Vance. Wolfe is eccentric, learned, standoffish, even rude. He is master of much esoteric and possibly useful information, little of which helps him to solve crimes. He specializes in noticing things others don't, and in being right when others are wrong.

Crime in Stout's books is nothing fancy, as it had tended to be in Van Dine and occasionally in Queen. People die by old-fashioned methods like knives, bullets, blunt instruments, or simple poisons, and for quite ordinary reasons like money, hatred, or power. Nor are Wolfe's methods unusual. They are essentially police methods (he has his own detectives as the police have theirs) and he often uses police information, since they have more manpower than he. Wolfe puts things together better than they do, and gets paid more for it.

No one, however, has ever approached the popularity of Erle Stanley Gardner's lawyer-detective Perry Mason. Gardner was admitted to the California bar at twenty-one and practiced law with great success for the next fifteen years in Ventura County. He was in his thirties when he began writing in earnest for the pulps, and within a few years was selling a million words a year while maintaining his practice. Since writing proved more interesting than law (though he was a noted trial lawyer) he quit the one and devoted himself to the other. In 1933, in *The Case of the Velvet Claws,* he introduced Perry Mason (who owed much to Melville Davisson Post) the lucky, likeable, clever, and slightly raffish lawyer-detective who won cases for his clients by solving seemingly open-and-shut cases through intuitive detection and legal legerdemain.

Gardner was undoubtedly the most widely read of all American writers. His first book sold twenty-eight million copies in its first fifteen years and was still on the market thirty-six years later. Seventy or more of his titles have exceeded a million; seventeen have exceeded two million; according to UNESCO's *Index Translationarum* he is the most widely translated author in the world. Since Gardner wrote under a number of names (A. A. Fair, Charles Kenny, Charleton Kendrake, and so on) his total production and sales are difficult to calculate. He had written close to two hundred books with sales probably in excess of one hundred and fifty million dollars; if, as publishers estimate, there are four to five readers for each copy of a detective book, it seems likely that the greater part of the American population might well have read a Gardner book at one time or another. Those who have not are more likely to have seen a Perry Mason movie (of which there were a dozen or more) or a Perry Mason television episode.

Mason is not an especially complex or well-developed character, nor are Gardner's plots marked by subtlety or sophistication. His five major characters—Mason; his devoted, attractive secretary Della Street; Paul Drake, his private investigator; Lieutenant Tragg of the police; and perennial adversary District Attorney Hamilton Burger—are so familiar to his readers that he rarely bothers to describe or characterize them. Dialogue is matter-of-fact, stylized, and comprises about three-quarters of the total wordage; what happens is nearly always talked about rather than observed. Locale is unimportant. Mason stories take place in California but there is little attempt to establish any sense of place. In *The Case of the Worried Waitress* (1966), a typical Gardner book, there are only three brief descriptive phrases applied to Mason, none to any other character, nor any reference to locale. After the opening sentence, "Perry Mason and Della Street were having lunch at Madison's Midtown Milestone," Gardner simply introduces the case at hand in the next fifteen lines.

Gardner's formula is predictably clear. Mason accepts an apparently hopeless or utterly confused case, tracks down the missing evidence, and often with the help of an obscure legal rule or ruse wins the case at the last minute. Each Mason plot is divided into seven recognizable sections: the case is introduced; Mason investigates; his client is wrongly arrested; he investigates further; the trial begins; Mason reverses the case by introducing new evidence; the true culprit is exposed in court. It is as formalized as Japanese Noh drama. Neither Gardner nor Mason philosophizes much about justice, nor does Mason worry about legal niceties. Mason wants to win cases and he always does; that he saves the innocent and sees justice done is incidental to his ingenious and imaginative solutions to the puzzle presented by a crime. District Attorney Hamilton Burger, who never wins a single case against Mason, means well but simply does not have the capacity to protect the innocent—something the general public may have felt about legal systems since Sumeria. What Mason does in the courtroom strikes a very deep response in the average mind.

The greatest change in the detective story since Poe came in 1926 with the emergence of the *Black Mask* school of fiction. *Black Mask,* a pulp magazine founded in 1920 by H. L. Mencken and George Jean Nathan, at first published quality detective stories with modest success. In 1926, under the editorship of Joseph Shaw, it began to specialize in tough, hard-boiled crime stories. He wanted, Shaw said, stories with a direct, straight plot line, "simplicity for the sake of stressing clarity, plausibility, and belief." They should emphasize action, "fast tempo," and should be written with objectivity, economy, restraint. Most important, to use Shaw's words, they should "set character before situation" with "recognizable characters in three-dimensional form." *Black Mask,* Shaw wrote later,

> . . . gave the stories over to the characters. . . . They did not themselves state that a situation was dangerous or exciting; they did not *describe* the characters as giants, dead shots, or infallible men. They *permitted* the actors on the stage to demonstrate all that. . . .

Shaw's formula, his exacting standards, and his obvious interest in creating a new kind of detective fiction attracted some of the better popular writers to *Black Mask* and its imitators—Dashiell Hammett, Carroll John Daly, Raoul Whitfield, Thomas Walsh, George Harmon Coxe, Paul Cain, Lester Dent, Raymond Chandler, and others. *Black Mask's* circulation rose and other magazines picked up the trend, among them *Double Detective, Detective Fiction Weekly, Action Detective, Black Aces,* and *Black Book Detective.* There were about twenty-four magazines specializing in tough-crime fiction by the middle thirties and at least forty "hard-boiled dicks" operating in them. These new detective stories dealt in violence, a great deal of it, but more important was the impression of realism they attempted to create. The point of the hard-boiled story was to create an authentic reflection of the kind of society in which the characters moved, a society, wrote Raymond Chandler, "hard and cynical about motive and character," a world filled with "the smell of fear."

The *Black Mask* story was a reaction against the whole Dupin-Holmes tradition, and against what the new writers believed was its essential falsity. They were trying, Chandler said, "to get murder away from the upper classes, the weekend houseparty, and the vicar's rose garden, and back to the people who were really good at it." They put crime into an environment where it really happened and for real reasons—fear, power, profit, sex, self-protection. There were situations, the stories implied, where the answer lay in guns rather than deductions; crime made messy problems which had untidy solutions. Murder in Sir Ronald's library, these writers believed, was not very important in terms of what went on in the real world of the twenties and thirties.

The sharpest distinction between the traditional detective story and the hard-boiled type lay in the character of the detective. The traditional amateur sleuth came from the professional classes and operated in the society of the country-house, the vicarage, the university, the suburban home. The new detective (who could also be a newspaperman, adventurer, or ex-crook like Gardner's Ed Jenkins) was more often than not a "private eye," a hired operative working on his own, separate from the police and occasionally in conflict with them. Hammett's middle-aged, nameless Continental Op (who worked for the Continental Detective Agency); Daly's Race Williams; Whitfield's Filipino Jo Gar; and others like Gardner's Lester Leith, Coxe's Casey, Cain's Shane, or Lybeck's Harrigan moved in a highly dangerous and violent world to earn their fees. These men tended to be cynical, well aware of the weaknesses of human nature, unsurprised and unmoved by them—though the Continental Op had a soft spot for Dinah Bland, a blowsy, pathetic, alcoholic call girl. Hard, violent, even cruel men, the detectives made their own code in order to cope with a society equally hard, violent, and cruel.

The tough-guy detective story concentrated, as Shaw said it should, on scene and situation rather than plot. The answer to "whodunit" was less important than the atmosphere, tone, and dramatics surrounding how it was done and for what reasons. The technical basis of the old-fashioned story, Chandler explained,

> was the relative insignificance of everything except the final denouement. What led up to it was more or less passage-work. The technical basis of the Black Mask type of story on the other hand was

that the scene outranked the plot, in the sense that a good plot was one that made good scenes. The ideal mystery was one you would read if the end was missing.

The hard-boiled school also handled the element of danger differently. In the older detective story the sense of danger was not really strong nor was the reader convincingly caught up with it. The mysterious red lamp that signaled another murder might glow in Mary Roberts Rinehart's dark old house, or the poisoner might strike again at the Rector's party, but the reader knew that there was some pattern behind it all and that the killer would eventually be exposed. In *Black Mask* stories this was not the case; danger was everywhere, nor was it rational. They were city stories, set in New York, or Los Angeles, or Chicago, where an innocent man might be caught in a street fight or the crooked cop might be on your street. As Chandler phrased it, in these new stories "the streets were dark with something more than night."

Certainly the impact of World War I and the unsettled, doubtful state of society after it had much to do with the theme and tone of the "hard-boiled" detective story, which provided, in Chandler's estimate, "the simplest and yet most complete pattern of the tensions in which we live in this generation." One of the reasons for the revolt against the old-style puzzle story (though it remained popular) was that the society of the twenties and thirties was no longer the orderly, self-confident, secure society of the prewar years. To some of those who survived The Great War, savagery lay close to the surface of life. The death of ten million men, wrote Robert Duffus in 1918, revealed to his generation that "there is no escape from the hideous chaos of struggle." About all one could do to survive, as Hemingway, James T. Farrell, James Cain, Horace McCoy, and other novelists recommended, was to play a counter-game against society.

The new-style detectives reflected this attitude. The society in which Vance, Queen, and even Charlie Chan operated was an essentially rational world in which crime could be solved by the man of logic. Postwar society was different. In a world of paid-off cops, corrupt politicians, rich crooks, expensive call girls, and contract murder, logic did not necessarily work. The question of who put the weedkiller in Aunt Hetty's bouillon was of little interest compared to that of who would (or could) break the power of a gangster czar. The hard-boiled dick lived in this world, where the puzzles had no answers nor could Dupin's elegant reasoning find any.

The most easily identifiable characteristic of the *Black Mask* story was its flat, terse, reportorial style. The writer tried to use language,

Chandler told Gardner, with a kind of controlled intensity, "similar to the control a great pitcher has over a ball." An early story of Paul Cain's handled violence without emphasis or emotion:

> The little man came into the room quickly and kicked the side of Kells' head very hard. Kells relaxed his grip on Rose and Rose stood up. He brushed himself off and went over and kicked Kells' head and face several times. He kicked Kells' head very carefully, drawing his foot back and aiming, and then kicking very accurately and hard. The kitten jumped off the desk and went to Kells' bloody head and sniffed delicately.

Raymond Chandler's description of the discovery of a body in *The High Window* was detailed and passionless:

> The floor of the bathroom was too short for him, so his knees were poked up and hung outwards slackly and his head was pressed against the wood-stone baseboard at the other end, not tilted up, but jammed tight. His brown suit was rumpled a little, and his dark glasses stuck out of his breast pocket at an unsafe angle. As if that mattered, his right hand was thrown across his stomach, his left hand lay on the floor, palm up, the fingers curled a little. There was a bloodcaked bruise on the right side of his head, in the blond hair. His open mouth was full of shiny crimson blood.

Surprising bits of metaphor surfaced (Stephen Crane fashion) in the prose of the better writers—a girl who "smelled the way the Taj Mahal looks by moonlight"; a man "with no more personality than a paper cup"; a woman "with a face like stale beer"; a sky "that was queer, with too much clarity in it, like something bitter in a glass of water." Chandler's description of death as "the big sleep" was used later by Eugene O'Neill.

There was sex in the stories, implicit rather than overt, not terribly important except as a reason for something else. Sex, it was assumed, was part of the tough, amoral society that produced crime; it had little to do with love. The love story and the detective story, in Chandler's estimation (Mary Roberts Rinehart notwithstanding) could not exist in the same book. To his detective Philip Marlowe, sex was as dangerous as a gun. In *The Little Sister* he is not even tempted, only wary and a bit amused.

> "Amigo," she said softly. She put her arms out. I took hold of her wrists and brought them together and made her palms touch. I played patacake with her for a moment. The expression in her eyes was languorous and fiery at the same time.
>
> I let go of her wrist, closed the door with my elbow and slid past her. It was like the first time.

"You ought to carry insurance on those," I said, touching one. It was real enough. The nipple was as hard as a ruby. I didn't look at her. I didn't want to look at her. I sat down on a davenport and rubbed a hand across my forehead. Slim, dark and lovely and smiling. Reeking with sex. Utterly beyond the moral laws of this or any other world I could imagine.

Hammett's Sam Spade, with full knowledge that the girl hoped to bribe him with her body, took the body but not the bribe in *The Maltese Falcon:*

> Her eyelids drooped. "Oh, I'm so tired," she said tremulously, "so tired of it all, of myself, of lying and thinking up lies, and of not knowing what is a lie and what is the truth. I wish I—" She put her hands up to Spade's cheeks, put her open mouth hard against his mouth, her body hard against his body. Spade's arms went around her holding her to him, muscles bulging his blue sleeves, a hand cradling her head, its fingers half lost among red hair, a hand moving groping fingers over her slim back. His eyes burned yellowly.

Dashiell Hammett began to develop the character of his private detective, the Continental Op, for *Black Mask* and in 1929 wrote him into a novel, *Red Harvest,* serialized in the magazine. The Op, a more complicated character than most of his companions, fortyish, a bit fat, and very tough—appeared again the same year in *The Dain Curse,* but in *The Maltese Falcon* (1930) Sam Spade replaced him. The investigator of *The Glass Key* (1931) was not a detective but Ned Beaumont, a racketeer's bodyguard. A study of character and brutality, it remains the most complex of Hammett's novels. *The Thin Man* (1934) shifted to Nick Charles, an exdetective who wanted only to be left alone to enjoy his bourbon and his pretty wife but who got involved in murder over his protest. The heart of Hammett's work lies in his first four novels, his three Sam Spade stories, and his early Continental Op series.

The Op, Spade, and Beaumont—Hammett's three versions of the tough hero—have similarities and differences. The Op is a professional, doing well what he is paid to do. He is scrupulously honest, not because of any ethical commitments but because his job demands it. He cleans up a corrupt city in *Red Harvest* because a man hired him to do it; that it will be just as corrupt five years hence matters not at all. "Emotions are nuisances during business hours," so he has none. Sex, hate, and anger divert the attention and impair efficiency; there is, he says, "hard skin over what's left of my soul . . . after twenty years of messing around with crime." His closest approach to introspection occurs in *Red Harvest,* when after causing sixteen deaths in a week he wonders briefly if he likes killing too much—"Play with murder enough, and it gets you one of two ways; it makes you sick or you get to like it. . . ."

Spade, described by Hammett as "a hard, shifty fellow, always able to take care of himself, able to get the best of anybody," is a more reflective man. A professional like The Op, Spade nevertheless has a large area of ambiguous gray in his character. Neither he nor the reader is sure he will deny himself the woman, reject the bribe, or find no pleasure in killing, nor does it really matter to him. Through Spade, Hammett came closer than anywhere else to a philosophical position—since life is disorderly and confused one cannot plan for it; one can only adjust to it, and in the end it is probably enough to have taken care of yourself.

Yet Spade does have an elementary if somewhat bruised belief in something positive. In his list of seven reasons for turning his bedmate Brigid O'Shaughnessy over to the police at the end of *The Maltese Falcon*, he cites first the fact that she had killed his partner—a man he hated, but still his partner. "When a man's partner is killed," he explains, "he's supposed to do something about it. It doesn't make any difference what you thought of him. You're supposed to do something about it." The Op's fidelity to his job and Spade's to his partner comprised Hammett's only positive statement before *The Glass Key* (the book he preferred) where loyalty was the major theme. Ned Beaumont's allegiance to Paul Madvig, a crooked politician who does not deserve it, brings him two of the most brutal beatings in literature and nearly brings him death.

Raymond Chandler's detective, Philip Marlowe, first appeared in *The Big Sleep* (1939), although Chandler had been developing the character since his first *Black Mask* story, "Blackmailers Don't Shoot," in 1933. Chandler, who did not begin writing until he was forty-five, experimented with Marlowe under several different names, gradually creating, he said, a detective interested in something more than money, "a man fit for adventure . . . , a complete man and a common man and yet an unusual man . . . , the best man in his world, and good enough for any world." That world presented itself to Marlowe much as it had to Spade. Deception is the only way to get along in it; everybody in it lies a little bit, some a lot. Nobody in a Chandler novel tells the whole truth, which makes finding any truth at all difficult, and nobody ever wins much.

"A lonely, proud man . . . , with rude wit, a lively sense of the grotesque, a disgust for sham, and a contempt for pettiness," Marlowe understands what the world is like, and somewhat cynically does what he can to change it a trifle. It is his willingness to involve himself that separates him from Spade and other private dicks of the period. "Marlowe has a personal conscience," Chandler once wrote. "He is a sympathetic man, and so will take up a personal cause for a lonely person." He is a professional and proud of it—"I told you I was a detective," he says. "I work at it, lady, I don't play at it"—but he also cares. "I hear voices crying in the night," he told Bernie Ohls, who asked him in *The Long Goodbye* why he makes his living as he does, "and I go to see what's the matter. You don't make a dime that way."

Chandler's contribution to the hard-boiled detective story was that he made it something more than a story about solving and punishing crime. It was equally important to him and Marlowe that someone care sufficiently about justice to risk danger to see that it *is* done. Marlowe solves murders, but he also protects those who need protection, saves what he can from the wreckage, and now and then feels compassion for the guilty, the dead, and those voices crying in the night. Chandler wrote seven novels: *The Big Sleep*, 1939; *Farewell, My Lovely*, 1940; *The High Window*, 1942; *The Lady in The Lake*, 1943; *The Little Sister*, 1949; *The Long Goodbye*, 1954; and *Playback*, 1958, written not long before his death and different from its predecessors. These and his twenty-three short stories exerted a strong influence on the course of the detective novel, which since his time has been overrun with tough private eyes.

Ross Macdonald's Lew Archer, who arrived in 1949 in *The Moving Target*, followed by fourteen others down to *The Goodbye Look* (1969), is by far the most literate and stylish of Marlowe's descendants. Like Hammett and Chandler, Macdonald has an imaginative metaphoric style; there are "eyes that change like lenses in a sophisticated camera," "the heartbroken lewdness that only very young girls are capable of," "a brilliant smile, that faded like an optical illusion," a man "with an air of desperate failure that hung about him like a personal odor."

The flat, reportorial style, echoing with impressionistic overtones, Macdonald uses with great skill, as exemplified by his description of young surfers in a roadside diner at a California beach:

> The overcast was burning off. A sun like a small watery moon appeared behind it. The muffled horizon gradually cleared, and the sea changed from grey to greyish blue. The surf had begun to thump so hard I could hear it.
>
> Two or three cars had come up from the cluster of beach houses, but there had been no sign of Harriet's green Buick. I started in on my second cup of coffee. Refills were only ten cents.
>
> A zebra-striped hearse with a broken headlight came in off the highway. It disgorged, from front and rear, four boys and two girls who all looked like siblings. Their hair, bleached by sun and perox-

ide, was long on the boys and short on the girls so that it was almost uniform. They wore blue sweatshirts over bathing suits. Their
faces were brown and closed.

They came in and sat in a row at the counter, ordered six beers,
drank them with hero sandwiches which the girls made out of
French loaves and other provisions brought in in paper bags. They
ate quietly and voraciously. From time to time, between bites, the
largest boy, who carried himself like their leader, made a remark
about big surf. He might have been talking about a tribal deity.

They rose in unison like a platoon, and marched out to their
hearse. Two of the boys got into the front seat. The rest of them sat
in the back beside the surfboards. One of the girls, the pretty one,
made a face at me through the side window. For no good reason, I
made a face back at her. The hearse turned down the blacktop toward the beach.

"Beach bums," the woman behind the counter said.

Macdonald (Kenneth Millar) uses Archer to explore the gaudy, unreal, restless society of Southern California, probing into the darkness
beneath the suntanned good life. Like Marlowe, Archer is hired for a routine job—a missing boy, a runaway bride, a jewel theft—which opens up
a whole unexpected basket of snakes. Each discovery leads him deeper
into evil. People lie to him, as he expects them to; they try to divert him
and bribe him, and sometimes they try to kill him, but Archer plods on
until the truth is out, hating what he sees people doing to each other. And
the truth, when he finds it, is wryly ironic. The people involved have often
done their terrible things not out of greed, or lust, or desire for power,
but from love, which as Archer suspects, is perhaps the most deadly motive of all.

Archer of course makes a living out of crime, but it is not that that
impels him into other people's lives. He is a thoughtful, compassionate
man, fascinated by the why of evil and murder and by the sick, sad, violent society that produces it. He is involved with his fellow beings and
cannot help it, with "all the long hairs and short hairs, the potheads and
the acid heads, draft dodgers and dollar chasers, swingers and walking
wounded, idiot saints, hard cases, and foolish virgins." Novels like *The
Zebra-Striped Hearse* (1962), *The Galton Case* (1964) and *Black Money*
(1966) survive comparison with Chandler and Hammett at their best.

After Archer, however, the curve goes down. John D. MacDonald's
dozen or so books about private detective Travis McGee mix sex and
brutality in increasing proportions. A professional who had forty novels
on the lists before he invented McGee in 1963, MacDonald has sold some
twenty-five million books and five hundred shorter pieces. McGee, de-

scribed as a "soldier of fortune, thinking man's Robin Hood . . . , amiable skeptic, freelance knight in slightly tarnished armor," is Spade and Marlowe set at stud in Florida's playboy paradise. Rape, torture, savage beatings, and death in especially gruesome form are standard fare in the McGee books, with at least one detailed description of orgasm per book. *Bright Orange for a Shroud* (1966) for example, contained nine sex acts, a suicide, four killings, and an especially obscene rape. *Dress Her in Indigo* (1969) involved five acts of intercourse, homosexuality, lesbianism, gang-rape, drug addiction, and nine killings. The focus of a McGee novel is almost always sexual, although the crime that catalyzes the action may be something else, and the retribution is often appropriately terrifying. One brutal rapist dies by being accidentally impaled through the crotch by a piece of driftwood after leaping from a boat; another is blinded, then the skin of his genitals carefully flayed. Violent as his books are, MacDonald writes with a strong narrative drive, handles character and motivation skillfully, and gives his locale a strong sense of Miami's bustling, boosterish, faintly decadent society.

Among the dozen or so hard-boiled dicks who have followed the Spade-Marlowe tradition, the ultimate degradation of it belongs to Mickey Spillane's Mike Hammer, who burst on an unsuspecting public in *I, The Jury*, in 1947, written in nine days. Since then none of Spillane's seventeen books (by 1969) have sold less than a million. Most have appeared in first printings of two million, while his total sales exceed fifty million.

Inept, vulgar, savage, the Hammer books nevertheless command a huge and devoted audience. As Charles Rolo pointed out, Spillane combines the comic strip (he once wrote for them), the pulp story, the sex magazine, and the blue movie with cops, robbers, and blood.

Hammer is by all odds the toughest character in modern fiction. He is not out to enforce the law or to serve justice. He is his own law (as *I, The Jury* makes clear), his own judge, prosecutor, and executioner. He has nothing against the police, but since they are handcuffed by such things as due process and constitutional rights, he punishes crimes that they cannot. People talk to him when they won't talk to the police, Hammer explains, "because they know what I'll do to them if they don't." His motives are morally simple. He never kills anyone who isn't "someone who needed knocking off bad." The way to handle a crook when the law can't is to "plunk one right in his gut and when he's dying on the floor kick his teeth in." Thus Hammett's recognition of ambiguity and chance, and Chandler's feel for human involvement, have been reduced by Spillane to nothing but killing.

Sex and death lie at the bottom of all Spillane books. His first five contained forty-eight killings, twenty-one beatings, and twenty-one sex acts. To Hammer all women are available; he never seduces any of them, since they proposition him immediately and are often forced to wait a bit. Eventually the women virtually attack him, asking only gratification, for which they are tearfully thankful:

> She was there in my arms again, softly at first and hungry-mouthed again. Her fingers were velvet cat-claws, kneading me gently, searching and finding. When I touched her, things seemed to melt away until there was only the warmth of flesh and a giddy sensation of being overpowered by a runaway emotion. As I lay there time ceased to exist and as she came down on top of me she murmured little things that only the mind heard. . . .

And along with sex is always death, sometimes quick and brutal:

> He opened his mouth wide and I shot him right through the gaping hole in his face and he slammed headfirst into the wall splattering his blood and brains all over the place.

Sometimes carefully, almost lovingly described:

> Their eyes always get that way when they knew they were about to die. It was a dull, glassy look and a slack expression and no words because they realized that the one on the other end of the gun had the same conscience factor as they had themselves and would shoot for the fun of it if they had to. They could hardly talk with the fear, so they couldn't lie at all. They could only hope that it would be over fast and painlessly and not with a gigantic hole in their intestines that would leave them living in hours of agony before the merciful blackness came. A long string of saliva came out of his mouth. He swallowed, wiped his mouth, and let his lips come shut. Then I swung the .45 and laid it across the side of his head so hard the scalp split and blood and tissue splashed over my hand. He went down without a sound, falling so that he was almost kissing the faceless body of the one by the radiator.

All this is justified by Hammer's moral judgment. In Spillane's system, evil people deserve what they get; anything they get is justifiable. Gangsters, dishonest politicians, narcotics peddlers, blackmailers, pornographers, Communists and the like ought to be beaten, tortured, and killed off. What Hammer calls his "kill lust" is aimed at them and others like them. The sex-and-guts formula of the Hammer books (and of Hammer's successors, a half-reformed hoodlum named Ryan and a "counterspy" named Tiger Mann) does not in itself explain Spillane's popularity.

He offers a simple, direct answer to some of society's more frustrating problems—the Mafia, crooked cops, big graft, foreign spies, gangsters, and the like. In other words, he gets results.

The detective mystery of the sixties and seventies divides into six fairly clear categories: the older tradition of detection; the "private eye" story; the "spy" novel of international intrigue; the domestic-sentimental mystery; the Gothic-suspense school; and the recent, offbeat "black humor" story which has not yet fully developed its own style. Most prolific and still the most popular are the traditional novels of formal detection, involving the familiar amateurs, professionals, and combinations thereof. The indomitable Ellery Queen still leads this category, but except for Helen McCloy's psychiatrist-detective Basil Willing and Helen Reilly's Inspector McKee the field is otherwise dominated by foreign imports, chiefly British, among them Agatha Christie's Belgian detective, Hercule Poirot, Ngaio Marsh's elegant Sir Roderick Alleyn, Michael Innes's (John Innes Mackintosh Stewart) Inspector Appleby, and J. J. Maric's (John Creasey) Inspector Gideon.

The most original and skillful American product of the police-procedure school is the realistic "87th Precinct" series by Ed McBain (Evan Hunter), opening with *Cop Hater* (1956) and the central figure of Detective Steve Carella, continuing through eighteen subsequent books. Tautly written, tightly plotted, and imaginatively conceived, Hunter's stories are by far the best of the police-procedure-detective type published in the fifties and sixties.

The "hard-boiled dick" story, in terms of sales, probably ranks second, the two best-selling authors in the category being John D. MacDonald's McGee (thirty million) and Donald Hamilton's Matt Helm (fourteen million). Macdonald's Archer, Prather's Shell Scott, Miller's Max Thursday, Garrity's Peter Braid, Richard Smith's John Kincaid, and Thomas Dewey's Mac appear regularly in the paperback racks. Harold Masur's Scott Jordan is a tough lawyer, something like Mason, but operates as a private eye. George Harmon Coxe's Casey, from *Black Mask* days, was still taking cases in the sixties and Brett Halliday's (David Dresser) Mike Shayne, who works in Miami Beach, handled his fiftieth case in 1968.

The spy novel, a detective variant, has been almost exclusively a British monopoly. The grandfather of them all was Arthur Sarsefield Wade (or Warde) who as Saxe Rohmer created the evil, inscrutable Dr. Fu Manchu in 1913 and carried his adventures through forty books. Rohmer was so steeped in Oriental lore that he was convinced he had existed in Egypt in a previous incarnation; he also studied painting, wrote music and plays, and invented an improved mothball. His creative life, however, was given over largely to Fu Manchu and his eternal lust for world domination, foiled each time only at the last moment by the intrepid British agent, Denis Nayland Smith of the Foreign Service.

Fu Manchu possessed the greatest array of weapons known to man, including death-rays, poisons that turned men green, television receivers that fitted the palm, and drugs in assortments and guises such as the pharmacopeia never knew. Not the least of his weapons were sloe-eyed exotic girls named Fah Lo See or Wah Lee Sin, who never tempted Smith but wreaked havoc with his staff. When Smith, at the beginning of the story, shouted, "Great issues are at stake! Blow the lock out with a carbine! The fate of a nation hangs on it!" the reader knew he was in for a tale of intrigue and danger such as the world had never known.

Nayland Smith's most popular grandson was Ian Fleming's James Bond (Secret Agent 007) whose books were incredibly successful in the fifties and sixties, approaching nine million in sales and culminating in a series of highly lucrative movies. Almost burlesques of themselves, the late Fleming stories fell off in quality. John Le Carré, another Britisher, burst into the market with *The Spy Who Came In from the Cold* (1963), his fellow-countryman Len Deighton with *The Ipcress File* (1962) and four others. Taking advantage of the James Bond phenomenon, American publishers resuscitated Nick Carter as a "Killmaster Spy" who through thirty-six books reveled in sex and violence like an international Mike Hammer. Donald Hamilton's Matt Helm, another "international agent," is essentially the tough-guy private eye in the espionage business, and so is Michael Avallone's Ed Noon. The most distinguished practitioner of the type in any era is Eric Ambler, a novelist of superior talent, whose *Background to Danger* (1937) was the first of nine superb novels; several, especially *A Coffin for Dimitrios* and *Journey into Fear*, have become classics in the field.

The mark of Mary Roberts Rinehart remained strong on the domestic mystery, which continues to hold a large, devoted audience. Helen McCloy, Mabel Seeley, Rae Foley (Elinore Denniston), and at least twenty other female authors supply the rental and public library shelves with hundreds of such novels. Richard and Frances Lockridge, a husband-and-wife writing team, introduced a husband-and-wife detective team, Mr. and Mrs. North, in 1936. The bright, attractive Norths, a kind of upper-class Blondie and Dagwood combination, blunder into a crime, help the police solve it, and blunder out once more into tennis, cocktails, suburbia, and trips to the theater. An immensely popular combination of humor, domesticity, danger, and cuteness, the North books moved into movies, radio, and television with great success. (Audrey) Kelly Roos's

Jeff and Haila, another couple, are cut to the same pattern. Emma Lathen, who entered the field in the late sixties with *A Stitch in Time* (1967), is probably the most expert and sophisticated of the contemporary female group. Choosing an unlikely field of specialization—big business and banking—and an equally unlikely amateur sleuth—a conservative, middle-aged investment banker named J. P. Thatcher—she nevertheless produced a witty and suspenseful series of books that still kept faith with the old-fashioned rules.

The writer who most closely approaches Mrs. Rinehart's skill, however, is Mignon G. Eberhart, who can produce the same mixture nearly as expertly as the Queen herself. Mrs. Eberhart began with *The Patient in Room 18* (1929) and at last count in 1969 had published over forty more. Nearly all her novels have appeared first as serials in women's magazines; many have been successful movies and television scripts; and she has produced a long list of short stories. The wife of an engineer, she has traveled widely and draws upon her travels for what she calls "authentic, interesting backgrounds." *Message from Hong Kong* (1969) provides an excellent example of her professional mixture of a trace of Gothic, a slender thread of romance, a not-too-dangerous mystery, and an exotic locale. Marcia Lowry, whose unwholesome husband Dino disappeared into the Far East, wishes to marry again but must establish her husband's existence. She begins a rather aimless search of Hong Kong and finds him murdered; with her intended second husband she begins a search for the criminals which eventually both solves the mystery and opens the way for a happy marriage.

If any new trend has appeared in the detective-mystery novel during the sixties, critic Anthony Boucher once remarked, it has been the appearance of humor—black and otherwise. Jacob Hay's "The Opposite Number," a clever spoof on the CIA and similar spy organizations that appeared in *Ellery Queen's Mystery Magazine* in 1966, for example, was really neither mystery nor detective in the ordinary sense at all, but a tour de force of sophisticated humor. Allen Kim Lang's "Murder Is a Gas," published by *The Saint Magazine* in 1967, about a series of murders in a wildly zany research-and-development corporation called Loki Laboratories, would probably have been steered toward a science fiction magazine a decade earlier.

George Baxt's *A Queer Kind of Death* (1967) introduced not only a nightmarish plot but a homosexual detective. Stanley Crawford's *Gascoyne* (1967) featured a sleuth who lives on (not near but *on*) a superhighway, and who pursues a criminal dressed as a Giant Panda. Chester Himes's Negro police detectives, Gravedigger Jones and Coffin Ed Johnson, barely escape grotesquery, while Himes's plots are loaded with odd-ball incidents and ironic in-jokes. *Blind Man with a Pistol* (1968), for example, is a kind of Virgilian journey through a Harlem netherworld that features a hundred-year-old man who lives with a dozen prostitutes in a funeral home, the murder of a white homosexual by black ones, the church of a self-styled Black Jesus, and assorted riots and violences. Where all this may lead the detective story of the seventies boggles the mind.

There is no doubt of the permanent popularity of detective-mystery stories in whatever form. Since they have never been regularly listed in best-seller computations, and since they frequently appear as reprints (some of Spillane's have had seventy-five reprintings) their sales can only be estimated. One of every four books published and reprinted in the United States each year is a detective-mystery; they make up half or more of the books stocked by the 50,000 rental libraries in the country and probably account for a third of all public library borrowings. Erle Stanley Gardner, whose books have sold upwards of 135 millions, stands first among all authors; Ellery Queen, at one hundred millions, precedes Mickey Spillane at fifty millions. Of all varieties of popular literature, the detective-mystery and its variants undoubtedly occupy first place with the mass reading public.

The reasons for such popularity are not hard to discover. People like to unravel riddles, and the detective-mystery at bottom, whatever its variation, is always a puzzle. It tells a story, nothing more; it doesn't involve symbols, multileveled interpretations, underlying myth-ritual patterns, nor elaborate psychologizing. Rarely does it grasp the reader inwardly, nor are its components realistically presented. To die by poison is horrible, but in most detective stories it is usually quick and offstage, nor does the reader ever see the gas chamber, the electric chair, the solitary cell. And the reader, of course, can have his satisfaction both ways. He can identify with the criminal to experience the vicarious thrill of crime, and then change places with the detective to search out and punish the culprit. Having long ago achieved a social status denied the Western, the comic, and the love story (Mary Roberts Rinehart was proud that her books were read by four Presidents) detective-mystery stories are ideally fitted to a popular market that wants the excitement of fiction without the sophistications and complexities of the formalized, higher-level novel.

THE FUTURE AS HISTORY: SCIENCE FICTION

The chief malady of man is a restless curiosity about things which he cannot understand.

— PASCAL, *Pensées*

Science fiction is a relatively recent branch of popular literature, since the scientific elements on which it is based are themselves recent. Only after it was generally agreed—during the eighteenth century—that science was an important influence on society, could science's relation to the future be written about. To the nineteenth century science was an imaginatively exciting and somewhat disturbing element of life; what the future might be, or what the present ought to be, in the light of science's ability to change things, fascinated the thinkers of the age. Fiction of fantasy—that is, of the unexplained impossibility—is of course as old as fairy tale and myth. Fiction of science—of the explicable possibility—depended on the post-Newtonian world's faith in science's ability to explain and shape experience. Whereas legend, myth, fantasy, and fairy tale utilized magic to invoke believability, the nineteenth century substituted science, to create a new and differently credible kind of tale.

Science fiction (as opposed to fantasy) concerns itself with possible future events, founded on an accurate knowledge of the present real world and based on a thorough understanding of the nature and limits of science's achievements. The writer, after choosing his premise, must logically develop his narrative without violating known fact, "except when the violation itself," as Fletcher Pratt has pointed out, "constitutes the basis of the story and a plausible explanation for the violation is furnished." Baum's *Wizard of Oz* is fantasy; Wells' *Invisible Man* is science fiction. Sam Moskowitz' definition of the genre locates its boundaries precisely:

> Science fiction is a branch of fantasy identifiable by the fact that it eases the "willing suspension of disbelief" on the part of its readers by utilizing an atmosphere of scientific credibility for its imaginative speculations in physical science, space, time, social science, and philosophy.

When people generally agreed that science caused continuous, inevitable, and perhaps desirable changes in the quality of life, modern science fiction took shape. As H. Bruce Franklin has explained, nineteenth-century literature was pervaded by an interest in science, and in the problems it brought as well as in those it seemed to solve. Charles Brockden Brown, Cooper, Hawthorne, Simms, and others used science as a symbolic vehicle for fiction. Poe, more than anyone of his time, experimented with it with skill and seriousness, using science and pseudoscience as tools with which to explore the recesses of the mind—*The Adventures of Hans Pfaal, The Narrative of A. Gordon Pym, The Balloon Hoax, The Case of M. Valdemar, A Tale of the Ragged Mountains,* and others. Poe established the essential difference between fantasy fiction and science fiction (though he wrote both) by ruling that every departure from the norm of behavior of men and matter must be explained rationally and must be scientifically plausible—a distinction ultimately of great importance.

In Victorian England and in France the science-fiction novel bloomed swiftly. Jules Verne, strongly influenced by Poe, in 1863 began a series of novels centered on journeys to the unusual, exotic, and unknown—*Five Weeks on a Balloon, A Journey to the Center of the Earth, From Earth to the Moon, Twenty Thousand Leagues under the Sea*—producing nearly fifty books in all. Verne speculated about the possibilities of time machines, space guns, star ships, submarines, rockets, and other devices, introducing a mechanical element into science fiction that it never lost. H. G. Wells in England gave science fiction meaning, symbols, and allegory—*The Time Machine* (1895), *The Invisible Man* (1897), *War of the Worlds* (1898), *The First Man on the Moon* (1901)—and established at least four plot-lines soon to become classic themes—stellar travel, alien invasion, time-warps, and the fourth dimension.

By 1900 science fiction was a well developed form of popular literature in Europe. The London *Strand Magazine* (which had an American edition) specialized in it, publishing Haggard, Verne, the fantasies of M. P. Shiel, and Conan Doyle's "Professor Challenger" stories; so too did *Pearson's, Blackwood's,* and other magazines. An American magazine,

The Black Cat, founded in 1895, published both science fiction and fantasy, likewise Munsey's *Argosy* and Street and Smith's *Popular Magazine.* Working from the formula polished by Verne and Wells, American science fiction writers by 1915 had tested most of the themes of the European variety and had established a number of distinct categories. There were stories of marvelous machines (tanks, robots, balloons, ships, aircraft, rockets, and the like); of space travel to other worlds (Mars, Venus, and especially the moon); of catastrophes (Manhattan splits in half, fogs poison New York and London, aliens invade, gravity inverts); of genetic monster creatures (men, plants, animals, cells); of mental aberrations and sensory extensions (telepathy, telekinesis, extrasensory perception, somnambulism); end-of-the-world and last-man stories of Armageddon; and time-displacement tales, plus endless variations and combinations of them all. Most writers, following Poe and Verne, exploited the journalistic mode, aimed at hoaxing the reader into the belief that what he read was a report of actual events.

The great boom in American science fiction started in 1912 with the publication in *All-Story* of a serial, "Under the Moons of Mars," by Edgar Rice Burroughs. Burroughs, who had been a cowboy, soldier, policeman, goldminer, storekeeper, and aluminum salesman, had gone rather unsuccessfully into advertising. After placing some copy in a pulp magazine, he wondered if he could write stories of the kind he read there, and immediately found he had a flair for popular fiction. Whether or not there was life on Mars was a favorite barroom argument; Burroughs' handling of the concept was shrewd and uncomplicated.

A natural storyteller, Burroughs had a real gift for suspense—holding the reader's attention. And he had just enough "message" to impress the reader with the seriousness of his story so that it seemed something more than merely adventure. Most of all, Burroughs had a genuine gift for characterization, unusual among pulp writers, that marked him at once as a success. John Carter, the explorer-narrator of the Mars novels, is a memorable, identifiable person. Tarzan remains the greatest popular character creation of all time—but one also does not forget the solid reality of jungle people like Tantor the elephant, Numa the Lion, Hista the Great Snake, and Tarzan's ape-mother, gentle Kala.

Burroughs wrote another Martian novel before he wrote *Tarzan of The Apes,* which he sold to *All-Story* in 1912. He said later that he invented the character one sleepless night as a variation on the Romulus and Remus legend, though he may also have drawn on Kipling's Mowgli and Rider Haggard's Africa. Burroughs knew little about Africa, and never bothered to find out much more. Nor did anyone care. After once accepting the premise that an abandoned child could be raised to maturity by apes, readers were prepared to accept anything else derived from that premise within the realm of possibility.

Tarzan's Africa, of course, was not really Africa at all, as both Burroughs and his readers knew. Having created a continent of his own, he made it his own world, with its own history, anthropology, genetics, language, and psychology. Accurate factual information would have spoiled it; instead of being one of the most imaginatively real creations of its kind, it would have been only a poor travelogue. Fundamentally Tarzan was science fiction, combining the superbeing theme, the lost-world theme, the Utopia theme, and the time-warp device.

Tarzan of the Apes sold so well that the A. C. McClurg Company put it out in book form, with the second in the series, *The Return of Tarzan,* following quickly. Estimates of the sales of the Tarzan series vary from twenty to fifty millions—and as Alva Johnston once wrote, the nation's trees resounded for years with Tarzan cries and the snapping of youthful collarbones. The ape-man has never been absent from at least one of the popular entertainment media since. Except for Mickey Mouse, Tarzan is undoubtedly the best-known fictional character in the world.

Yet Burroughs never surrendered to Tarzan. He continued his Martian series, alternating them with Tarzan books, eleven in all. Later he wrote seven "Pellucidar" novels, recounting adventures at the earth's core, and a series of Venusian novels. Of Burroughs' fifty-nine books, twenty-four, less than half, belong to Tarzan. His range was surprisingly broad. He wrote an imitation Jack London, *The Cave Girl;* a story about synthetic people, *Monster Men;* a Hollywood exposé, *The Girl from Hollywood;* a business novel, *The Efficiency Expert;* a Farrellish story about a Chicago slum youth, *The Mucker;* and a historical novel, *The Outlaw of Torn;* as well as two separate science fiction novels, *Moon Maid* and *The Land That Time Forgot.* Noticeably, he returned in his last and one of his best books, *Llana of Gathol,* written just before his death in 1950, to Mars and John Carter, the land and the man he liked best.

During the twenties, however, the nature of science fiction changed drastically with the emergence of a talented group of writers who served as a bridge from the older tradition of Poe, Verne, and Wells to a newer style. Science fiction of the twenties, after all, was read by an audience that grew up with the automobile, the airplane, X rays, and radios, had algebra, physics, and chemistry in high school, and knew all about Steinmetz, Mme. Curie, and Marconi. It demanded science in its science fiction. A. (Abraham) Merritt, whose stories first appeared in 1917, combined real science with older fantasy in a series of classic tales, many still in print, including *The Moon Pool* (1919), *The Meta Monster* (1920), and *The Ship of Ishtar* (1924). Murray Leinster (William Fitzgerald Jenkins), a learned amateur scientist with an inventive mind, turned out stories with production-line speed.

The man who was generally recognized as the progenitor of the new trend was Hugo Gernsback, who published the first radio magazine, *Modern Electrics*, in 1908 and later edited *Science and Invention*. Gernsback used a few stories based on science in his magazines and coined the rather awkward label "scientifiction" to describe the type. *Argosy* ran some such stories in the early twenties, but Gernsback's *Amazing Stories*, founded in 1926, was the first magazine devoted entirely to science fiction in modern dress. Selling at twenty-five cents, a fairly high price, it achieved a newsstand sale of 100,000 per issue, a large circulation for a specialized popular magazine.

Interest in *Amazing Stories* attracted other publishers. Gernsback lost control of it and founded three others which merged into *Wonder Stories* in 1930, along with *Astounding Stories of Super Science, The Planet, Startling Stories, Thrilling Wonder Stories, Astonishing Stories, Marvel Science*, and *Science Fiction*, mostly with circulations of 20,000 to 30,000 per issue. The big boom came in the fifties, when there were thirty-odd magazines in the field.

Running parallel was the "weird" magazine, publishing fantasy tales with a high science content, exemplified best by *Weird Tales*, founded in 1923. The theories of Charles Fort, an Albany businessman who collected reports of inexplicable happenings to show that there were problems beyond reason's limits, attracted a small group of writers who used Fort's *Book of the Damned* (1919) as a base for stories that crossed supernatural with scientific. H. P. Lovecraft, the master of the macabre, judged by many to be the equal of Poe, dominated this type; Edward Hamilton, a dedicated Fortean, probably ranked next in popular appeal.

Science fiction of the thirties focused on the "gadget" or "gimmick," as one writer called it, which served as the hook on which the narrative hung. It might be a space ship, or a gravitational shift, or a mind-machine, or a time-slip, but whatever it was it was the story's most important element. Characters and plot served chiefly to elucidate the central scientific point; subtlety of motivation or niceties of craftsmanship were of less value than the "science factor" on which the narrative pivoted. Science fiction in these years, as author and critic Judith Merril described it, was "a kind of educational evangelism, preaching Space Flight, Technology, Progress and the Rule of Reason"; its aim often seemed to be to convince the public of the beneficial potentials of science as much as to tell a story.

By the close of the thirties it seemed that the limits of scientific ingenuity had been reached, and that *scientific* interest in science fiction was wearing thin.

The second change in the nature of science fiction came with John W. Campbell's appointment as editor of *Astounding Science Fiction* in 1937. Campbell, who had written a good deal of it himself, had clear and definite ideas of what he wanted. Instead of concentrating on machines and methodology, he advised writers to emphasize character, style, and the dramatic possibilities of the genre. To him, and to the group of writers he encouraged, science fiction should be not only concerned with scientific and technological change, but with its social and cultural implications as well.

Campbell's ideas reinforced what many younger writers already felt, and they encouraged them to explore science fiction's broader potentials. If interplanetary travel might put mankind in touch with superior races that could read human minds, Robert Heinlein could build a story about the issue of whether or not such telepathic knowledge could be used as evidence in a murder trial. Fletcher Pratt wondered how, if radiation caused genetic change, a young couple two thousand years hence might plan a family; Rigort Smith wrote a short story about the problem of buying used space-cars from a sharp secondhand auto dealer. Interest shifted from the story-line to the characters, from science *per se* to the problems it might create, from technological progress to its effect on humanity. His stories, wrote A. E. Van Vogt, were not so much fiction about science as about "something happening to, or being made to happen by, people who were human beings first, and only secondly participants in some gigantic experiment."

This change in focus opened up a new area in which science fiction writers could work, bringing them closer to the techniques of traditional fiction. Lester Del Rey (who also edited *Space Fiction*), L. Sprague de Camp, A. E. Van Vogt, and Theodore Sturgeon, among others, pursued new lines of inquiry in science fiction with ingenuity and distinction. Robert Heinlein, interested in the philosophical and political implications of scientific change, created a "Future History" where the problems of man, society, and government in today's world could be brought under analysis.

G. Stanley Weinbaum developed the interplanetary novel; Philip Wylie worked with the superman theme; Edward Smith, who in 1928 published *The Skylark of Space*, one of the first "cosmic" stories, in 1937–38 published a four-part 400,000 word novel dealing with a future space society, including *The Grey Lensman*, on the "superrace" theme, and *Galactic Patrol*, a "space police" classic. Olaf Stapledon, a disciple of

Hegel and Spinoza, whose *Last and First Man* (1930) is still one of the best "last man" stories, created a "galactic empire" in *Star Maker* (1937). During the thirties and forties the science fiction writer aimed his stories at the point at which science impinged on society.

"Science fiction," wrote Isaac Asimov, one of the new school, "is that branch of literature which is concerned with the impact of scientific advance upon human beings." His own novel, *I, Robot,* was a sensitive probing of future relationships of man with machine implied by an increasingly computerized, mechanized civilization. Robert Bloch's "Almost Human," in which human beings corrupt an innocent robot, was a bitterly ironic comment on contemporary ethics. Heinlein's *Puppet Masters,* a variant of the alien-invader theme in which a race of terrifying and repulsive polyps very nearly enslave mankind, was a thinly veiled allegory of dictatorship. Van Vogt's *Slan,* in addition to being a provocative study of genetic selection, was also a quietly effective parable about individuality and conformity. Eando Binder's "A Teacher From Mars," dealing with a gentle, intelligent Martian's experiences on earth, was written specifically, Binder said, "to show the evils of discrimination and intolerance." Arthur Clarke's *Childhood's End,* an echo of the Edenic myth, was a story of humanity's rebirth and loss of innocence in a future interplanetary society.

The appeal of the new science fiction was immediately reflected in the market. Whereas there were only four science fiction magazines in 1937, there were thirteen in 1939, twenty-two in 1941 (dropping to eight in the war years), increasing to thirty in the fifties, coincident with interest in atomic energy, automation, rocketry, electronics, and the real possibilities of space travel. Two new and important magazines appeared, *The Magazine of Fantasy and Science Fiction* (1949), edited by Anthony Boucher (William A. P. White) and *Galaxy Science Fiction* (1950), edited by Herbert Gold, both emphasizing sophisticated plots, stylistic polish, and social-psychological materials.

The trend toward flexibility, breadth, and variety continued into the fifties. Writers who knew Jung and Freud, Joyce and Kafka, Frazer and Raglan, introduced psychiatry, philosophy, religion, sociology, and myth into science fiction. The focus of interest shifted from physical science to psychology, from engineering to biophysics, from lunar flight to extrasensory perception; authors asked imaginative questions about scientific theories and explored traditional philosophical and ethical assumptions.

"We take all the universe as our province," wrote Robert Silverberg, "and there are many ways of exploring that universe, from the bang-bang space opera to the abstruse excursion into inner space." Theodore Sturgeon (an admirer of William Blake and William Morris) specialized in monster stories; Isaac Asimov, a biochemist, introduced the detective formula in stories about R. Daneel Olivaw, the Robot Detective; Clifford Simak, a Minneapolis newspaperman, emphasized the bizarre and fantastic; Fritz Leiber toyed with time and witchcraft. Van Vogt invented the "slan," a genetically superior being, to study social and ethical issues raised by genetic manipulation.

Arthur C. Clarke, a British scientist, whose *Exploration of Space* was the first book of its kind to be chosen by the Book-of-the-Month Club, wrote *Childhood's End* (1953), *Earthlight* (1955), and *Moondust* (1961), books far above the average in concept, style, and maturity. Optimistic in outlook, Clarke's work has made him one of the best-known science fiction authors of the times. Ray Bradbury's novels, while science-based, have disturbing emotional, psychological, and political overtones that place them closer to fantasy. A careful craftsman and consummate stylist, Bradbury burst into notice with *The Martian Chronicles* (1950) and *The Illustrated Man* (1951), continuing with two collections, *Golden Apples of the Sun* (1953) and *A Medicine for Melancholy* (1959) and two novels, *Fahrenheit 451* (1953) and *Something Wicked This Way Comes* (1962). With sales of over ten million books, Bradbury is the best-selling science fiction writer of the present, by a clear margin.

Science fiction has standardized its plots into four broad categories: space travel to and from distant planets, involving galactic wars, alien races, new societies and extraterrestrial empires; time travel, to the future, past, "alternate universes," and "the world of IF" (if Hitler had won, if atomic war destroyed the earth, if Martians came) including the perennial "last man on earth" plot; the hazards of science—robots, monsters, computers, psychological and biological mutation; and the superman or superrace themes, serving the purposes of allegory and social criticism. Beneath the plots lie certain value patterns which seem to hold consistently throughout the spectrum of modern science fiction. They have deep faith in man's ability to improve his world and his future, an almost eighteenth-century, deistic conviction that science means progress, if properly used.

There is also in the more thoughtful stories a recognition of the need for human values in a nonhumanistic world, and sometimes too a sense of the pathos of the human experience. The mood is not always optimistic; there is room for failure. There is in science fiction, scientist Fred Hoyle writes, a "deep problem" that stays unanswered, the question of what lies beneath and behind science—"How is it decided how matter shall behave, how are the laws of physics determined, why these laws and no others? Is the universe purposive, or random, and why so? What moves it?"

Science fiction has never been as popular as the detective-mystery, the Western, or the love story, but its appeal over the years has been surprisingly consistent. It can be used as a covert protest against the inadequacies and inanities of things as they are; it offers the future as an indirect attack on the present. If reader and writer do not like the world as it is, they can vicariously make a better one; fiction which deals in alternative futures will always tend to attract those who have strong opinions about the world as it is and as it might be.

Robert Heinlein has suggested that science fiction provides a means for exploring and testing alternatives for organization and action that are too dangerous to attempt in actuality; by building models and projecting behavioral options into them, one can determine and evaluate effects and results in ways otherwise impossible. His own *Green Hills of Earth*, a modern classic built about the interplanetary travel theme, is an excellent example of how he uses speculations about future human behavior in space as a device for projecting changes in the present. Like Heinlein, Manly Wade Wellman has constructed in over a hundred stories a thirtieth-century civilization on an artificial planetoid, complete with its own history, government, technology, manners, and morals, so that he could analyze objectively his own twentieth-century society. And of course, science fiction appeals directly to the pervasive human desire for something new.

Science fiction maintained a stable audience through the sixties; in 1967, for example, there were 319 original science fiction books published and twenty collections (a yearly figure that holds fairly constant), and about twenty science fiction magazines continue to maintain combined circulations of 300,000 to 400,000 per year. The average well-stocked paperback bookstand in 1969 displayed about 200 to 250 science fiction books, and there are usually one or two movies each year made from the better ones. Science fiction entered the movies in the thirties with *Deluge, Invisible Man,* and *Things to Come;* continuing into the forties and fifties with *Rocket Ship X–M, Destination Moon, When Worlds Collide,* H. G. Wells's *War of the Worlds, The Day the Earth Stood Still;* and into the sixties with Stanley Kubrick's imaginative *2001*. Television picked it up quite early; Rod Serling's *Twilight Zone* held high ratings, and so did programs like *The Invaders, Land of the Giants, Voyage to the Bottom of the Sea,* and the literate, creative *Star Trek*. The United States space program, culminating in the Apollo Eleven moon landings of July, 1969, drew national attention to science fiction and science fiction writers, who rather complacently pointed out that space travel was but one of the things they had been writing about for years, and that, in fact, much of what Apollo

Raymond Chandler. HOUGHTON MIFFLIN COMPANY.

Two illustrations from an early edition of H. G. Wells's *War of the Worlds* (1898).
THE BETTMANN ARCHIVE INC.

Edgar Rice Burroughs using an early dictaphone. CULVER PICTURES, INC.

Zane Grey. CULVER PICTURES, INC.

did and found they had predicted. Significantly, Arthur C. Clarke, Isaac Asimov, Frederick Pohl, Rod Serling, Ray Bradbury, and Robert Heinlein all appeared as commentators on national television, accorded equal space with scientists. Sales of science fiction books—especially extraterrestrial novels—leaped in volume, bookstores reporting a ten-fold increase in sales a week after Apollo's flight. Whether in books, television, or movies, science fiction was obviously destined to become the folk literature of the space age in the seventies.

Except for the burst of popularity of space novels, the most marked trend of science fiction in the late sixties was its increased interest in psychological phenomena, with stories about personality transfers, identity shifts, and behavioral and emotional problems. The most obvious evidence of this has been the intrusion of sex. Traditionally out of bounds for science fiction, sex appeared in a few stories of the thirties, notably C. L. Moore's "Shambleau" (1933) in which Northwest Smith, a hard-boiled space adventurer, experienced the ultimate sensuality in the embracing coils of a Medusa-like Martian girl. Theodore Sturgeon, in the forties, experimented carefully with sexually-aware characters, while Philip José Farmer's story "The Lovers," published in 1952 in *Startling Stories,* was frankly sexual. Today it is not uncommon to find sophisticated sex in first-rate science fiction like Robert Silverberg's "Eve and the Twenty-three Adams," which concerns a pretty Crew Girl who services the entire personnel of a spaceship during a long voyage, or his amusing "Bride Ninety-One," which deals with the marital problems of one earthman who unwittingly marries eighteen alien spacegirls. It is also, unfortunately, not uncommon to find sex used blatantly and quite unscientifically in something like Farmer's *Flesh* (1968), in which aptly-named Space Commander Stagg, on discovering a new planet, is "invested with the pure sex power of fifty bulls and turned loose on a screaming frenzy of fired-up virgins."

SIXSHOOTER COUNTRY

The purpose is to create a distinct, individual character and pit him against a specific human problem and see how he meets it. If he misses, the academic pinheads call it art, a complex human document full of ambiguities. Mine don't miss, because I make a living at it.

—WESTERN WRITER.

The West of American fiction is a creation of the closing years of the eighteenth century. The seventeenth-century colonists, who came from an orderly, controlled civilization, saw the continent as chaotic and the land as savage and dangerous. To Michael Wigglesworth, New England poet and divine, it was

> A waste and howling wilderness
> Where none inhabited
> But hellish fiends, and brutish men,
> That devils worshipped.

Nature could kill—by starvation, climate, accident, disease, Indians—and it was not to be trifled with. The frontier from the first had to be controlled and civilized before it was livable.

From the point of view of the British government, the wilderness west of the Appalachians was merely blank. So little was known of the country to the west that the Governor of Virginia, as late as 1737, optimistically commissioned a single surveying party to map the colony "from sea to sea," as the colony's charter said. Except for furs it offered little of importance, and as the British Council of Trade concluded in 1721, trade with the Indians would never amount to much. After the defeat of the French, the British even proclaimed a western boundary beyond which migration should not go, proposing that settlers be diverted instead to Nova Scotia or Georgia, "where they would be useful to their Mother Country."

The colonists, however, by mid-eighteenth century, began to think of the country to the west in quite different terms. The prospect of an almost infinite expanse of unused, arable land, filled with resources, fired the American imagination. Jonathan Carver, who explored the Great Lakes in the 1760's, conceived of the West as the future "seat of a great empire" where "mighty kingdoms will emerge from the wilderness." Jefferson, of course, caught a glimpse of this vision, and sent Lewis and Clark west in 1804 to pursue it.

The great push westward after the Revolution was in part motivated by this concept of an emergent American empire. The area beyond the mountains was filled in swiftly. By the end of the Mexican War emigrants were already moving across the plains over trails laid out by Lewis and Clark, Zebulon Pike, John Charles Frémont, and others. William Becknell opened the Santa Fe Trail in 1821–22, William Ashley reached Yellowstone in 1823, and Jedidiah Smith, that intrepid mountain man, led the first overland crossing to California in 1826.

All this found its way into the books. There was an extensive popular literature of the West by the forties, built up out of an astonishing number of travel narratives, pioneer accounts, memoirs, autobiographies, and guidebooks, all available to an eager public that was anxious to know more about this new, exciting land. Lewis and Clark's journals, published in 1814, were reprinted many times before the Civil War. Hall Kelley, who founded the American Society for Encouraging the Settlement of the Oregon Territory in 1826, published a stream of informative pamphlets that made good reading for the East. Osborne Russell's *Journal of a Trapper,* Thomas Farnham's *Travels in the Great Western Prairies,* Rufus Sage's *Rocky Mountain Life,* and other books were hardly enough to satisfy the growing market. Young Francis Parkman's trip from St. Louis to Fort Laramie in 1846 resulted in one of the first Western classics, *The Oregon Trail,* in 1849. Discoveries at Sutter's Fort a year earlier (which proved, one guidebook said, "that gold exists all through the region" with fortunes "in the very sands of the streams") made best sellers out of highly colored, inaccurate journals and guidebooks like Lansford Hastings' *Emigrant's Guide to Oregon and California.*

The first great creation of Western fiction was Daniel Boone, born in Pennsylvania in 1734, who emigrated to Kentucky in 1767. A gentle man, Boone's life was as adventurous as any novelist could have made it, and he knew Kentucky's "dark and bloody ground" better than anyone before him. He helped bring about the Treaty of Sycamore Shoals, which marked the end of Indian claims in Kentucky; he blazed the Wilderness Trail over which thousands of emigrants moved westward; he founded

Boonesborough, the first settlement in Kentucky; and he survived a decade of dangerous Indian warfare.

After John Filson inserted an imaginative biography of Boone in his *Present State of Kentucky* (1784) the legend of Daniel Boone prospered until he became a combination of Rousseau and Launcelot. (Byron knew about Boone, and put him into *Don Juan*.) Timothy Flint's biography of him, published in 1833, furnished the pattern for the Boone myth in most of its subsequent manifestations. There were five more biographies of him in the next fifty years, including a revision of Flint's and a very popular one by Edward S. Ellis, the dime-novel specialist. The myth of Boone and his fabulous rifle, Tick-licker, soon became standard in fiction (as in Cooper's Leatherstocking novels) and Boone himself was one of the best-known heroes of American folklore.

After Boone came Davy Crockett, born in Tennessee in 1786, a frontier hunter and a scout for Andrew Jackson's campaign against Tecumseh. Crockett (who was barely literate) dictated a number of popular books, all of which contributed to the public image of Crockett the wise, honest, humorous, roughhewn man of the people—*Sketches and Eccentricities of Colonel David Crockett* (1833), *A Narration of the Life of David Crockett* (1834), *An Account of Colonel Crockett's Tour* (1834)— and a series of "Crockett Almanacs" in the thirties.

Crockett's death among the defenders of the Alamo in 1836 practically canonized him in Western lore. He appeared and reappeared in popular fiction and drama over the next century (with a great recrudescence on television in the nineteen-fifties) as the tough, brash, "ringtailed roarer" frontiersman. Crockett's narrative style, far different from that of the inflated biographies of Boone, was swift, spare, vivid, and humorous, an example of American vernacular prose at its early best, as in the story of his fight with a cougar in the swamp:

> The gun was now of no use, so I threw it away and drew my hunting knife, for I knew we should be at close quarters before the fight should be over. This time he succeeded in fastening on my left arm, and was just beginning to amuse himself by tearing the flesh off with his fangs, when I ripped my knife into his side and he let go his hold, much to my satisfaction. He wheeled about and came at me with increased fury, occasioned by the smarting of his wounds. . . . He pressed me close, and as I was stepping backwards my foot tripped in a vine and I fell to the ground. He was down on me like a nighthawk upon a June bug. He seized hold of the outer part of my right thigh, which afforded him considerable amusement; the hinder part of his body was toward my face; I grasped his tail with my left hand

and tickled his ribs with my hunting knife, which I held in my right. Still, the critter wouldn't let go his hold. I stuck my knife into his side and summoned all my strength to throw him over. He resisted, and was desperate heavy, but at last I got him so far down the declivity that he lost his balance and he rolled over and over until he landed on the margin of the river; but in his fall he dragged me along with him. Fortunately I fell uppermost, and his neck presented a fair mark for my hunting knife. Without allowing myself time even to draw breath, I aimed one desperate blow at his neck and the knife entered his gullet up to the handle and reached his heart. He struggled a few moments and died. I have had many fights with bears but that was mere child's play; this was my first fight ever with a cougar and I hope it may be the last.

There existed, then, by the middle of the nineteenth century, the materials for a significant body of popular fiction about the West. James Fenimore Cooper had the imagination and the talent to use it to create the first Western hero, Natty Bumppo (also known under the names of Leatherstocking, Hawkeye, Deerslayer, and Pathfinder) whose descendants, though they might wear cowboy garb instead of deerskin, are still with us. Natty, when he appeared as a youth in his first adventure in *The Deerslayer* (1841) was "about six feet in his moccasins, but his frame was comparatively light and slender, showing muscles, however, that promised unusual agility, if not unusual strength." He was young, guileless, his demeanor marked by "an earnestness of purpose . . . , sincerity of feeling, and air of integrity" that attracted trust. He loved the woods "for their freshness, their sublime solitudes, their vastness"; he was resolute in war, respectful of his enemy, loyal to his friends, and bound always by the code of honorable battle. Cooper also introduced in the Leatherstocking series a number of fictional conventions familiar to a century and a half of readers—the shifty, treacherous Indian; the kidnapped heroine; the single-handed duel; the arrival of the troops just in time; and most of all, the classic formula of chase, capture, escape, chase, and rescue.

Cooper's popularity made the Western novel known the world over. In the late thirties, even before the *Leatherstocking Tales* were complete, there were thirty-four European publishers at work reprinting them; Samuel F. B. Morse, touring the Middle East in 1833, bought copies in Turkish, Persian, and Arabic. Street and Smith published them for ten cents as late as 1920, while in 1969 the complete series was still available in inexpensive paper editions.

Cooper's success did not go unnoticed. Robert Montgomery Bird's *Nick of the Woods* (1937) was almost equally popular but his artistic sights were set substantially lower. Instead of Deerslayer, Nature's forest nobleman, Bird created Nathan Slaughter, or "Bloody Nathan," who spent his life murdering Indians, tracking them down with his dog Peter, who could smell a savage a half-mile away. A brutal, bitter book, *Nick of the Woods* went through twenty-four American editions and six abroad; turned into a play in 1838, it remained a popular melodrama for years. Bird's picture of the Indian in what he called "his natural barbaric state, as a barbarian," provided the model for the dime-novel treatment of the Indian a generation later. Bird's book was the first extended popular treatment of "the only good Indian is a dead Indian" theme. To Bird, the conflict of red and white civilization was irreconcilable,

> . . . a mortal feud, never destined to be really ended but with the annihilation, or civilization, of the American race, first begun between the savage and the white intruder. It was and is a measure of retaliation, compelled, if not justified, by the ferocious example of the red man.

The book was so well known that Mark Twain could mention it in *Life on the Mississippi* in 1883 without explaining the reference, assuming that all his readers knew it.

Bird never followed up his novel's success, but others rushed to supply the demand for more novels like it, among them Charles Webber, who gave up the ministry to join the Texas Rangers. Webber published *Jack Long, or Shot in the Eye* in 1846 and his best-known book, *Old Hicks the Guide,* in 1848, based on a trip of his own to the headwaters of the Trinity River in Texas. He wrote a great deal more for the magazines, turning out a succession of Western stories such as *The Gold Mines of the Gila, The Wild Girl of Nebraska, The Prairie Scout,* and *The Romance of Forest and Prairie Life.* Awkwardly written, naïve, and melodramatic, Webber's books nevertheless were widely praised as authentic Western documents.

Though Emerson Bennett's books were not much better than Webber's, they sold well—*The League of the Miamis, The Prairie Flower,* and *Leni-Leoti,* among others. The best Westerns written in the mid-century years were those by an Irish soldier of fortune and poet, Captain Mayne Reid, who drifted to the United States in 1840, fought in the Mexican War, and turned to novel writing in 1850 with a good adventure story, *The Rifle Rangers.*

A prodigious workman, Reid turned out ninety books, a dozen or so on the West, among the better ones *The Scalp Hunters* (1851) and his last, *The Free Lances* (1884). Reid took writing seriously; beneath his stiff and artificial style lay a real understanding of and respect for the Western experience. In his preface to *The Rifle Rangers* Reid urged American artists to turn their eyes westward and use what they saw there:

> Poet! You shall find themes for poesy worthy of its loftiest strains. Painter! for you there are pictures fresh from the hand of God. Writer! there are stories here still untold by the author-artist—legends of love and hate, of gratitude and revenge, of falsehood and devotion, of noble virtue and ignoble crime—legends redolent of romance, rich in reality!

As Daniel Boone exemplified the ideal Western hero in the first, or forest, phase of the westward movement, so Kit Carson became the model for the hero in his second, or prairie, manifestation. The literature about Carson, in fact, exceeded that about Boone by the late sixties. A Kentucky-born woodsman who went west, Carson made one of the first crossings of the Mojave Desert in 1830 and had a reputation as the Southwest's best guide. An unassuming man, Kit became to his surprise the subject of a stream of wildly imaginative stories. An Army surgeon, Dr. DeWitt Peters, wrote down a brief autobiography dictated by Carson (who later said Dr. Peters "laid it on a little too thick") which appeared in 1858 under the grandiloquent title of *The Life and Adventures of Kit Carson, The Nestor of the Rocky Mountains.* Peters' book was followed by others, such as Burdett's *Life of Kit Carson, The Great Western Hunter and Guide,* John S. C. Abbott's *Christopher Carson, Familiarly Known as Kit,* and so on. Carson furnished for fiction a real life replacement for Boone and Bumppo, a hero who, as one biography described him, was

> . . . one of the best of those noble and original characters that have from time to time sprung up on and beyond our frontier . . . , drawing from association with uncultivated nature, not the rudeness and sensualism of the savage, but genuine simplicity and truthfulness of disposition, and generosity, bravery, and singleheartedness to a degree rarely found in society.

The force that irrevocably changed the course of the Western novel, however, was the appearance of the cheaply produced book for the mass market. The materials and the formula already developed by Cooper, Bennett, Bird, and others gave the dime novel exactly what it required, better suited to its needs than the outworn robber and pirate tales. Western fiction had villains, heroes, danger, gore, chases, captures, wild animals, exotic landscapes, and all the other elements of sensationalism. Astute publishers recognized this at once, nor was it accidental that the first two novels of the House of Beadle and Adams, which opened the floodgates of the dime novel—Ann Stephens's *Malaeska* and Edward Ellis's *Seth Jones*—used exactly these materials.

The predominant hero of the early dime-novel Westerns was a continuation (as Seth Jones was) of the noble forest hunter, transferred to the plains complete with fur cap, buckskin shirt, and moccasins. The description of Harry Hawkeye, from an 1892 novel, exemplified the type:

> . . . straight as an arrow, fair and ruddy as a Viking, with long, flowing golden hair which rippled over his massive shoulders, falling nearly to his waist; a high, broad forehead beneath which sparkled a pair of violet blue eyes, tender and soulful in repose, firm and determined under excitement. His entire face was a study for a sculptor with its delicate aquiline nose, straight in outline as though chiselled from Parian marble, and its generous, manly mouth, with full crimson and arched lips, surmounted by a long, silken blonde mustache, through which a beautiful set of even white teeth gleamed like rows of lustrous pearls.

The dime-novel public, however, demanded more action and violence than the noble scout could normally supply. The insouciant Davy Crockett and bloody Nathan Slaughter fitted the needs of cheap fiction better than Leatherstocking's philosophizing. The new favorites were nerveless, cool killers with nothing of the knight errant in them—Deadshot Dave, Young Wild West, Roaring Ralph Rockwood the Reckless Ranger, Red River Bill, Daring Dick the Apache Killer. Deadwood Dick, created in the eighties by Edward Wheeler, for example, maintained a vaguely ambiguous position inside and outside the law. An ex-bandit who had presumably reformed, Dick reverted to type at least once and (the reader suspected) might again; his relations with women placed him some distance from Leatherstocking. For that matter, Wheeler's Wild West women, Calamity Jane, Edna the Girl Brigand, and Hurricane Nell, all drank whisky, played cards, and swore, undoubtedly among other things.

The trouble was that the dime-novel writers never took the West seriously; the flood of cheap fiction they poured out simply inundated and invalidated any meaning implicit in the Western experience. Practically none of the authors who mass-produced Westerns knew the West or bothered to find out about it. Thomas Harbaugh, who wrote dozens of Westerns as "Captain Howard Holmes," lived in Casstown, Ohio, and it is doubtful if he ever got west of Piqua. Cornelius Shea, who ground out Westerns for Norman Munro under various names, wore a wide-brimmed hat, a stickpin of rattlesnake rattles, and ran a tobacco store on Staten Island. Gilbert Patten, who wrote under the name of Wyoming Bill, admitted he had once gone through Wyoming on a train.

Ellis, Wheeler, Judson, and the others had little acquaintance with Western history, society, or geography. They gave the country, in millions and millions of words over half a century, an utterly false picture of the West, much of which remained fixed in the public mind forever after. By 1890 the stereotypes of Western fiction were so strong that it seemed doubtful they could ever be changed: the resourceful scout, the two-gun sheriff, the murderous Indian, the deceitful Mexican, the gallant outlaw, the humorous old trapper or prospector, the hanging judge, and so on. (But not yet the cowboy.)

Nevertheless, some writers used the West with respect and not a little art. Bret Harte's California stories, collected in *The Luck of Roaring Camp* (1870), and Twain's *Roughing It* (1871) were not only popular but influential in shaping the public's interest. Alfred Henry Lewis's "Old Cattleman" stories and his "Wolfville" series (1897–1908), like O. Henry's later *Heart of the West* (1907) represented serious attempts to use Western materials seriously.

More important, Theodore Roosevelt, who lived on and operated a ranch in Dakota Territory, published *Hunting Trips of a Ranchman* in 1885, *Ranch Life and the Hunting Trail* in 1888, and his four-volume *Winning of the West* between 1889 and 1896. A gentleman and scholar of repute, Roosevelt was neither amateur nor tenderfoot. He treated Western life and history with understanding, and what dime-novels and melodrama had degraded, he respectified. His importance in the development of the Western novel should not be overlooked.

Western fiction found a new hero, the cowboy, exactly when it needed one. Sensationalism in the dime novel of the eighties soon reached the point of absurdity; plots wore thin, characters repeated themselves. More and more, dime novel publishers admitted, they were forced to aim at the juvenile trade; there was not much, quite literally, in Western fiction by the nineties that an adult could read. The rise of the cattle empire in the Southwest provided writers with a new, untouched reservoir of material—cowboys, rustlers, sod busters, trail bosses, cattle drives, cow towns, ranch life—for use in Western fiction. Curiously enough the cattle business, hard, dirty, risky and lonesome work at best, suddenly became glamorous and the cowboy, who was (as Eugene Manlove Rhodes described him) no more than "a hired hand on horseback," turned into a romantic hero.

Part of the reason lay in the popularity of the Wild West Show, Buffalo Bill Cody's invention, which featured authentic cowboys like Buck Taylor, the first cowboy star and the subject of an admiring "biography" by dime-novel specialist Colonel Prentiss Ingraham, *Buck Taylor, King of the Cowboys; or Raiders and Rangers,* in 1887. Ingraham wrote several more books about Taylor, fixing the new picture of the cowboy firmly in the public mind—with a great deal of help, of course, from other Wild West shows and a multitude of imitators. Negro cowboys, of whom there were many, as Philip Durham has shown, of course never made it into the books or the shows at all.

Ingraham's and Cody's cowboys bore little relation to the real thing. (Charley Siringo's cowboy classic, *A Texas Cowboy, or Fifteen Years on the Hurricane Deck of a Spanish Pony,* published in 1885, went virtually unnoticed.) Trail towns did not welcome them, for as one city official put it, their "interests were chiefly women, cards, and whiskey." Yet the character obviously had appealed to the imagination of the reading public. According to the popular myth, the cowboy led a free, independent life outside society (like Boone and Natty), rode a horse (like a knight), carried a gun (like a lance), and wandered the West from ranch to ranch, working when he wished, living close to a beautiful but dangerous Nature. He loved horses, open country, campfires in the dusk, plain food, and desert sunsets. He had plenty of enemies (bad men, rustlers, Indians, storm, flood, wild animals) but he took care of himself and handled his own justice. Though in actuality the cowboy era in the West was short— from the trail drives of the sixties to the completion of the railroads that doomed them in the eighties—it was long enough to create a useful fictional myth.

The writer, as he looked at the West in 1900, could see there a large and eminently usable stock of materials. There were character types in plenty, plots in profusion. He had Indians, cowboys, sheriffs, dudes, outlaws, miners, judges, dance-hall girls, scouts, soldiers, gamblers, and a dozen more; he had Wells Fargo, the Pony Express, the railroad, the Oregon Trail, the covered wagon, Custer's Last Fight, the pursuit of Geronimo, range wars, the gold rush, and more history than he could use. And he had scenery such as few other authors ever had—mountain, desert, prairie, rivers, lakes, and the endless, savage beauty of the land. The essentials of popular fiction were there for the taking.

Owen Wister took them—the old plots, places, and people—put them into new relationships and perspectives, and made a new kind of Western novel. Born into a wealthy family, Wister studied music and painting in Europe, worked in a bank, and in the mid-eighties spent summers on a Wyoming ranch for his health. He graduated from Harvard Law School with Theodore Roosevelt and began writing stories about the West for the quality magazines. *The Virginian,* which appeared in 1902, changed the course of the Western novel. It went through six printings in six weeks, sold 300,000 copies its first two years, appeared as a movie four times, and as late as 1968 was not only still in print but was the basis for a television serial. Its sales passed the million mark in 1920 and approached two million in 1968.

The Virginian mentioned Indians once or twice, had a great deal of adolescent horseplay, stuffy dialogue, and exactly one four-line reference to cowboys at work, but none of that was important. Wister put into one package most of the old conventions and used them somewhat more imaginatively than his predecessors, but that wasn't important either. He did two things that were very important: he invented the cowboy, and he introduced love.

The Virginian was a natural nobleman—or as the Eastern narrator instantly recognized, "a gentleman"—right out of Scott and Cooper except for his dress:

> Lounging there at ease against the wall was a slim young giant, more beautiful than pictures. His broad, soft hat was pushed back; a loose-knotted, dull-scarlet handkerchief sagged from his throat; and one casual thumb was hooked in the cartridge-belt that slanted across his hips. He had plainly come many miles from somewhere across the vast horizon, as the dust upon him showed. His boots were white with it. His overalls were gray with it. The weather-beaten bloom of his face shone through it duskily, as the ripe peaches look upon their trees in the dry season. But no dinginess of travel or shabbiness of attire could tarnish the splendor that radiated from his youth and strength.

It was immediately evident that he was courteous, courageous, and everything that the code of the antebellum South required him to be. His lady-fair, a refined Yankee "schoolma'm" out of the sentimental-domestic novel, Miss Mary Stark of Bennington, Vermont (who read Dickens, Jane Austen, and Browning to the ranch hands) recognized in the Virginian the elements of true worth.

The plot involved ranchers versus rustlers, a villain named Trampas, a lynching party (which Wister had a hard time rationalizing), and the transforming power of a good woman's love. There was not much new except the manner in which Wister blended it all together. He did, however, fix the walkdown firmly in western tradition, that is, the climax in which two gunmen approach each other on an empty street until one draws. (George Ward Nichols had used it as early as 1867, describing Wild Bill Hickok's gun battle with Dave Tutt.) Zane Grey brought this device to its fullest perfection and bequeathed it to Hollywood.

The ironic fact was, however, that Wister wrote The Virginian with an axe to grind, and not as a contribution to Western fiction. A dedicated conservative, socially and politically, Wister thought he saw the aristocratic America he loved disappearing in the flood of immigrants (especially Jews) arriving in the nineties; the country's values, he believed, were fast sinking in a morass of materialism and radicalism. Hopefully, Wister thought, if the culture of the East was doomed, the West might remain the repository of the old virtues, "the true America, with thought, type, and life of its own." In his view, the cowboy represented "the last of the freedom-loving Americans," the West the last bastion of defense against "the debased and mongrel city . . . , crawling with alien vermin." He made this quite clear in his romanticized version of what it was like in a Wyoming saloon:

> There was scarce a face among them that had not something in it very likeable. Here were lusty horsemen ridden from the heat of the sun, and the wet of the storm, to divert themselves a while. Youth untamed sat here for an idle moment, spending easily its hard-earned money. City saloons rose to my vision, and I instantly preferred this Rocky Mountain place. More of death I undoubtedly saw, but less of vice, than its New York equivalents. . . . Even where baseness was visible, baseness was not uppermost. Daring, laughter, endurance, these were what I saw upon the countenances of the cowboys. . . . Something about them, and the idea of them, smote my American heart . . . ; in their spirits sat hidden a true nobility, and often beneath its unexpected shining their figures took on a heroic stature.

The Virginian represented a new American chivalry; to Wister "the Knight and the cowboy are nothing but the same Saxon, of different environments, the nobleman in London and the nobleman in Texas."

The public missed most of this, even though Wister in the 1911 edition wrote a new preface, emphasizing that his novel was "an expression of the American faith," currently under attack from "enemies both in Wall Street and in the Labor Unions." The thousands who went on buying it, to Wister's frustration, remembered the strong, silent, handsome hero with a wide-brimmed hat, cowboy boots, and ready six-gun; they remembered the gunfight, the wild beauty of the upland West, and the blooming of love in Medicine Bow, Wyoming.

Whatever else Wister did, he treated the materials of Western fiction with respect. With him and after him came other writers who also knew the West, loved it, and used it well. Stewart Edward White, whose two novels, *The Westerners* and *The Claim Jumpers,* preceded *The Virginian,* published *Arizona Nights* in 1907, a superb collection of stories. Two real cowboys, Andy Adams and Eugene Manlove Rhodes, also published books not long after Wister's. Adams's *Log of a Cowboy* (1903), *A Texas Matchmaker* (1904), and *Cattle Brands* (1906) were less fiction than autobiography; Adams tried fiction, but found he could not match the professionals and eventually gave up. Rhodes, Nebraska-born and both ranch hand and ranch owner, did not begin writing until he was forty. After the *Saturday Evening Post* began publishing his stories in 1910, Rhodes became the center of a cult of Western fans. His cowboys were hired hands with callouses and saddle sores who talked and acted as the real article did, but the *Post* unfortunately convinced him that he needed to insert a love interest and a noble social message into what was otherwise first-rate Western fiction. He published a number of books and collections, among them *West is West* (1917), *Paso por Aquí* (1926, considered by most readers his best), and *The Trusty Knaves* (1933).

Bertha Sinclair, one of the few women writers of Westerns under the name of B. M. Bower, created one of the better known cowboys of the period, Chip of the Flying U, in 1906. Chip, a prairie gentleman somewhat like the Virginian, philosophized and quoted Shakespeare, but he avoided women. The Flying U outfit provided Mrs. Sinclair with a cross section of ranch characters whose fortunes she followed in novel after novel, marrying them off one by one, and finally Chip himself. The conflict of cowman and farmer furnished the theme of her series. Believing firmly that farmers were villains and the West belonged to ranchers, she never drew a bad cowboy or a good sheepman, or displayed the slightest embarrassment about her prejudice.

Clarence Mulford, who lived in Maine, took much of his information about the West from books, but he was one of the most well-informed writers of his time on Western matters. Though his library of Americana was extensive and his knowledge of Western lore encyclopaedic, he never visited the West until seventeen years after his first book about it, *Bar-20 Range Years,* in 1907. In this novel he introduced Hopalong Cassidy, a tough, resourceful, humorous, and unpolished cowhand with a limp. Hopalong and his somewhat raffish friends, Shorty, Johnny, and Mesquite Jenkins, were working cowboys with none of Chip's or the Virginian's gentility. However, when Paramount Pictures put actor William Boyd into Hopalong Cassidy movies in 1934 they changed the character considerably. Television later gave him wavy gold hair, a white hat and boots, a gold saddle, and pretty girl friends, all of which would have made the original snort with disgust. For the real, unadorned Hopalong, the reader must return to *The Roundup, Trail Dust, Me'n Shorty, Hopalong Sits In,* or *On the Trail of the Tumbling T.*

W. C. Tuttle, whose father was a famous Western sheriff, and Henry Herbert Knibbs, who spent his life in the Southwest, published millions of words in the Western pulps. Knibbs's Young Pete, the Ridin' Kid from Powder River, won the admiration of thousands of readers for his "deadly accuracy, lightning-like swiftness, appalling freedom from accident, ostrich-like stomach, and camel-like ability to go without water." Charles Alden Seltzer wrote a number of stories before his first novel, *Range Riders,* in 1911, then a long series of successful books (forty-six of them, the last in 1941) and movie scripts for William S. Hart, Buck Jones, and Tom Mix. Although he knew Western life at first hand, he produced novel after novel full of clichés, tailored to the popular taste—*The Two Gun Man, Boss of the Lazy Y, Valley of the Stars,* and so on down to *Silver Spurs,* published in 1935 but essentially the same book as his first in 1911. Surprisingly, Seltzer's stories contained a strong element of real violence; he was fascinated by the professional killer, "the hardened, embittered, merciless demon of a gunman," and in *Range Boss* (1916) he inserted a brutally near-successful rape.

William McLeod Raine, as B. M. Bower did, used the rancher-sheepman conflict as his basic plot-line. He knew the West intimately and what he wrote was authentic. He served as a young man with the Arizona Rangers before his first novel, *Wyoming,* in 1908, averaging two books a year with titles like *Mavericks, Oh You Tex!,* and *Brand Blotters,* for the next forty years, his last in 1953, a year before his death. Unlike most of his contemporaries, Raine allowed more than a suggestion of sex in his novels. One of his heroines, an Eastern schoolma'm, he described as "slim and lissome, the dew of childhood on her lips and the mist of it in her eyes," and when she looked at the cowboys it was not the lure of the open range that interested them or the reader. In another Raine novel, when the hero clasped the girl to him for protection as the shooting began, he "suddenly knew the sweet delight of contact with her supple, surrendered figure," but was too busy to pursue that line of thought.

Emerson Hough was a cut above Raine, Knibbs, and Tuttle. Hough was an Iowa farm boy who went to New Mexico in the eighties, loved the country, and soon began writing about it in the newspapers and magazines. His *Story of the Cowboy* (1897), a semi-historical book, earned Roosevelt's praise; he continued with *The Way to the West* (1903), *The Story of the Outlaw* (1906), and *Fifty-four Forty or Fight* (1909). He had already published twenty-five books when the *Saturday Evening Post,* for which he wrote hunting and fishing stories, suggested that he write a novel about the westward migrations. The result was *The Covered Wagon,* published in 1922, a soundly-researched account of the Oregon

Trail and a runaway best seller that Hollywood turned into the first Western "epic" in film history. He followed immediately with *North of 36* (1923), an equally successful novel about the cattle drives.

Hough was a serious novelist but not a particularly talented one; he had little skill at characterization and a limited range of invention. Since the *Post* wanted him to follow Wister's formula of action plus love, he intruded an awkwardly-handled love interest into novels that were capable of standing on their own as excellent historical studies of the West. Few of his contemporaries could have matched his description of the great wagon train slowly moving west on the Oregon Trail:

> Slow, swaying, stately, the ox teams came on, as though impelled by and not compelling the fleet of white canvas sails. The teams did not hasten, did not abate their speed, but moved in an unagitated advance that gave the massed column something irresistibly epochal in look. The train, foreshortened to the watchers at the rendezvous, had a well-spaced formation—twenty wagons, thirty, forty, forty-seven— as Jesse Wingate mentally counted them. There were outriders; there were clumps of driven cattle. Along the flanks walked tall men, who flung over the low-headed cattle an admonitory lash whose keen report presently could be heard, still faint and far off. A dull dust cloud arose, softening the outlines of the prairie ships. . . . Lean boys, brown barefooted girls flanked the trail with driven stock. Chickens clucked in coops at the wagon sides. Uncounted children thrust out tousled heads from the openings of the canvas covers. Dogs beneath, jostling the tar buckets, barked in hostile salutation. Women in slatted sunbonnets turned impassive gaze from the high front seats, back of which, swung to the bows by leather loops, hung the inevitable family rifle. Now, at the tail gate of every wagon, lashed fast for its long journey, hung also the family plow.

It remained for Zane Grey, a dentist from Zanesville, Ohio, to put together everything that had been done and do it better than anyone before him and most of them after him. His publishing record has never been equaled among Western writers and may never be. He found the right formula with his fourth book, *Riders of the Purple Sage,* in 1912, and until his death in 1939 published novels as fast as he could write them. Any book he wrote had a guaranteed sale of at least half a million; since devoted readers kept the old ones selling while new ones appeared, from 1917 to 1926 there was at least one Zane Grey book on every year's best-seller list. He wrote fifty-four novels and left twenty more in manuscript, so that his books kept appearing for twenty years after his death. In 1969 his total sales passed twenty millions, twenty-two Grey books were still available in inexpensive editions, and complete sets of his novels were still for sale.

His popularity was neither accidental nor undeserved. Few popular novelists have possessed such a grasp of what the public wanted and few have developed Grey's skill at supplying it, though he wrote somewhat piously in the preface to *The Last Man*, in 1922,

> My long labors have been devoted to making stories resemble the times they depict. I have loved the West for its vastness, its contrast, its beauty and color of life, for its wildness and violence, and for the fact that I have seen how it developed great men and women who died unsung.

What he wrote did not necessarily turn out this way. He combined adventure, action, violence, crisis, conflict, sentimentalism, and sex in an extremely shrewd mixture, adding just enough history, scenery, and seriousness to give it the unmistakable stamp of a Zane Grey story.

Action came first. A master of the chase, the Indian ambush, the gunfight, the stampede, the fistfight, and the walkdown, Grey weaved them together with consummate skill and sufficient restraint to keep them believable. All the classic conflicts appeared in his novels: rancher and settler, sheriff and outlaw, gunman and gunman, cowboy and Indian, Indian and white, Eastern "culture" and Western society. His most notable contribution to the roster of characters was the gunfighter, the good-bad man who might be on either side of the law—rootless, lonely, a doomed wanderer through a society which had no place for him, like Pecos Smith, "whose real name was unknown, his past a mystery, and wherever he went there was trouble," or Buck Duane, son of a gunman and a gunman himself, tragically aware of the "tiger instinct" within him. Though the term existed in the seventies, Grey was the first writer of popular Westerns to seize and to capitalize on the "gunfighter" image. After he created the original model a hundred novelists and scriptwriters began producing it in quantity.

In an unobtrusive way the action in Zane Grey's work was surprisingly violent. *The Lone Star Ranger* (1915) contained one near-rape and two offstage rapes, ten killings by the hero, five by others, and two fistfights. In *The U. P. Trail* (1918), which contains nine killings, the heroine survives an Indian massacre, is kidnapped once by outlaws and twice by Sioux, is held prisoner in a Montana brothel, and escapes an Indian raid. But Grey's real skill lay in his ability to ring changes on standard plots, combining them with sufficient historical data to make them plausible. *Riders of the Purple Sage* placed a pretty, headstrong girl together with an outlaw gunman in the Mormon-Gentile wars of the seventies. *The U. P. Trail* set a handsome, young construction engineer and an orphaned girl against the background of the building of the transcontinental railroad. *Western Union* used the building of the first transcontinental telegraph, Indians, a prairie fire, a buffalo stampede, a flood, and a bandit gang to provide interest. In *The Vanishing American* and *Heritage of the Desert* Grey introduced and then edged away from a problem he apparently preferred to evade: the first suggests "passionate and unconventional love" between a young Indian chief and golden-haired Marian Warner from the East, the second something of the same sort between a rich Eastern boy and a half-Indian girl.

Grey gave his novels a powerful sense of place. He wrote description well, as in his evocation of the feel of a Western boom town, Fort Benton, in the seventies:

> Beyond Medicine Bow the grass and the green failed and the immense train of freight-cars and passenger coaches, loaded to capacity, clattered into arid country. Gray and red, the drab and fiery colors of the desert lent the ridges character—forbidding and barren. . . . Benton lay in the heart of barrenness, alkali, and desolation, on the face of the windy desert, alive with dustdevils, sweeping along yellow and funnel-shaped—a huge blocked-out town, and set where no town could ever live. Benton was prey for sun, wind, dust, drought, and the wind was terribly and unsupportably cold. No sage, no cedars, no grass, not even a cactus bush, nothing green or living to relieve the eye, which swept across the gray and the white, through the dust, to the distant bare and desolate hills of drab. . . . The train clattered and jolted to a stop. Neale, carrying his bags, stepped off into a half a foot of dust. He saw a disintegrated crowd of travelers that had just arrived, and of travelers ready to depart—soldiers, Indians, Mexicans, negroes, loafers, merchants, tradesmen, laborers, an ever-changing and ever-remarkable spectacle of humanity. He saw stage-coaches with hawkers bawling for passengers bound to Salt Lake, Ogden, Montana, Idaho; he saw a wide white street—white with dust where it was not thronged with moving men and women, and lined by tents and canvas houses and clapboard structures, together with the strangest conglomeration of painted and printed signs that ever advertised anything in the world. A woman, well clad, young, not uncomely, but with hungry eyes like those of a hawk, accosted Neale. He drew away. In the din he had not heard what she said. A boy likewise spoke to him; a greaser tried to take his luggage; a man jostling him felt at his pocket; and as Neale walked on he was leered at, importuned, jolted, accosted, and all but mobbed. So this was Benton.

Wister introduced love to the Western. Grey introduced sex, good and bad. Good women, he emphasized, were the best of all creatures this side of heaven, and their pure love the world's greatest ennobling force. At the same time they pulsated with promise; the final love scene of *The Lone Star Ranger* covered three and a half pages, opening thus:

> He stood holding her tight, with the feel of her warm, throbbing breast and the clasp of her arms as flesh and blood realities to fight a terrible fear. He felt her, and for the moment the might of it was stronger than all the demons that possessed him . . . , and now, with this woman in his arms, her swelling breast against his, he bent under the storm of passion and joy. . . . Their lips met in their first kiss. The sweetness, the fire of her mouth seemed so new, so strange, so irresistible. . . . She met him half-way, returned kiss for kiss, her face scarlet, her eyes closed, till her passion and strength spent, she fell back upon his shoulder. Presently she recovered, and she only drew the closer, and leaned upon him with her face upturned. He felt her hands on his, and they were soft, clinging, strong, like steel under velvet. He felt the rise and fall, the warmth of her breast. A tremor ran through him.

Grey's bad girls exuded mind-numbing sensuality, like Ruby the dance-hall girl in *The U. P. Trail:*

> Her arms were bare, her dress cut very low. Her face offered vivid contrast to the carmine on her lips. It was a soft, round face, with narrow eyes, dark, seductive, bold. She tilted her head to one side and suddenly smiled at Neale. It startled him. It was a smile with the shock of a bullet. The girl took hold of the lapels of his coat. She looked up. Her eyes were dark with what seemed like red shadows in them. She had white teeth. The carmined lips curled in a smile— a smile impossible to believe, of youth and sweetness, that disclosed a dimple in her cheek. She was pretty. She was holding him, pulling him a little toward her.
>
> "I like you!" she exclaimed.
>
> He felt her, saw her as in a dream. Her face possessed a peculiar fascination. The sleepy seductive eyes; the provoking half-smile, teasing, alluring; the red lips, full and young through the carmine paint. All of her seemed to breathe a different kind of power than he had ever before experienced—unspiritual, elemental, strong as some heady wine. She represented youth, health, beauty, terribly linked with evil wisdom, and a corrupt and irresistible power, possessing a base and mysterious affinity for man. The breath and the charm and the pestilence of her passed over Neale like fire.

Such things were not at all common in Western fiction in 1918.

Grey drew women better than he did men, though he leaned heavily for both on stereotypes taken out of the popular novel. Except for his gunmen, his heroes tended to be bland, a trifle too noble, a bit too upper class, like Richard Gale in *Desert Gold,* Wayne Cameron in *Western Union,* or Warren Neale in *The U. P. Trail.* More interesting were his semioutlaws—Lassiter, the doomed gunman in *Riders of the Purple Sage;* Nopahie, the bitter young Nopah warrior in *The Vanishing American;* Buck Duane, the agonized killer of *Lone Star Ranger* and the cold, tawny gunfighter Poggin, in the same novel. Some of Grey's women, excluding the prevalence of schoolma'm types and Eastern heiresses, could be interesting—Beauty Stanton, the regally-beautiful madam in *The U. P. Trail;* Fay Larkin, "fair as a Sago lily," the captive girl of *Rainbow Trail;* Mescal, the half-Navajo girl of *Heritage of the Desert,* purchased as a toy; Jane Wit111ersteen, the proud Mormon girl of *Riders of the Purple Sage.*

Beginning in the thirties, the Western novel took three directions. One group of writers saw in the Western experience the potential materials of a significant, artistic fiction. Harvey Fergusson's historical trilogy of the Southwest, *Blood of the Conquerors* (1921), *Wolf Song* (1927), and *In Those Days* (1929) was the first attempt at the serious Western novel. Paul Horgan, beginning with *Men At Arms* in 1931, continued to write novels about the Southwest into the forties, although he was perhaps better known as a Pulitzer-Prize-winning historian.

Edwin Corle's *Mojave* (1934), *Fig Tree John* (1935), and *Billy the Kid* (1953), and H. L. Davis's story of the Oregon frontier, *Honey in the Horn* (1935), were distinguished though not popular novels. Conrad Richter's four novels, *Sea of Grass* (1937), *The Trees* (1940), *The Fields* (1946), and *The Town* (1950), tracing the development of pioneer society from settlement to city, won him a Pulitzer Prize. Frederick Manfred's trilogy, *Lord Grizzly* (1954), *Riders of Judgment* (1957), and *Conquering Horse* (1959), represented another kind of effort to impose artistic patterns on historical materials. Walter Van Tilburg Clark's *Ox-Bow Incident* (1940), an anti-Western novel that destroyed most of the genre's most cherished conventions, and his symbol-loaded study of evil, *The Track of the Cat* (1949), remain probably the most stylish and sophisticated of artistically-oriented Westerns.

The second trend represented a continuation of the pulp-commercial Western stories written to a formula, described by one professional as "no undue strain on the brain, lots of action, lots of clichés—you can't sell it without clichés—good guy, bad guy, girl." Eugene Cunningham, who hit the market with *Riders of the Night* in 1932 and wrote two dozen more like it, many for the movies, was one of the more successful practitioners of the type. No one, however, approached Frederick Faust, who wrote most of his Westerns under the name of Max Brand. (He had nineteen other names for other types of fiction.) Faust, the Western's version of Erle Stanley Gardner, did the equivalent of a book every ten days for years (a lifetime total of 530 books) for a market ranging from *Harper's* to *Dime Detective,* in addition to thirty film scripts and a television series. He sold through five publishers, one of whom announced after Faust's death in 1944 that he had sufficient manuscript on hand to supply the market for another century.

Faust made no pretense of writing for any other purpose than profit. He knew and cared little about the West except at secondhand (most of his work was done in Italy) and he simply repeated his formula over and over in more than a hundred Westerns. His books were particularly adaptable to Hollywood treatment. *Destry Rides Again,* a desperado story, was made into a movie three times (starring Tom Mix, James Stewart, and Audie Murphy); *The Untamed* sold a million copies and made two movies; *Singing Guns* sold a million and a half and made another. Faust's West was essentially Hollywood's, a one-dimensional, scriptwriter's West decked out with sales tricks and attention-getters. He made a good deal of money and sold many books—sixteen of the Brand books and ten done as "Evan Evans" were still in print a quarter-century after his death—and others followed his example.

The Brand type is evident in the majority of the books in the paperback racks that advertise "an action-packed Western filled with kill-crazy outlaws, roaring sixguns, and hot lead," or "a tense novel about the Raiders from Hell, sixty horsemen dressed in black, gunning men down with savage cruelty." In them, as in Faust's novels, the West furnishes little more than a backdrop for rubberstamped adventure fiction. Beginning about 1960, however, action was not enough. One book in 1966 promised "a ruthless hunt across the burning land of that wild country among untamed men of brutal lusts"; in another in 1968, "he returned to his ranch to find his wife ravaged and beaten senseless, out of her mind with shock and terror"; another advertised that "he never spoke a word as he carried her to the shack and raped her again and again." Thus Mike Hammer and Travis McGee came to the West.

The third strain of the mid-century Western lies somewhere between the multileveled symbolism of Clark and the specious commercialism of the production-line hack. The Western Writers of America, an association formed in 1952 to preserve the integrity of the popular literary tradition against encroachment from above and below, eventually drew into its membership most of the best mass-market Western writers, among them

Nelson Nye (Clem Colt), Clifton Adams (Clay Randall), Wayne Over-
holser (John Daniels, Lee Leighton, Dan Stevens, Joseph Wayne), Steve
Frazee, L. P. Holmes (Matt Stewart), Frederick Glidden (Luke Short),
Ray Gaulden, Robert McLeod, and Louis L'Amour.

The Western story's prose, like that of the detective story, lost a great
deal of its sentimentalism and ornament in the thirties. The better Western writers learned to produce direct, concrete, fast-moving narrative, not
infrequently equal in skill to any done by the "quality" writers. Ernest
Haycox's vignette of the heat, dust, and emptiness of a prairie cattle-town
in the seventies is first-rate description:

> The town had a name but no shape, no street, no core. It was simply
> five buildings, flung without thought upon the dusty prairie at the
> eastern edge of Dakota, and these stood gaunt and hard-angled
> against the last of the day's streaming sunlight. The railroad, which
> gave the town a single pulse beat once a day, came as a black ribbon
> out of emptiness, touched this Corapolis with hurried indifference,
> and moved away into equal emptiness. The five buildings were alone
> in a gray-yellow space which ran outward in all directions, so empty
> that the tiring eye never saw where the earth ended and sky began.
> There were no trees in this world, no accents, no relieving inter-
> ruptions; nothing but the gray soil rolling on and short brown
> grass turned crisp and now ready to fade when winter temperatures
> touched it.

Will Henry's explanation of why the Cheyenne made war is simple,
moving, and succinct:

> The Cheyenne was in many ways the most admirable of Indians;
> indeed, of men. Kind to the old and the afflicted, gentle with the lost
> of mind, loyal to friend, devoted to all children, honoring the given
> word, punishing the broken vow, he was a man who did not under-
> stand the forked tongue of the white brother until far too late.
>
> When at last he saw how he had been cheated, and realized that
> he must fight or languish in the bondage of the reservation system,
> the Cheyenne chose his way with the dignity and courage which were
> his prairie birthrights.
>
> If it was a harsh way that he chose, it was noble too, and it was
> necessary. For there remained but little time to him—scarce time, in-
> deed, to run in the ponies, oil the old guns, make the medicine signs
> and mutter the sacred prayers to the Allfather.
>
> The white man was demanding war or peace, and peace at the
> price of slavery. The Cheyenne would not pay that price; he would
> never live unfree. He would follow the uncaught wind. He would
> range with the eagle and the wolf. He would live as Maheo had in-

tended him to live, a free thing, out there, under the wide blue sky. And he would fight for that freedom. He would fight until his people were no more, until the last buffalo had disappeared, until the last warrior had grown old and gone forever upon the last warpath. Then, perhaps, the grass would grow where he had been, but not before.

Luke Short's account of a two-man night ambush at an outlaw cabin is tightly-written, controlled action, its climax deliberately understated:

He steadied himself, his gun on the rock, and waited for the man in the cabin to shoot again. When he did, Traf put three swift shots in the direction of the gun flash, and a shot came from the man forted up across the way. Traf heard it hit in front of him and richochet off into the night. Then Dickey opened up on his rifleman and was answered by a shot that came from the top of the wall of the cabin. Both Dickey and Traf answered that shot.

Suddenly it was still, but only for a moment. From the cabin came a wild yell of "Pull out! Pull out!"

Traf waited, listening. He could hear somebody from the cabin going over the stony ground in the direction of the horses. A few minutes later he heard the circling of the man who had been forted up behind the rock, and he too was headed for the horses. Traf still waited. Then he caught the sound of cursing, undoubtedly triggered by the discovery that the horses were missing. This was followed by silence.

The men in the attacking party were afoot now. Would they wait until the moon rose to hunt for their horses, or would they leg it back to camp, hoping their horses had returned? Traf didn't know and didn't care. He waited some minutes longer and then, judging it was safe, gave the call of an owl. He got one in return and came out from behind the rock.

But curiosity was prodding him. Moving closer to the slope, he walked slowly until the slope began to lift off the flats. Traveling the line where the slope and the flats met, he had gone less than twenty yards when his boot touched a yielding object. He halted, knelt, reached out, and felt the body of a man. His hand came away wet. He wiped it on the man's clothing and reached in his pocket for a match and struck it. He was looking at a dead man, and he recognized him.

Popular Western fiction, as it is written for the mass market of the later twentieth century, must operate under clear and specific rules if it is to be commercially successful. It must involve the reader with a strong sense of locale; the Western novel is, above everything else, about a place and a time. As a matter of fact, the Western is fairly well restricted to the area west of Missouri and east of the Rockies, from west Texas, Arizona, and New Mexico to the Canadian border. Its time limits are approximately 1865 to 1890, that is, the cowboy and trail town era, beginning with the early cattle drives and ending with the completion of the railroad network in the Plains states. Stories laid in Mexico, East Texas, or California (except for the forty-niner era) do not go well; nor do stories with trucks, telephones, or cameras.

Second, the plot of the popular Western, according to Nelson Nye (who has written nearly a hundred) "should spring from the environment, the history, and the tradition of the locale. It should be germane to the country." The narrative of the Western must be believable and characteristic of the West; the setting is itself a generating force, not merely a backdrop for action that could have occurred anywhere else. For this reason the major characters are almost always cowhands, law officers, ranchers, or cavalry soldiers involved in some kind of action directly related to life in the seventies and eighties. Frank Gruber, who has written over a forty-year span Western, novels, movie scripts, and radio and television programs, has reduced them all to seven basic plot-lines, of which the majority of Westerns since Zane Grey (who developed many of them) have been variations. The "Union Pacific Story," he explains, deals with such things as the construction of a railroad, telegraph line, stage route, and so on in the face of obstacles presented by Indians, terrain, politics, or natural disasters. (The "journey story," like Hough's *Covered Wagon* or Haycox's "Stage to Lordsburg," belongs in this category.) The "Ranch Story" is simply rustlers versus ranchers, cattlemen versus nesters, sheepmen, drought, the perils of the trail, and other hazards. The "Empire Builder" plot is built about the figure of the Western imperialist, the visionary pioneer who wrests a kingdom out of the West and his struggle to retain it against the advance of civilization, the coming of law and order, government encroachment, and the like. The "Revenge Story" concerns the relentless pursuit of the evildoer by a Nemesis (as in Charles Portis's recent success, *True Grit*, told with humor and irony), the punishment of wrong, the redress of grievance—best illustrated by Zane Grey's classic *Riders of the Purple Sage*. The "Custer's Last Stand" story may not always concern Custer, but pits cavalry against Indian in a conflict to be retold over and over in various guises. The "Marshal Story" of the dedicated lawman or heroic sheriff (popular on television in *Gunsmoke* and its imitators) may be combined occasionally with the seventh type, the "Outlaw Story," in which the conflict between good and bad may be set against real history (as in the numerous treatments of Billy the Kid) or which may be itself the focus of good man turned bad or, as in Grey's *Lone Star Ranger,* bad man turned good.

Third, the conflict in the Western must be clear and unambiguous; it must have a clean-cut resolution. Vengeance, retribution, restoring the balance of right and wrong—these are favorite themes, expressed often in terms of the struggle of good men against power wrongly used, the liberation of a community from gang rule, the feud, and so on. The popular Western's plot, precisely defined by Henry Wilson Allen (Will Henry, Clay Fisher) "presents a precut slice of homespun life which is a gallant trial of good against evil in a perilous place and time where bravery and clean intent will not be matched by cowardice and dishonor." The contemporary popular Western tolerates strong man-woman relationships, but not overt sex. Love "must have a definite part in the motivation," writes Nye, "and must participate in the action"; sexual relationships occasionally (but only occasionally) may occur if demanded by the plotline. But the Western remains traditionally conservative on sexuality.

In effect, the West of popular fiction is a deceptive fairyland, an illusion maintained by an unspoken agreement between reader and writer never to shatter it. The reader wants the Old West, writes Allen, "so let him live there."

> Let him keep his illusions. Beguile him. Stir him up. Give him boots and spurs and a gun and a good fast horse, and let him ride with you. Let him hear the bullet whine, the wind sing, the coyote cry on the mountainside. Don't tell it like it was. Tell it like it ought to have been. Lift it up a few human levels so that it leaves the reader a better life in a better land that never really existed, but should have.

Without intending to slight the work of Frederick Glidden (Luke Short, the best of the action-Western writers), Alan LeMay (*The Searchers*), or Theodore V. Olsen (*The Stalking Moon*) it would be justifiable to select Allen, Jack Schaefer, A. B. Guthrie, and Ernest Haycox as the most distinguished writers of popular Westerns since the thirties. Allen has blended history with fiction in an unusually effective combination. Convinced that the frontier past deserved more truthful telling than most Western novels and movies gave it, he began in 1950 to buttress the classic Western-story conventions with solid historical research and sympathetic understanding. Each of his major books is based on an actual historical situation or character. *Yellow Hair* and *The Brass Command* (done as Clay Fisher) dealt with Custer and the cavalry campaigns; *Land of the Mandans, No Survivors,* and *The Last Warpath* were sensitive studies of the Indian wars; *The Fourth Horseman* derived from the Tonto Basin troubles in Arizona in 1887; *Alias Butch Cassidy* was an account of a real outlaw, George LeRoy Parker, who never killed anybody. Allen's forty novels, taken as a unit, constitute a significant body of traditional Western writing.

A. B. Guthrie's *The Big Sky*, published in 1947, received immediate popular and critical acclaim. A story of mountain men laid in the 1840's, it was written with accuracy, realism, and not a little poetic aura. *The Way West* (1949) won a Pulitzer Prize for fiction, again an expertly-told narrative of emigrant trains on the Oregon Trail in 1847. His novel about early Montana, *Three Thousand Hills* (1956) became a successful movie. Jack Schaefer, whose output has not been large (seven novels), wrote the perfect gunfighter story in *Shane* (1949).

In quantity and quality Ernest Haycox, who died in 1950, stands alone among contemporary Western authors. (The Western Writers of America's annual award is named an "Ernie" in his memory.) Haycox published twenty-five novels and over three hundred short stories, many of them successfully translated into movies. "Stage To Lordsburg" became *Stagecoach*, in its original 1939 version the best Western movie ever made; *Trouble Shooter* became *Union Pacific* (1939); *Trail Town* became *Abilene* (1946), among others. A careful, conscientious craftsman, Haycox infused the standard Western with new energy and breathed freshness into old conventions. *Bugles in the Afternoon* (considered by Haycox admirers to be his best) is another version of the Custer story; *Trail Smoke* is a replay of Grey's *Lone Star Ranger, Clint* a variant of the drifter-adventurer, *Trail Town* a straight cattle-drive story. Though there is hardly an original plot-pattern in any of his books, Haycox's skill at characterization and his strong sense of locale bring his books alive and keep the reader engaged.

The purpose of the popular Western novel is to entertain, and it is effective only insofar as it succeeds in doing so. It is written neither to shock nor titillate; it is neither myth nor epic nor multileveled symbolic narrative. It is an adventure story, good or bad only as it succeeds or fails to come alive as adventure and communicate the Western experience accurately and honestly. Fashionable academic criticism, beginning about 1945, saddled the Western novel with hero myths, fertility rites, quests, ritual killings, and phallic symbolism, very nearly smothering it in a fog of footnotes.

But it is not and never was, as Henry Allen has said, "mythic or Gothic or parapsychological or a meaningful social document." It is an adventure story which deals with a romantic, exciting, and colorful period

of American history. Life in the Western's West is simple, with easily defined enemies and clear-cut victories and defeats. In it the old-fashioned
virtues prevail—courage, integrity, pride, honor, stamina—in an unambiguous, uncompleted, uncomplicated society where success and failure,
good and evil, bravery and cowardice, can be clearly identified and
measured.

The popular Western novel runs about 60,000 words; its average sale
in paperback form (only a few appear in hard covers) seldom exceeds
100,000 copies, in exceptional cases 500,000. In 1967 there were 127 new
Western titles published and ninety-one reprints, a substantial increase
over previous years. In total sales, Zane Grey is first with five of the first
twelve all-time best-selling Westerns; his books have sold about twenty-
eight million copies. William McLeod Raine, Ernest Haycox, Max Brand,
Luke Short, Jack Schaefer, and Louis L'Amour belong in the first ten top
sellers, although exact sales figures are not easy to ascertain. Sales of Westerns in recent years have fallen somewhat behind those of detective-
mysteries, exposé novels, and sexual-historical romances, but the Western
will most probably endure. It contains too much of the American heritage,
and embodies too well the American frontier myth, ever to disappear.

PART FIVE

LET THE PEOPLE SING: POPULAR MUSIC

We make our songs easy to remember and easy to sing, songs the guy in the locker room and the woman in the farmhouse can sing without a piano.

—JULIUS STYNE, 1946

BALLADS TO BLUES

You can really reach people's souls with those D-flat blues.

—ORNETTE COLEMAN

The history of American popular music begins with the songbooks of the seventeenth century, brought from England by the earliest settlers who loved music, played and sang it, and had neither prejudice against it nor distaste for it, myths to the contrary. The Puritan respected music equally as much as any other seventeenth-century Englishman; he also believed that music had certain uses that were more important than others, and he did not believe in overemphasizing its secular purposes. John Playford, who was not a Puritan, in 1655 summarized the contemporary attitude toward music by explaining that priorities had to be kept straight:

> The first and chief Use of Musick is for the Service and Praise of God, whose gift it is. The second Use is for the Solace of Men . . . , as a temporary Blessing to recreate and cheer Men after long study and weary labor. . . .

That the New England Calvinists sang psalms should not obscure the fact that they liked singing, psalms or otherwise. The colonies imported songbooks by the shipload; "singing meetings" were common diversions and as colonial life grew less austere and more affluent, people bought instruments and formed orchestras. In the eighteenth century "singing schools" trained not only church choirs but secular choruses, some of them quite polished performers. Hymns as well as psalms were sung in the churches, some of them so well known as to constitute a kind of popular music themselves. Elias Mann's Northampton *Collection of Sacred Harmony* (1797), for example, was a tasteful collection whose religious content was less important than its general musical appeal.

At the same time, throughout the eighteenth century, ballads and broadsides—the popular songs of England transferred to colonial shores— provided another strain of popular music. Though their aim was to disperse information and news (of disasters, crimes, political events, and other items of public interest) they were also, in a sense, mass music. With new lyrics set to a traditional tune, as John Dickinson's revolutionary "Liberty Song" (1768) was set to the old English "Hearts of Oak," they were especially useful weapons during the argument with England. As Joel Barlow wrote in 1775, "I have great faith in the influence of songs . . . ; one good song is worth a dozen addresses or proclamations." William Billings' rousing "Chester," a defiant war song set to an old psalm tune, was more popular than "Yankee Doodle," itself adapted from an earlier English ballad. The words of these ballads, of course, counted much more than the music, which tended to use familiar tunes again and again. The "Anacreon" tune of "The Star-Spangled Banner" had already been used twenty-six times when Key took it for his lyrics in 1814.

There was, therefore, by the close of the Revolution, a well-developed secular, popular music in America, drawn from English and native sources. When Benjamin Carr put together his "Federal Overture" for public musical performance in 1794 he included, as a cross section of current popular taste, "Yankee Doodle," "Oh Dear, What Can The Matter Be?" "The Irish Washerwoman's Reel," "The President's March," "La Carmagnole" (a Spanish ballad), "Rose Tree" (a sentimental English ballad), and "La Marseillaise."

Music books, known as "songsters" or "musical miscellanies" always included patriotic and political songs, ballads, hymns, and play songs. Alexander Reinagle's 1789 songbook, for example, contained "Drink To Me Only With Thine Eyes," "How Happy the Soldier," "The Blue Bell of Scotland," "Johnny and Mary," and imported songs like "John Peel" and "Bonnie Doon." The pattern was repeated in many other collections, such as *The Musical Cavacanet, The Virginia Warbler, The United States Songster,* and *The Missouri Songster* (1808), one of the most widely used, which Lincoln remembered singing from as a boy. Among the favorites they reprinted were "Hail Columbia!" (also known as "The New Federal Song"); Robert Burns's "Auld Lang Syne," to a traditional Scottish air; John Rolfe's popular "Mary's Dream," imported from London in 1793 and used over and over; and Michael Arne's "Lass With the Delicate Air" (also known as "Young Molly Who Lives At the Foot of the Hill").

Matthew Lewis's "Crazy Jane," with words by John Davy, was a great favorite in 1800. Such collections proliferated from the 1790's well into the nineteenth century, supplying the main source of American popular music.

The songbooks gave singable, simple songs to a wide public, songs "well adapted to the family circle . . . , tender, eloquent, and chaste," as one editor said, suited to current tastes and to every conceivable interest. There were a good many sentimental "parlor songs" for family or individual use—"Rosalie the Prairie Flower," "Nobody's Darling," "Little Nellie," "Amber Lee." There were songs about current events, like Samuel Woodworth's lyrics for Jackson's campaign song of 1824, "The Hunters of Kentucky," a real rouser; and James Hewitt's "Tammany Quickstep" and "Lawrence the Brave." Woodworth, who wrote the lyrics for "The Fortune I Crave," "Love's Eyes," and "The Old Oaken Bucket," was the most successful songwriter of the period. No American, however, approached the popularity of Irish poet Tom Moore, who wrote lyrics for traditional Irish tunes. Moore's *Selections of Irish Melodies* (1807, 1813) contained such favorites as "The Harp That Once Through Tara's Halls," "Believe Me If All Those Endearing Young Charms," "Oft in the Stilly Night," and "The Last Rose of Summer"; at least a dozen of his songs sold steadily for the next twenty years.

Other songwriters also knew what the public liked. John Braham wrote "On This Cold Flinty Rock" and "The Beautiful Maid"; Charles Dibdin wrote "Poor Jack" and "Tom Truelove's Knell"; Charles Horn's "I've Been Roaming" was a popular tenor solo; James Hook wrote over two thousand songs before his death in 1847. The era's greatest hit was "Home, Sweet Home," John Howard Payne's collaboration with Englishman Henry Bishop, introduced in the opera *Clari* in 1823. Not far behind in popularity was John Mill Hewitt's ballad, "The Minstel's Return From the Wars," published in 1827.

It was obvious in the eighteen-thirties that there was a large demand for popular music, and that those who satisfied it stood to make substantial profits. The first composer to take full advantage of the market was Lowell Mason, a musically-inclined banker, whose hymnbook, published in 1822, returned him at least $60,000 profit. Mason became choirmaster of the Reverend Lyman Beecher's Boston church in 1827, helped to found the Boston Academy of Music, and revolutionized the teaching of music in the schools. He also continued to issue collections at handsome profits; his *Carmina Sacra* (1841) earned more than $100,000, an incredible amount for the times.

Mason mostly wrote hymns, but they were good songs, four of them among the most popular of all time—"Nearer My God to Thee," "From Greenland's Icy Mountains," "Blest Be the Tie That Binds," and "Work, for the Night Is Coming." He had an unusual gift for combining honest, earnest lyrics with simple melody in a way that the public appreciated and understood. William "Singing Billy" Walker's *Southern Harmony and Musical Companion* (1835), nearly as popular as Mason's collections, sold 600,000 copies over the next thirty years.

Mason's and Walker's hymnbooks, though their audience was by no means exclusively religious, did not fully exploit the great market for secular, especially sentimental, songs. Henry Russell, an English concert baritone who arrived in the United States in the 1830's, immediately perceived the potential profits, deliberately aimed at the popular market, and hit his target exactly. Russell had a hand in more than eight hundred songs, many of them well known, which he promoted by singing them himself on tour. Working with a number of good lyricists, especially with George Pope Morris, Russell wrote direct, melodic songs, using a minimum of notes in a limited range, dealing with fundamental emotions and popular tastes—"Life on the Ocean Wave," "Woodman, Spare that Tree," "The Old Armchair" (the first "mother song" hit), "The Old Family Clock," "Those Locks, Those Ebon Locks," "Baby Mine," and others which, he said, "made music the vehicle of grand thoughts and noble sentiments" precisely as the public desired.

A consummate showman, Russell used to pause dramatically near the close of his star number, "Woodman, Spare that Tree," encouraging the audience to shout, "Did he spare it?" at which point he would complete the song. Others mined the vein that Russell uncovered—J. P. Knight with "Rocked in the Cradle of the Deep"; Thomas Bayley with "Long, Long Ago"; Frederick Crouch with "Kathleen Mavourneen"—filling the songbooks with ballads to be sung around the parlor melodeon, in concerts by touring tenors, by young ladies at singing schools, and in the minstrel shows. Another medium for selling such songs was the "singing family," in which everybody from grandfather to grandchild made up a chorus which toured as a unit, like the sixteen Hutchinsons of New Hampshire, the Bakers, the Barbers, the Reiners, the Cheneys, the Blakeleys, and the Housers.

They were chiefly "story" songs, narratives which like popular poetry and novels dealt with home, family, love requited and unrequited, death and melancholy, hope and sorrow, designed for an audience quite different from that which bought Walker and Mason. "Eliza" was rather daring, since it involved a quite physical kiss:

> The shadows of eve 'gan to steal o'er the plain,
> To Eliza my heart I confess'd,
> Love sanctioned the moment, she smiled on my pain,
> On her lips a soft kiss I impress'd.

"My Mother" gave an unusual twist to the mother song in the lament of a girl whose marriage had been blocked by parental disapproval:

> The World may think me gay, for my feelings I smother,
> Oh thou hast been the cause of this anguish, my mother!

"Encompass'd in An Angel's Frame" mourned a lost lover in morbid metaphor:

> With yew and ivy round me spread
> My Anna there I'll mourn:
> For all my soul—now she is dead—
> Concentres in her urn.

The books which contained such songs appeared by dozens and sold in the thousands. Music for the popular market, written to its taste, was profitable business by the forties.

Minstrel shows, the most popular form of musical entertainment during the middle years of the nineteenth century, provided the chief vehicle for the performance of popular music. Not all minstrel tunes (and fewer as time passed) were so-called "darky" songs, although originally they formed the core of the show. Actually, "darky" songs such as "The Dinner Horn," "I Must Go To Richmond," or "Way Down in Cairo" were only partly Negro-based; Dan Emmett's great ballads and walkarounds, "Old Dan Tucker," "Blue Tail Fly," "Walk Along John," and "Dixie," were not really Negro songs at all. Minstrel shows drew from anywhere, using Irish jigs, Scotch airs, parodies, humor songs, "girl" songs ("Baltimore Belle," "Melinda May," "Angela Baker") and many, many sentimental ballads like "Go to Jane Glover and Tell Her I Love Her," "Nora McShane," "The Old Sexton," "Peaceful Slumbering," "The Midshipman's Farewell," and "Jennie":

> I've wealth and I've rank, I've lawns and I've deer,
> I've mansions and grounds, but all these without her,
> What are they to me? What are they to me?

Henry Russell, songbooks, singing families, parlor melodeons, minstrel shows, and touring tenors opened the ballad era of American popular music, nor has it yet closed. The basis of the ballad was the hymn

Title page of the first edition of "My Old Kentucky Home," from the Foster Hall Collection. CULVER PICTURES, INC.

Label from a popular 1908 Victor recording. RCA RECORDS.

Rosario Burdon conducting the Victor Orchestra, circa 1914. RCA RECORDS.

The Paul Whiteman orchestra. CULVER PICTURES, INC.

Duke Ellington at a 1945 recording session. CULVER PICTURES, INC.

Song publications of the
early forties, featuring Bing Crosby
and Frank Sinatra.
BOWLING GREEN STATE UNIVERSITY.

tune, out of the seventeenth-century hymnbook, out of Mason and Walker, out of this long and powerful American churchly tradition. Quite different from its European counterpart, the American ballad style can be clearly heard through all nineteenth and early twentieth century popular music— the thirty-two-bar evangelical hymn pattern, built of harmonically related eight-bar phrases divided into introduction, verse, and refrain. In common with most Western music, it used the *AABA* song form; that is, a musical statement, followed by its repetition with variation, followed by a "release" or "bridge" forming a transition to a restatement or conclusion. That the hymn tune and the *AABA* form lie at the root of the popular ballad may be illustrated merely by listening to "Swanee River," for example, or "Old Uncle Ned" (Foster did it extremely well in its simplest form), while many of the ballad songs themselves were directly adapted from "sacred miscellanies" or hymn collections.

By the middle of the nineteenth century the ballad was the characteristic form of American popular music, an essentially vocal music derived from a secularized version of the hymn. On this model songwriters evolved a standardized tune pattern that was easy for an untrained voice to sing (within an octave range), easy to play (using the four principal chords and most familiar positions), and easy to remember. Actually, the form quickly became so standardized that, as Sigmund Spaeth once demonstrated, it was possible to play "Dixie," "Yankee Doodle," and "Home Sweet Home" simultaneously in rather pleasing counterpoint.

The king of the early ballad era was Stephen Collins Foster, the doomed young genius whose tunes and lyrics became so deeply imbedded in the American popular heritage. Born in 1826 near Pittsburgh, Foster studied music as a boy and knew the ballad tradition well. He played guitar and flageolet (a kind of flute) with more than average skill, began writing songs at fourteen, and published his first ballad, "Open Thy Lattice, Love," at sixteen. Like most young songwriters, he knew a good many minstrel blackface tunes, but his contact with Negroes and Negro music was slight; since minstrel shows paid money for songs, he began writing for them in the mid-forties, though he was more interested in music of a more genteel kind. When "Old Uncle Ned" and "Oh Susannah!" were great hits Foster found himself a success in what he called "the Ethiopian field." Though minstrel songs continued to stream from his pen, he received small payment for them and often allowed others (including minstrel leader E. P. Christy) to publish them under their own names. In 1850 he signed a contract with a publishing company and made arrangements to write chiefly for Christy.

Foster wrote nearly four hundred songs, not all of them good or popular, including comic songs, "mother" songs, tearful ballads, war songs, temperance songs, hack ballads, and (after he succumbed to alcoholism in the sixties) anything that would bring him a few dollars. His best work came in the fifties. The great minstrel songs—"Old Folks at Home" (or "Swanee River"), "My Old Kentucky Home," "Old Black Joe," "Massa's in de Cold, Cold Ground" (his only dialect song), "Camptown Races"— were known everywhere. "Old Folks at Home," introduced by Christy's Minstrels in 1852, was such a hit that its publishers ran two presses around the clock for several days to satisfy the demand for sheet music. The majority of his songs, however, belonged in the sentimental ballad tradition and his best ones were almost as popular as his minstrel show tunes: the delicate "Jeannie with the Light Brown Hair," "Come Where My Love Lies Dreaming," "Beautiful Dreamer," "Gentle Annie," "Our Bright Summer Days Have Gone."

Though he died at thirty-seven with a few cents and the manuscript of "Beautiful Dreamer" in his pocket, Foster was and still is the most popular of all American songwriters. Known then and now by practically every American, his songs struck some responsive chord in the popular mind. Musically, he wrote a clean melodic line with simple harmonies— the tonic, dominant, sub-dominant pattern of the hymn and ballad—with interesting though uncomplicated variations. Beyond his really great talent for melody, Foster's effectiveness lay also in the close integration of his lyrics with his music, and in their content, which dealt with the verities of home, love, peace, security, and nostalgia.

There were other popular ballad writers, some nearly as good as Foster and most of them more financially successful. Every living room usually had at least one songbook in it, and if it had a piano, perhaps six. Publishers of the sixties and seventies recognized certain salable categories, such as love, family, reform or moral ("The Drunkard's Child," "A Pack of Cards," "All That Glitters Is Not Gold"), religious, comedy ("Where Was Moses When the Lights Went Out?"), minstrel-type "darky," specialty (railroad, sports, etc.), tragedy ("A Faded Rosebud in Our Bible"), and topical. Writers and publishers joined in a business arrangement in which writers tried to locate public preferences and write for them, while publishers attempted to anticipate the market and supply it.

War songs, of course, dominated the sixties. Dan Emmett's minstrel "walk-around" "Dixie" became the Confederacy's favorite. Julia Ward Howe's version of an old camp meeting rouser, "Say, Brother, Will You

Meet Us?" which became "The Battle Hymn of the Republic" in 1862 (and also "John Brown's Body") emerged as the most powerful song of the war. Bandmaster Patrick Gilman's "When Johnny Comes Marching Home," based on an Irish tune; George G. Root's "Tramp, Tramp, Tramp the Boys Are Marching" and Henry Clay Work's "Marching Through Georgia" were songs of great vitality. The war produced popular sentimental ballads too—Walter Kittredge's "Tenting Tonight on the Old Camp Ground," Root's "Just Before the Battle, Mother," and the hymn-like love song adopted by soldiers in both armies, H. D. Webster's haunting "Lorena."

The most successful songwriter of the mid-century years was George Frederick Root, whose ballads were no less popular than his war songs. "Rosalie, the Prairie Flower" (1855) alone earned him royalties of $3,000 a year. Henry Clay Work, who did "Father, Dear Father, Come Home With Me Now," the best known of all temperance songs, also wrote "Grandfather's Clock," still a barbershop favorite. Will S. Hayes wrote three hundred songs which sold twenty million copies. After "The Drummer Boy of Shiloh," his first wartime success, he published at least one 50,000-copies seller per year for twenty years. Hart Pease Danks wrote more than a hundred songs, but he needed only one, "Silver Threads Among the Gold" (1873) to make him a success. Each year certain writers hit the market exactly right: George Allen's "Bury Me Not on the Lone Prairie" (1850); H. S. Thompson's "Lily Dale" (1852), the most popular of the brokenhearted lover songs; Septimus Winner's "Listen to the Mocking Bird" (1855); Benjamin Russell Hanby's "My Darling Nelly Gray" (1856); and so on.

Most popular of all were topical songs which dealt with current events and reflected the tastes of the times. The public seemed to want songs about everything that happened, about the stock market, city life, politics, country life, elections, scandals, deaths, fads and fashions, anything of interest. Musicologist Paul Glass has calculated that between 350,000 and 400,000 such songs probably appeared between 1830 and 1910. Major events like the antislavery crusade, the California gold rush, or presidential elections naturally called forth dozens of songs, but so did matters of passing and lesser interest. Mrs. Frances Trollope's book, *Domestic Manners of the Americans* (1832), an attack on American culture, elicited "The Mrs. Trollope Quick Step." Darwin's *Origin of Species* brought "Darwin's Little Joke." Edward Payson Weston's record-breaking walk from Maine to Chicago in 1867 was immortalized in "March to Chicago." "The Bloomer's Complaint" satirized Mrs. Bloomer's attempt at dress reform; "Velocipediana" celebrated the bicycle craze of 1869.

Songwriters followed politics with items like "The Veto Galop"; "The Silver Knight of the West" (Bryan); "How Are You, Greenbacks?"; and "Follow the Plow," a Populist song. "I've Struck Ile" commemorated the discovery of oil in Pennsylvania; "The Express Galop" the first run of the Adams Express Company; "The Highway in the Air" the opening of the Brooklyn Bridge. In the older broadside tradition publishers brought out "Lost on the Lady Elgin" on the steamboat tragedy of 1860; "Homeless Tonight" on the Boston fire of 1872; "Bring Back My Darling" on the Charley Ross kidnapping of 1874; and "The Torrents Came Upon Them" on the Johnstown Flood of 1884. This was the music business at its most businesslike.

The link between the popular songs of the sixties, and the commercialized product of the nineties is best represented by the music of James Bland, born of free Negro parents in New York, musically well educated, a brilliant graduate of Howard University. He joined a Negro minstrel show company (of which there were not many) and wrote more than seven hundred songs for minstrel use, copyrighting only a few. Equaled perhaps only by Foster in his gift for melody, Bland turned out good songs by the score, many published under others' names.

"Carry Me Back to Old Virginny" (1878) alone was enough to place Bland with the popular immortals. "In the Evening By the Moonlight" remains one of the best harmony songs ever written; "Oh Dem Golden Slippers" and "Hand Me Down My Walkin' Cane" have such an authentic touch of the spiritual that most people still believe they are; "They Gotta Quit Kickin' My Dog Aroun'" was a comedy favorite for years. When Bland's troupe visited London in 1884 he stayed there to enjoy a highly successful career on the English stage. When he returned twenty years later the minstrel shows were nearly gone and he could not write what vaudeville wanted. Like Foster, he died broke and alone in 1911.

In the nineties the commercialization of popular music entered its final—and modern—phase. The market for songs was huge, increasing each year. The introduction of mass production methods in piano manufacture made the instrument a fixture in every middle-class home, bringing in the voice-and-piano age of song. Pianos, pump organs, and pianolas (soon to be followed by player pianos) were priced within the range of families with moderate means, which meant that music was a normal daily activity in millions of homes. A piano in the parlor and music lessons for the children were marks of refinement and respectability, the family a center for both musicmaking and listening. The same mass production methods, applied to mandolins, banjos, guitars, and other instruments, added thousands of people, who could make their own music, to the market for popular songs.

Writing songs to order for the mass market was not new, but both song publishing and song promotion, until the nineties, was a more or less unorganized business. There soon appeared a group of clever men, with a keen sense for the public taste and the ability to exploit it, who proceeded to write and publish a majority of the nation's songs. Paul Dresser, Charles K. Harris, Gussie Davis, Edward Marks, Joseph Shelly, Harry Kennedy, Charles Graham, Monroe Rosenfeld, later Harry Von Tilzer, Gus Edwards, and Ernest Ball, to name the better known, dominated the popular field and controlled its publishing. They wrote literally thousands of songs, all of them contrived for swiftly changing public tastes and almost all of them ephemeral—but they made a great deal of money. The patterns and techniques of commercialization which they established between 1890 and 1910 still remain fundamentally the same.

The career of Charles K. Harris, sometime minstrel singer and banjo-ist, serves as an example. Harris, who lived in Milwaukee, hung out a sign, "Songs Written to Order," and opened an office to supply vaudeville performers on a production-line basis. In 1892 he wrote "After The Ball" and persuaded J. Aldrich Libbey, a popular baritone, to insert it into the musical play "A Trip To Chinatown"; the song broke up the performance and eventually sold five million copies. Harris then moved to New York, since it provided a better base. The three big houses of Woodward, Witmark, and Stern-Howley-Harrison, were already there and by the late nineties most of the music publishers were concentrated in the Union Square area where, naturally, songwriters took up residence too. Over the next decade or so the business gradually moved uptown to 28th Street, known as "Tin Pan Alley."

Under the spur of fierce competition the music publishing houses developed rudimentary methods of market research, testing trends of the public taste and trying to anticipate them, and also evolved new methods of promoting or "plugging" songs by inducing performers to use them. Vaudevillians, singing waiters, musical comedy writers, anybody who might give a song publicity were either importuned or bribed. (Libbey received $500 and a percentage for using "After The Ball.") By 1914 it could take as much as $14,000 to get a song before the public; in 1915 a famous vaudeville quartet used twelve songs in its act, collecting for each at the rate of one hundred dollars a song.

The men who wrote the popular songs were shrewd, expert judges of public preferences. Harris, known for "After The Ball" and "Just Break the News to Mother," wrote an unbroken succession of hits year in and year out. Gussie Davis, a Negro, had at least fifteen hits to his credit among the dozens he wrote, the most successful "In The Baggage Coach Ahead" and "The Fatal Wedding." James Thornton wrote "'My Sweetheart's The Man in The Moon" and "When You Were Sweet Sixteen," written as a love song for his wife. H. W. Petrie had "I Don't Want to Play in Your Yard," Charles Graham "Two Little Girls in Blue." Paul Dresser, Theodore Dreiser's talented, high-living brother, who flamed like a rocket through the era's popular music, wrote not only the famous "My Gal Sal" and "On the Banks of the Wabash," but dozens more that the nation hummed and sang in close harmony; in 1896 he had ten hits, six in 1897, sixteen in 1898, and at least five best-selling songs each year until his death in 1906.

These songs were nearly all sentimental ballads, some less lachrymose than others—"In the Good Old Summertime," "Ida, Sweet as Apple Cider," "Shine on, Harvest Moon," "The Band Played On," "A Bicycle Built for Two." Since they were made for singing, they emphasized a simple melody line, simple chording, and a restricted range. Since they were also written for vaudeville and concert singers, like Aldrich, Libbey or Edward Marks and were often part of a larger act, they told a story that held the audience's attention. "After The Ball," for example, was a rather complicated story of estranged lovers; so too with songs like "Sweet Adeline," "Down By the Old Mill Stream," "Dear Old Girl," and "I Wonder Who's Kissing Her Now." Since the verse carried the narrative, they usually had sixteen-bar verses and eight-bar choruses.

Somewhat different were the "parlor songs" constructed for around-the-piano home talent. These tended to resemble either hymns or the more maudlin ballads. Countless young ladies tackled "My Isle of Golden Dreams," "Lullaby Land," "Mighty Lak a Rose," "There's a Long Long Trail A'Winding," "In the Sweet Long Ago," "The Day When You'll Forget Me," or "Only a Pansy Blossom." The most successful writer in this genre was Carrie Jacobs-Bond, the widow of a physician in Northern Michigan who moved to Chicago to make a living. She found she had a talent for songwriting, and in 1896 made arrangements with a printer to publish songs which her son peddled on his bicycle to music stores. They caught on after she began to sing them herself on vaudeville programs, and with "Just A'Wearyin' For You" (1901) she had a hit.

Prominent concert singers like Jessie Bartlett Davis, Chauncey Olcott, David Bispham, and Madame Schumann-Heink featured Mrs. Bond's songs, like "I Love You Truly," "God Remembers When the World Forgets," "A Little Pink Rose." After "A Perfect Day" (1910), her sheet music was on half the pianos in the country. Undoubtedly the most popular

woman composer in American musical history, she was a White House
guest of Roosevelt, Harding, and Coolidge, for whom she sang her famous
lyrics,

> When you come to the end of a perfect day,
> And you sit alone with your thought,
> While the chimes ring out with a carol gay,
> For the joy that the day has brought.

It was Herbert Hoover who wrote the epitaph for her grave in California's
Forest Lawn Cemetery.

But the nineties also introduced a tough, overtly sexual element into
popular music, reflecting the changed manners and mores of an urbanizing, polyglot, acquisitive, and increasingly sophisticated society. This derived partly from the dialect "coon song," from the white minstrel show,
and partly from the ragtime songs from Negro honky-tonk low life. The
minstrel show developed a comic song based on the caricature of the
chicken-stealing, cakewalking "high yaller" city Negro, done by white
men in blackface; Paul Allen's "New Coon in Town" (1883) and Leon
Berg's "Coontown Billimane" (1892) were popular songs of this kind.
Ben Harney, a "coon shouter" and ragtime piano player, became famous
in vaudeville during the nineties for coon songs; Ernest Hogan, himself
a Negro, wrote "All Coons Look Alike To Me" in 1896, a song bitterly
resented by Negroes and which Hogan was sorry he wrote.

Some ribald songs came from the black cabarets and clubs in the
cities, on the wrong side of the tracks. Babe Connors' Castle Club in
St. Louis, for example, featured "the prettiest and lightest girls from New
Orleans" who danced on a huge mirror clad only in shoes and stockings.
Babe also featured Mamma Lou, a powerful black woman who belted
out songs like "There'll Be a Hot Time in the Old Town Tonight" and
"Ta-ra-ra-boom-der-é" (which had variant spellings), both of which became popular with the white public in much-sterilized versions. The
"coon song" suddenly became a nineties fad (some six hundred of them
were written between 1890 and 1900) with one called "Coon! Coon!
Coon!" representing the ultimate. Many had ribald, frankly sexual implications—"I Got Mine," "You Don't Have to Marry the Girl," "I Don't Like
No Cheap Man," "Pump Away Joseph," or "A Red Hot Member" (who's
"cooler than December" and "can surely sting like a bumble-bee.")

Bull-voiced May Irwin and Maggie Cline, both vaudeville favorites,
specialized in rough-and-tumble songs like "Throw Him Down McCluskey," "Down Went McGinty," and "The Bully Song." More sophisticated
songs reflected the same trend, with titles like "In The Naughty Alto-

gether," "Won't You Fondle Me?" "Cuddle Up a Little Closer," and the double entendre of "You Can Go As Far As You Like With Me in My Merry Oldsmobile" of 1906.

The New York *Dramatic Mirror* complained about the morality of popular songs, citing

Every day I go for a lark in the park—and Johnny goes too—
Every night I come home to my bed, and Johnny comes too—

while the 1913 Ziegfeld Follies featured "Everybody's Doing It" (which turned out to be a new dance, the turkey trot). Popular on the stage were aggressive female singers, like Blanch Ring, Marie Cahill, Eva Tanguay, Sophie Tucker, Nora Bayes. Noticeably, for the first time heavy drinking was treated as comic material, in contrast to the temperance songs of the seventies, with songs like "The Old Man's Drunk Again," "The Bottle's Empty," and "Fizz, Glorious Fizz!"

The most important musical fact of the nineties, however, was the introduction of ragtime into popular music. The product of a number of elements, ragtime owed something to the "coon song," the Negro work-song, and the minstrel show tune. Negroes who could not get work in white minstrel shows made their own music in imitation, using tunes and styles from the waterfront dives and barrelhouses, Negro dances, and borrowed ballad tunes. The result was a genuine, unique, black music called "ragtime," a slang term for syncopation. During the seventies and eighties cities with large Negro populations like St. Louis, Memphis, and New Orleans were already active black music centers.

Ragtime was rhythmic rather than melodic, instrumental rather than vocal, an adaptation of dance music made particularly for piano and strongly influenced by march rhythm. Musically it featured a syncopated right-hand treble melody line (sometimes triple time) set against a driving, steady, regularly accented left-hand bass, usually 2/4 time. Early rags were played at march tempo, but later piano players speeded up the tempo and added melodic embellishments in the treble line. A rather formal music, ragtime was intended to be played as written, although more musically trained composers like Scott Joplin included a section near the close, labeled "Stomp," for improvisation. Rags sometimes had several themes (Joplin's "Maple Leaf Rag" had four) with complex formal developments.

Ragtime moved across the line into white music during the nineties. The first published rag was probably "Mississippi Rag" in 1897, which set off a sheet music explosion. Within five years or so practically all popular songs except waltzes and two-steps were rag-influenced, attacked as "vulgar, filthy, and suggestive music" by critics, and decried by the American Federation of Musicians in 1901 as "musical trash." Nevertheless, ragtime was fresh, vital music that the public liked. Even Dvořák and Debussy used it, albeit somewhat self-consciously and without real understanding. Everybody played and sang ragtime songs, like Shelton Brooks's classic, "The Darktown Strutter's Ball," with its famous opening lines, "I'll be down to get you in a taxi, honey . . . ," and stores sold instruction books so that young ladies who practiced Czerny for their music teachers could learn ragtime on their own. Ragtime's lower-class origins made it attractive to sophisticated white audiences; its validity and vigor provided a welcome relief from sentimental ballads and parlor songs.

Scott Joplin was the best known and the best of the ragtime writers. A Texas-born Negro with sound musical training, Joplin played with a troupe at a Sedalia, Missouri, club owned by a music publisher, John Stark, who liked rags. In 1899 Stark published "Maple Leaf," an immediate hit, and Joplin went into the business. He published thirty-nine rags of his own, an instruction book for ragtime pianists, a ragtime opera (never staged) and another unsuccessful one, *Treemonista* (1911) which did not appeal to a public accustomed to Victor Herbert. Others entered the field quickly; there were at least thirty first-rate ragtime writers publishing between 1900 and 1914, a number of ragtime piano schools, ragtime vaudeville acts, and ragtime singers like James J. Morton who sang nothing else.

Joe Lamb, George Botsford, Charlie Johnson (famous for "Dill Pickle Rag" and "Swanee Rag") and Percy Wenrich were white ragtime specialists whose songs sold in the thousands. Tom Turpin, James Scott, and Louis Chauvin were Negro ragtime piano stars; so were New Orleans pianists Tony Jackson and Jelly Roll Morton. The craze was nearly over by 1914, by which time ragtime had been thoroughly commercialized (as in Irving Berlin's spurious "Alexander's Ragtime Band" of 1911). Ragtime's influence on popular music, however, both in style and content, was permanent—for it became one of the major strands in American jazz.

The production line at Tin Pan Alley continued to turn out popular songs the standard formula after 1900, ragtime-tinged and somewhat more raucous than those of the nineties. Every five-and-dime store had a music section, where a bored girl banged out sample selections on a tinny piano. The right kind of song could easily sell a million copies, the best a great many more. There were forty-two million-copy sellers in 1907; "Meet Me Tonight in Dreamland" (1909) sold over five million that year, "Let Me Call You Sweetheart" (1910) over eight million.

The men who wrote songs for this mass market knew exactly how to do it. Ernest R. Ball, who had a talent for tearjerkers that still endears him to tenors, wrote them out by the dozen—"Dear Little Boy of Mine," "Till The Sands of the Desert Grow Cold," and of course "When Irish Eyes Are Smiling" and "Mother Machree." Percy Wenrich, classically-trained like Ball, did "Put on Your Old Gray Bonnet," "When You Wore a Tulip," and "On Moonlight Bay," among others. Gus Edwards had a half-dozen or more in the million bracket—among them "School Days," "By The Light of the Silvery Moon," "Sunbonnet Sue," and "Way Down Yonder in the Cornfield." Joseph McCarthy wrote the gracefully lyrical "Alice Blue Gown" and "I'm Always Chasing Rainbows." They were all good songs, made for people to sing and hear, dealing honestly and simply with common themes.

The most prolific of the early twentieth century ballad makers was unquestionably Harry Von Tilzer (born Harry Gumm), who wrote fifteen songs that went over the million mark in sheet music and a dozen others that approached it. Working on commission from vaudevillians, singers, and band leaders, he could fabricate ballads, tap dance tunes, comic songs, coon songs, ragtime, or almost anything else in a matter of hours. (He liked the tinny sound of a piano with paper across the strings, hence the name "Tin Pan Alley" for the street where he had his studio.) His "Old Irish Mother of Mine" combined the mother song with the Irish song into a virtuoso piece for vaudeville tenors. "Only a Bird in a Gilded Cage," written at a Chicago roadhouse party, reduced the establishment to tears with the story of a pretty girl whose

> beauty was sold, for an old man's gold,
> Just a bird in a gilded cage,

a vaudeville standard for years. Von Tilzer, who produced songs for twenty-seven years, once calculated he had written at least eight thousand —among them such familiar parlor favorites as "Wait Till The Sun Shines, Nellie"; "Take Me Out to The Ball Game"; "On a Sunday Afternoon"; and "I Want a Girl Just Like the Girl Who Married Dear Old Dad."

Irving Berlin (Izzy Baline) exceeded Von Tilzer and everyone else. By any count the most successful of modern American popular songwriters, Berlin moved with the times over a span of fifty years, maintaining remarkably consistent touch with the musical tastes of a rapidly changing society. As a singing waiter in a New York restaurant near Tony Pastor's, Berlin began by writing lyrics for others, then in 1909 writing entire songs on commission for vaudeville singers. "Alexander's Ragtime Band," done first as a piano rag in 1909, gave him a reputation as a ragtime writer.

Turning to the sentimental ballad style, "When I Lost You," (written after the death of his young wife and still one of his best) showed his talent in that field. Taking a worn-out and meretricious musical style, the Tin Pan Alley love song, Berlin infused it with a new emotional validity to which the public immediately responded. No other songwriter has approached Berlin in this genre: millions knew and still know "All By Myself," "What'll I Do?" "All Alone," "Always," "Remember," "How Deep Is the Ocean?" "Say It Isn't So," "The Song Is Ended."

Beginning with *Watch Your Step* in 1914, Berlin established himself in musical comedy and later in Hollywood with a long succession of melodic, witty, and sophisticated tunes like "A Pretty Girl is Like a Melody," "Isn't This a Lovely Day," "Let's Have Another Cup of Coffee," "Cheek to Cheek," "I'm Putting All My Eggs in One Basket," "Count Your Blessings," and a dozen others. Three Berlin songs attained the status of national classics—"Easter Parade," "God Bless America" (which received a Presidential Citation in 1945 and is perennially proposed as a national anthem), and "White Christmas," second only to "Silent Night" as the nation's favorite Christmas song with record sales over thirty million.

The operetta, a popular form of musical entertainment after 1900, aimed at a different audience than that attracted by ragtime or the ballad, but its music was no less commercial, designed to draw the largest possible crowds into the theater and to sell the largest volume of sheet music. Risky ventures that could lose thousands or pay off handsomely, expensive to stage and maintain, operettas depended wholly on their songs for success. If people went to the theater to hear the tunes, remembered them, bought the music and sang them around the piano, writers and singers and musicians and producers made money. Harry Von Tilzer and Victor Herbert wrote music for exactly the same reason, and Herbert dominated his field as Von Tilzer did his.

Willard Spencer's imitation Gilbert and Sullivan, *The Little Tycoon*, ran for five hundred performances in 1886, an indication of the operetta's box-office potential. Reginald De Koven, American-born but European-trained, wrote *The Begum* (1887) and then *Robin Hood* (1890), whose featured song, "Oh, Promise Me!" still remains a wedding standard. Woolson Morse's *Wang* (1891) and William Furst's *Isle of Champagne* (1891) were moderate successes, but Herbert's *Prince Ananias* (1894) established him at once as the best of the operetta-writers.

Herbert's librettos meant little; his shows depended quite properly on his songs. He simply wrote good ones, very good ones—graceful, melodic, romantic, singable—and a lot of them. Working sometimes on four productions at once, he produced fifty operettas in forty years, whose songs were sung and whistled and played by millions—from *Babes in Toyland* (1903), *Mlle. Modiste* (1905, featuring Fritzi Scheff), *The Red Mill* (1906), *Naughty Marietta* (1910), down to *Orange Blossoms* (1922), and in them such favorites as "Kiss Me Again," "Ah, Sweet Mystery of Life," "A Kiss in the Dark," "Sweethearts," "I'm Falling in Love With Someone," "Thine Alone," "Gypsy Love Song." Though not all of Herbert's operettas were successful, songs from his failures often survived after the production was forgotten. Music critics dismissed him as "second-rate Strauss" and "the poor man's Gounod," but no other light-opera composer ever matched his popularity.

Gustave Kerker, Gustave Luders, Karl Hochsna, and others came from Europe to cash in on the operetta fad. Czech-born Rudolf Friml, arriving in 1912, wrote four of the more popular, *The Firefly, The Vagabond King, Rose Marie,* and *The Three Musketeers,* featuring songs like "Only a Rose," "Ma Belle," and "If I Were King." Sigmund Romberg, a Viennese, wrote 175 songs for other people's shows and in 1915 wrote his own, *Blue Paradise,* followed by a series of successes into the twenties, *Blossom Time* (1921), *The Student Prince* (1924), *Desert Song* (1926), to the posthumous *Girl in Pink Tights* (1954). Romberg never wrote a witty or sophisticated song, but for sentimental romanticism he had no superior, *vide* "Song of Love," "Deep In My Heart," "Lover Come Back Back to Me," "One Kiss," and "Softly, As in a Morning Sunrise."

The invention and perfection of the phonograph changed everything in the popular music industry. Developed originally as a business machine (like the telephone and telegraph) a steady series of improvements made the phonograph (or gramophone) a commercial reality by 1900. Edison and Columbia dominated the market until 1901 when the Victor Talking Machine Company entered the field. The large sale of purely entertaining recordings in the nineties convinced these companies that the future of the machine lay in the market for mass entertainment, with an emphasis on music. What the largest segment of the public wanted, the phonograph companies would record and sell; what they recorded and sold would also have the largest public exposure. The phonograph, therefore, both met and made public taste.

Records ruined the sheet music business and nearly ruined the piano business. Prices of sheet music went down—from forty cents in 1902 to ten cents in 1916—for sheet music sales no longer really mattered. Record sales alone could make a song a hit, and in 1919 exactly that happened; George Stoddard's "Mary," turned down by three publishers, sold 300,000 copies in three months as a Victor record, which forced its publication in sheet music.

The phonograph made music available to anyone, almost anywhere, almost any time; to produce music with a phonograph required no skill, no lessons, no major outlay of money. People who could neither hum, sing, whistle, play piano, nor attend the theater or music hall were now included in the biggest market popular music had ever known. In 1910 the sales of popular songs, in all forms, exceeded two *billion* dollars.

The effects on popular music were revolutionary. Songs of the nineties and the early 1900's were written for playing and singing by amateurs at home; now songs were written for performance by experts on recordings to be listened to by a nonparticipating audience. Since professionals did the recordings, the music they used could be much more complicated, arrangements more intricate, harmonies and ranges suited to better-trained musicians. "A Bicycle Built for Two," with its simple melody, easily-managed lyrics, and uncomplicated harmony, was tailored for the market of 1892. It bore little relation to "Stardust" (1929) which did not even have lyrics in its original version. A record made by professionals to listen or dance to at home required a quite different kind of song than that made for a quartet to sing around the pianola. The phonograph record invited better writers and musicians to attempt something more challenging, with octave jumps and harmonic arrangements suitable to skilled performers. Malvin Schonberger's "Whispering" (1920) or Creamer and Layton's "After You've Gone" (1918) were songs that presumed some skill in musicianship on the part of the performer.

Furthermore, since the time of a record was established at three minutes, more or less, songwriters and arrangers had to work with about two and one-half choruses, the standard unit for years until the arrival of long-playing records. The narrative song, with its sixteen-bar verse, did not fit this format; what the lyric said had to be terse and direct. Since early recording equipment took brass better than strings, loud rhythmic music was best; since ragtime and jazz music recorded well, companies issued jazz records and reinforced the acceptance of jazz. Brash, blasting vocalists like Billy Murray, Elsie Janis, Will Dillon, and Sophie Tucker, or piercing tenors like Henry Burr, found the new medium much to their liking.

The introduction of the "blues" into popular music was, however, the most important musical influence since ragtime appeared a generation earlier. Blues songs evolved as a variety of Afro-American folksong in the mid-nineteenth century (possibly earlier) South; by the eighties this music (unnamed, since the "blues" title came a decade later) was an established song style among Negro singers and musicians. It was strongly melodic music, made to be sung. Its melancholy or wryly humorous lyrics depended on a series of three-line stanzas, the second line repeating the first, the third making a resolution or conclusion:

> Sent for you yesterday, and here you come today,
> Sent for you yesterday, and here you come today—
> If you can't do better, might as well stay away.

Blues singers slid or wavered notes, a style easily adaptable (as it proved) to piano and other solo instruments. Instead of the usual eight- or sixteen-bar melody, blues had a twelve-bar melody of three four-bar phrases, flatting the third and seventh notes (the "blue" notes) in the major diatonic scale. Its customary chord progression was from the common chord of the tonic, to the common chord of the sub-dominant, to the chord of the dominant seventh, with a return to the tonic, much like folksong. Rhythmically, the blues came to depend on a heavy, lagging accent on the second and fourth beats of 4/4 time. During the eighties Negro "blues singers" wandered through the South, singing verses they borrowed, adapted, or improvised, to the accompaniment of guitars or harmonicas at bars, picnics, street corners, funerals, or wherever they were welcome.

Everybody in the South knew about the blues, but it was W. C. Handy, a Negro minister's son from Alabama, who transferred them from regional, racial music into the mainstream of American popular song. Handy, who learned to play guitar and trumpet as a youth, joined a company of traveling minstrels against his father's wishes, turned himself into an expert musician and arranger, and organized a first-rate band of his own. He knew blues music well, and in 1909 wrote a campaign song for "Boss" Crump of Memphis in the blues style, which he published as a piano piece called "Memphis Blues." A shrewd New York publisher bought it for fifty dollars, and issued it with lyrics in 1913, and reaped considerable profit.

Handy then wrote another, "St. Louis Blues" (turned down by three publishers who could see no market for it), which Handy himself finally printed in 1914. Sophie Tucker introduced it on Broadway, Victor made a record of it, and soon the song was well on its way to becoming the most famous blues ever written—recorded more than a thousand times, fifty years after its publication still earning $25,000 a year in royalties. Handy's firm became the leading publisher of blues music, and Handy himself continued to write blues songs—"Beale Street," "Joe Turner,"

"John Henry," and many others. He neither "invented" the blues nor did he claim to have done so. What he did was to put together the elements of a vital, powerful, indigenous musical tradition and make it available to a new, different, and much wider public, a contribution of considerable importance in the history of popular music.

After Handy, writers like Clarence Williams ("Royal Garden Blues") and Perry Bradford ("Crazy Blues") entered the blues field. Bessie Smith, who began recording in 1923, made the blues singing style popular, selling over two million records her first year. Possessed of a rich, controlled contralto, Bessie smoothed out the roughnesses of the "talking blues" into something more sophisticated and stylish; she also widened the range of the blues, from the wit of her "rent party" songs to the naked emotion of her versions of older folk-blues. She became the model for a strong tradition of black singers, including such contemporaries as Alberta Hunter and Chippie Hill, followed by Lizzie Miles, Ethel Waters, Billie Holiday, and others down to the Mo-town singers of the sixties.

CHAPTER FOURTEEN

THE BIG BAND ERA

It Don't Mean a Thing If It Ain't Got that Swing

—WORDS BY IRVING MILLS, MUSIC BY DUKE ELLINGTON,
PUBLISHED BY GOTHAM MUSIC SERVICE, 1932

The expanding record market of the World War I years created a tremendous demand for musicians, arrangers, and songwriters; in a field rapidly becoming professionalized, there was little place for the man who picked out a catchy tune with one finger. What the nineties made into a business was now big business, one in which success meant a great deal of money. A hit record could sell two million copies in a matter of months; the Victor Company, for example, in exactly two years, 1913–15, nearly doubled its assets from thirteen million to twenty-three million dollars. Records became a rich source of revenue for songwriters, a potent means for reaching the public with new songs. Stars like Eddie Cantor, who signed a five-year contract with Brunswick Records in 1920 at a yearly guarantee of $200,000, could make a hit overnight with a single recording. Popular music was no place for amateurs.

The trouble was that despite the huge profits from record sales, anybody's songs could be used without permission or payment. Copyright laws of course forbade this, but complete enforcement of the law was nearly impossible. After 1909 songwriters collected two cents a record, but there seemed to be no way to collect for nonrecorded performances. In 1914 Victor Herbert, hearing an orchestra playing one of his songs free for the fifteenth time in a week, organized a meeting out of which grew the American Society of Composers, Authors, and Publishers. ASCAP, to collect fee payments, instituted test suits which were eventually successful in the Supreme Court in 1917. By establishing a system of ratings and performances, the organization began to distribute royalties to song-writers and lyricists on a percentage basis—in 1963 it divided about thirty-three million dollars. (Stephen Foster, who died with thirty-eight cents, under this system would have drawn about $20,000 per year).

The dance craze of the years 1900 to 1920 served to modify the style of popular music and to influence its market. The waltz and two-step, the two basic types of ballroom dancing, were suddenly displaced by the fox-trot, Gotham gobble, toddle, Gaby glide, turkey trot, grizzly bear, kan-garoo dip, and the bunny hug:

> As snug as a bug in a rug,
> Stop, Stop, that bunny hug!

Current Opinion noted in 1913 that any restaurant that hoped to draw customers had to have a dance floor. Dancing parties were fashion-able among the smarter set; junior proms began; cabarets flourished; and the public ballroom soon blossomed. Songwriters emphasized the dance-able qualities of a tune rather than its melody or lyrics, so that rhythm, preferably combined with melody but not necessarily so, took precedence for the first time in popular music. Even sheet music intended for vocal performance carried dance orchestrations with it, nor did the words of popular dance tunes to make sense—"Shake that Thing," "I'm So Happy, Honey," "By Heck," "Doin' the Drag."

Vernon Castle (real name Blythe) and his wife Irene, who starred in a series of "dance teas" in New York in 1912, became the most famous dance team in the nation. A handsome and stylish couple, they made dancing not only respectable but fashionable and glamorous. Irene Castle, an exceptionally beautiful woman, was the first star to bob her hair, the first to make fashion styles for the wealthy society set, and she became a model for the sophisticated twenties woman. They created their own step, The Castle Walk, and introduced a number of others, among them the tango, the lame duck, the Maxixe, the half-and-half, the Castle rag, and attracted thousands of people on to the dance floor.

For the amateur who stumbled through a fox-trot (the one two-step variation that lasted) the Castles provided inspiration and example. For the next fifty years dancing—whether it be the Charleston, the Black Bottom, the Big Apple, the Lindy Hop, or the twist and bougaloo—was inextricably linked with the record business and popular songs. A Victor advertisement of the twenties summarized the situation well:

You cannot resist dancing when the music is provided by His Mas-ter's Voice. The tunes are fascinating and have a snap which only those famous dance orchestras that record for Victor can give them. You can dance whenever you like.

As the phonograph record dominated the popular market in the decade following World War I, so the motion picture and the radio dominated it in the twenties and early thirties. Silent films, of course, used popular songs as accompaniment; during the twenties film companies distributed extensive piano, organ, and orchestra scores for each picture. "Theme songs" like "Weary River" (Richard Barthelmess), "The Sheik of Araby" (Rudolph Valentino), and "Pagan Love Song" (Ramon Navarro) rocketed to popularity along with the movie. Long before sound movies, theater organists hammered home theme music to the audience; it was customary in larger movie houses to feature an entire organ concert, composed entirely of theme music, before or after the film.

The introduction of sound in 1926 expanded the music market immeasurably. Since every sound film needed new songs, tailored to the mood and narrative of the picture, Tin Pan Alley began a swift move to Hollywood. Major film companies established their own record and sheet music companies; Metro-Goldwyn-Mayer, at one point in the twenties, owned half the year's best-selling songs. Movies made song hits overnight—"Diane" from *Seventh Heaven* (1927), Jolson's "Sonny Boy" from *The Singing Fool* (1928), "Jeannine" from *Lilac Time* (1928)—and still do. *Sunny Side Up* (1929), with Janet Gaynor and Charles Farrell, the first of the great musicals, introduced four immediate hits—"Sunny Side Up," "Turn on the Heat," "If I had a Talking Picture of You," and the little shop girl's dream song, "I'm a Dreamer, Aren't We All?"

Radio, introduced in the twenties and organized into an industry by the thirties, completed the transition in popular music from consumer-as-participant to consumer-as-listener, a trend begun by the player-piano, later reinforced by phonograph and movie soundtrack. Trained to listen professionally by the demands of these media, the public immediately accepted the new one. Radio music was even more available than music on records; it was there in a flick of a dial, and best of all, it was free.

Combined with the phonograph and the talking film, radio opened a huge new market to exploitation, making older techniques of songwriting and selling obsolete, providing a quick and efficient way of bringing songs to the public. A radio star, like a recording star (and they were often the same person) could put a song into the million-copy class by a single presentation; what Jessica Dragonette, Lanny Ross, Morton Downey, Kate Smith, Rudy Vallée, Dick Powell, Connie Boswell, or Bing Crosby sang one week was on "Your Hit Parade" (a program that lasted for twenty-five years) the next. Radio also brought prominence and pros-

perity to bands that played the popular tunes; millions of people listened
to Isham Jones, Wayne King, Ted Weems, Jan Garber, Guy Lombardo,
Kay Kyser, Sammy Kaye, and Benny Goodman, all of whom, like the popular singers, could make songs into hits.

Although it first seemed that radio and the depression doomed the
record business—sales of popular songs dropped from one hundred and
seven million records in 1927 to six million in 1932—record companies
bounced back by selling phonograph "pickups" which used the radio
amplifier as a reproduction device. Simultaneously, improved electrical
recordings and better equipment gave the listener a wilder and truer spectrum of sound than before, leading to the *LP* or long-play microgroove
record in the late forties. Meanwhile coin phonographs or "juke boxes,"
which both bought and sold records, put the product in every conceivable public place; there were half a million of them scattered over the
country by 1940, doing a five-hundred-million-dollar a year business. In
1946 there were 775 record companies in the market selling about three
hundred million records a year, and a million jukeboxes each averaging
a take of thirty dollars a week. The appearance of the radio "disc jockey,"
a term coined by *Variety* in 1937 to describe an announcer who played
records, added another sales factor. There were 1,200 disc jockeys regularly scheduled on radio in 1965.

The burgeoning of popular music in the twenties and thirties through
phonograph, films, and radio brought popular songwriters the greatest
prosperity they had ever known. There were fads and fashions in tunes,
such as a sudden burst of zany songs ("Yes, We Have No Bananas," "It
Ain' Gonna Rain No More," "I Couldn't Get To It in Time," "The Farmer
Took Another Load Away"), and a "mammy" craze ("Carolina Mammy,"
"Don't Leave Me Dear Old Mammy," "No One Loves You Better than
Your M-A-Double M-Y," "I Want My Mammy," and plain "Mammy"),
until it seemed that almost anything would sell.

Tin Pan Alley music prospered—simple, tuneful songs in the popular
manner perfected by the turn-of-the-century writers, updated for con-
temporary tastes. Milton Ager and Jack Yellen did this kind of song well—
"Ain't She Sweet," and "Happy Days Are Here Again," and so did Con
Conrad with tunes like "Margie," "Ma, He's Makin' Eyes at Me," and
"Lonesome and Sorry." Harry Warren, who worked with lyricist Al
Dubin, wrote some of the best, among them "You Must Have Been a
Beautiful Baby," and "I Found a Million Dollar Baby"; he also had a
surprisingly elegant lyrical gift that showed in love ballads like "I Only
Have Eyes For You" and "September in the Rain." Richard Whiting, who

worked for Remick Publishers, entered the market in 1918 with "Till We Meet Again" to continue with "Sleepy Time Gal," "Japanese Sandman," and "Louise," among others. Even more prolific was Walter Donaldson, who except for Berlin remains the biggest seller; in 1932 the Leo Feist Company sold five million copies of sheet music, four million of it by Donaldson. He wrote "How Ya Gonna Keep 'Em Down on the Farm" in 1919 and "Mammy" for Jolson in 1921, then turned out a dozen hits a year for twenty years—"Yes Sir, That's My Baby," "At Sundown," "Love Me or Leave Me," "After I Say I'm Sorry," "My Blue Heaven" (which sold four million records in 1927), and "Little White Lies."

These were the older generation of songwriters, whose products still sold well. However, newer, more sophisticated, and more musically complicated songs were beginning to catch the popular taste about 1920. Until then, popular songs were usually restricted to an octave range, built about four basic chords, with simple lyrics, written primarily for the home pianist and amateur vocalist. As the public became accustomed to professional, polished performances on records and radio, it also learned how to listen to what popular composers, arrangers, and artists could do. More and more popular songwriters were musically trained; their arrangements used wider ranges, advanced harmonies, more difficult intervals, longer melody lines.

The twenties trend in ballad writing was exemplified in the career of Jerome Kern, who studied at the New York College of Music and in Europe; served an apprenticeship in Tin Pan Alley; and took his first stage assignment in 1910 with a score for *Mr. Wix of Wickham*, a routine musical comedy. Kern's score seemed so fresh and original that critics and audiences watched for new Kern tunes, in which time after time he broke up the old song formulas—"Old Man River," "Smoke Gets in Your Eyes," "Why Was I Born," "Make Believe," "The Way You Look Tonight," "The Last Time I Saw Paris"—using altered chords, parallel fifths, delayed resolutions, and other devices quite unknown to men like Warren, Conrad, and Donaldson.

Nearly as influential as Kern, and perhaps more so in the orchestral field, was Duke Ellington, whose music was made for dancing and whose lyrics were difficult even for professionals to sing. Moving away from the blues-based jazz idiom of Harlem's Cotton Club, where his band's precise musicianship and powerful music made it one of the world's best-known musical organizations, Ellington introduced a series of artfully controlled, skillfully arranged songs into the popular field, among them "Mood Indigo," "Sophisticated Lady," "In a Sentimental Mood," and "Solitude." One need only compare "Yes Sir, That's My Baby" with Kern's "Smoke

Gets in Your Eyes," and "Ain't She Sweet" with Ellington's "I Let a Song
Go Out of My Heart" to recognize the arrival of a new kind of popular
song.

Kern and Ellington were only two of a group of musically trained,
sophisticated professionals who had no interest whatever in the "Hey
Baby" style of Tin Pan Alley. There were also Gershwin tunes which
musicians still find interesting—"Bidin' My Time," "I Got Rhythm,"
"Somebody Loves Me," "Embraceable You"—and those of Nacio Herb
Brown, a California real estate broker who drew on his own symphonic
work for "Temptation," "You Stepped Out of a Dream," "Pagan Love
Song," "You Are My Lucky Star," and "You Were Meant For Me." Jimmy
McHugh, who as rehearsal accompanist for The Boston Opera played
for Mary Garden and Caruso, wrote Harlem Cotton Club shows; with a
young schoolteacher, Dorothy Fields, he wrote a series of good-natured
songs like "I Can't Give You Anything But Love," "The Sunny Side of the
Street," and gentle love ballads like "I'm In The Mood For Love" and
"How Blue the Night."

Hoagy (Hoagland) Carmichael, an Indiana college boy, began as a
"blues" writer ("Washboard Blues," "Riverboat Shuffle") and in 1927
wrote the melody for what became in 1929, with lyrics by Mitchell Parish,
the perennial Junior Prom favorite, "Stardust." He continued with "Lazy
Bones," "Lazy River," "Two Sleepy People," "In the Cool of the Evening," and "Rockin' Chair," all of them musically sophisticated, highly
professional songs. Ray Henderson (real name Brost) studied at Chicago
Conservatory, took a song plugger's job, subsequently published over
two hundred songs, and wrote the music for five shows and half a dozen
movies. He joined lyricists Lew Brown and Buddy DeSylva in a prosperous publishing house which produced two dozen hits—among them, "Five
Foot Two," "Sitting on Top of the World," "The Best Things in Life Are
Free," "Just a Memory," "Together," "Button Up Your Overcoat," and
"Bye Bye Blackbird." Brown, DeSylva, and Henderson songs, with their
bright melodies and flip lyrics, suited the mood of the period perfectly.

Though the etymology of "jazz" is not clear, there is reason to believe
that the word springs from either French or African origins via American
Negro dialect, in which it has sexual connotations. It begins to appear in
print about 1914 (sometimes spelled "jass"), although the term was
known in New Orleans as early as the 1880's. The *Literary Digest* in
1917 noted the spread of "a strange word, jazz, used mainly as an adjec-
tive descriptive of a band." Whatever its etymology, "jazz" described a
kind of popular music that developed in lower-class Southern society

(most visibly in New Orleans) out of French, Spanish, African, Caribbean, and American elements. The music drew from all the current popular forms: marches, quadrilles, waltzes, polkas, hymns; from the European heritage of formal music; from Afro-American work songs and gospel songs; from minstrel shows and popular ballads; and especially from blues and ragtime music. "Tiger Rag," for example, was adapted from a quadrille; "High Society" from a French band piece; "When the Saints Go Marching In" from a gospel hymn.

The swift evolution of jazz music in the late nineteenth century came as a result of the black man's opportunity to secure musical instruments after the Civil War, cheaply and in quantity, allowing him to transfer the music he had long created out of harmonicas, jugs, homemade guitars, washboards, and crude banjos, to conventional instrumentation. New Orleans, a highly musical city with singing societies, string orchestras, music groups, and operatic companies, was also famous for balls, banquets, parades, and riverboat excursions. Especially well known were the city's marching bands, both black and white, sponsored by fraternal, labor, and civic groups. Street bands, common in the 1870's at funerals, weddings, holidays, election days, and other festive occasions, proliferated in the eighties. At the memorial funeral procession for President Garfield in 1881 there were more than a dozen Negro bands.

Since New Orleans' cosmopolitan society had more tolerant racial attitudes than any other Southern city, it was a mecca for black musicians. Storyville, the city's gaudy bordello and cabaret district, catered to pleasure seekers of all races. Pete Lala's, Tuxedo Hall, The 101 Ranch, and Tom Anderson's Annex, to name a few of the better-class establishments, drew the best musicians in the South, while polite society's banquets and balls provided additional employment for them.

New Orleans, then, offered the jazz musician his first paying audiences; its musical climate contained all the elements which, combined by talented black and white musicians, could produce a new and distinctive musical idiom. When the strong melodic lines and cadences of street band music merged with the tonality of blues and worksongs and ragtime's syncopation—with the whole translated into dance music in the nineties— jazz entered the mainstream of American popular music.

New Orleans jazz bands adapted the vocal traits of the blues and the rhythmic effects of ragtime to traditional orchestral music, retaining something of all three. By choosing cornet and clarinet (occasionally trombone) as voice-line instruments, jazz musicians imposed the vocal style of the blues singer on the orchestral form, augmenting the standard rhythms with ragtime effects from piano, drums, banjo, mandolin or guitar, using the trombone as bass-line counterpart. Buddy Bolden's famous band, for example, had five to seven pieces, built around the basic instrumentation of cornet, clarinet, trombone, guitar, and drums.

By 1915 the personnel of the standard jazz band was more or less divided into a melodic section and a rhythm section, a pattern maintained over the next forty years. Jack Laine's Ragtime Band, Tom Brown's Dixieland Band, and the Original Dixieland Jazz Band were white; Buddy Bolden's, King Oliver's, Freddy Keppard's, and Jelly Roll Morton's were black. Though both played much the same kind of music, white bands developed their own "dixieland" style, using cornet and clarinet as melody leads, voiced so that the cornet lead was carried lower than the clarinet, which usually carried a harmony an octave and a third above its normal chord position and always above the lead.

Jazz, then, was *vocalized* music. Its harmonies were relatively simple, borrowed from hymns and marches; its chordal structure was based on the tonic, subdominant, and dominant seventh chords (C-major, F, and G-seventh in the key of C) with flatted notes used in the blues manner. The themes were in 4/4 time, expressed in eight to twelve-bar choruses, holding a steady beat throughout. However, the unique characteristic of jazz lay in its rich variety of rhythmic variation, in shifting accents, adjustments, and changes of the beat.

Jazz also placed great importance on improvisation, on the musician's ability to extemporize around the melody and its underlying chord structure. Jazz improvisation was not, however, an impromptu every-man-for-himself affair; players improvised within a loose but implicitly unified form, knowing where they had to be melodically and harmonically, at the right moment. This has been, in fact, one of the lasting criteria in judging a jazz musician's ability—his improvisational adeptness in "making the changes," in expressing himself within the structure of the piece.

The city officials of New Orleans and the United States Army closed down Storyville in 1917, but its music would have moved out anyway. Negro migrations toward Kansas City, St. Louis, Detroit, New York, and particularly Chicago in the period after World War I created large black communities in Northern cities and new employment opportunities for jazz musicians. White jazz bands like Tom Brown's, the Original Dixielanders, and the New Orleans Rhythm Kings went North soon after the war; King Oliver left New Orleans in 1917 or 1918; Jelly Roll Morton in the early twenties. In Chicago, black and white musicians worked at the new music, shaping and probing, testing its potentials—Louis Armstrong, Earl Hines, Bix Beiderbecke, Jimmy McPartland, Bud Freeman, Frank Teschemacher, Muggsy Spanier. New York drew musicians from Chicago, the South and the Southwest as well—Red Nichols, Jack Teagarden, Fats Waller, Duke Ellington, young Benny Goodman, Count Basie (from New Jersey, however).

By the mid-twenties jazz music had a secure commercial base in every major Northern city, to the dismay of many who mistrusted its lower-class origins and associations. Titles like "Jazz Me Blues" led to accusations that the music represented a demoralizing social influence. The Reverend John Roach Straton, for example, denounced jazz in the twenties as "intellectual and spiritual debauchery"; Daniel Mason, a respected musical educator, called it "a meaningless stirabout, a commotion without purpose"; a New York physician claimed it "gave the same results as whiskey or any other alcoholic drink."

Nevertheless, despite objections, jazz was the most popular form of music—bands played it, songwriters wrote it, movies featured it (as in Al Jolson's *Jazz Singer* of 1927, which had little to do with jazz), people danced to it and listened to it. What orchestra leaders and songwriters considered "jazz" ranged over a wide spectrum. Some created something called "hot jazz," emphasizing fast, loud, trumpet-led, rackety tunes like "Dardanella," "Runnin' Wild," and "At The Jazz Babies' Ball." Vincent Lopez, one of the earliest converts to jazz among orchestra leaders, called his "sweet Jazz," emphasizing lyrical songs, saxophone, piano, and muted brass, a style perfected by Guy Lombardo's Royal Canadians, who advertised "the sweetest music this side of heaven." Paul Whiteman, who organized a dance band after World War I, hired Ferdie Grofé as arranger and made "sweet jazz" into "symphonic jazz," which reached its climax in Whiteman's Aeolian Hall concert of 1924, intended to illustrate "the tremendous strides which have been made in popular music from the day of discordant Jazz . . . to the really melodious music of today." Whiteman featured George Gershwin at the piano in his own "Rhapsody in Blue," and closed the concert in unconscious irony with Elgar's "Pomp and Circumstance."

Since the two most lucrative markets for jazz music were dancehalls and records (later theater appearances) composers, arrangers, and musicians emphasized its adaptability to dancing and listening. The trend, therefore, was toward larger, better disciplined bands who played more or less arranged music; in turn, the increasing use of arranged music called for musicians who could read and play technically difficult passages. The relaxed, spontaneous early New Orleans style began to disappear before the "big-band style," which by the thirties developed its own musical characteristics: "riffing," steady repetition of a terse melodic phrase in an extended series with slight variations; explosive solo impro-

visations set against tightly-written backgrounds; complex harmonies and
strident tone colors; a powerfully driving, insistent combination of
rhythm and melody called "swing," which depended on an almost im-
perceptibly hurried accent on the second and fourth beats, as well as on
a personal response to rhythm that could not be written in musical nota-
tion. Swing rhythms tended to emphasize (in both solo and ensemble)
a "triplet feeling," so that a passage notated in standard 4/4 form was to
be interpreted thus:

Improvisation remained a key element of big-band swing, but less spontaneous, more confined within the arrangement's framework. Arrangers
like Ellington, Fletcher Henderson, Don Redman, Jimmie Lunceford,
and Sy Oliver became as necessary to the band as its soloists, working out
techniques that soon became swing-band trademarks: brass, reeds, and
rhythm section voiced as separate units with intricate interplay among
them; solo instruments set against shifting riff and blues-break patterns;
a heavy pulsing beat superbly suited to dance floor and recordings.

The bands of the thirties, when swing was at its height—Ellington,
Shaw, Lunceford, the Dorseys, Basie, Woody Herman, Glen Gray, Glenn
Miller, Goodman—sold millions of records, had millions of radio listeners,
appeared in films, and brought popular songs to a huge public market.
Whatever its popularity, there were still those who suspected swing's
impact on the young; the music critic of *The New York Times* in 1938
warned of its "dangerously hypnotic influence" which led dancers straight
toward "moral weakness" and "the breakdown of conventions." Nevertheless, when Benny Goodman's orchestra appeared at Carnegie Hall in concert that year, playing music hardly twenty-five years away from the New
Orleans street bands, it was certain that jazz had become an integral
and important part of American popular music.

The tremendous popularity of thirties big-band jazz over the air
(when college students stayed up till early morning to hear Benny Good-

man's "Let's Dance" program from the West Coast) did not escape the notice of song publishers and record companies. Songwriters wrote music that was adapted to big-band swing and big-band singers; Decca Records, formed in 1934, specialized in dance records at thirty-five cents, and sold them by the thousands. Victor alone put out 900,000 dance records in 1936, accounting for 80 per cent of its total output. The thirties were perhaps popular music's most prosperous era, through movies, radio, records, jukeboxes, clubs, and dance halls; a band like Goodman's or Dorsey's could gross half a million dollars a year.

It was also obvious that singers could do the same, or even better. Rudy (Hubert Prior) Vallée, a journeyman saxophonist who formed his own band in 1929, was one of the first to discover the great commercial potential of the new media. His rendition of "I'm Just a Vagabond Lover," via radio and records, started him on a tumultuously successful career in 1929 that led to his own radio hour, at least twelve hit records in ten years, and a long movie contract. Vallée made the important discovery that what went into a microphone did not necessarily come out of the radio or phonograph speaker the same way; his "crooning" vocal style fitted radio and records perfectly, and he quickly capitalized on it. (Nick Lucas, radio's "Whispering Troubador," found this out in 1925, but never developed the style as Vallée did.) "The voice that starts its strange journey at the microphone hardly more than banal," remarked a radio columnist, "fills the air at its destination with that rarest charm of beauty —uniqueness, novelty." Vallée's success with sentimental ballads like "Deep Night," "Good Night, Sweetheart," "Lover, Come Back to Me," and "Marie" illuminated the fact that the microphone, properly used, was an instrument in its own right and something much more than mere amplification.

Vallée found it difficult to adapt to changing musical styles, sang less after 1940, and eventually carved out an eminently successful career as an actor. Bing (Harry Lillis) Crosby, one-third of The Rhythm Boys vocal group with Paul Whiteman's orchestra, did some solo work in 1931 and in 1932 became a star with his record of "I Surrender, Dear." Crosby, who also knew how to use a microphone, had considerable musicianship, excellent vocal equipment, and an unerring sense of popular taste. After he packed the Paramount Theater for twenty consecutive weeks in 1933 he began making movies, entered radio, and in the early fifties went into television, thereby covering all the mass entertainment media. Probably no other entertainer has approached Crosby's success—thirty-three hit records (his version of Berlin's "White Christmas" alone has sold twenty-one million copies), forty-odd films, fifteen times listed among the ten highest-paid persons in the entertainment world. Nearly every subsequent popular male vocalist, with few exceptions, has been influenced in some way by Crosby's techniques and example.

George T. Simon, in his historical summary of the swing era, listed over three hundred big swing bands of national reputation in the thirties and early forties, with two journals (*Metronome* and *Downbeat*) devoted wholly to the band business. In 1940 it was apparent that the swing wave was receding. Nineteen forty-five was the last good year. In 1946 eight of the most successful bands broke up, and by the late forties few of the larger organizations remained. There were a number of reasons: a wartime shortage of musicians; the imposition of a 20 per cent amusement tax on dance halls and performances; the rise of improved home recording systems; the postwar trend among musicians themselves away from swing patterns. Most of all, certainly, there was a shift in popular taste from the public performance toward the personalized, intimate media of radio, records, and television, all ideally suited to small-group music and particularly to the vocalist.

Singers replaced big bands as the chief purveyors of popular songs. Vallée and Crosby started it, and they had many followers—Frank Sinatra, Perry Como, Dick Haymes, Tony Bennett, Dinah Shore, Peggy Lee, Ella Fitzgerald, Jo Stafford, and others. Frank Sinatra, who began with Tommy Dorsey's orchestra almost exactly a decade after Crosby made his first record, emerged as a popular star in 1942, entered films in 1943, and by the fifties was well established in television. Influenced by Dorsey's trombone phrasing and Crosby's tone quality, Sinatra developed a restrained but intensely emotional vocal style of his own. Studying his craft carefully and thoughtfully, he exploited microphonic and recording techniques more expertly than any of his predecessors; and as few popular singers have been able to do, adapted to changing musical fashions so well that he dominated his field for nearly a quarter century. Bennett, less well known than Sinatra but like him a meticulous craftsman and highly-trained musician, proved to be one of the most durable of the male vocalists who appeared in the fifties.

The second great change in jazz music came during the Second World War years. The break between the musical style of the thirties and the forties was a result of changes inherent in the constantly shifting nature of jazz music itself, as well as of alterations in the nature and tastes of society. Differences were already visible among a number of musicians in the thirties who felt constricted by the commercially viable patterns of swing. In the late thirties musicians like saxophonists Lester

Young and Charlie Parker, drummers Jo Jones and Kenny Clarke, and guitarist Charlie Christian were already pushing against the limits of big-band jazz. Drawing from ever-wider experiments, musicians in the forties put together a kind of jazz called at first "bebop" or "rebop," later merely "bop," something virtually unintelligible both to older musicians and the general public.

Bop was a deliberate break with all the familiar jazz patterns, a rejection of almost everything that had gone before. As developed by men like Parker, trumpeter Dizzy Gillespie, pianist Bud Powell, and others, it abandoned the familiar swing rhythms for a tangle of rhythmical complexities; cymbals were used as time keeping instruments, drums mainly for accents, piano and guitar (when used at all) for fragmented chord progressions and single note lines.

The bop soloist, instead of improvising a new melody line on the chord sequences of a popular tune, took off on long, irregular lines free of the standard progressions. Parker explained it by saying that, bored with the usual solo line when playing "Cherokee" one night in 1939 with guitarist Biddy Fleet, he "tried higher intervals of a chord as a melody line, and backed them with related changes." This innovation meant that the new musical style was primarily harmonic rather than melodic. A typical "bop" reworking of a standard tune, such as "Lady Be Good," might be

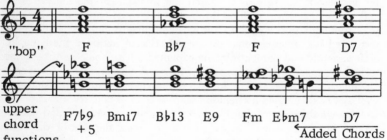

Harmonically, the new style was intricate and involved; soloists used longer phrases, played more notes, used unexpected pauses. It demanded great instrumental virtuosity and technically advanced musicianship, and it had little to offer the general music-buying public or the dance hall.

Bop jazz did not last long—perhaps five years at the most—for it was far too complicated and esoteric to attract audiences or even traditional musicians. It was introspective, "inside" music; it could not be danced to, or sung, or even listened to except by the most knowledgeable. Bop musicians, affecting goatees, dark glasses, berets, and unusual names and antics, seemed determined to reject the public—some refused to allow applause, others played with their backs to audiences in a gesture of contempt. It was not popular music nor was it ever intended to be; in terms of commercial success, it never was. Yet, despite its exaggerations and absurdities, the bop revolution opened up another new stream of jazz, the so-called "cool" music which followed it in the fifties.

The term "cool" was (and still is) used in a number of contradictory senses, but it originally designated both an instrumental and an arranging style. In the first sense it meant a style of solo improvisation opposed to the "hot" of the thirties and twenties; that is, it described an understated, relaxed, deliberately restrained manner. Saxophonist Lester Young's approach to his solos—a light, clear breathy sound without vibrato—influenced a number of younger musicians toward his "cool" style, especially young white saxophonists and trumpeters.

In a related sense "cool" meant a specific kind of ensemble sound, exemplified in the forties by Claude Thornhill's and a few other bands, musicians, and arrangers—Gil Evans, John Lewis, Johnny Carisi, Thelonious Monk. Based on a vibratoless sound, with the addition of controlled brass, augmented woodwinds, and light percussion, it produced a delicate, pensive, richly-colored music. Adapted and developed by musicians such as Gerry Mulligan, Lee Konitz, Julian Adderley, Miles Davis, and Shorty Rogers, cool music used not only the harmonic complexities of the forties—flatted fifths, augmented ninths, and the like—but tried to absorb into jazz certain classical elements like fugal and contrapuntal styles.

Cool arrangers wrote for unusual instruments like Flügelhorn, cello, and French horn; they strove for the so-called "conservatory" sound, a vibratoless, light, pure instrumental sound that no longer imitated the blues-vocal style. Their aim was to break out of the dominant-to-tonic resolution that had restricted jazz musicians, they felt, for years; whatever had to be done to open jazz music up, they were willing to do. The cool school encouraged such "free form" experimenters as Ornette Coleman and John Coltrane, both saxophonists, who abandoned chord changes, bar structures, key signatures, regular rhythm, and arranged themes to improvise not within a chord structure but only within the general area of the pitch. Some jazz musicians are still exploring the paths opened by Coltrane and Coleman and other experimenters with modes, scales, and time.

The trend of bop and cool jazz was obviously away from the popular audience. None of the cool groups sold records in significant quantities;

"liner notes" on album jackets imitated academic musical criticism in terms unintelligible to the general public; jazz critics themselves evolved a specialized vocabulary copied from academic music and art criticism. The group that came closest to popular acceptance was Stan Kenton's "progressive" band. A big, brassy, cool-influenced and (among musicians) controversial outfit, its records sold better than those of any other of the larger orchestras during the years 1946–51; in 1948 Kenton's was the only band ever to earn a million dollars in one twelve-month period.

But by 1952 nearly all of the bop-cool bands—Herman, Gillespie, Barnet, Ventura—were gone. It was interesting and challenging music, certainly, but it was not popular music. In 1963 John Wilson, jazz critic of *The New York Times*, could not recall a single jazz record over the preceding decade that could have been called a "hit." The best-selling records were those by bands, and especially vocalists, who learned their trade in the thirties and early forties, such as Sinatra, Ella Fitzgerald, Crosby, Como, or new "rock and roll" singers like Elvis Presley.

Fifties jazz was listening music, demanding specialized, highly literate musicians and audiences. It was intended to be a serious art form, free of any of the usual elements of popular entertainment. Interestingly, in fifty years or less at least one strain of jazz thus reversed its social and artistic placement, from below the middle level of popular taste and artistic value to far above it; from lower-class music to music of great sophistication.

Yet if jazz in the fifties was no longer a "popular" art in the mass sense, it did strongly influence the character and sound of other popular music—especially film, television, and concert jazz—in its tonal colorings, harmonic complexities, and imaginative instrumentation. The general public, by the late fifties, was ready to accept music it could never have understood in the thirties, amply illustrated by the work of such arrangers as Henry Mancini, Nelson Riddle, Johnny Mandel, Evans, Billy May, and André Previn.

COUNTRY, BLUEGRASS, AND BEATLES

I wanted to scream, and when it was over I hurt. It was an answer to something, something I don't even understand.

—INTERVIEW WITH A GIRL AFTER A BEATLES CONCERT

"Country" music, though its commercial success came late, was long part of the American popular music tradition. English, Irish, and Scottish folk ballads, chanteys, and work songs furnished one strand of its development; Protestant hymnals, particularly of the evangelical variety, another strand; the popular sentimental ballad of the turn-of-the-century years a third. Merging these elements produced music that was predominantly Southern, rural, vocal, and white. Of the thirty most popular "country" singers in 1967–68, all were white, rural, and Southern-born, except one from Arizona. As Roy Acuff, who sold twenty-two million records, once said, "If you aren't a country boy, you can't write or sing country music." Hank Williams put it somewhat more bluntly by saying, "You got to have smelt a lot of mule manure before you can sing like a hillbilly."

Fiddling Bob Haines recorded a few Edison cylinders in the early nineteen-hundreds, but country music had no recognized name until the Okeh Record Company placed it under "Old Time Records" in its 1915 catalogue, to separate it from Negro "race records" and gospel hymns. *Variety*, in 1926, seems to have been among the first to call it "hillbilly music," but the great increase in its sales and popularity encouraged the use of the name "country music" in the thirties. Minnie Pearl (Sarah Ophelia Colley Cannon), one of its leading female singers, once remarked that the big difference between "hillbilly" and "country" was that country singers could afford mink coats.

Radio and records spread country music over an ever-increasing market. WSB in Atlanta began to program "hillbilly bands" like Gid Tanner's Skillet-Lickers in the early twenties. Chicago's WLS "Barn Dance" program, introduced in 1924, broadcast regularly for four and a half hours every Saturday night for the next thirty-six years. Nashville's "Grand Ole Opry" over WSM, started in 1925, is still on the air; its studio and theater audiences alone have been estimated at over fifteen million. WLW's "Renfro Valley Barn Dance," begun in 1939, continued for years. The extent of country music's popularity may be inferred from the fact that in the sixties one of every two single records sold belong in the country category; that 2,200 radio stations program some country music every day; and that 260 radio stations broadcast no other kind of music at all.

By the forties there were millions of country records sold each year by such stars as Hank Snow, Ernest Tubbs, Red Foley, Jimmy Wakeley, Riley Puckett, Webb Pierce, Rod Brasfield, Rex Allen, Chet Atkins, Slim Wilson, Spade Cooley, and Red Fletcher; and by groups like The Hoosier Hot Shots and The Sons of the Pioneers. Jimmie Davis, composer of "You Are My Sunshine" and "It Makes No Difference Now," eventually became Governor of Louisiana. Hank Williams' "Cold Cold Heart," "Jambalaya," "Your Cheatin' Heart," and his hymn-styled "I Saw The Light" made him the nation's best-selling country singer (he wrote 125 songs in all) at the time of his death in 1953. Acuff's "Wabash Cannonball," "Great Speckled Bird," and others put him into a million-dollar-a-year publishing business. Eddy Arnold, who began his career in 1946, never made a record which sold less than a quarter million copies, while his total sales in 1968 reached forty-six million. Arnold in 1969 received over a half-million dollars for county fair appearances alone.

Country singers did equally well in the fifties and sixties—Porter Wagoner, The Wilburn Brothers, Marty Robbins, Jimmy Dickens. Johnny Cash, who was working a full day in the Arkansas cotton fields at twelve, owned two corporations at thirty-seven, grossing two million dollars a year. He has sold twelve million records, a million tapes, written nine million-copy hits; he broke the attendance record at London's Palladium in 1968; and he had his own television program in prime time in 1969. Tennessee Ernie Ford, who had several best-selling albums of hymns, left country ranks to become a television personality. Roger Miller, who sang with ironic wit as well as country sentiment, wrote at least twenty million-copy songs, among them "King of the Road," "Dang Me," "Little Green Apples," and "You Can't Rollerskate in a Buffalo Herd." Jimmy Dean, Jim Reeves, and Glen Campbell, who were also successful as television and nightclub ballad-singers, came from country backgrounds but appealed to wider urban audiences. Country music also developed a number of popular women vocalists; in addition to the redoubtable Minnie Pearl, there was also Brenda Lee, Liz Anderson, Loretta Lynn, June Carter, Kitty Wells, and Dotty West.

The relationship of so-called Western music to country music is close and difficult to estimate. Some early country singers were Texans—Eck Robertson, Carl Sprague, and Vernon Dalhart, for example—while the Southwest drew heavy settlement from the Southeast, the migrants bringing their music with them and adapting its lyrics to cotton- and cattle-country life. Carl Sprague recorded some ranch songs for Victor in 1924, becoming probably the first "singing cowboy," while Jules Verne Allen, Goebel Reeves, Mac McClintock, and others broadcast "cowboy" music in the twenties and thirties. Otto Gray's Oklahoma Cowboys Band, organized in 1924, played tunes like "Song of the Dying Cowboy" and "When The Work's All Done This Fall," which were musically no different whatever from "country" music. The Beverly Hill Billies band, organized in Los Angeles in 1928 and the most influential of the early Western-type bands, was in fact an excellent country-music orchestra. Although Gene Autry, Texas-born and Oklahoma-raised, was billed on his early records as a "singing cowboy," he also was a headliner on the WLS Barn Dance program with the usual repertory of country tunes.

When the introduction of sound to the movies raised the question of what kind of music should accompany Westerns, "old time" or "hillbilly" seemed to fit best, although it was essentially Southern rural music transferred into Southwestern settings, its lyrics dealing with dogies, prairies, sagebrush, roundups, and the like. Ken Maynard, who could play fiddle, sang four songs in *Songs of the Saddle* in 1930; his movie *Strawberry Roan* in 1933 was the first Western to feature a song as part of the plot. Gene Autry, already a radio star, moved to Hollywood in 1934, the first of the famous cowboy singing stars to have the film written especially to display his talents. Audiences waited for Autry to use his songs to foil crooks, send messages to a pal in prison (as Blondel did to Richard the Lion-Hearted), quell mobs, and resolve any and all crises. Western movie audiences of the thirties learned to accept forty-piece backup orchestras suddenly audible behind the corral or on the empty prairie; and highly skilled cowboy musicians who could sing in complex harmony and play instruments professionally. The character of the Western movie itself changed swiftly and drastically; Buck Jones, an authentic old-time cowboy actor, once complained that in the movies of the thirties and forties "all you need to stop Indians or rustlers is a loud voice and a guitar."

Leonard Slye of Duck Run, Ohio, a member of a very good singing group called The Sons of the Pioneers, changed his name to Roy Rogers to become the movies' "King of the Cowboys," and others appeared. Warner Brothers, in fact, had ten singing cowboy stars under contract at one time, lending new meaning to the term "horse opera." Autry, however, dominated the field with records, radio programs, and a successful cycle of movies. His appearance in Dublin in 1939 drew a crowd of 750,-000 into the streets; the town of Berwyn, Oklahoma, officially changed its name to Gene Autry in 1941; Autry later organized his own movie company, record company, several music publishing houses, and bought hotels, motels, restaurants, and a chain of businesses.

Since movies made this kind of music a more marketable commodity than ever, songs written for Westerns were fed into the radio and record market and doubled their sales. The introduction of Billy Hill's "Last Roundup" (he also wrote "Wagon Wheels" and "Empty Saddles") into the score of the Ziegfeld Follies of 1934 marked the symbolic climax of country music's acceptance into the popular music market. The movies, curiously enough, also provided country musicians with a kind of gaudy Western-style uniform which they wore with magnificent irrelevance, since country music was not and had never been Western. In recent years, however, younger country musicians have tended to replace canary-yellow sequined coats, ruffled shirts, red boots, and ten-gallon hats with quiet, expensively tailored formal clothes with perhaps a touch of Western flavor.

What the public knew as "Western" music via the movies during the thirties and forties was not produced by cowboys nor did it have anything to do, musically, with the West. Its only recognizable difference from country music, if any, lay in its greater use of voice and violin and less emphasis on instrumentation. A distinctive form of "Western-type" music did appear, however, in the twenties and after, under various names such as "Okie music," "Tex-Mex jazz," and finally "Western swing," used to describe a music built on blues, square dance and foxtrot tunes, and popular ballads. Bands like The Hi-Flyers, The Texas Ramblers, and The East Texas Serenaders played "Five Foot Two" and "Stardust" as well as square-dance breakdowns and ragtime pieces; some of the bands showed strong Dixieland and swing influences and the larger ones added reeds, brass, and string bass. Spade Cooley, Bob Wills and his Texas Playboys, Ernest Tubbs, Buck Owens' Buckaroos—these and dozens of other bands like them have drawn thousands to theaters and dance-halls through the Midwest, Southwest, and West for the last thirty years. What they play is really neither country nor Western, but it is a vital, exciting, and highly expert form of popular music.

Country music since the forties has been composed, arranged, and performed for a mass market by skillful men who knew exactly what they were doing; none of it was naïve or unstudied. Until the mid-forties record companies made recordings anywhere, but in 1945 when Decca set up facilities in Nashville, already a country music center, other companies followed suit. Fred Rose, himself a highly-skilled composer and performer, had established the first influential country music publishing house in Nashville; within ten years the city was the nation's third largest recording center (after New York and Los Angeles) and by the sixties was selling seventy million records each year—composing a hundred-million-dollar-a-year business. (The Armed Forces Network's "Hillbilly Gasthaus" program, beamed from Germany, drew 12 million listeners from 22 countries in 1956.) Nashville in the mid-sixties had 1,100 professional musicians, one hundred and eleven music publishers, two hundred songwriters, and twelve booking agencies. It is also the source of a personal appearance network which grosses ten million dollars a year from over 15,000 engagements.

The increasing sophistication and commercialization of country music evoked a counteraction from portions of its original audience. "Bluegrass," which emerged in the thirties, was a deliberate return to country music's rural, Southern folk-song roots, best exemplified in the recordings made by Bill Monroe and His Blue Grass Boys in 1945. Earl Scruggs of North Carolina, who played for Monroe, joined Lester Flatt of Tennessee in 1948 to form The Foggy Mountain Boys, followed by the Stanley Brothers, The Carter Family, The Clinch Mountain Boys, and others, about forty major bluegrass groups in all.

Unlike country, which is guitar-based, bluegrass is banjo-based, a descendant of the nineteenth-century string bands, built about nonelectrified bass, rhythm guitar, fiddle, banjo, dobro, and mandolin, though some groups have occasionally added drums, harmonica, or accordion, much to the disapproval of the purists. Bluegrass music is light and fast, instrumental rather than vocal, usually in three-part or duet harmony with seldom more than five chord changes in a song. It is built on a four-line verse, in simple 2/4 or 4/4 time for vocal music and a fast 4/4 for instrumentals.

Close to their folk origins, blugrass lyrics tend to be traditional. The Foggy Mountain Boys' most popular album, for example, featured tunes like "Heaven," "Mama's and Daddy's Little Girl," "Big Black Train," "Old Folks," and "Goin' Home." Though bluegrass records rarely sold in the "top twenty" class, they have maintained a steady nationwide market, since they represent the Southern white's protest against urbanization and commercialization—a quiet musical protest against the move to Detroit or

Chicago to look for work—and furnish him with some sense of his cultural roots wherever he lives.

Country music in fully developed form uses the standard thirty-two-bar song form (occasionally a twelve-bar blues) with the usual "blues" chord order. It does not ordinarily use flatted blues notes, nor does it emphasize syncopation. Its instrumentation is usually nonamplified guitar, steel guitar, violin, accordion, and string bass (sometimes piano and drums), emphasizing a strong one and three beat in 4/4 time. The country vocal style is consciously nasal, with an exaggerated Southern or Southwestern accent; older country singers may slip into falsetto, yodel, or quaver, though younger ones tend to avoid both nasality and dialect. Since the narrative element in country lyrics is important, vocalists are practically a necessity for any band.

Country songs always tell a story or make a point, sometimes sentimental (as in Marty Robbins' "Hello Heartache," or Hank Snow's "A Faded Petal"), sometimes realistic, as in Harlan Howard's "Busted" or Merle Travis' coalmine classic, "Sixteen tons":

> You load sixteen tons, what do you get?
> Another day older and deeper in debt.
> Saint Peter don't you call me 'cause I can't go,
> I owe my soul to the company store.

The matter of country lyrics is direct and honest stuff—love, death, sorrow, rejection, faith, home, marriage—with nothing of the "Cocktails for Two" or "Ain't She Sweet" element. Johnny Cash, for example, among his forty major hit records, sang "I Walk the Line," "The Long Black Veil," and "Don't Take Your Guns to Town." Tammy Wynette, famous for her songs of troubled love, recorded "I Don't Wanna Play House," "Your Good Girl's Gonna Go Bad," "I Stayed Long Enough," and "D-I-V-O-R-C-E." Country music concerns itself with trucking, mining, farming, vagrancy, poverty, prison, and the troubles of life:

> As long as ole bacon stays at thirty cents a pound,
> I'm a-gonna eat rabbit if I have to run him down,

or:

> Left my gal in the mountains, left her standin' in the rain,
> Went down to the railroad, caught myself a midnight train,
> Beat my way to Georgia, landed in a gamblin' town,
> Got myself in trouble, shot a county sheriff down.

Country music, however, covers a wide spectrum of tastes, mirroring the increasing complexity of American nonurban life and the growing sophistication of its audience. The Country Music Association's awards for 1968 clearly reflected the genre's diversity by featuring Pat Boone's version of Red Foley's hymn-like "Peace in the Valley"; Glen Campbell's expertly tailored, commercially arranged ballad, "By the Time I Get to Phoenix"; and Johnny Cash's rocking, twanging "Folsom Prison Blues," straight out of the backcountry South. The 1969 awards were almost a repeat performance, with Campbell singing a stylish sentimental ballad, "Galveston," and Cash a camp-meeting rouser called "Daddy Sang Bass."

The rhythm and blues revival of the fifties represented almost precisely the opposite of cool jazz. Meaning exactly what the name implied— a combination of older blues harmonies with a basic jazz beat—it drew from everywhere: from gospel, folk, country, and white and black popular music. It was less a new style than an amalgamation of many styles, but it derived most heavily from two major traditional sources.

First, the blues singing style, which entered black church music in the early years of the century, matured into "gospel" music by the fifties, beautifully exemplified by Mahalia Jackson. The gospel blues style also strongly influenced secular jazz-oriented singers like Clara Ward, Dinah Washington, Sara Vaughan, and Aretha Franklin; jazz instrumentalists like Milt Jackson (vibra-harp), Horace Silver (piano), T-Bone Walker (guitar); and singer Ray Charles, who with his band and supporting female trio, the "Raelettes," came to represent best the rhythm and blues sound. This was primarily black music in a return to its "soul" origins and to its emotional content. Horace Silver said he hoped to "create tunes with a blues feeling and a hell of a beat and a melody that is meaningful." Art Blakey, a drummer in a group called The Jazz Messengers, called it "having the spirit hit you . . . , getting the message."

Second, the old blues-singer tradition, kept alive by Southern "race records," came North with the post-World War II waves of Negro migration. Blues "shouters" and musicians from the Delta South, Oklahoma, Texas, and Arkansas came to Chicago and Detroit, where the big black ghettoes were, bringing the blues with them—now electrified and amplified—music which young black and white musicians found elemental, powerful, and challenging. Howlin' Wolf, Muddy Waters, Sonny Terry, John Lee Hooker, Little Walter, Memphis Slim, Bo Diddley, and their music could hardly have supplied a greater contrast to the cerebral remoteness of the cool school. In fact, the emergence of electrified "soul" blues began to displace the "cool" style even among sophisticated musicians like Miles Davis and Gerry Mulligan, who included rhythm and blues "rockers" in their big band albums.

Rhythm and blues music released a great burst of creativity in popular music. Hundreds of artists were attracted to the new idiom and hundreds of recording companies sprang up to take commercial advantage of it. It was tough music, going back to the beat-and-blues vocal style of older jazz, for rhythm and blues, with its strong vocalized solo line, either featured a singer or implied one. It was urbanized, explicitly rhythmic blues, to which electrical amplification and advanced recording techniques added new dimensions and effects. It was singable, danceable, participatory music, especially attractive to the younger generation. It was unrestrained and direct, aimed at involving the listener physically and emotionally; rhythm and blues audiences stamped, clapped, and danced in the aisles as in the days of swing. Lyrics were direct, sometimes suggestive (like the old blues), as in Willie Dixon's "Back Door Man":

> Hey all you people
> You tryin' to sleep,
> I'm out to get you with my
> Midnight creep, cause I'm a
> Back door man, I'm a
> Back door man.
> The men don't know, but the
> Little girls understand.

It was also highly salable music. Good rhythm and blues bands drew crowds of fifteen thousand and filled auditoriums everywhere.

Current popular dances, when the rhythm and blues revival began, were usually extensions of the Big Apple and other forties styles like the Chicken and the Dirty Boogie. Faced with a new music which these dances did not fit, and by a public (primarily white) which did not know how to dance to it, the recording industry in the late fifties (with much help from public relations promotion) literally invented the Twist, to fill the need. Popularized by Chubby Checker, Joey Dee, Fats Domino, and other "twist bands," the Twist had no orderly series of steps, a peculiarly sexless avoidance of bodily contact, and it left the individual freedom to move as he wished within a simple pattern. It was based, actually, on traditional black dancing styles hardly fitted to the popular market; but the Twist was easy to do and mildly daring—not enough to get high school students ejected from Saturday night dances; simple enough for the white night club trade. Eventually, the Twist disappeared in favor of modifications of the black originals such as The Slop, The Mashed Potato, The Monkey, and so on, all danced to rhythm and blues music.

Rhythm and blues used the twelve-bar blues structure and the blues scale, with a basic I-IV-V7-I chord progression. Its rhythmic pattern was standard blues 4/4 time with heavily-accented, lagging second and fourth beats and occasional excursions into "shuffle" or "twist" rhythms (eight eighth notes, evenly and lightly accented). Whether sung or played, the melody line was handled in vocalized blues style, flatting, wavering, or "worrying" notes, sometimes with falsetto, shouts, or spoken lyrics.

At the center of rhythm and blues instrumentation was the rhythm section—guitar, drums, piano, bass, all powerfully amplified—with solo brass and reeds added as arrangements increased in complexity. Ray Charles, born in Florida but trained in the Chicago-Detroit jazz mainstream, summarized most of the characteristics of mature rhythm and blues as it emerged in the early sixties with his gospel-influenced, blues-shouter singing style, "soul" piano, tightly balanced harmonies, sophisticated use of vocal and rhythmic backgrounds, and driving, pulsating, overriding blues rhythms.

"Rock and Roll" music, a rhythm and blues variant, erupted in 1954 with Bill Haley's recording of "Rock Around the Clock," which eventually reached the incredible sale of sixteen million copies. Rock and roll used a I-vi-vii-V7-I chord structure and the same heavily accented, driving rhythm and blues beat. Singers like Chuck Berry, Carl Perkins, Buddy Holly, and the Everly Brothers (originally a country duet) drew capacity audiences across the country and in Europe, but none approached the popularity of Elvis Presley, a young white truck driver from Tupelo, Mississippi, whose wild, intense vocal style (influenced by blues-shouters Bo Diddley and Joe Turner) swept everything before him. His record of "Heartbreak Hotel" (1956) became the number-one best seller in every popular musical category, the first ever to do so. His succession of hits seemed endless, as month after month Presley records stayed at the top of the lists—"Hound Dog," "I Got A Woman," "Long Tall Sally," "Gonna Sit Right Down and Cry."

His appearance on Milton Berle's television show in 1956 elicited a flood of protests (Jack Gould of The New York Times said he behaved "like a sex maniac"), so for his next show NBC made him wear white tie and tails and restricted him to a minimum of above-the-hips contortions. Presley complained that this hurt his work a good deal, but it hurt his popularity not at all. His trademarks—sideburns, tight pants, powerful shouting style, even the presumably suggestive motions—influenced his whole generation of rock and roll singers. Twelve years after "Heartbreak Hotel" he had sold two hundred million records, starred in twenty-nine movies (at an average salary of $850,000 each) and drew $100,000 a week for infrequent club appearances. Presley's audience was almost wholly adolescent; estimates of his market have ranged from 80 per cent to 95 per cent in the teen-age bracket. Yet he has had greater impact on recent singing styles in popular music than any other single personality.

Rock and roll's success among teenagers led immediately to its commercialization in that wide open, multimillion-dollar market. Songwriters and arrangers, especially the team of Lieber and Stoller, took the genre's musical ideas, reduced them to stereotyped patterns, smoothed out the rougher elements, and produced a repeatable formula, known in the trade as "the hit sound." Tommy Boyce and Bobby Hart, who turned out tunes for popular groups like The Monkees, between 1964 and 1969 wrote three hundred songs which sold a total of forty-two million records, most of them barely above the bubblegum level and hardly distinguishable from one another, using the same introductions, the same chord progressions, and the same general combination of sounds. Sold by millions to an average fifteen-year-old market, these records, relentlessly pushed by disc jockeys, dominated the airways and the jukeboxes in the fifties and sixties, month in and month out.

The popularity of rock and roll movie music brought a Hollywood style known as "surfing music" by association with the sport of the same name, which de-emphasized the black connotations of the type and featured clean-cut white singing groups like Jan and Dean and The Beach Boys. Other manifestations followed under various names, sometimes produced by publicity men and not all of them marking any real changes in musical style. "Folk-rock," a term coined by record companies, showed the influence of Bob Dylan and popular folksingers, using folk-materials in rhythm and blues manner. "Acid-rock," another journalistic term, was chiefly a matter of lyrics dealing with fantasy and the drug experience. The main stream of rhythm and blues music, however, continued in the singers and in the recording and backup bands of musicians like B. B. King, Sam Cooke, Chuck Jackson, Ike and Tina Turner, and others.

European tours by Buddy Holly, Bill Haley, and other American groups in the late fifties, combined with the enormous foreign sale of American records, created a tremendous market for rhythm and blues and rock and roll in England and on the continent. Four young Liverpool musicians, George Harrison, Paul McCartney, John Lennon, and Ringo Starr (Richard Starkey), under the influence of Holly, Haley, Presley, and the Everly Brothers, formed "The Beatles" and quickly attracted a large audience in England during 1962 and 1963. (The title is probably formed from "beat," though Lennon spoofed reporters by claiming that a large bearded figure rose from the sea and said, "You're the Beatles, with an A.")

The Beatles' record of "I Want to Hold Your Hand" appeared in December, 1963 with over a million prerelease orders; its American release caused small riots in record stores, while their first album, "Meet The Beatles," sold two million copies in thirty days. Newspapers coined the word "Beatlemania" to describe the hysterical response of adolescents to the music, while the popular music field spawned literally hundreds of imitators. (There were 1,500 of them in England alone in 1964.) Practically every musical group in England, Europe, and the United States after 1963 reflected something of the Beatle influence.

While the Beatles' audience might be preponderantly pubescent, at the same time their musical ideas attracted and influenced serious, sophisticated, professional musicians. A substantial part of their popularity among the young was perhaps more sociological than musical, and it seems safe to assume that a large number of teen-age Beatle enthusiasts had little or no concept of the musical content of their recordings. Their exuberant vitality, their delicate handling of sentimentality, and their real lyrical gifts offered something new and fresh to popular music. At the same time, their topical, carefully-coded lyrics, with concealed references to sex, drugs, and rebellion, captivated restless and uncertain youth everywhere. (Although their rebelliousness has proved to be partly ironic, and not half so destructive as their critics have assumed.) Their extravagantly eccentric dress, wild hair styles, and public antics implied a lifestyle which proved instantly attractive to the adolescent. Amateur and professional sociologists, psychologists, and commentators, fascinated by Beatlemania among the young, tried to account for it in terms of its covert sexuality, its satisfaction of the adolescent need for group solidarity, and its function as a focus for lonely, alienated, uncertain, and rebellious youth. John Lennon, however, undoubtedly made the final statement on the group's social significance by writing that "when people start 'appreciating' our music, getting deep things out of it, making a thing out of it, then it's a lot of - - - -."

The Beatles' importance to popular music, however, had little to do with screaming adolescents, for they brought to it a fund of ideas and a musical style that have since exerted enormous influence on the field. Whatever their eccentricities of dress and behavior, they were, as a musical organization, highly skilled, imaginative, daring, and thoroughly competent professionals. Musically, they borrowed from a number of sources.

Their rhythm was originally Haley-based; Starr, never an imaginative

drummer, used mainly shuffle and twist rhythms with the usual variations. However, the group was among the first to make sheer volume an
essential ingredient of rhythm and blues music, taking full advantage of
all the potentials of electronic amplification. Loudness, which the Beatles
emphasized from the start, remained a vital factor in the total rhythmic
impact of the genre for another decade. Their vocal style was adapted in
part from the Everly Brothers, who sang in perfect fourths, and from
Presley's blues-shouting, Delta-based style. Their instrumentation was
basically country—lead guitar, rhythm and steel guitar, drums, bass—
augmented for recordings by horns, strings, extra percussion, and various
exotic instruments. None of this was particularly original. The qualities
of inventiveness, freshness, and excitement that they contributed to
rhythm and blues music came from their handling of harmony and form.

They broke the standard chord progressions of rhythm and blues into
much more complex and sophisticated patterns, using common tone and
parallel tone progressions, the II-V-I sequence, and nondiatonic modula-
tions, devices not new to music but quite new to rhythm and blues.
Equally important, they broke out of the thirty-two-bar *AABA* song form
familiar to popular music for a century and a half; their recording of
"Yesterday" (1963) was the first million-copy record to shatter the standard format of eight-bar units repeated with variations. The Beatles made
irregularity of form not only possible, but popular and familiar to the
public ear. It is hard to match the imaginativeness and lyric delicacy of
such early Beatle tunes as "Michelle" and "Norwegian Wood," in modern popular music.

The financial returns from The Beatles' American tour of 1964 led
the British government to classify them as a national economic resource,
and all of them were awarded M. B. E. citations by the Queen, though
Lennon later returned his. Their American sales alone in 1964–65 reached
fifteen million dollars, to which endorsements of sweatshirts, guitars, ash-
trays, and the like added another fifty million. Their film, *A Hard Day's
Night,* well received by critics, grossed more than one and a half million
in its first week, single records from the sound track sold at 10,000 per day,
and the sound track album itself sold two million within the year. Their
1965 tour of twenty-four cities in thirty-three days, though less enthusi-
astically received than their first, netted over a million dollars' profit.

The Beatles' fee of $150,000 for one appearance in Kansas City, in
fact, set the record for a single show to that time; their 1964–65 sales, one
hundred million discs in one year, still stands as another record. Their
album, *Sergeant Pepper's Lonely Hearts Club Band,* sold three and a half
million copies in 1967–68. "Hey Jude," in 1968, sold three million

copies in two months, their seventeenth single record to sell over a million. That same year, for the sixth successive time, the record industry voted The Beatles the most commercially valuable musical property in the world. Their 1968 album sold the incredible number of 1,900,000 copies in the United States in one week of November alone—a retail value of twenty-two million dollars.

The Beatles made rhythm and blues into a complex, challenging, open-ended musical genre. Lennon, McCartney, and Harrison proved to be talented and ingenious musicians who surprised the public with new ideas in every record release. By their use of startling rhythmic devices such as abrupt time changes, metrical alterations, and extended rubatos; by instrumental experimentation involving baroque trumpet, harpsichord, organ, celli, or sitars; by daring chord progressions, dissonances, shifting key signatures and the like, they extended the boundaries of popular music. Their success—both musical and commercial—encouraged a creative, spontaneous, and exciting kind of music for a new generation of composers and performers. "When people ask to re-create the mood of the sixties," remarked composer Aaron Copland in 1968, "they will play Beatle music."

Developments in rhythm and blues music, especially as derived from The Beatles, had obvious effects on popular music aimed at older age groups who had more traditional tastes. Rhythm and blues affected the singing styles of entertainers like Andy Williams, Tony Bennett, Dean Martin, and Sinatra himself; it appeared in musical arrangements for movies and television, in records by arrangers like Mancini, Keyes, Costa, and Mersey, and especially in the popular arranging team of Bert Bacharach and Hal David. All popular music other than country and semiclassical, after the mid-fifties, reflected in one way or another the impact of The Beatles' use of rhythm and blues: increased emphasis on modal approaches to improvisation; subtler and more intricate harmonic relationships; greater use of irregular song forms; harmonic and rhythmic experimentation. For convincing proof of the shift in the public's acceptance of this new, popular musical idiom, one need only to listen to the music of the television commercials of the late sixties.

Partly in response to the Beatles' use of topical lyrics, dozens of groups capitalized on the desire for personal involvement The Beatles' music aroused in the younger generation. The rhythm and blues vocal style was especially adaptable to singers, and to singing groups who provided their own backup music. Recognizing the publicity value of odd names and unusual dress, a number of post-Beatle musicians vied for honors

in eccentricity. The strange, sometimes witty, often irreverent names—
The Bubble Gum Machine, The Union Gap, The Quicksilver Messenger
Service, Country Joe and the Fish, Big Brother and the Holding Company, The Iron Butterfly, The Jefferson Airplane, Blue Cheer (both of
which derive from drug slang), The Rotary Connection, Canned Heat—
and various modes of dress (Civil War uniforms, Salvation Army clothes,
Spanish boleros, Edwardian trousers, army surplus) are in themselves a
unique musical phenomenon, indicative of how large an influence public
relations and nonmusical factors played in the popularity of their music.
Even The Beatles, whose talent was more than sufficient to make it
unnecessary, felt constrained to resort to similar publicity tricks.

Vocalists of the sixties like Bob Dylan, Joan Baez, Janis Ian, Sonny
and Cher, and Simon and Garfunkel, whose music was derived more from
the folk tradition than from rhythm and blues, emphasized the social
message of the lyrics over musical values, serving as commentators as well
as entertainers. Dylan, for example, was strongly influenced by folksinger
Woody Guthrie, country-singer Hank Williams, and rhythm and blues
singers Chuck Berry and Buddy Holly. His pleas for social justice, "The
Times They Are a'Changin'," "Blowin' in the Wind," and his satire on
sentimentality in "It Ain't Me Babe," were all in the million-seller bracket.
More directly influenced by The Beatles were such groups as The Cream,
The Doors, and The Mamas and the Papas, who continued to experiment with rhythm and blues sounds. Recognizing the potential of the
"teeny-bopper" or early-adolescent market, a number of groups aimed
their product at that age group in pale imitation of The Beatles—The
Monkees, The Dave Clark Five, Herman's Hermits, Paul Revere and the
Raiders, among others.

Other groups tested the limits of taste and legality with lyrics of
violence, sex, drug addiction, and vulgarity. Employing costumes and
language designed to repel and disgust the "straight" public, groups such
as The Savages and The Fugs (some of whose records were banned by
the mass media) consistently sold albums in the 100,000 bracket, chiefly
to young adults. The lyrics of "Honey Rock," a hard-rock love song that
sold a million copies, for example, simply repeated over and over, "I
want it"; The Fugs occasionally chanted obscenities in unison behind the
music; Janis Joplin's hit album was first titled *Sex, Dope, and Cheap
Thrills,* later shortened to *Cheap Thrills.* In addition, a number of
bands backed their concerts with a "light show," or exhibition of flashing
lights in imitation of the effects produced by psychedelic drugs. Certainly
a substantial part of the popularity of such groups lay in their appeal to
the least mature segment of the market for reasons which bore no rela-

tion to music, something not at all unknown in the history of popular music over the past century.

Individual vocalists like James Brown, José Feliciano, and Johnny Rivers continued the "soul" and blues-shouting tradition through the sixties, the most popular being Jimi Hendrix of The Jimi Hendrix Experience, somewhat grandiloquently chosen by *Melody Maker* magazine in 1968 as "The World's Number One Musician." In many ways a traditional blues singer, soundly grounded in musical technique, Hendrix based a good deal of his audience appeal on his attention to the psychedelic experience. His performances, which bordered on hysteria, occasionally required special police to maintain a semblance of audience order. Janis Joplin, a Southern white girl who developed her frantic singing style from the black blues-shouting tradition, drew tremendous audiences in 1968 by pushing the rock-blues style to its limits, screaming and stamping out songs while drinking a liqueur called Southern Comfort. Interestingly enough, neither Hendrix nor Joplin were particularly effective on records; Big Brother and the Holding Company, Janis's backup band, was a less-than-mediocre musical group, hardly to be compared with the Hendrix band. The impact of both singers, an undeniably powerful one, was at least partly visual and derived a great deal from the personality of the performance, perhaps as much as from the music.

Two important strains of post-Beatle rhythm and blues, however, represented a return to the earlier blues-style music of the fifties. The first, called "The Motown Sound" after the Detroit recording company which introduced it, featured black instrumental and vocal groups like Aretha Franklin, Diana Ross and the Supremes, Smokey Robinson and The Miracles, The Four Tops, Little Stevie Wonder, The Temptations, and the Marinettes. Relatively uninfluenced by The Beatles, Motown groups brought the rhythm and blues style smoothness, sophistication (both musical and emotional), considerable harmonic complexity, and an urbanized, black, "high-society" polish lacking in its earlier practitioners like B. B. King or Muddy Waters. The Detroit-based groups were by no means naïve or spontaneous; their music, though still blues-oriented, was controlled, disciplined, knowledgeable. They represented a thoroughly Negro music which had grown up in the Northern cities since the forties, still as self-consciously racial as old-time jazz but transformed into a mid-twentieth-century black idiom.

Coexistent with the urbanized sophistication of the Motown blues style, which possibly reached the climax of its popularity in 1968, was the rebirth of the older blues—but as reinterpreted by white musicians such as Blood, Sweat and Tears, Steppenwolf, Canned Heat, Eric Clapton's

English groups, and others. After The Beatles and their followers had explored the potentials of rock into psychedelic blind alleys, and the "inside" referential music of the extremist groups had begun to lose its appeal, young white musicians returned to a loud, harsh, raw (but basically blues) music that recalled the rock of the fifties, amplified, electrified, and exaggerated far beyond the bounds of the original. A circuit of music halls sprang up around this music in 1968 and 1969—Detroit's Grande Ballroom, Philadelphia's Electric Factory, Boston's Psychedelic Supermarket, San Francisco's Fillmore West—drawing audiences almost wholly white, middle class, and sixteen to twenty-five. At such major ballrooms a top-rated band could demand $20,000 to $30,000 for a weekend engagement and attract crowds of 10,000. (The Woodstock festival in 1969, in fact, featuring this music outdoors, drew 300,000 people, perhaps the largest number in the United States to hear a live performance directly.) Ironically, black audiences generally found these white blues-rock bands unacceptable.

The impact of electrical amplification and new recording techniques on popular music after 1950 was nothing less than revolutionary. Amplification made the guitar an important melodic instrument, audible even in a large band, and created new solo artists—Charlie Christian, Wes Montgomery, Eric Clapton, and others. It also actually did create a new instrument, the electric organ; the addition of the electric bass and the bass guitar (or Fender bass) added tremendous power to amplified rhythms. The shock of amplified sound, sometimes pushed beyond the limits of auditory tolerance, involved the listener physically; the actual bodily participation of an audience in a theoretically infinite amplification of sound was an important element in the music's effect. Hendrix, for example, with a group of three, used twelve giant amplifiers containing a total of forty-eight large speakers.

New recording techniques made the sound engineer an influential musical factor, since he could quite literally create music by changing the nature of the recorded sounds. He could modify sound in endless alterations; he could combine music made on different days, by instruments played separately, into a unified performance that never occurred; by "overdubbing" he could produce sounds that did not exist before. The total effects of electronic recording techniques on popular music have yet to be estimated. But it is clear that it has been possible, for over a decade, to make music from prerecorded tapes in the studio without an audience or musicians. It is also possible to create a perfect performance by combining portions of tapes of previous performances, thus adapting to music the revision process hitherto available only to writers and painters.

Beginning in the forties, the average age of the popular-record buyer dropped sharply. The enormous sales of Presley, rock and roll groups, the Beatles, and the rest, have been primarily among the young, and even more spectacularly, among the very young. Eighty per cent of all single records and fifty per cent of all albums are purchased by persons under twenty-five; of that amount almost three-quarters are purchased by buyers under eighteen. Popular music has been in the curious position since World War II of being very nearly an adolescent monopoly. For one reason, the population growth rate since the postwar years created a great new teen-age and adolescent market that shows no signs of receding—affluent, ready for exploitation, and like all youthful markets, eager for novelty and innovation. For another, the perfection of small, cheap, transistorized radios and phonographs put millions of music-making devices into the hands of youngsters who never had them before. Record companies, radio disc jockeys, and musical performers take dead aim at this huge market, one much more lucrative over the long run than the adult segment.

Very few of the best-selling performers and musical groups since the fifties have been familiar to anyone over twenty-five. The "best of 1968," chosen by several record columnists, included Richard Harris, José Feliciano, the Bee Gees, Otis Redding, The Rascals, Julie Driscoll, and Dion. "Top artist" of the year was Aretha Franklin, whose sale of eleven million records made her the best-selling female vocalist in popular music's history. "Top groups" were The Cream and The Beatles, the latter the only name recognizable, no doubt, to the average American adult. Nowhere else in the popular arts is the gulf between generations (not even in television or the movies) so evident. To the over-thirty group, the best-selling recording orchestras in 1968 were Lawrence Welk (with a television following of millions) and the Glenn Miller Band—the former playing updated thirties music, the latter using many of the same arrangements left by Miller at his death during World War II.

Paradoxically, popular music has always been both a business and an art; there are arguments for making it either, but stronger ones for making it both. Its primary aim, obviously, is to be popular; its success is measured by the profit it brings in the marketplace. Popular music is therefore a business, selling a commercial product which satisfies the public taste for musical entertainment. But it is also a form of art, one which furnishes an aesthetic experience for millions of people. The necessities of the market restrict or conventionalize what they do, but however commercial their purpose, the songwriter and performer strive to do the most proficient and satisfying job they can within the limits imposed. They cannot, no matter how skillful their control of the medium or how cunning their contrivance, guarantee that the product will meet the market's test. A song's acceptance is not simply a matter of market research or hard-sell advertising; 98 per cent of all songs, notably, are not hits, despite the desperate efforts of publishers, agents, and public relations men. Popular music must have, somehow and somewhere within it, an indefinable something—which may be called art by some, artifice by others—that moves people to respond to it.

What *does* make popular music popular? It must have, of course, a rhythmic basis, a quality of sound, and melodic attraction, but it must also have emotion, an idea, a point of view which includes both the person listening and the person performing. It must in some way fit and express the current cultural pattern of the public to which it appeals, align itself with the median taste, relate to the tone, needs, and values of the age. The lachrymose parlor songs of the eighteen-forties did not fit the nineties; the ingenuous ballads of the nineties did not fit the nineteen-twenties; the jingling Tin Pan Alley tunes of the twenties did not fit the thirties; the slick, tailored songs of the thirties and forties did not fit the ironic, rebellious mood of the fifties and sixties. Each era chooses its own songs to express itself; the popular song is popular because it does precisely that.

PART SIX

MEDIA HOT AND COOL: MOVIES, RADIO, AND TELEVISION

If we listened to the eggheads, we'd be out of business in six months.

—ROBERT SARNOFF, CHAIRMAN
NATIONAL BROADCASTING COMPANY

CULTURE AT THE BIJOU: THE WIDE WORLD OF FILM

The cinema is a ribbon of dreams

—ORSON WELLES

The possibility of taking pictures that moved attracted many curious and ingenious men during the later years of the nineteenth century, among them Thomas Alva Edison, who had already captured sound on his phonograph in 1877. Much of the work on his moving picture project he turned over to his assistant, William Kennedy Dickson, who evolved a camera in 1889 after eight years of experimentation, using film strips recently developed by George Eastman. (French inventors, however, had already successfully made moving pictures.) Edison applied for patents in 1891 on both the camera and a projector, a black box with a peephole lens through which one peered at a moving film strip lighted from behind by an electric lamp.

Enterprising operators installed Edison's Kinetoscopes, as he named them, in amusement parks, reaping profits at a penny a look. After the first successful picture arcade opened in New York City in April, 1894, others quickly followed. Lasting about thirty seconds, the showings were sometimes geared to a phonograph to provide a crude sound movie. To keep the peepshows supplied with film Edison built a tar-paper shack at his New Jersey laboratories as a "studio," but others swiftly entered the business. The films were at first merely bits of scenery and action— acrobats, dancers, boxers, fire engines, parades, mountains, waterfalls, and so on. Later arcade films were brief skits, usually comic, sometimes risqué. Producers soon found that "What the Bootblack Saw," or "Taking a Bath" drew more pennies than "View of the Falls" or "Otters at

Play," and they adjusted their films accordingly. The first faint glimmer of censorship, in fact, came after the showing of "Dolorita's Passion Dance" at an Atlantic City arcade in 1895; the offending film was promptly removed.

It was perfectly clear, since a Kinetoscope could handle but one customer at a time, that if the picture could be projected on a screen a number of people could see it at once. Improved projectors which appeared in the nineties, with names like Bioscope, Vitascope, and Cinématograph, were immediately put to use by arcade owners who merely hung a sheet at one end of a room, put in chairs, and made theaters out of vacant stores. Such theaters (called "nickelodeons" although the prices were often ten cents) appeared in New York, Los Angeles, Atlanta, and Chicago as early as 1895, proliferating wildly over the next few years. By 1905 there were roughly three thousand such theaters in operation, by 1910, 10,000. "In almost every case," the New York *Herald* reported in 1907, "a long, narrow room, formerly used for business purposes, has been made over. . . . At the rear a stage is raised. Before the curtain is placed a piano, which does service for an orchestra. Packed into the room as closely as they can be placed are chairs for spectators, who number from a few to four hundred and fifty." The films lasted for twenty to thirty minutes, after which the house was cleared and the program repeated, sometimes from eight in the morning until midnight.

Regular theaters began showing moving pictures too. The first public film projection in an American theater occurred at Koster and Bial's Music Hall in New York on April 23, 1896, an event the *Times* found "wonderfully real and singularly exhilarating." Music halls and vaudeville theaters immediately began using films as "openers" to begin programs and as "chasers" to clear the house. In 1908 two enterprising owners in Pennsylvania remodeled their arcade, bought new equipment, put in regular seats and a piano, and designed their building especially for movie showings. Soon similar theaters appeared in hundreds of towns and cities—with names like "Bijou," "Lyric," "Fairyland," "Dreamland," and "Comique"—with ticket offices, lobbies, ushers, popcorn and peanuts, and different priced seats.

An early program was a mixed bag of short films, depending on a supply turned out in frantic haste by numbers of fledgling companies. There were comic films like "Watering the Garden" (in which an unsuspecting gardener is sprayed by a hose) and "The Coachman and the Boy" (in which a mischievous boy bedevils the servant); travelogues of the Alps or Borneo; trick films about trips to the moon; and so on. Koster and Bial's original program listed "Sea Waves," "Umbrella Dance," "Burlesque Boxing," "Venice," "Kaiser Wilhelm Reviewing Troops," "Butterfly Dance," and six other shorts. A Tacoma program of 1900 showed little change: "Sleigh Riding in Central Park," "The Elopement," "Trained Horses," "The Bowery at Night," "A Narrow Escape on the Baltimore and Ohio Railroad," and "The Ups and Downs of Army Life," mixing thrills, scenery, romance, and comedy in a popular assortment.

Sex entered the films quickly, via various "Arab" or "Moorish" dances and especially with a short film called "The Kiss," done in 1896 by May Irwin and John Rice, which covered forty-two feet of film and created a good deal of talk. Within the next few years theaters offered items like "The Gaieties of Divorce," "Cupid's Barometer," "Who's in the Bedroom?" and "The Maid's Guest," many of them based on slightly laundered vaudeville and burlesque skits. One of the first long films to be shown as a single program was the Corbett-Fitzsimmons fight of 1897 which ran 11,000 feet; the next hit, the same year, was a filmed version of the entire Passion Play. Sex, action, religion, and the spectacular entered the movies at the same time.

Five, ten, and fifteen cent prices brought theatrical entertainment to audiences that neither vaudeville nor the popular stage had ever touched. Nickelodeons and cheap movie houses, located in the city's poorest and most congested districts, supplied exactly what the urban masses wanted. Families went to the movies together, local merchants advertised on their screens, audiences sang together from song slides, people met and socialized—all for nickels and dimes. (Subtitles, of course, taught thousands of immigrants to speak English.) A city movie house could gross a thousand dollars a week with ease in 1908, and by that time every major city had a hundred or more of them.

There were between eight thousand and ten thousand movie theaters in the country in 1909. *Survey* magazine reported that New York City had 340 theaters, with a quarter-million daily attendance and a half-million on Sundays. Chicago in 1911 had four hundred movie houses that showed 3,255 different movies that year; nationally, *Survey* estimated, there were 13,000 theaters attracting daily audiences of five to seven million people. "In the tenement districts," the magazine wrote, "the moving picture has well nigh driven other forms of entertainment from the field." Movies were mass entertainment aimed at the lowest common audience denominator, and they never pretended otherwise. "If you're tired of life," ran an advertising jingle, "go to the picture show,"

> If you're sick of troubles rife, go to the picture show;
> You'll forget your unpaid bills, rheumatism and other ills,
> If you'll stow away your pills, and go to the picture show.

As theaters demanded more and more pictures studios ground them out by the scores. By 1900 it was obvious that longer narrative films, rather than bits and pieces of skits and scenes, were what audiences wanted. Plot and characterization appeared—farmers, firemen, rascally kids, old maids, lovers, police, and so on—put together in scenes to produce a continuous narrative with a beginning, middle, and end. The movie was now a play, created by editing, cutting, selecting, and joining scenes; imaginative cameramen and studio directors experimented constantly with the new medium, testing its possibilities and potentials. Edwin S. Porter, an Edison cameraman, made *The Life of an American Fireman* in late 1902 or early 1903. In his next movie, *The Great Train Robbery* (1903), he moved the camera outdoors and put together what was probably the first motion picture in the modern sense—that is, an entire film governed by a single narrative conception, created by combining all the techniques of directing, editing, cutting, and filming known to that time. In addition, Porter put into his picture nearly all the elements (except sex) that were to dominate the content of the film for generations to come—action, violence, speed, suspense, a chase, good guys versus bad guys, all leading to an anticipated ending.

The early movies drew their plots from everywhere, but most naturally from currently popular books and plays. All the schoolroom classics went on film—*Uncle Tom's Cabin, Oliver Twist, Romeo and Juliet, The Scarlet Letter, Ramona, Ben Hur, Evangeline*—and stage successes like *The Bandit King, Fools of Fate, Just Gold, The Crooked Banker, The Schoolma'm and the Cowboy, Judith of Bethulia, Way Down East,* and dozens of other tried-and-true plays and novels. There were crime and mystery movies like *The Rogue of Paris, The Mysterious Criminal, The Ex-Convict;* problem movies like *The Path of Folly* or *Why Girls Leave Home* or *The Suffragette;* comedies and farces like *Maid's Night Out* and *The Drummer's Trip Home.* Beginning in 1912 studios produced so-called feature films, that is, relatively long movies (five reels or more, a reel running from eleven to fifteen minutes) which cost more to make and for which theaters charged increased prices. *Quo Vadis*, a nine-reeler imported from Italy in 1913, reinforced the trend. As longer movies became increasingly complicated in plot, they demanded much more skill and polish from cameramen, directors, and actors. *Oliver Twist* (1912) ran five reels; *Queen Elizabeth* (1912, starring the great Sarah Bernhardt) was seven reels; *The Spoilers,* adapted from Rex Beach's popular novel in 1914, ran nine reels and two hours; Griffith's *Birth of a Nation* (1915) was twelve reels long. In 1915 Paramount alone produced 104 feature-length films; in 1916 the industry's total was 647; in 1918, 841.

By 1915 movies were different because audiences had changed. Film producers no longer aimed at the ten-cent trade in the tenement district, for there were movie houses spread out in hamlets and cities all over the country. Profits were where the audiences were—in the huge middle class—which demanded not only different kinds of movies but different kinds of theaters. The industry had little competition (by 1917 American studios made 97 per cent of all the films in the world), an audience of millions, and no foreseeable limits to an expanding market. No popular art had ever had quite so entrancing a prospect before. From vacant stores movies moved into "palaces" like Mitchel Mark's New York Strand that opened in 1914 with thick rugs, lounges, chandeliers, paintings, comfortable seats, an organ, a thirty-piece orchestra, and a corps of cadet-trained ushers. In 1916 there were 21,000 new theaters built over the country, asking prices up to $1.50, with an established program pattern of comedy, newsreel, and travelogue, followed by the feature picture.

Studios in the pre-World War I period had the same problems that faced other producers of popular art—how to cover the broadest possible spectrum of the market by appealing to the most and offending the least; and how to make the most profit with the least risk. To solve the first they made two kinds of pictures, one with first-rate actors and sophisticated stories for "class" audiences, the other routine movies with lesser-known actors and formularized plots for the mass trade. Working with primitive and highly intuitional market research methods, movie makers divided production schedules into conventionalized categories and produced a certain number each year in each category. The so-called B picture was an industry staple as early as 1914.

To solve the second they did exactly what Henry Ford had done in the auto industry—standardize the product along lines of proved audience appeal so that it could be turned out with a minimum of cost and risk. The "star" was the key factor in the "A" or quality picture, since he or she stabilized the picture's appeal. The "B" picture's market depended less on the star than the story; people came to see a comedy or an action picture not because of who was in it, but because they wanted to see that kind of picture. It was nothing more than dime-novel, stage-melodrama production technique carried over into a new but similar medium.

In Hollywood (where the industry began to concentrate about 1909) movie-makers settled on nine major categories of films which, experience showed, consistently made money, all of them types transferred from popular drama and fiction: the epic-spectacular; the adventure-romance; farce and comedy; the Western; the melodram..; the problem play; the love-sex story; the "classic"; the mystery-crime play. Epics like *The Life of Moses* (1913), *Samson* (1914), *Daughter of the Gods* (1916), and *Joan of Arc* (1916) pointed toward the "super colossals" of the twenties; Kalem Studio's *Ben Hur* was judged by critics to be the "most superb moving picture ever made." There were adventure movies like *The Count of Monte Cristo* (featuring an aging, fat James O'Neill), *Graustark*, *The Prisoner of Zenda, Under Royal Patronage, An Enemy to the King, To Have and To Hold,* and so on.

Recognizing that film did a much more effective job than the stage in presenting exotic, romantic adventure, films put their plots in places like the frozen North, the mighty Alps, the burning sands of the desert, the mysterious East, the languorous South Seas, or anywhere set-builders could transport them. Comedies, many straight out of vaudeville, came by dozens—*Happy-Go-Lucky, The Win(k)some Widow, Maisie Puts One Over, Susie Snowflake, Pretty Mrs. Smith, The Bachelor Husband.* Most of the melodramas quickly reappeared in the movies—*Uncle Tom's Cabin* (three times), *The Two Orphans* (three times), *St. Elmo, A Dixie Mother, The Engineer's Sweetheart, A Ragged Girl, Michael Strogoff, The Princess from the Poorhouse, The Kiss of Hate, The Blind Fiddler.* For "A" audiences studios ransacked the classics—*Carmen, Rip Van Winkle* (which Joseph Jefferson filmed in 1896), *Oliver Twist* (three times), *Vanity Fair, Enoch Arden* (twice), *Ivanhoe, Robinson Crusoe, The Deerslayer, Hiawatha, Camille,* and Shakespeare. Mystery-crime stories were as popular in the movies as on the stage: *The Cracksman, The Conspiracy, The Broken Coin, The Black Box, The Severed Hand, The Crimson Stain, The Dragon's Claw,* and of course Sherlock Holmes himself.

There were a good many "problem" movies such as *The Common Law* (marriage), *The Secret Sin* (adultery), *Sins of the Parents* (juvenile delinquency), and *The Weakness of Man* (women). *Traffic in Souls* (1913), for example, was advertised as a "$200,000 spectacle in 700 scenes with 801 players, showing the traps cunningly laid for young girls by vice agents." Love stories clogged screens everywhere (*Love's Sunset, Wildflower, The Dawn of a Romance, Salomy Jane, Helen of the Chorus*) until in 1914 Elinor Glyn's novel, *Three Weeks,* put sophisticated sex into the movies with great style: later the explosive debut of Theda Bara (a tailor's daughter from Cincinnati named Theodosia Goodman) in *A Fool There Was,* gave the movies their first "bad woman" heroine.

The Western movie came early, since it could draw on an already powerful tradition in fiction and drama. *The Great Train Robbery* introduced the first cowboy hero, "Bronco Billy" Anderson (Max Aronson), a portly little man who could not ride a horse very well but who made four hundred one-reelers before 1914. Most of the early Westerns were made in the New Jersey flats, dozens of them with names like *Across the Plains* or *Stranger at Coyote; The Virginian,* made for the first time in 1914, represented the type's highest early development.

Tom Mix, a real cowboy, made the first of over sixty feature Westerns in 1917, while William S. Hart, whose career began a year earlier, became the best-known and most highly paid Western star of early films. Hart, already an accomplished Shakespearean actor, took the Western seriously, insisted on absolute authenticity of characterization and locale, and used nothing but adult, mature plots. His favorite character was the "good-bad" hero (sketched out in fiction by Zane Grey) which he played over and over for twelve years—in shows like *Two-Gun Hicks, Bad Buck of Santa Inez, The Desert Man, The Narrow Trail, Tumbleweeds,* and others. Hart also transferred to the screen other Western conventions adapted from stage and fiction—the bad girl, the lonely gunfighter, the saloon brawl, the walkdown—and he also made the hero's horse a character. Hart never kissed a horse, as legend claimed, but once his horse *did* kiss him.

The most original film work came in comedy. Although the vaudeville skit and the stage farce translated fairly well into movie terms, the new medium gave writers and actors so much more visual freedom and so many more comic opportunities that good comedians immediately took advantage of it. John Bunny, a superb pantomimist, developed silent comedy to a high art; so too did Chaplin, Buster Keaton, Fatty Arbuckle, Ben Turpin, Harry Langdon, Charlie Chase, Mack Swain, Chester Conklin, Larry Semon, Ford Sterling, Marie Dressler, and Mabel Normand. Most of the great early comedians could make an entire film without a single subtitle, so highly skilled were they as pantomimists.

Mack Sennett, who came to Hollywood in 1909 out of burlesque, vaudeville, and the circus, made two comedies a week from 1910 through 1912, when he organized the Keystone Company. He made one hundred and forty that year alone, a storehouse on which movies and television still draw. Sennett gathered a group of tremendously talented actors and turned them loose, creating a gentle, zany world of comedy in which all laws of reason and reality were suspended, where cops chased everybody and caught nobody, autos fell apart and rejoined after a train cut them in half, a man robbed a bank with a vacuum cleaner, floods swept through bathrooms, trains roared through parlors, and the most violent weapon was a banana cream pie. What Sennett and others like him accomplished in the Golden Age of comedy has never been equaled since.

The serial furnished the clearest example of how the movies appropriated a popular entertainment form and adapted it to their purposes. Movie serials, which flourished from 1912 to the 1930's, simply put the old melodramas and dime novels on film—suspense, danger, a barrage of horrors, a suggestion of sex. The trick of using each episode of fifteen to thirty minutes for a complete section of a longer narrative, like chapters in a book, had great advantages for the movie theater (as it did later for radio and television) since it kept the audience coming back and helped fill the house on ordinarily slow Saturday afternoons. The French made a serial about Nick Carter in 1908, but the first American serial was probably *What Happened to Mary?* (1912), a twelve-part story of a foundling girl's adventures from orphanage to marriage. The real thing, however, came in 1913 with *The Adventures of Kathlyn,* thirteen episodes starring Kathlyn Williams, a well-proportioned blonde who lived with her father in India, where she daily faced danger from wild animals on the one hand and on the other the blandishments of Umballa, an odious rajah determined to add her to his harem. The hero (played by Tom Santschi) always appeared in time to save her from either or both.

The incomparable Pearl White appeared first in *The Exploits of Elaine,* in 1914, followed by *The New Exploits of Elaine* and *The Romance of Elaine.* The famous *Perils of Pauline* series, which ran for only twenty episodes, appeared also in 1914, but Miss White continued a number of other series, finally retiring in the late twenties with two million dollars and a home on the Riviera. With her soft, innocent face and cloud of golden hair, she could look terrified more convincingly than any other actress. Helen Holmes, another durable heroine, made *The Hazards of Helen* in an incredible one hundred and nineteen installments; Ruth Roland made *The Adventures of Ruth, The Red Circle, Ruth of the Range,* and nine others.

Serials came in all kinds and lengths, but the most popular were Westerns, mysteries, detective-crime stories, and adventure (pirate, jungle, war, etc.), with some mixtures. They ran to titles like *The Black Secret, The Haunted Valley, The Lightning Raiders, The Diamond from the Sky,* and *The Fatal Drug. The Fighting Trail* and *The Valley of Vanishing Men* were obviously Westerns; *Neal of the Navy* and *Vultures of the Sea* adventure; *The Green Archer* (adapted from Edgar Wallace stories) crime-mystery; *The Mysterious Pilot* air-adventure. *The Million Dollar Mystery* (twenty-three episodes) played in seven thousand theaters and grossed two million dollars, a tremendous sum for the times. As the stage had done, the serials capitalized on names in the news, starring celebrities like Bill Elliott, Jack Dempsey, Gene Tunney, Captain Frank Hawks, and Red Grange. Tarzan appeared serially in 1928, Flash Gordon in 1936, followed by Jack Armstrong and other comic-strip radio characters. The boom years were 1914 to 1926, when the industry produced about twenty serials each year; after that the total slowly diminished. The last true serial, probably, was *Blazing the Overland Trail* in 1956.

The vital element in the serial was simply the conflict of good and evil, stated in unequivocal, easily-grasped terms of hero (or heroine) versus villain (or villains). Pearl White's *Elaine* series featured three villains—a master criminal, a wily Oriental, and a German baron (this last played by Lionel Barrymore). Writers of "Hazards," "Perils," and "Adventures" serials with female leads dangled their girls from airplanes, trapped them in caves and snake pits, hung them over cliffs and waterfalls, and sank them in quicksands. (Many actresses did their own stunt work.) Writers vied in putting them in impossible positions and then rescuing them the next Saturday. Ruth Roland was once caught in a cave with flood waters rising around her, chained to a wall, an axe hung over her head by a slim cord, surrounded by giant spiders. She was rescued in two minutes, however, in the next episode.

The second major element was the chase, or as Miss White called it, the pursuit of the "weenie." The heroine, she explained, had the weenie, that is, something of value—a map of a mine, a will, a secret formula—that the villains wanted. Their pursuit of it and her could then be extended indefinitely, depending on the ingenuity of writers and the durability of actresses. In *The Mysteries of Myra*, Myra inherited a number of documents from her father, who had once been (but recanted) a member of a secret criminal group called "The Black Brothers," which would expose and convict them all if turned over to the police. The Brothers were not only criminals possessed of the usual weapons, but were also actual wizards who used ghosts, vampires, werewolves, monsters, and mysterious mental aberrations against her. Fortunately, her fiancé, Dr. Alden, was not only a physician but an "occult scientist" who gave the Brothers as good as he got for thirty-six episodes. He finally beat them with a machine that hypnotized *their* hypnotic machine which he then turned against *them*.

In less than two decades, the movies developed technically and creatively with amazing swiftness. Of the movies produced in this period, six may be chosen to represent the early film at its best, each the progenitor of a long line of descendants. *The Spoilers* (1914), directed by Colin Campbell, was the first classic of violence, featuring a fight between Dustin Farnum and villain Tom Santschi that lasted for a complete reel. A straight adventure story laid in the Yukon goldfields, it became the standard by which he-man pictures were judged for thirty years. (Milton Sills and Noah Beery remade it in 1927, William Boyd and Gary Cooper in 1932, and Randolph Scott and John Wayne in 1942.)

D. W. Griffith's handling of Civil War scenes in *The Birth of a Nation* (1915), the most important film in the early history of the film, furnished the grammar, technique, and style of the movie epic for generations to come. Griffith put together a number of devices—close-up and long shot, cross-cutting (shifting from one place to another to show simultaneous action), "Rembrandt" lighting (shadow and profile), cameras in motion—to set a pattern still valid for the type. (He also introduced souvenir programs, full orchestral accompaniment, special music, reserved seats, a two-dollar admission fee, and all the publicity tricks of a "premiere.")

Hell's Hinges, starring William S. Hart and directed by him, contained elements quite alien to the standard Western—the degradation of a weak-willed frontier minister by a bar-girl, as well as his subsequent drunkenness and suicide; a realistically drawn portrait of the trollop who seduces him; few fisticuffs, little violence, only one riding sequence; and the most powerful mob scene filmed up to that time. Hart played Blaze Tracey, a moody, dangerous gunman with his own code of ethics whose bittersweet love affair with the heroine is unusually underplayed for the period. Tracey's gradual reformation contrasts with the parallel disintegration of the minister, superbly played by Jack Standing, while the prostitute's attractive evil contrasts with the virtue of the heroine. Hart's insistence on realism made the locale a picture of a seedy, dusty, unlovely town, quite unlike anything out of the popular Western novel. D. W. Griffith's *Broken Blossoms* (1919), a violent, ugly story of a young Chinese (Richard Barthelmess), a London street waif (Lillian Gish), and a brutal sadist (Donald Crisp), ending in murder and suicide, was superlative melodrama transferred to the screen with great skill. Douglas Fairbanks' *Mark of Zorro* (1920) represented the adventure-romance at its good-natured best, with Fairbanks as a gay Mexican Robin Hood and Noah Beery as a jovial villain. Paramount's *Dr. Jekyll and Mr. Hyde* (1920) with John Barrymore as the tragic doctor, a tremendously effective Grand Guignol shocker (with sloe-eyed Nita Naldi supplying a sex interest Stevenson left out) was the first of the horror-mystery cycle that stretched over the next forty years. Certainly in 1920 the movies were not only big business and a lucrative popular art, but a highly-developed and skilled one.

It was thoroughly understood in the "industry" (a term in use as early as 1906), that a motion picture was a commercial venture, not an art, and that while it was desirable to make good pictures, it was absolutely essential to make profitable ones. From the first movie-makers knew that they had to please as many people as possible by giving them what they wanted. Hollywood was a business, and nobody in authority pretended otherwise. It had nothing against art and hoped to produce some of it, but what stood out clearly on the books was profit or loss. The industry knew by the twenties that in the long run (and in this it was no different from any other popular art) that the best it could do was to reflect as directly and completely as it could the interests, values, anxieties, and illusions of its customers. To appeal to a mass audience the movies therefore accepted certain conventions which, experience taught, lost money for the industry when disregarded and made money for them when followed. Like any other business man, Budd Schulberg wrote later, the producer "aimed to please as many people as possible while minimizing risks and standardizing production." The conflict between art and profits (in which art almost always lost) was endemic in the industry from the first.

Nevertheless, producers and directors, working within the restrictions imposed by these conventions, explored ideas and techniques with imagination and skill. So too did actors and writers. "Movie" acting, as distinct from stage acting, emerged as a separate style, understated, aimed at a camera rather than an auditorium, direct, intimate, less "stagey." Writers who recognized that a movie script and a stage play were two quite different things learned how to write for the camera and around its specialized uses—cutting, fading, close-up, montage, and the like.

After the first Vitascope showings everyone agreed that the new medium would have a powerful influence on American life ("a most potent factor in shaping national mind and morals," *Harper's Weekly* said), though few could be sure to what end. *The Independent* in 1910 praised movies as "a new form of fine art not unworthy to rank with the older arts." William Dean Howells, the nation's most respected literary critic, thought the film had great potential but wondered "what it *ethically* may become." *The Nation* in 1913 hailed the motion picture as Whitman's dream of a democratic art come true, "a real and truly popular art . . . , created for the masses and largely by them"; *The Bookman* in 1915 called it "authentic democratic art, straight from the hearts of the humble classes."

Others were not so sure. *The Outlook* wondered if too many movies might destroy the audience's sense of reality, encouraging them to substitute illusion for life. Joseph Fulk of the University of Nebraska, com-

pleting a study for the National Education Association in 1912, thought
that the movies were dominated too much by "the sensational . . . , the
growing desire for emotional excitement . . . , and too many ready-
made interpretations and conclusions." Some critics found little to praise.
Good Housekeeping in 1910 called the theater "a primary school for criminals . . . , teaching obscenity, crime, murder, and debauchery for a
nickel." William C. De Mille, Cecil B. De Mille's older brother and a well-
known actor and playwright, believed movies "a cheap form of entertainment for cheap people" (though he later went to Hollywood himself)
while *The Independent* in 1916, compiling a brief for debates on the
question "Resolved, that motion pictures offer desirable amusement,"
could do no better than offer six points for and six against.

Calls for censorship came quite early. Chicago began to censor films
in 1907; New York established a censorship board in 1909; Pennsylvania
passed state laws controlling movie stories in 1911. The New York board
looked for "prolonged love scenes . . . , close dancing,"

> displays of the person, portrayal of crime . . . , gruesome or sug-
> gestive acts, undue violence, and acts which arouse rather than mini-
> mize passion, tend to perpetuate double standards of morality, and
> easy ways of gratifying desire.

Refusing, it said, to accept "as a standard the New York stage or its complicated, liberal, and abnormal life," the board condemned fifty-three
movies in 1913 and censored parts of four hundred and one others, without, however, much effect on future productions.

Whatever their art or lack of it, or morality or lack of it, the movies
by 1920 had completely changed the style of popular entertainment.
Their effect on theaters and vaudeville was devastatingly swift; movie
houses simply drew away audiences by millions. Old-style theater closed
up, except for the traveling tent shows, which offered little competition
to the movies. Vaudeville died and its stars went on film; the stage attracted smaller audiences of élite tastes and ceased to be a popular art.
Film was the dominant, pervasive, nearly exclusive form of popular
dramatic entertainment.

Culturally, during the twenties the motion picture brought the mass
audience to a level of sophistication in manners, speech, dress, morals,
and social and ethical attitudes utterly unknown—and utterly undreamed
of—by the preceding generation. The movies did not gradually become a
mirror of life; rather, life became a mirror of the movies. People copied
what they saw on the screen, making the conventions of the film the conventions of the style of life they lived in imitation of it. A theater adver-

tisement in 1922 said it accurately and succinctly: "Before you know it you are *living* the story! All the adventure, all the romance, all the excitement you lack in your daily life are in pictures!" (which supplied them to millions every night of the week).

At the end of World War I the motion picture had arrived as commercialized popular art, popular beyond the early producers' wildest dreams. Movie-making was the fifth largest industry in the country, its techniques of production and distribution fully developed. Hollywood dominated the world market; film company stock was listed on Wall Street; Hollywood's payroll by 1920 ran twenty million dollars yearly. There were directors and critics and actors who considered the cinema an art form, but few others had such illusions; it was a highly lucrative form of popular entertainment, aimed at a mass market. Studios were complicated film factories with high production costs; stars were expensive but absolutely necessary. "Safe" stars whose names sold films could call the tune on salaries as they wished. In 1926 the weekly salaries of the most expensive reached astronomical proportions: Harold Lloyd, $40,000; Chaplin, $30,000; Fairbanks, $24,000; Gloria Swanson, $19,400; Tom Mix, $19,000; Marion Davies, $10,000. William S. Hart drew two and a quarter million for nine films in two years.

With millions riding on each major picture, studios could afford few mistakes; like other industries they had to standardize the product to minimize risks and maximize profits. One method was to construct the film about a star of guaranteed box-office value. Another was to standardize the story, using only tried-and-true materials like Westerns, crime, the Civil War, historical "spectacles," love, music, children, home life, and sex. A predictable number of people, for example, would pay to see Mary Pickford in *Daddy Long-Legs;* an equally predictable number would pay to see movies titled *Blind Husbands* or *Guns on the Range* with anybody. Another was to deal in escape, to sell audiences the fairy tales they wanted to believe—the Milquetoast turns hero, the rich heiress marries the commoner, the right man finally comes along, the boy-next-door wins out over the city slicker, the plain secretary is really a ravishing beauty with her glasses off. Hollywood, Budd Schulberg wrote later, put "standard-brand stars in standard-brand stories that stood the test of ordeal-by-box-office." The possibilities of profit if they hit the right formula were enormous, and producers knew it.

Any Mary Pickford picture, for example, grossed about three times its production cost. A standard De Mille comedy cost about $25,000 to make and grossed $300,000. The Western epic, *The Covered Wagon* (1923) cost $750,000 and took in $4,000,000; *The Big Parade* (1925), the last of the war epics, cost $200,000 and collected five and a half million. With profits like this, Hollywood was anxious to give the public whatever it wanted. If it wanted Latin lovers like Rudolph Valentino, it gave them Ramon Navarro, Rod LaRocque, and Ricardo Cortez too; or he-men like Douglas Fairbanks, Milton Sills, and Richard Dix; or strong Westerners like Hart, Mix, Hoot Gibson, Buck Jones; or femmes fatales like Nita Naldi, Pola Negri, and Greta Garbo (who also had great talent); or comics like Chaplin and Lloyd and Keaton; or "flappers" like Clara Bow, Colleen Moore, Sue Carol, and Joan Crawford; or animals like Rin-Tin-Tin the dog. Stars lived like stars, the way the public wanted them to, larger than life. Clara Bow, the original "It" girl, queen of the "Jazz Babies," received 100,000 fan letters a year, gave parties for whole football squads, owned a Kissel roadster (colored red to match her hair) with two red Irish setters trained to ride on the running boards, earned four thousand dollars a week and spent it all.

Movies changed with the public mood. Mary Pickford's *Pollyanna* was too simpleminded for the taste of a wartime generation. Stories turned tougher, flavored with satire, sex, ambiguity, irony, and straight sensationalism. Theda Bara, who made her first "vamp" picture in 1915, made almost forty more, cut to the same suggestive pattern. Sexual problems and moral issues appeared on the screen: infidelity, broken homes, divorce, abortion, illegitimacy, prostitution, sadism. New heroines reflected new sophistication—Alla Nazimova, Norma Talmadge, Mae Murray, Pola Negri, Gloria Swanson. Movies featured sensual display and sexual suggestiveness. "The ruined woman," said Cecil B. De Mille, "is as out of style as the Victorian who used to faint," while titles like *Twin Beds, Forbidden Fruit, Scrambled Wives,* and *The Other Woman's Husband* appeared on marquees. Sex in the twenties could be exotic, as in Valentino's *The Sheik* and its imitators like *Burning Sands, The Tents of Allah, One Stolen Night;* frantic as in *Lying Lips, Mad Love, Modern Maidens,* or *The Mad Whirl;* or falsely moral as in *Reckless Mothers, Old Wives for New, Flapper Wives,* and *Blind Husbands.*

"Films featured the lust for youth," writes Lewis Jacobs of the twenties, "fed the romantic desire for 'freedom,' stumped for the mercenary business psychology of the day . . . , and showed that money talked, clothes were an index of position in life . . . , material success mattered." There were films with go-get'em titles like *Putting It Over, It Pays to Advertise,* and *Money! Money! Money!* Bootleggers, gangsters, and mistresses seemed on the screen to be people of excitement and glamour; pictures about bad girls came by dozens—*Rag Doll, Ladies of Pleasure, The Joy Girl, Trifling Women, Ladies of the Night*—showing the sinful fun of rolled stockings, hip flasks, and petting. One movie, according to a near-hysterical public-relations man, gave the audience "brilliant men, beautiful jazz babies, champagne baths, midnight revels, petting parties in the purple dawn, all ending in a terrific smashing climax that makes you gasp!" What the movies did, and what the people wanted them to do, was to show life as an exciting, sensational adventure, to create for the millions, as the Lynds said in their sociological study of "Middletown," "a happy, sophisticated, make-believe world" that was better to live in than the one they had. The function of the popular movie was not to reflect reality, but to blur and glamorize it. This drew the crowds, and still does.

The director in the twenties who realized most clearly that movies were commercialized entertainment—not art—and that the best movies were those that satisfied the most people, was Cecil B. De Mille. A genius at matching his films to the widest public taste, De Mille started out in 1914 with *The Squaw Man,* a Western combined with the same Indian-white love story that had pleased audiences since Pocahontas. He moved into superpatriotic war films during World War I, and afterwards was among the first in Hollywood to sense the changed mood of postwar society. He shifted at once to gilt-edged, double-entendre films of sex and high-life with names like *Male and Female, Wives and Lovers,* and *The Golden Bed.*

De Mille recognized that if one portion of the audience was interested in the clothes the actress took off, the other was interested in the clothes she put on. He used actresses like clotheshorses, their lingerie, coiffures, shoes, hats, and clothes done by the best New York and Paris houses. He set off Gloria Swanson's icy beauty with clothes that few women dared to wear but all hoped to; if his publicity releases can be believed, Lillian Rich, in *The Golden Bed,* used twenty-eight different kinds of perfume alone. He also made the bath, complete with tantalizing glimpses of thigh and breast, a standard movie feature.

When he felt that the public had had enough, De Mille quickly switched to piously moralized, covertly suggestive biblical epics, beginning with *The Ten Commandments* (1923) which illustrated with great flourish the sinfulness forbidden by each commandment. De Mille managed to work sex and clothes into almost everything, employing hundreds of scantily-draped maidens for bath scenes and Roman orgies, tracing the temptations of adultery and fornication with great effectiveness. (Without bedrooms and bathrooms, one critic remarked, nothing would happen in a De Mille picture.) He did, of course, only what popular novelists and playwrights had done for years—tell about sin so that it could be avoided. *The Ten Commandments* played almost continuously for ten years and was still in theaters in 1936; *The King of Kings* (1927), its successor, was on theater bills as late as 1957. His remake of *The Ten Commandments* (1956) was just as successful as the first version.

The twenties also introduced the "big" picture, a trend started by Griffith's *Birth of a Nation,* which showed that a star plus "a cast of thousands" and a story set in an exciting locale would draw millions. There were Valentino's *Sheik* and *Four Horsemen;* Francis X. Bushman and Ramon Navarro in *Ben Hur;* Westerns like *The Covered Wagon* and *The Iron Horse;* war pictures like *The Big Parade* and *Wings,* the ancestor of all airplane epics. There were Lon Chaney's magnificent horror epics, *The Hunchback of Notre Dame* and *The Phantom of the Opera.* There was *Flesh and the Devil,* John Gilbert's and Greta Garbo's steamy "love-epic." Sometimes expertly done and sometimes merely pretentious, the "feature" film dominated the industry. Hart's stained, lonely hero was superseded by less interesting but more reliable box-office cowboys like Tom Mix, Hoot Gibson, Ken Maynard, and Buck Jones.

At the opposite pole were the good-natured, dash-and-derring-do adventure movies of Douglas Fairbanks, holdovers, really, from simpler prewar times. Done lightheartedly, with wonderful chase sequences, tremendous sword battles in which no one was hurt, and very pretty heroines in dire danger, they were perhaps the most stylish pictures made in the twenties. Thousands of boys fenced with pieces of lath, leaped over walls, and swung from ropes after seeing *The Mark of Zorro, The Three Musketeers, The Thief of Baghdad,* or *The Black Pirate.* Fairbanks's films never took themselves seriously; in *Zorro,* in fact, the villainous Noah Beery, constantly frustrated by the ingenious bandit chief, finally threw down his sword, swore to be good, and joined the hero's jolly robber crew. For sheer enjoyment, his movies were surpassed only by the great comedy of the era.

Mack Sennett and Hal Roach kept the two-reeler comedy going for a long time, but in the early twenties the best comedians moved into full-length features of their own. Charles Chaplin, Harold Lloyd, and Buster Keaton built unforgettable characters into their films—the tramp with the battered derby, malacca cane, and funny walk; the fresh-faced, bespectacled, innocent American boy; the deadpan little man with the flat hat and the rubber-ball bounce. Keaton's *Sherlock Junior* (1924), Lloyd's *The Freshman* (1925), and Chaplin's *Gold Rush* (1925) touched a high point that movie comedy never reached again.

In 1926, probably the movies' best year, there were about 20,000 theaters in the United States, with new ones under construction at the rate of a thousand a year. The industry produced seven to eight hundred films a year for an audience that reached seven million daily and nine million on Sunday. Approximately five hundred of these theaters cost a million dollars, the great "palaces" in the cities much more. If the public wanted dreams on the screen, it needed dream palaces to show them in. "We visualize and dream," wrote one theater architect, "a magnificent amphitheater under a glorious moonlit sky in an Italian garden, in a Persian court, in a Spanish patio, or in a mystic Egyptian templeyard, all canopied by a soft moonlit sky." The costumed doorman, military-trained ushers, Grand Lobby, banks of softly-colored lights, "mighty Wurlitzer" organ, and gold leaf and Moorish architecture were all part of the ambiance of escape and splendor with which the movies surrounded themselves. Harold Rambosch, whose firm built and decorated some of the biggest theaters, saw them as

> . . . social safety valves in that the public can partake of the same luxuries as the rich and use them to the same full extent. No kings or emperors have wandered through such luxurious surroundings.

Rambosch specialized in a mixture of Moorish, Gothic, and Renaissance styles, with much gold leaf. John Eberson, another well-known designer, created an "atmospheric effect" with starlit skies and floating clouds, combined with French and Italian garden-style interiors. S. L. Rothafel's New York City Roxy, built in 1927 (demolished in 1960), represented the ultimate in movie-theater architecture: a rotunda roof fifty-eight by forty-one feet that weighed four tons; a lobby for two thousand people; 6,214 seats; 3 organ consoles and a 110-piece orchestra; 125 ushers; a ballet corps, hospital, and catering service.

The choice of the word "cathedral" to describe the Roxy was more apt than the public-relations man knew, for the public accepted the movies with an ardor and commitment granted to no other form of popular art. Nor could the critics decide if what the theaters showed was really "art." Kenneth McGowan, writing in 1921, thought they were not but could be; Thomas Craven, an art historian of note, thought they were a great democratic *American* art, "as indigenous as ice-water and the Red Indian . . . , an art that reaches the heart of the people." Stage actor Otis Skinner wrote in *The Ladies Home Journal* that movies could never be artistic; Charlie Chaplin replied that they were already "great popular art"; Cecil B. De Mille, whose article in the same series was titled "The Public Is Always Right," did not care one way or the other.

The silent film was really never silent, since a pianist or organist or orchestra always provided accompaniment and sound effects to match the action. Obviously films needed sound, however, before they could become a complete medium; action demanded sound, simply because in actual life nothing happened without it. Everyone in the industry experimented with sound from Edison on. A swift succession of technological improvements, after Lee DeForest produced a successful sound film in 1923, brought it to Hollywood quickly. William Fox leased the Swiss Tri-Ergon system in 1925 and released a Movietone sound short in 1926. Warner Brothers, using a system developed by Bell Telephone Laboratories, presented the first bill of talking and musical shorts at the Manhattan Opera House on August 6, 1926, together with *Don Juan*, a John Barrymore–May McAvoy silent feature accompanied by synchronized music. Then on October 16, 1927, Al Jolson's *The Jazz Singer* opened, really a silent film with four musical sequences. After finishing a song, Jolson (so the story goes) ad libbed the lines, "Wait a minute, wait a minute—You ain't heard nothin' yet folks, listen to this," and started the great Hollywood revolution. *The Jazz Singer* was such a hit that Warner's hastily put together an "all-talking" feature, *Lights of New York*, in 1928, which immediately broke *The Jazz Singer's* box-office record. Other studios frantically converted their silents into "talkies," while Fox in 1929 proclaimed *In Old Arizona* to be the first "all-talking movie filmed *outdoors*."

The effect on Hollywood was immediate. In 1927, the last year the silent film predominated, paid admissions for movies were $60,000,000. In 1929, when "talkies" began to replace silents, paid admissions reached $110,000,000—almost double. Throughout the worst of the depression years, there still seemed to be enough money left in the public's pocket to keep audience attendance up and films profitable. The changeover was amazingly swift; by late 1928, 1,300 theaters had installed sound; by late 1929, 10,000. During 1930 Hollywood produced 335 sound films, 95 more with sound sequences, and 175 silents. In 1931 there were exactly two silents—*Tabu* and Chaplin's *City Lights*.

The impact of sound simply shattered the industry. It added a realistic dimension to movies hitherto impossible to attain, since the audience heard as well as saw the action and was simultaneously involved in it. Everything audible was now available to the director, the writer, the actor—footsteps, raindrops, explosions, street noises, trains, laughter, screams, sobs, the whole range of the human voice and the whole spectrum of the world's sounds. A picture with a descriptive subtitle was clearly an imitation of experience; picture and sound together made the illusion almost the real thing. Sound speeded up the narrative, naturally, since information would be conveyed by sound and speech instead of by subtitles and pantomime. Sound also changed acting styles overnight; the exaggerations of expression and movement needed to project emotions from the silent screen were no longer necessary. An actor who could not use his voice could use only half his skill; seeing *and* hearing him closed the gap that subtitles always left between actor and viewer.

Understated, low-key acting became the order of the day; the contortions of the older Hollywood generation seemed ridiculous when combined with speech. Sound ruined some actors and actresses: Emil Jannings (Teutonic accent), Vilma Banky (Hungarian accent), Mae Murray (lisp), John Gilbert (high-pitched), Corrine Griffith (nasal), Clara Bow (rich Brooklynese). Sound also made actors and actresses (especially those who knew their trade) into stars more quickly than ever before: Bette Davis, Spencer Tracy, Clark Gable, Humphrey Bogart, Cary Grant, James Stewart, Myrna Loy, William Powell, Norma Shearer, Greta Garbo, Joan Crawford, various Barrymores, Gary Cooper, Frederic March, Charles Laughton, Claudette Colbert, Charles Boyer, Katherine Hepburn, Leslie Howard—among others. The public of the thirties accepted the new galaxy with an eagerness that made even the idolatry of the twenties seem tame; their names were, without exaggeration, household words.

Sound films not only added a powerful new member to the production crew—the sound engineer (*Broadway Melody* had to have fifteen of them) who had almost as much power as the director—but made the writer more important than he was before. Movies needed good dialogue and a great deal of it; not only was there no way to save a bad script, but a good one might save a bad picture. Meanwhile, the task of the director, always difficult, now demanded tremendous talent. He not only had to handle sound, but he had to know how to use all the techniques sound brought with it—dubbing, simultaneous sound, background sound, and a hundred new tricks that could add immeasurably to the films' effectiveness. Lewis Milestone's use of a distant birdsong to contrast with the deadly silence of the trenches in *All Quiet on the Western Front,* or Rouben Mamoulian's use of words echoing imposed over a close-up of Sylvia Sidney's agonized face in *City Streets,* showed what an inventive director could do with his new tools. And since sound tripled and sometimes quintupled the cost of a picture, studios could afford few mistakes. The tendency was, naturally, to make standardized films that would be sure to make money, so that while the introduction of sound might stimulate directors, writers, and actors to explore and experiment, it also forced front offices to look on experimentation with suspicion.

The film industry thus tended to develop certain commercially tested kinds of films and to stick with them. Within their boundaries actors, writers, and directors could (and often did) move brilliantly, making the most of the opportunities sound presented. Hollywood of course remade the classics again with *Tale of Two Cities, David Copperfield,* and *Wuthering Heights,* and (like popular drama) translated best-selling novels like *The Good Earth* and *Gone With the Wind* into cinematic hits. The "horror" movie, popularized by Lon Chaney's fifteen silent films, found sound much to its advantage. Bela Lugosi as Dracula, adapted from Bram Stoker's nineteenth-century shocker, and Boris Karloff as Frankenstein's monster, based on Mary Shelley's old gothic thriller, set the pattern for an interminable line of successors down to tongue-in-cheek potboilers like *Son of the Monster, Bride of Frankenstein, Frankenstein Meets the Wolfman,* and *I Was a Teenage Werewolf.* As late as 1960 Hollywood was still producing a hundred horror films a year.

Since sound obviously meant music too, Hollywood (at first ineptly) hastened to transfer musical comedies from stage to screen by the dozens —*The Vagabond King, Desert Song, Sunny,* and so on—emphasizing as the stage did tunes, costumes, girls, pretentious production numbers, and inconsequential plots, well represented by the filmed operettas starring Jeannette MacDonald and Nelson Eddy, beginning with *Rose Marie* in 1936. Metro-Goldwyn-Mayer's *Broadway Melody* in 1929 inaugurated a cycle of "all-talking, all-singing, all-dancing!" musicals while Busby Berkeley, who choreographed Eddie Cantor's *Whoopee!* in 1930, created a pattern for opulent staging that lasted for over a decade. Later Broadway dancer Fred Astaire, usually teamed with Ginger Rogers as his partner, developed a stylish, sophisticated film in which story line, music, dancing, and cleverly understated camera work were integrated into a skillful new kind of movie musical. Pictures like Astaire's *Top Hat* (1935), *Swingtime* (1936), and *Carefree* (1938) have rarely been equaled for grace and lightness of touch.

The effects of sound on comedy were swift. The silents depended on pantomime and slapstick, emphasizing the humor of character and situation. Since sound added a whole new dimension, the wisecrack became as important as the sight-gag. Comics like Keaton, Langdon, Lloyd, and even Chaplin, who had brought silent comedy to a high art, were suddenly crowded out by stand-up Broadway comics like Ed Wynn, Lou Holtz, Bobby Clark, Jimmy Durante, Bob Hope, and the Marx Brothers. W. C. Fields, one of the few who made the transition, made it because he was also an uncommonly good actor. Hope, who was never particularly good at visual comedy but who epitomized the wisecracker, proved to be the most durable of all.

Sound naturally brought the "singing Western," with heroes whose chief weapons were guitars and thirty-piece orchestras, like Gene Autry, Roy Rogers, Tex Ritter, and others. Rogers and Autry, who made six to eight pictures a year, each sure to gross $650,000, were among Hollywood's safest investments. "Action" Westerns, perennially popular, appeared with routine titles like *Blazing Guns* or *Sundown Canyon*. These so-called oaters, singing or nonsinging, returned 50 per cent or more profits so consistently that in 1946 over a quarter of all films produced were Westerns.

Three "gangster" films, Edward G. Robinson's *Little Caesar* (1930), James Cagney's *Public Enemy* (1931), and Paul Muni's *Scarface* (1932) set off a series of hard-boiled movies which reflected the same public mood as the popular "hard-boiled dick" and "private eye" novels. Their clipped, pungent dialogue, realistic sets, and newsreel quality left marks on movie-making styles throughout the thirties. Fifty gangster films were released in 1931 alone; when the flood of violence provoked a public reaction, Hollywood simply turned the plot over and made "G-Men" the heroes. Much of the same hard, realistic approach characterized the "message" pictures of the socially-conscious thirties, among them *I Am a Fugitive from a Chain Gang* (1932), *Wild Boys of the Road* (1933), Paul Muni's *Pasteur, Zola,* and *Juarez* (1935, 1937, 1939), *Dead End* (1937), and *The Grapes of Wrath* (1939).

By the end of the decade, many directors had learned how to use sound, and how to put together all the elements of filmmaking in original, creative ways. John Ford, in *The Informer* (1935), *Stagecoach* (1939), *The Grapes of Wrath* (1939), and *The Long Voyage Home* (1940), produced a distinguished series of films that still remain among the classics. Alfred Hitchcock, an English import, created a psychological-horror thriller at the opposite pole from the Chaney-Lugosi-Karloff screamers. His *Thirty-Nine Steps* (1935) introduced a finely-honed, elegantly terrifying kind of movie which became his personal property. The mark of the "Hitchcock Style" has appeared on hundreds of movies since. Frank Capra's brand of light comedy with social overtones set another style—*It Happened One Night* (1934, Gable and Colbert); *The Thin Man* (1934, William Powell and Myrna Loy); *Nothing Sacred* (1937, Gable and Carole Lombard); *You Can't Take It With You* (1938, Lionel Barrymore and others); *Bringing Up Baby* (1938, Cary Grant). As a kind of summary of everything that went on in the Hollywood of the thirties, Orson Welles made *Citizen Kane* (1941), one of the half-dozen most technically influential films ever released.

It was chiefly through the adaptation of sound (and later color) to the animated cartoon that it emerged in the thirties as an unusually popular and profitable form of film entertainment. Experiments in the nineties produced successful cartoons in the early 1900's; Winsor McKay's *Gertie the Dinosaur* (1910) which used 10,000 sketches, and a number of other comic strip characters were transferred to the screen without attracting much attention. The most imaginative cartoonist to work exclusively with film was Max Fleischer, who created a series in the twenties, *Out of the Inkwell*, starring Koko the Clown, Billy Boop, and Betty Boop, all quite popular—and when revived on television forty years later, amazingly deft and skillfully done. By the thirties the cartoon was a standard program item, usually following the newsreel before the feature.

Walt Disney, who began making animated cartoons in the twenties, drew Mickey Mouse in 1928 in a short called *Steamboat Willie*, the first such film to coordinate music, dialogue, and sound effects with the drawings, which made all the difference. As Pluto, Goofy, Donald Duck and others followed, Disney's cartoons became the best-known on the screen. Convinced that the cartoon had wider possibilities, Disney introduced color, used more sophisticated plots, and improved animation. In 1937 he produced *Snow White and the Seven Dwarfs*, the first feature-length cartoon, which required six hundred artists, two million drawings, and four years to make. After that Disney dominated the field with productions of *Fantasia, Pinocchio, Bambi*, and *Sleeping Beauty*, moving to live features in 1948.

In the forties a number of younger artists tried to break out of the pattern Disney had imposed on the cartoon, among them Norman McLaren and Mary Ellen Bute, who tried some interesting experimental adult cartoons, while Stephen Bosustow's *Mr. Magoo* and *Gerald McBoing-Boing*, beginning in the fifties, set off in a new direction. To a large extent, however, Disney's shadow continued to dominate the form. He won thirty Academy awards (more than anyone else in movie history) and made his name synonymous with cartooning. No other single character in the film industry—except possibly Chaplin's little tramp—was ever so widely known in the world as Mickey Mouse. Hailed by some critics as a cinematic genius and rejected by others as no more than a child's showman, Disney had an unfailing instinct for the right touch at the right moment, and an infallible identification with the illusions, dreams, and values of the average man. What he did best, of course, was the fairy tale, the oldest and most universally human of all forms of popular entertainment, using the tremendous resources of film to tell it as no one had ever been able to tell it before. The number of people who have seen a Disney cartoon defies calculation. *Snow White* alone played theaters somewhere in the world continuously for thirty-one years and still does, its sound track dubbed in fourteen languages.

During the late thirties and early forties just about everybody went to the movies, which reached and remained on what seemed to be a permanent plateau of popularity. In 1939, 65 per cent of the national population went to the movies at least once a week. The industry employed 282,000 people, produced fourteen short subjects and ten feature films a week. The love affairs of Clark Gable and Carole Lombard, or Robert Taylor and Barbara Stanwyck, were vicariously shared national passions; the Los Angeles Museum of History, Science, and Art, with a fine sense of historicity, in 1939, added to its collections the very sarong worn by Dorothy Lamour in *Her Jungle Lover*.

The introduction of radio, despite predictions, hurt movie attendance little at first and shortly not at all. Television, however, was a quite different matter. There were marketable sets in 1939, but they did not appear in quantity until after the close of World War II—with shattering effects on Hollywood. Movie attendance in 1947 averaged eighty-five to ninety million a week; in 1957 it was half that. At the same time the number of television sets in the country increased from 200,000 in 1947 to twelve million in 1951 to twenty million in 1952, and so on. In 1945 there were 20,000 movie theaters; in the early sixties half that. A statistical study in Southern California showed that in 1946 the average moviegoer attended a theater four times a month; in 1950 three and two-tenths times, in 1951 two and three-tenths, in 1952 one and three-tenths times. Instead of going to the movies, millions of people were staying home to watch television—free.

The movie industry at first shrugged it off, barring the televised use of film strips, forbidding stars to appear on television programs, trying to buy stations themselves. Samuel Goldwyn, writing in 1951, believed that television would actually create larger audiences for movies by encouraging Hollywood to make bigger and better films, but he was whistling in the dark. Even double and triple features failed to bring them in. More theaters closed each year, although the construction of "drive-in" movies kept up attendance figures that otherwise would have plummeted. Movies had been shown outside in 1914, but the drive-in derived from Richard Hollingshead's experimental four-hundred-car outdoor theater in Camden, New Jersey, which opened in June, 1933. Appealing to the family trade ("Kar and Kiddies Free!") drive-ins provided prizes, playpens, popcorn, and privacy in addition to movies. Interestingly enough, an analysis of the movie trade in the mid-fifties showed that a large percentage of receipts (in the case of drive-ins, over half) came from sales of food and soft drinks. A poor man's theater after the fashion of the old nickelodeons, drive-ins demanded simple, inexpensive, grade-B movies like *Lost Girls, Blood on the Saddle, Dracula Meets the Son of Frankenstein,* or *A Marriage of Shame,* which Hollywood hastened to make.

Television's inroads on movie audiences amounted almost to catastrophe. In 1946 people were going to the movies at the number of eighty-two million a week; by 1950 only about thirty-six million Americans went weekly, and even by the early sixties, despite a large increase in population, attendance reached not much more than half of what it had been at its peak. As a result, Hollywood needed to make only two hundred pictures a year in the mid-fifties instead of the five hundred to eight hundred it needed to fill the theater screens in its prosperous days. With each film a costlier and riskier gamble, studios could not afford to take chances. Even "safe" older types—crime, Western, sex, comedy, historical epic—cost $800,-000 and up, so Hollywood made them by the dozens, strictly to formula. On the assumption that more of the same (that is, more stars, more extras, more scenery, more sex, and more cost) would guarantee success Hollywood turned to spectacular "blockbusters" like *My Fair Lady* (1952, five and a half million), De Mille's remake of his *Ten Commandments* (1956, thirteen and a half million), *Ben Hur* yet again (1959, fifteen million), *Mutiny on the Bounty* (remade 1962, eighteen million), and *Cleopatra* (1963, four hours and thirty-three minutes, thirty-seven million).

Elizabeth Taylor's and Richard Burton's *Cleopatra* was the last of the old-style spectaculars—overheated publicity, astronomical costs, "cast of thousands," opulent sets, elephants and soldiers, and a torrid off-screen affair between the stars. Investments of this size discouraged experimentation and innovation; neither did they always make profits. Hoping to engage the audience in contemporary issues, Hollywood turned also to "message" movies about things like juvenile delinquency, alcoholism, race prejudice, religious bigotry, and the like, with *Gentlemen's Agreement, Pinky, Crossfire, Lost Weekend, Boomerang,* and others. In addition, striking at television's most obvious weakness, its small screen, the industry developed wide-screen, three-dimensional processes like Cinerama, Vista-Vision, and Todd-AO.

The film industry reached a kind of uneasy stability in the mid-sixties, when attendance settled down to a yearly average of about forty million customers per week (in 1949 it was seventy million) and the number of theaters, including drive-ins, remained at about 21,000. Noticeably, however, the national population increased by fifty-two million over the years from 1949–69, and the 21,000 theaters represented less than four-fifths of the movie houses open in the late forties. Major producers and independent studios turned out less than half the number of films in 1968 as in 1948—180 as against 366—but the smaller weekly audience, reflecting the affluent society from which it derives, paid in considerably more money for movie admissions; one and one-tenth billion dollars, an increase of over one-third. Significantly, the films never regained the "mature audience" they lost in the fifties to television and other attractions. An American Research Bureau report in 1969 on Detroit's moviegoing audience (no doubt duplicated in other cities) showed that the greatest potential audience for films lay in the twelve to thirty-plus age group, especially in its sixteen to twenty-two segment. Similar nationwide surveys indicate that fifty-two per cent of the movie audience remains under the age of twenty, seventy-two per cent of it under thirty. Successful theater managers, therefore, tend to pay little attention to the movie critics, who in their estimation view films in terms of an older, inconsequential audience. "The true test of a big picture," remarked Martin Shafer of Detroit's Suburban Theaters, Inc., "is its gross. Our job is to determine what the public wants." Since Hell's Angels, 1969 outdrew by more than four times a picture unanimously acclaimed by the critics, The Lion in Winter, in his theaters in 1969, his attitude is understandable.

Since Hollywood always made money from sex and sensation, films of the sixties were no exceptions. After an innocuous comedy The Moon Is Blue failed to receive approval of the industry's review board and did well at the box office, studios emphasized the sexual and the sensational. Between 1960 and 1966 American movies either featured or suggested drug addiction, rape, incest, prostitution, nymphomania, voyeurism, homosexuality, lesbianism, cannibalism, and necrophilia, nor has the trend showed signs of lessening. Meanwhile Pillow Talk (1959) reinstated the sophisticated sex comedy, popularized thirty years earlier by Lubitsch and De Mille. The "problem" or "message" movie remained standard fare, particularly those dealing with racial prejudice like Nothing But a Man, Black Like Me, One Potato, Two Potato, Guess Who's Coming to Dinner, and In the Heat of the Night. Somewhat surprisingly, films also got into politics, a topic they had always avoided, with Dr. Strangelove, Seven Days in May, The Best Man, and The Manchurian Candidate, among others.

Spectaculars in the sixties did fairly well (Genghis Khan, Spartacus, Exodus, The Alamo, Lawrence of Arabia, The Greatest Story Ever Told); so did war pictures (King Rat, Battle of the Bulge, Von Ryan's Express). A whole cycle of "spy" pictures, encouraged by the success of Ian Fleming's "James Bond" novels, appeared later (Dr. No, Goldfinger, Casino

Royale, Thunderball); sophisticated crime (*In Cold Blood, Bonnie and Clyde*, updated versions of the gangster films of the thirties) did very well indeed.

Of the traditional types, Westerns and musicals stood their ground best. The fifties and sixties abounded with good Westerns—Alan Ladd's *Shane*, Gregory Peck's *The Gunfighter*, John Wayne's *The Searchers* and his later *True Grit*, Henry Fonda's *The Tin Star*; James Stewart's *Shenandoah*, Kirk Douglas's *Lonely Are the Brave*, and at least a dozen others. The "big" musicals of the fifties—*An American in Paris, My Fair Lady, Band Wagon, The King and I*—attracted large audiences, but *West Side Story* (1961) set off a chain of successes. *West Side Story* showed a profit of 32.5 million dollars by 1969, *Mary Poppins* 48.6 million, *Thoroughly Modern Millie* 30 million. *The Sound of Music* (1965), based on the story of the singing Trapp family, had the largest box-office gross in film history: 112 million dollars in its first four years. As of January, 1969, Hollywood had sixteen new musicals in the making or ready to release.

While some (but by no means all) of the "big" pictures make money, steady, safe returns lie in the low budget pictures done for the drive-in, triple-feature trade, the films that titillate, enthrall, and amuse mass audiences at cheap prices just as the melodrama, vaudeville, farce, popular novel, and dime shocker always have. Out of Hollywood's total yearly production of films probably not more than one-quarter have ever been high-budget "A" films with well-known stars. The rest have been routine bread-and-butter productions designed to fill in between "Spectaculars" and "Blockbusters," providing the night-to-night bills needed to keep the house partly filled on Tuesdays and Thursdays.

Great stars made only a limited number of films per year; the rest of the time screens were occupied by undistinguished movies with minor players. These routine "B" movies were the cinematic equivalents of the cheap novel on the newsstand, the sentimental melodrama in the tent show, the mass-produced magazine serial; they were and are stylized popular art aimed at nothing but transitory entertainment. They stayed with the trends, took no risks, disturbed nobody, raised no problems, simplified issues, and gave the public entertainment and not "art." Although they represent by far the majority of films produced over the years, their titles and the people who played in them are long forgotten, and appear in none of the many histories of the movies.

To examine what movie theaters actually played, week in and week out, over the years shows how much of that which appeared on the screen was simple, mass-produced entertainment. 1919, for example, featured a number of well-done "A" films, among them Richard Barthelmess's *Bro-*

ken Blossoms. On the other hand, during the first week of May, 1919, most of the movie houses in St. Louis were showing film versions of Harold Bell Wright's best-selling novels, *The Shepherd of The Hills* and *The Eyes of the World,* three Westerns, five sex shows (*The Parisian Tigress, The Home Breaker, Spotlight Sadie, Are You Fit to Marry?,* and *The Amazing Wife*), and three crime-mysteries (*Help, Help, Police!, Shadows of Suspicion, One of the Finest*). Not one could be called, by any stretch of the critical imagination, distinguished cinema. Ten years later, when *The Virginian* and *In Old Arizona* drew crowds and *Broadway Melody* was chosen "outstanding film of the year," all were playing in St. Louis in early May, but three-quarters of theaters were showing action pictures like *The Duke Steps Out* (four theaters); crime-suspense like *Alias Jimmy Valentine* (three theaters); a great deal of sex—*Not Quite Decent, His Captive Woman, Why Be Good, Scandal, Girls Gone Wild, The Wild Party, Shady Lady* (seven theaters)—and four Westerns.

Washington in May, 1939, did about the same. This was the year of *All the King's Men, Dark Victory,* and *Champion,* all first-rate movies; but of the city's thirty-eight theaters, twenty-four were showing films like *Come On Rangers, Lawless Valley, Thundering West, Boy Trouble, Woman's Doctor, Off the Record, Burn 'Em Up O'Connor,* and *Blondie,* adapted from Chic Young's comic strip. There was not much change in movie fare in St. Louis in May, 1949, where there were thirty-five drive-ins alone, not one playing an "A" picture. Audiences could see *The Younger Brothers,* a particularly violent Western, at thirty-six theaters; six showed gangster-crime pictures (*Race Street, Junior G-Men, Jinx Money, Dillinger,* and so on); *Smart Girls Don't Talk, Confessions of a Nudist,* and *Ladies of the Street* furnished sex interest; one could also see *The Bowery Boys* (four theaters) or an air-epic, *Eagle Squadron.*

In New York in May, 1959, sixteen theaters had *Al Capone;* twenty-six presented a double feature, *The Horrors of the Black Museum* and *The Headless Ghost.* Detroit's movies, in May, 1969, represented the range of modern Hollywood. There were two award-winning films on view (*Charly, The Lion in Winter*) but forty-eight theaters were showing horror, sex, crime, and Westerns: *Dracula Has Risen from the Grave* (seven), *Hang 'Em High* (Western, four), *Assignment to Kill* (spy-crime, eight), *Hammerhead* (private eye, six), *Monica's Thing* (sex, six), *The Degenerates* (six), *The Wicked Die Slow* (Western violence, six), and an assortment that included *Raw Weekend, Busty Brown, Chamber of Horrors, A Woman's Urge, Her Odd Tastes, Makeout Suburban Style,* and *Corridors of Blood.* It is not likely that the memory of any of these will survive, yet they and others like them provide one-half or more of American cinematic entertainment year after year.

These kinds of movies have furnished entertainment for mass audiences for seventy-five years. Dore Schary, a successful producer and thoughtful student of films, once pointed out that most durable, and in the long run the most profitable, movies are those which conventionalize basic popular tastes and present them simply and clearly in an acceptable context. Sex, suspense, violence, and sentiment have sold and will continue to sell movies as they have books, plays, comic strips, and everything else in the popular arts. The film, then, represents the transference to a new medium of much the same fictional and dramatic materials which have always characterized the entertainment industry. The motion picture is not and never was a new *kind* of popular art, but only a new way of presenting the same stuff to a wider audience in more effective terms. Books and plays have always been Hollywood's primary sources of materials, translated (often with great skill) to the screen; so few movies have used original scripts that the answer, "No, but I saw the movie," supplies its own question. Like any other popular art, motion pictures are made to make money; like the Elizabethan revenge play, the Restoration comedy, and the nineteenth-century melodrama, they deal with dramatic themes and in dramatic patterns that can be repeated profitably and indefinitely. What *Current Opinion* said in 1922 about Hollywood still holds true, that "movies are business in bulk, sold and oversold . . . like soap and motorcars." "It's not our business to promote the culture of the country, or to make art films," Herbert Solow, head of M-G-M's production told a reporter in 1969, "It's to make money for the studio."

THE AUDIBLE BECOMES VISIBLE: RADIO AND TELEVISION

What have you done with my child?

—LEE DE FOREST, INVENTOR OF THE AUDION, IN 1947

A number of experiments with the wireless transmission of sound during the latter years of the nineteenth century, culminating with Lee De Forest's invention of the audion tube in 1906, brought radio. Its chief use, it was assumed, would be commercial, replacing the telegraph and telephone, but its lack of privacy (anybody who had a receiver could listen) discouraged that. De Forest, as early as 1909, speculated that the public nature of radio might really be its greatest strength, for it might furnish, he wrote, "a means by which opera can be brought into every home; someday the news, and even advertising, will be sent out to the public on wireless telephone." He said nothing of entertainment, but young David Sarnoff, working for the Marconi Wireless Company in 1916, recognized the possibilities very clearly. He sent a memo to his superiors recommending the manufacture of a radio music box "which would make radio a household utility in the same sense as the piano or phonograph. The idea is to bring music into the house by wireless."

By the time Sarnoff became commercial manager for the Radio Corporation of America in 1920, his suggestion was a reality. Experimental stations were already broadcasting news, records, and market reports, and there were stations in Pittsburgh, Detroit, Chicago, Newark, and other cities. Pittsburgh's KDKA sent out the first preadvertised, scheduled broadcast on November 2, 1920. Eight more stations went on the air that year; there were five hundred three years later, and General Electric sold eleven million receivers that year. (An eight-tube RCA with five dials and a speaker cost $275.)

Early performers on radio received no fee or a token one, a state of affairs which lasted very briefly. The pressing problem for stations, obviously, was how to pay for broadcasts. Manufacturers of receivers at first considered subsidizing stations in order to stimulate the sale of sets, a plan that proved unworkable. When WEAF in New York sold ten minutes of air time on August 28, 1922, to a real estate company to advertise an apartment house named Hawthorne Court, it set the course of radio financing. Although Herbert Hoover, Secretary of Commerce, believed that "the American people will never stand for advertising on the air," it was soon certain that they would, and that it was the easiest and most profitable way of paying for radio. (By way of contrast, the Pepsi-Cola commercial song, "Pepsi-Cola hits the spot . . . ," was played 296,426 times in 1941, which apparently remains the record.) The question of whether or not radio should be privately-owned and financed by advertising, or a publicly-owned system financed by subsidy, was never considered by Congress or any other body. Radio was considered from the first to be private enterprise.

If the "commercial" was radio's first foundation stone, centralization was the other. As stations competed for talent and costs climbed, it was good business to combine a number of stations into a "network" so that expenses could be divided. Making it possible for each station to carry the same program at the same time to a mass audience had also the added advantage of disseminating the commercial message more widely. American Telephone and Telegraph set up a small network in 1923; in 1926 RCA announced the formation of the National Broadcasting Company (nineteen stations); the Columbia chain emerged in 1927. The Federal government, caught by surprise by the swift development of this powerful and tremendously profitable communication industry, had no way of supervising it except under the terms of an inadequate act dating from 1912. Not until 1927 with the creation of the Federal Radio Commission and a licensing act did the industry come under any meaningful control. By that time the two basic principles on which radio was based—advertising and consolidation—were firmly established. The whole process, from eight rather tentative stations, more or less, in 1920, to three hundred stations and two chains, took almost exactly nine years.

The twenties was a decade of firsts, during which radio—chiefly by trial and error—developed its own patterns of content and methods of operation. Coverage of the Dempsey-Carpentier fight in 1921 showed its great potential for sports; Graham McNamee started broadcasting baseball games in 1923; the first cross-country hookup broadcast the Rose Bowl game in 1927. (Worried about the suitability of a football game as the occasion for this epoch-making event, the networks scheduled the New York Symphony for the same evening.) Broadcasting the national party conventions of 1924 showed radio's political possibilities. When stage comic Ed Wynn, hired for a program in 1922, found that he could not work before a microphone in an empty studio, the staff hastily assembled scrubwomen, passersby, and employees for the first "studio audience." Gimbel's sponsored the first hour-long musical broadcast in 1922; the first "remote" danceband pickup, of Vincent Lopez's orchestra from the Hotel Pennsylvania in 1921, brought so many people to the hotel that the manager called the police. Vaughn de Leath, the first female radio singer, sang softly into the microphone in order not to strain the station's delicate equipment and invented "crooning," radio's distinctive vocal style.

Radio's artists, producers, and sponsors probed the medium's boundaries through the early twenties, finding out what it could do well and what it could not. Radio's great appeal was its simultaneity, the sense it gave the listener of having heard things exactly as they happened when they happened, a "now" quality it shared with no other medium. Radio closed the time-gap between event and audience as neither film nor record could—to use a favorite announcers' phrase, it was "up-to-the-minute." Second, radio had a person-to-person quality that gave an illusion of private, face-to-face communication. Though an audience might number millions, each individual listened separately, not in a crowd but at home, in familiar surroundings, possibly alone. Third, in radio the listener constructed the picture that went with the sound however he liked; since the set gave him none, he created a perfect one, seeing the speaker, event, or situation as he wished it to be. Radio could improve on actuality itself, something that film (and even television) could not do.

Radio provided sound, the listener filled out the rest in his mind. The loudspeaker made an illusion real by music, voice inflections, sound effects; with its help the audience could make a castle from a few bars of song, a city street from taxi-horns and street cries, a forest from a wind machine and a few bird chirps. The actual sound of snapping bones was never so authentic as soda crackers crunched near the microphone; a knife stuck into a cabbage head was a very real stab in the heart. The Cavern of the Great Worm in "Lights Out," the Lone Ranger's "fiery horse with the speed of light," and the excited bustle of first-night at "The Little Theater Off Times Square" could be seen in the mind as they never could on film or in a book.

Taking advantage of its unique quality of contemporaneity, early radio emphasized "special events" broadcasts—a William Jennings Bryan speech, the Army-Navy game, the Scopes trial in Tennessee, election returns of 1924 and 1928, the World Series, the arrival of the *Graf Zeppelin*, the Chicago Opera, Lindbergh's flight. "Special broadcasts" sometimes bordered on the ridiculous—the sound of an egg frying on a sidewalk in hot weather, a baby robin's first cheep, the roar of Niagara Falls—which a good sound effects man could do better. Nevertheless, audiences never seemed to tire of the delight of hearing things, not even when one desperate announcer, caught with a short script, held the microphone out the window and announced, "Ladies and gentlemen, the sounds of the city, brought to you directly as they happen!"

Like the movies, radio quickly produced "stars." Announcers like Graham McNamee, Milton Cross, Phillips Carlin, Frank Gallop, Norman Brokenshire, and James Wallington commanded large salaries and enthusiastic followings. (McNamee received 50,000 letters after the 1925 World Series; Leo Fitzpatrick in Kansas City enrolled two million listeners in his Nighthawk Club.) Comedians like Wynn, Cantor, and Will Rogers; orchestra leaders like Lopez, Wayne King, and Paul Tremaine; singers like Arthur Tracy ("The Street Singer") and Joseph White ("The Silver Masked Tenor," who wore a sterling silver mask in public) had millions of fans.

Jessica Dragonette, who sang on the Cities Service Hour, drew 150,-000 people to Chicago's Grant Park for a personal appearance, and 15,-000 in Minneapolis during a below-zero blizzard and a taxi strike. The year 1929, which marked the appearance on radio of Kate Smith, Bing Crosby, Rudy Vallée, and Freeman Gosden's and Charles Correll's "Amos and Andy" show, opened radio's golden age of popularity. With the help of the movies, radio ruined what was left of traditional "show business." Practically every vaudeville and stage star who could do so shifted to radio, where money and sponsors waited; "show business," wrote *Variety* in 1925, "is helpless against radio," for as *Broadcasting* magazine said, "You can get Eddie Cantor on the air for nothing."

The decade of the thirties, when everybody listened to radio and few criticized, was radio's own. Since one-third of all Americans owned at least one radio, the potential audience for a program was figured at sixty million. It was most assuredly big business, the value of air time measured in seconds; an hour on NBC in 1931 cost a minimum of $10,000; more for the best time. Program ratings, designed to measure audiences, appeared in 1931, the first attempt to put the problem of cost in relation to effectiveness on a business basis. If a program had a huge audience

("Amos and Andy," for example, once held two-thirds of the entire listening audience) it naturally charged more for sponsorship, until many became so expensive that they were syndicated and recorded for re-broadcasts. With thousands of dollars involved in a single program (Eddie Cantor cost one hundred dollars a minute) it was obvious that stations could not handle the business by themselves. Instead agencies sold "packaged" shows—stars, script, production, direction, sound effects—to sponsors, a business operation that remained the same for thirty years and was passed intact into television.

Agencies developed radio shows like pieces of merchandise, made to sell to as many people as possible. Successful shows tended to sound alike because they were; sponsors, in fact, suspected too much originality since it might detract from the effectiveness of their "brief message" and since it involved risks which could be financially disastrous. The sponsor and the agency, then, began quite early to determine the trend of radio entertainment and nobody had illusions otherwise. "American radio," said J. Harold Ryan, president of the National Association of Broadcasters in 1925,

> . . . is the product of American business. If the legend still persists that a radio station is some kind of art center, a technical museum, or a little piece of Hollywood transplanted strangely to your home town, then the first official act of the second quarter century should be to list it along with the local dairies, banks, bakeries, and filling stations.

The comedian was king in the thirties, his popularity cutting across all age and interest groups. A survey in 1935 showed that 65 per cent of radio's listeners preferred comedies over any other programs, and the air was filled with them. Eddie Cantor, Ed Wynn, Jack Benny, Fred Allen, Bob Burns, Fanny Brice, Bob Hope, Jimmy Durante, Jack Pearl, Joe Cook, Lou Holtz, Joe Penner, and Milton Berle, to name a few, came from vaudeville or the nightclub circuit. Comedy teams—Burns and Allen, Fibber and Molly, Easy Aces, Vic and Sade, Myrt and Marge, Lum and Abner, and of course Amos and Andy—were all surefire.

Musical programs came next in audience preference: the Cliquot Club Eskimos, Ralph Ginsburg and his Palmer House Ensemble, Phil Spitalny and his All-Girl Orchestra (featuring Evelyn and her Magic Violin), the Lady Esther Serenade, the Bell Telephone Hour, the indomitable A. and P. Gypsies. Remote broadcasts from nightclubs, hotels, and dance halls were standard late-evening programs that brought dozens of bands into prominence—George Olsen, Abe Lyman, Peter Van Steeden,

Leo Reisman, Harry Sosnik, Blue Barron, Jan Garber. It was the best of all possible worlds for musicians. Almost every station of consequence had an announcer who said at 11:30 P.M.:

> And now, from the beautiful Bamboo Room of the Hotel Belton in the heart of downtown Des Moines, WHO sends you the dancing music of Joe Spivak and his Serenaders, featuring Scotty Smith and his golden sax, with their theme song . . .

Thousands of youths stayed up late to hear the Coon-Sanders Night-hawks from Kansas City, Art Kassel and Wayne King from the Trianon-Aragon, Hal Kemp from the Blackhawk, Larry Clinton from the Glen Island Casino, or the Dorseys from Frank Daly's Meadowbrook. With a little imagination they were there, and it was exciting.

Radio in the thirties developed the news report to a high point of popularity. Floyd Gibbons, who wore an eye-patch and talked faster than any man in radio, was the first "personality" reporter, followed by "com-mentators" who interpreted and editorialized on the news—doom-voiced Boake Carter, precise H. V. Kaltenborn, stagey Gabriel Heatter ("There's good news toNIGHT!"), chatty Lowell Thomas, professorial Edwin C. Hill, and later a younger group of professionals, Shirer, Trout, Swing, Murrow. Surveys taken in the early forties showed that 40 per cent of the listeners preferred radio to newspapers for news reporting.

"Gossip reporters," transferred from the newspapers, like Walter Winchell and Jimmie Fidler, had large followings; so did "girl talk" shows with "Martha Deane," "Beatrice Fairfax," "Betty Moore," and, under her own name, Mary Margaret McBride. Contest, audience participation, panel, and "game" shows were wildly popular: Professor Quiz, Dr. I.Q. ("I have a lady in the balcony, Doctor"), Hobby Lobby, True or False. A Brooklyn cabdriver named Lester Kroll, using the name of "Mr. Anthony," discovered what the "confession" magazines had long known; that everybody loves somebody else's misery. His "Goodwill Hour," dur-ing which he interviewed people with pathetically difficult personal prob-lems and gave them crude advice, brought him three thousand dollars a week and made "And what is your problem, Madam?" a national catch-line. His agony program had many imitators and successors, like "Queen for a Day," "Welcome Travellers," and "Strike It Rich."

The daily audience's greatest devotion, however, was reserved for the serial drama or "soap opera" (so-called because of the number of soap company sponsors), which reached its climax in the late thirties when a housewife could listen to them for seven consecutive hours daily. It was, wrote James Thurber in nostalgic recollection,

   . . . a kind of sandwich, whose recipe is simple enough, although it took years to compound. Between thick slices of advertising, spread twelve minutes of dialogue, add predicament, villainy, and female suffering in equal measure, throw in a dash of nobility, sprinkle with tears, season with organ music, cover with a rich announcer sauce, and serve five times a week.

The serial drama came in episodes of fifteen minutes to a half hour, from one to five times a week; a sequence usually took three to four weeks to complete, with the next section introduced as a subplot about the third week. Each sequence began and closed with trouble, with a week of tranquility in the middle. (One serial was frankly titled "Trouble House" and another "Lonely Women.") Serials had no beginning or end, for they simply began or ended with the sponsorship. Happy serials never succeeded; a three-day listening sample in 1938 disclosed stories dealing with adultery, divorce, illegitimacy, forgery, greed, possible incest, arson, murder, robbery, suicide, alcoholism, mental illness, bigamy, embezzlement, and accidental death. Studies showed that the more personal problems the listener had, the more serials she (almost all listeners were women) listened to. The average housewife listened to 6.6 regularly; those who listened least heard two; the most twenty-two.

   Each serial sequence followed much the same format: thirty seconds of organ music, followed by a synopsis of the plot ending with a lead-in to today's episode—"Can Eve tell Mark that the chances of proving his innocence are slim, now that Mary will testify against him if Harry dies, and if Elizabeth stays in Chicago with Aunt Hester?" The episode ended with another question, "What will Eve say when Cousin Lionel tells the District Attorney what he saw that night at the country-club dance?" with the tag-line, "Listen again tomorrow at the same time." A good many actors and actresses played in nothing else; Fran Carlin played in six serials year after year, J. Allan Smythe played Father Barbour on "One Man's Family" for twenty-seven years. Jim Backus, Tyrone Power, Frank Lovejoy, Martha Scott, Don Ameche, Art Carney, and Mercedes McCambridge, among other young actors, made a living in them.

   Serial dramas were mass-produced by assembly-line techniques, much like the older popular novels. Frank and Anne Hummert, who formed a corporation to write them, had a stable of writers who turned out episodes at $125 a week for a five-week series. At one time they had sixty-seven shows a week on the air, worth nine million dollars in air time; in 1938 Hummert serials totaled five million words, the equivalent of fifty-five novels. The Hummerts did "Our Gal Sunday," and a dozen others, including "Other Wife" (a businessman, his wife, and his secretary). Charles Andrews wrote "Just Plain Bill" (a small-town barber-philosopher) and "Mary Noble, Backstage Wife" about a plain girl married to a famous actor. (Comedians Bob and Ray had a boisterous parody titled "Mary Backstage, Noble Wife," about a girl married to an actor-heel named Harry Backstage.) Elaine Carrington wrote "When a Girl Marries" and "Pepper Young's Family"; Irma Phillips wrote "Road of Life" and "The Right to Happiness"; Sandra Michael "Against the Storm," and Carleton Morse the best of them, "One Man's Family." Polls showed that listeners believed serials gave them valuable guidance toward solving their own problems, and that they felt better able to bear their own troubles after hearing others'. "I can get through the day better," one woman wrote, "when I hear they have sorrows too."

Except for variety-comedy shows, much of the evening programming was given over to drama. The "First-Nighter" programs (1929–53), which seemed always to star two competent veterans, Barbara Luddy and Les Tremayne, was exceptionally durable. De Mille's Lux Radio Theater, Grand Central Station, The Philip Morris Playhouse, The Texaco Theater, and others specialized in expertly presented professional theater, often with "name" stars. The dramatic staple, however, was the quarter- or half-hour adventure-detective-crime-suspense show with a continuing cast—detectives Sam Spade, Martin Kane, Boston Blackie, Mr. Keen, The Fat Man, The Thin Man; Jack Armstrong, Captain Midnight, Sky King, Renfrew of the Royal Mounted, Sergeant Preston of the Yukon; Gang-busters, Mr. District Attorney, G-Men; Inner Sanctum and Mystery Theater; and the greatest adventure dramas of them all, The Lone Ranger and The Green Hornet, both created by Fran Striker and George W. Trendle.

Radio did little new in the forties, with the exception of the "disc jockey" show, the first of a number of small clouds on the industry's horizon. A court decision of 1940 made it possible for radio to use phonograph records on the air without special licensing, thus providing cheap, ready-made music. Martin Block's "Makebelieve Ballroom" in New York (begun in 1935), a program devoted wholly to "chatter and platters," within a year had twenty-three sponsors and drew 12,000 fan letters a month. According to one sponsor, Block's commercials increased the sale of his doughnuts 432,000 a week in two months. At about the same time an industry-wide ruling removed the limit to the number of commercials such programs might make each hour, a combination soon to affect radio's future irrevocably.

Beyond this, radio remained much the same. Clever use of the give-away gimmick, already employed successfully by Professor Quiz, Dr. I.Q., and other shows, made Take It or Leave It (1943) featuring "the $64 Question," into the first really popular "quiz" show. (Later, of course, the question on television was worth $64,000.) Truth or Consequences, the audience-participation hit of 1944, was a version of the old parlor game in which contestants paid "consequences" for failing to answer a question. Since the questions were silly and unanswerable, willing contestants performed silly stunts, punctuated by master-of-ceremonies Ralph Edwards shouting archly, "Aren't we devils?" These led to a rash of panel, quiz, and audience-participation shows, including the literate Information Please and the interesting juvenile genius show, The Quiz Kids.

Stop the Music!, originated by Lewis Cowan, who also created The Quiz Kids, was among the first of the big giveaway shows during the late forties, during radio's frantic competition with television. Harry Salter's orchestra played popular songs which were interrupted by Bert Parks's shout of "Stop the Music!" The program then placed a phone call at random, and if the person at home could identify the song he was showered with gifts—matched pearls, refrigerators, trips to Hawaii—to the value of $20,000 to $30,000. After twenty years of depression, deprivation and wartime austerity, Stop the Music! struck exactly the right chord for a consumption-conscious, affluent society. For the next several years, game shows showered blizzards of gifts on radio audiences—Hit the Jackpot, Go For the House, Chance of a Lifetime, Shoot the Moon, and so on, until television took over.

Through the same years, Toscanini conducted the NBC Symphony; Arthur Godfrey made the big time as host, salesman, and entertainer; Basil Rathbone re-created a stylish Sherlock Holmes; "Meet the Press," a new show in 1946, combined the traditional talk and forum shows. The older bands and singers were challenged by Glenn Miller, Harry James, Dinah Shore, The Andrews Sisters, Frank Sinatra, while "Your Hit Parade" tried frantically to find new ways of presenting the same "hit" songs week after week.

The daily program format changed little during the decade, for no one saw any reason to tamper with success. On April 6, 1949, NBC offered twenty serial dramas, four comedy shows, two dramatic hours, six musical programs, a mystery program, and an audience-quiz program. CBS differed only in distribution: fifteen serials, six comedies, one play, one mystery, three musical programs, and seven audience-quiz-panel shows. The industry was fat and lazy, giving the public exactly what ten years of success showed it wanted. Radio presented 22,000 different programs a day, seven and a half million yearly, over nearly a thousand stations, most of them making money. Lee De Forest, inventor of the audion that helped make radio a reality in 1921, wrote despairingly in 1947 what could have been "a potent instrumentality for culture, fine music, and the uplifting of America's mass intelligence," had instead become "a laughing stock, resolutely kept the average intelligence of thirteen years." Six months later a CBS vice-president, almost as if in reply, remarked, "The masses like comic books, Betty Grable, broad comedy, simple drama—it's fast, vulgar, simple, fundamental," and radio kept it that way.

But during these years, from 1935–50, radio was at the height of its wealth, power, and public acceptance. It invented practically nothing new. The vast majority of its programs were simply transferred from movies, stage, and fiction, using the same staple materials that had supported popular art for generations, cast into shapes compatible with the new medium. Radio was merely a new way to do old things. It actually contributed only three new kinds of programs: the audience participation show (including the panel, quiz, and giveaway); the documentary (chiefly for news); and the talk-discussion or forum show (actually a carry-over from the lyceum and Chautauqua), none of them really classifiable as entertainment. Everything else was borrowed, but nevertheless, it was skillfully done, effective, and occasionally brilliantly entertaining.

An analysis of 908 nationally-rated, regularly scheduled programs over the period 1920–50 reveals eleven major types of programs, all of them fully developed by 1935. Drama was by far the most numerous: 278 dramatic programs, of which 168 were serials with a continuing sequential narrative and more or less permanent cast; and 110 (like The Silver Theater, Studio One, The Screen Guild Theater) presenting plays complete in themselves with different casts. Next came comedy, 104 programs consisting of those built around the personality of a star (fifty-nine), or "situation" comedy with a continuing narrative line (forty-five). Among the first were such stars as Jack Benny, Fred Allen, Edgar Bergen, Milton Berle, Joe Penner, and others with "comedy hours"; among the latter were Ozzie and Harriet (Nelson), The Great Gildersleeve (Hal Peary), the Aldrich Family (Ezra Stone), Life with Riley (William Bendix), My Friend Irma (Marie Wilson), My Favorite Husband (Lucille Ball), and Life With Luigi (J. Carroll Naish). Crime-detective-mystery shows came third (eighty-three), adventure next (seventy-six), musical shows next (seventy-one), The Fitch Bandwagon, Camel Caravan, The Chesterfield Supper Club, Let's Dance. Quiz, panel, and audience-participation programs accounted for sixty-nine (Pot o' Gold, Beat the Band, Stop the Music, Blind Date, Candid Microphone, Truth or Consequences, Twenty Questions); and "variety" shows, constructed on a vaudeville format with a "personality host" for fifty-seven, among them Rudy Vallee's "Fleischmann Hour," Bing Crosby's "Kraft Music Hall," Ed Wynn's "Texaco Theater," "Al Pearce's Gang," Eddie Cantor's "Chase and Sanborn Hour," and of course Ed Sullivan's "Toast of the Town." These seven types accounted for all but seventy-nine of the list, the rest scattered among discussion-forum programs (twenty-eight, such as People's Platform, Round Table of the Air, America's Town Meeting, and the American Forum), children's shows (twenty-five), religious programs (fourteen), documentaries (six), and "human interest" shows (six).

Not surprisingly, radio drama, comedy, and variety avoided sex far more than the movies did. For one thing, radio was part of the home environment, listened to by families, most of its programs designed to cover a broad spectrum of age, taste, education, and sophistication. While sex lay beneath the surface of a good deal of serial drama, it was not there if the listener preferred not to recognize it; its presence was simply part of the "real life" illusion the audience presumed. Equally important was the fact that radio programs had sponsors who were extraordinarily sensitive to criticism that might influence sales. Paradoxically, the same story and comedy materials that brought people into movie theaters by millions were taboo over the air; the film could do easily what radio did not dare. Audiences would not accept at home many of the more candid expressions of sex they readily accepted in the theater or on the printed page. Both performer and sponsor quickly learned the penalties of crossing the narrow boundaries of public tolerance in such matters.

Clearly, radio took few chances. Whatever was popular in other media it took for its own use, absorbing or imitating it. (Of 110 adventure, drama, and comedy shows, twenty-eight were taken directly from popular novels and thirty-one from comic strips.) Serial drama, the most popular of all radio types, was nothing more than sentimental-domestic novel-melodrama, "true confession" material cut up into episodes, aimed at the same female audience. (There was, in fact, both a "True Confessions" serial and a "True Story Hour.") They divided into five easily-recognizable, highly-traditional types: family, guide-figures, marriage, "woman alone" or career girl, and "helping hand" or homely philosophy.

Better known family-type serials included "Pepper Young's Family," "Today's Children," "Bachelor's Children," "The Stepmother," "The O'Neills," "Those We Love," "Painted Dreams," and so on. "One Man's Family," written by Carleton E. Morse during its entire life of twenty-seven years (1932–59), was by far the most literate, the most adult in conception, and (except for "Ma Perkins") the most durable. Built about the Barbour family of San Francisco—father, mother, and five children—it was done with restraint, realism, and superb characterization. Characters made mistakes, parents were not always wise, children got into trouble, people fell in love with the wrong people, unto the third generation. At the same time there were marriages that turned out well, problems finally solved, and as real families did, somehow they got along fairly well. During its better years, as a half-hour-weekly program until 1950, "One Man's Family" was a notable exception to the soap-opera stereotype.

Guide-figure types were usually doctors and nurses (occasionally lawyers) paralleling the "doctor novel" of popular fiction—"Young Doctor Malone," "Dr. Christian," "Woman in White," "Joyce Jordan, Girl Intern," "Road of Life" ("Dr. Brent, call surgery . . . ! Dr. Brent, call surgery . . . !"). Serials about marriage, especially the pain of it, exceeded all others: "Backstage Wife," "Claudia and David," "John's Other Wife," "Stella Dallas," "Dear John," "Orphans of Divorce," "Second Husband," and thirty-two more. "Our Gal Sunday" asked the question, "Can this girl from a little mining town in the West find happiness as the wife of a wealthy, titled Englishman?" As wife to Lord Henry Brinthorpe and mistress of Black Swan Castle, Sunday did find it difficult, but she persevered.

Women who had to make it alone had many interesting adventures: "Young Widder Brown," "Mary Marlin," "Arnold Grimm's Daughter," "Brenda Curtis," and so on. Portia, of "Portia Faces Life," was a lady lawyer who kept suitors at arm's length, or half-an-arm's length, throughout a long and successful legal career. Mary Marlin, a brilliant Senator, did the same. Young Widder Brown, who ran a tea shop in Smithville, kept the handsome local doctor at bay for years. "The Romance of Helen Trent," which understandably had millions of listeners in the over-thirty group, told "the story of a woman who set out to prove what so many other women long to prove in their own lives . . . , that romance can live on at thirty-five . . . , and beyond. . . ." Homely philosophers and Good Samaritans abounded: "Just Plain Bill" (a Hartsville barber), "Lorenzo Jones" (a wise garage mechanic) and his wife Belle, "Scattergood Baines" (a crackerbarrel pundit), "The Guiding Light" (a kindly minister), "Big Sister" and various Aunt Marys, Jennies, and others. "Ma Perkins," the champion of all helpers, owned a lumberyard in Rushville Center and gave advice continuously for twenty-seven years—the series eventually involved ninety-seven characters.

Crime, adventure, mystery, and detective stories, straight from the pulps and comics, loomed large in daily programming. Practically every detective in popular fiction showed up on the air—Sam Spade, Nero Wolfe, Philip Marlowe, Charlie Chan, Ellery Queen, Perry Mason, Philo

Vance, Nick Carter, along with private eyes created especially for radio, like Martin Kane, Pat Novak, The Fat Man, Thatcher Colt, and Richard Diamond. So too did The Saint, Jimmy Valentine, Boston Blackie, and Bulldog Drummond. "Call the Police," "This is Your FBI," "Crime Clues," "Crime Fighters," "The Lineup," and "20,000 Years in Sing Sing" took care of police drama. "Gangbusters," written by Phillip Lord, capitalized on the headlines of the gang-ridden thirties; "Mr. District Attorney," also by Lord, was modeled on the career of Thomas Dewey in New York City. "Mr. District Attorney" was one of the few programs that moved directly from radio to television intact, including the star, Jay Jostyn.

The air was filled with adventure shows like "The Cisco Kid," "The Falcon," "The Man Called X," "Johnny Dollar," and transfers from the comics like "Terry and the Pirates," "Smilin' Jack," "Don Winslow," "Jungle Jim," "Mandrake," "Superman," and of course "Tarzan." Rimsky Korsakov's "Flight of the Bumblebee" music always introduced Brett Reid, who as "The Green Hornet" fought crime weekly all over the world. (Brett Reid's father Dan Reid, was a nephew of The Lone Ranger, whose real name was Reid; in fact, Brett's father was named after the Lone Ranger's older brother. The show was written by the same team that produced The Lone Ranger, hence the relationship.) "The William Tell Overture" meant the greatest of them all, The Lone Ranger himself, with the breathless introduction that closed with the words that thousands of men will always remember, "And now, from out of the past come the thundering hoofbeats of the great horse SILVER . . . *The Lone Ranger rides again!*" The sponsors of Jack Armstrong, "the Alllllll-American Boy," whose theme song was "Wave the Flag for Hudson High, Boys!" gave away whistling rings, hike-o-meters, secret decoders, and Norden bombsights. When Jack joined the Scientific Bureau of Investigation in later years, it became just another police-adventure story.

Mystery-suspense shows were made to order for radio, where the listener's imagination plus studio sound effects could create tensions and horrors impossible in picture or print. The sound of the squeaking door that opened "The Inner Sanctum," one of the best, thrilled millions with anticipation of ghosts, vampires, mad scientists, zombies, terror, and death in strange forms. "The Hermit's Cave," which featured "Ghost stories! WEIRD Stories! and murders TOO!" was straight fantasy-fiction from the pulps. "Mystery Theater," "Secret City," and "The Shadow" all had devoted listeners. "Suspense," narrated by "The Man in Black," featured actors like Orson Welles, Ida Lupino, Cary Grant, Agnes Moorhead, and Lucille Ball as guest stars. Arch Oboler's "Lights Out," a polished, expertly-tailored program, specialized in shatteringly real sound effects. A generation of listeners never forgot the wet sound of Donovan's disembodied brain throbbing in its chemical bath, or the sizzle of the drop of acid that still may be eating its way through the vitals of the earth, or the soft, smothered smack of the bit of growing chicken-heart tissue that escaped the laboratory and engulfed the world.

The most spectacular instance of radio's powers of verisimilitude derived from Orson Welles's adaptation of H. G. Wells's science-fiction novel, *War of the Worlds,* presented on the Mercury Theater's broadcast of October 30, 1938—at eight o'clock on Hallowe'en. Welles produced the program as a simulated news broadcast with on-the-spot announcers, interviews, and the whole range of radio's arsenal of sound effects. Beginning with the announcement of the landing of a meteor near Grover's Mills, New Jersey, which turned out to be a spaceship containing Martians armed with death-ray guns, the program spread panic through the New York and New Jersey area and soon to other parts of the nation. Although the program opened with the announcement that it was a play, and three more announcements repeated the fact during the broadcast, apparently few listeners paid attention. Cars were racing along highways on the East Coast before the program ended, sailors were recalled from shore leave, National Guardsmen dug out World War I gas masks, people evacuated homes in Brooklyn, New Jersey farmers formed a home-guard. CBS began to make periodic announcements at 9:15 P.M. that it had been only a play, the Associated Press sent out reassuring bulletins, and metropolitan police stations tried vainly to cope with hundreds of frantic calls, but it all did little good—particularly when a few stations broadcast interviews with people who had actually *seen* the Martians while others reported rumors on additional landings elsewhere in the country. Hysteria hit the Midwest and West within hours (a power failure in the state of Washington helped) and not for another forty-eight hours did the country regain its sanity.

The most singular of the adventure-mystery type was Carleton Morse's "I Love a Mystery," which combined elements of the better hardboiled dick story and the adventure pulps. The series traced the adventures of tough, pragmatic Jack Packard, a woman-chasing Texan named Doc Long, and a powerful Englishman, Reggie York, all of whom ran the A-1 Detective Agency, "no job too tough, no mystery too baffling." There was violence, blood, tough talk, and overtones of sex in Morse's scripts that appeared nowhere else, along with real skill at dialogue and characterization. Over their five best years (1939–44) the trio had thirty-eight adventures, among them such classics as "Blood on the Cat"; "The Thing

Wouldn't Die;" "Twenty Traders of Timbuktu;" "No Ring, No Ring Finger, No Husband." Morse's plots were tough. Cherry Martin's sexually-demented assailant slashed her lightly with a razor in the dark while he cried like a baby. The Maestro turned his beautiful assistant Natushka at night into a werewolf which drank the blood of the lovers she charmed by day. Anybody who loved pretty Sunny Richards burst into flame when she was near him; Jack, who hated emotional entanglements, had to get himself engaged to Sunny to solve that one, and immediately left her when he did. There was nothing else on the air quite like "I Love a Mystery."

Rather surprisingly, there were few fantasy-science-fiction programs on radio, except for Buck Rogers and Flash Gordon, who made the transition from comic books unimpaired. "Dimension X," an excellent but short-lived show, had some scripts by Ray Bradbury. Nor were there many Westerns, since radio could never impart the powerful sense of place and time, as film and fiction could, that the Western needed. "The Lone Ranger" rang with echoes of Zane Grey, of course, but there was nothing in him of the good-bad man, the gunslinger, or the lonesome cowboy; he was, more accurately, Lancelot in a ten-gallon hat. Gene Autry and Roy Rogers merely played the same singing cowboys before the microphone they did on film. "Hopalong Cassidy," played by blondined William Boyd in a white, bespangled cowboy suit, bore no resemblance whatever to the original.

"The Sheriff," "Six Shooter," and "Death Valley Days" simply dramatized stories from the Western pulps, not very well. "Tom Mix," next to "The Lone Ranger" the most popular Western, was really a juvenile adventure story that owed little if anything to the Western tradition. (Mix himself never appeared on the program, and only at the end of each episode did the listener know that he was "impersonated.") Tom pursued rustlers and international spies, and outwitted city gangsters and master criminals, all of whom seemed to converge somehow on the small town of Dobie, surely one of the most harassed settlements in frontier history.

The forties were flush times, but radio's roof began to cave in late in the decade. The signs were visible in 1948, when even though there were only a million television sets as against seventy-five million radios, observers in network offices noted a downward trend. "If I weren't mildly suspicious of the word," wrote John Crosby, a leading radio critic, "I'd say it was the beginning of an epoch and the end of another." Yet 1950 looked like a good year. There were 108 programs that had been on the air for ten years, twelve of them for twenty years; the same leaders (Jack Benny, Bing Crosby, first in ratings for over fifteen years); $183,000,000 in network sales, and profits up. But by December, 1950, there were over five million television sets in American homes with the same dramas, quiz shows, detective-crime stories, serials, comedies, and variety shows as radio, using radio's performers. After 1950 it was all downhill for radio. Ratings on Fred Allen's popular comedy show dropped from 28.7 (that is, 28.7 per cent of the available listening audience) to 11.2 and finally went off the air; Bob Hope's went from 23.8 to 5.4 and off the air. "Lux Radio Theater," radio's highest-rated dramatic show, reached eleven million homes in 1949 and less than three million in 1955. Most damaging of all, sponsors swiftly shifted their money to television, which despite its higher costs, got better results. In 1948 radio sold $137,500,000 worth of advertising; in 1955 $76,000,000. Television meanwhile in 1955 sold $320,-000,000, and almost doubled that by 1957–58. In 1954 there were only thirty-five sponsored half-hour shows left on radio; in 1960 three.

Radio could not compete and made no real attempt to do so. It did not die, by any means—there were radios in 96 per cent of American homes in 1956—but since it could not do what television did it shifted its aims entirely. Radio had mobility, as television did not, and its sense of simultaneity still worked to its advantage; wherever the listener went radio could go with him, especially in his automobile. By 1960 70 per cent of all autos had radios; the transistor, which made radio even more easily portable, increased the listening public by millions. These things helped to hold radio's daytime audience while television usurped evenings.

Looking for new kinds of listeners, stations changed to "service" programming. Since it did music and news well, radio concentrated on them; since it could cover regional and local affairs cheaply and quickly, it specialized in such things as "on-the-spot" events, background music, weather, and traffic reports, local interviews, public service announcements, and the like. Individual stations directed programs at local minority audiences like teenagers, racial groups, serious-music lovers. Having lost its huge entertainment potential, radio developed a continuous audience for all-day and sometimes all-night "talk" shows interspersed with a few spots for records, commercials, and news. It developed also a variation on the audience-participation show in which listeners phoned in for conversations with the interviewer; shows like Long John Nebel's, Barry Gray's, Jean Shepherd's, and Barry Farber's drew literally millions of calls. CBS once recorded 1,070,000 attempted calls to one of its talk-and-phone shows in one month over six stations. Meanwhile the local disc jockey, with his "Top Twenty Tunes of the Week," interrupted by dozens of commercials, continued to dominate radio.

In effect, radio since the mid-fifties has been successful at what it does, which has been essentially to serve the community as a kind of adjunct newspaper. As an index of its success, it is noticeable that the number of stations increased from two thousand in 1950 to over five thousand in 1965; there are still one hundred million sets in American homes, fifty million in autos, and perhaps ten million more in public places such as restaurants, filling stations, and stores. Radio provides information, services, and advertising but not entertainment—or at least little, and that to specialized audiences. The net result is that radio is no longer mass popular entertainment.

A series of successful experiments with wireless transmission of pictures led to the first television (a word not yet invented) broadcast in 1927, when a talk by Secretary of Commerce Herbert Hoover in Washington was seen and heard in New York, two hundred miles away. Both RCA and General Electric operated experimental stations in the early thirties; the British Broadcasting Company initiated regularly scheduled programs in 1936 and NBC put its experimental W2XBS on the air in 1939. NCB's telecast of President Roosevelt's address at the opening of the 1939 New York World's Fair is usually accepted as the beginnings of American television. Commercials were not far behind. The Bulova Watch Company, on July 1, 1941, sponsored the first commercial telecast over WNBT in New York, a one-minute time signal that cost nine dollars. World War II, however, halted the construction of stations and the manufacture of sets. At the close of the war, television was firmly in the hands of the same companies that controlled radio. NBC's WNBT and CBS's WCBW (both in New York), the first licensed commercial stations, were in effect radio stations with pictures.

Television intruded into American life with shattering suddenness. In 1946 there were only seven thousand sets in the country; in 1948 there were 172,000; in 1950 more than five million. Between 1949 and 1952 sets entered American homes at the rate of a quarter million a month. Radio audiences, during radio's most swiftly-growing years, increased at the rate of two million a year; television's grew five million a year during the fifties and early sixties. The medium's phenomenal growth never paused— in 1952 there were seventeen million sets in American homes; in 1954 thirty-six and a half million; in 1958 forty-eight and a half million (that year CBS Radio introduced "bargain advertising rates"); in 1965 seventy million; in 1968 seventy-nine million. Significantly, in 1948 television stations increased their advertising rates by fifty per cent or more, but despite the increased costs, *Time* reported, 94 per cent of advertisers who bought air time preferred to buy it on television rather than on radio. By

THE EDISON KINETOSCOPE

An Unsurpassed Moving Picture Machine from every point of view. "Once used, always used."

The motion picture show is fast becoming the biggest factor in the amusement field—the biggest money-maker for the men who are playing the game with both eyes open. Go into the business now, while it's still young, but be sure to start with the right machine. A cheap machine is a bad investment and a losing proposition from the beginning.

The Edison Kinetoscope projects the clearest, steadiest pictures, is the simplest machine to operate, is absolutely safe and will outwear any other motion picture machine made. Write us to-day for a catalog and a copy of the Edison Kinetogram.

COMING EDISON FILMS
Tell your exchange you want them.

May 10—*"Treasure Island," by Robert Louis Stevenson. 1,050 feet. Drama.
" 11—*"Every Rose Has Its Stem," by Ethel Browning. 1,000 feet. Comedy-Drama.
" 14—*"The Bank President's Son," by Marion Brooks. 1,000 feet. Drama.
" 15—*"A Personal Affair." 1,000 feet. Comedy.
" 17—*"The Convict's Parole," by Melvin G. Winstock. 1,000 feet. Drama.
" 18—*"A Romance of the Ice Fields." 635 feet. Drama.
"Scenes in Delhi, India " 365 feet. Descriptive.
" 21—*"Their 'Hero,' from "At Good Od Siwash," by George Fitch. 1,000 feet. Comedy.
" 22—*"The Artist and the Brain Specialist," by Harry Furniss. 1,000 feet. Comedy-Drama.
" 24—*"The Sunset Gun," by Bannister Merwin. 1,000 feet. Drama.
" 25—*"A Western Prince Charming," from "A Chaparral Prince," by O. Henry. 1,000 feet. Drama.
" 28—*"Jim's Wife." 1,000 feet. Drama.
" 29—*"The Passion Flower." 1,000 feet. Comedy.
" 31—*"Views in Calcutta, India " 1,000 feet. Descriptive.

* Posters furnished by A. B. C. Co.

Thomas A. Edison

237 Lakeside Ave.,   Orange, N. J.

UNDERWRITERS' TYPE "B"

Special Features:

Adjustable Outside Revolving Shutter, Chain Take-up, Extra Large House with square condenser holder, Double Magazine Rollers, Heavy Brass Terminals on connecting cords, set of Heavy Extension Legs, four of which are 1 1-4 inches in diameter. A very substantial stand.

Price, with Rheostat, 110 volt, 25-40 amperes, $225.00
Price, with 110 volt, 60 cycle Transformer, $245.00

1913 Advertisement for "The Edison Kinetoscope."
CULVER PICTURES, INC.

A movie house of the early twenties showing Buster Keaton in *Sherlock Jr.* CULVER PICTURES, INC.

Dustin Farnum in *The Squaw Man*. CULVER PICTURES, INC.

Lillian Gish in *Birth of a Nation*. CULVER PICTURES, INC.

"One Man's Family": Minetta Ellen as Fanny, Bernice Erwin as Hazel, Michael Rafetto as Paul, Barton Yarborough as Cliff, Page Gilman as Jack, Kathleen Wilson as Claudia, and J. Anthony Smythe as Henry. CULVER PICTURES, INC.

Milton Berle, one of the few comedians to make a successful transition from radio to television. CBS RADIO.

1950 television's advertising receipts were over 170 million dollars, by 1955 over one billion, and by 1967 over two billion.

Observers of the contemporary scene were well aware of television's initial impact on American society; some were less sanguine than others about the result. Bishop Fulton Sheen, who enjoyed a wide reputation as a radio speaker, saw it as "a blessing. Radio is like the Old Testament . . . , hearing wisdom without seeing; television is like the New Testament, because in it the wisdom becomes flesh and dwells among us." Gilbert Seldes, long a skeptical critic of radio and film, saw it as "a golden hope, away from the fallacy of mass entertainment and toward a great communications and entertainment medium in a democratic society." Others were not so certain, but all agreed that, as John Houseman wrote in 1950, television would soon be "the dominant medium of mass communication in the world . . . because of its incontestable technical superiority over all other existing means of communication."

There was much to support Houseman's view. Television was radio with eyes, a newspaper without print, movies individualized. It involved its audience totally and instantaneously with a compelling combination of sight, sound, and motion that no other medium provided. Television fostered the illusion of intimacy—seen at home, individually or in a small group, positing a one-to-one relationship between the figure on the screen and the viewer at the set. Television also fostered the illusion of realism (like radio but more completely) because it showed what happened *when* it happened, visibly and audibly, with neither time-lag nor intervening agency. Films, newspapers, and the phonograph always involved intermediaries—a cameraman, a cutter or editor, a reporter, a selection of events, a choice of information—which television barely inferred. What appeared on the television screen (despite the fact that it was edited) appeared to be "the real thing." As philosopher-critic Marshall McLuhan pointed out, television is a "cool" medium in that as part of a new communications system (as opposed to "hot" or "linear" media like print) it makes the viewer a participant rather than a spectator. It is television's "all inclusive *nowness*," McLuhan wrote in *Understanding Media*, which makes it very nearly the ultimate "instantaneous electronic environment . . . , a total field of instantaneous data in which . . . involvement is mandatory."

Television's most overwhelming characteristic is the size of its audience, always measured in millions, which makes it the greatest shared popular experience in history. Its life blood from the first was advertising, designed to sell products to a mass audience which in turn (as in other mass media) forced it toward conformity and standardization. Television is primarily a selling machine of great efficiency if properly handled. NBC's two-year study of its impact on the buying habits of a Midwestern town showed that advertising could increase sales from 48 per cent to 200 per cent (depending on the type of product) within a few weeks. (One recipe, presented on the Kraft Music Hall, almost immediately brought a half-million requests.) Television's grasp of its audience is all-encompassing. In 1967 95 per cent of all households owned at least one set while 25 per cent had two or more. During the peak viewing season (January and February) the average set is on forty-four hours a week; the potential audience for any single program is calculated at eighty-three–eighty-five million. (The "TV Dinner," that most McLuhanesque of culinary innovations, appeared in 1954.) The average American male at age sixty-five has spent three thousand days, or nearly nine years, watching television; a five-year-old American child has spent more hours before the set than a student spends in class during four years of college.

Television must therefore always see its audience not only as an audience but as a market; what it presents is not only entertainment but advertising. Nothing can be done on television without consideration of both sets of conditions. Studies have shown that a program that requires too much thought, elicits too much excitement, or stirs up too much controversy is likely to make the viewer neglect the sponsor's message; the element of mediocrity thus has a certain importance in programming.

Costs are far greater than those of film, radio, or print and therefore tend also to control programs. Television must produce each year over four hundred times as many hours of entertainment as Hollywood did during its prosperous era; television in ten days presents more hours of drama than Broadway in a year. Each network must fill about twenty-five to thirty hours of evening "prime time" each week with approximately fifty to seventy-five shows which cost from $130,000 to $500,000. Arthur Miller's play, "Death of a Salesman," produced by CBS in 1966, cost the network $880,000, of which the sponsor, Xerox, paid only $250,000. Television's question in producing any program, therefore, is always how much does it cost to reach how many millions of viewers most effectively, and what will be the result to the sponsor in increased sales? As Robert Kintner of NBC said in 1960, "The ultimate responsibility [for television programs] is ours, but the ultimate power has to be the sponsor's, because without him you couldn't run a network."

Television took over radio's format quickly: fifteen minute, half-hour, and hour segments; distribution of the day into morning (talk and games), afternoon (serials), and evening (prime time); commercial breaks in exactly the same places in the same language; the same programs in the same ratios—that is, 75 per cent entertainment, 25 per cent public service, informational, religious, educational, and children's programs. By the late fifties television had evolved a permanent day-to-day pattern which it has maintained without appreciable change. On May 1, 1959, channels available to New York City viewers carried, between 6:30 A.M. and 6 P.M. the following: six children's programs, five cartoons, eight situation comedies, eleven movies, four talk shows, two musical programs, five comedy-drama shows, five Western-police adventure shows, eleven serial dramas, and thirteen audience-participation-game shows. On May 1, 1969, the pattern was precisely the same, except for a slight increase in the proportion of situation comedies and "talk shows": children's programs (six), cartoons (six), situation comedies (fourteen), movies (nine), talks (twelve), music (two), comedy-drama (five), adventure-police-Western (seven), serial dramas (fourteen), audience-participation games (thirteen). Having once found an acceptable pattern, television is not likely to change it.

Television soon developed its two major program concepts, the "special" or "spectacular," and the serial. The special, a single program of particular importance or quality, may be built about a topic, performer, or narrative. In 1968 the industry programmed 235 specials ranging from "Man and His Universe" through "Sinatra" to "Heidi" and "Peanuts." The serial, as in radio, is a regularly scheduled show built about the presence of performer or "host," a continuing narrative, a repeatable format, a semipermanent cast, or some other unifying device. Television's entertainment programs from the beginning divided easily into the same categories as radio's—that is, dramatic, musical, variety, comedy, game and audience participation, talk and discussion—with the addition of movies.

Since the medium is especially well-adapted to it, drama has been a television staple. The "playhouse" or "theater" program was transferred directly from radio, complete with "host" or "hostess," beginning with the Kraft Theater, The Philco Playhouse, and the experimental Studio One in 1948. Others appeared in the fifties: The General Electric Theater, The Ford Star Jubilee, The Alcoa Theater, Producer's Playhouse, and Playhouse Ninety, the first to break the half-hour or hour format by playing an hour-and-a-half. A large number of adventure, police, and detective programs came directly from radio, the comics, movies, and novels—Ellery Queen, Martin Kane, The Thin Man, Mr. and Mrs. North, Dragnet, Big Town, Perry Mason, and so on. Like radio audiences, television viewers like private eye, police, and crime dramas: Richard Diamond, M-Squad, NYPD, Naked City, Meet McGraw, 77 Sunset Strip, Peter Gunn (an updated Philo Vance who appreciated good jazz and sophisticated girls), Hawaiian Eye, The FBI, Lineup, Mannix, Hawaii Five-O, The Untouchables (one of the most violent on television), to name a few. The indestructible Tarzan naturally moved into television, along with Zorro, Robin Hood, Jungle Jim, Steve Canyon, and Sheena, Queen of the Jungle. Cut to the same pattern were Sea Hunt, Riverboat, The Alaskan, The Fugitive, Dangerman, F-Troop, and a dozen more. The popularity of spy novels created spy shows (Five Fingers, I Spy, The Man from UNCLE, The Girl from UNCLE, among others) as well as two antispy shows, Get Smart (a spoof) and Mission Impossible (a highly sophisticated, ironic parody).

Mystery and suspense, exemplified in "Alfred Hitchcock Presents" and "Suspense" were no less popular on television than on radio. Fantasy-science-fiction shows, curiously enough, were never numerous; Rod Serling's expertly-done "Twilight Zone" and the later "Star Trek" were imaginative adaptations of standard science fiction fare. Unlike radio, television introduced a few dramatic series which dealt with current issues, among them East Side West Side (urban social problems), Mr. Novak (juvenile delinquency), Slattery's People (politics), and The Defenders (courts of justice).

Television immediately made the Western its 'own. "Kid Westerns" like Hopalong Cassidy, Tom Mix, Gene Autry, and The Lone Ranger came over from radio early; the first "adult" Western, aimed at a broader and more mature public was probably Wyatt Earp in 1955, the same year that Rifleman and Gunsmoke (television's only real classical Western) also appeared. After that they came in floods: Zane Grey Theater (1956), Maverick, Cheyenne, Tombstone Territory, Trackdown, Wagon Train, Sugarfoot, Restless Gun, Colt .45, Have Gun, Will Travel (all 1957); The Texan, Wanted Dead or Alive, Lawman, Bat Masterson, Cimarron City (all 1958); Bronco, The Deputy, Rawhide, Wichita Town, Bonanza (all 1959); and so on. There were by actual count twenty-two Western series on television during the peak years, 1958–60, a number gradually reduced as the wave receded.

By the mid-sixties television has developed three major types of Western drama: the soap-opera Western; the classic Western; and the isolated-hero Western, deriving from the "good-bad" man concept that radio had never really accepted. Bonanza, the best-written of the soap-opera variety, depended on what was essentially the daily serial format, following the fortunes and troubles of a tightly-knit motherless ranch family dominated by a strong, kindly, wise father (reminiscent of Just Plain Bill and Father Barbour), emphasizing strongly-etched characterizations and a story line shrewdly compounded of sentimental-adventure elements. Bonanza's locale and action happened to be Western; the series would survive equally as well were it laid somewhere else, since its Western elements were never vital to its wide appeal. (So too such "Westerns" as Big Valley and The Guns of Will Sonnett.)

Gunsmoke, on the other hand, embodied the classic Western theme of conflict between frontier and civilization, lawlessness and order, settlement and range. Sheriff Matt Dillon (played expertly for years by James Arness) of Dodge City, a town just turning the corner of civilization, with the help of deputies, doctors, lawyers, blacksmiths, storekeepers, and an attractive, somewhat ambiguous lady saloon-owner, protects the community from danger from without and subversion from within. Almost every episode in Gunsmoke's long span begins with the town's values in danger, and ends with the danger averted. Aided by sound acting, excellent production, and intelligent writing, Gunsmoke has managed to maintain every convention of the classic Western without falling into cliché or boredom, handling the traditional materials with respect and restraint.

When it adopted real characters like Earp, Carson, Masterson, and Billy the Kid, and fictional ones like Brett Maverick, Sugarfoot, and The Rifleman, television also accepted the knight-errant, good-bad figure already fully developed in both movies and fiction, the outsider who (like Shane and Buck Duane) when the community has lost its struggle for law, order, and justice, rides in, sets things right, and rides away again. Some of these came to depend on sheer violence, a trick device (Masterson's cane), or a "gimmicked" character (a Wells-Fargo detective), and the majority of them were uninspired imitations of the better movie Westerns. The best was Have Gun, Will Travel, built on the character of Paladin, a roving, black-clad gunman, played with subtlety and skill by actor Richard Boone. A kind of anti-Zane Grey gunman, Paladin was a wandering knight-errant, true, but he was also a cold-blooded, professional "hired gun" who worked for pay. Obviously a success with pretty girls, Paladin drank the best wines, lived in the best San Francisco hotels, and cultivated expensive tastes; given to quoting poetry (and quite aptly) he was a well-educated, thoughtful man with his own style and a saving sense of the absurd. Personally impeccable and ironically detached, he operated within—but always aloof from—a hard, violent, realistically dirty West with tough, pragmatic effectiveness. During its decade on the air, Have Gun, Will Travel was undoubtedly the most literate and sophisticated of television Westerns.

The majority of television musical shows were lifted intact from radio—The Voice of Firestone, The Bell Telephone Hour, Your Hit Parade, and others. Singers and bands out of radio and records took over the musical-variety shows—Crosby, Sinatra, Kate Smith, Perry Como, Dinah Shore, Cugat, Lopez. Liberace, strictly a television phenomenon, made his debut in 1952; Lawrence Welk and his "over-forty" musical hour started in 1955. Radio's "comedy hour" format fitted television perfectly; all that had to be done was to film it. Since many of radio's comedians were veterans of vaudeville and night clubs they simply dusted off and modernized their old routines; Milton Berle's record of four hundred successive stand-up comedy shows still remains a television record.

Everybody was working in the early fifties—Sid Caesar, Jackie Gleason, Benny, Red Skelton, Wynn, Hope, Phil Silvers, Martha Raye, and all the familiar names. A younger group followed them in the sixties (Phil Foster, Louis Nye, Tom Poston, Jerry Lester, Joey Adams, Steve Allen, Rowan and Martin) while Ed Sullivan's "Toast of the Town," which made its debut in 1948, was no more than vaudeville on the small screen. Satire, developed to a high art in radio by such luminaries as Will Rogers and Fred Allen, never fitted television's concept of comedy or its sensitivity toward sponsors. A few stand-up comedians tried it (Hope, Alan King, Shelley Berman) but few did it well. The only extensive attempt at satirically edged social commentary, that of the Smothers Brothers in 1968, proved inept and immature.

Situation comedy was as popular in television as it had been in radio. Amos and Andy, Life With Riley, The Aldrich Family, and My Favorite Husband (soon to become Lucille Ball's fabulously successful I Love Lucy) all came over from radio and attracted dozens of imitators. From 1964 to 1968 there were over sixty regularly scheduled situation comedies (many with "canned" or recorded laughter) of which not more than a half-dozen survived. Lucille Ball's, Dick Van Dyke's, and Phil Silver's "Sergeant Bilko" series, among the best of their kind, probably represented the closest television ever came to the great radio and movie comedies of the twenties and thirties. Beverly Hillbillies, an ingenuous one-joke series involving comic mountaineers in Hollywood, and Gomer Pyle, an equally unsophisticated show about a dumb Marine recruit, lasted longer but were never in the same class. As Paul Henning, who wrote Beverly Hillbillies and two others, once explained, situation comedies derived their popularity from the fact that they are "pure escape, something you can laugh at and not have to think about your mother's operation." They deal in neither sex, nor issues, nor problems, but only laughter.

Games, panels, quizzes, and audience-participation shows have probably occupied more hours of television than any other kind of program. Radio proved that people like the vicarious experience of winning a prize, beating the experts, or listening to another's troubles, whereas television made it all visible. What's My Line, the longest-lived of the panel shows, started in 1950; the next five years saw seventeen of them, including such perennials as People Are Funny, Truth or Consequences, Down You Go, Beat the Clock, and Twenty Questions. The $64,000 Question opened up the big money in 1955 and introduced the "isolation booth" device for added suspense; The Big Surprise raised the prize to $100,000; Twenty-One hit $200,000; and finally Break the Bank made it an even quarter-million. Accusations of collusion, however, closed most of the big ones down in 1958–60, but the concept remained a daytime favorite. At least twenty-five were on the air in 1969, television's single original contribution to popular entertainment.

Radio's staple soap opera, One Man's Family, came into television in 1949, followed by Portia Faces Life, From These Roots, and other favorites. CBS tried a new twist, The Verdict Is Yours, in which actors improvised in a courtroom equipped with real lawyers, but the housewife still preferred stories of troubled people told in interminable episodes. There were never so many serial dramas in television as on radio, the result of fewer channels and higher costs, but there were enough to occupy any housewife's afternoons. As the World Turns, Search for Tomorrow, Guiding Light, Another World, The Edge of Night have all reached the twenty-year mark; The Doctors, Days of Our Lives, and Secret Storm are not far behind. Dark Shadows, a relatively recent entry, reflects the influence of Popular "Gothic" fiction; Love Is a Many-Splendored Thing, aimed at young marrieds, is a good deal more stylish than most and a bit more sophisticated in its narrative. General Hospital and The Doctors of course are merely extensions of "doctor-nurse" paperbacks and radio plays; Days of Our Lives, set in the split-levels, is calculated to appeal to the suburban housewife. Prime time for serials is from about 11:00 A.M. to 4:00 P.M., that is, from the children's lunch until school is out. A housewife in Detroit in 1969 would choose among eighteen serials during these hours, or could listen to eleven consecutively.

Television's serials are copied directly from radio's—plot, characters, themes, structure. Like radio's, they move slowly, in three-to-four week episodes, with a major plot and two minor plots in each episode. As the major plot approaches its interminable but inevitable conclusion, one of the minor plots emerges to replace it, the other moves up to first minor position, and a new minor plot is introduced. Everything is done to give the serial the illusion of veracity; writers work from a map of the town in which the events take place and a list of previous characters and plots so that the scripts are internally consistent and chronologically and geographically accurate. Since the development of each episode moves slowly, a viewer can miss a day or two without losing the thread of the narrative. Robert Aaron, who supervised daytime programming for NBC, explained that the aim of the serial is to give the viewer (almost always a housewife) constant reassurance,

> . . . that her middle-class values are fine, that giving up what she thought of as a career in favor of marriage is fine, that life's little problems are the ones that really count, that apple pie is not really fluoridated.

As the World Turns, which commands one of the largest audiences (about eight million) on daytime television, is written by Irma Phillips and Agnes Nixon. Miss Phillips learned her trade on radio in the twenties; Mrs. Nixon, who entered the field later, handles three other shows. The plot of the serial, according to the producer,

> . . . deals with the loves and lives—no, lives and loves in that order —and ups and downs of two families who are good friends, covering all the related experiences that any two families might encounter. . . . The viewers identify with the characters, this rapport, this identity, is what holds an audience.

The two families, the Hughes and the Lowells and their children, combine with friends, acquaintances, in-laws, and neighbors into incredibly complex episodes that seem to defy rational analysis. The common theme is trouble; few sequences end happily, and those that do prepare for those that do not. To understand one episode in 1967, the viewer must have familiarized himself with this background synopsis:

> Young Dr. Bob Hughes, who was blinded by flying glass in a laboratory explosion, faces eye surgery. The accident happened the day that his wife, Sandy, ran away from home. Sandy ran away because she was upset at having lost custody of her son, Jimmy, who was born in prison while she was serving a sentence for having helped her ex-husband Roy rob a store. Sandy's flight was unnecessary, had she known it, because Roy had already decided to return Jimmy to her. This so upset Penny, Dr. Bob's sister, who had married Roy to make a home for Jimmy, that she left for New York. Dr. Bob's exwife Lisa has just had a child, Chuckie, out of wedlock. Chuckie's father is Dr. Michael, who was married to Clare, the alcoholic mother of Ellen, who herself once had a child out of wedlock, who was adopted by Dr. David. When Dr. David's wife died, he married Ellen; the boy, who grew up to be Dr. Dan, never knew Ellen was his real mother. Dr. David's housekeeper, however, hated Ellen and threatened to tell Dr. Dan; Ellen in a rage hit her with a statue and the housekeeper died. Ellen served a term for manslaughter, and met Sandy in jail.

Characters in television serials are almost exclusively middle-class, white, suburban, professional or near-professional people, although identifiably ethnic and racial characters began to appear in the sixties. Television soap opera, however, deals much more frankly than radio ever did with issues such as drugs, rape, abortions, adultery, and mental illness. As the World Turns pioneered what the trade called "the Ellen Story," or out-of-wedlock child; while sex may be treated frankly, homosexuality and kidnapping (matters of real terror to mothers) are still taboo. Profanity, nudity, and obscenity are forbidden, and despite their occasional directness, serial dramas remain quite consciously moral. Peyton Place, the television version of Grace Metalious' best-selling novel, though advertised as an "earthy, frank, frequently shocking story," did better as a nighttime show than as a daytime serial.

Discussion and "talk" shows proved to be even more popular on television than on radio. Seeing the talkers, plus the intimacy and immediacy of the medium, added greatly to their effectiveness; in addition, such programs were inexpensive, simple to produce, and easily adapted to frequent commercials. The Today Show, begun in 1953, patterned on a magazine format, has been the most ambitious and well-designed of the type. Discussion programs like Meet the Press, Face the Nation, and American Forum of the Air have fairly large followings. "Girl-talk" shows for women tend to occupy morning hours as serials do the afternoon; Wendy Barrie, Margaret Allen, Peggy Fitzgerald, Sheilah Graham, Virginia Graham, Dr. Joyce Brothers, Arlene Francis, and Faye Emerson are among those who have at one time or another led the ratings. Monsignor (now Bishop) Sheen's "Life Is Worth Living" (first on the screens in 1952) dominated religious discussion shows for years; Edward R. Murrow's interviews (Person to Person, Small World) were among television's most literate. Steve Allen's Tonight Show, begun in 1954, showed how late-hour time could be put to highly profitable use with a combination of music, comedy, and talk, a kind of potpourri format later developed by Jack Parr and Johnny Carson. With a few notable exceptions (among them Today, Murrow, Sheen, and the press interviews) the aim of such programs has been entertainment, not information, for rather specialized audiences—women, celebrity-hunters, time-killers, late-night viewers.

Television's problem, like those of radio and Hollywood (and of every other form of mass popular entertainment) has been that its critics have attacked it violently for not being something that it never intended to be, or could be. Walter Lippmann at its outset thought it "debasing and degrading"; Norman Cousins called it "an assault upon the human mind"; Vance Packard judged it "blatant bad taste"; David Susskind (himself a television personality) labeled it "a travesty, a gigantic ho-hum, a huge comic strip." Such accusations can be multiplied by tens in any given month, and all miss the point, which Dick Powell of Four Star Television Productions made crystal clear: "People think this is an art. It's a business."

Neither radio nor movies nor television nor popular fiction intend to corrupt the public taste, but create for it. Television is a mass medium which depends on advertising for its profit. Since it is not profitable to consider the tastes of individual members of the audience, television aims to give reasonable satisfaction to all elements of it; television (like any other mass medium) will serve the desires of any group large enough to constitute a profitable market. As Robert Salant of CBS once explained:

> Broadcasting is a mass medium; it has to be. Unless it can enlist and hold the interest of most of the people, a good part of the time, it is just too expensive to survive. It must have something—even the great majority of its material—that will appeal not just to thousands or hundreds of thousands but to millions and tens of millions.

The industry's point is to make a profit; the most successful programs are those which do so. As in any other medium of mass entertainment, financial risks are large, and so is the potential profit. In television's early days the annual income was 170 million dollars; for the first half of 1967 the three major chains alone (not counting six hundred independent stations) reported advertising revenues of seven hundred million dollars. A television station can be worth between six and ten million dollars a year to the fortunate owner.

Television, therefore, has a right to do what the public wants it to do, and as nearly all observers agree, the public wants diversion and entertainment, as its choice of the so-called top ten programs illustrates each year. (In 1969 these included six situation comedies, two comedy-variety shows, and two Westerns.) "We're not lousing up America, we're giving it what it demands," wrote Perry Lafferty of CBS in 1968. "Our job is to entertain the masses." No matter what the index of measurement, the viewing public overwhelmingly considers television as popular entertainment. Audiences will always choose, Leo Rosten has explained,

> . . . the frivolous as against the serious, escape as against reality, the lurid as against the tragic . . . , fiction as against fact, the diverting as against the significant.

In making these choices, television's mass audience (or radio's, or Hollywood's, or the paperback publisher's) is no different from any other.

THE POPULAR ARTS AND
THE CRITICS

When a medium becomes a depth experience, the old categories of classsical and popular, or of highbrow and lowbrow, no longer obtain.

—MARSHALL MC LUHAN

Critical attitudes toward the study of American popular culture began to form in the years after World War I. Looking at twentieth century mass society and its powerful and pervasive new media of communication, critics found future prospects frightening. Ortega y Gassett's concept of mass man, in his *Revolt of the Masses* (1930, translated 1932), argued with considerable conviction that the patronage of the masses vulgarized taste, dehumanized standards, and destroyed art. The emergence of mass society seemed to imply that if the arts were to exist and flourish as before, control of artistic standards could not be left to public policy. T. S. Eliot, in his *Notes Toward a Definition of Culture* (1948), saw culture threatened by the values of the marketplace, finding a basic, eternal conflict between art and equalitarianism. F. R. Leavis, in England in the thirties, came to similar conclusions. Popular acceptance, it was argued, dooms art; popular art by definition is mediocre, false, or bad.

The trend of elitist criticism was persuasively summarized by Dwight Macdonald in a series of essays culminating in "Masscult and Midcult" (1960), which exerted a strong influence on critical attitudes toward popular culture among literary critics. Locating three cultural levels— High, Mid, and Mass—Macdonald warned that that "collective monstrosity," the mass audience, was well on the way toward burying true culture beneath an avalanche of "fabricated . . . , homogenized" popular art which had "not even . . . the theoretical possibility of being good." The dominance of mass man in modern society, in Macdonald's

view, changed the audience for culture "from a small body of connois-
seurs into a large body of ignoramuses." Culture had always been the
property of a cultivated *cognoscenti;* once it spread into the *ignoscenti* it
automatically deteriorated. Similarly Richard Hoggart in England, following Leavis and Macdonald, exclaimed that mass culture was dangerously attractive to mass man, since it was "full of a corrupt brightness, of
improper appeals and moral evasions." Marxist critics of the thirties and
after, however, taking an almost opposite tack, argued that the problem
lay with the control of popular art by an aristocratic elite who duped and
exploited the masses by feeding it bad art.

Critics of popular culture, facing the future with trepidation, were
uncertain of the next step. Followers of Ortega y Gassett (like Ernest van
den Haag) believed that the only way to preserve high art was somehow
to reestablish the vanished line between aristocracy and lower classes,
thus to bring art under aristocratic control, safe from popular intrusion.
A few, like Hoggart, felt that perhaps "official interference" in the form
of government control of the media might be justified as a way of containing "dangerous cultural developments." Others, like Macdonald, finding such solutions unrealistic in a society in which mass culture was already firmly established, placed greater faith in the creation of a subelite
of critics (most of whom would apparently live in New York) who, by
reason of their positions in the artistic community and their access to the
communications media, could exert a counterforce against mass vulgarity.

On the other hand, there were those who saw the diffusion of culture
through modern society in a more optimistic light. Gilbert Seldes, who
had observed the advance of the popular arts since the twenties, was
hopeful of a "reasonably possible future" for them, since they do have,
after all, "the power to communicate directly with everyone"; his primary
objection stemmed from the fact that, he believed, they do not sufficiently reflect the ethics and aspirations of a democracy." Popularity,
argued Alvin Toffler, was neither necessarily dangerous to qualify in the
arts nor degrading to the artist; the dissemination of the arts to ever wider
audiences could powerfully influence both the level of public taste and
the relevance of art to the public need. A narrow elitism, wrote Norman
Podhoretz, condemns the arts to "an eternal isolation . . . that would
finally end in sterility, disassociation, and mandarinism." Edward Shils, in
an essay titled "Daydreams and Nightmares: Reflections on the Criticism
of Mass Culture" (1957) attacked the concept on which elitist criticism
was based:

> . . . The major error of the analysts of popular culture is their be-
> lief that it has succeeded to something which was intrinsically

worthy, that man has sunk into a hitherto unknown mire because of it, and that this is a necessary prelude to the further degradation, and perhaps ultimate extinction, of high culture. . . . It would be far more correct to assume that mass culture is now less damaging to the lower classes than the dismal and harsh existence of earlier centuries had ever been. The reading of good books, the enjoyment of superior music and painting, although perhaps meager, is certainly more widespread now than in previous centuries, and there is no reason to believe that it is less profound or less genuine. Only the frustrated attachment to an impossible ideal of human perfection, and a distaste for one's own society and for human beings as they are, can obscure this.

In addition, it became evident by the mid-sixties that none of the elitists' proposals to control and direct popular taste had met with marked success. Neither the British nor the French experience in governmentally controlled radio and television offered much encouragement. The influence of New York critics on popular taste proved minuscule indeed. At the same time Macdonald's masscult-midcult theory revealed obvious limitations. First of all, the generally-accepted assumption that presumed a helpless mass audience and a powerful set of manipulators proved overly simplistic as a model of the complicated, subtle relationship that actually existed between the communications media and the public. "Recent research," writes John Cawelti, has "stressed the influence of social reference groups which intervene between the media and the audience, shaping the public's perception and reaction to communication in many ways." Furthermore, the specter of an ignorant mass culture overwhelming all "good" art failed to materialize. Research seemed to indicate that penetration of the mass media into society was accompanied by increased participation in (and possibly appreciation of) the arts at all levels. Modern media, concluded David Manning White, may "hold out the greatest promise to the average man of cultural richness no previous age could give him." Finally, it became clear that to the younger generation popular culture constituted a richly substantial part of their experience which called forth vital, rewarding responses. To a generation that found in The Beatles, Bogart movies, Marvel Group Comics, and Peanuts a new parameter of experience, the warnings of the older critics that popular culture was false and dangerous meant little.

In the meantime, Marshall McLuhan's provocative conjectures concerning communications, beginning with *The Mechanical Bride* (1951) and continued through *Understanding Media* (1964), provided wholly new ways of examining contemporary culture and of evaluating the impact of modern media on the arts. Elitist critics like Macdonald objected most strongly to the *content* of the popular arts; to McLuhan content or "message" was much less important than the medium itself, that is, than the total experience in depth. "Anything that is approached in depth," he wrote in *The Medium Is the Massage* (1967) "acquires as much interest as the greatest matters." There is thus no longer "high-brow" or "low-brow," nor does content count—"depth means insight, not point of view, and insight is a kind of mutual involvement in a process that makes the content of the item quite secondary."

Deriving partly from McLuhan's observations on communications theory and culture, and partly from a searching reexamination of the whole body of elitist criticism, a reevaluation of the position of popular culture in modern critical thought is currently in process. Philosopher Abraham Kaplan, for example, in a sensible essay in 1966, suggested that popularity and validity are not mutually exclusive; that there have been accomplishments of considerable merit in the popular arts; and that they may not yet have reached their full potential. Susan Sontag, in *Against Interpretation* (1966), questioned the usual distinction between "high" and "low" art as highly dubious. Rejecting the traditional model of art as form imposed on content, like McLuhan she saw art instead as neither elite nor popular, neither high nor low, but simply as art, "a new kind of instrument . . . for modifying consciousness and organizing new modes of sensibility."

Whatever its manner of expression, popular culture and the arts included in that culture can no longer be treated with contempt or dismissed as unworthy of study. Instead of the rigid divisions (despite disclaimers, obviously based on politically and economically drawn lines) among high-, mid-, and low-class art established by the elitist critics over the past forty years, it has become more reasonable to view the arts as one long continuum, to consider all levels of artistic accomplishment as related rather than disparate. "Perhaps the best metaphorical figure," writes Ray Browne,

> for all art is that of a flattened ellipsis, or lens. In the center, largest in bulk and easiest seen through is popular art, which includes mass art. On either end of the lens are high and folk art. . . . All four derive in many ways and to many degrees from one another, and the lines of demarcation between any two are indistinct and fluid.

To erase the boundaries, created by snobbery and cultism, that have so long divided the arts means, in the long run, greater understanding of them. Thus involved with the vast, unknown terrain of popular culture, critics and public alike may explore and discover patterns of the American experience which will help to expand our knowledge and control of it.

BIBLIOGRAPHY AND SOURCES

It would be time-consuming and, in a way, impossible to acknowledge my debt to all the authors whose works I have used, in one form or another, in putting this book together. I have tried, however, in these chapter bibliographies to indicate the sources of most of my materials, and to indicate as well in what sources the reader may pursue matters further. To those whose contributions I may have inadvertently overlooked in these credits I offer apologies; to all I offer deep appreciation.

INTRODUCTION

I have avoided the distinction between "mass" and "popular" art as essentially irrelevant here. For considerations of these and other terms, see Edward Shils, "Mass Society and Its Culture," and Oscar Handlin, "Mass and Popular Culture," in Norman Jacobs, ed., *Culture for the Millions?* (Princeton, 1961); Henry Nash Smith, preface to *Popular Culture and Industrialism, 1865–1890* (Garden City, 1967); Roy Harvey Pearce, "Mass Culture, Popular Culture: Notes for a Humanistic Primer," *College English,* XXIII (March, 1962) 417–432.

Beginning in the early nineteen sixties, critics began to use the German word "kitsch" to describe certain aspects of popular art. Clement Greenberg defined it as "ersatz culture . . . , designed for those who, insensible to the values of genuine culture, are hungry nonetheless for the diversion that only culture of some sort can provide," *Art and Culture* (Boston, 1961), pp. 9–15. See also Harold Rosenberg, "Pop Culture and Kitsch Criticism," *Dissent*, V (1958), 14–19. "Camp," a term coined in the mid-sixties, is applied to popular art aesthetically so tasteless as to be amusing to the sophisticated; see Susan Sontag's "Notes on Camp," in *Against Interpretation* (New York, 1966).

PART ONE

For the general history of book publishing and merchandising, the more useful books include: H. Lehman-Haupt, L. C. Wroth, and Rollo Silver, *The Book in America* (New York, 1952); William Charvat, *Literary Publishing in America 1790–1850* (New York, 1959); Roger H. Smith, ed., *The American Reading Public* (New York, 1963); Raymond H. Shore, *Cheap Book Production in the United States, 1870–1891* (New York, 1937); William Miller, *The Book Industry* (New York, 1949); John C. Oswald, *Printing in the Americas* (New York, 1937); and the histories of various publishing houses, among them Roger Burlingame's about Scribner's *Of Making Many Books* (New York, 1946); Joseph Harper, *The House of Harper* (New York, 1912); David Kaser, *Messrs. Carey and Lea* (Philadelphia, 1957); and John Wiley and Sons, *The First One Hundred and Fifty Years* (New York, 1957). For the life and times of the book clubs, see James D. Hart, *The Popular Book*, pp. 273–275; Henry Seidel Canby, "How the Book-of-the-Month Club Began," *Atlantic Monthly* (May, 1947), pp. 131–35; Joseph Kappel, "Book Clubs and the Evaluation of Books," *Public Opinion Quarterly*, XII (1948) 243–52; and John Hutchens, "For Better or Worse, The Book Clubs," *New York Times Book Review* (March 31, 1948). The paperbound book's history is more than adequately covered in Freeman Lewis, *Paperbound Books in America* (New York, 1952); John Tebbel, *Paperback Books: a Pocket History* (New York, 1964); Kurt Enoch, "The Paperbound Book," *Library Quarterly* (July, 1954) pp. 211–25; C. Hugh Holman, "Cheap Books and the Public Interest: Paperbound Book Publishing in Two Centuries," in Ray Browne, ed., *Frontiers of American Culture* (Purdue, Indiana, 1968) pp. 25–35; and Walter Clemons, "Ten Little Pocket Books and How They Grew," *New York Times Book Review* (June 15, 1969) pp. 4–5.

The two general sources on which the portions of this chapter dealing with fiction have leaned most heavily are Frank Luther Mott's pioneering study, *Golden Multitudes* (New York, 1947) and James D. Hart's comprehensive *The Popular Book* (Berkeley, 1961). Good studies of the early novel are: Lily D. Loshe, *The Early American Novel* (New York, 1902); Herbert Brown, *The Sentimental Novel in America* (Durham, North Carolina, 1940);

Alexander Cowie, *The Rise of the American Novel* (New York, 1948); and G. H. Orians, "Censure of Fiction in American Magazines and Romances 1789–1810," *PMLA*, LII (March, 1937), 195–215. Mid-nineteenth-century popular fiction is treated in: Helen Papashavily, *All The Happy Endings* (New York, 1956); Mary Noel, *Villains Galore: The Heyday of the Popular Story Weekly* (New York, 1954); Dorothy C. Hockey, *The Good and The Beautiful: A Study of Best-Selling Novels in America, 1865–1920* (Western Reserve University dissertation, 1947); Warren French, "Joseph Holt Ingraham," *Journal of Mississippi History*, XI (July, 1949), 155–71; and Joseph Satterthwaite, "The Tremulous Formula: Form and Technique in Godey's Fiction," *American Quarterly*, VIII (Summer, 1956) 99–113. For later nineteenth-century fiction, see Quentin Reynold's *The Fiction Factory* (New York, 1955); Alexander Cowie, "The Vogue of the Domestic Novel," *South Atlantic Quarterly*, XLI (October, 1942), 416–25; and Beatrice Hofstadter, "Popular Culture and the Romantic Heroine," *American Scholar* (Winter, 1960–61), pp. 98–116. Alice P. Hackett, "Forty Years of Best Sellers," and "Do You Remember?", *Saturday Review*, XLVII (August 29, 1964), 92–95, 109–125; and her *Seventy Years of Best Sellers* (Philadelphia, 1968) provide the best single source of information on sales, content, and distribution of twentieth-century popular books. Professor Irving Hart's periodical studies in *Publishers' Weekly*, especially "Fiction Fashions 1895–1925," (February 5, 1927), and "The Most Popular Authors of Fiction in the Postwar Period" (March 12, 1927), furnish invaluable information.

Professor Hart's analyses of publisher's lists show that in the years 1895–1920 the twelve best-selling authors, in addition to the five listed in the text, include George Barr McCutcheon, Eleanor Porter, Alice Hegan Rice, Booth Tarkington, Florence Barclay, Mrs. Humphrey Ward,, and Rex Beach. The twelve best sellers for the period 1919–1926 include, in addition, James Oliver Curwood, Sinclair Lewis, A. S. M. Hutchinson, Peter B. Kyne, Rafael Sabatini, Joseph C. Lincoln, Edna Ferber, Kathleen Norris, and E. Phillips Oppenheim. Information on recent novelists is most easily obtained from *Contemporary Authors,* periodically revised.

Other useful analyses are: Harrison Smith, "Twenty-five Years of Best Sellers," *English Journal*, XXXIII (October, 1944), 402–408; and Frederick Lewis Allen, "Best Sellers 1930–35," *Saturday Review of Literature* (December 7, 1935). Additional information and speculation may be found in: D. T. Turner, "Ambivalent Values in Recent Best Sellers," *Journal of Human Relations*, X (1962) 163–80; Edward Weeks, "What Makes a Book a Best Seller?", *The New York Times Book Review* (December 20, 1936); John Harvey, "The Content Characteristics of Best Sellers," *Public Opinion Quarterly*, XVII (Spring, 1953) 91–113; Granville Hicks, "The Mystery of the Best Seller," *English Journal*, XXIII (October, 1934) 621–29; and George Stevens's delightful *Lincoln's Doctor's Dog* (Philadelphia, 1938). The library of the Kinsey Institute at Indiana University contains the best collection of exposé literature used in this chapter.

Gary Jennings, "Heathcliff Doesn't Smoke L and M's," *The New York Times Book Review* (July 27, 1969) is a delightful study of the Gothics, while the details of the "Penelope Ashe" hoax appeared in Associated Press wire stories of August 7 and 8, 1969.

There are separate studies of some of the popular poets, among them such excellent sources as Gordon Haight's *Mrs. Sigourney* (New York, 1935), but by far the greater amount of information is to be found in literary surveys and compilations such as: E. H. and G. L. Duyckinck, *Cyclopaedia of American Literature* (Philadelphia, 1875); James Onderdonk, *American Poetry* (Boston, 1896); James Abernathy, *American Literature* (New York, 1913); Brander Mathews, *Introduction to American Literature* (Boston, 1911); F. V. M. Painter, *Introduction to American Literature* (Boston, 1897); and Howard Cook, *Our Poets of Today* (New York, 1919). Ola Winslow's *American Broadside Verse* (New Haven, 1930) gives excellent early examples of the type; Edgar Wolf, *American Song Ballads, Ship Ballads, and Poetical Broadsides 1850–1870* (Philadelphia, 1963) provides information on later types. James Hart's *The Popular Book* (Berkeley, 1961) and Frank L. Mott's *Golden Multitudes* (New York, 1947) give some consideration to popular poetry, though they are chiefly concerned with fiction. Among the collections used in this study, the most useful are: George B. Cheever, *The American Common-Place Book of Poetry* (Boston, 1831); Bryant's various editions of his *Library of Poetry and Song*; Charles A. Dana, ed., *The Household Book of Poetry* (New York, 1903); Henry T. Coates, *The Fireside Encyclopaedia of Poetry* (Philadelphia, 1879); The Standard Library, *Favorite Poems* (Buffalo, 1907); Frank McAlpine, *Popular Poetic Pearls* (Dallas and San Francisco, 1885); Anne Brackett and Ida Elliott, *Poetry for Home and School* (New York, 1876); Charles Gayley and Martin Flaherty, *Poetry of the People* (Boston, 1904); Walter F. Rice, *The Humbler Poets* (Chicago, 1911); Slason Thompson, *The Humbler Poets* (Chicago, 1886); Bliss Carman, *The World's Greatest Poetry* (New York, 1904, ten volumes); Berton Braley, *The World's Thousand Best Poems* (New York, 1929, ten volumes); Thomas Clark and E. A. Gillespie, *A Thousand Quotable Poems* (New York, 1937); Hazel Felleman, *The Best Loved Poems of the American People* (New York, 1936); Burton Stevenson, *The Home Book of Verse* (New York, 1922 and subsequent editions); James T. Fields, *Household Friends for Every Season* (Boston, 1864); E. C. Stedman, *An American Anthology* (Boston, 1900); David George, *The Family Book of Best Loved Poems* (New York, 1952); and P. E. Ernest, *A Family Album of Favorite Poems* (New York, 1959). For remarks on Gibran, see Anthony Ferris, ed., Kahlil Gibran, *Thoughts and Meditations* (New York, 1960). Lee Steinmetz, *The Poetry of the Civil War* (East Lansing, 1960) is the only critical anthology of wartime verse, edited with skill and perception, although one should also consult Claudius M. Capps, *The Blue and the Gray* (Boston, 1943). Athie Sales Davis's newspaper verse anthologies appeared from 1920 to 1942, published in New York. For poetry of World War I, see

T. S. Moore, *Our Soldier Poets* (London, 1919) and William Allan Brooks, *The Soldier's Collection of Poems and Ballads* (New York, 1941), as well as the *Stars and Stripes* collection of 1926. Geoffrey Hellman's profile of Service, in *The New Yorker* (March 30 and April 6, 1946), is delightful. *Scribner's*, January 16, 1917, contains an essay on Seeger. *Time* gives a brief estimate of McKuen's popularity in the May 16, 1969 issue.

There is no adequate study of juvenile literature in the United States, though there are a number of studies of Horatio Alger. The two most comprehensive biographies are John Tebbel, *From Rags to Riches* (New York, 1963) and Ralph Gardner, *Horatio Alger and the American Hero Era* (Mendota, Illinois, 1964). Other studies, historical and critical, of Alger used in this chapter, are: Thomas Meeken, "A Forgettable Centenary," *The New York Times Magazine* (January 28, 1964); Robert Falk, "Notes on the Higher Criticism of Horatio Alger," *Arizona Quarterly*, XIX (Summer, 1963), 151–71; Fred Schroeder, "America's First Literary Realist," *Western Humanities Review*, XVI (Spring, 1963), 129–38; Marshall Fishwick, "The Rise and Fall of Horatio Alger," *Saturday Review* (November 17, 1956); Frederick Lewis Allen, "Horatio Alger Junior," *Saturday Review of Literature* (September 17, 1938); Henry F. Pringle, "The Rebellious Parson," *Saturday Evening Post* (February 10, 1957). Henry Hinsdale and Tony London, *Frank Merriwell's Father* (Norman, Oklahoma, 1964) is the major source of information on Gilbert Patten; other articles include Stewart Holbrook, "Frank Merriwell at Yale," *Lansing State Journal* (October 22, 1964), Barney Lefferts, "The Return of Frank Merriwell," *The New York Times Magazine* (August 19, 1956); and John L. Cutler, "Gilbert Patten and the Merriwell Saga," *University of Maine Studies* (Orono, Me., 1934) series 2, no. 31. An excellent survey of the Stratemeyer syndicate is "For It Was Indeed He," *Fortune*, IX (April, 1934) 86 ff. Robert Cantwell's "A Sneering Laugh With the Bases Loaded," *Sports Illustrated* (April 23, 1962), is a delightful study of the athletic school; Jim Treloar, "The Search for the Lost Books of Childhood," Detroit *Free Press* (May 1, 1966), is another, dealing with the Merriwells and Rovers. Arthur Praeger's "The Secret of Nancy Drew," *Saturday Review* (January 25, 1969), is excellent.

PART TWO

There is no single, general study of the popular theater in America, but there are a number of useful, compendious histories of American drama. Arthur H. Quinn, *American Drama* (two volumes, New York, 1955 ed.) is of course the standard reference. Oral M. Coad and Edwin Mims, Jr., *The American Stage* (New York, 1929) though old, is useful and contains information unavailable elsewhere. Glenn Hughes, *A History of the American Theater* (New

York, 1951) is the best one-volume history. Richard Moody's *Dramas from the American Theater* (Cleveland, 1960), a collection of popular American plays with excellent introductory material and bibliographies, is an essential source; Moody's study of Romantic drama, *America Takes the Stage* (Bloomington, Indiana, 1955), is basic to an understanding of the nineteenth-century popular drama. Other useful sources are: Daniel Blum, *A Pictorial History of the American Theater* (New York, 1956); Barnard Hewitt, *Theater USA: 1668 to 1957* (New York, 1959); Howard Taubman, *The Making of the American Theater* (New York, 1967); Hugh F. Rankin, *The Theater in Colonial America* (Chapel Hill, 1965); Lloyd Morris's chatty *Curtain Time* (New York, 1953), chiefly about actors; and Abe Laufe, *Anatomy of a Hit: Long Run Plays* (New York, 1966).

Specialized studies used in this chapter include: Daniel Grimsted, *Melodrama Unveiled: American Theater and Culture, 1800–1850* (Chicago, 1968), an excellent book of cultural history with extensive bibliographies; Francis Hodge, *Yankee Theater: The Image of America on the Stage, 1825–1850* (Austin, Texas, 1964), a study of the Yankee character in the theater; Philip Graham, *Showboats, The History of an American Institution* (Austin, Texas, 1951); Elizabeth Leonard and Julia Goodman, *Buffalo Bill, King of the Old West* (New York, 1955); Dan Leonard, *Lives and Legends of Buffalo Bill* (Tulsa, 1960); and Jay Monaghan, "The Stage Career of Buffalo Bill," *Journal of the Illinois Historical Society*, XXXI (December, 1938), 411–23. Myron Matlaw's *The Black Crook and Other Nineteenth-Century Plays* (New York, 1967) not only reprints eight popular plays but has excellent introductory materials and useful notes.

The history of vaudeville may be traced in Joe Laurie Jr., *Vaudeville from the Honky-Tonks to the Palace* (New York, 1953), Bernard Sobel, *A Pictorial History of Vaudeville* (New York, 1961); Douglas Gilbert, *American Vaudeville: Its Life and Times* (New York, 1940); Abel Green and Joe Laurie, Jr., *Show Biz: From Vaude to Video* (New York, 1951); and Albert McLean, *American Vaudeville as Ritual* (Lexington, Kentucky, 1965). Burlesque is treated by Irving Zeidman, *The American Burlesque Show* (New York, 1967); Bernard Sobel, *Burleycue* (New York, 1931); and Sobel's *A Pictorial History of Burlesque* (New York, 1956). Marian Spitzer's *The Palace* (New York, 1969), a nostalgic reminiscence by the theater's press agent, is an entertaining source of information.

The history of *Uncle Tom's Cabin* and the Tom shows derives from Moody, Quinn, Hewitt, and Hughes, above; Henry Birdoff, *The World's Greatest Hit* (New York, 1947) is a thorough study of the various companies and actors. W. L. Lawrence, "The Rise of Spectacle in America," *Theatre Arts Magazine*, XXV (1917), 44–45 provides interesting materials on the spectaculars; Roy Boe, "The Panoramas of the Mississippi," *Mississippi Quarterly*, XVI (1963), 203–19, furnished information on this type of exhibition. The circus has been thoroughly covered by Wilson Disher, *The Greatest Show on Earth* (New York, 1937); Earl May, *The Circus from Rome to Ring-*

ling (Chicago, 1932); George L. Chindahl, *The Circus in America* (Caldwell, Idaho, 1959); Gene Plowden, *Those Amazing Ringlings* (Caldwell, Idaho, 1967); and John Durant, *The Pictorial History of the American Circus* (New York, 1957).

Much of the material concerning the tent show is drawn from the collection of scripts, playbills, and clippings owned by Harold Rosier of the Rosier Shows, Jackson, Michigan. For additional information, see George Eels, "The Barnstormers," *Diners Club Magazine* (June, 1965), 6–15; and Vance Johnson, "Hits in the Tall Corn," *Collier's* (August 20, 1949) 56 ff. The Toby show is treated in Neil Schaffner and Vance Johnson, *The Fabulous Toby* (New York, 1968), and Jere C. Mickel, "The Genesis of Toby," *Journal of American Folklore* (1967) pp. 334–40.

The rise of the minstrel show is documented in Gilbert Chase, *America's Music* (New York, 1955); Daniel Paskman and Sigmund Spaeth, *Gentlemen, Be Seated!* (New York, 1928); Carl Wittke, *Tambo and Bones: A History of the American Minstrel* (New York, 1930); Hans Nathan, *Dan Emmett and Early American Minstrelsy* (Norman, Oklahoma, 1961); and Moody, above. The account of the history of musical comedy derives chiefly from Lehman Engel, *The American Musical Theater* (New York, 1967); Gilbert Chase, *America's Music* (New York, 1955); David Ewen, *The Story of America's Musical Theater* (Philadelphia, 1961); Cecil Smith, *Musical Comedy in America* (New York, 1950); and Abe Laufe, *Broadway's Greatest Musicals* (New York, 1969).

PART THREE

A classic and still useful study of dime novels is Edmund Pearson, *Dime Novels* (Boston, 1919); the definitive study of the most prolific publishers is Albert Johannsen, *The House of Beadle and Adams* (two volumes, Norman, Oklahoma, 1950). *Dime Novel Roundup*, a monthly magazine for authors, collectors, and libraries, is indispensable for any student of the genre; Charles Bragin's *Bibliography: Dime Novels 1860–1964* (Brooklyn, 1964) is an equally indispensable bibliographical source. Two thoughtful essays are Mary Noel, "Dime Novels," *Amercian Heritage*, VII (February, 1956) 50–56 ff.; and Merle Curti, "Dime Novels and the American Tradition," *Yale Review* (June, 1937) 761–70. Gilbert Patten's "Dime Novel Days," *Saturday Evening Post* (February 28, 1931), 6–7, 74–78; and (March 7, 1931), 36–38, 45–50, are useful accounts by one of the most prolific of the writers.

There are a number of useful studies of the comics: Colton Waugh, *The Comics* (New York, 1947); Stephen Becker, *Comic Art in America* (New York, 1960); Walter Murrell, *A History of American Graphic Humor* (New York, 1933, 1938); Martin Sheridan, *Comics and Their Creators* (New York,

1942); Thomas Craven, *Cartoon Cavalcade* (New York, 1943); and Pierre Couperie, Maurice Horn, et. al., *A History of the Comic Strip* (New York, 1968), on which this portion has drawn considerably. David Manning White and Robert Abel edited an excellent collection of essays, *The Funnies* (New York, 1963), and Jules Feiffer's *The Great Comic Book Heroes* (New York, 1965) is brightly written and informative. Leslie Fiedler's essay, "Comic Books," in *No! in Thunder* (New York, 1962) and Leo Gurko's "Folklore of the American Hero," in *Heroes, Highbrows, and the Popular Mind* (New York, 1959) are stimulating discussions; *The Journal of Educational Sociology*, XVII (December, 1944), Harvey Zorbaugh, ed., is given over to analyses and speculations about the place of comics in culture, while Dr. Frederic Wertham's *The Seduction of the Innocent* (New York, 1954) outlines the original attacks on them. Leo Bogart's study, "Comic Strips and Their Adult Readers," in Bernard Rosenberg, and David White, eds., *Mass Culture* (Glencoe, 1957); the report of Edward Robinson and David White, "Who Reads Comics?" and Francis Barhus, "The World of the Sunday Comics," in White and Abel, above, are studies of readership. Ken Michaels' interview with Charles Schulz, "You're a Good Man, Charlie Schulz," is in the *Chicago Tribune Magazine* (May 18, 1969); see also Schulz's essay, "But a Comic Strip Has to Grow," *Saturday Review* (April 2, 1969), 73–74.

PART FOUR

Standard studies of the detective story are Howard Haycraft's *The Art of the Mystery Story* (New York, 1946) and *Murder for Pleasure* (New York, 1941). W. O. Aydelotte, "The Detective Story as a Historical Source," *Yale Review*, XXXIX (Fall, 1949), 76–95 is a good brief review of the genre to 1930. Studies of the recent detective-mystery include *Tough Guy Writers of the Thirties*, David Madden, ed. (Carbondale, Illinois, 1968); Philip Durham's excellent study of Chandler, *Down These Mean Streets a Man Must Go* (Chapel Hill, 1966), and his unpublished dissertation, "The Objective Treatment of the 'Hardboiled Hero' in American Fiction" (Northwestern University, 1949). On the private eye novels, John Paterson, "A Cosmic View of the Private Eye," *Saturday Review of Literature* (August 22, 1953), was especially useful. A brilliant analysis of Spillane's mixture of sentimentality, pornography, and violence, with reference to the Hammett-Chandler tradition, is John Cawelti's "The Spillane Phenomenon," *University of Chicago Magazine*, LXI (1969), 18–25. The best book on Dashiell Hammett, both biographical and critical, is William F. Nolan, *Dashiell Hammett: A Casebook* (Santa Barbara, California, 1969) which includes a complete checklist of Hammett's work and an excellent bibliography of source materials. Additional sources are Raymond Chandler's introduction to and his title essay in *The Simple Art of Murder*

(New York, 1950); Harold Orel's unpublished paper, "The American Detective Hero" and "Raymond Chandler's Last Novel," *Journal of the Midwest American Studies Association*, II (Spring, 1961), 59–63; Herbert Ruhm, "In Rat's Alley," *Carleton Miscellany*, VIII (Winter, 1967), 118–23; Alva Johnston's study of Spillane, "Death's Fairhaired Boy," *Life* (June 23, 1952); Christopher LaFarge, "Mickey Spillane and his Bloody Hammer," *Saturday Review* (November 4, 1954); Charles J. Rolo, 'Spillane and Simenon," *New World Writing #4* (New York, 1952); *The Hardboiled Dicks*, Ron T. Goulart, ed. (New York, 1967); and Joseph T. Shaw's introduction to *The Hardboiled Omnibus* (New York, 1946). For recent trends in the genre, see the introductions to the series, *Best Detective Stories of the Year*. An excellent essay on Kenneth Millar's work is that by William Goldman in his review of *The Goodbye Look*, *The New York Times Book Review* (June 1, 1969).

The most thorough studies of science fiction, on which this essay has leaned heavily, are those of Sam Moscowitz, *Explorers of The Infinite* (Cleveland, 1963); *Seekers of Tomorrow* (Cleveland, 1966); and *Science Fiction by Gaslight* (Cleveland, 1968). Additional useful studies are Kingsley Amis, *New Maps of Hell* (New York, 1960); Reginald Bretnor, *Modern Science Fiction* (New York, 1953); J. O. Bailey, *Pilgrims Through Space and Time* (New York, 1947); Basil Davenport, *An Inquiry into Science Fiction* (New York, 1955); *The Science Fiction Novel*, Basil Davenport, ed. (New York, 1959); Damon Knight, *Essays on Modern Science Fiction* (Chicago, 1956); and H. Bruce Franklin's historical study, *Future Perfect: American Science Fiction of the Nineteenth Century* (New York, 1966). Donald Day, *Index to the Science Fiction Magazines 1926–50* (Portland, Oregon, 1952); its continuation, *Index to the Science Fiction Magazines 1961–65* (Cambridge, Massachusetts, 1966); and W. R. Cole, *A Checklist of Science Fiction Anthologies* (New York, 1964) are indispensable bibliographies. John W. Campbell's *Collected Editorials* for *Analog* (Garden City, 1966) provide valuable insights; Robert Silverberg's "Diversity in Science Fiction," *Fantastic* (February, 1969), outlines the contemporary pattern. Relevant articles include Arthur C. Clarke, "In Defense of Science Fiction," *UNESCO Courier*, XV (November, 1962), 14–17; Isaac Asimov, "The Sword of Achilles," *Bulletin of the Atomic Scientists*, XIX (November, 1963), 17–19; Robert West, "Science Fiction and Its Ideas," *Georgia Review*, XV (Fall, 1961), 276–86; R. Gordon Kelly, "Ideology in Some Modern Science Fiction Novels," *Journal of Popular Culture*, I (Fall, 1968), 24–35; Reuel Denney, "Reactors of the Imagination," in *The Astonished Muse* (Chicago, 1957); Fletcher Pratt, "From the Fairy Tale of Science to the Science of the Fairy Tale," *Pacific Spectator*, II (Spring, 1948), 193–206; Alva Johnson, "Tarzan, or How to Become a Great Writer," *Saturday Evening Post* (July 29, 1939); Alan Townsend, "Soviet Science Fiction," *The Listener* (October 24, 1963); Judith Merril, introduction to *Path into the Unknown* (New York, 1968).

The bibliography of the Western novel, as distinct from the Western movie, radio serial, and television play, is less extensive than might be supposed. The most comprehensive and useful study is that of Francis R. Hodgins, *The Literary Emancipation of a Region: The Changing Image of the American West in Fiction,* unpublished Ph.D. dissertation (Michigan State University, 1957). Bernard DeVoto, "Western Fiction," *Harper's Magazine,* CCIX (December, 1954), 10–14; and W. R. Hutchinson, "Virgins, Villains, and Varmints," *Huntington Library Quarterly,* XVI (August, 1953), 381–93, are also useful articles. An excellent essay is John R. Milton, "The Western Novel," *Chicago Review,* XVI (Summer, 1963), 74–100; good brief treatments of the popular Western are Horace Gregory, "Guns of the Roaring West," *Avon Book of Modern Writing* (New York, 1954) pp. 217–35; and Harry E. Maule, preface, *The Pocket Book of Western Stories* (New York, 1945). A provocative scholarly study is Joseph Waldmeir, "The Cowboy, The Knight, and Popular Taste," *Southern Folklore Quarterly,* XXII (September, 1958), 113–20; John Williams, "The Western: Definition of a Myth," *The Nation* (November 18, 1961); and John Evans, "Modern Man and the Cowboy," *Television Quarterly,* I (May, 1962), 31–36, are treatments of the genre in cinema and television. There are a number of studies of the cowboy in fiction: Levette Davidson, "Fact or Formula in Western Fiction," *Colorado Quarterly,* III (Winter, 1955), 278–87; Carey McWilliams, "Myths of the West," *North American Review,* CCXXXII (November, 1931), 424–32; Joe B. Frantz, *The American Cowboy: Myth and Reality* (New York, 1955); Harry E. Lichter, "The Western Hero in Fact and Fancy," *Wisconsin Magazine of History,* XL (Autumn, 1955), 52–58; John G. Cawelti, "Cowboys, Indians, and Outlaws," *The American West,* I (Spring, 1964), 29–35, 77–79; Owen C. Ulp, "Cowhands, Cowhorses, and Cows," *The American West,* III (Winter, 1966), 64–71; Clifford P. Westmaier, "The Cowboy: Sinner or Saint," *New Mexico Historical Review,* XXV (April, 1950), 89–108. Especially important in the history of the Western novel are E. Douglas Branch, *The Cowboy and His Interpreters* (New York, 1926); James K. Folsom, *The American Western Novel* (New Haven, 1966); and Andy Adams's article, "Western Interpreters," *Southwest Review,* X (October, 1924), 70–74. Philip Durham, "The Negro Cowboy," *American Quarterly,* VII (Fall, 1955), 291–301, is a pioneer study of an area long neglected by Western novelists and historians. Joseph G. Rose's *The Gunfighter: Man or Myth?* (Norman, Oklahoma, 1968), effectively disposes of the gunman legend and contains much information in its development in fiction. Frank Gruber's book of reminiscences, *The Pulp Jungle* (Los Angeles, 1967), by a man who spent forty years in the detective-Western factories, is both charming and informative.

For a study of the modern popular Western, there is no better source than *Roundup,* the official journal of the Western Writers of America, edited in Tucson, Arizona. James Fargo, "The Western and Ernest Haycox," *Prairie Schooner,* XXVI (Summer, 1952) 65–72, is an excellent estimate; Mary Davison Rhodes, *The Hired Man on Horseback* (Boston, 1938), the life of Eugene Rhodes, is another useful study of the early Western. Frederick Faust is treated in Danell Richardson, *Max Brand: The Man and His Work* (New York,

1963). On the significance of academic criticism of the Western, see C. L. Sonnichsen, "The Wyatt Earp Syndrome," *Roundup*, XVI (September, 1968), 4–7; and William Turner, "Notes on Western Fiction," *Roundup*, XVI (February, 1968), 1–4. For examples of significant scholarly criticism see Alexander Miller, "The Western: A Theological Note," *Christian Century* (November 27, 1957); Martin Nussbaum, "Sociological Symbolism of the Adult Western," *Social Forces*, XXXIX (October, 1960), 25–28; and David B. Davis's amusingly naïve "Ten Gallon Hero," *American Quarterly*, VI (Summer, 1954), 11–25. Especial thanks is due to Nelson C. Nye, of Tucson, Arizona, and Henry Wilson Allen, of Encino, California, for invaluable information about the modern Western novel and for assistance in evaluating it.

PART FIVE

For general information about popular music and musicians, the most useful reference works are Irwin Stambler, *The Encyclopedia of Popular Music* (New York, 1965), and Julius Mattfeld, *Variety Music Cavalcade: Musical-Historical Review 1620–1961* (Englewood Cliffs, New Jersey, 1966). *Variety's* list of the "Golden One Hundred" popular songs of all time, from "After You've Gone" to "Zing, Went the Strings of My Heart," is reprinted in Mattfeld, xiv. Nick Kenny, *How To Write, Sing, and Sell Popular Songs* (New York, 1946) and Arthur Korb, *How To Write Songs That Sell* (New York, 1949) provide interesting information on commercial songwriting methods.

There are a number of excellent studies of popular music: James J. Field, *American Popular Music 1875–1950* (Philadelphia, 1956); Harry Dichter and Elliott Shapiro, *Early American Sheet Music* (New York, 1941); Sigmund Spaeth's pioneering volumes, *Read 'Em and Weep* (New York, 1926) and *Weep Some More My Lady* (New York, 1927), and his larger study, *A History of Popular Music in America* (New York, 1948); and Isaac Goldberg, *Tin Pan Alley* (New York, 1930). David Ewen's *American Popular Songs* (New York, 1966) and *Panorama of American Popular Music* (Englewood Cliffs, New Jersey, 1957) are invaluable. Douglas Gilbert, *Lost Chords* (Garden City, 1942); Elizabeth Montgomery, *The Story Behind Popular Songs* (New York, 1960); and Edward B. Marks, *They All Sang* (New York, 1934) are helpful to any student of the genre. Marks's book, by one of the more successful early songwriters, lists 1,545 songs, 300 musical names, and 500 musical vaudeville acts of the period 1890–1920. Helen Kaufman, *From Jehovah to Jazz* (New York, 1937) and Lester Levy, *Grace Notes in American History: Popular Sheet Music from 1820–1900* (Norman, Oklahoma, 1967) are useful; Larry Freeman, *The Melodies Linger On* (Watkins Glen, New York, 1951) is one of the most informative studies of the period 1900–1950. The economics of music publishing is explained by David Dachs, *Anything Goes: The World of Popular*

Music (Indianapolis, 1964). The meaning of the phonograph for American cultural life is discussed in Roland Gelatt, *The Fabulous Phonograph* (New York, 1955). The Civil War period of music is treated by Irwin and Jerry Silberman, *Songs of the Civil War* (New York, 1960), and Willard Heaps and William Porter, *The Singing Sixties* (Norman, Oklahoma, 1960). The best study of Stephen Foster is John Howard Tasker, *America's Troubador* (New York, 1962). Carol Brink, *Harps in the Wind* (New York, 1947) is a study of the Hutchinson Family Singers.

For information on country-and-western music, major sources are Linnell Gentry, *A History and Encyclopaedia of Country, Western, and Gospel Music* (Nashville, 1961), Billboard's *The World of Country* (November, 1963; November, 1964, New York) and Robert Shelton and Burt Goldblatt, *The Country Music Story* (Indianapolis, 1966). Informative scholarly articles are Archie Green, "Hillbilly Music, Source and Symbol," *Journal of American Folklore*, LXXVIII (July–September, 1965) 204–29; L. Mayne Smith, "An Introduction to Bluegrass," *ibid.*, pp. 245–57; and D. K. Wilgass, "Introduction to the Study of Hillbilly Music," *ibid.*, pp. 195–204. "Country Music, Nashville Style," in *McCall's*, LXXXVIII (April, 1961), 92–96; and "Roger Miller Day," The Detroit *Free Press* (December 4, 1968), furnish additional information.

Articles on popular songs, jazz, ragtime, rhythm and blues, and trends since 1960 include Bruce Jay Freedman, "The New Sound of Rock and Roll," *Holiday* (July, 1965), pp. 44–98; Daniel Hoffman and Dave Brubeck, "Two Views of Jazz," *Perspectives USA* (Spring, 1956), pp. 29–42; Albert Goldman, "The Emergence of Rock," *New American Review*, #3 (Spring, 1968); Marshall Stearns, "New Directions in Jazz," *Yale Review*, XLIX (Autumn, 1959), 54–60; Nat Hentoff, "Jazz and the Intellectuals," *Chicago Review*, IX (Fall, 1955) 110–21; Gene Lees, "The Decline of the American Popular Song," *Hi Fi and Stereo Review* (January 1964), pp. 59–63; H. F. Mooney, "Songs, Singers, and Society, 1890–1954," *American Quarterly*, VI (Fall, 1954) 221–32, and "Popular Music Since 1920," *ibid.*, XX (Spring, 1968), 67–85; and James Morris, "Monarchs of the Beatle Empire," *Saturday Evening Post* (August 27, 1966), pp. 23–30. For current trends in popular records consult the annual *GO Pop Annual*, Pyramid Books.

General histories of jazz and its various phases are: André Hodeir, *Toward Jazz* (New York, 1962); Rudi Blesh and Harriet Janis, *They All Played Ragtime* (New York, 1966); Gunther Schuller, *Early Jazz* (New York, 1968); Samuel Charters, *Jazz: New Orleans 1885–1957* (New York, 1958); Marshall Stearns, *The Story of Jazz* (New York, 1956); Barry Ulanov, *A History of Jazz in America* (New York, 1952); Rudi Blesh, *Shining Trumpets* (New York, 1946); and the series edited by Martin Williams, the first volume of which is *Jazz Masters of New Orleans* (New York, 1967). Later developments are treated in John S. Wilson, *Jazz: The Transition Years* (New York, 1966); Leonard Feather, *Inside Be-Bop* (New York, 1949); Irving Kolodin and Benny Goodman, *The Kingdom of Swing* (New York, 1939); John S. Wilson, *Collector's Jazz: Modern* (New York, 1959); George T. Simon, *The Big Bands*

(New York, 1967); and particularly well by John Rublowsky, *Popular Music*
(New York, 1967). Two studies of the Beatles appeared in 1968; Hunter
Davies, *The Beatles* (New York, 1968), and Julius Fast, *The Beatles: The
Real Story* (New York, 1968): see also Alan Beckett, "The Stones," *New Left
Review* (Jan.–Feb. 1968) pp. 24–29; and *Rock*, Jonathan Eisen, ed. (New
York, 1969). It is also possible to buy a collection of sayings and jests by the
Beatles—Rick Friedman, *The Beatles: Words Without Music* (New York, 1968)
—and to subscribe to several journals which deal with rock music, drugs, racial
confrontations, etc., among them *Changes, Crawdaddy, Pop Cycle*, and *Rolling
Stone*. Current trends may be followed in the annual editions of *FLIP'S Groovy
Guide* and the *GO POP Annual*, which furnish information on the personnel,
musical characteristics, and current status of eighty to one hundred groups.
Lillian Roxon, *The Rock Encyclopedia* (New York, 1969) contains biographical and commercial information about all major groups, artists, managers, and
recordings.

Acknowledgment must be made for the valuable assistance in this chapter
of Ron English, Detroit musician, arranger, and composer, and particularly of
Peter Nye of Eastern Michigan University, who read and supervised the portions dealing with popular music since 1930, though neither, of course, are to
be held responsible for the opinions therein.

PART SIX

There are dozens of critical essays and books on the movies; among the
more recent are: Gilbert Seldes, *The Great Audience* (New York, 1950) and
The Public Arts (New York, 1960); Parker Tyler, *Three Faces of Film* (New
York, 1960); Frank Getlein and Harold Gardiner, *Movies, Morals and Art*
(New York, 1961); Ezra Goodman, *The Fifty-Year Decline and Fall of
Hollywood* (New York, 1961); Robert Warshaw, *The Immediate Experience*
(Garden City, 1962); and Judith Crist, *The Private Eye, The Cowboy, and
The Very Naked Girl* (New York, 1968). Among historical studies the fol-
lowing are especially useful: Lewis Jacobs, *The Rise of the American Film*
(New York, 1939); Daniel Blum, *A Pictorial History of the Silent Film* (New
York, 1953); Richard Griffith and Arthur Mayer, *The Movies* (New York,
1957); Arthur Knight, *The Liveliest Art* (New York, 1957); Joe Franklin,
Classics of the Silent Screen (New York, 1959); Albert R. Fulton, *Motion
Pictures* (Norman, Oklahoma, 1960); Paul Rotha, *The Film Till Now* (New
York, 1960 ed.); Terry Ramsaye, *A Million and One Nights* (New York, 1964
ed.); Richard Schickel, *Movies: The History of an Art and an Institution*
(New York, 1964); Kenneth McGowan, *Behind the Screen* (New York, 1965
ed.); and Daniel Blum and John Kobal, *A New Pictorial History of the Talkies*
(New York, 1968). The International Film Guide Series volumes, David

Robinson, *Hollywood in the Twenties;* John Baxter, *Hollywood in the Thirties;* and Charles Higham and Joel Greenberg, *Hollywood in the Forties,* furnish additional information on these years. Paul Michael, *The American Movies Reference Book* (Englewood Cliffs, 1968) is a helpful source of information.

There are several interesting specialized studies to be consulted for a wider view of the popular film: Kalton Lahue, *Winds of Laughter: The Comedy Short* (Norman, Oklahoma, 1960); G. N. Fenin and William Everson, *The Western* (New York, 1962); William Everson, *The Bad Guys: A Pictorial History of the Movie Villain* (New York, 1944); Kalton Lahue and Terry Brewer, *Kops and Kustards: The Legend of Keystone Film* (Norman, Oklahoma, 1968); and three nostalgic books on old movies, Charles Beaumont's *Remember! Remember!* (New York, 1963); Kevin Brownlow, *The Parade's Gone By* (New York, 1968); and Edward Wagenknecht, *Movies in the Age of Innocence* (Norman, Oklahoma, 1962). Kelton Lahue's *Continued Next Week: A History of the Movie Serial* (Norman, Oklahoma, 1964) is superb. Excellent articles on movie theaters are C. G. Rinehart, "Halls of Illusion," *Saturday Evening Post* (May 11, 1929), pp. 16–17 ff.; and Ben Hall, "The Best Ree-maining Seats," *American Heritage,* XII (October, 1961), 42 ff.

Over the years literally hundreds of articles and essays on the movies have been published in newspapers and magazines. Of two hundred checked for this study, the following seemed sufficiently useful to cite: "The Movies," *Survey* (April 3, 1909), pp. 8–9; "Drama of the People," *Independent* (September 29, 1910), pp. 713–14; "The Moving Picture, Primary School for Criminals," *Good Housekeeping* (August, 1910), pp. 184–186; W. D. Howells, "The Cinematographic Show: Its Essence and Influence," *Harpers* (September 1912), pp. 634–37; Joseph Fulk, "The Effect on Education and Morals of the Moving Pictures Shows," *National Education Association, Proceedings and Addresses* (Ann Arbor, Michigan, 1912) pp. 456–61; "Moving Pictures, The Good and Bad of It," *Outlook* (July 13, 1912); Olivia Howard Dunbar, "The Lure of the Films," *Harper's Weekly* (January, 1913), pp. 20–22; "Democratic Art," *Nation* (August 28, 1913), p. 193; "Cultural Values of the Movies," *Review of Reviews* (July, 1914), pp. 103–105; "New Art Being Developed," *Current Opinion* (June, 1914), pp. 66–67; "Censoring the Five-Cent Movie," *Survey* (June 27, 1914), p. 5; "Movie Manners and Morals," *Outlook* (July 26, 1916), pp. 27–30; "Movies Create Art," *Harper's Weekly* (April 29, 1916), p. 456; "Democracy and the Movies," *Bookman* (May, 1918), pp. 235–39; "Influence of the Kinematograph on National Life," *Nineteenth Century* (April, 1921), 661–72; "Arraignment and Defense of the Movies," *Current Opinion* (March, 1922), pp. 353–55; "Movies and the People," *Outlook* (May 16, 1923), p. 27; "The Menace of the Movies," *Christian Century* (April 16, 23, 1930). *The Annals of the American Academy of Political and Social Science,* CXXVIII (1926) published (pp. 1–175) a symposium, "The Motion Picture in its Economic and Social Aspects," and twenty years after, in November, 1947, Vol. CCLIV, another, pp. 1–172, "The Motion Picture Industry," both important and informative.

Ladies Home Journal, 1922–1927, ran a series of excellent articles on the movies by stars, producers, and directors, among them Chaplin, Fairbanks, Otis, Skinner, De Mille, and Mary Pickford. Irving Thalberg and H. Weir, "Why Movies Cost So Much," *Saturday Evening Post* (November 4, 1933), pp. 27 ff. is a thorough explanation of movie budgeting. Other informative articles during the forties are J. P. McEvoy," Fear Over Hollywood," *Readers' Digest* (January 1941), pp. 62–65; "Top Years for Oaters," *Time* (April 29, 1946), p. 94; John Houseman, "Today's Hero," *Hollywood Quarterly,* II (January, 1947) 61–65, on changing trends; "Public Taste in Entertainment," *Fortune* (March, 1949), pp. 39–40; "Horse Opera," *Life* (October 7, 1949), pp. 93–97; R. L. Henry, "The Cultural Influence of the Talkies," *School and Society* (February 2, 1949), pp. 149–50. Budd Schulberg's thoughtful essay, "Movies in America: After Fifty Years," is in the *Atlantic Monthly* (November, 1947), pp.115–21. For the state of the medium in the fifties and sixties, see, among others, J. Dinant, "Movies Take to the Pastures," *Saturday Evening Post* (October 14, 1950); Samuel Goldwyn, "Is Hollywood Through?" *Colliers* (September 29, 1951); Milton Mackaye, "Big Brawl, Hollywood versus Television," *Saturday Evening Post* (January 19, 26; February 2, 1952); "Big Change in Hollywood," *Saturday Review* (December 21,1957); "The Vanishing Moviegoer," *Time* (February 10, 1958); Richard Ardrey, "What Happened to Hollywood?" *Reporter* (January 24, 1957); Arthur Knight, "The New Frankness in Films," *Saturday Review* (December 19, 1959); George Bluestone, "The Changing Cowboy," *Western Humanities Review, XIV* (Summer, 1960) 331–37; "Gold in the Hills, Films for TV," *Time* (November 25, 1966); "Hollywood Rides Again," *Fortune* (November, 1966); and Dore Schary, "Our Movie Mythology," *Reporter* (March 3, 1960), pp. 39–42.

Television and Radio, Giraud Chesley, Garnet Garrison, and Edgar Willis, eds. (New York 1963) provides a useful general introduction to the media. Eric Barnouw's two-volume study, *A History of Broadcasting in the United States* (New York, 1965, 1968) is the most complete historical treatment of radio; the files of *Radio Broadcast Magazine* (1920–30) and its successor, *Radio Digest* (1931–33) provide detailed information. There are a number of excellent reminiscences: Sam Slate and Joe Cook, *It Sounds Impossible* (New York, 1963); Fred Buxton and Bill Owen, *Radio's Golden Age* (New York, 1949); Robert J. Landry, *This Fascinating Radio Business* (Indianapolis, 1946); Francis Chase, *Sound and Fury: An Informal History of Broadcasting* (New York, 1947). Mary Jane Higby's study of radio soap operas, *Tune in Tomorrow* (New York, 1968) and Jim Harmon's study of serials, *The Great Radio Heroes* (New York, 1967) are superb. Paul Lazarfeld's study, *Radio Listening in the United States* (New York, 1948) contains useful statistics; Irving Settel, *A Pictorial History of Radio* (New York, 1967) is entertaining and informative. "Public Taste in Entertainment," *Fortune,* XXXIX (March, 1949), 43–44 is an interesting survey of radio taste; R. A. Smith, "TV, The Coming Showdown," *Fortune,* L (September, 1954) 138–39, considers the radio-TV conflict.

The history of television is considered in Leo Bogart, *The Age of Television* (New York, 1966); Daniel Blum, *A Pictorial History of Television* (New York, 1959). Marshall McLuhan, *Understanding Media* (New York, 1964) is the most provocative effort to place mass communication media, including television, into cultural and historical perspective. Other studies include *Television's Impact on American Culture*, William Elliott, ed. (East Lansing, 1956); *The Meaning of Commercial Television*, Stanley Donner, ed. (Stanford, 1966); Lotte Bailyn, "The Uses of Television," *Journal of Social Issues*, XVIII 1962), 1–61. Charles Sopkin's *Seven Glorious Days, Seven Funfilled Nights* (New York, 1968) is a sardonic commentary on TV programming; Harold Mehling, *The Great Timekiller* (Cleveland, 1962) is a study of program content. The problem of costs and profits is treated in Wayde Ogden, *The Television Business* (New York, 1961), and in a number of articles, among them "The Economic Squeeze on TV," *Reporter* (April 29, 1960); "Television," *Chicago Tribune Magazine* (June 2, 1968); Andy Lewis, "Budgets, Machinery, and the Question of Art," *Reporter* (May 2, 1965); Richard Merlman, "Power and Community on TV," *Journal of Popular Culture*, II (Summer 1968) 63–81. The debates over television's function, tastes, appeal, and aims is interminable. Yale Roe, *The Television Dilemma* (New York, 1962) is a summary; early discussions include Marya Mannes, "The Right to be Entertained," *Reporter* (June 30, 1955); Bernard Smith, "There Ought to be a Law," *Harper's* (September, 1948, pp. 34–42; Vance Packard, "New Kinds of TV," *Atlantic* (October, 1963), pp. 69–74; Walter Lippmann in The Chicago *Sun-Times* (January 17, 1960); W. S. Schlamm, "A Critical Look at Television," *American Mercury* (October, 1959), pp. 70–73. The symposium in *Harper's*, "TV and Its Critics" (July–October, 1959), summarizes most of the issues and arguments. From the industry, Robert Sarnoff's article, "What Do You Want from TV?" *Saturday Evening Post* (July 1, 1961), is by far the best-reasoned, practical reply. Joan Barthel's study of "As The World Turns" and current serials is delightful—"The World Has Turned More than 3,200 Times," *The New York Times Magazine* (September 8, 1968); see also Leslie Millin, "Every Afternoon," Toronto *Globe and Mail* (June 9, 1969), which includes an interview with Robert Aaron of NBC. *Sight, Sound and Society* (Boston, 1968), David Manning White and Richard Averson, eds., is a collection of essays dealing with motion pictures and television as mass media, and their effects on elections, children, minority groups, education, etc.

POSTSCRIPT

A useful summary of the debate over the validity and meaning of popular culture is Gifford Phillips, *The Arts in a Democratic Society* (Santa Barbara, California, 1966). British trends in elitist thinking are exemplified in F. R.

Leavis and Denys Thompson, *Culture and Environment* (London, 1933); and *Discrimination and Popular Culture*, Denys Thompson, ed. (London, 1964); and particularly in Richard Hoggart's *The Uses of Literacy* (London, 1957). Dwight Macdonald developed and revised his theories in "A Theory of Popular Culture," *Politics* (February, 1944) pp. 20–24; "A Theory of Mass Culture," *Diogenes* (Summer, 1953) pp. 1–17; and his essay, "Mass Cult and Midcult," in *Against the American Grain* (New York: 1962). William Gass, "Even If By All the Oxen in the World," representing the most uncompromising elitist position, is in *Frontiers of American Culture*, Ray Browne, *et al.*, eds. (Lafayette, Indiana, 1968). For opposing views, see Norman Podhoretz in *Show Magazine* (December, 1962), pp. 41–45; Alvin Toffler, *The Culture Consumers* (New York: 1964), particularly chapters I and XIV; and David Manning White, "Mass Culture in America: Another Point of View," in Bernard Rosenberg and D. M. White, eds., *Mass Culture: The Popular Arts in America* (New York: 1957). Susan Sontag's essay, "On Culture and the New Sensibility" is in her collection, *Against Interpretation* (New York 1966); Abraham Kaplan's "The Aesthetics of the Popular Arts" is in *The Journal of Aesthetics and Art Criticism*, XXIV (Spring, 1966), 351–64. Two excellent commentaries on the modern view of popular culture are John Cawelti's essay-review in *American Quarterly*, XX (Summer, 1968) 254–59; and Ray Browne's preface to Arnold Rampersand, *Melville's Israel Potter* (Bowling Green, Ohio, 1969). John Cawelti's brilliant essay, "Beatles, Batman, and The New Aesthetics," *Midway* (Autumn, 1968), pp. 49–70, is by far the most thoughtful analysis of recent changes in approaches to popular culture, and of its relationships to philosophical positions and communications theory; it is required reading for anyone concerned with the popular arts.

"Chester," 307
Chester, Frank and Harry, 78
Chesterfield Supper Club, The, 399
Chestnut Street Theater, 142
Cheyenne Charlie, 205–206
Cheyennes, war against, 299, 410
Chicago, Ill., 146, 173, 192, 257, 347–348; censorship in, 373; meatpacking industry in, 35; musical opportunities in, 331, 333, 393; radio station, 343–344; vaudeville theaters in, 169–170
Chicago American, 218, 237
Chicago Daily News, 124
Chicago Exposition of 1893, 185
Chicago Tribune, 52, 219–220
Chicago: Wicked City, 31
Chicken, type of dance, 349
Chief Ponteach, 148
Child and Baby Care, 54
Child of Passion, The, 30
Childhood, guides to, 26; and psychology, 83; theme of, 104, 117
Childhood's End, 276–277
Children of The King, 33
Children, entertainment for, 228, 247, 400, 409
Children's Hour, The, 101, 137
"Childs First Impression of a Star, A," 109
Childs, Lydia Maria, 22
China, 50
China and Japan, 187
Chinatown in New York City, 176
Chip the Cave Child, 200
Chip of the Flying U, 291
Choate, Rufus, 21
Choir Invisible, The, 36
Choral effects, 164
Christian, Charlie, 338, 357
Christian ideals and faith, 15, 36, 39, 46, 66, 156, 160
Christian Spectator, The, 16
Christianity, affirmation of, 32; early, 47
Christie, Agatha, 250, 265
"Christmas Bells," 120
Christopher Carson, Familiarly Known as Kit, 285
Christy, Edwin P., 163, 165, 311; Minstrels of, 126, 166, 312
Chronicles, popularity of, 10
"Chubby Checkers," 349
Church choirs, 164, 306; traditions of, 311
Church Street Theater, 142
Church, Benjamin, 90
Churchill, Winston, 34, 40, 54
Cibber, Colley, 141
Cigarette Maker's Romance, A, 33
Cimarron, 48, 410
Cincinnati, Ohio, 144

Cinematograph, 363
Cinerama, 385
Circuits, organization of, 173
Circular Staircase, The, 247–248
Circulation and distribution of publications, 5, 238, 255, 274, 278
Circus, the, entertainment by, 3, 172, 186, 188–195, 368
"Cisco Kid, The," 402
Cities Service Hour, 393
Citizen Kane, 382
City, the: burgeoning of, 37, 140, 150; entertainment in, 189, 196, 257, 364; politics and politicians in, 36, 159–160, 333; typical type of, 62, 68, 151
"City Beside the Golden Gate, The," 187
City Lights, 379
City Streets, 380
Civic organizations and celebrations, 97, 166
Civil War: effect of, 32, 43–44, 116, 147, 167, 188, 194, 202, 374; novels, 29, 34, 239; poetry, 105, 110, 113–114
Civil War Book Club, 56
Civil War Series by Stratemeyer, 78
Claim Jumpers, The, 290
Clairvoyance and mesmerism, 168
Clapton, Eric, 357
"Clarence Young," 77
Clari, 308
Clarissa, 17
Clark, Bobby, 171, 381
Clark, George Rogers, 33
Clarke, Arthur C., 276–277, 279, 298
Clarke, C. W., 153
Clarke, Kenny, 338
Class: lower, 1, 151, 319, 331, 419–420; middle, 1–2, 63, 67, 145–146, 155, 160, 168, 171, 212, 366; professional, 256; snobbish of, 3, 140, 146, 178, 421
Classicism, 294, 366, 382; in comics, 240; on film, 365; in music, 146, 354; in novels, 273; Western, 281, 410–411
"Claudia and David," 401
Clay, Bertha M., 202
Clayton, Bessie, 176, 215
Cleopatra, 385
Clerk, A. Piker, 218
Clinch Mountain Boys, The, 346
Cline, Maggie, 171, 317
Clint, 303
Clinton, Larry, 395
Cliquot Club Eskimos, 394
Clowns, performance of, 188–189
Clubs, book, 43, 55–56, 277; service, 166; social, 317, 336
"Clue in the Jewel Box, The," 86
Coachman and the Boy, The, 363
Coates, Henry M., 94
Cobb, Sylvanus T., 29, 35, 200

"It's Me, Dilly," 229
Ivanhoe, 21, 367
"I've Been Roaming," 308
"I've Struck Ile," 314

Jabot, M., 216
Jack Long, or Shot in the Eye, 284
Jack Out West, 71
Jack The Runaway, 78
Jack, Sam T., 173
"Jacket of Gray, The," 111
Jack's Creoles, 165
Jackson, Andrew, 109, 152, 282, 308
Jackson, Chuck, 351
Jackson, Joe, 169
Jackson, Mahalia, 348
Jackson, Milt, 348
Jackson, Peter, 154
Jackson, Stonewall, 104–105
Jackson, Tony, 319
"Jackson Twins," 229
Jacobs, Lewis, 375
"Jambalaya," 343
James Adams, 195
"James Bond" novels, 386
James Boys, The, 206
James, Frank, 193
James, Harry, 398
James, Henry, 33
James, Jesse, 73, 196, 203
"Jane Arden, Girl Reporter," 229
Janice Meredith, 33
Janis, Elsie, 171, 323
Janney, Russell, 46
"Japanese Sandman," 330
Jazz, American origin and etymology of, 319, 323, 330–340, 348
"Jazz Me Blues," 334
Jazz Messengers, The, 348
Jazz Singer, 178, 334, 379
"Jeannie with the Light Brown Hair," 312
"Jeannine," 328
"Jedidiah Homebred,"
Jefferson Airplane, The, 355
Jefferson, Joseph, 146–147, 150, 157, 198, 281, 367
Jeffries, James J., 148
Jelly Roll Morton, 319, 333
Jemmy Daily, or, The Little News Vendor, 22
Jenkins, Ed, 256
Jenkins, Mesquite, 291
Jenkins, William Fitzgerald, 274
Jenks, George, 206
"Jennie," 310
Jennings, Emil, 380
"Jeremiah Saddlebags," 237
Jerry Leemy, 230
Jersey prison ship, 19–20

Jewish Book Club, 56
Jews, the, 74–75, aggressiveness of, 87; comics, 169; history of, 96; types of, 151, 168
Jiggs and Maggie, 236
"Jim," 115
"Jim Bludsoe," 126
"Jim Bowie," 77
"Jim Crow," 163
Jimi Hendrix Experience, The, 356
Jimmie Davis-Neil Schaffner Players, 197
Jimmy Valentine, 402
Jinx Money, 388
Joan of Arc, 189, 367
"Joaquin," (Cincinnatus Heine) Miller, 126
"Joe Palooka," 227, 230
"John Brown's Body," 313
John Martin's Secret, 159
"John Peel," 307
"Johnny Dollar," 402
"Johnny Hazard," 228
"Johnny and Mary," 307
"John's Other Wife," 401
Johnson, Charlie, 319
Johnson, Coffin Ed, 267
Johnson, Crockett, 231, 233
Johnson, Ferd, 223
Johnson, Sam, 1
Johnston, Alva, 273
Johnston, Mary, 33, 45
Johnstown Flood of 1884, 314
Jolson, Al, 170, 177–179, 328, 330, 334, 379
"Jonathan Ploughboy," 149
Jonathan Wild, 30, 244
Jones, Buck, 292, 344, 375, 377
Jones, H. Bedford, 210
Jones, Isham, 329
Jones, James, 51
Jones, Jo, 338
Jones, Joe, 149
Joplin, Janis, 355–356
Joplin, Scott, 318
Jordan, Scott, 265
José, Philip, 279
Journal (Indianapolis), 117
Journal (Milwaukee), 157
Journal of a Trapper, 281
Journals and journalism, 10–11, 14, 89, 92, 115, 188, 244–245
Journey to the Center of the Earth, A, 271
Journey into Fear, 266
Journey to the Gold Diggins, 237
Journey through the Holy Land, 187
Journey on the Rhine, A, 187
"Journey Story," The, 301
Joy Girl, The, 375
Joy in the Morning, 47